# The Oxford
# Harriet Beecher Stowe
# Reader

❧

Edited
with an Introduction
by

## Joan D. Hedrick

New York • Oxford
OXFORD UNIVERSITY PRESS
1999

**Oxford University Press**

Oxford  New York
Athens  Auckland  Bangkok  Bogotá  Buenos Aires  Calcutta
Cape Town  Chennai  Dar es Salaam  Delhi  Florence  Hong Kong  Istanbul
Karachi  Kuala Lumpur  Madrid  Melbourne  Mexico City  Mumbai
Nairobi  Paris  São Paulo  Singapore  Taipei  Tokyo  Toronto  Warsaw

and associated companies in
Berlin  Ibadan

Copyright © 1999 by Oxford University Press

Published by Oxford University Press, Inc.
198 Madison Avenue, New York, New York 10016
http://www.oup-usa.org

Oxford is a registered trademark of Oxford University Press

**Library of Congress Cataloging-in-Publication Data**

Stowe, Harriet Beecher, 1811–1896.
   [Selections.  1999]
   The Oxford Harriet Beecher Stowe reader / edited with an
introduction by Joan D. Hedrick.
     p.  cm.
   Includes bibliographical references.
   ISBN 0-19-509117-5 (acid-free paper)
   1. Antislavery movements—United States—Literary collections.
2. Plantation life—Southern States—Fiction.   3. Afro-Americans—
Southern States—Fiction,   4. Slavery—Southern States—Fiction.
5. Slaves—Southern States—Fiction.   6. Political fiction,
American.   7. Didactic fiction, American.   I. Hedrick, Joan D.,
1944-  .  II. Title.
PS2952.H43  1999               97-32020
813'.3—dc21               CIP

9 8 7 6 5 4 3 2 1
Printed in the United States of America
on acid-free paper.

# The Oxford
# Harriet
# Beecher
# Stowe
## Reader

# CONTENTS

❧

III. Domestic Culture and Politics

# A NOTE ON THE TEXT

❧

Unless otherwise noted, the source of each text in this edition is the first printed edition of that text. A few small corrections of punctuation were made silently to these. The following stories, sketches, and editorials were not collected in book form in Stowe's lifetime: "Modern Uses of Language," "Uncle Enoch," "The Old Meeting-House," "To the Editor of the *Cincinnati Journal and Luminary*," "The Freeman's Dream," "An Appeal to Women of the Free States of America," "What Is to Be Done With Them?" "Will You Take a Pilot?" and "The True Story of Lady Byron's Life." The magazine sources in these cases are indicated in the headnote. For unpublished letters and addresses, the archive where the original or copy may be found is indicated at the foot of the document. The spelling and punctuation in Stowe's letters remain as she wrote them. The text of *Uncle Tom's Cabin* is the one established for the Library of America collection of Stowe's novels, and is used with the publisher's permission.

# ACKNOWLEDGMENTS

❧

I am grateful to the editors at Oxford University Press for suggesting and supporting this project, to Ann Morrissey for expert assistance with annotations, and to the following libraries for their assistance: the Boston Public Library, the John Hay Library at Brown University, the Schlesinger Library in Cambridge, Massachusetts, the Sterling Memorial Library at Yale University, the Watkinson Library at Trinity College, Trinity College Library Interlibrary Loan, and Dr. Williams's Library in London. I thank the President and Trustees of Trinity College for a research leave which allowed me to work on this. For permission to quote from Stowe's unpublished letters I am grateful to the Harriet Beecher Stowe Center. I thank the Connecticut Historical Society for permission to quote "An Affectionate and Christian Address," and the Library of America for permission to use the text of *Uncle Tom's Cabin* established for their edition of Stowe's novels. I am particularly grateful to the Northeast Nineteenth-Century American Women Writers Group for suggestions on what to include in this reader, and to Jane Nadel-Klein, Margo Perkins, and Barbara Sicherman for reading several versions of my introduction and making helpful criticisms.

# CHRONOLOGY

❦

| | |
|---|---|
| 1811 | Harriet Beecher born on June 14 in Litchfield, Connecticut, the seventh child of Lyman Beecher and Roxana Foote. |
| 1816 | Death of Roxana Foote. |
| 1819 | Enters the Litchfield Female Academy. |
| 1824 | Enters the Hartford Female Seminary, where she will remain until 1832. |
| 1825 | Experiences first conversion. |
| 1827 | Becomes teacher at the Hartford Female Seminary. |
| 1828 | Writes "Modern Uses of Language." |
| 1832 | Leaves New England for Cincinnati, Ohio, where she will live for eighteen years. |
| 1833 | Publishes *Primary Geography for Children*, a widely adopted text. Joins the Semi-Colon Club, a literary society. Publishes essays and stories in the *Western Monthly Magazine*. Teaches in Catharine Beecher's Western Female Institute. |
| 1835 | Publishes "Uncle Enoch." |
| 1836 | Marries Calvin Ellis Stowe, clergyman and professor of the Bible and church history at Lane Seminary in Cincinnati. Writes "To the Editor of the *Cincinnati Journal and Luminary*." Gives birth to twin daughters, Eliza and Harriet. |
| 1838 | Birth of son Henry. |
| 1840 | Publishes "The Old Meeting-House: Sketch from the Note-Book of an Old Gentleman" |
| 1840 | Birth of son Frederick. |
| 1841 | Publishes "The Canal-Boat." |
| 1843 | Suicide of brother George Beecher. Birth of daughter Georgiana. Second conversion experience. |
| 1845 | Publishes "Uncle Sam's Emancipation: A Sketch," the germ of *Uncle Tom's Cabin*. |
| 1846–47 | Takes the water cure at Brattleboro, Vermont. |
| 1848 | Birth of son Samuel Charles (Charley). |

1849        Death of Charley

1850        Moves to Brunswick, Maine, where Calvin Stowe takes position at Bowdoin College. Birth of son Charles Edward. Publishes "The Freeman's Dream: A Parable" and other sketches in the antislavery weekly the *National Era*.

1851        Serializes *Uncle Tom's Cabin* in the *National Era*.

1852        *Uncle Tom's Cabin* published by J. P. Jewett. Dispute with the Rev. Joel Parker. Moves to Andover, Massachusetts, where Calvin Stowe accepts position at Andover Theological Seminary.

1853        Publishes *A Key to Uncle Tom's Cabin* and tours the British Isles. Receives the "Affectionate and Christian Address" at Stafford House.

1854        Publishes "An Appeal to Women of the Free States of America, on the Present Crisis in Our Country" in an attempt to defeat the Kansas-Nebraska Act. Also *Sunny Memories of Foreign Lands*, based on the journal her brother Charles kept of her trip to the British Isles.

1856        Publishes *Dred*, her second antislavery novel. Second tour of Europe.

1857        Death of Henry Ellis, a freshman at Dartmouth College, who drowns swimming the Connecticut River. Helps found the *Atlantic Monthly*.

1859        Publishes *The Minister's Wooing*, her first New England novel. Leaves in August for third tour of Europe.

1862        Publishes *The Pearl of Orr's Island*, her second New England novel, and *Agnes of Sorrento*, her Italian novel.

1863        Calvin Stowe retires.

1864        Moves into "Oakholm," her first Hartford house.

1865        Publishes *House and Home Papers* and *Little Foxes*, from columns on domestic subjects written for the *Atlantic Monthly*.

1867        Publishes two collections of children's stories, *The Daisy's First Winter, and Other Stories*, and *Queer Little People*. Also a volume of *Religious Poems*. First of annual migrations to Mandarin, Florida.

1868        Publishes *The Chimney-Corner*, the third collection of her domestic columns, and *Men of Our Times; or, Leading Patriots of the Day*.

1869        Publishes *Oldtown Folks*, her third New England novel. Also "The True Story of Lady Byron's Life." Co-edits *Hearth and Home* with Ik Marvel.

1870        Publishes *Lady Byron Vindicated*. Also *Little Pussy Willow*, children's stories originally published in *Our Young Folks*.

1871        Disappearance of son Frederick. Publishes *My Wife and I; or, Harry Henderson's History* and *Pink and White Tyranny: A Society Novel*, the first of her New York novels.

1872        Publishes *Oldtown Fireside Stories*, originally published in the *Atlantic Monthly*. Reading tour in New England.

1873        Publishes *Palmetto-Leaves*, sketches of Florida. Reading tour in the

West. Buys Forest Street house in Hartford, where she and Calvin will live the rest of their days.

1874 Publishes *Woman in Sacred History*.

1875 Publishes *We and Our Neighbors; or, The Records of an Unfashionable Street*, the third of her New York novels.

1876 Publishes *Betty's Bright Idea*. Also, *Deacon Pitkin's Farm*, and *The First Christmas of New England*.

1877 Publishes *Footsteps of the Master*.

1879 Publishes *Poganuc People: Their Loves and Lives*, fictionalized reminiscences of growing up in Litchfield.

1884 Publishes *A Dog's Mission; or, The Story of the Old Avery House, and Other Stories*.

1886 Calvin Stowe dies on August 6.

1887 Georgianna May Stowe dies.

1889 Suffers major decline in health.

1896 Dies on July 1 in Hartford.

# The Oxford
# Harriet
# Beecher
# Stowe
## Reader

# Introduction

Harriet Beecher Stowe had a profound effect on nineteenth-century culture and politics, not because her ideas were original, but because they were common. Somewhat paradoxically, she remains one of the most controversial writers America has produced. What makes Stowe so radical is that she insisted upon putting her ideas into action. As Jane Tompkins has written about *Uncle Tom's Cabin*, "Stowe's very conservatism—her reliance on established patterns of living and traditional beliefs—is precisely what gives her novel its revolutionary potential."[1]

Whether describing a trip by canal boat, the lawful brutalities of slavery, or the arrangements of a parlor, Stowe elevated the ordinary. Journalist, pamphleteer, novelist, preacher, domestic advice-giver, Stowe aimed to reach the broad mass of mothers, fathers, brothers, and sisters who read. She spoke for motherhood and the flag and apple pie, but she made her readers uncomfortable eating that pie unless others were eating it too. She used the written word as a vehicle for religious, social, and political purposes—often mixing these with entertainment. Had she been a theologian or philosopher—occupations effectively denied her because of her sex—she would have poured her ideas into different molds. As it is, she often clothed her ideas in narrative form.

The object of this reader is to present a sampling of Stowe's literary production suggesting her range, rhetorical strategies, and cultural designs on the world. Selected with an eye to what will be useful in the classroom, the readings are divided into three categories: Early Sketches, Antislavery Writings, and Domestic Culture and Politics. There is inevitably some overlap among these categories. Early Sketches include the best work of her literary apprenticeship, pieces that chart important future directions. In Antislavery Writings, *Uncle Tom's Cabin* is included entire. Its brilliance and popularity have overshadowed the considerable body of antislavery writing Stowe produced. The section on Antislavery Writings restores *Uncle Tom's Cabin* to that body, and includes a generous selection from *A Key to Uncle Tom's Cabin*, a companion volume to her novel. The section on Domestic Culture and Politics attempts to represent the range of her thinking on the Victorian home, for which she was a major propagandist. Both the complexity and political nature of this writing are suggested by the inclusion here of "The True Story of Lady Byron's Life." Stowe's expose of male debauchery and incest at the heart of the nineteenth-century home illustrates her willingness to take on the most challenging of social and political issues of her time.

❦ ❦ ❦

Harriet Beecher was born in Litchfield, Connecticut, on June 14, 1811, the seventh child of Lyman Beecher and Roxana Foote Beecher. One of the most famous clergymen of the early nineteenth century, Lyman Beecher was determined to have a role in shaping the culture of the new nation and was a powerful model for his children, most of whom had distinguished public careers as reformers, educators, and preachers. At a time when religion and politics were closely intertwined, all of Stowe's brothers became ministers. Early recognizing the genius of his daughter, Lyman Beecher remarked that he would give $100 if Harriet were a boy and Henry Ward a girl.[2]

Stowe's mother was Roxana Foote of Guilford, Connecticut, who embodied what the nineteenth century thought of as "True Womanhood." She was as private and retiring as her husband was public and commanding. After bearing nine children, she died at the age of forty-one of tuberculosis—not an unusual reward for the true woman of her time. Desiring the approbation of her famous father and yet loyal to the image of her perfectly self-denying and domestic mother, Stowe negotiated the boundary between the private and the public spheres through the act of writing. A woman picking up her pen in the privacy of the parlor did not depart from woman's conventional social role; yet when parlor writing was published, it reached a wide public and had the power to change the course of history.

Stowe was prepared for her career by an education which, in its rigor and classical depth, may be compared to that of her contemporary, Margaret Fuller. Like Fuller, Stowe studied Latin and was a precocious student. Both were drawn as young women to Madame de Stael's *Corinne*—a romantic antidote to their highly disciplined intellectual lives. But unlike Fuller, whose education took place at home under the instruction of her intensely demanding father, Stowe had the benefit of the moral and social atmosphere of two of the finest female seminaries in the nation.

At Sarah Pierce's Litchfield Female Academy, located one block from the Beecher parsonage, Harriet Beecher rubbed shoulders with girls from all over the United States, Canada, and the West Indies, thus obtaining a national experience rare for the time. Entering at age eight, she received an education roughly equivalent to that of a young man. Although Sarah Pierce taught music, dancing, singing, and embroidery—the "ornamental" subjects demanded by parents who were concerned that their daughters be marriageable—she also provided unusually thorough training in ancient and modern history and geography. With the addition to the staff of her nephew, John P. Brace, the curriculum was expanded to include chemistry, astronomy, botany, Latin, and moral philosophy. A typical course of study in Harriet Beecher's day was "Morse's Geography, Webster's Elements of English Grammar, Miss Pierce's History, Arithmetic through Interest, Blair's Lectures, Modern Europe, Ramsey's American Revolution, Natural Philosophy, Chemistry, Paley's Moral Philosophy, Hedge's Logic and Addison [i.e., Allison] on Taste."[3] Sarah Pierce's educational goal was to teach the art of thinking, her larger purpose, to "vindicate the equality of female intellect."[4] While she preached feminine modesty and prepared her students to embrace a conventional social role, her school was organized around a military model that stressed competition and prizes.[5]

Stowe recalled particularly the excitement generated by John Brace, whose methods of teaching composition she later imitated as a teacher at the Hartford Female Seminary. Before asking his students to write on a subject, Brace first led lively discussions that brought various points of view to the fore. Reduced to its elements, his method was to convince students they had something to say before they took up their pens. Harriet Beecher was an eager writer in what Brace called this "literary loving school."[6] Her first assignment was an essay on "The Difference between the Natural and Moral Sublime"—a topic, Stowe noted, "not trashy or sentimental, such as are often supposed to be the style for female schools." At age nine she volunteered to write weekly essays; at age thirteen she won the honor of having her composition read aloud at the annual school exhibit, where it made her father sit up and ask who the author was. When the answer came, "Your daughter, sir," Stowe experienced what she later called "the proudest moment of my life."[7]

That year, 1824, Harriet Beecher left Litchfield for Hartford, where she would stay until 1832, first as a student and then a teacher at the school founded by her sister. Under Catharine Beecher's leadership, the Hartford Female Seminary became a testing ground for women's "moral influence." It provided Harriet Beecher's first lectern and pulpit, an opportunity to test her power to influence others. In this women's culture Harriet Beecher tentatively tried out her vocations of teacher, preacher, and writer.

## Early Essays and Sketches

At age fourteen Stowe became the editor of the Hartford Female Seminary school newspaper and three years later produced for it a remarkably mature satire, "Modern Uses of Language." Taking as her target the abstruse language of philosophical tracts and school texts in use at the Hartford Female Seminary, she presented the "modern" approach to language: "1st. to conceal ideas. 2d. To conceal the *want* of them" (23). After referring to examples her students would recognize, she pungently analyzed the politics of this convoluted use of the English language: "Some ignorant persons may, perhaps, wonder what is the object of wrapping up ideas in obscure and mystical language; but, is it not perfectly evident that there is a need of a constant succession of great men? a need that they should write? and, that they should have something to write about?" (24). Murky language provides the great men opportunity to engage in clarifications, rejoinders, and discoveries of commonalities that would have been self-evident were they expressed in plain English. It also disciplines the common reader: "This use of language . . . serves to convince common-sense people of their own insufficiency and ignorance. . . . Did you ever read 'Coleridge's Aids to Reflection?' if you have, you must have *reflected* something in this strain. 'What an insignificant insect I am! I thought I could read the English language, but I was mistaken! Not one word of all this great book can I understand! What a great mind the man must have to say things so incomprehensibly!'" (25).

This youthful essay displays an intellectual courage and confidence that would carry its author into turbulent waters at one of the most sectarian and contentious periods in American history. Stowe imbibed a goodly portion of the Beecher family scrappiness, but unlike her father, who expended his prodigious energies in intricate theological debates and heresy trials, Stowe stayed attuned to popular opinion and cultivated a plain style of speech that was widely accessible.

In 1832 Lyman Beecher moved his family from New England to Cincinnati, Ohio, where he hoped to "save the West" from the increasing numbers of Roman Catholics and infidels who were settling in the Mississippi Valley and threatening Beecher's vision of a Protestant evangelical commonwealth. Twenty-one-year-old Harriet Beecher approached the West in a more tolerant and open spirit. While her father campaigned to wipe out the cultural diversity of the Mississippi Valley, she observed new customs, listened to the international accents spoken at the Cincinnati landing, and began writing sketches and stories stimulated by her new surroundings. The West was the cradle of her career. Her discovery of the West was also a discovery of New England, for she could not appreciate the uniqueness of her birthplace until she left it.

Her first stories were written for the Semi-Colon Club, a distinguished and well-informed group of Cincinnati's leading citizens. The Semi-Colons met regularly on Monday evenings for dancing, socializing, courting, and the reading aloud of specially prepared stories, poems, and reminiscences. The pieces Stowe wrote for these gatherings were often nostalgic and humorous sketches of New England life and characters, like "The Old Meeting-House," (36) from which would later grow her New England novels. From her vantage point in the West, Stowe could discern the outlines of regional types. She began capturing distinctive voices and dialects in stories such as "Uncle Enoch," a temperance tale (26). "The Canal-Boat," found among the Semi-Colon Club's papers, suggests the combination of entertainment and description that characterized these domestic literary productions. Stowe's amusing sketch of this new form of national transportation not only helped the Semi-Colons to pass an enjoyable evening together; it educated the unschooled as to what to expect when they stepped foot into one of these human sardine cans. Her delight in colloquial speech is illustrated by her summary comment on the discomforts of the travelers: "Truly, as Sam Slick says, 'there's a *sight of wear* in human natur'" (43). Her Western voice clearly emerges here, just as surely as Sam Clemens's would a generation later. Stowe's ability to hear and translate local accents to a national audience was the first step toward creating a national literature.

## Antislavery Writings

Given her prominent role in the slavery controversy, it is striking that up until the time she wrote *Uncle Tom's Cabin* Stowe was not active in antislavery—unlike, for example, her brother Edward, who had been with Elijah Lovejoy when he had been murdered defending his abolitionist newspaper in Alton, Illinois, or like her sister Catharine, who wrote an *Essay on Slavery and Abolitionism with Reference to the Duty of American Females* (1837). As these examples suggest, Stowe was exposed to the controversy by virtue of being a Beecher. In 1834 her father was caught in a crossfire of public opinion when the students at Lane Seminary, where he was president, held the famous Lane Debates. For eighteen days they debated the best way to end slavery, first listening to arguments for colonization, then for "immediate abolition." The colonizationists advocated sending the slaves back to Africa; until such arrangements could be put in place, the institution of slavery should be tolerated. The students voted overwhelmingly for the more radical position of immediate abolition, and Theodore Weld led a walkout of the student body to Oberlin, whose president, Charles Grandison Finney, took a more clear-cut position on the slavery issue than his rival evangelist, Lyman Beecher.

Harriet Beecher was drawn into the controversy in 1836, the summer after she married Calvin Stowe, a biblical scholar who taught at Lane Seminary. That summer the office in Cincinnati where James G. Birney printed his abolitionist paper, *The Philanthropist*, was broken into and his press damaged. When Birney refused to cease publication, some of Cincinnati's most distinguished citizens conspired to form a mob against him. During this period the regular editor of the *Cincinnati Journal and Luminary* was out of town and Stowe's brother Henry Ward Beecher was editor pro tem. Using the pseudonym "Franklin," Stowe wrote a letter to the editor meant to provide her brother the opportunity to make some remarks on the subject (49). Like the Lane Debates, this was at heart a free speech issue, and Stowe threw her energies into defense of that American constitutional right. This letter and the story "Uncle Sam's Emancipation" (52), published nine years later, are among the few writings before *Uncle Tom's Cabin* to touch on the issue of slavery. Both make prominent use of dialogue to carry her points; dramatizing different points of view in different characters would remain a staple of her writing. What is most striking about both "Franklin" and "Uncle Sam's Emancipation" is Stowe's calm appeal to logic and reason. In *Uncle Tom's Cabin* she would not abandon these, but she combined them with a powerful emotional appeal rooted in her experience as a mother who had lost a child.

The birth of twins in 1836 plunged Stowe into a busy but by all accounts happy domesticity. By employing the help of several immigrant "girls" whose labor could be had for barely more than their board, Stowe managed to keep on writing. Her stories and sketches appeared in the *Western Monthly Magazine*, the *New-York Evangelist*, and *Godey's Lady's Book*. In 1843 Harper and Brothers brought out a collection of her work entitled *The Mayflower*. Buoyed by this recognition, Stowe wrote to her husband, "On the whole, my dear, if I choose to be a literary lady, I have, I think, as good a chance of making profit by it as any one I know of."[8] Calvin Stowe's response was less equivocal than Harriet's, and typical of the support he offered her in their marriage of fifty years. To the woman who had been signing her stories "Mrs. H. E. Beecher Stowe" he wrote,

You must be a *literary woman*. It is so written in the book of fate. Make all your calculations accordingly. Get a good stock of health and brush up your mind. Drop the

E out of your name. It only encumbers it and stops the flow and euphony, and write yourself only and always, *Harriet Beecher Stowe*, which is a name euphonous, flowing, and full of meaning; and my word for it, your husband will lift up his head in the gate, and your children will rise up and call you blessed.[9]

The intellectual companionship the Stowes enjoyed was tested and stretched thin in the following decade by the stresses of poverty, ill health, frequent childbearing, and attempts to limit their family size through sexual abstinence.

In the summer of 1849 Stowe's sixth child, Samuel Charles, died in a cholera epidemic in Cincinnati. With the death of eighteen-month-old "Charley," Stowe experienced one of the most common and profound events of nineteenth-century family life. At a time when childhood diseases such as whooping cough regularly claimed young lives, most families had lost at least one child. Stowe responded to the loss of her baby by transforming her grief into an engine of prophecy and redemption. "There were circumstances about his death of such peculiar bitterness," she later wrote to Eliza Cabot Follen, "of what might seem almost cruel suffering, that I felt that I could never be consoled for it, unless it should appear that this crushing of my own heart might enable me to work out some great good to others . . ." (71). By focusing in *Uncle Tom's Cabin* on the separation of children from parents, Stowe tapped the overwrought feelings of white, middle-class parents and enlisted their sympathies for slave parents through the powerful metaphors of an evangelical religion shaped by both loss and bondage. "It was at *his* dying bed and at *his* grave," she wrote of Charley, "that I learnt what a poor slave mother may feel when her child is torn away from her" (71).

The passage of the Fugitive Slave Law the following year implicated the North in just such family separations. Called by Theodore Parker the Government Kidnapping Act, the Fugitive Slave Law commanded citizens "to aid and assist in the prompt and efficient execution of this law, whenever their services may be required." Under section seven, persons who gave shelter, food, or assistance to an escaping slave were liable to a fine of one thousand dollars and six months in prison. The Fugitive Slave Law effectively abrogated individual rights such as habeas corpus and the right of trial by jury and provided what abolitionists called bribes to commissioners by awarding them ten dollars for every alleged fugitive they remanded to slavery, but only five dollars for every one they determined to be free.[10]

The letters Stowe wrote during this period to her brother and sisters show her increasing anger and frustration at the indifference with which the majority of public opinion met each new incident of forcible reenslavement of fugitives. She was particularly infuriated by the mealymouthed responses of Christian ministers. Must they "make it a moment to be exceedingly cool!" she burst out to her brother Henry. "I feel as if my heart would burn itself out in grief and shame that such things are." She longed to "do something even the humblest in this cause" (64). When she found her way, she would paint graphic pictures that brought the sufferings of individual bondmen and bondwomen into the parlors of white America. When she finished with her readers, many would be weeping, and none would be cool.

As it happens, Stowe had just received one hundred dollars from Gamaliel Bailey, editor of the *National Era*, with a note urging her to continue supplying his magazine with material.[11] Bailey had a long association with antislavery, having taken over the editorship of the *Philanthropist* in 1838 when James G. Birney gave it up. Since removing to Brunswick, Maine, where Calvin Stowe had taken a professorship at Bowdoin College, Stowe had published four pieces in his paper, including, on August 1, 1850, a response to the Fugitive Slave Law (57). On March 9, 1851 Stowe wrote to Bailey that she had embarked on

> a series of sketches which give the lights and shadows of the "patriarchal institution", written either from observation, incidents which have occurred in the sphere of my personal knowledge, or in the knowledge of my friends. I shall show the *best side* of the thing, and something *faintly approaching the worst.*

Whether she was defending free speech or approaching the truly dangerous issue of slavery, Stowe was always attuned to the best ways to persuade an audience; now she proposed to Bailey a bold use of narrative—of "pictures"—for rhetorical purposes. "There is no arguing with *pictures*, and everybody is impressed by them, whether they mean to be or not." She knew this story would be "a much longer one than any I have ever written," and warned Bailey that it might "extend through three or four numbers" (66). In fact, *Uncle Tom's Cabin* would run weekly in the *National Era* for nearly a year, from June 5, 1851 to April 1, 1852, with Stowe writing sometimes just ahead of printers' deadlines.

The July 10, 1851 edition of the *National Era* carried the most memorable episode of *Uncle Tom's Cabin*. Eliza's crossing of the Ohio River with the slave catchers in close pursuit of her little Harry takes just two paragraphs to recount, yet it came for many to symbolize the movement of the entire liberation epic. When the novel was put on stage, a hush fell on the audience at the National Theatre in New York as Eliza escaped from her pursuers and reached the northern side of the river. An observer who turned to look was astonished to see that the entire audience, from the gentlemen and ladies in the balconies to the rough-shirted men in the galleries, was in tears.[12] Stowe knew that if she could evoke this response on behalf of "property," if she could bring her readers to see the heroism of a slave, she had begun a revolution in sentiment. Many things about this scene were tailored for her white audience: Eliza is so light-skinned she can pass for white (like many slaves who in fact escaped; see the attention to skin color in the ads for runaway slaves in *A Key to Uncle Tom's Cabin* (444). Like a true woman, Eliza runs away not because she desires freedom for herself, but to save her child. But the very ambiguity of her skin tone and Stowe's inclusion of a black woman in the cult of true womanhood worked to break down the racial categories that contained moral feeling.

*Uncle Tom's Cabin* had a huge following and sold over 300,000 copies in this country during the first year after it was published in book form by J. P. Jewett in 1852. The impact of *Uncle Tom's Cabin* on the conscience of the nation, already tender from the outrages of the Fugitive Slave Law, was such that when Stowe came to the White House in 1862, Abraham Lincoln is said to have greeted her with the words, "So you're the little woman who wrote the book that started this great war."

The effect of *Uncle Tom's Cabin* on American literature was, to foreign observers, equally striking. In a public meeting held in Stowe's honor in Scotland, one of the testimonial speakers credited Stowe with having revolutionized the British view of American literature:

> We have long been accustomed to despise American literature—I mean as compared with our own. I have heard eminent *litterateurs* say, "Pshaw! the Americans have no national literature." It was thought that they lived entirely on plunder—the plunder of poor slaves, and of poor British authors. [Loud cheers.] Their own works, when they came among us, were treated either with contempt or with patronizing wonder— yes, the "Sketch Book" was a very good book to be an American's. To parody two lines of Pope, we
>
> > "Admired such wisdom in a Yankee shape,
> > And showed an Irving as they show an ape."
>
> [Loud cheers.] . . . Let us hear no more of the poverty of American brains, or the barrenness of American literature. Had it produced only Uncle Tom's Cabin, it had evaded contempt just as certainly as Don Quixote, had there been no other product of the Spanish mind, would have rendered it forever illustrious.[13]

In a similar vein, Charles Kingsley called the book "a really healthy indigenous growth, autochthonous, & free from all that hapless second & third-hand Germanism, & Italianism, & all other unreal-isms which make me sigh over almost every American book I open." Kingsley quoted a critic who found *Uncle Tom* "the greatest novel ever written," reminiscent "in a lower sphere" of Shakespeare "in that marvellous clearness of insight and outsight, which makes it seemingly impossible for her to see any one of her characters without shewing him or her at once as a distinct individual man or woman, different from all others."[14] The British saw that the originality of the book sprang from Stowe's grasp of the nationality of her material: an epic theme—republican ideals in conflict with a feudal institution—was enshrined in a narrative bristling with regional types.

Writing after a century of neglect in which Stowe's national reputation had been eclipsed, Ellen Moers observed:

> We have forgotten that *Uncle Tom's Cabin* won its vast public here and abroad not only for its slavery matter, but also for its dedication to the American Real, its priceless evocation of the national character and daily ways. We have forgotten that the first time the phrase "The Great American Novel" was used, *Uncle Tom's Cabin* appeared to its inventor, John William DeForest, to have been the only pretender to the title, because of its "national breadth." Writing in *The Nation*, in 1868, DeForest said Mrs. Stowe's antebellum novel was the "single tale which paints American life so broadly, truly, and sympathetically that every American of feeling and culture is forced to acknowledge the picture as a likeness of something which he knows."[15]

Stowe's success in creating the American Real has made her novel the touchstone of racial politics. The immediate response was "Anti-Tom" counterpropaganda, such as the proslavery *Aunt Phyllis's Cabin; or, Southern Life As It Is*, by Mary H. Eastman. When emancipation made slavery a moot issue, the racial politics of *Uncle Tom's Cabin* continued around the issue of Stowe's characterizations of black people. Her success in imprinting Tom and Topsy and Eliza and George Harris on the national imagination made *Uncle Tom's Cabin*, in Richard Yarborough's words, "the epicenter of a massive cultural phenomenon, the tremors of which still affect the relationship between blacks and whites in the United States." As he remarks, the "extraordinary synthesizing power" of *Uncle Tom's Cabin* quickly elevated its black characters "to the status of literary paradigms and even cultural archetypes with which subsequent writers—black and white—have had to reckon."[16]

Stowe's intention to study "the negro character" (66) was probably in her mind an undertaking similar to her shrewd sketches of regional types. It is true, as she told Bailey, that she had "had ample opportunities for studying" African Americans; she did not consider, however, that her evidence was garnered mainly in domestic settings in which her position as white mistress to black servants (many of them former slaves) radically compromised her perceptions. In *Uncle Tom's Cabin* her generalizations about African Americans repeatedly assume their childlike dependence—a posture or "mask" that could be accounted for by the economic and psychological exigencies of the mistress–servant relationship. "You see how this subject has laid hold of me," she wrote to her brother Henry,

> but I have known a great many slaves—had them in my family known their history & feelings and seen how alike their heart beats to any other throbbing heart & above all what woman deepest feels I have seen the strength of their instinctive and domestic attachments in which *as a race* they excel the anglo saxon. The poor slave on whom the burden of domestic bereavement falls heaviest is precisely the creature of all Gods creatures that feels it deepest. [65]

Stowe's attribution of deeper feeling to African Americans "as a race" was consistent with what George Fredrickson has called "romantic racialism," a blend of philanthropic and paternalistic attitudes. One of the earliest formulators of this ideology was Alexander Kinmont, who, in his 1837–1838 lectures in Cincinnati, proclaimed the moral superiority of African Americans: "All the sweeter graces of the Christian religion appear almost too tropical and tender plants to grow in the Caucasian mind; they require a character of human nature which you can see in the rude lineaments of the Ethiopian." It is highly likely that Harriet Beecher Stowe, living in Cincinnati at the time Kinmont delivered his lectures, was exposed to his ideas. Such romantic racialism was widespread by 1851.[17] The complexity and contradiction of Stowe's novel lie in her use of a common theory of racial difference to effect a revolution in sentiment about the institution of slavery.

While many African Americans then and now have complained that Stowe made her hero, Tom, too good to be true, the South complained about her highly colored picture of slavery, and a Presbyterian clergyman threatened to sue her for quoting him by name as endorsing proslavery sentiments (67). Stowe responded to this array of complaints in characteristic fashion: she wrote another book. In *A Key to Uncle Tom's Cabin*, whose subtitle promised to *[Present] the Original Facts and Documents Upon which the Story is Founded, Together with Corroborative*

*Statements Verifying the Truth of the Work*, Stowe acknowledged that her fiction was being judged not as a work of art but as fact. Stowe disarmed her critics by admitting that her work fell short of the truth—but for the reason "that slavery, in some of its workings, is too dreadful for the purposes of art. A work which should represent it strictly as it is would be a work which could not be read" (412). In her novel Stowe spares her readers the details of Legree's torture of Tom, who refuses to reveal Cassy and Emmeline's path of escape; in *A Key to Uncle Tom's Cabin* Stowe cites instances of torture by whipping, fire, and the pouring of hot pepper pods over fresh wounds.

Parts of *A Key to Uncle Tom's Cabin* originated in her dispute with the Rev. Joel Parker, whom she quoted in Chapter XII, "Select Incident of Lawful Trade." In the passage to which he objected, Tom witnesses a slave auction:

> Tom had watched the whole transaction from first to last, and had a perfect understanding of its results. To him, it looked like something unutterably horrible and cruel, because, poor, ignorant black soul! he had not learned to generalize, and to take enlarged views. If he had only been instructed by certain ministers of Christianity, he might have thought better of it, and seen in it an every-day incident of a lawful trade; a trade which is the vital support of an institution which an American divine tells us has *"no evils but such as are inseparable from any other relations in social and domestic life."* [175]

A footnote attributed this quotation to Dr. Joel Parker of Philadelphia. "After painting a scene of shocking inhumanity," Parker complained to her, "you hold me up to the public, in an odious light, by representing me as uttering sentiments that seem to justify or, at least to palliate the cruelties which you have described."[18] Since Stowe was quoting from a newspaper account in which Parker had been quoted to this effect—without producing any challenge from him—she thought his indignation odd. In her reply she reminded him of this and said that if she had taken his sentiments to be proslavery, the reading public had doubtless formed a similar view and it was to them that he owed an explanation. "In the chapter in which your remark occurs I considered myself as the advocate of the poor & uneducated against the educated & the powerful," she told him, articulating a stance that was increasingly to take her into anticlerical positions.[19]

What Parker had actually said in the *Christian Observer* of December 25, 1846, was: "What then are the evils inseparable from slavery? There is not one that is not equally inseparable from depraved human nature in other lawful relations."[20] Although the words were different, the sentiment of this syntactically treacherous sentence was the one Harriet had attributed to Parker: hold the double negatives still, and slavery is equated with other legal institutions, such as marriage. Stowe's insistence on holding this minister accountable for his slippery language is of a piece with her satire on the "great men" in her youthful "Modern Uses of Language." When Parker challenged her to prove her statement that the proslavery views she quoted were a concise digest of the position of many American Protestant churches, she gleefully complied, enlisting her ministerial brothers as research assistants. When Parker and the proslavery *New York Observer* failed to live up to their bargain to publish these materials, Stowe showcased the proslavery pronouncements of synods and annual conferences of churches in Part IV of *A Key to Uncle Tom's Cabin*.

*A Key to Uncle Tom's Cabin* also puts before the reader in shocking detail the legal status of the slave and the abuses to which this led in specific cases. "I must confess, that, until I commenced the examination necessary to write this," she told Eliza Cabot Follen, "much as I thought I knew before, I had not *begun* to measure the depth of the abyss." She was particularly affected by reading the legal cases. "The laws, records of courts, & judicial proceedings are so incredible, as to actually make me doubt the evidence of my own eyesight" (75).

Stowe's critics had pounced on Legree's murder of his own slave as a totally unrealistic event; it was a crime expressly forbidden by slave law, as decided in *Souther v. the Commonwealth*. In Part II of the *Key* Stowe responded by presenting case after case of slave justice, including *Souther v. the Commonwealth* (429), the details of which were more graphic than anything she had put in her book, confirming, as she told a correspondent, that "if my representations have erred anywhere, it is by being under rather than overcolored."[21]

In the meantime, Uncle Tom leapt from the pages of Stowe's novel onto the boards of the theater almost as soon as it was published. Even relatively mild versions, such as George Aiken's script, featured white actors in black face. *Uncle Tom's Cabin* ran continuously for ninety years, making it the longest running play in American history. As enterprising promoters of the play attempted to distinguish their productions from others, they adopted more sensational and circus-like features. If one Topsy was good, two were better. The doubling of characters, the introduction of live bloodhounds, and the pandering to racist sensibilities moved the play closer to the minstrel tradition upon which it was grafted. Stowe had no control over these productions, yet they shaped views of her novel for many twentieth-century spectators.

What Stowe did have a considerable role in shaping was her own public image. She was careful to do nothing that would set her apart, in word or deed, from her natural power base: the women. After the publication of *Uncle Tom's Cabin*, Stowe did much to cultivate an outward posture of true womanhood. One of the most polished examples of this retired and womanly species of self-promotion was the famous letter she wrote to Eliza Cabot Follen in response to her request for some information about the author of *Uncle Tom's Cabin* (71). This letter, copied and passed hand to hand among the British abolitionists, won the hearts of the women and assured them that Stowe was not carried away with her own importance.

Although the phenomenal success of *Uncle Tom's Cabin* made Stowe's voice the most powerful on behalf of the slave, by the canons of true womanhood she was prohibited from speaking in public. During her triumphal tour of the British Isles in 1853, she was met by huge crowds in city after city, but at the large soirees held in her honor she would sit in silence while her husband or brother made a speech. Denied both voice and vote, women in the British Isles collected over half a million signatures and attached them to an "Affectionate and Christian Address" (451) to their sisters in the United States of America urging upon them the duty, as wives, mothers, and sisters, of ending the abomination of slavery.

The following year the impending passage of the Kansas-Nebraska Act moved Stowe to political action. Stephen Douglas, the senator from Illinois, in an attempt to ensure that the transcontinental railroad would run through his state, introduced in January of 1854 a bill effectively repealing the Missouri Compromise of 1820. Those who had argued against appeasing the South with the Fugitive Slave Law now saw their worst fears confirmed: the slave power, emboldened by a sympathetic president, the self-interest of politicians like Douglas, and the craving of the country for more land, argued that the time had come to do away with the Compromise that had kept slavery out of all territories to the north of 36° 30'. In an attempt to defeat the bill, Stowe used money collected on her British tour to organize a petition campaign. She also published in the *Independent* an "Appeal to the Women of the Free States" (452). Clearly modeled on the example of the British women's "Affectionate and Christian Address" and published on the eve of the Senate vote on the Nebraska bill, Stowe's "Appeal" urged women to action: "Women of the free States! the question is not, shall we remonstrate with slavery on its own soil? but are we willing to receive slavery into the free States and territories of the Union?" She urged women to petition, to organize lectures, and to pray, citing the example of the British women's organization to outlaw the slave trade. "Seventy thousand families refused the use of sugar, as a testimony to their abhorrence of the manner in which it was produced" (454).

In spite of Stowe's "Appeal" and the inundation of Congress with petitions, including several Stowe helped organize, the Kansas-Nebraska Act passed on May 26, 1854. The bloody struggles that ensued were the first battles of the Civil War, as settlers in Kansas fought among themselves to determine whether the territory should be free or slave. Antislavery voices called for emigrants from the free states to settle in Kansas and declare it free soil. The "Emigrant Aid Society" was formed and sent settlers to establish antislavery communities, including a significant one in Lawrence, Kansas. But every time an election was held in Kansas, "Border Ruffians" poured in from Missouri and put proslavery men in power. Henry Ward Beecher's Plymouth Church sent boxes of Sharpe's rifles, known as "Beecher's Bibles," to help the antislavery settlers protect themselves from proslavery forces. The sectional warfare that prevailed in Kansas between 1854 and 1858 was most intense between December 1855 and September 1856—the period during which Harriet Beecher Stowe wrote her second antislavery novel: *Dred: A Tale of the Great Dismal Swamp*.[22]

The escalating violence of the 1850s led her to choose a hero very different from Uncle Tom: Dred is presented as the son of Denmark Vesey, the historical figure hanged in South Carolina in 1822 for fomenting rebellion among the slaves, allegedly through his work with the African Methodist church. Like Uncle Tom, Dred's identity is defined by religion; but Tom's New Testament Christian pacifism is replaced in *Dred* by a militant invocation of the Old Testament prophets who called for "a day of vengeance." The insurrectionary purpose to which the Bible was put in "secret meetings of conspirators" (467) bore out the worst fears of slaveowners who believed that liberating a slave's mind was the first step toward liberating his body. Dred compares himself to Moses among the Egyptians and imagines "that, like Moses, he was sent as a deliverer" (466). The Garrisonian nonresistance movement was plagued by the question, "Was the Negro who epit-omized the doctrine [of non-resistance] bereft of means to liberate himself?"[23] In this novel Stowe tentatively approached this question, imbued with a much stronger sense than *Uncle Tom's Cabin* conveyed of a slave culture of resistance. The generalizations about the African race that Stowe freely sprinkled through-out *Uncle Tom's Cabin* are, with a few exceptions, replaced in *Dred* by more par-ticular attention to African ancestry; Dred is part Mandingo, "one of the finest of African tribes, distinguished for intelligence, beauty of form, and an indomitable pride and energy of nature" (465). Stowe incorporates in her narrative long pas-sages from the printed reports of Denmark Vesey's conspiracy, including a de-scription of Gullah Jack, a coconspirator with enormous power over his fellow Africans by virtue of his sorcery and charms. The Denmark Vesey story assumes but inverts the story of the faithful Uncle Tom, for all the leaders of the conspir-acy, except Gullah Jack, enjoyed the "highest confidence" of their owners (465).

In addition to using fiction to dramatize the national crisis, beginning in 1853 Stowe was a columnist for the *Independent,* a religious, antislavery weekly, where she was usually featured on the front page. She continued her columns through the beginning of the Civil War, during which she was a strong advocate for im-mediate emancipation. In "What Is to Be Done With Them?" Stowe undertook to reason with whites who feared the aftermath of freedom. Appealing to this coun-try's experience with the pauper population of Europe, whom the Old World pre-dicted "would swamp our free institutions," Stowe asked, "what did we do with them? . . . We simply treated them as equal men and women—free to come and live, trade, work, buy, sell, in our land, as long as they behaved themselves, and liable if they did not behave to be imprisoned and punished like any of the rest of us" (470). Stowe's unequivocal endorsement of the equal rights tradition is con-sistent with similar rhetorical moves in *Uncle Tom's Cabin,* but in "What Is to Be Done With Them?" it is unalloyed with paternalism. In this essay Stowe also dis-avows colonization, a position she was criticized for taking in the "Concluding Remarks" to *Uncle Tom's Cabin.*

Stowe also joined her voice to those who were urging President Lincoln to act. In July of 1862, unbeknownst to the public, Lincoln met with his cabinet and proposed to free the slaves. His Emancipation Proclamation would be kept secret for several more months as he waited for a Union victory before unveiling it. In the meantime, pressure mounted to push the president in this direction. On August 20, 1862, Horace Greeley's "The Prayer of Twenty Millions" editorial in the influential New York *Tribune* urged emancipation.[24] Lincoln held fast. He re-sponded to Greeley's editorial by announcing

> My paramount object in this struggle *is* to save the Union, and is *not* either to save or destroy Slavery. If I could save the Union without freeing *any* slave, I would do it; . . . What I do about slavery and the colored race, I do because I believe it helps to save the Union; and what I forbear I forbear because I do *not* believe it would help to save the Union.

Stowe publicly challenged Lincoln on this famous utterance. In a passage that displays to advantage the anarchic impulse of her best social and political thought, she rewrote Lincoln's words to reflect the priorities of "the King of kings":

My paramount object in this struggle is to set at liberty them that are bruised, and *not* either to save or destroy the Union. What I do in favor of the Union, I do because it helps to free the oppressed; what I forbear, I forbear because it does not help to free the oppressed. I shall do less for the Union whenever it would hurt the cause of the slave, and more when I believe it would help the cause of the slave. [472]

## Domestic Culture and Politics

Like her view of racial difference, Stowe's view of woman's sphere was rooted in a popular ideology—that woman's place was in the home. Being a Beecher, she used that ideology in a national, political context—as Catharine Beecher had done in her *Treatise on Domestic Economy*, which was reprinted nearly every year from 1841 to 1856. When it was reprinted in enlarged form in 1869 under the title *The American Woman's Home* it bore the names of both Catharine Beecher and Harriet Beecher Stowe, but in fact Stowe had written only several chapters on home decoration. Stowe's writing on the home is more accurately and fully represented by the domestic columns she wrote for the *Atlantic Monthly*. Four of these columns compose the bulk of the section on Domestic Culture and Politics.

This domestic writing allowed Stowe to reach a wide audience of women for whom home and family were central concerns. As her classic letter to Sarah Buckingham Beecher demonstrates, Stowe knew in intimate detail the complexities of the white, middle-class woman's work (483). She was not, however, a particularly adept housekeeper. She was better at writing about domestic tranquillity than in bringing it about. Calvin Stowe was a neat and orderly man who wanted only a predictable household routine. He was most at peace when his wife was away. During these respites, Calvin would write glowingly of the order that descended: meals were on time and there was little in the way of broken crockery, nor was the house littered with "old shoes nor old bonnets, nor old petticoats nor cast off dresses, nor papers, nor books, nor letters taped here & there and every where."[25] Stowe admitted "the importance of system and order in a family," but urged on her husband the fact that both she and her "help," a young English woman, "labor under serious natural disadvantages on the subject." She observed, "It is not all that is necessary to feel the importance of order and system, but it requires a particular kind of talent to carry it through a family. Very much the same kind of talent, as Uncle Samuel said, which is necessary to make a good prime minister."[26]

Stowe was right that her talents did not lie in domestic management. The good home manager must keep her eyes and ears alert to the motions and doings of a dozen people and contrivances; she must know that that thumping noise means that the dog has gotten into the garbage pail; she must keep the calendars of husband, children, servants, and shopkeepers in her head; the coordination of such detail requires attention to many things at once. Harriet Beecher Stowe's nature was different. Calvin Stowe created a memorable portrait of her in one of his letters of domestic complaint:

When your mind is on any particular point, it is your nature to feel and act as if that were the only thing in the world; and you drive at it and make every thing bend to it, to the manifest injury of other interests. For instance, when you are intent on raising flowers, you are sure to visit them and inspect them very carefully every morning; but your kitchen could go for two or three days without any inspection at all, you would be quite ignorant of what there was in the house to be cooked, or the way in which the work was done.[27]

Stowe's kitchen probably more closely resembled Dinah's in *Uncle Tom's Cabin* than it did Rachel Halliday's. But like Horatio Alger, who dropped out of Harvard and then wrote stories of success, she had everything she needed: she knew intimately the desires and dreams and frustrations of her readers.

From her early story, "Trials of a Housekeeper" (479) to her columns of domestic advice in the *Atlantic Monthly* (488), Stowe's writings on the home and domesticity spoke to a burgeoning middle class uncertain how to manage the stresses of the emerging nuclear family and the increasing elaborateness of the Victorian home. Stowe's most significant elaboration of Victorian domesticity lay in the series she wrote for the *Atlantic Monthly* during and immediately after the Civil War. Her *House and Home Papers* in 1864 and *The Chimney-Corner* for 1865 and 1866 provided monthly advice columns on topics ranging from carpets to servants and domestic politics.

Stowe explicitly undertook the *House and Home Papers* to escape from the horror and death of the Civil War battlefield. She described them as "a sort of sprightly writing that I feel I need to write in these days to keep from thinking of things that make me dizzy & blind & fill my eyes with tears so that I cant see the paper." She told her editor, James Fields, "It is not wise that all our literature should run in a rut cut thro our hearts & red with our blood—I feel the need of a little gentle household merriment & talk of common things—to indulge which I have devised this."[28]

As is appropriate to a series written during this country's national struggle for survival, Stowe's ideology of the home is closely linked with her notions of American nationality. The American home, as Stowe elaborates it, becomes an occasion to celebrate American distinctiveness. This concept is like Catharine Beecher's belief in the importance of "the family state" to the American experiment, but whereas Catharine "saw social relations as a series of hierarchies" and repeatedly reminded her readers of "the duties of subordination,"[29] Stowe, while not free of class bias, made democratic individualism a touchstone. Whether she is advising on choosing household furnishings or the management of help, Stowe contrasts the class system of Europe with its elaborate domestic establishments to a doctrine of "the plain average" and a more realistic view of what is possible in a democratic country lacking a permanent class of servants. However, Stowe recognized that it was increasingly difficult to live simply and economically in the midst of the plethora of consumer goods being pumped into the market. The affluence that was threatening American ideals made it all the more imperative to shore them up.

Stowe chose to narrate these domestic talks in the voice of a man, "Christopher Crowfield," who writes papers in response to discussions with his wife and two daughters—a setting that mimics her own parlor apprenticeship. In her male persona, Stowe urged women to confine their heroism to the home. "We have heard much lately of the restricted sphere of woman," pontificates Christopher Crowfield in *House and Home Papers.*

> We have been told how many spirits among women are of a wider, stronger, more heroic mould than befits the mere routine of housekeeping. It may be true that there are many women far too great, too wise, too high, for mere housekeeping. But where is the woman in any way too great, or too high, or too wise, to spend herself in creating a home?

Reworking the ideology of Republican Motherhood to fit the Civil War, Crowfield continues, "From such homes go forth all heroisms, all inspirations, all great deeds. Such mothers and such homes have made the heroes and martyrs, faithful unto death, who have given their precious lives to us during these three years of our agony!" (493). In contrast to the conservatism of these sentiments, Christopher Crowfield opines that there is no reason "why a woman's vote in the state should not be received with as much respect as in the family" (498). The Civil War and Emancipation created one of the most radical moments in American history. As the nation "dedicated to the proposition that all men are created equal" battled to determine whether "any nation so conceived and so dedicated, can long endure," woman suffrage took on a new life; Stowe, ever attuned to the course of public opinion, moved with the times.

In contrast to her first year's columns, the "Chimney-Corner for 1865" examined not the ideology but the psychology of the home. These sketches are particularly sensitive to the jarring of temperaments that occurs within the home as people of very different disposition are thrown together in daily intercourse. Indeed, in their psychological realism they are much more revealing of the home than her idealization of that institution in her first set of papers. The voice of Christopher Crowfield is also less obtrusive; Stowe appears to forget for long stretches that he is the narrator and her own voice assumes its characteristic turns. She describes the home as "a place not only of strong affections, but of entire unreserves; it is life's undress rehearsal, its backroom, its dressing-room, from which we go forth to more careful and guarded intercourse, leaving behind us much *debris* of cast-off and every-day clothing."[30] Combining dialogue, vignette, and authorial comment, much as she would in her society novels of the 1870s, these columns fall somewhere in between journalism, domestic sermon, and fiction.

The combination of indirection and courage Stowe brought to women's issues led to what is surely one of the oddest documents in American literary history: her revelation, in the pages of the *Atlantic Monthly*, of "The True Story of Lady Byron's Life" (531). In a private interview four years before her death, Lady Byron revealed to Stowe the real reason for her separation from Lord Byron: before and during their marriage, Lord Byron had engaged in an incestuous affair with his half sister, Augusta Leigh. The publication of a one-sided memoir by Byron's mistress, Countess Guiccioli, prompted Stowe to reveal Lady Byron's secret.

When the press heaped a torrent of abuse upon Stowe for daring to speak publicly of incest, Stowe wrote a supporter, "Such a scoffing at Christs spirit in a professed Christian country I have not seen since I saw half the professed

Christians of America on their knees before the fugitive slave law."[31] She may have imagined that her defense of Lady Byron would be the *Uncle Tom's Cabin* of women's sexual slavery, but Stowe's politics were too inchoate and her platform too narrow for this to happen. Defending Lady Byron's reputation, Stowe herself was skewered on the contradictions inherent in the cult of true womanhood.

It is notoriously difficult to establish the truth in cases of sexual misconduct, because the only witnesses, as a rule, are the accuser and the accused. The credibility of each depends heavily on the credibility of their sex, for in a sexual crime, sexual stereotypes are often more powerful lenses than individual characters. Stowe's depiction of Lady Byron as an "angel," a type of the suffering Christ, suggests that she was seeing her as an idealization of Victorian womanhood, invested with all the power and nobility of that type. When skeptics asked why Lady Byron would stay with Lord Byron long after her discovery that her husband was regularly committing incest, Stowe responded that she did so out of concern for the state of Lord Byron's soul; she martyred herself in the hope of reclaiming him. To the *Nation*, this made Lady Byron ridiculous. Stowe responded, "What would Christ say to that? Did not Christ for three years bear daily contact with what he calls an evil and adulterous generation . . .?"[32] To claim that Lady Byron would have fled in horror from the crime is to expect, said Stowe, that she would act like a "common correct English wife," an expectation which "does no justice to her."[33] Stowe's elevation of Lady Byron above self-interest, moral outrage, and jealousy was of a piece with the Victorian strategy of "passionlessness," a strategy that increased nineteenth-century woman's power by insulating her from her husband's sexual demands.[34] But Stowe was inadvertently confirming the very portrait of Lady Byron she aimed to combat: that of the cold and aloof wife who drove her husband into the arms of others. From the point of view of the woman's movement, Stowe's strategy was also seriously flawed; she could not simultaneously hold up Lady Byron as a type of universal womanhood and yet make that womanhood dependent on her superiority to the common English wife. Stowe's maiden attempt at sexual speech was riven by deeply held class assumptions.

Yet it was precisely because Stowe articulated the contradictions of "the plain average" that her voice was so powerful. She reached a broad audience of middle-class Americans concerned about home and family and American values. By passionately espousing the ideal of democracy that supported this bourgeois culture, Stowe also gave voice to the radical promise on which this country was founded, and which a civil war was fought to realize. Although she is thought of as a sentimentalist, she was also a realist. Her insistence on describing the common and ordinary gave her a powerful arsenal of sentimental tools with which to raise the conscience of the nation to the everyday brutalities of slavery. With this same attention to the details of everyday life, to particular accents and local customs, she laid the planks of an American national literature.

## Notes

1. Jane Tompkins, "Sentimental Power: *Uncle Tom's Cabin* and the Politics of Literary History," in *Sensational Designs: The Cultural Work of American Fiction, 1790–1850* (New York: Oxford University Press, 1985), 145.

2. Lyman Beecher to George Foote, January 24, 1819, Foote Collection, Harriet Beecher Stowe Center Library (formerly Stowe-Day Memorial Library), Hartford, Conn. The biographical material in this introduction is adapted from Joan D. Hedrick, *Harriet Beecher Stowe: A Life* (New York: Oxford University Press, 1994).

3. Emily Noyes Vanderpoel, *More Chronicles of a Pioneer School: From 1792 to 1833* (New York: The Cadmus Book Shop, 1927), 9.

4. Mary Beth Norton, *Liberty's Daughters: The Revolutionary Experience of American Women, 1750–1800* (Boston and Toronto: Little, Brown & Company, 1980), 272.

5. Lynn Brickley, "Sarah Pierce's Litchfield Female Academy, 1792–1833," diss., Graduate School of Education, Harvard University, 1985, 576.

6. Brickley, "Litchfield Female Academy," 213.

7. *The Autobiography of Lyman Beecher*, 2 vols., ed. Barbara M. Cross (Cambridge, Mass.: Harvard University Press, 1961), 1:399.

8. Forrest Wilson, *Crusader in Crinoline: The Life of Harriet Beecher Stowe* (Philadelphia: J. B. Lippincott, 1941), 213.

9. Calvin Ellis Stowe to HBS, April 30, 1842, Acquisitions, Harriet Beecher Stowe Center Library, Hartford, Conn.

10. The text of the bill may be found in the *National Era*, October 3, 1850, pp. 160, 158.

11. HBS to Calvin Ellis Stowe, January 27 [1851], Acquisitions, Harriet Beecher Stowe Center Library, Hartford, Conn.

12. Thomas F. Gossett, *"Uncle Tom's Cabin" and American Culture* (Dallas: Southern Methodist University Press, 1985), 270.

13. HBS, *Sunny Memories of Foreign Lands* (Boston: Phillips, Sampson, and Company, 1854), 2 vols., 1:xxxviii.

14. Charles Kinglsey to HBS, August 12, 1852, folder 242, Beecher-Stowe Collection, Schlesinger Library, Cambridge, Mass.

15. Ellen Moers, *Harriet Beecher Stowe and American Literature* (Hartford, Conn.: Stowe-Day Foundation, 1978), 11.

16. Richard Yarborough, "Strategies of Black Characterization in *Uncle Tom's Cabin* and the Early Afro-American Novel," in Eric Sundquist, *New Essays on "Uncle Tom's Cabin"* (Cambridge: Cambridge University Press, 1986), 46, 47.

17. George M. Fredrickson, *The Black Image in the White Mind: The Debate on Afro-American Character and Destiny, 1817–1914* (New York: Harper & Row, Publishers, 1971), 97-129, especially 104-105 and 110. The quotation, from Kinmont's *Twelve Lectures on the Natural History of Man* (Cincinnati, 1839), is quoted by Fredrickson on p. 105.

18. Joel Parker to HBS, May 19, 1852, Beecher Family Papers, Sterling Memorial Library, Yale University.

19. HBS to Joel Parker, [May 1852], Beecher Family Papers, Sterling Memorial Library, Yale University.

20. "The Grounds of Offense in Uncle Tom's Cabin," by G., New York *Independent*, October 21, 1852, p. 171.

21. HBS to Lord Denman, January 20, 1853, Huntington Library, San Marino, California.

22. See Michael Fellman, "Rehearsal for the Civil War: Antislavery and Proslavery at the Fighting Point in Kansas, 1854–1856," in Lewis Perry and Michael Fellman, eds., *Antislavery Reconsidered: New Perspectives on the Abolitionists* (Baton Rouge and London: Louisiana State University Press, 1979), 287–307.

23. Lewis Perry, *Radical Abolitionism: Anarchy and the Government of God in Antislavery Thought* (Ithaca and London: Cornell University Press, 1973), 234.

24. Horace Greeley, "The Prayer of Twenty Millions," New York *Tribune*, August 20, 1861.

25. Calvin Ellis Stowe to HBS, October 6, 1856 and December 30, 1856, both in Acquisitions, Harriet Beecher Stowe Center Library.

26. HBS to Calvin Ellis Stowe, September 1846, in C. E. Stowe, *Life of Harriet Beecher Stowe, Compiled from her Letters and Journals* (Boston: Houghton, Mifflin and Co., 1889), 115.

27. Calvin Ellis Stowe to HBS, September 30, 1844, folder 61, Beecher-Stowe Collection, Schlesinger Library, Cambridge, Mass.

28. HBS to James T. Fields, October 12, 1863, University of Virginia Library; HBS to James Fields, October 27, [1863], Huntington Library, San Marino, California.

29. Jeanne Boydston, Mary Kelley, and Anne Margolis, *The Limits of Sisterhood: The Beecher Sisters on Women's Rights and Woman's Sphere* (Chapel Hill: The University of North Carolina Press, 1988), 19, 130.

30. Harriet Beecher Stowe, *Little Foxes* (Boston: J. R. Osgood, 1865), 9.

31. HBS to the Rev. R. Patton, September 10, 1869, Authors Collection, Smith College.

32. HBS to Dr. Patton, September 2, 1869, Acquisitions, Harriet Beecher Stowe Center Library, Hartford, Conn.

33. HBS to Henry Ward Beecher, n.d. [1869], Beecher Family Papers, Sterling Memorial Library, Yale University.

34. See Nancy F. Cott, "Passionlessness: An Interpretation of Victorian Sexual Ideology, 1790–1850," *Signs: Journal of Women in Culture and Society* 4(Winter 1978):219–236.

# PART 1

# Early Essays and Sketches

# Modern Uses of Language

"Modern Uses of Language" first appeared in the Hartford Female Seminary *Levee Gazette*, a handwritten magazine to which the seventeen-year-old "Miss Harriet Beecher" had just assumed editorship. Like many of the essays in the school newspaper, the tone of this precocious essay is satirical. Reflecting her experience with textbooks such as the opaque but much-used Joseph Butler's *Analogy of Religion*, Stowe's incisive critique of obscurantist language and the posturing of "great men" strikes a clear note that echoes throughout her career.

"Modern Uses of Language" was published in the *Western Monthly Magazine* in March 1833.

> Words, words, words!
> *Hamlet*

he use of words, in all antiquated dictionary and grammar books, is stated to be, *'to convey ideas.'* It is the fear that some of our readers, on such obsolete authority, should take up this very absurd notion, which leads us to discuss a subject, which might otherwise be deemed too abstruse.

Let it then be understood, that in these days of marvellous light, words are no longer used, as in ruder ages, to convey *ideas*. Examples of this antiquated manner of employing them are now so rare, that they can only be cited as exceptions to general practice. The wisdom of modern days has employed language for a much wider purpose and given it a twofold use.

1st. To *conceal* ideas. 2d. To conceal the *want* of them. Let every one who sits down to read a book, establish in his own mind the conviction, that if the author can help it, he is to know nothing of its meaning; since if there be ideas, it will be the object to conceal them; and if there be not, to conceal the want of them.

We shall offer a few remarks on both these usages, and specify some of the works which will illustrate them.

Let us first consider the use of language in *concealing ideas*. This mode of language has not been entirely peculiar to modern days. Occasional specimens of it have been found from the time of Egyptian hieroglyphics to this day. This method is generally employed in all philosophical, mathematical, metaphysical, and theological works; indeed, in all works where the subject is important, and people might be supposed to wish to know something about it. Philosophers have always seemed disposed to verify the declaration of scripture, 'we are the people, and wisdom shall die with us;' since it is no fault of theirs, if after they are dead, any one ever finds out what they mean. In illustration of this, we will request our readers to examine the chapters written by the celebrated Dugald Stewart on *Abstraction*, for the purpose of finding out the meaning of Nominalism and Conceptualism; or his chapters on the double meaning of analysis and synthesis, and if they find out his ideas, they will have much clearer heads than the writer could possibly have apprehended.[1]

Brown, too, though he in some cases has had the misfortune to state his ideas with pitiable clearness, has yet contrived by a judicious intermixture of flowers, figures, allusions, and quotations, to produce quite as philosophical a jumble as his less ornamented brother. On the whole, we think that if the secrets of the craft are ever made manifest, it will not be by means of either of these writers.

We might mention many other examples to illustrate this hieroglyphical use of language. We would, however, recommend to our readers, if they would *realize* the fact, to attempt an English version of Butler's Analogy; or to read the prose works of Milton, where they will find a comma once in two pages, and a full-stop once in ten. Or we would more especially recommend to them, a great proportion of schoolbooks, whose express object is to *convey knowledge*.

The rules in Daboll's Arithmetic are beautiful specimens. Any poor child who has been doomed to find out how to learn multiplication, by reading the *'preambulatory'* discourse which precedes it, has doubtless discovered a most judicious adaptation of words for concealing the sense.

Some ignorant persons may, perhaps, wonder what is the object of wrapping up ideas in obscure and mystical language; but, is it not perfectly evident that there is need of a constant succession of great men? a need that they should write? and, that they should have something to write about? Now, it is well known to all who have any thing to do with philosophical treatises, that their writers take up a great part of them, either in showing the mistakes into which the learned Dr. K——, or the elegant and ingenious Professor S——, or the celebrated Mr. Somebodyelse, have fallen, in consequence of misapprehension of language; or else in combating with astonishing intrepidity, opinions which nobody ever thought of advancing, because they have mistaken the meaning themselves. For example, Mr. Locke, or Bishop Berkeley, advance an opinion, harmless and rational enough, if it only were put into good English. But from some obscurity in the language, Dr. Reid discerns in it a manifest absurdity. Here is a fine opportunity for writing chapter on chapter, to hunt down this unlucky idea, till at last he kills it stone dead, in a 'reductio ad absurdum.' Mr. Stewart then comes and 'conceives, that Dr. Reid has so thoroughly disposed of it, that there is no need for *him* to say a word,' and then goes on to give us fifteen or twenty pages, on the same subject, as a sort of funeral requiem.

But after this solemn death and burial, lo!

---

[1]Dugald Stewart (1753–1828) was a student of Thomas Reid (1710–1796), a Scottish "common sense" philosopher who challenged the skepticism of Hume and Berkeley.

'John Barleycorn gets up again,
To sore surprise them all.'

For now, Brown appears to raise it from the dust, and stoutly to maintain that Locke, and Berkeley, and Reid, and Stewart, all held it, and thought just alike, *only*, they *did* misunderstand each other's language.

Now it is clear, that if men of great and acute minds, who must have understood the principles of the science, had been thoughtless enough to state them in precise language, a great part of the materials for profound speculation must have failed.

This use of language is also advantageous in a *moral* point of view; it promotes humility; it serves to convince common-sense people of their own insufficiency and ignorance. Great minds are humble by constitution. The weight of their own talent keeps them down. Little ones need ballast, and therefore, great ones give it. My dear friend, whoever you are, blessed only with *common sense*, and a tolerably comfortable opinion of your powers, have you never experienced this power of a great mind to utterly puzzle and confound you? Did you ever read 'Coleridge's Aids to Reflection?' if you have, you must have *reflected* something in this strain. 'What an insignificant insect I am! I thought I could read the English language, but I was mistaken! Not one word of all this great book can I understand! What a great mind the man must have to say things so incomprehensibly!'

We now proceed to illustrate the use of words in concealing the *want of ideas*.

We have many ingenious specimens of this style of writing in the newspaper and souvenir literature of the day, especially in the poetry. Some honest readers need to be admonished that many things written in our language mean absolutely *nothing*. They are a sort of glorious, bewildering, bewitching, covering of *vacuum*. Any one who will analyze this sort of production, will discern that the art of concealing the want of ideas has arrived at a desirable degree of perfection. There are certain cant phrases, technics of the art, and he who would be a poet, or a fine writer, has only to intersperse them with common words, at judicious distances, and he will attain thereunto. As examples we give the words, 'rich,' 'deep,' 'bright,' 'beautiful,' 'glorious.' We have 'beautiful thoughts,' 'rich, deep feelings;' 'rich, deep tones;' 'rich, rushing prayers,' and the like. Then we have 'glorious forms,' 'glorious souls,' 'glorious brows,' and 'glorious, flashing eyes.' We have, moreover, 'burning thoughts,' 'burning feelings,' 'burning tears,' and a variety of other conflagrations, indicating that the literary epidemic of the day is highly inflammatory.

Should any person be antiquated enough to wish to find some key for understanding language, as used in the two ways now illustrated, we recommend the following rules.

1st. Never to *expect sense*, in productions professedly nonsensical, such as modern elegant literature. Let him just allow the words to slide easily through his head, without agitating himself to ask what they mean, and he will find that he is, in general, most 'beautifully affected.'

2d. In philosophical treatises, and other works where one might expect to find ideas concealed, let him make up his mind what the author *ought to say*, and in nine cases out of ten, he can make all the words jingle along in the most accommodating way in the world.

3d. All obstinate phrases, that will not bear this mode of operating, let him pass over as a sort of philosophical chorus, like the word "*Selah*,' in the Psalms, which nobody understands.

4th. In a fashionable party, let him suppose, that all the noise he hears means nothing, of course; and regard it simply as the clatter of multitudes of talking machines.

'Vox, et præterea, *nihil!*'

'noise, and *nothing but* noise!'

If he will observe these rules, particularly the third, we can assure him he will find no difficulty in understanding the current literature of the time:

'Unto his eye
The midnight darkness will be broad noonday,'

and philosophy and poetry will alike appear to him to be what in truth they are, words.

B.

❦ ❦ ❦

# Uncle Enoch

One of several temperance tales Stowe wrote, "Uncle Enoch" is an early attempt to use fiction to advance a national reform. An excellent example of Stowe's skill in drawing colloquial types and sustaining a didactic story through dialogue, "Uncle Enoch" reflects Stowe's preoccupation with how best to persuade people of a new idea. Rather than preaching about the "national sin" of drunkenness, as her father did in his *Six Sermons on Intemperance* (1827), Stowe appeals primarily to physiology, practicality, logic, and Yankee self-improvement. Her tale is spiced with incisive realistic touches, such as the "medicinal" drinking of the women.

"Uncle Enoch" appeared in the *New-York Evangelist* on May 30, 1835.

ew people have passed many hours in Elliston without hearing, at least, of Uncle Enoch. Enoch Mullins was his original name, but the latter part had long since fallen into desuetude, and Enoch, with the affectionate prefix of Uncle, was the title by which he was universally known and addressed.

At the time that our history commenceth he was about fifty years of age—his form well proportioned, and his hair slightly sprinkled with grey. His countenance had the lines of intelligence common to the first class of New England farmers, and a benevolence so marked that it attracted the attention even of the casual observer.

Uncle Enoch's countenance was a true index of his soul. He was the patriarch of the place, universally reverenced and beloved, even by the immoral. Though his morality was of the strictest kind, yet it carried nothing of sourness or severity towards others. Though he was a reprover of sin, yet it was for the most part in secret, and with such kindness that the offender was commonly melted if not reformed.

Uncle Enoch lived directly opposite the meeting house in which he was a constant worshiper. No person in the congregation could remember the day on which his seat was vacant. When the second bell began to toll, he would lay aside his big Bible and take from the upper shelf in the closet his white beaver hat, and having given it a few careful strokes with a brush kept for the especial purpose, place it reverently on his head and proceed with great gravity to the meeting house, and wait in the vestibule till the minister came. Having given him a warm shake of the hand, he would leave him, to pursue his way up the broad aisle to the pulpit, himself taking the side one, though his pew joined the pulpit stairs. By this movement he thought he gave his minister due precedence, and arrived at his seat at the same time the minister gained the pulpit.

It was the custom of the bell-ringer to cease ringing as soon as the minister entered the meeting house. As the broad aisle was not so immediately within the scope of his vision as the side one, he used to look out for Uncle Enoch, and whenever he saw him moving up with measured steps and slow, to take it for granted that the minister had come: nor is it known that he ever erred in consequence of following this rule.

Uncle Enoch's wife, Tabitha, had been dead about twelve years, and the ancient maidens and bereaved spouses had long since come to the conclusion that he would never change his condition, though no declaration to this effect seems ever to have escaped him.

He had three unmarried daughters, the oldest of whom had not passed the age when certain inquiries are disagreeable, and answers apocryphal; and the youngest was but twelve. They were handsome, industrious, and benevolent, and were universally esteemed. Many a roguish young fellow walked the straiter, especially in the presence of Uncle Enoch, for their sakes.

In the afternoon of a pleasant Sabbath in October, 18—, the minister gave notice that the Rev. Mr. N.—— would preach in the evening on the subject of temperance.

This was a new thing under the sun, and occasioned some remarks. Elliston was a retired place, and the hue and cry raised by the temperance folks elsewhere had not disturbed its quiet. The retailer measured out his doses without reproof, and the drinkers followed one another to the grave without interruption, and the distillery daily sent up its black smoke to heaven, and none thought it other than a blessing.

"I wonder," said Dea. May's wife to her neighbor, Mrs. Brooks, as they walked home from meeting, "I wonder what the man would be about? He a going to preach about our tempers!" [It should be remarked that Mrs. May had been enjoying her usual nap during divine service, and was not fully awake when the notice respecting the evening sermon was given.] "What does he know about our tempers? I shouldn't be much afraid to say that he has'nt a good temper himself. They say the devil reproves sin."

"Aye," said a young buck on horseback who had heard her remarks, "and when he gets tired he sets Deacon May at it."

"Who be you, you wicked varmint, that dares talk saucy to me? If I had the handling of you, I would pretty soon fetch the tallow out of your hair."

By this time the graceless loon had passed beyond hearing, and the conversation which had been so unceremoniously interrupted was renewed.

"You did not exactly hear what Mr. Forbes said," remarked Mrs. Brooks, "he said the minister would preach on *temperance,* meaning I suppose about drunkards."

"Well, may be he did, but he might as well stay away, I guess. Won't you stop in and rest a bit?"

The invitation was accepted. As soon as Mrs. May had put by her things, she produced a bottle from the closet, and with the aid of some brown sugar and water, prepared a potion *to keep the wind out of their stomachs.* A little more was urged on Mrs. Brooks as she was about to go away, *to keep her from taking cold,* and Mrs. May also took some, not because she *really needed it,* but for company's sake. Mrs. B. thus effectually guarded against the cold of a pleasant October afternoon, arrived safely at home, and, as was not uncommon when she stopped at Mrs. May's, in a very cheerful frame of mind. Her heart was enlarged towards her husband and children, and the table was spread with a profusion of cakes and sweetmeats that had long reposed in secresy and darkness.

"Mr. Brooks, I wish you had been to meeting; such an excellent sermon as Mr. Forbes preached—I've not been so refreshed I don't know when."

"Not since the last time you stopped at mother May's," said Mr. Brooks. Mr. B. was a very worthy man, who had adopted the notion that religion consists only in justice and kindness to our fellow men, and that there is no obligation to attend on the public worship of God, or openly to profess obedience to him. "What was the sermon about?" continued he.

"Why I dont just remember all of it, but it was all very good, and there is going to be a meeting to-night, and Mr. Somebody from away off down east is going to preach on temperance."

"I think it is about time there was a sermon or something else on that subject."

"What makes you think so? There are a good many drunkards about the Still, and over in Ash-Hollow, but not many around here. There is only old Jenkins, and Friover, and Widow Clemson, and Sam Dingley, and—

"At least ten in this district where there are only eighteen families; two more than one half. I counted them up to-day," said Mr. Brooks.

"Well I dont think it very good business for Sunday, to be hunting up your neighbors' faults."

"I han't told you all, for of the eight that's left, four of them have more than once been seen the worse for liquor."

"There is Esq. Thome I know sometimes takes a little too much on election and training days, when there is so much treating going on among you men—but there is no danger Esq. Thome will ever be a drunkard. And Mr. James, when he gets tired of staying in the store all the time, takes a little to keep up his spirits, and sometimes takes enough to show it—but I ought not to find fault, for once I went to buy some tea, and he was so good natured and silly, that he gave me back more change than I gave him at first; and when I told him of it, he only laughed and said it was all right, and made me keep it; so that I got my tea for nothing, and nine-pence into the bargain. Mr. James is one of the nicest men in town, and I'll hear nobody say he drinks too much."

"He'll die a drunkard within five years," said her husband somewhat warmly.

"Hey-diddle-diddle, so I've got a prophet for a husband. Well, we read there shall be false prophets. You'd make out that every body is a drunkard, for every body in town drinks more or less. I reckon you will go and hear the man preach."

"I mean to get in about sermon time."

The time for evening service at length arrived. As it was a new thing, the house was well filled. The speaker was a man of sense, and resolved not to defeat his object by pushing it too fast. He dwelt on the evils of intemperance in a most powerful manner, and showed in general, its increase and its cost. There he rested his first appeal, but not however till his vivid picture had led the inquiry to arise in more than one mind, *What can be done?* Before he closed, he stated that, if the people desired it, he would speak on the subject again on Tuesday evening. As it seemed to be their desire, a meeting was accordingly appointed.

Among the first that raised the inquiry, *What can be done?* was Uncle Enoch. He had always been a temperate man, in the old sense of the word; he even went so far as to establish the rule that no man who once got drunk in his employ should ever be hired again. Still he used it occasionally himself, and furnished it to his hands, especially in haying time.

Uncle Enoch had seen the fearful progress of drunkenness since the erection of the distillery, but could think of no remedy; and had perhaps been led in consequence to turn off his mind from the subject. But when the evil was eloquently set forth, and urged on his attention, he could not but ask with a good deal of feeling, *What can be done?* Early on Monday morning, the Rev. Mr. N——— called at his house. Uncle Enoch soon got into the subject.

"You told us last night nothing but what we knew before, only you set it out rather better; but what good will it all do if we can't help it?"

"I don't see as it will do any good," said Mr. N———, wishing to lead Uncle Enoch on.

"If I see my house tumbling down, and it can't be helped, it isn't worth while to make a fuss about it. And so if we can't stop the flood of drunkenness, it isn't worth while to make a fuss: but if any thing *can* be done, it ought to be."

"Did you ever know any body to get drowned in the pond out yonder?" said Mr. N———, looking through the window towards the pond, as if it had just attracted his attention.

"Yes—two of neighbor Wright's boys, not long ago."

"How did it happen?"

"They went to play in the water, and got beyond their depth, and were drowned."

"If they had never gone near the pond they wouldn't have been drowned, would they?"

"Certainly not; but I want to talk on the subject you preached about."

"Oh, very well. You find the number of drunkards increasing in your town?"

"Yes, very fast."

"Ah, how does that happen?"

"Why they get whisky so easy and so cheap that they take more and more, till at last they give up and become sots."

"None of them become drunkards all at once?"

"No, I never heard of such a case."

"Nor I neither. Then if these men hadn't begun to drink at all, they would never have become drunkards, any more than Mr. Wright's boys would have been drowned if they hadn't gone near the pond?"

"I guess your doctrine is that a man shouldn't drink at all. Is that your creed?"

"I would have a man drink every thing that will do him good. But I tell you I don't believe ardent spirits do a man any good."

"If you could *prove that*, then you would get your case, for then a man ought not to drink at all, and so he would never become a drunkard, that's clear. But I don't think you *can* prove it. A little spirit is good sometimes. When a man's tired it gives him strength."

"Let us see. When you are tired, you take some, and for a little while you feel stronger. So when your horse is tired and you spur him up, he goes faster for a little time, but he hasn't any more strength."

"Stop, Mister, your argument won't hold. The horse goes faster, but he doesn't feel less tired; whereas when any one is tired, a little spirit makes him *feel* stronger."

"Consider how we get strength. Our food passes into the stomach, is dissolved, and part is taken up by certain small vessels and goes to increase the blood and nourish the body. But all physicians know that rum does not suffer any change, that no part of it goes to form the fluid which nourishes. In ardent spirit there is not a particle of nourishment, and hence it can't give any real strength. Every physician will tell you what I've said is true."

"That I don't dispute, but you haven't convinced me yet. *I know* that I have felt the stronger for taking spirit."

"Now I will show you that that is possible without any additional nourishment. Suppose you come home from work at night, very tired. A person asks you to walk four or five miles. You are so tired that you really don't feel as if you had strength enough to do it. He then offers you ten dollars to go, and it rouses you up, and you feel as if you can go, and you walk off quite smart. The stimulus is equal to a glass of rum. But the promise of money didn't give the body any real strength. It only gathered together the little strength that remained, and when that was spent, you were weaker than before. Now that is the way that spirits work, only they strain the body more, and besides they act as a slow poison."

Mr. N——— then went on to give the testimony of many of the first physicians to the uselessness of spirits, and their injurious effects on the constitution when used even in small quantities. He showed that all kinds of work, as had been found by actual experiment, could be done better without spirits than with, and hence drew the conclusion, that as there was no necessity for it, men ought *not to go near the pond.*

"Well," said Uncle Enoch, "may be you'r right, and I hope you are. Mr. Newel's meadow is next to mine, and his hands have as much again rum as mine, and they don't do much more than half as much work, and not more than half as well. It may be that mine would do as much and as well without rum."

"You were speaking of your distillery; I think you said drunkenness had increased since it was built."

"Yes, greatly."

"It is no great benefit to the town then, for it deprives the town of a great deal of labor, for drunkards won't work, so there's so much lost. Then it taxes those who *do work*, to support those who *won't.*"

"It has been of some benefit by affording a market for grain; it has raised the price a good deal."

"A man raises grain and has it turned into rum to make drunkards with. Now don't the increase of taxes it has occasioned more than equal the increase of the price of grain?"

"I don't know but it does."

"And don't nearly all who sell grain take part of their pay in rum, and so become, sooner or later, drunkards?"

"A great many do."

"Well, then, the distillery gives a man a market for his rye: he gets, say five cents more on a bushel than if there were no distillery. In the mean time he drinks up ten cents on a bushel, if not more; and in four or five years becomes a drunkard. He therefore raises no more rye, and the town must be taxed to support his family. This don't look much like a benefit to the town, does it?"

"No, it don't."

"You said men became drunkards because it was so handy, the distillery being near: now if it were fifty miles off the danger would not be so great?"

"No."

"If it were 500 miles off, still less?"

"Yes."

"If a thousand, less yet? now if it were so far off as to be altogether beyond their reach, would it not be for the best? For instance, at the bottom of the sea?"

"I see you are for a war of extermination against spirits, and I believe you are not far from right. I don't know as I fully see through the subject yet though. You wouldn't have any body sell spirits then?"

"Not unless I wanted to raise up a crop of drunkards."

"Humph. Well, I don't want to talk any more now. I'll think it over. Come and take some supper with us to-night, and I'll let you know what I think then."

Mr. N——— called in the evening, and Uncle Enoch went over pretty much the same ground as in the morning, and proposed all the objections he could think of. By this means he became, although a convert of a day, pretty well acquainted with the subject, and prepared to reason and act.

"Now," said Uncle Enoch, "I'm ready to take hold and do all I can. What I want you to do tomorrow night is, to say over again all you said about pauperism and crime, and the cost of drinking, and then say all you've said to me, leaving out the distillery and stores. We'll get at them by and by."

The preacher succeeded to the satisfaction of Uncle Enoch, who told him that he had made out a stronger case than he had to him. "I think," said he, "we can start some of them now."

A constitution for a temperance society was then read. Mr. N——— remarked that he had no wish to press the formation of a society unless it was heartily desired, and that he might know the minds of the people, he would proceed no farther then, but wait to see how many on reflection should desire it. "Our good friend on the right," said he, turning to Uncle Enoch, "will be able to inform me whether it is desired that I should stay and attend to the formation of a society."

Uncle arose and said, "My friends, this is a new plan, and worth thinking of. We live in a country where they are continually finding out new things, and when a man has invented a new machine, if it's useful, we praise him and pay him too. Now if they have found out a way that will stop the increase of drunkards, if it appears to be a good invention, *let us try it*, especially as it don't cost any thing. I'm for trying it, as I was the patent rake that saved me the work of ten men. I want to see if it won't save money, and characters, and lives."

The meeting was then dismissed.

Though the influence made on the audience was deep and strong, yet not a few repaired to the tavern to discuss what they had heard, with the aid of ardent spirits.

"Landlord," said one, "a gill of West India;" he took it in his hand, and holding it up to the light to admire its color, began his comments on the address:

"I don't approve the way he proposes at all. His object is a good one—I despise a drunkard"—

"You despise a drunkard, do you?" said a giant of a fellow who had come for the purpose of getting drunk, but had proceeded but a comparatively small way in the business.

"Yes," said the first speaker rather timidly.

"Take that then," said the toper, suiting the action to the word, and driving the uplifted glass into the face of his fellow, so as to forever deprive him of an eye.

There was no disposition on the part of the former to continue the contest, after the loss of so important a member. He retired somewhat in doubt, it may be thought, as to the benefits of moderate drinking.

The next morning, Uncle Enoch started out bright and early to see how many names he could get to the constitution. He knew pretty well whom he would be likely to find ready, and shaped his course accordingly. In an hour's time he had nearly fifty names. Some scandal-loving people said that Sally Squires and Widow Baily would not have joined the society if any body else had asked them but Uncle Enoch, nor then, if he had not been a widower, but people *will talk*.

Uncle Enoch at length called at Mr. Brooks', and proposed the subject.

"I'll join right off," said he, "I made up my mind to, as soon as I heard what the man had to say. I was afraid before I went last night that it would turn out to be some Presbyterian trick, but it's a true bill. Let me have the paper."

"Will your wife join?" said Uncle Enoch, looking for an answer to Mrs. B.

"Law, Uncle Enoch, what makes you ask *me*? you don't think *I* drink, do you?"

"We want all them to join that don't, or won't drink."

"What good will it do for *a woman* to join? and I don't think it looks well either."

"I think it looks as well as it does for them to drink, and a good deal better. It will do this good: They will give their influence to temperance, they can bring up their children to let rum alone, and they may save their husbands from being drunkards."

"But can't a body do this without joining a society? It seems like saying a body can't let it alone without signing a promise. It takes away a person's liberty."

"It takes away a person's liberty of getting drunk, the liberty of hurrying the body to the grave, and the soul to hell—that's the liberty it takes away; but if you want to keep it, you can."

"Well, I shan't join you just now, I want to think upon it."

"It will be too late before a great while," thought Uncle Enoch, as he left the house. [It should have been remarked that Mr. Brooks left them at the beginning of the conversation, probably in order that Uncle Enoch might have free scope.]

He next called at Squire Goodell's. The old Squire was about the richest man in Elliston. He had bought a large farm when he came into the place, and left it to the management of his three sons, all of whom took to drink and died young. The cause was not fully suspected even when the enormous bills for whisky were presented for payment. He thought that work went on in proportion to the amount of whisky used, and so one kind of work did, viz: the work of death. Uncle Enoch found the Squire and his family prepared to do every thing in their power to promote the cause of total abstinence. A tear fell down the old man's cheek as he subscribed his name. "Ah," said he, "if this had been known ten years ago, my poor boys might have been alive now."

The daughters hesitated to give their names, for fear lest they should exceed the bounds of propriety and delicacy.

"I can't see," said Uncle Enoch, "why any woman need be ashamed to do that which will tend to make sober men of their brothers and husbands. It isn't thought indelicate for a female to tend on a sick brother or friend. Now if it isn't indelicate for a woman to do a great deal to save a man's *body from the grave*, sure it can't be to do a little to save not only his body from the grave, but *his soul from hell*. The case is to me as clear as day light."

The young ladies then put down their names.

Uncle Enoch next went to Deacon May's. The Deacon was a good man; had always been a temperate drinker; was never known to have taken *too much*, as the phrase went. He was a very industrious man, and was somewhat active in doing good, *provided he started the plan himself*, or was the *first one consulted* about it. In this case he thought he had been neglected, and hinted as much to Uncle Enoch.

"Bless your heart, Deacon, don't you always do what's right? The man thought *you* would take hold without asking."

"I don't know," said the Deacon, "about this binding one's self. I think it's best to abstain, but I think I can do more good out of the society than in it."

"That's what I was just saying to Mr. May," said his hopeful spouse.

"In what way, Deacon?"

"Why, if I see a man going to drink, and I talk to him, he will answer, *you are a member of the temperance society*, and wont mind what I say; but if I can tell him I am not, I can get some hold on him."

"Well, then you ought not to join the church, for when you go to reprove a Sabbath breaker, he will say, *you belong to the church*, and will not mind what you say. If you could tell him you *don't* belong to the church, would you get any better hold of him? No, no, Deacon; your argument proves too much. I'll tell you just how it will work if you don't join. When I see a man ready to become a drunkard, and urge him to join the society that he may be saved, he will say, there's Deacon May hasn't joined, and he is a good man; I'll do as he does. Now that is just the way it will work. It will be just as it is in religion, when a man tries to please the wicked by going over to them, they won't mind what he says."

"If folks don't drink enough to hurt them," said Mrs. M. "why should they deny themselves for the sake of those who *will get drunk?*"

"If for no other, that which moved Paul when he declared he would eat no meat while the world stood if it caused his brother to offend. He was willing to give up not only rum, which does no good, but meat, which does."

"Well, I think a little spirit does good sometimes. When I've been washing, I think it really has done me good."

"You heard the proof Mr. N. brought on the subject, and you can't get away from it. It don't give a woman any strength; it don't make her eye look any clearer; it don't make her breath any sweeter; it don't do her any good at all."

The Deacon began to think that the subject was coming too near home. Moreover his judgment was convinced, and his prejudices alone stood in the way. These he overcame, and took the pen and wrote his name, and handed it to his wife.

"If Mrs. May don't think it's best, she had better not sign now," said Uncle Enoch.

"*I think it's best,*" said the Deacon emphatically.

She took the pen and added her name, saying she was always glad to follow Mr. May's example, for then she knew she was right. Uncle Enoch doubted her good will in the deed, notwithstanding this dutiful speech.

Uncle Enoch next visited the principal store in the place. The merchant was a member of the church, and one of the most consistent and esteemed of the number. Like all his brother merchants at that time, he kept a supply of ardent spirits. Uncle Enoch reckoned that it would not take long to bring him around, because, said he, "he is made of the right sort of stuff." He went to the store not intending to address him at first, but to talk over the subject with others in his hearing. Among a number of citizens there collected, he found a young man who professed infidel principles, a Mr. Heron. He was a fluent talker, and was always rating about the evils done by priest-craft and religion.

"Mr. H," said Uncle Enoch, "you are a great friend to society, according to your tell, I want you to sign this paper."

"I'll not have any thing to do with your priest-craft," said Heron.

"You like to see drunkenness flourish then, do you? may be you want drunkards to increase, in order to keep your ranks full?"

"It's all priest-craft."

"How do you *prove that*? come, you talk a great deal about *proving things*, you want every thing to be *proved* before you believe it, you say: now I want you to prove what you have said, and I'll believe it."

"I don't want to dispute with you."

"Now, young chap, that wont do: just stick to your text. You say it's all priest-craft. I say, *prove it*, or the folks will know how much weight to give to what you say against religion; and I guess they do know pretty well now."

The young man was silent.

"Now you pretend that all you say against religion is out of good will to people; why don't you show your friendship in something besides talk? You can't deny but that religion gives people *some comfort*. If Christians have selfish motives, as you pretend, they do many charitable things; this you cannot deny. Why don't your folks do better things? They *must* before they can get the people to leave our doctrine for theirs. It is just about like this: There is a man starving to death, and I give him a piece of bread; you cry out to him, Don't take it, for he means to make you pay for it by and by; but you don't offer him any thing to keep him from starving. What shall the poor man do, if he throws away the bread I give him? He must die, and so would all the world for all your sort of folks would do for them. If you care as much about your fellow creatures as you pretend, why don't you help to do them good?"

"The priests have got them under their thumbs so that there is no chance."

"Well, here's a chance, why don't you seize upon it?"

"I'm not going to give up my rights. No man has a right to deprive me of my liberty by making me sign a bond like that."

"You won't give up your right to get drunk, and make other folks drunk, will you? You are a liberty man I see. Sometimes men a'nt willing to give up the liberty of helping themselves to their neighbors' property, and the liberty of going to state's prison. These sorts of liberty are pretty much a like."

"Well, I shant join the society."

"I reckoned you would'nt from the first; but I thought I would reason the matter with you, and let folks see what your principles are."

"Hav'nt you got through? for I want to be going."

"Yes, all but one thing, and that you will at last find out to be true. Remember, young man, it's a tough thing to carry on war against God Almighty."

The young man departed without making any reply. The company present, including the merchant, joined the society.

"Uncle Enoch," said he, as he put down his name, "there a'nt nothing said about *selling* in the pledge, but I hold it binds me to stop."

"I reckon it does; there can't be no doubt of it."

"What can I do with the spirits I have on hand? I can't well afford to lose it."

"Why seeing this is a public object, and that it was bought ignorantly, I'll bear a part, and I guess 'Squire Goodell will do the same, and we'll keep it till we have a meeting, and then pour it out down in the hollow and set fire to it."

"It will make some mouths water to see it go so," said one.

"It ought to make 'em think of where they are going to if they don't turn about."

Uncle Enoch then went home in high spirits, and showed his list of names to his daughters.—"I'm nearly sure," said he, "that all that's here will hold out but one—I should'nt wonder if she drinks before night. When a woman gets the taste for spirits, it's no easy thing to cure her.—A she drunkard is about the worst two-legged thing I know of, and there is a good many more of them in every place, than most persons think for."

❦ ❦ ❦

# The Old Meeting-House: Sketch from the Note-Book of an Old Gentleman

One of Stowe's first village sketches of New England, "The Old Meeting-House" strikes a nostalgic note common among pieces prepared for the Semi-Colon Club, whose members were strongly represented by New Englanders transplanted to the Ohio Valley. Stowe's adoption of the persona of an Old Gentleman is consistent with disguises she adopted on such occasions, where members' contributions were read anonymously.

The contrast between the high setting and Stowe's graphic depiction of human and canine behavior in the "The Old Meeting-House" makes for a gentle humor and strongly etched portraits of village types. She would go on to develop this material in her New England novels, especially *Oldtown Folks*. "The Old Meeting-House" was published in *Godey's Lady's Book* in August 1840, and appears in the Riverside collection of her *Writings*, volume 15.

ever shall I forget the dignity and sense of importance which swelled my mind when I was first pronounced old enough to go to meeting. That eventful Sunday I was up long before day, and even took my Sabbath suit to the window to ascertain by the first light that it actually was there, just as it looked the night before. With what complacency did I view myself completely dressed! How did I count over the rows of yellow gilt buttons on my coat! how my good mother, grandmother, and aunts fussed, and twitched, and pulled, to make everything set up and set down, just in the proper place! how my clean, starched white collar was turned over and smoothed again and again, and my golden curls twisted and arranged to make the most of me! and, last of all, how I was cautioned not to be thinking of my clothes. In truth, I was in those days a very handsome youngster, and it really is no more than justice to let the fact be known, as there is nothing in my present appearance from which it could ever be inferred. Everybody in the house successively asked me if I should be a good boy, and sit still, and not talk, nor laugh; and my mother informed me, *in terrorem*, that there was a tithing man, who carried off naughty children, and shut them up in a dark place behind the pulpit; and that this tithing man, Mr. Zephaniah Scranton, sat just where he could see me. This fact impressed my mind with more solemnity than all the exhortations which had preceded it—a proof of the efficacy of facts above reason. Under shadow and power of this weighty truth, I demurely took hold of my mother's forefinger to walk to meeting.

The traveler in New England, as he stands on some eminence, and looks down on its rich landscape of golden grain and waving cornfield, sees no feature more beautiful than its simple churches, whose white taper fingers point upward, amid the greenness and bloom of the distant prospects, as if to remind one of the overshadowing providence whence all this luxuriant beauty flows; and year by year, as new ones are added to the number, or succeed in the place of old ones, there is discernible an evident improvement in their taste and architecture. Those modest Doric little buildings, with their white pillars, green blinds, and neat inclosures, are very different affairs from those great, uncouth mountains of windows and doors that stood in the same place years before. To my childish eye, however, our old meeting-house was an awe-inspiring thing. To me it seemed fashioned very nearly on the model of Noah's ark and Solomon's temple, as set forth in the pictures in my Scripture Catechism—pictures which I did not doubt were authentic copies; and what more respectable and venerable architectural precedent could any one desire? Its double rows of windows, of which I knew the number by heart, its doors with great wooden quirls over them, its belfry projecting out at the east end, its steeple and bell, all inspired as much sense of the sublime in me as Strasbourg Cathedral itself; and the inside was not a whit less imposing.

How magnificent, to my eye, seemed the turnip-like canopy that hung over the minister's head, hooked by a long iron rod to the wall above! and how apprehensively did I consider the question, what would become of him if it should fall! How did I wonder at the panels on either side of the pulpit, in each of which was carved and painted a flaming red tulip, bolt upright, with its leaves projecting out at right angles! and then at the grapevine, bas-relieved on the front, with its exactly triangular bunches of grapes, alternating at exact intervals with exactly triangular leaves. To me it was an indisputable representation of how grapevines ought to look, if they would only be straight and regular, instead of curling and scrambling, and twisting themselves into all sorts of slovenly shapes. The area of the house was divided into large square pews, boxed up with stout boards, and surmounted with a kind of baluster work, which I supposed to be provided for the special accommodation of us youngsters, being the "loop-holes of retreat" through which we gazed on the "remarkabilia" of the scene. It was especially interesting to me to notice the coming in to meeting of the congregation. The doors were so contrived that on entering you stepped down instead of up—a construction that has more than once led to unlucky results in the case of strangers. I remember once when an unlucky Frenchman, entirely unsuspicious of the danger that awaited him, made entrance by pitching devoutly upon his nose in the middle of the broad aisle; that it took three bunches of my grandmother's fennel to bring my risibles into anything like composure. Such exhibitions, fortunately for me, were very rare; but still I found great amusement in watching the distinctive and marked outlines of the various people that filled up the seats around me. A Yankee village presents a picture of the curiosities of every generation: there from year to year, they live on, preserved by hard labor and regular habits, exhibiting every peculiarity of manner and appearance, as distinctly marked as when they first came from the mint of nature. And as everybody goes punctually to meeting, the meeting-house becomes a sort of museum of antiquities—a general muster ground for past and present.

I remember still with what wondering admiration I used to look around on the people that surrounded our pew. On one side there was an old Captain McLean, and Major McDill, a couple whom the mischievous wits of the village designated as Captain McLean and Captain McFat; and, in truth, they were a perfect antithesis, a living exemplification of flesh and spirit. Captain McLean was a mournful, lengthy, considerate-looking old gentleman, with a long face, digressing into a long, thin, horny nose, which, when he applied his pocket-handkerchief, gave forth a melancholy, minor-keyed sound, such as a ghost might make, using a pocket-handkerchief in the long gallery of some old castle.

Close at his side was the doughty, puffing Captain McDill, whose full-orbed, jolly visage was illuminated by a most valiant red nose, shaped something like an overgrown doughnut, and looking as if it had been thrown at his face, and happened to hit in the middle. Then there was old Israel Peters, with a wooden leg, which tramped into meeting, with undeviating regularity, ten minutes before meeting time; and there was Jedediah Stebbins, a thin, wistful, moonshiny-looking old gentleman, whose mouth appeared as if it had been gathered up with a needle and thread, and whose eyes seemed as if they had been bound with red tape; and there was old Benaiah Stephens, who used regularly to get up and stand when the minister was about half through his sermon, exhibiting his tall figure, long, single-breasted coat, with buttons nearly as large as a tea plate; his large, black, horn spectacles stretched down on the extreme end of a very long nose, and vigorously chewing, meanwhile, on the bunch of caraway which he always carried in one hand. Then there was Aunt Sally Stimpson, and old Widow Smith, and a whole bevy of little, dried old ladies, with small, straight, black bonnets, tight sleeves to the elbow, long silk gloves, and great fans, big enough for a windmill; and of a hot day it was a great amusement to me to watch the bobbing of the little black bonnets, which showed that sleep had got the better of their owners' attention, and the sputter and rustling of the fans, when a more profound nod than common would suddenly waken them, and set them to fanning and listening with redoubled devotion. There was Deacon Dundas, a great wagon load of an old gentleman, whose ample pockets looked as if they might have held half the congregation, who used to establish himself just on one side of me, and seemed to feel such entire confidence in the soundness and capacity of his pastor that he could sleep very comfortably from one end of the sermon to the other. Occasionally, to be sure, one of your officious blue flies, who, as everybody knows, are amazingly particular about such matters, would buzz into his mouth, or flirt into his ears a passing admonition as to the impropriety of sleeping in meeting, when the good old gentleman would start, open his eyes very wide, and look about with a resolute air, as much as to day, "I was n't asleep, I can tell you;" and then setting himself in an edifying posture of attention, you might perceive his head gradually settling back, his mouth slowly opening wider and wider, till the good man would go off again soundly asleep, as if nothing had happened.

It was a good orthodox custom of old times to take every part of the domestic establishment to meeting, even down to the faithful dog, who, as he had supervised the labors of the week, also came with due particularity to supervise the worship of Sunday. I think I can see now the fitting out on a Sunday morning— the one wagon, or two, as the case might be, tackled up with an "old gray" or an "old bay," with a buffalo skin over the seat by way of cushion, and all the family, in their Sunday best, packed in for meeting; while Master Bose, Watch, or Towser stood prepared to be an outguard, and went meekly trotting up hill and down dale in the rear. Arrived at meeting, the canine part of the establishment generally conducted themselves with great decorum, lying down and going to sleep as decently as anybody present, except when some of the business-loving bluebottles aforesaid would make a sortie upon them, when you might hear the snap of their jaws as they vainly sought to lay hold of the offender. Now and then, between some of the sixthlies, seventhlies, and eighthlies, you might hear some old patriarch giving himself a rousing shake, and pitpatting soberly up the aisles, as if to see that everything was going on properly, after which he would lie down and compose himself to sleep again; and certainly this was as improving a way of spending Sunday as a good Christian dog could desire.

But the glory of our meeting-house was its singers' seat—that empyrean of those who rejoiced in the divine, mysterious art of fa-sol-la-ing, who, by a distinguishing grace and privilege, could "raise and fall" the cabalistical eighth notes, and move serene through the enchanted region of flats, sharps, thirds, fifths, and octaves.

There they sat in the gallery that lined three sides of the house, treble, counter, tenor, and bass, each with its appropriate leaders and supporters; there were generally seated the bloom of our young people; sparkling, modest, and blushing girls on one side, with their ribbons and finery, making the place where they sat as blooming and lively as a flower garden, and fiery, forward, confident young men on the other. In spite of its being a meeting-house, we could not swear that glances were never given and returned, and that there was not often as much of an approach to flirtation as the distance and the sobriety of the place would admit.

Certain it was, that there was no place where our village coquettes attracted half so many eyes or led astray half so many hearts.

But I have been talking of singers all this time, and neglected to mention the Magnus Apollo of the whole concern, the redoubtable chorister, who occupied the seat of honor in the midst of the middle gallery, and exactly opposite to the minister. Certain it is that the good man, if he were alive, would never believe it; for no person ever more magnified his office, or had a more thorough belief in his own greatness and supremacy, than Zedekiah Morse. Methinks I can see him now as he appeared to my eyes on that first Sunday, when he shot up from behind the gallery, as if he had been sent up by a spring. He was a little man, whose fiery red hair, brushed straight upon the top of his head, had an appearance as vigorous and lively as real flame; and this, added to the ardor and determination of all his motions, had obtained for him the surname of the "Burning Bush." He seemed possessed with the very soul of song; and from the moment he began to sing, looked alive all over, till it seemed to me that his whole body would follow his hair upwards, fairly rapt away by the power of harmony. With what an air did he sound the important fa-sol-la in the ears of the waiting gallery, who stood with open mouths ready to seize their pitch, preparatory to their general *set to!* How did his ascending and descending arm astonish the zephyrs when once he laid himself out to the important work of beating time! How did his little head whisk from side to side, as now he beat and roared towards the ladies on his right, and now towards the gentlemen on his left! It used to seem to my astonished vision as if his form grew taller, his arm longer, his hair redder, and his little green eyes brighter, with every stave; and particularly when he perceived any falling off of time or discrepancy in pitch; with what redoubled vigor would he thump the gallery and roar at the delinquent quarter, till every mother's son and daughter of them skipped and scrambled into the right place again!

Oh, it was a fine thing to see the vigor and discipline with which he managed the business; so that if, on a hot, drowsy Sunday, any part of the choir hung back or sung sleepily on the first part of a verse, they were obliged to bestir themselves in good earnest, and sing three times as fast, in order to get through with the others. 'Kiah Morse was no advocate for your dozy, drawling singing, that one may do at leisure, between sleeping and waking, I assure you; indeed, he got entirely out of the graces of Deacon Dundas and one or two other portly, leisurely old gentlemen below, who had been used to throw back their heads, shut up their eyes, and take the comfort of the psalm, by prolonging indefinitely all the notes. The first Sunday after 'Kiah took the music in hand, the old deacon really rubbed his eyes and looked about him, for the psalm was sung off before he was ready to get his mouth opened, and he really looked upon it as a most irreverent piece of business.

But the glory of 'Kiah's art consisted in the execution of those good old billowy compositions called fuguing tunes, where the four parts that compose the choir take up the song, and go racing around one after another, each singing a different set of words, till, at length, by some inexplicable magic, they all come together again, and sail smoothly out into a rolling sea of song. I remember the wonder with which I used to look from side to side when treble, tenor, counter, and bass were thus roaring and foaming,—and it verily seemed to me as if the psalm was going to pieces among the breakers,—and the delighted astonishment with which I found that each particular verse did emerge whole and uninjured from the storm.

But alas for the wonders of that old meeting-house, how they are passed away! Even the venerable building itself has been pulled down, and its fragments scattered; yet still I retain enough of my childish feelings to wonder whether any little boy was gratified by the possession of those painted tulips and grapevines, which my childish eye used to covet, and about the obtaining of which, in case the house should ever be pulled down, I devised so many schemes during the long sermons and services of summer days. I have visited the spot where it stood, but the modern, fair-looking building that stands in its room bears no trace of it; and of the various familiar faces that used to be seen inside not one remains. Verily, I must be growing old; and as old people are apt to spin long stories, I check myself, and lay down my pen.

❦ ❦ ❦

# The Canal-Boat

Entertaining, witty, and deftly drawn, "The Canal-Boat," like many of Stowe's early sketches and stories, was originally written for the Semi-Colon Club. With wonderful equipoise, Stowe announces her lowly subject, assuming the importance of the ordinary. She proceeds with sureness of tone and comic precision of detail to provide a realistic and amusing sketch of this national mode of transportation. It is likely she wrote this piece shortly after she traveled from Cincinnati by stage and canal boat to attend her brother Henry Ward Beecher's graduation from Amherst College in 1834.

"The Canal-Boat" was published in *Godey's Lady's Book* in October 1841, and collected in her first anthology, *The Mayflower* (1843).

f all the ways of travelling which obtain among our locomotive nation, this said vehicle, the canal-boat, is the most absolutely prosaic and inglorious. There is something picturesque, nay, almost sublime, in the lordly march of your well-built, high-bred steamboat. Go take your stand on some overhanging bluff, where the blue Ohio winds its thread of silver, or the sturdy Mississippi makes its path through unbroken forests, and it will do your heart good to see the gallant boat walking the waters with unbroken and powerful tread, and, like some fabled monster of the wave, breathing fire, and making the shores resound with its deep respirations. Then there is something mysterious, even awful, in the power of steam. See it curling up against a blue sky some rosy morning—graceful, fleeting, intangible, and to all appearance the softest and gentlest of all spiritual things—and then think that it is this fairy spirit that keeps all the world alive and hot with motion; think how excellent a servant it is, doing all sorts of gigantic works, like the genii of old; and yet, if you let slip the talisman only for a moment, what terrible advantage it will take of you! and you will confess that steam has some claims both to the beautiful and the terrible. For our own part, when we are down among the machinery of a steamboat in full play, we conduct ourself very reverently, for we consider it as a very serious neighborhood; and every time the steam whizzes with such red-hot determination from the escape valve, we start as if some of the spirits were after us. But in a canal-boat there is no power, no mystery, no danger; one cannot blow up, one cannot be drowned, unless by some special effort: one sees clearly all there is in the case—a horse, a rope, and a muddy strip of water—and that is all.

Did you ever try it, reader? If not, take an imaginary trip with us, just for experiment. "There's the boat!" exclaims a passenger in the omnibus, as we are rolling down from the Pittsburg Mansion House to the canal. "Where?" exclaim a dozen of voices, and forthwith a dozen heads go out of the window. "Why, down there, under that bridge; don't you see those lights?" "What! that little thing?" exclaims an inexperienced traveller; "dear me! we can't half of us get into it!" "We! indeed," says some old hand in the business; "I think you'll find it will hold us and a dozen more loads like us." "Impossible!" say some. "You'll see," say the initiated; and, as soon as you get out, you *do* see, and hear too, what seems like a general breaking loose from the Tower of Babel, amid a perfect hailstorm of trunks, boxes, valises, carpet-bags, and every describable and indescribable form of what a Westerner calls "plunder."

"That's my trunk!" barks out a big, round man. "That's my bandbox!" screams a heartstricken old lady, in terror for her immaculate Sunday caps. "Where's my little red box? I had two carpet-bags and a—My trunk had a scarle—Halloo! where are you going with that portmanteau? Husband! husband! do see after the large basket and the little hair trunk—oh! and the baby's little chair!" "Go below—go below, for mercy's sake, my dear; I'll see to the baggage." At last, the feminine part of creation perceiving that, in this particular instance, they gain nothing by public speaking, are content to be led quietly under hatches, and amusing is the look of dismay which each new-comer gives to the confined quarters that present themselves. Those who were so ignorant of the power of compression as to suppose the boat scarce large enough to contain them and theirs, find, with dismay, a respectable colony of old ladies, babies, mothers, big baskets, and carpet-bags already established. "Mercy on us!" says one, after surveying the little room, about ten feet long and six high, "where are we all to sleep to-night?" "O me! what a sight of children!" says a young lady, in a despairing tone. "Poh!" says an initiated traveller; "children! scarce any here; let's see: one—the woman in the corner, two—that child with the bread and butter, three—and then there's that other woman with two—really, it's quite moderate for a canal-boat: however, we can't tell till they have all come."

"All! for mercy's sake, you don't say there are any more coming!" exclaim two or three in a breath; "they *can't* come; *there is not room!*"

Notwithstanding the impressive utterance of this sentence, the contrary is immediately demonstrated by the appearance of a very corpulent elderly lady, with three well-grown daughters, who come down looking about them most complacently, entirely regardless of the unchristian looks of the company. What a mercy it is that fat people are always good-natured!

After this follows an indiscriminate raining down of all shapes, sizes, sexes, and ages—men, women, children, babies, and nurses. The state of feeling becomes perfectly desperate. Darkness gathers on all faces. "We shall be smothered! we shall be crowded to death! we *can't stay* here!" are heard faintly from one and another; and yet, though the boat grows no wider, the walls no higher, they do live, and do bear it, in spite of repeated protestations to the contrary. Truly, as Sam Slick says, "there's a *sight of wear* in human natur'."

But, meanwhile, the children grow sleepy, and divers interesting little duets and trios arise from one part or another of the cabin.

"Hush, Johnny! be a good boy," says a pale, nursing mamma, to a great, bristling, white-headed phenomenon, who is kicking very much at large in her lap.

"I won't be a good boy, neither," responds Johnny, with interesting explicitness; "I want to go to bed, and so-o-o-o!" and Johnny makes up a mouth as big as a teacup, and roars with good courage, and his mamma asks him "if he ever saw pa do so," and tells him that "he is mamma's dear, good little boy, and must not make a noise," with various observations of the kind, which are so strikingly efficacious in such cases. Meanwhile, the domestic concert in other quarters proceeds with vigour. "Mamma, I'm tired!" bawls a child. "Where's the baby's nightgown?" calls a nurse. "Do take Peter up in your lap, and keep him still." "Pray get out some biscuits to stop their mouths." Meanwhile, sundry babies strike in "con spirito," as the music-books have it, and execute various flourishes; the disconsolate mothers sigh, and look as if all was over with them; and the young ladies appear extremely disgusted, and wonder "what business women have to be travelling round with babies!"

To these troubles succeeds the turning-out scene, when the whole caravan is injected into the gentlemen's cabin, that the beds may be made. The red curtains are put down, and in solemn silence all, the last mysterious preparations begin. At length it is announced that all is ready. Forthwith the whole company rush back, and find the walls embellished by a series of little shelves, about a foot wide, each furnished with a mattress and bedding, and hooked to the ceiling by a very suspiciously slender cord. Direful are the ruminations and exclamations of inexperienced travellers, particularly young ones, as they eye these very equivocal accomodations. "What! sleep up there! *I* won't sleep on one of those top shelves, *I* know. The cords will certainly break." The chambermaid here takes up the conversation, and solemnly assures them that such an accident is not to be thought of at all; that it is a natural impossibility—a thing that could not happen without an actual miracle; and since it becomes increasingly evident that thirty ladies cannot all sleep on the lowest shelf, there is some effort made to exercise faith in this doctrine; nevertheless, all look on their neighbours with fear and trembling; and when the stout lady talks of taking a shelf, she is most urgently pressed to change places with her alarmed neighbour below. Points of location being after a while adjusted, comes the last struggle. Everybody wants to take off their bonnet, to look for their shawl, to find their cloak, to get their carpet-bag, and all set about it with such zeal that nothing can be done. "Ma'am, you're on my foot!" says one, "Will you please to move, ma'am?" says somebody, who is gasping and struggling behind you. "Move!" you echo. "Indeed, I should be very glad to, but I don't see much prospect of it." "Chambermaid!" calls a lady, who is struggling among a heap of carpet-bags and children at one end of the cabin. "Ma'am!" echoes the poor chambermaid, who is wedged fast, in a similar situation, at the other. "Where's my cloak, chambermaid?" "I'd find it, ma'am, if I could move." "Chambermaid, my basket!" "Chambermaid, my parasol!" "Chambermaid, my carpet-bag!" "Mamma, they push me so!" "Hush, child; crawl under there, and lie still till I can undress you." At last, however, the various distresses are over, the babies sink to sleep, and even that much-enduring being, the chambermaid, seeks out some corner for repose. Tired and drowsy, you are just sinking into a doze, when bang! goes the boat against the sides of a lock, ropes scrape, men run and shout, and up fly the heads of all the top shelf-ites, who are generally the more juvenile and airy part of the company.

"What's that! what's that!" flies from mouth to mouth; and forthwith they proceed to awaken their respective relations. "Mother! Aunt Hannah! do wake up; what is this awful noise?" "Oh, only a lock!" "Pray be still," groan out the sleepy members from below.

A lock!" exclaim the vivacious creatures, ever on the alert for information; "and what *is* a lock, pray?"

"Don't you know what a lock is, you silly creatures? Do lie down and go to sleep."

"But say, there ain't any *danger* in a lock, is there?" respond the querists. "Danger!" exclaims a deaf old lady, poking up her head, "what's the matter? There ha'n't nothin' burst, has there?" "No, no, no!" exclaim the provoked and despairing opposition party, who find that there is no such thing as going to sleep till they have made the old lady below and the young ladies above understand exactly the philosophy of a lock. After a while the conversation again subsides; again all is still; you hear only the trampling of horses and the rippling of the rope in the water, and sleep again is stealing over you. You doze, you dream, and all of a sudden you are started by a cry, "Chambermaid! wake up the lady that wants to be set ashore." Up jumps chambermaid, and up jumps the lady and two children, and forthwith form a committee of inquiry as to ways and means. "Where's my bonnet?" says the lady, half awake, and fumbling among the various articles of that name. "I thought I hung it up behind the door." "Can't you find it?" says poor chambermaid, yawning and rubbing her eyes. "Oh, yes, here it is," says the lady; and then the cloak, the shawl, the gloves, the shoes, receive each a separate discussion. At last all seems ready, and they begin to move off, when, lo! Peter's cap is missing. "Now where can it be?" soliloquizes the lady. "I put it right here by the table-leg; maybe it got into some of the berths." At this suggestion, the chambermaid takes the candle, and goes round deliberately to every berth, poking the light directly in the face of every sleeper. "Here it is," she exclaims, pulling at something black under one pillow. "No, indeed, those are my shoes," says the vexed sleeper. "Maybe it's here," she resumes, darting upon something dark in another berth. "No, that's my bag," responds the occupant. The chambermaid then proceeds to turn over all the children on the floor, to see if it is not under them, in the course of which process they are most agreeably waked up and enlivened; and, when everybody is broad awake, and most uncharitably wishing the cap, and Peter too, at the bottom of the canal, the good lady exclaims, "Well, if this isn't lucky! here I had it safe in my basket all the time!" and she departs amid the—what shall I say?—execrations?—of the whole company, ladies though they be.

Well, after this follows a hushing up and wiping up among the juvenile population, and a series of remarks commences from the various shelves, of a very edifying and instructive tendency. One says that the woman did not seem to know where anything was; another says that she has waked them all up; a third adds that she has waked up all the children too; and the elderly ladies make moral reflections on the importance of putting your things where you can find them— being always ready; which observations, being delivered in an exceedingly doleful and drowsy tone, form a sort of subbass to the lively chattering of the upper shelfites, who declare that they feel quite wide awake—that they don't think they shall go to sleep again to-night—and discourse over everything in creation, until you heartily wish you were enough related to them to give them a scolding.

At last, however, voice after voice drops off; you fall into a most refreshing slumber; it seems to you that you sleep about a quarter of an hour, when the chambermaid pulls you by the sleeve: "Will you please to get up, ma'am; we want to make the beds." You start and stare. Sure enough, the night is gone. So much for sleeping on board canal-boats.

Let us not enumerate the manifold perplexities of the morning toilet in a place where every lady realizes most forcibly the condition of the old woman who lived under a broom: "All she wanted was elbow room." Let us not tell how one glass is made to answer for thirty fair faces, one ewer and vase for thirty lavations; and, tell it not in Gath! one towel for a company! Let us not intimate how ladies' shoes have, in the night, clandestinely slid into the gentlemen's cabin, and gentlemen's boots elbowed, or, rather, *toed* their way among lady's gear, nor recite the exclamations after runaway property that are heard. "I can't find nothin' of Johnny's shoe!" "Here's a shoe in the water pitcher—is this it?" "My side-combs are gone!" exclaims a nymph with dishevelled curls. "Massy! do look at my bonnet!" exclaims an old lady, elevating an article crushed into as many angles as there are pieces in a minced pie. "I never did sleep *so much together* in my life," echoes a poor little French lady, whom despair has driven into talking English.

But our shortening paper warns us not to prolong our catalogue of distresses beyond reasonable bounds, and therefore we will close with advising all our friends who intend to try this way of travelling for *pleasure,* to take a good stock both of patience and clean towels with them, for we think that they will find abundant need for both.

# PART 2
# Antislavery Writings

# To the Editor of the *Cincinnati Journal and Luminary*

On July 12, 1836, the office in Cincinnati where James G. Birney printed his anti-slavery paper, *The Philanthropist*, was broken into and the press damaged. When Birney refused to cease publication, some of Cincinnati's most distinguished citizens conspired to form a mob against him. During this period the regular editor of the *Cincinnati Journal and Luminary* was out of town and Stowe's brother Henry Ward Beecher was editor pro tem. Using the pseudonym "Franklin," Stowe wrote a letter to the editor meant to provide her brother the opportunity to make some remarks on the subject. In her first public remarks on the slavery controversy, Stowe mounts a vigorous defense of the principle of free speech and subtly appeals to the self-interest of the property-owning mob. Her letter appeared in the *Cincinnati Journal and Luminary* on July 21, 1836.

**M**r. Editor:—A few days ago at the dinner table of a friend, a man of sense and intelligence, the following conversation took place—"So," said Mr. L—, flourishing his carver, "I hear Birney's press is broken open at last,—I knew it must be so, well, I can't say that I am sorry— it will teach him better than to be setting these ultra measures on foot in our city."—"You are glad of it!" said I, "you, a Christian man and a lover of good order, not sorry that the laws of the city have been violated, and the rights of private property invaded!—my good sir, I am astonished at you!"

"Why, no," said my friend, looking somewhat puzzled, "I disapprove of mobs and unlawful proceedings of every kind;—no man more;—but then Birney and these fellows are so ultra and immoderate, and their measures are so calculated to throw community into a ferment!—"

"And breaking into houses and destroying property are measures indicative of so much more moderation, and so eminently tranquilizing in their influence on community, that you patronize them, as the least of two evils!"

"Why, no, certainly," said Mr. L., "I would *patronize* no such thing; I disapprove of the *infraction of law* in this case, though I cannot say I am sorry that the thing has been done."

"But my good friend, by uttering just such a sentence as you have now, you do as much to patronize mobs and unlawful proceedings as any of their leaders could desire. Suppose the leaders of a mob knew that after they had broken the

laws of the city, all respectable citizens would calmly put their hands in their pockets, and say 'well, I'm glad they did the thing, though I seriously object to this
breaking of the laws,' do you think that this metaphysical reservation at the end
of the sentence would have any effect in deterring from the next outrage!"

My friend was silent and went on eating his beef for some moments with
great solidity and then resumed—"But you must allow that it is very undesirable
to have that Birney here sending out these inflammatory things!"

"Why! what harm do they do?"

"*Why?*—they inflame community."

"Well, and what harm is there in inflaming community?"

"Why, it makes men furious, gives rise to popular commotions and distur-
bances, and *mobs*, &c.," said he hastily, beginning to see where his own logic was
taking him.

"And is it because you are so fearful that Birney will create mobs and excitement, that you are not sorry that there was a mob last night to tear down his
printing press? It seems to me that it is not so consistent an arrangement of principles as might be made; now my friend, do you think the liberty of the press is
a good thing?"

"Certainly—to be sure."

"And you think it a good article in our constitution, that allows every man
to speak, write, and publish his own opinions, without any other responsibility
than that of the laws of his country?"

"Certainly I do."

"Well then, as Mr. Birney is a man, I suppose you think it's right to allow *him*
to do it in particular?"

"But Mr. Birney's opinions are so dangerous!"

"That is to say, so *you* think them; there are a large class of people in the nation, who are just as sure that they are not, now how is the constitution to be
worded:

"Every man in the state may speak, write, print, and publish his own sentiments on any subject, provided that nobody in the nation thinks they are dangerous."

"Pshaw! said my friend—of course no law could run in that way, but there is
a point you know, where all men of sense are pretty much agreed."

"Then," said I, "perhaps you would recommend that the constitution should
provide that every man may print and publish his sentiments, except in cases
where all men of sense are *pretty much agreed* that they are dangerous."

"Why," said my friend, after an uneasy silence of a few moments, "really you
are getting to be quite a warm abolitionist—I had no idea that you were so much
inclined to favor Birney—it was only a month ago that I heard you lamenting that
he would come here and set up his paper."

"So I did," said I, "and so I do now, but that has nothing to do with the question. The question is—is the article in our constitution that allows freedom of the
press, a good one? either say it is a good one, and allow Birney, or any other man
(be his opinions what they may) the benefit of it, or say it is *not* good, have it
struck out, and take the consequences."

"Well," said my friend, "you are right I believe, but what is to be done! there must be some restraint on these fellows."

"Perhaps that is a difficult question, Mr. L———, but one thing is certain: the encouraging of mobs is *not* the thing to be done. I have been perfectly shocked to hear sensible christian men making just such remarks on several occasions as you have made to-day. Why just suppose that there was a train of gunpowder extending under every house in the city, and the incendiaries had begun to explode it under some unsightly old buildings which specially disfigure the place—you stand on a hill top and look down with great complacency—"That's right—can't say I'm sorry!—glad to see those ugly old things blown sky high!" "You fool," says a man running up, out of breath—"don't you know that the same train of powder runs under your house and mine, and every house in the city; let it go twenty minutes longer and they will all go together!" Now this is precisely the case with these mobs. Every man is glad of a mob that happens to fall in with his views, without considering that if the mob system gets once thoroughly running, it may go *against*, as well as *for* them.

There is a mob at Vicksburgh against the gamblers; "I'm glad of it," say some well disposed people, "t'will put a stop to this gambling." But what next? Why next there is a mob to tear down a church, or tar and feather a minister; and now the good people are shocked at this mobbing system!—what an awful thing it is! There is a mob to-night to tear down an abolition press; "glad of it," say many respectable men, this abolition is a bad thing—ought to be stopped. But at the heels of this follow a Jackson mob and a Harrison mob, a mob of workmen for wages, a mob on rail-road companies, and a mob on water companies;—one man's house is torn down for one thing, and another's factory burns for another, till all begin to doubt whether abolition*ism* or any other *ism* is not better than mob*ism*— and all this comes of every man patronising in the beginning, the particular mob that happened to suit his own taste. Now the only way to prevent all this, is for every man to stand sternly up for the principles of law, and frown with indignation on every violation of them even though they accidentally accomplish something that he thinks desirable. The minister and christian must treat with as much severity a mob against gambling as a mob against ministers and churches. The patriot statesman frowns alike on the mob that advances as on that that retards his plans, and all lovers of good order must declare with one voice, that they will regard nothing with approbation, compromise with nothing, and accept of nothing as a good deed that is purchased by outrages endangering those rights of property and of free opinion which are the pride and treasure of every American citizen.

FRANKLIN

# Uncle Sam's Emancipation

A SKETCH

Appearing in the New-York *Evangelist* on January 2, 1845, under the title "Immediate Emancipation," this "true story" of Cincinnati rehearses materials Stowe would develop in a different direction in *Uncle Tom's Cabin*. Making excellent use of dialect and dialogue, Stowe adopts the strategy that would make *Uncle Tom's Cabin* effective with a wide audience. She deliberately attacks slavery as a system, thus avoiding what she calls "[t]he great error of controversy," its readiness "to assail *persons* rather than *principles*." Recognizing the lineaments of Auguste St. Clare in the reasonable master of this story, Stowe referred to this incident in her "Concluding Remarks" to *Uncle Tom's Cabin*.

This story was reprinted in 1853 as "Uncle Sam's Emancipation" in a collection bearing that title.

It may be gratifying to those who desire to think well of human nature, to know that the leading incidents of the subjoined sketch are literal matters of fact, occurring in the city of Cincinnati, which have come within the scope of the writer's personal knowledge—the incidents have merely been clothed in a dramatic form, to present them more vividly to the reader.

In one of the hotel parlors of our queen city, a young gentleman, apparently in no very easy frame of mind, was pacing up and down the room, looking alternately at his watch and out of the window, as if expecting somebody. At last he rang the bell violently, and a hotel servant soon appeared.

"Has my man Sam come in yet?" he inquired.

The polished yellow gentleman to whom this was addressed, answered with a polite, but somewhat sinister smirk, that nothing had been seen of him since early that morning.

"Lazy dog! full three hours since I sent him off to B——— street, and I have seen nothing of him since."

The yellow gentleman remarked with consolatory politeness, that "he hoped Sam had not *run away*," adding, with an ill-concealed grin, that "them boys was mighty apt to show the clean heel when they come into a free State."

"Oh, no; I'm quite easy as to that," returned the young gentleman; "I'll risk Sam's ever being willing to part from me. I brought him because I was sure of him."

"Don't you be too sure," remarked a gentleman from behind, who had been listening to the conversation. "There are plenty of mischief-making busybodies on the trail of every southern gentleman, to interfere with his family matters, and decoy off his servants."

"Didn't I see Sam talking at the corner with the Quaker Simmons?" said another servant, who meanwhile had entered.

"Talking with Simmons, was he?" remarked the last speaker, with irritation; "that rascal Simmons does nothing else, I believe, but tote away gentlemen's servants. Well, if Simmons has got him, you may as well be quiet; you'll not see your fellow again in a hurry."

"And who the deuce is this Simmons?" said our young gentleman, who, though evidently of a good natured mould, was now beginning to wax wroth; "and what business has he to interfere with other people's affairs?"

"You had better have asked those questions a few days ago, and then you would have kept a closer eye on your fellow; a meddlesome, canting, Quaker rascal, that all these black hounds run to, to be helped into Canada, and nobody knows where all."

The young gentleman jerked out his watch with increasing energy, and then walking fiercely up to the coloured waiter, who was setting the dinner table with an air of provoking satisfaction, he thundered at him, "You rascal, you understand this matter; I see it in your eyes."

Our gentleman of colour bowed, and with an air of mischievous intelligence, protested that he never interfered with other gentlemen's matters, while sundry of his brethren in office looked unutterable things out of the corners of their eyes.

"There is some cursed plot hatched up among you," said the young man. "You have talked Sam into it; I know he never would have thought of leaving me unless he was put-up to it. Tell me now," he resumed, "have you heard Sam say anything about it? Come, be reasonable," he added, in a milder tone, "you shall find your account in it."

Thus adjured, the waiter protested he would be happy to give the gentleman any satisfaction in his power. The fact was, Sam had been pretty full of notions lately, and had been to see Simmons, and in short, he should not wonder if he never saw any more of him.

And as hour after hour passed, the whole day, the whole night, and no Sam was forthcoming, the truth of the surmise became increasingly evident. Our young hero, Mr. Alfred B——, was a good deal provoked, and strange as the fact may seem, a good deal grieved too, for he really loved the fellow. "Loved him!" says some scornful zealot; "a slaveholder *love* his slave!" Yes, brother; why not? A warm-hearted man will love his dog, his horse, even to grieving bitterly for their loss, and why not credit the fact that such a one may *love* the human creature whom custom has placed on the same level. The fact was, Alfred B—— did love this young man; he had been appropriated to him in childhood; and Alfred had always redressed his grievances, fought his battles, got him out of scrapes, and purchased for him, with liberal hand, indulgences to which his comrades were strangers. He had taken pride to dress him smartly, and as for hardship and want, they had never come near him.

"The poor, silly, ungrateful puppy!" soliloquized he, "what can he do with himself? Confound that Quaker, and all his meddlesome tribe—been at him with their bloody-bone stories, I suppose—Sam knows better, the scamp—halloa, there," he called to one of the waiters, "where does this Simpkins—Simon—Simmons, or what d'ye call him, live?"

"His shop is No. 5, on G. street."

"Well, I'll go at him, and see what business he has with my affairs."

The Quaker was sitting at the door of his shop, with a round, rosy, good-humoured face, so expressive of placidity and satisfaction, that it was difficult to approach in ireful feeling.

"Is your name Simmons?" demanded Alfred, in a voice whose natural urbanity was somewhat sharpened by vexation.

"Yes, friend; what dost thou wish?"

"I wish to inquire whether you have seen anything of my coloured fellow, Sam; a man of twenty-five, or thereabouts, lodging at the Pearl street House?"

"I rather suspect that I have," said the Quaker, in a quiet, meditative tone, as if thinking the matter over with himself.

"And is it true, sir, that you have encouraged and assisted him in his efforts to get out of my service?"

"Such, truly, is the fact, my friend."

Losing patience at this provoking equanimity, our young friend poured forth his sentiments with no inconsiderable energy, and in terms not the most select or pacific, all which our Quaker received with that placid, full-orbed tranquillity of countenance, which seemed to say, "Pray, sir, relieve your mind; don't be particular, scold as hard as you like." The singularity of this expression struck the young man, and as his wrath became gradually spent, he could hardly help laughing at the tranquillity of his opponent, and he gradually changed his tone for one of expostulation. "What motive could induce you, sir, thus to incommode a stranger, and one who never injured you at all?"

"I am sorry thou art incommoded," rejoined the Quaker. "Thy servant, as thee calls him, came to me, and I helped him, as I would any other poor fellow in distress."

"Poor fellow!" said Alfred, angrily; "that's the story of the whole of you. I tell you there is not a free negro in your city so well off as my Sam is, and always has been, and he'll find it out before long."

"But tell me, friend, thou mayest die as well as another man; thy establishment may fall into debt, as well as another man's; and thy Sam may be sold by the Sheriff for debt, or change hands in dividing the estate, and so, though he was bred easily, and well cared for, he may come to be a field hand, under hard masters, starved, beaten, overworked—such things do happen sometimes, do they not?"

"Sometimes, perhaps they do," replied the young man.

"Well, look you, by our laws in Ohio, thy Sam is now a free man; as free as I or thou; he hath a strong back, good hands, good courage, can earn his ten or twelve dollars a month—or do better. Now taking all things into account, if thee were in his place, what would thee do—would thee go back a slave, or try thy luck as a free man?"

Alfred said nothing in reply to this, only after a while he murmured half to himself, "I thought the fellow had more gratitude, after all my kindness."

"Thee talks of gratitude," said the Quaker, "now how does that account stand? Thou hast fed, and clothed, and protected this man; thou hast not starved, beaten, or abused him—that would have been unworthy of thee; thou hast shown him special kindness, and in return he has given thee faithful service for fifteen or twenty years; all his time, all his strength, all he could do or be, he has given thee, and ye are about even." The young man looked thoughtful, but made no reply.

"Sir," said he at last, "I will take no unfair advantage of you; I wish to get my servant once more; can I do so?"

"Certainly. I will bring him to thy lodgings this evening, if thee wish it. I know thee will do what is fair," said the Quaker.

It were difficult to define the thoughts of the young man, as he returned to his lodgings. Naturally generous and humane, he had never dreamed that he had rendered injustice to the human beings he claimed as his own. Injustice and oppression he had sometimes seen with detestation, in other establishments; but it had been his pride that they were excluded from his own. It had been his pride to think that his indulgence and liberality made a situation of dependence on him preferable even to liberty.

The dark picture of possible reverses which the slave system hangs over the lot of the most favoured slaves, never occurred to him. Accordingly, at six o'clock that evening, a light tap at the door of Mr. B.'s parlor, announced the Quaker, and hanging back behind him, the reluctant Sam, who, with all his newly-acquired love of liberty, felt almost as if he were treating his old master rather shabbily, in deserting him.

"So, Sam," said Alfred, "how is this? they say you want to leave me."

"Yes, master."

"Why, what's the matter, Sam? haven't I always been good to you; and has not my father always been good to you?"

"Oh yes, master; very good."

"Have you not always had good food, good clothes, and lived easy?"

"Yes, master."

"And nobody has ever abused you?"

"No, master."

"Well, then, why do you wish to leave me?"

"Oh, massa, I want to be a free man."

"Why, Sam, ain't you well enough off now?"

"Oh, massa may die; then nobody knows who get me; some dreadful folks, you know, master, might get me, as they did Jim Sanford, and nobody to take my part. No, master, I rather be free man."

Alfred turned to the window, and thought a few moments, and then said, turning about, "Well, Sam, I believe you are right. I think, on the whole, I'd like best to be a free man myself, and I must not wonder that you do. So, for ought I see, you must go; but then, Sam, there's your wife and child." Sam's countenance fell.

"Never mind, Sam. I will send them up to you."

"Oh, master!"

"I will; but you must remember now, Sam, you have got both yourself and them to take care of, and have no master to look after you; be steady, sober, and industrious, and then if ever you get into distress, send word to me, and I'll help you." Lest any accuse us of over-colouring our story, we will close it by extracting a passage or two from the letter which the generous young man the next day left in the hands of the Quaker, for his emancipated servant. We can assure our readers that we copy from the original document, which now lies before us:

DEAR SAM—I am just on the eve of my departure for Pittsburg; I may not see you again for a long time, possibly never, and I leave this letter with your friends, Messrs. A. and B., for you, and herewith bid you an affectionate farewell. Let me give you some advice, which is, now that you are a free man, in a free State, be obedient as you were when a slave; perform all the duties that are required of you, and do all you can for your own future welfare and respectability. Let me assure you that I have the same good feeling towards you that you know I always had; and let me tell you further, that if ever you want a friend, call or write to me, and I will be that friend. Should you be sick, and not able to work, and want money to a small amount at different times, write to me, and I will always let you have it. I have not with me at present much money, though I will leave with my agent here, the Messrs. W., five dollars for you; you must give them a receipt for it. On my return from Pittsburg, I will call and see you if I have time; fail not to write to my father, for he made you a good master, and you should always treat him with respect, and cherish his memory so long as you live. Be good, industrious, and honourable, and if unfortunate in your undertakings, never forget that you have a friend in me. Farewell, and believe me your affectionate young master and friend.

ALFRED B———.

That dispositions as ingenuous and noble as that of this young man, are commonly to be found either in slave States or free, is more than we dare to assert. But when we see such found, even among those who are born and bred slaveholders, we cannot but feel that there is encouragement for a fair, and mild, and brotherly presentation of truth, and every reason to lament hasty and wholesale denunciations. The great error of controversy is, that it is ever ready to assail *persons* rather than *principles*. The slave *system*, as a system, perhaps concentrates more wrong than any other now existing, and yet those who live under and in it may be, as we see, enlightened, generous, and amenable to reason. If the *system* alone is attacked, such minds will be the first to perceive its evils, and to turn against it; but if the system be attacked through individuals, self-love, wounded pride, and a thousand natural feelings, will be at once enlisted for its preservation. We therefore subjoin it as the moral of our story, that a man who has had the misfortune to be born and bred a slaveholder, may be enlightened, generous, humane, and capable of the most disinterested regard to the welfare of his slave.

# The Freeman's Dream

A PARABLE

Written in response to the passage of the Fugitive Slave Law, "The Freeman's Dream" makes a direct link between Christianity and civil disobedience. It was published in the *National Era* on August 1, 1850, just before Stowe began for that abolitionist publication the sketches that would become *Uncle Tom's Cabin*.

I t seemed to him that it was a fair summer evening, and he was walking calmly up and down his estate, watching the ripening grain and listening to the distant voices of his children, as they played by his door, and the song of his wife as she rocked her babe to rest, and the soul of the man grew soft within him, and he gave God thanks with a full heart.

But now there came towards him in the twilight a poor black man, worn and wasted, his clothes rent and travel-soiled, and his step crouching and fearful. He was one that had dwelt in darkness, and as one that had been long dead; and behind him stood, fearfully, a thin and trembling woman, with a wailing babe at her bosom, and a frightened child clinging to her skirts; and the man held out his hand wistfully, and begged for food and shelter, if only for one night, for the pursuer was behind him, and his soul failed him for fear.

The man was not hard, and his heart misgave him when he looked on the failing eye and toil-worn face—when he saw the worn and trembling hands stretched forth; but then he bethought him of human laws, and he feared to befriend him, and he hardened his heart, and set his face as a flint, and bade him pass on, and trouble him not.

And it was so that after he passed on, he saw that the pursuers came up with him, and the man and the woman could not escape, because they were weary and footsore, and there was no more strength in them. And the man heard their screams, and saw them bound and taken by them that would not show mercy.

And after these things the man dreamed, and it seemed to him that the sky grew dark, and the earth rocked to and fro, and the heavens flashed with strange light, and a distant rush, as of wings, was heard, and suddenly, in mid heavens, appeared the sign of the Son of Man, with his mighty angels. Upward, with countless myriads, dizzied and astounded, he seemed to be borne from the earth towards the great white throne and Him that sat thereon, before whose face the heavens and the earth fled away.

Onward, a resistless impulse impelled him towards the bar of the mighty

Judge, and before him, as if written in fire, rose in a moment all the thoughts and words and deeds of his past life; and as if he had been the only son of earth to be judged, he felt himself standing alone and trembling before that all-searching Presence. Then an awful voice pierced his soul, saying—"Depart from me ye accursed! for I was an hungered, and ye gave me no meat; I was thirsty, and ye gave me no drink; I was a stranger, and ye took me not in." And, terrified and subdued, the man made answer, "Lord, where?" And immediately rose before him these poor fugitive slaves, whom he had spurned from his door; and the Judge made answer—"Inasmuch as ye did it not to one of the least of these my brethren, ye did it not to me." And with that, terrified and affrighted, the man awoke.

Of late, there have seemed to be many in this nation, who seem to think that there is no standard of right and wrong higher than an act of Congress, or an interpretation of the United States Constitution. It is humiliating to think that there should be in the church of Christ men and ministers who should need to be reminded that the laws of their Master are above human laws which come in conflict with them; and that though heaven and earth pass away, His word shall not pass away.

Are not the hungry, the thirsty, the stranger, the naked, the prisoner, and every form of bleeding, suffering humanity, as much under the protection of Christ in the person of the black as the white—of the bond as the free? Has he not solemnly told us, and once for all, that every needy human being is His brother, and that neglect of his wants is neglect of Himself?

Shall any doubt if he *may* help the toil-worn, escaping fugitive, sick in heart, weary in limb, hungry and heartsore—let him rather ask, shall he dare refuse him help? To him, too, shall come a dread hour, when a lonely fugitive from life's shore, in unknown lands, he must beg for shelter and help. The only Saviour in that hour is Him who has said, "Inasmuch as ye did it not to the least of these my brethren, ye did it not to *me!*"

❦ ❦ ❦

# To Frederick Douglass, July 9, 1851

In the midst of writing *Uncle Tom's Cabin,* Stowe seeks information from eloquent abolitionist Frederick Douglass, whose narrative of his life as a slave had appeared in 1845. In addition to asking Douglass to provide her details about slavery, Stowe attempts to change his views of the American clergy, rehearsing arguments she would soon use in Part IV of *A Key to Uncle Tom's Cabin.* Here, however, she makes no mention of the proslavery pronouncements of synods and conferences. There are no known replies to this letter.

Frederick Douglass Esq

Sir—

You may perhaps have noticed in your editorial readings a series of articles that I am furnishing for the Era under the title of "Uncle Tom's Cabin or Life among the lowly"—In the course of my story, the scene will fall upon a cotton plantation—I am very desirous here to gain information from one who has been an actual labourer on one—& it occurs to me that in the circle of your acquaintance there might be one who would be able to communicate to me some such information as I desire—I have before me an able paper written by a southern planter in which the details & modus operandi are given from *his* point of sight—I am anxious to have some now from another stand point—I wish to be able to make a picture that shall be graphic & true to nature in its details—Such a person as Henry Bibb,[1] if in this country might give me just the kind of information I desire you may possibly know of some other person—I will subjoin to this letter a list of questions which in that case, you will do me a favor by inclosing to the individual with a request that he will at earliest convenience answer them—

For some few weeks past, I have received your paper[2] thro the mail—& have read it with great interest—& desire to return my acknowledgements for it—It will be a pleasure to me at some time, when less occupied to contribute something to its columns—

—I have noticed with regret, your sentiments on two subjects,—the church—& African Colonization—& with the more regret, because I think you have a considerable share of reason for your feelings on both these subjects—*but* I would willingly if I could modify your view on both points

—In the first place you say the church is "pro slavery"—There is a sense in which this may be true—The American church of all denominations taken as a body—comprise the best & most conscientious people in the country—I do *not* say it comprises *none but these*—or that more such are found out of it—but only that if a census were taken of the purest & most high principled men & women of our country the *majority* of them would be found to be professors of religion in some of the various christian denominations—

—This fact has given to the church great weight in this country—the general & predominant spirit of intelligence & probity & piety of its majority has given it that degree of weight—that it has the *power* to decide the great moral questions of the day—Whatever it unitedly & decidedly sets itself against as a moral evil it *can* put down—

---

[1] Henry Bibb recounted his experiences under slavery and his escape from it in *Narrative of the Life and Adventures of Henry Bibb, Written by Himself* (New York: Published by the author, 1849).

[2] Douglass began publishing *The North Star* in 1847. In 1851 he changed the name of his paper to *Frederick Douglass's Paper* to distinguish it from all the other papers that had "stars" in them.

In this sense the church is responsible for the sin of slavery—Dr Barnes has beautifully & briefly expressed this on the last page of his work on slavery when he says "Not all the force *out* of the church could sustain slavery an hour if it were not sustained *in* it"—[3]

It then appears that the church has the *power* to put an end to this evil—& does not do it—In this sense she may be said to be *pro slavery*—But the church has the same power over intemperence & sabbath breaking—& sin of all kind— no doubt if the moral power of the church were brought up to the N Testament point it is sufficient to put an end to all these too

But I would ask you would you consider it a fair representation of the christian church in this country to say it is prointemperence—pro, sabbath breaking & pro every thing which it might put down if it was in a higher state of moral feeling?—

—If you should make a list of all the abolitionists of the country I think you would find a majority of them in the church—certainly some of the most influential & efficient ones are ministers—

—I am a ministers daughter—a ministers wife & I have had six brothers in the ministry—(one is in Heaven)—& I certainly ought to know something of the feelings of ministers—I was a child in 1821—when the Missouri question was agitated[4] & some of the strongest & deepest impressions on my mind were my fathers sermons & prayers—& the anguish of his soul for the poor slave at that time—I remember his preaching drawing tears down the hardest faces of the old farmers—I remember his prayers night & morning in the family for "poor oppressed bleeding Africa" that the time of her deliverance might come prayers offered with strong crying & tears, & which indelibly impressed my heart & made me what I am from my soul the enemy of all slavery—Every brother I have has been in his sphere a leading anti slavery man—one of them was to the last hour of his life the bosom friend & counsellor of Lovejoy[5]—& all have been known & read of all men—As for myself & husband we have lived on the border of a slave state,—& we have never for years shrunk from the fugitive—we have helped them with all we had to give— I have received the children of liberated slaves into a family school & taught them with my own children—& it has been the influence that we found *in the church* & by the altar that has made us all do this—Gather up all the sermons that have been published on the offensive & unchristian Law & you will find that those against it are numerically more than those in its favour—& yet some of the strongest opponents have not published their sermons—out of thirteen ministers who meet with

[3]Dr. Albert Barnes (1798–1870), a Presbyterian clergyman and a colleague of Lyman Beecher.

[4]The Missouri Compromise of 1820 (not 1821, as Stowe misremembered) proposed admission of Maine as a free state and of Missouri as a slave state and excluded slavery from the Louisiana Purchase north of 36° 30'.

[5]Edward Beecher was with Elijah Lovejoy (1802–1837) when he was murdered in Alton, Illinois, while defending his abolitionist newspaper. Lovejoy was the most important abolitionist martyr before John Brown. Stowe includes a long account of his experiences in Part IV of *A Key to Uncle Tom's Cabin*.

my husband weekly for discussion of moral subjects only three are found who will acknowledge or obey this law in any shape—

—After all my brother, the strength & hope of your oppressed race does lie in the *church*—In hearts united to Him of whom it is said He shall spare the souls of the needy—precious shall their blood be in his sight—Every thing is against you—but *Jesus Christ* is for you—& He has not forgotten his church misguided & erring tho it be—I have looked all the field over with despairing eye—

I see no hope except in Him—This movement must & will become a purely religious one—the light will spread in churches—the tone of feeling will rise—christians north & south will give up all connection with & take up their testimony against it—& thus the work will be done—

[Harriet Beecher Stowe Center Library, Hartford, Connecticut]

❦ ❦ ❦

# To Catharine Beecher, n.d. [1850 or 1851]

In this letter to her sister Stowe vents her increasing wrath over the coolness of the nation in the face of the Fugitive Slave Law. Her tea table disagreement with Professor Upham demonstrates that women and children—who could not vote—debated the laws of the United States in that domestic sphere of power, the parlor, and found them wanting. Her dispute with Professor Upham—whose resolve wavered when faced with an actual fugitive slave—parallels the experience of Senator Bird in the chapter in *Uncle Tom's Cabin* entitled "In Which It Appears that a Senator Is but a Man."

DEAR SISTER

Your last letter was a real good one, it did my heart good to find somebody in as indignant a state as I am about this miserable wicked fugitive slave business

Why I have felt almost choked sometimes with pent up wrath that does no good—Not so much at the southerners who very naturally are blinded by their interests but at those who as OConnel[1] says "having no interest at all in the matter for an apology must do it from sheer disinterested love of wickedness"—Not that I think that this language does really apply to them for many of them are very good people, but they certainly lay themselves open to the worst of suppo-

[1]Daniel O'Connell (1775–1847), Irish political leader who fought for Catholic emancipation and the repeal of the union with England.

sitions, who can want to hush up & salve over such an outrage on common humanity to say nothing of religion

—The Union!—Some unions I think are better broken than kept & to a union cemented on such terms might apply the text "Tho hand join in hand &c

Well now would you believe it here is Proff Upham[2] talking somewhat in this way—He has got his mind filled with an idea of the negroes having been brought into this country in order to acquire civilization & christianity & be sent back to evangelise Africa & that our nation ought to buy them with the public money & send them off—& until that is done he is for bearing every thing in silence—stroking & saying "pussy pussy" so as to allay all prejudice & avoid all agitation!

He & and I had over the tea table the other night that sort of an argument which consists in both sides saying over & over just what they said before, for any length of time—but when I asked him flatly if he would obey the law supposing a fugitive came to him Mrs. Upham[3] laughed & he hemmed & hawed & little Mary Upham broke out "I wouldnt I know"

Well the next day there comes a long a fugitive bound for Canada and Smyth[4] sends him right up to Proff Upham who takes him into his study & hears his story, gives him a dollar & Mrs. Upham puts in bountifully in the provision line & then he comes here for lodging—Now our beds were all full & before this law passed I might have tried to send him somewhere else As it was all hands in the house united in making him up a bed in our waste room & Henry & Freddy & Georgy[5] seemed to think they could not do too much for him—There hasnt any body in our house got waited on so abundantly & willingly for ever so long—these negroes possess some mysterious power of pleasing children for they hung round him & seemed never tired of hearing him talk & sing He was a genuine article from the "Ole Carling State"

—Father E_____[6] of Bath, too, had been talking greatly about "sustaining the Union" & Smith sent the coloured br[other] to him also—& E_____ gave him a dollar & told him to put on for Canada—their hearts are better on this point than their heads

[Beecher Family Papers, Sterling Memorial Library, Yale University]

[2]Thomas Cogswell Upham (1799–1872), Professor of Mental and Moral Philosophy at Bowdoin College. An early supporter of the colonization movement and a life member of the American Colonization Society, he was described by one of his admiring students as having the fault of "excessive nervous timidity."
[3]Phebe Lord Upham of Kennebunk, Maine.
[4]William Smyth (1797–1868), Professor of Greek and Mathematics at Bowdoin College, well known for his support of temperance and antislavery. His home in Brunswick was said to be a station on the underground railroad.
[5]Stowe's children Henry Ellis, Frederick William, and Georgiana May.
[6]Rev. John W. Ellingwood, retired pastor of the Old North (Congregational) Church in Bath, Maine.

❦ ❦ ❦

# To Henry Ward Beecher,
# February 1, 1851

Stowe's brother Henry Ward Beecher was at this time an editor of the *Independent*, an antislavery religious weekly. Throughout her career Stowe relied on her network of well-connected siblings to provide her with information and access to organs of public opinion. As she responds to articles in Henry's paper and gives him suggestions, her impatience with second-hand participation in the Fugitive Slave Law debate is palpable.

Feby 1st & onward all along shore

DEAR HENRY

It is even so—you know and have said what is a deep yet not often spoken sorrow to me, how little there is to be of sympathy and communion on this side of the grave—in every way I see more and more how little this life amounts to, how little that we can hold to our heart for a moment and say *it is here*. Nevertheless I shall not willingly give up what little may be permitted—nor quickly let the multifarious *present* which is so mighty with you, elbow me out of every little nook and corner of your heart and memory. This eternal railroad whizz I protest against, quite perhaps to as much purpose as if I protested against a literal one under full head of steam.

Evening—To day I read over Storrs article in answer to the N York observer.[1] You dont know how my heart burns within me at the blindness and obtuseness of good people on so very simple a point of morality as this—Storrs piece is a very fine one—I thought it was yours till I got thro and saw the signature.

If I thank God for anything it is that you and Charles[2] are enlisted in this cause as you are heartily, wholly over shoes and stockings—Some of the defences of these principles are so very guarded and candid and cautious and sweet and

[1]Richard Storrs, "The Right of Self-Defense," *Independent*, January 30, 1851, p. 18. Storrs responds to the *Observer's* attack on the *Independent's* position that fugitive slaves have the right to defend themselves.
[2]Stowe's brother Charles Edward Beecher.

explanatory that they put me in mind of little Dr. Chillip laying his head on one side and saying "Do you know Mr. Copperfield—that I *dont* find Mr. and Miss Murdstone in the New Testament?"[3]

As if a man should get up and with great parade and begging a thousand pardons tell us that *he* really as an individual could not see his way clear to murder his father and mother in bed even tho required to do it by the laws of his country—that as far as he could see—he could not bring himself to think that any law could make that right. Must we forever keep calm and smile and smile when every sentiment of manliness and humanity is kicked and rolled in the dust and lies trampled and bleeding and make it a moment to be exceedingly cool! I feel as if my heart would burn itself out in grief and shame that such things are. I wish I had your chance, but next best to that it is to have you have it, so fire away, give them no rest day nor night.

I read your Shakspear Sabbath.[4] You feel a stronger sympathy with him than I do. So I have felt, but not so perhaps I should feel at that shrine. Martin Luthers grave might be a more likely spot. Why dont you publish your criticisms on the paintings I should like to have that. Bailey[5] sent me a check the other day for $100 and wanted me to furnish as much as I chose and what I chose for it next year. Can you furnish me suggestions and materials for some graphic sketches that shall have some bearing on the slave power and principle instead of a political idea.

Would to God I could do something even the humblest in this cause. I have actually and really found tears dropping on my pillow when I have thought of the wrongs and sorrows of those oppressed ones. Is it possible that Henry Long[6] is hopelessly sold and that in all this nation of freemen there is not one deliverer brave enough and strong enough to recover him—be delivered up by freemen and northern men and are there Christians that can find nothing better to do than cry peace when such things are done. How I detest that cool way of lumping together all the woes and crimes, the heart-breaks, the bitter untold agonies of thousand poor bleeding helpless hearts, many creatures with the bland expression its very sad to be sure—very dreadful—but we musn't allow our feelings to run away with us, we must consider &c., &c, &c.

I heard from Putnam that Father had been there preaching seven times a week. Well done, for him.

---

[3]In Dickens's *David Copperfield*, Dr. Chillip is a meek character who "carried his head on one side, partly in modest depreciation of himself, partly in modest propitiation of everybody else." Edward Murdstone is David's stepfather, who together with his sister Jane Murdstone cruelly punish and harass David.
[4]Henry Ward Beecher, "A Sabbath at Stratford-on-Avon," *Independent*, August 4, 1850, p. 14.
[5]Gamaliel Bailey, editor of the antislavery *National Era*. See next letter.
[6]In a celebrated example of the Fugitive Slave Law at work, Henry Long, a waiter at the Pacific Hotel in New York, was violently seized while waiting on table and taken to the U. S. clerk's office, where he learned that he was claimed by one John T. Smith. In spite of evidence that he was in New York months before he was supposed to have fled from Richmond, Virginia, Long was sent South to his claimant.

Now I take the Independent I seem to get a letter from you weekly so write away as much as ever you can and I will answer when I feel like it.

Don't fail to come this way as you intimated this spring. I need a days talk and I wish it would only be in season so that we could take a carriage and spend the day down by the sea among the beautiful islands and glorious scenery of our sea coast. Can you send me any thing that will give me the argument that Christians use who defend obedience to the slave law. I might perhaps feel more charity if I saw the other side—at present I cannot see or imagine what plausible thing can be said—except that might makes right.

What will the end be? *Will* this nation acquiesce in this horrid wrong? What do you see from your watch tower.

You see in this note how this subject has laid hold of me but I have known a great many slaves—had them in my family, known their history and feelings and seen how alike their heart beats to any other throbbing heart and above all what woman deepest feels I have seen the strength of their instinctive and domestic attachments in which *as a race* they excell the anglo saxon. The poor slave on whom the burden of domestic bereavement falls heaviest is precisely the creature of all Gods creatures that feels it deepest. Strive, pray labor Henry be the champion of the oppressed and may God defend and bless you.

One thing—why dont your papers publish the fugitive law—no comment is a greater libel. If I find universally that when I come to put this law directly at the unionist and say "would you not feed the hungry and clothe the naked slave" that they shrink and say this is not forbidden it is not against the law—I think it ought to be put in every Christian paper once a week that people may know what it is. I for one have never seen it and half the people I talk with never have.[7] Well I may as well stop here as anywhere.

AFFECTIONATELY YOURS,
HATTY

[Beecher Family Papers, Sterling Memorial Library, Yale University]

❦ ❦ ❦

# To Gamaliel Bailey, March 9, 1851

Written to the editor of the *National Era* while Stowe was in the initial stages of writing *Uncle Tom's Cabin*, this letter provides an excellent view of her rhetorical strategies and motives.

---

[7]The *Independent* printed the text of the Fugitive Slave Law on October 3, 1850.

Brunswick, March 9 [1851]
Maine

Mr. Bailey,

DEAR SIR:

I am at present occupied upon a story which will be a much longer one than any I have ever written, embracing a series of sketches which give the lights and shadows of the "patriarchal institution", written either from observation, incidents which have occurred in the sphere of my personal knowledge, or in the knowledge of my friends. I shall show the *best side* of the thing, and something *faintly approaching the worst*.

Up to this year I have always felt that I had no particular call to meddle with this subject, and I dreaded to expose even my own mind to the full force of its exciting power. But I feel now that the time is come when even a woman or a child who can speak a word for freedom and humanity is bound to speak. The Carthagenian women in the last peril of their state cut off their hair for bow strings to give to the defenders of their country, and such peril and shame as now hangs over this country is worse than Roman slavery, and I hope every woman who can write will not be silent. I have admired and sympathized with the fearless and free spirit of Grace Greenwood, and her letters have done my heart good.[1] My vocation is simply that of *painter*, and my object will be to hold up in the most lifelike and graphic manner possible slavery, its reverses, changes, and the negro character, which I have had ample opportunities for studying. There is no arguing with *pictures*, and everybody is impressed by them, whether they mean to be or not.

I wrote beforehand because I know that you have much matter to arrange, and thought it might not be amiss to give you a hint. The thing may extend through three or four numbers. It will be ready in two or three weeks.

A week or two ago I sent to Mrs. Bailey a story from one of my friends for her paper,[2] requesting also to have my name put down as a subscriber. I have since heard nothing from it. Should the story not prove suitable to her purposes, she will oblige me by redirecting it to me.
(Ms. illegible.)

YOURS WITH [SINCERE] ESTEEM,
H. STOWE
[Typescript copy, Boston Public Library]

[1] Journalist Grace Greenwood (Sara Jane Lippincott) published letters on travel and other subjects in Bailey's *National Era*. In 1850, beginning with a letter in March of that year on the abolition of slavery in the District of Columbia, Greenwood's letters became increasingly political.
[2] *The Friend of Youth*, a monthly newspaper edited by Margaret L. Bailey.

# To The Reverend Joel Parker, [New York], [May 22, 1852]

In Chapter 12 of *Uncle Tom's Cabin*, Stowe quoted a proslavery pronouncement by Joel Parker, a Presbyterian minister, and identified him by name in a footnote. Parker demanded a public retraction and threatened a $20,000 lawsuit. In this and her subsequent replies to Parker, Stowe refused to back down from her understanding of his position, though she had already attempted unsuccessfully to have the footnote removed, as it eventually would be. Stowe's rhetorical advantage in this letter to an ordained minister comes from her adoption of the innocent stance of a Christian who has no doubt of the evils of slavery.

Revd Joel Parker

DEAR SIR

Your letter, via Brunswick reached me in this city about a week since & only feeble health & the multiplied engagements of anniversary week have delayed my reply to this time.

Give me leave to assure you that you have entirely misapprehended the purpose & spirit with which I quoted the remark attributed to you with your name. It had nothing to do with personal feeling one way or the other. I simply quoted you as a well known leading man, who I supposed to be an acknowledged supporter of the pro slavery side of the question—& I quoted you in preference to any of the other clergymen on that side of the question simply because the remark attributed to you, was more neatly and pointedly expressed, & more summarily included the whole subject than any remark of others to the same general purport

My reason for considering you on the proslavery side of the question will be better appreciated by you by showing the manner in which I was led to that opinion It is considerably more than a year ago that I saw the sentence in question quoted in one of the leading papers of the day with your name. I said immediately that I did not believe you had said it—& that I knew you would contradict it—I searched the papers week after week with the eye of a friend for that denial—I only found the thing reaffirmed in paper after paper both religious & secular. It was embraced in a schedule of the sayings & sentiments of American Ministers in regard to slavery which was read at a public meeting in the World's

Fair & which formed a basis of some considerable discussion & action on the pro-priety of admitting American preachers without examination into English Pulpits—These papers in which all this was recorded were the leading religious prints—prints which I could not suppose you were not familiar with & I could not suppose that you would allow any sentiment to go the rounds of them, printed in capitals with your name in full, unless it were a sentiment to which you were fully committed & which you were determined to abide by & sustain—

I therefore with great regret, set you down in my mind as a leader on that side of the question & quoted you as such—and I think that I had reason to do so.

If you thought the imputation of this sentiment a "stain" on your character an injury to your christian & ministerial reputation—why have you never before contradicted it?—Why have you allowed it quoted & requoted from paper to paper proclaimed in a public meeting at the worlds fair—& returned in capitals to this country & not come out with the most earnest denial of which you were capable?—

Yet your note was the first *shadow* of any reason I have ever had for thinking that this opinion was *not* yours—& that you were not willing to be considered on that side of the question—

Under this attitude—you must perceive that it is not in *my* power to set you right before a Christian public who probably have formed their opinion from the same sources from which I formed mine.—The quotation of it in the book, is only one indication of that very general belief which attributes to you such sentiments & it is to the christian public generally as I apprehend, that your denial of such sentiments & expressions should be addressed & to them you should explain why you have allowed yourself to be so publicly & frequently & notoriously ranged on that side of the question, & why you have taken no notice of what you say you consider as a "libel"—when it has been so very publicly & for such a long time proclaimed in the ordinary channels of intelligence.

I need not say that a satisfactory explanation of this matter would give me pleasure. It is no pleasure to me to have it proved that any minister of the Saviour could have said such a thing & I should be sincerely glad to see you exhonerated before the public when you shall have satisfactorily explained the subject. I will with pleasure do any thing that may be in my power to obviate the misconcep-tions that have arisen from your long silence

TRULY YOURS
HB STOWE


In the chapter in which your remark occurs I considered myself as the advocate of the poor & uneducated against the educated & the powerful I have ever con-sidered the American Internal Slave trade as the vital support of the system that without which it would immediately become worthless in a pecuniary point of view & of course ceace to exist & therefore I confronted the sentiment with the dramatic reality of the slave trade

[Beecher Family Papers, Sterling Memorial Library, Yale University]

❦ ❦ ❦

# To Henry Ward Beecher,
# November 1, 1852

Thinking to call her bluff, Parker challenged Stowe to prove that the American Protestant churches had made public statements supporting slavery. Stowe gleefully accepted the challenge and enlisted her brothers as research assistants. Parker did not publish the resulting materials in the *New York Observer*. Stowe later included many of them in Part IV of *A Key to Uncle Tom's Cabin*.

Andover Nov 1 1852

DEAR HENRY

I suppose you have seen my solemn adjuration & citation in the New York Observer—well the man will have it—let him take it—I send you herein my acceptance of his challenge—Wait one week & if he does n't publish it—publish it in the Independent quoting beforehand his address to me. If he does publish, publish it no less, for your readers The man has no kind of idea what he has brought upon himself nor of the tremendous antislavery battery that he has pledged himself to erect in the sacred limits of the Observer if I only will be so good as to furnish him materials.

Edward who in his way is no fool particularly in exhuming all sorts of inconvenient declarations & arranging them in most uncomfortable proximities is already up to his chin in documents which he reads & makes notes of with that grave thoughtful smile peculiar to him we have a great abundance of declarations of Synods, Presbyteries & Ecclesiastical bodies of all denominations which are in their way considerably striking—All I want is a few declarations selected from the back files of the N. Y. Observer—I am very sure that that sentiment has been asserted there—also the back files of the Philadelphia Observer—I think the sentiment that slavery stands on the same ground with other lawful relations was pretty broadly asserted in a review of Uncle Tom in that paper—Ask Lewis Tappan[1] "that very active & persevering Secretary" (N. Y. O.) if he has any thing on his shelves—Let him write & tell *what he has* & if we have n't got it, he can

---

[1]Lewis Tappan (1788–1873) was a New York philanthropist who supported antislavery causes.

69

sent it to us. Documentary reports of Ecclesiastical bodies are the thing Back numbers of the Princeton Repertory—during the time of the controversy with Albert Barnes are specially requisite—I will write an article that shall cite the delinquents on this subject at the bar of public opinion every where from here to Leipsic & happy those who have always stood firm like Albert Barnes & some others I could name—Now if Tappan has the back numbers of the Princeton Repertory during that controversy let him send them by Express—

Cant you come on & see us—things are getting decidedly interesting. You will see by this article how much afraid I am—I would gladly have been silent, he would make me speak—now he shall hear me out & the world shall hear what atrocious things have been said in the name & authority of Christ by his church in this country—Mr Underwood of Kentucky told me the other day that one very consientous man in Kentucky after reading my book had bought land in Ohio & was about removing his slaves there to free them & of two others who had made their wills freeing their slaves at death. This is a commentary on the book's being hurtful to the slave It gives them liberty, which is a very bad thing—Henry—the battle is coming on—when it will end, I know not—I only hope every one feels as alert as I do—Do come & see us—do. Why dont Susy[2] write me? my autograph is worth something now-a-days & I wrote her & Essie a large letter with mine own hand which is more than I can do for you today having written the enclosed, *three times* with my own hand since yesterday morning—

The one to the Observer was mailed last night & before you publish it, it is as well to wait & see what they will do about it. The probability is that he will tell his readers that he has received a long & very scurrilous letter from Mrs Stowe which self respect will forbid him to publish or he may garble it for I notice that his mode of treating articles very much resembles our little black Trip's. he shakes them about in his mouth rolls them in the mud tears them to strips, & then holds them up as much as to say "See now what kind of an article this is"—It may be somewhat amusing to compare my piece after he has shaken it with the original article—I declare, it is a shame to laugh at him so, but as Brother Straels said to Mr Stowe—I cant cry— I would if I could." Dont pray show this for it really is too bad only between ourselves a little fun in this dismally solemn world is as good as a little wine for the stomach's sake.

GOODBYE   YOUR AFFECTIONATE SISTER<br>HATTY

Dont you admire the *closing* request in my letter.

[Beecher Family Papers, Sterling Memorial Library, Yale University]

[2]Susan Howard. John and Susan Howard were wealthy parishioners in Henry Ward Beecher's Plymouth Church in Brooklyn.

# To Eliza Cabot Follen, December 16, 1852

After the publication of *Uncle Tom's Cabin*, Eliza Cabot Follen, American author of numerous books for children, wrote to Stowe from England requesting that she supply some information about herself. Stowe's reply arrived shortly before her triumphal tour of the British Isles in 1853 and was doubtless thought of by both correspondents as something of a public relations ploy. It was copied numerous times and passed among the philanthropic and literary women of England. There are four surviving copies (each with slight variations). The original has been lost. The text here is from the copy in Dr. Williams's Library, London.

Andover, Dec. 16/52

My Dear Madam,

I hasten to reply to your letter to me the more interesting that I have long been acquainted with you, and during all the nursery part of my life, made daily use of your little poems for children. I used to think sometimes in those days that I would write to you & tell you how much I was obliged to you for the pleasure which they gave us all.

So you want to know something about what sort of a woman I am——well, if this is any object, you shall have statistics free of charge.

To begin then, I am a little bit of a woman—somewhat more than 40—about as thin & dry as a pinch of snuff—never very much to look at in my best days—& looking like a used up article now. I was married when I was 25 years old to a man rich in Greek & Hebrew, Latin & Arabic, & alas! rich in nothing else. When I went to housekeeping, my entire stock of china for parlour & kitchen was bought for 11 dollars, & this lasted very well for 2 years, till my brother who was married & brought in his bride to visit me & found upon review that I had neither plates nor teacups enough to set a table for my father's family, wherefore I thought it best to reinforce the establishment by getting me a tea-set which cost 10 dollars more, & this, I believe, formed my whole stock in trade for some years.

But then I was abundantly enriched with wealth of another kind. I had 2 little curly headed twin daughters to begin with, & my stock in this line has gradually increased till I have been the mother of 7 children, the most beautiful of which, the most loved, lies buried near my Cincinati residence. It was at *his* dying bed & at *his* grave, that I learnt what a poor slave mother may feel when her child is torn away from her. In the depths of sorrow, which seemed to me immeasurable, it was my only prayer to God that such anguish might not be suffered in vain! There were circumstances about his death, of such peculiar bitterness, of what might seem almost cruel suffering, that I felt I could never be consoled for it, unless it should appear that this crushing of my own heart might enable me to work out some great good to others. It was during the cholera summer, when in a circle of 5 miles around me, in the short space of 3 months, 9000 were buried around me, a mortality which I have never heard exceeded any where. My husband in feeble health was obliged to be absent the whole time, & I had sole charge of a family of 15 persons. He could not return to me because I would not permit it, for in many instances, where parents abroad had returned to their families in the infected atmosphere, the result had been sudden death, & the physicians warned me that if he returned it would be only to die. My poor Charlie died for want of medical aid timely rendered for in the universal confusion & despair that prevailed, it was often impossible to obtain assistance till it was too late.

I allude to this now, because I have often felt that much that is in this book had its root in the awful scenes & bitter sorrows of that summer. It has left now, I trust, no trace in any mind except a deep compassion for the sorrowful, especially for mothers who are separated from their children.

You have probably read the article in Frazer's Magazine.[1] It is in most respects a true history, tho' I think somewhat coloured. In looking it over, tho' I could not deny that the facts had all occurred, yet it struck me that there was more the air of romance about it than was really consistent with truth. In one respect he is mistaken. He seems to think that the Anti slavery collision in Lane Seminary was cause of the subsequent difficulties & embarassments, pecuniary & otherwise, which rendered our Western residence arduous & uncomfortable.[2] In this respect he is mistaken. The facts of the case were these. When we went out there, we found an Institution organized with that looseness of design & rudeness of conception which often attends enterprizes in a new country. All conceivable & contradictory impossibilities were to be accomplished by it. It was to embrace High School, College, Theological Seminary, & manual Labour Institution all together. My father & husband found a mixed multitude to the number of 300, of all ages & sizes from High School boys to men of 22 & 30 years, all mingling together in most admired disorder; everything to be done in the future, with no buildings or accommodations of any sort do it with. They took advantage of the Anti Slavery explosion to retrench & methodize this system of housekeeping. They cut off the Preparatory School & College, because there were an abundance of better ones in the immediate vicinity, & resolved to confine themselves to the one object of

[1]William Birney, "Some Account of Mrs. Beecher Stowe and Her Family," *Fraser's Magazine* 46(November 1852):518–525.
[2]Stowe refers to the famous Lane Debates of 1834 organized by Theodore Weld on the slavery question. Weld later led a walk-out in which fifty-one students followed him to Oberlin College. This was a public relations disaster for Lane Seminary.

preparing young men already educated, for the ministry. Of course the outward show of scholars greatly decreased, & it was said that there was but a handful of them, but there were as many theological students as there had been before, only the other departments were wanting. The object was now to get the proper buildings & endowments for a permanent Theological Institution, by which an educated, intelligent Protestant ministry should be disseminated thro' the Western valley. Then came on that great pecuniary pressure which was felt all thro' America;[3] banks & mercantile houses were failing all over the country, & the funds of our Institution were very seriously involved. My Father's whole support was lost in the failure of a mercantile house,[4] & he supported himself, while he performed his duties as President of the Seminary, by being at the same time Pastor of a neighbouring city church. The funds of Mr. Stowe's professorship were invested in banks which either failed or suspended payment, & our yearly income was reduced to a mere pittance. Still it was thought on all hands that we must not leave the position, but struggle on with what hope we might, till the Institution should be cleared from debt. It was the hardest trial of our life at this time, to be obliged to refuse continual invitations to return to New England, whose climate was more favourable to our health, & which was endeared to us as our native land, especially as these invitations were accompanied with offers of pecuniary competence.

During these long years of struggling with poverty & sickness, & a hot debilitating climate, my children grew up around me. The nursery & the kitchen were my principal fields of labour.

Some of my friends pitying my toils, copied & sent some of my little sketches to certain liberally paying annuals, with my name. With the first money that I earned in this way, I bought a *feather bed*! for as I had married into poverty & without a dowry, & as my husband had only a large library of books, & a great deal of learning, this bed & pillows was thought on the whole, the most profitable investment. After this, I thought I had discovered the philosopher's stone, & when a new carpet or a mattress was going to be needed, or when at the close of the year, it began to be evident that my family accounts, like poor Dora's,[5] *"wouldn't add up,"* then I used to say to my faithful friend & factotum Anna,[6] who shared all my joys & sorrows, "Now if you'll keep the babies & attend to all the things in the house for one day, I'll write a piece, & then we shall be out of the scrape;" & so I became an authoress. Very modest, at first I do assure you, & remonstrating very seriously with the friends who had thought it best to put my name to the pieces, by way of getting up a reputation, & if you ever get to see a

---

[3]The Panic of 1837.
[4]The mercantile house of Arthur Tappan, New York philanthropist who supported various antislavery causes, including Lane Seminary.
[5]Dora Copperfield, the "child-wife" in Dickens's *David Copperfield*.
[6]Anna Smith became Stowe's live-in household help in 1836, the year Stowe married and gave birth to twins. She stayed for the eighteen years of their Cincinnati sojourn, followed them to Brunswick in 1850, and left shortly thereafter to return to the midwest.

wood cut of me, with an inordinately long nose, on the cover of all the Anti Slavery almanacs I wish you to take notice that I have been forced into it, contrary to my natural modesty by the imperative solicitations of my dear 5000 friends & the public generally.

One thing I must say with regard to my life at the West, which you will understand better than many Englishwomen could.

I lived 2 miles from the city of Cincinati, in the country, & domestic service you know, not always to be found in the city, is next to an impossibility to be obtained in the country, even by those who are willing to give the highest wages. So what was to be expected for poor me who had very little of this world's good to offer? Had it not been for my inseparable friend Anna a noble hearted English girl, who landed on our American shores in destitution & sorrow, & who clave unto me as Ruth to Naomi, I had never lived through all the toil which this uncertainty & absolute want of Domestic service imposed on both; you may imagine therefore how glad I was when our Seminary property being divided into small lots, which were rented out at a low price, a number of poor families settled in our vicinity, from whom we could occasionally obtain domestic services.— About a dozen families of liberated slaves were among the number, & they became my favorite resorts in cases of emergency.—If any body wants to have a black face look handsome, let them be left as I have been, in feeble health, in oppressive, hot weather, with a sick baby in arms, & two or three other little ones in the nursery, and not a servant in the whole house to do a single turn: & then if they should see my good old aunt Frankie, coming in with her honest, bluff, black face, her long, strong arms, her chest as big & stout as a barrel, & her hilarious hearty laugh, perfectly delighted to take one's washing, & do it at a fair price, they would appreciate the beauty of black people—My cook, poor Eliza Buck (how she would stare to think of her name's going to England) was a regular epitome of slave life in herself, fat gentle, easy, loving & loveable, always calling my very modest house & door yard, "The Place" as if it had been a plantation with 700 hands on it.— Her way of arranging her kitchen was at first somewhat like Dinah's, though she imbibed our ideas more rapidly, & seemed more ready to listen to suggestions, than did that dignitary. She had lived through the whole sad story of a Virginia-raised slave's life. In her youth she must have been a very handsome mulatto girl. Her voice was sweet & her manner refined & agreeable. She was raised in a good family as nurse & sempstress. When the family became embarrased, she was suddenly sold onto a plantation in Louisiana; She has often told me how without any warning, she was suddenly forced into a carriage, & saw her little mistress screaming & stretching her arms from the window towards her, as she was driven away. She has told me of scenes on the Louisiana plantations & how she has often been out in the night by stealth, ministering to poor slaves, who had been mangled & lacerated by the whip.—Thence she was sold again into Kentucky, & her last master was the father of all her children. On this point she always maintained a delicacy & reserve, which, though it is not at all uncommon among slave women, always appeared to me remarkable—She always called him her husband, & spoke of him with the same apparent feeling with which any woman regards her husband, & it was not till after she had lived with me some years that I discovered accidentally, the real nature of the connexion.—I shall never forget how sorry I felt for her, nor my feelings at her humble apology—"You know, Mrs. Stowe, slave women can't help themselves." She had two very pretty quadroon daughters with beautiful hair & eyes, interesting children, whom I had instructed in the family school with my children. Time would fail me to tell you all that I learnt incidentally of the working of the slave system, in the history of various slaves, who came into my family and of the *underground railroad*, which I may say ran through our barn.[7] But I have made my labor already too long.—

You ask with regard to the remuneration which I have received for my work, here in America. Having been poor all my life, & expecting to be poor to the end of it, the idea of making anything by a book which I wrote just because I could not help it, never occurred to me. It was therefore, an agreeable surprise to receive ten thousand dollars as the first fruits of 3 months' sale. I presume as much more is now due.—Mr. Bosworth in England, the firm of Clark & Cº, & Mr. Bentley have all offered to me an interest in the sales of their editions in London. I am very glad of it, both on account of the value of what they offer, & the value of the example they set in a matter, wherein, I think, justice has been too little regarded.—

I have been invited to visit Scotland, & shall probably spend the summer there & in England.—I have very much at heart, a design to erect in some of the Northern States, a normal school, for the education of *coloured* teachers in the United States & Canada. I have very much wished that some permanent memorial of good to the coloured race, might be erected out of the proceeds of a work, which had so unprecedented a sale.—

My own share of the profits will be less than that of the publishers either English or American, but I am willing to give largely for this purpose, & I feel no doubt that the American & English publishers, will be willing to unite with me, for nothing tends more immediately to the emancipation of the slave, than the education & elevation of the free.—

I am now writing a work[8] which will contain perhaps an equal amount of matter with Uncle Tom's Cabin. It will contain all the facts & documents, on which that story was founded, & an immense body of facts, reports of trials, legal decisions & testimony of people living in the South, which will more than confirm every statement in it & show how much more fact than fiction it is.

I must confess that till I commenced the examinations necessary to write this, much as I thought I knew before, I had not *begun* to measure the depth of the abyss. The laws, records of courts & judicial proceedings are so incredible, as actually to make me doubt the evidence of my own eyesight, & fill me still with amazement, whenever I think of them.—It seems to me that the book cannot but

---

[7]There are two documented instances of the Stowe family's assisting runaway slaves. In 1839 an unnamed woman from Kentucky whom Stowe hired as a domestic turned out to be a runaway slave. When it was discovered that her master was in pursuit, they helped her to travel north (see selection from *A Key to Uncle Tom's Cabin*, 413). For the other instance, see Stowe's letter to Catharine Beecher (62).

[8]*A Key to Uncle Tom's Cabin.*

be felt—& that coming upon the sensibility awakened by the other, it must do something.—

I suffer excessively in writing these things. It may truly be said I write with *heart's blood*.—Many times in writing "Uncle Tom's Cabin" I thought my health w^d fail utterly, but I prayed earnestly that God would help me till I got thro'—& now I am pressed above measure, & beyond strength—This horror, this nightmare, abomination! can it be in *my* country! It lies like lead on my heart, it shadows my life with sorrow, the more so, that I feel, as for my own brothers, for the South— & I am pained by every horror that I am obliged to write, as one who is forced by an awful oath, to disclose in a court, some family disgrace! Many times I have thought I must die, & yet, I pray God that I may live to see something done.

I shall probably be in London in May.—shall I see you? It seems to me so odd & dream-like, that so many people want to see me—and I can't help thinking, that they will think that God hath "chosen the weak things of the world" when they do.—If I live till Spring, then I shall hope to see Shakespeare's grave & Britton's mulberry tree & the good land of my fathers—old, old England! May that day come

> YRS AFFECTLY
> H. B. STOWE
> [Dr. Williams's Library, London]

❦ ❦ ❦

# To William Lloyd Garrison, November 1853

On December 3 and 4, 1853, the American Anti-Slavery Society celebrated in Philadelphia its twentieth anniversary, marking the occasion with numerous speeches, many of them by women. William Lloyd Garrison, who presided over the commemoration, apparently invited Stowe to participate. In declining this overture, Stowe revealed her discomfort with Garrison's radicalism. In spite of their differences this exchange was the beginning of deep mutual regard that the two liberators carried to the end of their lives.

> Andover, Mass.
> Nov. 1853

DEAR SIR

The letter you were so kind as to address to me on my departure for Europe I was unable to read for sometime owing to ill health. When I could read I had not strength to reply to it.

In Switzerland, I projected the plan of a letter which I meant to have addressed to you publicly thro the columns of the Liberator[1]—that was never finished but I think I shall finish & offer it to your columns at some future time.

In regard to you, your paper & in some measure your party I am in an honest embarassment—I sympathise with you fully in many of your positions: others I consider erroneous, hurtful to liberty & the progress of humanity—nevertheless I believe you & those who support them to be honest & conscientious in your course & opinions

I am a constant reader of your paper & an admirer of much that is in it. I like its frankness fearlessness—truthfulness & independence—at the same time I regard with apprehension & sorrow much that is in it Were it circulated only among intelligent well balanced minds able to discriminate between good & evil I should not feel so much apprehension. To *me* the paper is decidedly valuable as a frank & able expose of the ultra progressive element in our times. What I fear is that it will take from poor Uncle Tom his bible & give him nothing in its place—you understand me—do you not?

In this view, I cannot conscientiously do any thing the which might endorse your party and your paper, without at the same time entering protest against what I consider erroneous & hurtful With this view I have written the letter of reply to your invitation—& I imagine that I give you the greatest possible proof of esteem & respect by thus frankly telling you my whole mind and expecting you to be well pleased with my sincerity.

For many reasons I should like to have an opportunity of free conversation with you Could you not come & make us a call one of these days if you will appoint a time I will be sure to be at home

VERY TRULY YOURS

H B. STOWE

[Antislavery Collection, Boston Public Library]

---

[1]Garrison's radical abolitionist newspaper.

❦ ❦ ❦

# Uncle Tom's Cabin;

OR,
LIFE AMONG THE LOWLY

## CONTENTS

### VOLUME I

*Uncle Tom's Cabin* by Harriet Beecher Stowe. Reprinted by permission of The Library of America, NY.

## VOLUME II

## *Preface*

he scenes of this story, as its title indicates, lie among a race hitherto ig-
nored by the associations of polite and refined society; an exotic race,
whose ancestors, born beneath a tropic sun, brought with them, and
perpetuated to their descendants, a character so essentially unlike the
hard and dominant Anglo-Saxon race, as for many years to have won from it only
misunderstanding and contempt.

But, another and better day is dawning; every influence of literature, of poetry and of art, in our times, is becoming more and more in unison with the great
master chord of Christianity, "good will to man."

The poet, the painter, and the artist, now seek out and embellish the common
and gentler humanities of life, and, under the allurements of fiction, breathe a humanizing and subduing influence, favorable to the development of the great principles of Christian brotherhood.

The hand of benevolence is everywhere stretched out, searching into abuses,
righting wrongs, alleviating distresses, and bringing to the knowledge and sympathies of the world the lowly, the oppressed, and the forgotten.

In this general movement, unhappy Africa at last is remembered; Africa, who
began the race of civilization and human progress in the dim, gray dawn of early
time, but who, for centuries, has lain bound and bleeding at the foot of civilized
and Christianized humanity, imploring compassion in vain.

But the heart of the dominant race, who have been her conquerors, her hard
masters, has at length been turned towards her in mercy; and it has been seen
how far nobler it is in nations to protect the feeble than to oppress them. Thanks
be to God, the world has at last outlived the slave-trade!

The object of these sketches is to awaken sympathy and feeling for the African
race, as they exist among us; to show their wrongs and sorrows, under a system
so necessarily cruel and unjust as to defeat and do away the good effects of all
that can be attempted for them, by their best friends, under it.

In doing this, the author can sincerely disclaim any invidious feeling towards
those individuals who, often without any fault of their own, are involved in the
trials and embarrassments of the legal relations of slavery.

Experience has shown her that some of the noblest of minds and hearts are
often thus involved; and no one knows better than they do, that what may be
gathered of the evils of slavery from sketches like these, is not the half that could
be told, of the unspeakable whole.

In the northern states, these representations may, perhaps, be thought carica-
tures; in the southern states are witnesses who know their fidelity. What personal
knowledge the author has had, of the truth of incidents such as here are related,
will appear in its time.

It is a comfort to hope, as so many of the world's sorrows and wrongs have,
from age to age, been lived down, so a time shall come when sketches similar to
these shall be valuable only as memorials of what has long ceased to be.

When an enlightened and Christianized community shall have, on the shores
of Africa, laws, language and literature, drawn from among us, may then the

scenes of the house of bondage be to them like the remembrance of Egypt to the Israelite,—a motive of thankfulness to Him who hath redeemed them!

For, while politicians contend, and men are swerved this way and that by conflicting tides of interest and passion, the great cause of human liberty is in the hands of one, of whom it is said:

> "He shall not fail nor be discouraged
>   Till He have set judgment in the earth."
> "He shall deliver the needy when he crieth,
>   The poor, and him that hath no helper."
> "He shall redeem their soul from deceit and violence,
>   And precious shall their blood be in His sight."

## VOLUME I

### I.
### *In Which the Reader Is Introduced to a Man of Humanity*

Late in the afternoon of a chilly day in February, two gentlemen were sitting alone over their wine, in a well-furnished dining parlor, in the town of P——, in Kentucky. There were no servants present, and the gentlemen, with chairs closely approaching, seemed to be discussing some subject with great earnestness.

For convenience sake, we have said, hitherto, two *gentlemen*. One of the parties, however, when critically examined, did not seem, strictly speaking, to come under the species. He was a short, thick-set man, with coarse, commonplace features, and that swaggering air of pretension which marks a low man who is trying to elbow his way upward in the world. He was much over-dressed, in a gaudy vest of many colors, a blue neckerchief, bedropped gayly with yellow spots, and arranged with a flaunting tie, quite in keeping with the general air of the man. His hands, large and coarse, were plentifully bedecked with rings; and he wore a heavy gold watch-chain, with a bundle of seals of portentous size, and a great variety of colors, attached to it,—which, in the ardor of conversation, he was in the habit of flourishing and jingling with evident satisfaction. His conversation was in free and easy defiance of Murray's Grammar, and was garnished at convenient intervals with various profane expressions, which not even the desire to be graphic in our account shall induce us to transcribe.

His campanion, Mr. Shelby, had the appearance of a gentleman; and the arrangements of the house, and the general air of the housekeeping, indicated easy, and even opulent circumstances. As we before stated, the two were in the midst of an earnest conversation.

"That is the way I should arrange the matter," said Mr. Shelby.

"I can't make trade that way—I positively can't, Mr. Shelby," said the other, holding up a glass of wine between his eye and the light.

"Why, the fact is, Haley, Tom is an uncommon fellow; he is certainly worth that sum anywhere,—steady, honest, capable, manages my whole farm like a clock."

"You mean honest, as niggers go," said Haley, helping himself to a glass of brandy.

"No; I mean, really, Tom is a good, steady, sensible, pious fellow. He got religion at a camp-meeting, four years ago; and I believe he really *did* get it. I 've trusted him, since then, with everything I have,—money, house, horses,—and let him come and go round the country; and I always found him true and square in everything."

"Some folks don't believe there is pious niggers, Shelby," said Haley, with a candid flourish of his hand, "but *I do*. I had a fellow, now, in this yer last lot I took to Orleans—'t was as good as a meetin, now, really; to hear that critter pray; and he was quite gentle and quiet like. He fetched me a good sum, too, for I bought him cheap of a man that was 'bliged to sell out; so I realized six hundred on him. Yes, I consider religion a valeyable thing in a nigger, when it 's the genuine article, and no mistake."

"Well, Tom's got the real article, if ever a fellow had," rejoined the other. "Why, last fall, I let him go to Cincinnati alone, to do business for me, and bring home five hundred dollars. 'Tom,' says I to him, 'I trust you, because I think you 're a Christian—I know you would n't cheat.' Tom comes back, sure enough; I knew he would. Some low fellows, they say, said to him—'Tom, why don't you make tracks for Canada?' 'Ah, master trusted me, and I could n't,'—they told me about it. I am sorry to part with Tom, I must say. You ought to let him cover the whole balance of the debt; and you would, Haley, if you had any conscience."

"Well, I 've got just as much conscience as any man in business can afford to keep,—just a little, you know, to swear by, as 't were," said the trader, jocularly; "and, then, I 'm ready to do anything in reason to 'blige friends; but this yer, you see, is a leetle too hard on a fellow—a leetle too hard." The trader sighed contemplatively, and poured out some more brandy.

"Well, then, Haley, how will you trade?" said Mr. Shelby, after an uneasy interval of silence.

"Well, have n't you a boy or gal that you could throw in with Tom?"

"Hum!—none that I could well spare; to tell the truth, it 's only hard necessity makes me willing to sell at all. I don't like parting with any of my hands, that 's a fact."

Here the door opened, and a small quadroon boy, between four and five years of age, entered the room. There was something in his appearance remarkably beautiful and engaging. His black hair, fine as floss silk, hung in glossy curls about his round, dimpled face, while a pair of large dark eyes, full of fire and softness, looked out from beneath the rich, long lashes, as he peered curiously into the apartment. A gay robe of scarlet and yellow plaid, carefully made and neatly fitted, set off to advantage the dark and rich style of his beauty; and a certain comic air of assurance, blended with bashfulness, showed that he had been not unused to being petted and noticed by his master.

"Hulloa, Jim Crow!" said Mr. Shelby, whistling, and snapping a bunch of raisins towards him, "pick that up, now!"

The child scampered, with all his little strength, after the prize, while his master laughed.

"Come here, Jim Crow," said he. The child came up, and the master patted the curly head, and chucked him under the chin.

"Now, Jim, show this gentleman how you can dance and sing." The boy commenced one of those wild, grotesque songs common among the negroes, in a rich, clear voice, accompanying his singing with many comic evolutions of the hands, feet, and whole body, all in perfect time to the music.

"Bravo!" said Haley, throwing him a quarter of an orange.

"Now, Jim, walk like old Uncle Cudjoe, when he has the rheumatism," said his master.

Instantly the flexible limbs of the child assumed the appearance of deformity and distortion, as, with his back humped up, and his master's stick in his hand, he hobbled about the room, his childish face drawn into a doleful pucker, and spitting from right to left, in imitation of an old man.

Both gentlemen laughed uproariously.

"Now, Jim," said his master, "show us how old Elder Robbins leads the psalm." The boy drew his chubby face down to a formidable length, and commenced toning a psalm tune through his nose, with imperturbable gravity.

"Hurrah! bravo! what a young 'un!" said Haley; "that chap's a case, I 'll promise. Tell you what," said he, suddenly clapping his hand on Mr. Shelby's shoulder, "fling in that chap, and I 'll settle the business—I will. Come, now, if that ain't doing the thing up about the rightest!"

At this moment, the door was pushed gently open, and a young quadroon woman, apparently about twenty-five, entered the room.

There needed only a glance from the child to her, to identify her as its mother. There was the same rich, full, dark eye, with its long lashes; the same ripples of silky black hair. The brown of her complexion gave way on the cheek to a perceptible flush, which deepened as she saw the gaze of the strange man fixed upon her in bold and undisguised admiration. Her dress was of the neatest possible fit, and set off to advantage her finely moulded shape;—a delicately formed hand and a trim foot and ankle were items of appearance that did not escape the quick eye of the trader, well used to run up at a glance the points of a fine female article.

"Well, Eliza?" said her master, as she stopped and looked hesitatingly at him.

"I was looking for Harry, please, sir;" and the boy bounded toward her, showing his spoils, which he had gathered in the skirt of his robe.

"Well, take him away, then," said Mr. Shelby; and hastily she withdrew, carrying the child on her arm.

"By Jupiter," said the trader, turning to him in admiration, "there 's an article, now! You might make your fortune on that ar gal in Orleans, any day. I 've seen over a thousand, in my day, paid down for gals not a bit handsomer."

"I don't want to make my fortune on her," said Mr. Shelby, dryly; and, seeking to turn the conversation, he uncorked a bottle of fresh wine, and asked his companion's opinion of it.

"Capital, sir,—first chop!" said the trader; then turning, and slapping his hand familiarly on Shelby's shoulder, he added—

"Come, how will you trade about the gal?—what shall I say for her—what'll you take?"

"Mr. Haley, she is not to be sold," said Shelby. "My wife would not part with her for her weight in gold."

"Ay, ay! women always say such things, cause they ha'nt no sort of calculation. Just show 'em how many watches, feathers, and trinkets, one's weight in gold would buy, and that alters the case, *I* reckon."

"I tell you, Haley, this must not be spoken of; I say no, and I mean no," said Shelby, decidedly.

"Well, you 'll let me have the boy, though," said the trader; "you must own I 've come down pretty handsomely for him."

"What on earth can you want with the child?" said Shelby.

"Why, I 've got a friend that 's going into this yer branch of the business—wants to buy up handsome boys to raise for the market. Fancy articles entirely—sell for waiters, and so on, to rich 'uns, that can pay for handsome 'uns. It sets off one of yer great places—a real handsome boy to open door, wait, and tend. They fetch a good sum; and this little devil is such a comical, musical concern, he 's just the article."

"I would rather not sell him," said Mr. Shelby, thoughtfully; "the fact is, sir, I 'm a humane man, and I hate to take the boy from his mother, sir."

"O, you do?—La! yes—something of that ar natur. I understand, perfectly. It is mighty onpleasant getting on with women, sometimes. I al'ays hates these yer screechin', screamin' times. They are *mighty* onpleasant; but, as I manages business, I generally avoids 'em, sir. Now, what if you get the girl off for a day, or a week, or so; then the thing 's done quietly,—all over before she comes home. Your wife might get her some ear-rings, or a new gown, or some such truck, to make up with her."

"I 'm afraid not."

"Lor bless ye, yes! These critters an't like white folks, you know; they gets over things, only manage right. Now, they say," said Haley, assuming a candid and confidential air, "that this kind o' trade is hardening to the feelings; but I never found it so. Fact is, I never could do things up the way some fellers manage the business. I 've seen 'em as would pull a woman's child out of her arms, and set him up to sell, and she screechin' like mad all the time;—very bad policy—damages the article—makes 'em quite unfit for service sometimes. I knew a real handsome gal once, in Orleans, as was entirely ruined by this sort o' handling. The fellow that was trading for her did n't want her baby; and she was one of your real high sort, when her blood was up. I tell you, she squeezed up her child in her arms, and talked, and went on real awful. It kinder makes my blood run cold to think on 't; and when they carried off the child, and locked her up, she jest went ravin' mad, and died in a week. Clear waste, sir, of a thousand dollars, just for want of management,—there's where 't is. It's always best to do the humane thing, sir; that's been *my* experience." And the trader leaned back in his chair, and folded his arm, with an air of virtuous decision, apparently considering himself a second Wilberforce.

The subject appeared to interest the gentleman deeply; for while Mr. Shelby was thoughtfully peeling an orange, Haley broke out afresh, with becoming diffidence, but as if actually driven by the force of truth to say a few words more.

"It don't look well, now, for a feller to be praisin' himself; but I say it jest because it's the truth. I believe I'm reckoned to bring in about the finest droves of niggers that is brought in,—at least, I've been told so; if I have once, I reckon I have a hundred times,—all in good case,—fat and likely, and I lose as few as any man in the business. And I lays it all to my management, sir; and humanity, sir, I may say, is the great pillar of *my* management."

Mr. Shelby did not know what to say, and so he said, "Indeed!"

"Now, I've been laughed at for my notions, sir, and I've been talked to. They an't pop'lar, and they an't common; but I stuck to 'em, sir; I've stuck to 'em, and realized well on 'em; yes, sir, they have paid their passage, I may say," and the trader laughed at his joke.

There was something so piquant and original in these elucidations of humanity, that Mr. Shelby could not help laughing in company. Perhaps you laugh too, dear reader; but you know humanity comes out in a variety of strange forms now-a-days, and there is no end to the odd things that humane people will say and do.

Mr. Shelby's laugh encouraged the trader to proceed.

"It's strange, now, but I never could beat this into people's heads. Now, there was Tom Loker, my old partner, down in Natchez; he was a clever fellow, Tom was, only the very devil with niggers,—on principle 't was, you see, for a better hearted feller never broke bread; 't was his *system*, sir. I used to talk to Tom. 'Why, Tom,' I used to say, 'when your gals takes on and cry, what's the use o' crackin on 'em over the head, and knockin' on 'em round? It's ridiculous,' says I, 'and don't do no sort o' good. Why, I don't see no harm in their cryin',' says I; 'it's natur,' says I, 'and if natur can't blow off one way, it will another. Besides, Tom,' says I, 'it jest spiles your gals; they get sickly, and down in the mouth; and sometimes they gets ugly,—particular yallow gals do,—and it's the devil and all gettin' on 'em broke in. Now,' says I, 'why can't you kinder coax 'em up, and speak 'em fair? Depend on it, Tom, a little humanity, thrown in along, goes a heap further than all your jawin' and crackin'; and it pays better,' says I, 'depend on 't.' But Tom could n't get the hang on 't; and he spiled so many for me, that I had to break off with him, though he was a good-hearted fellow, and as fair a business hand as is goin'."

"And do you find your ways of managing do the business better than Tom's?" said Mr. Shelby.

"Why, yes, sir, I may say so. You see, when I any ways can, I takes a leetle care about the onpleasant parts, like selling young uns and that,—get the gals out of the way—out of sight, out of mind, you know,—and when it's clean done, and can't be helped, they naturally gets used to it. 'Tan't, you know, as if it was white folks, that's brought up in the way of 'spectin' to keep their children and wives, and all that. Niggers, you know, that's fetched up properly, ha' n't no kind of 'spectations of no kind; so all these things comes easier."

"I'm afraid mine are not properly brought up, then," said Mr. Shelby.

"S'pose not; you Kentucky folks spile your niggers. You mean well by 'em, but 'tan't no real kindness, arter all. Now, a nigger, you see, what 's got to be hacked and tumbled round the world, and sold to Tom, and Dick, and the Lord knows who, 'tan't no kindness to be givin' on him notions and expectations, and bringin' on him up too well, for the rough and tumble comes all the harder on him arter. Now, I venture to say, your niggers would be quite chop-fallen in a place where some of your plantation niggers would be singing and whooping like all possessed. Every man, you know, Mr. Shelby, naturally thinks well of his own ways; and I think I treat niggers just about as well as it 's ever worth while to treat 'em."

"It's a happy thing to be satisfied," said Mr. Shelby, with a slight shrug, and some perceptible feelings of a disagreeable nature.

"Well," said Haley, after they had both silently picked their nuts for a season, "what do you say?"

"I 'll think the matter over, and talk with my wife," said Mr. Shelby. "Meantime, Haley, if you want the matter carried on in the quiet way you speak of, you 'd best not let your business in this neighborhood be known. It will get out among my boys, and it will not be a particularly quiet business getting away any of my fellows, if they know it, I 'll promise you."

"O! certainly, by all means, mum! of course. But I 'll tell you, I 'm in a devil of a hurry, and shall want to know, as soon as possible, what I may depend on," said he, rising and putting on his overcoat.

"Well, call up this evening, between six and seven, and you shall have my answer," said Mr. Shelby, and the trader bowed himself out of the apartment.

"I 'd like to have been able to kick the fellow down the steps," said he to himself, as he saw the door fairly closed, "with his impudent assurance; but he knows how much he has me at advantage. If anybody had ever said to me that I should sell Tom down south to one of those rascally traders, I should have said, 'Is thy servant a dog, that he should do this thing?' And now it must come, for aught I see. And Eliza's child, too! I know that I shall have some fuss with wife about that; and, for that matter, about Tom, too. So much for being in debt,—heigho! The fellow sees his advantage, and means to push it."

Perhaps the mildest form of the system of slavery is to be seen in the State of Kentucky. The general prevalence of agricultural pursuits of a quiet and gradual nature, not requiring those periodic seasons of hurry and pressure that are called for in the business of more southern districts, makes the task of the negro a more healthful and reasonable one; while the master, content with a more gradual style of acquisition, has not those temptations to hardheartedness which always overcome frail human nature when the prospect of sudden and rapid gain is weighed in the balance, with no heavier counterpoise than the interests of the helpless and unprotected.

Whoever visits some estates there, and witnesses the good-humored indulgence of some masters and mistresses, and the affectionate loyalty of some slaves, might be tempted to dream the oft-fabled poetic legend of a patriarchal institution, and all that; but over and above the scene there broods a portentous shadow— the shadow of *law*. So long as the law considers all these human beings, with beating hearts and living affections, only as so many *things* belonging to a master,—so long as the failure, or misfortune, or imprudence, or death of the kindest owner, may cause them any day to exchange a life of kind protection and indulgence for one of hopeless misery and toil,—so long it is impossible to make anything beautiful or desirable in the best regulated administration of slavery.

Mr. Shelby was a fair average kind of man, good-natured and kindly, and disposed to easy indulgence of those around him, and there had never been a lack of anything which might contribute to the physical comfort of the negroes on his estate. He had, however, speculated largely and quite loosely; had involved himself deeply, and his notes to a large amount had come into the hands of Haley; and this small piece of information is the key to the preceding conversation.

Now, it had so happened that, in approaching the door, Eliza had caught enough of the conversation to know that a trader was making offers to her master for somebody.

She would gladly have stopped at the door to listen, as she came out; but her mistress just then calling, she was obliged to hasten away.

Still she thought she heard the trader make an offer for her boy;—could she be mistaken? Her heart swelled and throbbed, and she involuntarily strained him so tight that the little fellow looked up into her face in astonishment.

"Eliza, girl, what ails you to-day?" said her mistress, when Eliza had upset the wash-pitcher, knocked down the workstand, and finally was abstractedly offering her mistress a long night-gown in place of the silk dress she had ordered her to bring from the wardrobe.

Eliza started. "O, missis!" she said, raising her eyes; then, bursting into tears, she sat down in a chair, and began sobbing.

"Why, Eliza, child! what ails you?" said her mistress.

"O! missis, missis," said Eliza, "there 's been a trader talking with master in the parlor! I heard him."

"Well, silly child, suppose there has."

"O, missis, *do* you suppose mas'r would sell my Harry?" And the poor creature threw herself into a chair, and sobbed convulsively.

"Sell him! No, you foolish girl! You know your master never deals with those southern traders, and never means to sell any of his servants, as long as they behave well. Why, you silly child, who do you think would want to buy your Harry? Do you think all the world are set on him as you are, you goosie? Come, cheer up, and hook my dress. There now, put my back hair up in that pretty braid you learnt the other day, and don't go listening at doors any more."

"Well, but, missis, *you* never would give your consent—to—to—"

"Nonsense, child! to be sure, I should n't. What do you talk so for? I would as soon have one of my own children sold. But really, Eliza, you are getting altogether too proud of that little fellow. A man can't put his nose into the door, but you think he must be coming to buy him."

Reassured by her mistress' confident tone, Eliza proceeded nimbly and adroitly with her toilet, laughing at her own fears, as she proceeded.

Mrs. Shelby was a woman of a high class, both intellectually and morally. To that natural magnanimity and generosity of mind which one often marks as characteristic of the women of Kentucky, she added high moral and religious sensibility and principle, carried out with great energy and ability into practical results. Her husband, who made no professions to any particular religious character, nevertheless reverenced and respected the consistency of hers, and stood, perhaps, a little in awe of her opinion. Certain it was that he gave her unlimited scope in all her benevolent efforts for the comfort, instruction, and improvement of her servants, though he never took any decided part in them himself. In fact, if not exactly a believer in the doctrine of the efficiency of the extra good works of saints, he really seemed somehow or other to fancy that his wife had piety and benevolence enough for two—to indulge a shadowy expectation of getting into heaven through her superabundance of qualities to which he made no particular pretension.

The heaviest load on his mind, after his conversation with the trader, lay in the foreseen necessity of breaking to his wife the arrangement contemplated,—meeting the importunities and opposition which he knew he should have reason to encounter.

Mrs. Shelby, being entirely ignorant of her husband's embarrassments, and knowing only the general kindliness of his temper, had been quite sincere in the entire incredulity with which she had met Eliza's suspicions. In fact, she dismissed the matter from her mind, without a second thought; and being occupied in preparations for an evening visit, it passed out of her thoughts entirely.

## II.
## The Mother

Eliza had been brought up by her mistress, from girlhood, as a petted and indulged favorite.

The traveller in the south must often have remarked that peculiar air of refinement, that softness of voice and manner, which seems in many cases to be a particular gift to the quadroon and mulatto women. These natural graces in the quadroon are often united with beauty of the most dazzling kind, and in almost every case with a personal appearance prepossessing and agreeable. Eliza, such as we have described her, is not a fancy sketch, but taken from remembrance, as we saw her, years ago, in Kentucky. Safe under the protecting care of her mistress, Eliza had reached maturity without those temptations which make beauty so fatal an inheritance to a slave. She had been married to a bright and talented young mulatto man, who was a slave on a neighboring estate, and bore the name of George Harris.

This young man had been hired out by his master to work in a bagging factory, where his adroitness and ingenuity caused him to be considered the first hand in the place. He had invented a machine for the cleaning of the hemp, which, considering the education and circumstances of the inventor, displayed quite as much mechanical genius as Whitney's cotton-gin.*

*A machine of this description was really the invention of a young colored man in Kentucky.

He was possessed of a handsome person and pleasing manners, and was a general favorite in the factory. Nevertheless, as this young man was in the eye of the law not a man, but a thing, all these superior qualifications were subject to the control of a vulgar, narrow-minded, tyrannical master. This same gentleman, having heard of the fame of George's invention, took a ride over to the factory, to see what this intelligent chattel had been about. He was received with great enthusiasm by the employer, who congratulated him on possessing so valuable a slave.

He was waited upon over the factory, shown the machinery by George, who, in high spirits, talked so fluently, held himself so erect, looked so handsome and manly, that his master began to feel an uneasy consciousness of inferiority. What business had his slave to be marching round the country, inventing machines, and holding up his head among gentlemen? He 'd soon put a stop to it. He 'd take him back, and put him to hoeing and digging, and "see if he 'd step about so smart." Accordingly, the manufacturer and all hands concerned were astounded when he suddenly demanded George's wages, and announced his intention of taking him home.

"But, Mr. Harris," remonstrated the manufacturer, "is n't this rather sudden?"

"What if it is?—is n't the man *mine*?"

"We would be willing, sir, to increase the rate of compensation."

"No object at all, sir. I don't need to hire any of my hands out, unless I 've a mind to."

"But, sir, he seems peculiarly adapted to this business."

"Dare say he may be; never was much adapted to anything that I set him about, I 'll be bound."

"But only think of his inventing this machine," interposed one of the workmen, rather unluckily.

"O yes!—a machine for saving work, is it? He 'd invent that, I 'll be bound; let a nigger alone for that, any time. They are all labor-saving machines themselves, every one of 'em. No, he shall tramp!"

George had stood like one transfixed, at hearing his doom thus suddenly pronounced by a power that he knew was irresistible. He folded his arms, tightly pressed in his lips, but a whole volcano of bitter feelings burned in his bosom, and sent streams of fire through his veins. He breathed short, and his large dark eyes flashed like live coals; and he might have broken out into some dangerous ebullition, had not the kindly manufacturer touched him on the arm, and said, in a low tone,

"Give way, George; go with him for the present. We 'll try to help you, yet."

The tyrant observed the whisper, and conjectured its import, though he could not hear what was said; and he inwardly strengthened himself in his determination to keep the power he possessed over his victim.

George was taken home, and put to the meanest drudgery of the farm. He had been able to repress every disrespectful word; but the flashing eye, the gloomy and troubled brow, were part of a natural language that could not be repressed,—indubitable signs, which showed too plainly that the man could not become a thing.

It was during the happy period of his employment in the factory that George had seen and married his wife. During that period,—being much trusted and favored by his employer,—he had free liberty to come and go at discretion. The marriage was highly approved of by Mrs. Shelby, who, with a little womanly complacency in match-making, felt pleased to unite her handsome favorite with one of her own class who seemed in every way suited to her; and so they were married in her mistress' great parlor, and her mistress herself adorned the bride's beautiful hair with orange-blossoms, and threw over it the bridal veil, which certainly could scarce have rested on a fairer head; and there was no lack of white gloves, and cake and wine,—of admiring guests to praise the bride's beauty, and her mistress' indulgence and liberality. For a year or two Eliza saw her husband frequently, and there was nothing to interrupt their happiness, except the loss of two infant children, to whom she was passionately attached, and whom she mourned with a grief so intense as to call for gentle remonstrance from her mistress, who sought, with maternal anxiety, to direct her naturally passionate feelings within the bounds of reason and religion.

After the birth of little Harry, however, she had gradually become tranquillized and settled; and every bleeding tie and throbbing nerve, once more entwined with that little life, seemed to become sound and healthful, and Eliza was a happy woman up to the time that her husband was rudely torn from his kind employer, and brought under the iron sway of his legal owner.

The manufacturer, true to his word, visited Mr. Harris a week or two after George had been taken away, when, as he hoped, the heat of the occasion had passed away, and tried every possible inducement to lead him to restore him to his former employment.

"You need n't trouble yourself to talk any longer," said he, doggedly; "I know my own business, sir."

"I did not presume to interfere with it, sir. I only thought that you might think it for your interest to let your man to us on the terms proposed."

"O, I understand the matter well enough. I saw your winking and whispering, the day I took him out of the factory; but you don't come it over me that way. It 's a free country, sir; the man's *mine*, and I do what I please with him,—that 's it!"

And so fell George's last hope;—nothing before him but a life of toil and drudgery, rendered more bitter by every little smarting vexation and indignity which tyrannical ingenuity could devise.

A very humane jurist once said, The worst use you can put a man to is to hang him. No; there is another use that a man can be put to that is WORSE!

### III.
### *The Husband and Father*

Mrs. Shelby had gone on her visit, and Eliza stood in the verandah, rather dejectedly looking after the retreating carriage, when a hand was laid on her shoulder. She turned, and a bright smile lighted up her fine eyes.

"George, is it you? How you frightened me! Well; I am so glad you 's come! Missis is gone to spend the afternoon; so come into my little room, and we 'll have the time all to ourselves."

Saying this, she drew him into a neat little apartment opening on the verandah, where she generally sat at her sewing, within call of her mistress.

"How glad I am!—why don't you smile?—and look at Harry—how he grows." The boy stood shyly regarding his father through his curls, holding close to the skirts of his mother's dress. "Is n't he beautiful?" said Eliza, lifting his long curls and kissing him.

"I wish he 'd never been born!" said George, bitterly. "I wish I 'd never been born myself!"

Surprised and frightened, Eliza sat down, leaned her head on her husband's shoulder, and burst into tears.

"There now, Eliza, it 's too bad for me to make you feel so, poor girl!" said he, fondly; "it 's too bad. O, how I wish you never had seen me—you might have been happy!"

"George! George! how can you talk so? What dreadful thing has happened, or is going to happen? I 'm sure we 've been very happy, till lately."

"So we have, dear," said George. Then drawing his child on his knee, he gazed intently on his glorious dark eyes, and passed his hands through his long curls.

"Just like you, Eliza; and you are the handsomest woman I ever saw, and the best one I ever wish to see; but, oh, I wish I 'd never seen you, nor you me!"

"O, George, how can you!"

"Yes, Eliza, it 's all misery, misery, misery! My life is bitter as wormwood; the very life is burning out of me. I 'm a poor, miserable, forlorn drudge; I shall only drag you down with me, that 's all. What 's the use of our trying to do anything, trying to know anything, trying to be anything? What 's the use of living? I wish I was dead!"

"O, now, dear George, that is really wicked! I know how you feel about losing your place in the factory, and you have a hard master; but pray be patient, and perhaps something—"

"Patient!" said he, interrupting her; "have n't I been patient? Did I say a word when he came and took me away, for no earthly reason, from the place where everybody was kind to me? I 'd paid him truly every cent of my earnings,—and they all say I worked well."

"Well, it is dreadful," said Eliza; "but, after all, he is your master, you know."

"My master! and who made him my master? That 's what I think of—what right has he to me? I 'm a man as much as he is. I 'm a better man than he is. I know more about business than he does; I am a better manager than he is; I can read better than he can; I can write a better hand,—and I 've learned it all myself, and no thanks to him,—I 've learned it in spite of him; and now what right has he to make a drayhorse of me?—to take me from things I can do, and do better than he can, and put me to work that any horse can do? He tries to do it; he says he 'll bring me down and humble me, and he puts me to just the hardest, meanest and dirtiest work, on purpose!"

"O, George! George! you frighten me! Why, I never heard you talk so; I'm afraid you 'll do something dreadful. I don't wonder at your feelings, at all; but oh, do be careful—do, do—for my sake—for Harry's!"

"I have been careful, and I have been patient, but it 's growing worse and worse; flesh and blood can't bear it any longer;—every chance he can get to insult and torment me, he takes. I thought I could do my work well, and keep on quiet, and have some time to read and learn out of work hours; but the more he sees I can do, the more he loads on. He says that though I don't say anything, he sees I 've got the devil in me, and he means to bring it out; and one of these days it will come out in a way that he won't like, or I'm mistaken!"

"O dear! what shall we do?" said Eliza, mournfully.

"It was only yesterday," said George, "as I was busy loading stones into a cart, that young Mas'r Tom stood there, slashing his whip so near the horse that the creature was frightened. I asked him to stop, as pleasant as I could,—he just kept right on. I begged him again, and then he turned on me, and began striking me. I held his hand, and then he screamed and kicked and ran to his father, and told him that I was fighting him. He came in a rage, and said he 'd teach me who was my master; and he tied me to a tree, and cut switches for young master, and told him that he might whip me till he was tired;—and he did do it! If I don't make him remember it, some time!" and the brow of the young man grew dark, and his eyes burned with an expression that made his young wife tremble. "Who made this man my master? That 's what I want to know!" he said.

"Well," said Eliza, mournfully, "I always thought that I must obey my master and mistress, or I could n't be a Christian."

"There is some sense in it, in your case; they have brought you up like a child, fed you, clothed you, indulged you, and taught you, so that you have a good education; that is some reason why they should claim you. But I have been kicked and cuffed and sworn at, and at the best only let alone; and what do I owe? I've paid for all my keeping a hundred times over. I *won't* bear it. No, I *won't*!" he said, clenching his hand with a fierce frown.

Eliza trembled, and was silent. She had never seen her husband in this mood before; and her gentle system of ethics seemed to bend like a reed in the surges of such passions.

"You know poor little Carlo, that you gave me," added George; "the creature has been about all the comfort that I've had. He has slept with me nights, and followed me around days, and kind o' looked at me as if he understood how I felt. Well, the other day I was just feeding him with a few old scraps I picked up by the kitchen door, and Mas'r came along, and said I was feeding him up at his expense, and that he couldn't afford to have every nigger keeping his dog, and ordered me to tie a stone to his neck and throw him in the pond."

"O, George, you did n't do it!"

"Do it? not I!—but he did. Mas'r and Tom pelted the poor drowning creature with stones. Poor thing! he looked at me so mournful, as if he wondered why I did n't save him. I had to take a flogging because I would n't do it myself. I don't care. Mas'r will find out that I'm one that whipping won't tame. My day will come yet, if he don't look out."

"What are you going to do? O, George, don't do anything wicked; if you only trust in God, and try to do right, he'll deliver you."

"I an't a Christian like you, Eliza; my heart 's full of bitterness; I can't trust in God. Why does he let things be so?"

"O, George, we must have faith. Mistress says that when all things go wrong to us, we must believe that God is doing the very best."

"That 's easy to say for people that are sitting on their sofas and riding in their carriages; but let 'em be where I am, I guess it would come some harder. I wish I could be good; but my heart burns, and can't be reconciled, anyhow. You could n't, in my place,—you can't now, if I tell you all I 've got to say. You don't know the whole yet."

"What can be coming now?"

"Well, lately Mas'r has been saying that he was a fool to let me marry off the place; that he hates Mr. Shelby and all his tribe, because they are proud, and hold their heads up above him, and that I 've got proud notions from you; and he says he won't let me come here any more, and that I shall take a wife and settle down on his place. At first he only scolded and grumbled these things; but yesterday he told me that I should take Mina for a wife, and settle down in a cabin with her, or he would sell me down river."

"Why—but you were married to *me*, by the minister, as much as if you 'd been a white man!" said Eliza, simply.

"Don't you know a slave can't be married? There is no law in this country for that; I can't hold you for my wife, if he chooses to part us. That 's why I wish I 'd never seen you,—why I wish I 'd never been born; it would have been better for us both,—it would have been better for this poor child if he had never been born. All this may happen to him yet!"

"O, but master is so kind!"

"Yes, but who knows?—he may die—and then he may be sold to nobody knows who. What pleasure is it that he is handsome, and smart, and bright? I tell you, Eliza, that a sword will pierce through your soul for every good and pleasant thing your child is or has; it will make him worth too much for you to keep!"

The words smote heavily on Eliza's heart; the vision of the trader came before her eyes, and, as if some one had struck her a deadly blow, she turned pale and gasped for breath. She looked nervously out on the verandah, where the boy, tired of the grave conversation, had retired, and where he was riding triumphantly up and down on Mr. Shelby's walking-stick. She would have spoken to tell her husband her fears, but checked herself.

"No, no,—he has enough to bear, poor fellow!" she thought. "No, I won't tell him; besides, it an't true; Missis never deceives us."

"So, Eliza, my girl," said the husband, mournfully, "bear up, now; and good-by, for I'm going."

"Going, George! Going where?"

"To Canada," said he, straightening himself up; "and when I 'm there, I 'll buy you; that 's all the hope that 's left us. You have a kind master, that won't refuse to sell you. I 'll buy you and the boy;—God helping me, I will!"

"O, dreadful! if you should be taken?"

"I won't be taken, Eliza; I 'll *die* first! I 'll be free, or I 'll die!"

"You won't kill yourself!"

"No need of that. They will kill me, fast enough; they never will get me down the river alive!"

"O, George, for my sake, do be careful! Don't do anything wicked; don't lay hands on yourself, or anybody else! You are tempted too much—too much; but don't—go you must—but go carefully, prudently; pray God to help you."

"Well, then, Eliza, hear my plan. Mas'r took it into his head to send me right by here, with a note to Mr. Symmes, that lives a mile past. I believe he expected I should come here to tell you what I have. It would please him, if he thought it would aggravate 'Shelby's folks,' as he calls 'em. I 'm going home quite resigned, you understand, as if all was over. I 've got some preparations made,—and there are those that will help me; and, in the course of a week or so, I shall be among the missing, some day. Pray for me, Eliza; perhaps the good Lord will hear *you*."

"O, pray yourself, George, and go trusting in him; then you won't do anything wicked."

"Well, now, *good-by*," said George, holding Eliza's hands, and gazing into her eyes, without moving. They stood silent; then there were last words, and sobs, and bitter weeping,—such parting as those may make whose hope to meet again is as the spider's web,—and the husband and wife were parted.

## IV.
## An Evening in Uncle Tom's Cabin

The cabin of Uncle Tom was a small log building, close adjoining to "the house," as the negro *par excellence* designates his master's dwelling. In front it had a neat gardenpatch, where, every summer, strawberries, raspberries, and a variety of fruits and vegetables, flourished under careful tending. The whole front of it was covered by a large scarlet bignonia and a native multiflora rose, which, entwisting and interlacing, left scarce a vestige of the rough logs to be seen. Here, also, in summer, various brilliant annuals, such as marigolds, petunias, four-o'clocks, found an indulgent corner in which to unfold their splendors, and were the delight and pride of Aunt Chloe's heart.

Let us enter the dwelling. The evening meal at the house is over, and Aunt Chloe, who presided over its preparation as head cook, has left to inferior officers in the kitchen the business of clearing away and washing dishes, and come out into her own snug territories, to "get her ole man's supper;" therefore, doubt not that it is her you see by the fire, presiding with anxious interest over certain frizzling items in a stew-pan, and anon with grave consideration lifting the cover of a bake-kettle, from whence steam forth indubitable intimations of "something good." A round, black, shining face is hers, so glossy as to suggest the idea that she might have been washed over with white of eggs, like one of her own tea rusks. Her whole plump countenance beams with satisfaction and contentment from under her well-starched checked turban, bearing on it, however, if we must confess it, a little of that tinge of self-consciousness which becomes the first cook of the neighborhood, as Aunt Chloe was universally held and acknowledged to be.

A cook she certainly was, in the very bone and centre of her soul. Not a chicken or turkey or duck in the barn-yard but looked grave when they saw her approaching, and seemed evidently to be reflecting on their latter end; and certain it was that she was always meditating on trussing, stuffing and roasting, to a degree that was calculated to inspire terror in any reflecting fowl living. Her corn-cake, in all its varieties of hoe-cake, dodgers, muffins, and other species too numerous to mention, was a sublime mystery to all less practised compounders; and she would shake her fat sides with honest pride and merriment, as she would narrate the fruitless efforts that one and another of her compeers had made to attain to her elevation.

The arrival of company at the house, the arranging of dinners and suppers "in style," awoke all the energies of her soul; and no sight was more welcome to her than a pile of travelling trunks launched on the verandah, for then she foresaw fresh efforts and fresh triumphs.

Just at present, however, Aunt Chloe is looking into the bake-pan; in which congenial operation we shall leave her till we finish our picture of the cottage.

In one corner of it stood a bed, covered neatly with a snowy spread; and by the side of it was a piece of carpeting, of some considerable size. On this piece of carpeting Aunt Chloe took her stand, as being decidedly in the upper walks of life; and it and the bed by which it lay, and the whole corner, in fact, were treated with distinguished consideration, and made, so far as possible, sacred from the marauding in-roads and desecrations of little folks. In fact, that corner was the *drawing-room* of the establishment. In the other corner was a bed of much humbler pretensions, and evidently designed for *use*. The wall over the fireplace was adorned with some very brilliant scriptural prints, and a portrait of General Washington, drawn and colored in a manner which would certainly have astonished that hero, if ever he had happened to meet with its like.

On a rough bench in the corner, a couple of woolly-headed boys, with glistening black eyes and fat shining cheeks, were busy in superintending the first walking operations of the baby, which, as is usually the case, consisted in getting up on its feet, balancing a moment, and then tumbling down,—each successive failure being violently cheered, as something decidedly clever.

A table, somewhat rheumatic in its limbs, was drawn out in front of the fire, and covered with a cloth, displaying cups and saucers of a decidedly brilliant pattern, with other symptoms of an approaching meal. At this table was seated Uncle Tom, Mr. Shelby's best hand, who, as he is to be the hero of our story, we must daguerreotype for our readers. He was a large, broad-chested, powerfully-made man, of a full glossy black, and a face whose truly African features were characterized by an expression of grave and steady good sense, united with much kindliness and benevolence. There was something about his whole air self-respecting and dignified, yet united with a confiding and humble simplicity.

He was very busily intent at this moment on a slate lying before him, on which he was carefully and slowly endeavoring to accomplish a copy of some letters, in which operation he was overlooked by young Mas'r George, a smart, bright boy of thirteen, who appeared fully to realize the dignity of his position as instructor.

"Not that way, Uncle Tom,—not that way," said he, briskly, as Uncle Tom laboriously brought up the tail of his *g* the wrong side out; "that makes a *q*, you see."

"La sakes, now, does it?" said Uncle Tom, looking with a respectful, admiring air, as his young teacher flourishingly scrawled *q*'s and *g*'s innumerable for his edification; and then, taking the pencil in his big, heavy fingers, he patiently recommenced.

"How easy white folks al'us does things!" said Aunt Chloe, pausing while she was greasing a griddle with a scrap of bacon on her fork, and regarding young Master George with pride. "The way he can write, now! and read, too! and then to come out here evenings and read his lessons to us,—it 's mighty interestin'!"

"But, Aunt Chloe, I 'm getting mighty hungry," said George. "Is n't that cake in the skillet almost done?"

"Mose done, Mas'r George," said Aunt Chloe, lifting the lid and peeping in,— "browning beautiful—a real lovely brown. Ah! let me alone for dat. Missis let Sally try to make some cake, t'other day, jes to *larn* her, she said. 'O, go way, Missis,' says I; 'it really hurts my feelin's, now, to see good vittles spilt dat ar way! Cake ris all to one side—no shape at all; no more than my shoe;—go way!'"

And with this final expression of contempt for Sally's greenness, Aunt Chloe whipped the cover off the bake-kettle, and disclosed to view a neatly-baked pound-cake, of which no city confectioner need to have been ashamed. This being evidently the central point of the entertainment, Aunt Chloe began now to bustle about earnestly in the supper department.

"Here you, Mose and Pete! get out de way, you niggers! Get away, Mericky, honey,—mammy 'll give her baby some fin, by and by. Now, Mas'r George, you jest take off dem books, and set down now with my old man, and I'll take up de sausages, and have de first griddle full of cakes on your plates in less dan no time."

"They wanted me to come to supper in the house," said George; "but I knew what was what too well for that, Aunt Chloe."

"So you did—so you did, honey," said Aunt Chloe, heaping the smoking batter-cakes on his plate; "you know 'd your old aunty 'd keep the best for you. O, let you alone for dat! Go way!" And, with that, aunty gave George a nudge with her finger, designed to be immensely facetious, and turned again to her griddle with great briskness.

"Now for the cake," said Mas'r George, when the activity of the griddle department had somewhat subsided; and, with that, the youngster flourished a large knife over the article in question.

"La bless you, Mas'r George!" said Aunt Chloe, with earnestness, catching his arm, "you would n't be for cuttin' it wid dat ar great heavy knife! Smash all down—spile all de pretty rise of it. Here, I 've got a thin old knife, I keeps sharp a purpose. Dar now, see! comes apart light as a feather! Now eat away—you won't get anything to beat dat ar."

"Tom Lincon says," said George, speaking with his mouth full, "that their Jinny is a better cook than you."

"Dem Lincons an't much count, no way!" said Aunt Chloe, contemptuously; "I mean, set along side *our* folks. They 's 'spectable folks enough in a kinder plain

way; but, as to gettin' up anything in style, they don't begin to have a notion on
't. Set Mas'r Lincon, now, alongside Mas'r Shelby! Good Lor! and Missis Lincon,—
can she kinder sweep it into a room like my missis,—so kinder splendid, yer
know! O, go way! don't tell me nothin' of dem Lincons!"—and Aunt Chloe tossed
her head as one who hoped she did know something of the world.

"Well, though, I 've heard you say," said George, "that Jinny was a pretty fair
cook."

"So I did," said Aunt Chloe,—"I may say dat. Good, plain, common cookin',
Jinny'll do;—make a good pone o' bread,—bile her taters *far*,—her corn cakes
is n't extra, not extra now, Jinny's corn cakes is n't, but then they 's far,—but, Lor,
comes to de higher branches, and what *can* she do? Why, she makes pies—sartin
she does; but what kinder crust? Can she make your real flecky paste, as melts
in your mouth, and lies all up like a puff? Now, I went over thar when Miss Mary
was gwine to be married, and Jinny she jest showed me de weddin' pies. Jinny
and I is good friends, ye know. I never said nothin'; but go long, Mas'r George!
Why, I should n't sleep a wink for a week, if I had a batch of pies like dem ar.
Why, dey wan't no 'count 't all."

"I suppose Jinny thought they were ever so nice," said George.

"Thought so!—did n't she? Thar she was, showing 'em, as innocent—ye see,
it 's jest here, Jinny *don't know*. Lor, the family an't nothing! She can't be spected
to know! 'Ta'nt no fault o' hern. Ah, Mas'r George, you does n't know half your
privileges in yer family and bringin' up!" Here Aunt Chloe sighed, and rolled up
her eyes with emotion.

"I 'm sure, Aunt Chloe, I understand all my pie and pudding privileges," said
George. "Ask Tom Lincon if I don't crow over him, every time I meet him."

Aunt Chloe sat back in her chair, and indulged in a hearty guffaw of laughter,
at this witticism of young Mas'r's, laughing till the tears rolled down her black,
shining cheeks, and varying the exercise with playfully slapping and poking Mas'r
Georgey, and telling him to go way, and that he was a case—that he was fit to kill
her, and that he sartin would kill her, one of these days; and, between each of these
sanguinary predictions, going off into a laugh, each longer and stronger than the
other, till George really began to think that he was a very dangerously witty fellow,
and that it became him to be careful how he talked "as funny as he could."

"And so ye told Tom, did ye? O, Lor! what young uns will be up ter! Ye
crowed over Tom? O, Lor! Mas'r George, if ye would n't make a hornbug laugh!"

"Yes," said George, "I says to him, 'Tom, you ought to see some of Aunt
Chloe's pies; they 're the right sort,' says I."

"Pity, now, Tom could n't," said Aunt Chloe, on whose benevolent heart the
idea of Tom's benighted condition seemed to make a strong impression. "Ye
oughter just ask him here to dinner, some o' these times, Mas'r George," she added;
"it would look quite pretty of ye. Ye know, Mas'r George, ye oughtenter feel 'bove
nobody, on 'count yer privileges, 'cause all our privileges is gi'n to us; we ought
al'ays to 'member that," said Aunt Chloe, looking quite serious.

"Well, I mean to ask Tom here, some day next week," said George; "and you
do your prettiest, Aunt Chloe, and we 'll make him stare. Won't we make him eat
so he won't get over it for a fortnight?"

"Yes, yes—sartin," said Aunt Chloe, delighted; "you 'll see. Lor! to think of some of our dinners! Yer mind dat ar great chicken pie I made when we guv de dinner to General Knox? I and Missis, we come pretty near quarrelling about dat ar crust. What does get into ladies sometimes, I don't know; but, sometimes, when a body has de heaviest kind o' 'sponsibility on 'em, as ye may say, and is all kinder 'seris' and taken up, dey takes dat ar time to be hangin' round and kinder interferin'! Now, Missis, she wanted me to do dis way, and she wanted me to do dat way; and finally, I got kinder sarcy, and, says I, 'Now, Missis, do jist look at dem beautiful' white hands o' yourn, with long fingers, and all a sparkling with rings, like my white lilies when de dew 's on 'em; and look at my great black stumpin hands. Now, don't ye think dat de Lord must have meant *me* to make de pie-crust, and you to stay in de parlor?' Dar! I was jist so sarcy, Mas'r George."

"And what did mother say?" said George.

"Say?—why, she kinder larfed in her eyes—dem great handsome eyes o' hern; and, says she, 'Well, Aunt Chloe, I think you are about in the right on 't,' says she; and she went off in de parlor. She oughter cracked me over de head for bein' so sarcy; but dar 's whar 't is—I can't do nothin' with ladies in de kitchen!"

"Well, you made out well with that dinner,—I remember everybody said so," said George.

"Did n't I? And wan't I behind de dinin'-room door dat bery day? and did n't I see de General pass his plate three times for some more dat bery pie?—and, says he, 'You must have an uncommon cook, Mrs. Shelby.' Lor! I was fit to split myself.

"And de Gineral, he knows what cookin' is," said Aunt Chloe, drawing herself up with an air. "Bery nice man, de Gineral! He comes of one of de bery *fustest* families in Old Virginny! He knows what's what, now, as well as I do—de Gineral. Ye see, there 's *pints* in all pies, Mas'r George; but tan't everybody knows what they is, or as orter be. But the Gineral, he knows; I knew by his 'marks he made. Yes, he knows what de pints is!"

By this time, Master George had arrived at that pass to which even a boy can come (under uncommon circumstances, when he really could not eat another morsel), and, therefore, he was at leisure to notice the pile of woolly heads and glistening eyes which were regarding their operations hungrily from the opposite corner.

"Here, you Mose, Pete," he said, breaking off liberal bits, and throwing it at them; "you want some, don't you? Come, Aunt Chloe, bake them some cakes."

And George and Tom moved to a comfortable seat in the chimney-corner, while Aunt Chloe, after baking a goodly pile of cakes, took her baby on her lap, and began alternately filling its mouth and her own, and distributing to Mose and Pete, who seemed rather to prefer eating theirs as they rolled about on the floor under the table, tickling each other, and occasionally pulling the baby's toes.

"O! go long, will ye?" said the mother, giving now and then a kick, in a kind of general way, under the table, when the movement became too obstreperous. "Can't ye be decent when white folks comes to see ye? Stop dat ar, now, will ye? Better mind yerselves, or I'll take ye down a button-hole lower, when Mas'r George is gone!"

What meaning was couched under this terrible threat, it is difficult to say; but certain it is that its awful indistinctness seemed to produce very little impression on the young sinners addressed.

"La, now!" said Uncle Tom, "they are so full of tickle all the while, they can't behave theirselves."

Here the boys emerged from under the table, and, with hands and faces well plastered with molasses, began a vigorous kissing of the baby.

"Get along wid ye!" said the mother, pushing away their woolly heads. "Ye 'll all stick together, and never get clar, if ye do dat fashion. Go long to de spring and wash yerselves!" she said, seconding her exhortations by a slap, which resounded very formidably, but which seemed only to knock out so much more laugh from the young ones, as they tumbled precipitately over each other out of doors, where they fairly screamed with merriment.

"Did ye ever see such aggravating young uns?" said Aunt Chloe, rather complacently, as, producing an old towel, kept for such emergencies, she poured a little water out of the cracked tea-pot on it, and began rubbing off the molasses from the baby's face and hands; and, having polished her till she shone, she set her down in Tom's lap, while she busied herself in clearing away supper. The baby employed the intervals in pulling Tom's nose, scratching his face, and burying her fat hands in his woolly hair, which last operation seemed to afford her special content.

"Aint she a peart young un?" said Tom, holding her from him to take a full-length view; then, getting up, he set her on his broad shoulder, and began capering and dancing with her, while Mas'r George snapped at her with his pocket-handkerchief, and Mose and Pete, now returned again, roared after her like bears, till Aunt Chloe declared that they "fairly took her head off" with their noise. As, according to her own statement, this surgical operation was a matter of daily occurrence in the cabin, the declaration no whit abated the merriment, till every one had roared and tumbled and danced themselves down to a state of composure.

"Well, now, I hopes you 're done," said Aunt Chloe, who had been busy in pulling out a rude box of a trundle-bed; "and now, you Mose and you Pete, get into thar; for we 's goin' to have the meetin'."

"O mother, we don't wanter. We wants to sit up to meetin',—meetin's is so curis. We likes 'em."

"La, Aunt Chloe, shove it under, and let 'em sit up," said Mas'r George, decisively, giving a push to the rude machine.

Aunt Chloe, having thus saved appearances, seemed highly delighted to push the thing under, saying, as she did so, "Well, mebbe 't will do 'em some good."

The house now resolved itself into a committee of the whole, to consider the accommodations and arrangements for the meeting.

"What we 's to do for cheers, now, I declar I don't know," said Aunt Chloe. As the meeting had been held at Uncle Tom's, weekly, for an indefinite length of time, without any more "cheers," there seemed some encouragement to hope that a way would be discovered at present.

"Old Uncle Peter sung both de legs out of dat oldest cheer, last week," suggested Mose.

"You go long! I'll boun' you pulled 'em out; some o' your shines," said Aunt Chloe.

"Well, it 'll stand, if it only keeps jam up agin de wall!" said Mose.

"Den Uncle Peter mus'n't sit in it, cause he al'ays hitches when he gets a singing. He hitched pretty nigh across de room, t'other night," said Pete.

"Good Lor! get him in it, then," said Mose, "and den he 'd begin, 'Come saints and sinners, hear me tell,' and den down he 'd go,"—and Mose imitated precisely the nasal tones of the old man, tumbling on the floor, to illustrate the supposed catastrophe.

"Come now, be decent, can't ye?" said Aunt Chloe; "an't yer shamed?"

Mas'r George, however, joined the offender in the laugh, and declared decidedly that Mose was a "buster." So the maternal admonition seemed rather to fail of effect.

"Well, ole man," said Aunt Chloe, "you 'll have to tote in them ar bar'ls."

"Mother's bar'ls is like dat ar widder's, Mas'r George was reading 'bout, in de good book,— dey never fails," said Mose, aside to Pete.

"I 'm sure one on 'em caved in last week," said Pete, "and let 'em all down in de middle of de singin'; dat ar was failin', warnt it?"

During this aside between Mose and Pete, two empty casks had been rolled into the cabin, and being secured from rolling, by stones on each side, boards were laid across them, which arrangement, together with the turning down of certain tubs and pails, and the disposing of the rickety chairs, at last completed the preparation.

"Mas'r George is such a beautiful reader, now, I know he 'll stay to read for us," said Aunt Chloe; " 'pears like 't will be so much more interestin'."

George very readily consented, for your boy is always ready for anything that makes him of importance.

The room was soon filled with a motley assemblage, from the old gray-headed patriarch of eighty, to the young girl and lad of fifteen. A little harmless gossip ensued on various themes, such as where old Aunt Sally got her new red head-kerchief, and how "Missis was a going to give Lizzy that spotted muslin gown, when she 'd got her new berage made up;" and how Mas'r Shelby was thinking of buying a new sorel colt, that was going to prove an addition to the glories of the place. A few of the worshippers belonged to families hard by, who had got permission to attend, and who brought in various choice scraps of information, about the sayings and doings at the house and on the place, which circulated as freely as the same sort of small change does in higher circles.

After a while the singing commenced, to the evident delight of all present. Not even all the disadvantage of nasal intonation could prevent the effect of the naturally fine voices, in airs at once wild and spirited. The words were sometimes the well-known and common hymns sung in the churches about, and sometimes of a wilder, more indefinite character, picked up at camp-meetings.

The chorus of one of them, which ran as follows, was sung with great energy and unction:

"Die on the field of battle,
Die on the field of battle,
Glory in my soul."

Another special favorite had oft repeated the words—

"O, I'm going to glory,—won't you come along with me?
Don't you see the angels beck'ning, and a calling me away?
Don't you see the golden city and the everlasting day?"

There were others, which made incessant mention of "Jordan's banks," and "Canaan's fields," and the "New Jerusalem;" for the negro mind, impassioned and imaginative, always attaches itself to hymns and expressions of a vivid and pictorial nature; and, as they sung, some laughed, and some cried, and some clapped hands, or shook hands rejoicingly with each other, as if they had fairly gained the other side of the river.

Various exhortations, or relations of experience, followed, and intermingled with the singing. One old gray-headed woman, long past work, but much revered as a sort of chronicle of the past, rose, and leaning on her staff, said—

"Well, chil'en! Well, I'm mighty glad to hear ye all and see ye all once more, 'cause I don't know when I 'll be gone to glory; but I 've done got ready, chil'en; 'pears like I 'd got my little bundle all tied up, and my bonnet on, jest a waitin' for the stage to come along and take me home; sometimes, in the night, I think I hear the wheels a rattlin', and I'm lookin'out all the time; now, you jest be ready too, for I tell ye all, chil'en," she said, striking her staff hard on the floor, "dat ar *glory* is a mighty thing! It 's a mighty thing, chil'en,—you don'no nothing about it,—it 's *wonderful*." And the old creature sat down, with streaming tears, as wholly overcome, while the whole circle struck up—

"O Canaan, bright Canaan,
I'm bound for the land of Canaan."

Mas'r George, by request, read the last chapters of Revelation, often interrupted by such exclamations as "The *sakes* now!" "Only hear that!" "Jest think on 't!" "Is all that a comin' sure enough?"

George, who was a bright boy, and well trained in religious things by his mother, finding himself an object of general admiration, threw in expositions of his own, from time to time, with a commendable seriousness and gravity, for which he was admired by the young and blessed by the old; and it was agreed, on all hands, that "a minister could n't lay it off better than he did;" that "'t was reely 'mazin'!"

Uncle Tom was a sort of patriarch in religious matters, in the neighborhood. Having, naturally, an organization in which the *morale* was strongly predominant, together with a greater breadth and cultivation of mind than obtained among his companions, he was looked up to with great respect, as a sort of minister among them; and the simple, hearty, sincere style of his exhortations might have edified even better educated persons. But it was in prayer that he especially excelled. Nothing could exceed the touching simplicity, the child-like earnestness, of his prayer, enriched with the language of Scripture, which seemed so entirely to have wrought itself into his being, as to have become a part of himself, and to drop from his lips unconsciously; in the language of a pious old negro, he "prayed right up." And so much did his prayer always work on the devotional feelings of his audiences, that there seemed often a danger that it would be lost altogether in the abundance of the responses which broke out everywhere around him.

---

While this scene was passing in the cabin of the man, one quite otherwise passed in the halls of the master.

The trader and Mr. Shelby were seated together in the dining room afore-named, at a table covered with papers and writing utensils.

Mr. Shelby was busy in counting some bundles of bills, which, as they were counted, he pushed over to the trader, who counted them likewise.

"All fair," said the trader; "and now for signing these yer."

Mr. Shelby hastily drew the bills of sale towards him, and signed them, like a man that hurries over some disagreeable business, and then pushed them over with the money. Haley produced, from a well-worn valise, a parchment, which, after looking over it a moment, he handed to Mr. Shelby, who took it with a gesture of suppressed eagerness.

"Wal, now, the thing's *done!*" said the trader, getting up.

"It 's *done!*" said Mr. Shelby, in a musing tone; and, fetching a long breath, repeated, "*It 's done!*"

"Yer don't seem to feel much pleased with it, 'pears to me," said the trader.

"Haley," said Mr. Shelby, "I hope you 'll remember that you promised, on your honor, you would n't sell Tom, without knowing what sort of hands he 's going into."

"Why, you've just done it, sir," said the trader.

"Circumstances, you well know, *obliged* me," said Shelby, haughtily.

"Wal, you know, they may 'blige *me*, too," said the trader. "Howsomever, I 'll do the very best I can in gettin' Tom a good berth; as to my treatin' on him bad, you need n't be a grain afeard. If there 's anything that I thank the Lord for, it is that I 'm never noways cruel."

After the expositions which the trader had previously given of his humane principles, Mr. Shelby did not feel particularly reässured by these declarations; but, as they were the best comfort the case admitted of, he allowed the trader to depart in silence, and betook himself to a solitary cigar.

## V.

### *Showing the Feelings of Living Property on Changing Owners*

Mr. and Mrs. Shelby had retired to their apartment for the night. He was lounging in a large easy-chair, looking over some letters that had come in the afternoon mail, and she was standing before her mirror, brushing out the complicated braids and curls in which Eliza had arranged her hair; for, noticing her pale cheeks and haggard eyes, she had excused her attendance that night, and ordered her to bed. The employment, naturally enough, suggested her conversation with the girl in the morning; and, turning to her husband, she said carelessly,

"By the by, Arthur, who was that low-bred fellow that you lugged in to our dinner-table to-day?"

"Haley is his name," said Shelby, turning himself rather uneasily in his chair, and continuing with his eyes fixed on a letter.

"Haley! Who is he, and what may be his business here, pray?"

"Well, he 's a man that I transacted some business with, last time I was at Natchez," said Mr. Shelby.

"And he presumed on it to make himself quite at home, and call and dine here, ay?"

"Why, I invited him; I had some accounts with him," said Shelby.

"Is he a negro-trader?" said Mrs. Shelby, noticing a certain embarrassment in her husband's manner.

"Why, my dear, what put that into your head?" said Shelby, looking up.

"Nothing,—only Eliza came in here, after dinner, in a great worry, crying and taking on, and said you were talking with a trader, and that she heard him make an offer for her boy—the ridiculous little goose!"

"She did, hey?" said Mr. Shelby, returning to his paper, which he seemed for a few moments quite intent upon, not perceiving that he was holding it bottom upwards.

"It will have to come out," said he, mentally; "as well now as ever."

"I told Eliza," said Mrs. Shelby, as she continued brushing her hair, "that she was a little fool for her pains, and that you never had anything to do with that sort of persons. Of course, I knew you never meant to sell any of our people,— least of all, to such a fellow."

"Well, Emily," said her husband, "so I have always felt and said; but the fact is that my business lies so that I cannot get on without. I shall have to sell some of my hands."

"To that creature? Impossible! Mr. Shelby, you cannot be serious."

"I 'm sorry to say that I am," said Mr. Shelby. "I 've agreed to sell Tom."

"What! our Tom?—that good, faithful creature!—been your faithful servant from a boy! O, Mr. Shelby!—and you have promised him his freedom, too,—you and I have spoken to him a hundred times of it. Well, I can believe anything now,— I can believe *now* that you could sell little Harry, poor Eliza's only child!" said Mrs. Shelby, in a tone between grief and indignation.

"Well, since you must know all, it is so. I have agreed to sell Tom and Harry both; and I don't know why I am to be rated, as if I were a monster, for doing what every one does every day."

"But why, of all others, choose these?" said Mrs. Shelby. "Why sell them, of all on the place, if you must sell at all?"

"Because they will bring the highest sum of any,—that 's why. I could choose another, if you say so. The fellow made me a high bid on Eliza, if that would suit you any better," said Mr. Shelby.

"The wretch!" said Mrs. Shelby, vehemently.

"Well, I did n't listen to it, a moment,—out of regard to your feelings, I would n't;—so give me some credit."

"My dear," said Mrs. Shelby, recollecting herself, "forgive me. I have been hasty. I was surprised, and entirely unprepared for this;—but surely you will allow me to intercede for these poor creatures. Tom is a noble-hearted, faithful fellow, if he is black. I do believe, Mr. Shelby, that if he were put to it, he would lay down his life for you."

"I know it,—I dare say;—but what 's the use of all this?—I can't help myself."

"Why not make a pecuniary sacrifice? I'm willing to bear my part of the inconvenience. O, Mr. Shelby, I have tried—tried most faithfully, as a Christian woman should—to do my duty to these poor, simple, dependent creatures. I have cared for them, instructed them, watched over them, and known all their little cares and joys, for years; and how can I ever hold up my head again among them, if, for the sake of a little paltry gain, we sell such a faithful, excellent, confiding creature as poor Tom, and tear from him in a moment all we have taught him to love and value? I have taught them the duties of the family, of parent and child, and husband and wife; and how can I bear to have this open acknowledgment that we care for no tie, no duty, no relation, however sacred, compared with money? I have talked with Eliza about her boy—her duty to him as a Christian mother, to watch over him, pray for him, and bring him up in a Christian way; and now what can I say, if you tear him away, and sell him, soul and body, to a profane, unprincipled man, just to save a little money? I have told her that one soul is worth more than all the money in the world; and how will she believe me when she sees us turn round and sell her child?—sell him, perhaps, to certain ruin of body and soul!"

"I 'm sorry you feel so about it, Emily,—indeed I am," said Mr. Shelby; "and I respect your feelings, too, though I don't pretend to share them to their full extent; but I tell you now, solemnly, it 's of no use—I can't help myself. I did n't mean to tell you this, Emily; but, in plain words, there is no choice between selling these two and selling everything. Either they must go, or *all* must. Haley has come into possession of a mortgage, which, if I don't clear off with him directly, will take everything before it. I 've raked, and scraped, and borrowed, and all but begged,— and the price of these two was needed to make up the balance, and I had to give them up. Haley fancied the child; he agreed to settle the matter that way, and no other. I was in his power, and *had* to do it. If you feel so to have them sold, would it be any better to have *all* sold?"

Mrs. Shelby stood like one stricken. Finally, turning to her toilet, she rested her face in her hands, and gave a sort of groan.

"This is God's curse on slavery!—a bitter, bitter, most accursed thing!—a curse to the master and a curse to the slave! I was a fool to think I could make anything good out of such a deadly evil. It is a sin to hold a slave under laws like ours,— I always felt it was,—I always thought so when I was a girl,—I thought so still more after I joined the church; but I thought I could gild it over,—I thought, by kindness, and care, and instruction, I could make the condition of mine better than freedom—fool that I was!"

"Why, wife, you are getting to be an abolitionist, quite."

"Abolitionist! if they knew all I know about slavery, they *might* talk! We don't need them to tell us; you know I never thought that slavery was right—never felt willing to own slaves."

"Well, therein you differ from many wise and pious men," said Mr. Shelby. "You remember Mr. B.'s sermon, the other Sunday?"

"I don't want to hear such sermons; I never wish to hear Mr. B. in our church again. Ministers can't help the evil, perhaps,—can't cure it, any more than we can,—but defend it!—it always went against my common sense. And I think you did n't think much of that sermon, either."

"Well," said Shelby, "I must say these ministers sometimes carry matters further than we poor sinners would exactly dare to do. We men of the world must wink pretty hard at various things, and get used to a deal that is n't the exact thing. But we don't quite fancy, when women and ministers come out broad and square, and go beyond us in matters of either modesty or morals, that 's a fact. But now, my dear, I trust you see the necessity of the thing, and you see that I have done the very best that circumstances would allow."

"O yes, yes!" said Mrs. Shelby, hurriedly and abstractedly fingering her gold watch,—"I have n't any jewelry of any amount," she added, thoughtfully; "but would not this watch do something?—it was an expensive one, when it was bought. If I could only at least save Eliza's child, I would sacrifice anything I have."

"I 'm sorry, very sorry, Emily," said Mr. Shelby, "I 'm sorry this takes hold of you so; but it will do no good. The fact is, Emily, the thing 's done; the bills of sale are already signed, and in Haley's hands; and you must be thankful it is no worse. That man has had it in his power to ruin us all,—and now he is fairly off. If you knew the man as I do, you 'd think that we had had a narrow escape."

"Is he so hard, then?"

"Why, not a cruel man, exactly, but a man of leather,—a man alive to nothing but trade and profit,—cool, and unhesitating, and unrelenting, as death and the grave. He 'd sell his own mother at a good per centage—not wishing the old woman any harm, either."

"And this wretch owns that good, faithful Tom, and Eliza's child!"

"Well, my dear, the fact is that this goes rather hard with me; it's a thing I hate to think of. Haley wants to drive matters, and take possession to-morrow. I 'm going to get out my horse bright and early, and be off. I can't see Tom, that 's a fact; and you had better arrange a drive somewhere, and carry Eliza off. Let the thing be done when she is out of sight."

"No, no," said Mrs. Shelby; "I 'll be in no sense accomplice or help in this cruel business. I 'll go and see poor old Tom, God help him, in his distress! They shall see, at any rate, that their mistress can feel for and with them. As to Eliza, I dare not think about it. The Lord forgive us! What have we done, that this cruel necessity should come on us?"

There was one listener to this conversation whom Mr. and Mrs. Shelby little suspected.

Communicating with their apartment was a large closet, opening by a door into the outer passage. When Mrs. Shelby had dismissed Eliza for the night, her feverish and excited mind had suggested the idea of this closet; and she had hidden herself there, and, with her ear pressed close against the crack of the door, had lost not a word of the conversation.

When the voices died into silence, she rose and crept stealthily away. Pale, shivering, with rigid features and compressed lips, she looked an entirely altered being from the soft and timid creature she had been hitherto. She moved cautiously along the entry, paused one moment at her mistress' door, and raised her hands in mute appeal to Heaven, and then turned and glided into her own room. It was a quiet, neat apartment, on the same floor with her mistress. There was the pleasant sunny window, where she had often sat singing at her sewing; there a little case of books, and various little fancy articles, ranged by them, the gifts of Christmas holidays; there was her simple wardrobe in the closet and in the drawers;—here was, in short, her home; and, on the whole, a happy one it had been to her. But there, on the bed, lay her slumbering boy, his long curls falling negligently around his unconscious face, his rosy mouth half open, his little fat hands thrown out over the bed-clothes, and a smile spread like a sunbeam over his whole face.

"Poor boy! poor fellow!" said Eliza; "they have sold you! but your mother will save you yet!"

No tear dropped over that pillow; in such straits as these, the heart has no tears to give,—it drops only blood, bleeding itself away in silence. She took a piece of paper and pencil, and wrote, hastily,

"O, Missis! dear Missis! don't think me ungrateful,—don't think hard of me, any way,—I heard all you and master said to-night. I am going to try to save my boy—you will not blame me! God bless and reward you for all your kindness!"

Hastily folding and directing this, she went to a drawer and made up a little package of clothing for her boy, which she tied with a handkerchief firmly round her waist; and, so fond is a mother's remembrance, that, even in the terrors of that hour, she did not forget to put in the little package one or two of his favorite toys, reserving a gayly painted parrot to amuse him, when she should be called on to awaken him. It was some trouble to arouse the little sleeper; but, after some effort, he sat up, and was playing with his bird, while his mother was putting on her bonnet and shawl.

"Where are you going, mother?" said he, as she drew near the bed, with his little coat and cap.

His mother drew near, and looked so earnestly into his eyes, that he at once divined that something unusual was the matter.

"Hush, Harry," she said; "must n't speak loud, or they will hear us. A wicked man was coming to take little Harry away from his mother, and carry him 'way off in the dark; but mother won't let him—she 's going to put on her little boy's cap and coat, and run off with him, so the ugly man can't catch him."

Saying these words, she had tied and buttoned on the child's simple outfit, and, taking him in her arms, she whispered to him to be very still; and, opening a door in her room which led into the outer verandah, she glided noiselessly out.

It was a sparkling, frosty, star-light night, and the mother wrapped the shawl close round her child, as, perfectly quiet with vague terror, he clung round her neck.

Old Bruno, a great Newfoundland, who slept at the end of the porch, rose, with a low growl, as she came near. She gently spoke his name, and the animal, an old pet and playmate of hers, instantly, wagging his tail, prepared to follow her, though apparently revolving much, in his simple dog's head, what such an indiscreet midnight promenade might mean. Some dim ideas of imprudence or impropriety in the measure seemed to embarrass him considerably; for he often stopped, as Eliza glided forward, and looked wistfully, first at her and then at the house, and then, as if reässured by reflection, he pattered along after her again. A few minutes brought them to the window of Uncle Tom's cottage, and Eliza, stopping, tapped lightly on the window-pane.

The prayer-meeting at Uncle Tom's had, in the order of hymn-singing, been protracted to a very late hour; and, as Uncle Tom had indulged himself in a few lengthy solos afterwards, the consequence was, that, although it was now between twelve and one o'clock, he and his worthy helpmeet were not yet asleep.

"Good Lord! what's that?" said Aunt Chloe, starting up and hastily drawing the curtain. "My sakes alive, if it an't Lizy! Get on your clothes, old man, quick!— there's old Bruno, too, a pawin' round; what on airth! I'm gwine to open the door."

And, suiting the action to the word, the door flew open, and the light of the tallow candle, which Tom had hastily lighted, fell on the haggard face and dark, wild eyes of the fugitive.

"Lord bless you!—I'm skeered to look at ye, Lizy! Are ye tuck sick, or what's come over ye?"

"I'm running away—Uncle Tom and Aunt Chloe—carrying off my child— Master sold him!"

"Sold him?" echoed both, lifting up their hands in dismay.

"Yes, sold him!" said Eliza, firmly; "I crept into the closet by Mistress' door to-night, and I heard Master tell Missis that he had sold my Harry, and you, Uncle Tom, both, to a trader; and that he was going off this morning on his horse, and that the man was to take possession today."

Tom had stood, during this speech, with his hands raised, and his eyes dilated, like a man in a dream. Slowly and gradually, as its meaning came over him, he collapsed, rather than seated himself, on his old chair, and sunk his head down upon his knees.

"The good Lord have pity on us!" said Aunt Chloe. "O! it don't seem as if it was true! What has he done, that Mas'r should sell *him*?"

"He has n't done anything,—it is n't for that. Master don't want to sell; and Missis—she's always good. I heard her plead and beg for us; but he told her 't was no use; that he was in this man's debt, and that this man had got the power over him; and that if he did n't pay him off clear, it would end in his having to sell the place and all the people, and move off. Yes, I heard him say there was no choice between selling these two and selling all, the man was driving him so hard. Master said he was sorry; but oh, Missis—you ought to have heard her talk! If she an't a Christian and an angel, there never was one. I'm a wicked girl to leave her so; but, then, I can't help it. She said, herself, one soul was worth more than the world; and this boy has a soul, and if I let him be carried off, who knows what 'll become of it? It must be right: but, if it an't right, the Lord forgive me, for I can't help doing it!"

"Well, old man!" said Aunt Chloe, "why don't you go, too? Will you wait to be toted down river, where they kill niggers with hard work and starving? I'd a heap rather die than go there, any day! There's time for ye,—be off with Lizy,—you've got a pass to come and go any time. Come, bustle up, and I'll get your things together."

Tom slowly raised his head, and looked sorrowfully but quietly around, and said,

"No, no—I an't going. Let Eliza go—it's her right! I would n't be the one to say no—'t an't in *natur* for her to stay; but you heard what she said! If I must be sold, or all the people on the place, and everything go to rack, why, let me be sold. I s'pose I can b'ar it as well as any on 'em," he added, while something like a sob and a sigh shook his broad, rough chest convulsively. "Mas'r always found me on the spot—he always will. I never have broke trust, nor used my pass no ways contrary to my word, and I never will. It's better for me alone to go, than to break up the place and sell all. Mas'r an't to blame, Chloe, and he'll take care of you and the poor—"

Here he turned to the rough trundle-bed full of little woolly heads, and broke fairly down. He leaned over the back of the chair, and covered his face with his large hands. Sobs, heavy, hoarse and loud, shook the chair, and great tears fell through his fingers on the floor: just such tears, sir, as you dropped into the coffin where lay your first-born son; such tears, woman, as you shed when you heard the cries of your dying babe. For, sir, he was a man,—and you are but another man. And, woman, though dressed in silk and jewels, you are but a woman, and, in life's great straits and mighty griefs, ye feel but one sorrow!

"And now," said Eliza, as she stood in the door, "I saw my husband only this afternoon, and I little knew then what was to come. They have pushed him to the very last standing-place, and he told me, to-day, that he was going to run away. Do try, if you can, to get word to him. Tell him how I went, and why I went; and tell him I'm going to try and find Canada. You must give my love to him, and tell him, if I never see him again,"—she turned away, and stood with her back to them for a moment, and then added, in a husky voice, "tell him to be as good as he can, and try and meet me in the kingdom of heaven."

"Call Bruno in there," she added. "Shut the door on him, poor beast! He must n't go with me!"

A few last words and tears, a few simple adieus and blessings, and clasping her wondering and affrighted child in her arms, she glided noiselessly away.

## VI.
### Discovery

Mr. and Mrs. Shelby, after their protracted discussion of the night before, did not readily sink to repose, and, in consequence, slept somewhat later than usual, the ensuing morning.

"I wonder what keeps Eliza," said Mrs. Shelby, after giving her bell repeated pulls, to no purpose.

Mr. Shelby was standing before his dressing-glass, sharpening his razor; and just then the door opened, and a colored boy entered, with his shaving-water.

"Andy," said his mistress, "step to Eliza's door, and tell her I have rung for her three times. Poor thing!" she added, to herself, with a sigh.

Andy soon returned, with eyes very wide in astonishment.

"Lor, Missis! Lizy's drawers is all open, and her things all lying every which way; and I believe she's just done clared out!"

The truth flashed upon Mr. Shelby and his wife at the same moment. He exclaimed,

"Then she suspected it, and she 's off!"

"The Lord be thanked!" said Mrs. Shelby. "I trust she is."

"Wife, you talk like a fool! Really, it will be something pretty awkward for me, if she is. Haley saw that I hesitated about selling this child, and he 'll think I connived at it, to get him out of the way. It touches my honor!" And Mr. Shelby left the room hastily.

There was great running and ejaculating, and opening and shutting of doors, and appearance of faces in all shades of color in different places, for about a quarter of an hour. One person only, who might have shed some light on the matter, was entirely silent, and that was the head cook, Aunt Chloe. Silently, and with a heavy cloud settled down over her once joyous face, she proceeded making out her breakfast biscuits, as if she heard and saw nothing of the excitement around her.

Very soon, about a dozen young imps were roosting, like so many crows, on the verandah railings, each one determined to be the first one to apprize the strange Mas'r of his ill luck.

"He 'll be rael mad, I 'll be bound," said Andy.

"*Won't* he swar!" said little black Jake.

"Yes, for he *does* swar," said woolly-headed Mandy. "I hearn him yesterday, at dinner. I hearn all about it then, 'cause I got into the closet where Missis keeps the great jugs, and I hearn every word." And Mandy, who had never in her life thought of the meaning of a word she had heard, more than a black cat, now took airs of superior wisdom, and strutted about, forgetting to state that, though actually coiled up among the jugs at the time specified, she had been fast asleep all the time.

When, at last, Haley appeared, booted and spurred, he was saluted with the bad tidings on every hand. The young imps on the verandah were not disappointed in their hope of hearing him "swar," which he did with a fluency and fervency which delighted them all amazingly, as they ducked and dodged hither and thither, to be out of the reach of his riding-whip; and, all whooping off together, they tumbled, in a pile of immeasurable giggle, on the withered turf under the verandah, where they kicked up their heels and shouted to their full satisfaction.

"If I had the little devils!" muttered Haley, between his teeth.

"But you ha'nt got 'em, though!" said Andy, with a triumphant flourish, and making a string of indescribable mouths at the unfortunate trader's back, when he was fairly beyond hearing.

"I say now, Shelby, this yer 's a most extro'rnary business!" said Haley, as he abruptly entered the parlor. "It seems that gal 's off, with her young un."

"Mr. Haley, Mrs. Shelby is present," said Mr. Shelby.

"I beg pardon, ma'am," said Haley, bowing slightly, with a still lowering brow; "but still I say, as I said before, this yer 's a sing'lar report. Is it true, sir?"

"Sir," said Mr. Shelby, "if you wish to communicate with me, you must observe something of the decorum of a gentleman. Andy, take Mr. Haley's hat and riding-whip. Take a seat, sir. Yes, sir; I regret to say that the young woman, excited by overhearing, or having reported to her, something of this business, has taken her child in the night, and made off."

"I did expect fair dealing in this matter, I confess," said Haley.

"Well, sir," said Mr. Shelby, turning sharply round upon him, "what am I to understand by that remark? If any man calls my honor in question, I shall have but one answer for him."

The trader cowered at this, and in a somewhat lower tone said that "it was plaguy hard on a fellow, that had made a fair bargain, to be gulled that way."

"Mr. Haley," said Mr. Shelby, "if I did not think you had some cause for disappointment, I should not have borne from you the rude and unceremonious style of your entrance into my parlor this morning. I say thus much, however, since appearances call for it, that I shall allow of no insinuations cast upon me, as if I were at all partner to any unfairness in this matter. Moreover, I shall feel bound to give you every assistance, in the use of horses, servant, &c., in the recovery of your property. So, in short, Haley," said he, suddenly dropping from the tone of dignified coolness to his ordinary one of easy frankness, "the best way for you is to keep good-natured and eat some breakfast, and we will then see what is to be done."

Mrs. Shelby now rose, and said her engagements would prevent her being at the breakfast-table that morning; and, deputing a very respectable mulatto woman to attend to the gentlemen's coffee at the side-board, she left the room.

"Old lady don't like your humble servant, over and above," said Haley, with an uneasy effort to be very familiar.

"I am not accustomed to hear my wife spoken of with such freedom," said Mr. Shelby, dryly.

"Beg pardon; of course, only a joke, you know," said Haley, forcing a laugh.

"Some jokes are less agreeable than others," rejoined Shelby.

"Devilish free, now I 've signed those papers, cuss him!" muttered Haley to himself; "quite grand, since yesterday!"

Never did fall of any prime minister at court occasion wider surges of sensation than the report of Tom's fate among his compeers on the place. It was the topic in every mouth, everywhere; and nothing was done in the house or in the field, but to discuss its probable results. Eliza's flight—an unprecedented event on the place—was also a great accessory in stimulating the general excitement.

Black Sam, as he was commonly called, from his being about three shades blacker than any other son of ebony on the place, was revolving the matter profoundly in all its phases and bearings, with a comprehensiveness of vision and a strict look-out to his own personal well-being, that would have done credit to any white patriot in Washington.

"It 's an ill wind dat blows nowhar,—dat ar a fact," said Sam, sententiously, giving an additional hoist to his pantaloons, and adroitly substituting a long nail in place of a missing suspender-button, with which effort of mechanical genius he seemed highly delighted.

"Yes, it 's an ill wind blows nowhar," he repeated. "Now, dar, Tom's down—wal, course der 's room for some nigger to be up—and why not dis nigger?—dat 's de idee. Tom, a ridin' round de country—boots blacked—pass in his pocket—all grand as Cuffee—who but he? Now, why should n't Sam?—dat 's what I want to know."

"Halloo, Sam—O Sam! Mas'r wants you to cotch Bill and Jerry," said Andy, cutting short Sam's soliloquy.

"High! what 's afoot now, young un?"

"Why, you don't know, I s'pose, that Lizy's cut stick, and clared out, with her young un?"

"You teach your granny!" said Sam, with infinite contempt; "knowed it a heap sight sooner than you did; this nigger an't so green, now!"

"Well, anyhow, Mas'r wants Bill and Jerry geared right up; and you and I 's to go with Mas'r Haley, to look arter her."

"Good, now! dat 's de time o' day!" said Sam. "It 's Sam dat 's called for in dese yer times. He 's de nigger. See if I don't cotch her, now; Mas'r 'll see what Sam can do!"

"Ah! but, Sam," said Andy, "you 'd better think twice; for Missis don't want her cotched, and she 'll be in yer wool."

"High!" said Sam, opening his eyes. "How you know dat?"

"Heard her say so, my own self, dis blessed mornin', when I bring in Mas'r's shaving-water. She sent me to see why Lizy did n't come to dress her; and when I told her she was off, she jest ris up, and ses she, 'The Lord be praised;' and Mas'r, he seemed rael mad, and ses he, 'Wife, you talk like a fool.' But Lor! she 'll bring him to! I knows well enough how that 'll be,—it 's allers best to stand Missis' side the fence, now I tell yer."

Black Sam, upon this, scratched his woolly pate, which, if it did not contain very profound wisdom, still contained a great deal of a particular species much in demand among politicians of all complexions and countries, and vulgarly de-nominated "knowing which side the bread is buttered;" so, stopping with grave consideration, he again gave a hitch to his pantaloons, which was his regularly organized method of assisting his mental perplexities.

"Der an't no sayin'—never—'bout no kind o' thing in *dis* yer world," he said, at last.

Sam spoke like a philosopher, emphasizing *this*—as if he had had a large ex-perience in different sorts of worlds, and therefore had come to his conclusions advisedly.

"Now, sartin I 'd a said that Missis would a scoured the varsal world after Lizy," added Sam, thoughtfully.

"So she would," said Andy; "but can't ye see through a ladder, ye black nig-ger? Missis don't want dis yer Mas'r Haley to get Lizy's boy; dat 's de go!"

"High!" said Sam, with an indescribable intonation, known only to those who have heard it among the negroes.

"And I 'll tell yer more 'n all," said Andy; "I specs you 'd better be making tracks for dem hosses,—mighty sudden, too,—for I hearn Missis 'quirin' arter yer,—so you 've stood foolin' long enough."

Sam, upon this, began to bestir himself in real earnest, and after a-while appeared, bearing down gloriously towards the house, with Bill and Jerry in a full canter, and adroitly throwing himself off before they had any idea of stopping, he brought them up alongside of the horse-post like a tornado. Haley's horse, which was a skittish young colt, winced, and bounced, and pulled hard at his halter.

"Ho, ho!" said Sam, "skeery, ar ye?" and his black visage lighted up with a curious, mischievous gleam. "I'll fix ye now!" said he.

There was a large beech-tree overshadowing the place, and the small, sharp, triangular beech-nuts lay scattered thickly on the ground. With one of these in his fingers, Sam approached the colt, stroked and patted, and seemed apparently busy in soothing his agitation. On pretence of adjusting the saddle, he adroitly slipped under it the sharp little nut, in such a manner that the least weight brought upon the saddle would annoy the nervous sensibilities of the animal, without leaving any perceptible graze or wound.

"Dar!" he said, rolling his eyes with an approving grin; "me fix 'em!"

At this moment Mrs. Shelby appeared on the balcony, beckoning to him. Sam approached with as good a determination to pay court as did ever suitor after a vacant place at St. James' or Washington.

"Why have you been loitering so, Sam? I sent Andy to tell you to hurry."

"Lord bless you, Missis!" said Sam, "horses won't be cotched all in a mimit; they 'd done clared out way down to the south pasture, and the Lord knows whar!"

"Sam, how often must I tell you not to say 'Lord bless you, and the Lord knows,' and such things? It 's wicked."

"O, Lord bless my soul! I done forgot, Missis! I won't say nothing of de sort no more."

"Why, Sam, you just *have* said it again."

"Did I? O, Lord! I mean—I did n't go fur to say it."

"You must be *careful*, Sam."

"Just let me get my breath, Missis, and I 'll start fair. I 'll be berry careful."

"Well, Sam, you are to go with Mr. Haley, to show him the road, and help him. Be careful of the horses, Sam; you know Jerry was a little lame last week, *don't ride them too fast*."

Mrs. Shelby spoke the last words with a low voice, and strong emphasis.

"Let dis child alone for dat!" said Sam, rolling up his eyes with a volume of meaning. "Lord knows! High! Did n't say dat!" said he, suddenly catching his breath, with a ludicrous flourish of apprehension, which made his mistress laugh, spite of herself. "Yes, Missis, I 'll look out for de hosses!"

"Now, Andy," said Sam, returning to his stand under the beech-trees, "you see I would n't be 't all surprised if dat ar gen'lman's crittur should gib a fling, by and by, when he comes to be a gettin' up. You know, Andy, critturs *will* do such things;" and therewith Sam poked Andy in the side, in a highly suggestive manner.

"High!" said Andy, with an air of instant appreciation.

"Yes, you see, Andy, Missis wants to make time,—dat ar 's clar to der most or'nary 'bserver. I jis make a little for her. Now, you see, get all dese yer hosses loose, caperin' permiscus round dis yer lot and down to de wood dar, and I spec Mas'r won't be off in a hurry."

Andy grinned.

"Yer see," said Sam, "yer see, Andy, if any such thing should happen as that Mas'r Haley's horse *should* begin to act contrary, and cut up, you and I jist lets go of our'n to help him, and *we 'll help him*—oh yes!" And Sam and Andy laid their heads back on their shoulders, and broke into a low, immoderate laugh, snapping their fingers and flourishing their heels with exquisite delight.

At this instant, Haley appeared on the verandah. Somewhat mollified by certain cups of very good coffee, he came out smiling and talking, in tolerably restored humor. Sam and Andy, clawing for certain fragmentary palm-leaves, which they were in the habit of considering as hats, flew to the horse-posts, to be ready to "help Mas'r."

Sam's palm-leaf had been ingeniously disentangled from all pretensions to braid, as respects its brim; and the slivers starting apart, and standing upright, gave it a blazing air of freedom and defiance, quite equal to that of any Fejee chief; while the whole brim of Andy's being departed bodily, he rapped the crown on his head with a dexterous thump, and looked about well pleased, as if to say, "Who says I have n't got a hat?"

"Well, boys," said Haley, "look alive now; we must lose no time."

"Not a bit of him, Mas'r!" said Sam, putting Haley's rein in his hand, and holding his stirrup, while Andy was untying the other two horses.

The instant Haley touched the saddle, the mettlesome creature bounded from the earth with a sudden spring, that threw his master sprawling, some feet off, on the soft, dry turf. Sam, with frantic ejaculations, made a dive at the reins, but only succeeded in brushing the blazing palm-leaf afore-named into the horse's eyes, which by no means tended to allay the confusion of his nerves. So, with great vehemence, he overturned Sam, and, giving two or three contemptuous snorts, flourished his heels vigorously in the air, and was soon prancing away towards the lower end of the lawn, followed by Bill and Jerry, whom Andy had not failed to let loose, according to contract, speeding them off with various direful ejaculations. And now ensued a miscellaneous scene of confusion. Sam and Andy ran and shouted,—dogs barked here and there,—and Mike, Mose, Mandy, Fanny, and all the smaller specimens on the place, both male and female, raced, clapped hands, whooped, and shouted, with outrageous officiousness and untiring zeal.

Haley's horse, which was a white one, and very fleet and spirited, appeared to enter into the spirit of the scene with great gusto; and having for his coursing ground a lawn of nearly half a mile in extent, gently sloping down on every side into indefinite woodland, he appeared to take infinite delight in seeing how near he could allow his pursuers to approach him, and then, when within a hand's breadth, whisk off with a start and a snort, like a mischievous beast as he was, and career far down into some alley of the wood-lot. Nothing was further from Sam's mind than to have any one of the troop taken until such season as should seem to him most befitting,—and the exertions that he made were certainly most heroic. Like the sword of Cœur De Lion, which always blazed in the front and thickest of the battle, Sam's palm-leaf was to be seen everywhere when there was the least danger that a horse could be caught;—there he would bear down full tilt, shouting, "Now for it! cotch him! cotch him!" in a way that would set everything to indiscriminate rout in a moment.

Haley ran up and down, and cursed and swore and stamped miscellaneously. Mr. Shelby in vain tried to shout directions from the balcony, and Mrs. Shelby from her chamber window alternately laughed and wondered,—not without some inkling of what lay at the bottom of all this confusion.

At last, about twelve o'clock, Sam appeared triumphant, mounted on Jerry, with Haley's horse by his side, reeking with sweat, but with flashing eyes and dilated nostrils, showing that the spirit of freedom had not yet entirely subsided.

"He 's cotched!" he exclaimed, triumphantly. "If 't had n't been for me, they might a bust theirselves, all on 'em; but I cotched him!"

"You!" growled Haley, in no amiable mood. "If it had n't been for you, this never would have happened."

"Lord bless us, Mas'r," said Sam, in a tone of the deepest concern, "and me that has been racin' and chasin' till the sweat jest pours off me!"

"Well, well!" said Haley, "you 've lost me near three hours, with your cursed nonsense. Now let 's be off, and have no more fooling."

"Why, Mas'r," said Sam, in a deprecating tone, "I believe you mean to kill us all clar, horses and all. Here we are all just ready to drop down, and the critters all in a reek of sweat. Why, Mas'r won't think of startin' on now till arter dinner. Mas'r's hoss wants rubben down; see how he splashed hisself; and Jerry limps too; don't think Missis would be willin' to have us start dis yer way, no how. Lord bless you, Mas'r, we can ketch up, if we do stop. Lizy never was no great of a walker."

Mrs. Shelby, who, greatly to her amusement, had overheard this conversation from the verandah, now resolved to do her part. She came forward, and, courteously expressing her concern for Haley's accident, pressed him to stay to dinner, saying that the cook should bring it on the table immediately.

Thus, all things considered, Haley, with rather an equivocal grace, proceeded to the parlor, while Sam, rolling his eyes after him with unutterable meaning, proceeded gravely with the horses to the stable-yard.

"Did yer see him, Andy? *did* yer see him?" said Sam, when he had got fairly beyond the shelter of the barn, and fastened the horse to a post. "O, Lor, if it warn't as good as a meetin', now, to see him a dancin' and kickin' and swarin' at us. Did n 't I hear him? Swar away, ole fellow (says I to myself); will yer have yer hoss now, or wait till you cotch him? (says I). Lor, Andy, I think I can see him now." And Sam and Andy leaned up against the barn, and laughed to their hearts' content.

"Yer oughter seen how mad he looked, when I brought the hoss up. Lord, he 'd a killed me, if he durs' to; and there I was a standin' as innercent and as humble."

"Lor, I seed you," said Andy; "an't you an old hoss, Sam?"

"Rather specks I am," said Sam; "did yer see Missis up stars at the winder? I seed her laughin'."

"I 'm sure, I was racin' so, I did n't see nothing," said Andy.

"Well, yer see," said Sam, proceeding gravely to wash down Haley's pony, "I 'se 'quired what yer may call a habit o' *bobservation*, Andy. It 's a very 'portant habit, Andy; and I 'commend yer to be cultivatin' it, now yer young. Hist up that hind foot, Andy. Yer see, Andy, it 's *bobservation* makes all de difference in niggers. Did n't I see which way the wind blew dis yer mornin'? Did n't I see what Missis wanted, though she never let on? Dat ar 's bobservation, Andy. I 'spects it 's what you may call a faculty. Faculties is different in different peoples, but cultivation of 'em goes a great way."

"I guess if I had n't helped your bobservation dis mornin', yer would n't have seen your way so smart," said Andy.

"Andy," said Sam, "you 's a promisin' child, der an't no manner o' doubt. I thinks lots of yer, Andy; and I don't feel no ways ashamed to take idees from you. We oughtenter overlook nobody, Andy, cause the smartest on us gets tripped up sometimes. And so, Andy, let 's go up to the house now. I 'll be boun' Missis 'll give us an uncommon good bite, dis yer time."

## VII.
### The Mother's Struggle

It is impossible to conceive of a human creature more wholly desolate and forlorn than Eliza, when she turned her footsteps from Uncle Tom's cabin.

Her husband's suffering and dangers, and the danger of her child, all blended in her mind, with a confused and stunning sense of the risk she was running, in leaving the only home she had ever known, and cutting loose from the protection of a friend whom she loved and revered. Then there was the parting from every familiar object,—the place where she had grown up, the trees under which she had played, the groves where she had walked many an evening in happier days, by the side of her young husband,—everything, as it lay in the clear, frosty starlight, seemed to speak reproachfully to her, and ask her whither could she go from a home like that?

But stronger than all was maternal love, wrought into a paroxysm of frenzy by the near approach of a fearful danger. Her boy was old enough to have walked by her side, and, in an indifferent case, she would only have led him by the hand; but now the bare thought of putting him out of her arms made her shudder, and she strained him to her bosom with a convulsive grasp, as she went rapidly forward.

The frosty ground creaked beneath her feet, and she trembled at the sound; every quaking leaf and fluttering shadow sent the blood backward to her heart, and quickened her footsteps. She wondered within herself at the strength that seemed to be come upon her; for she felt the weight of her boy as if it had been a feather, and every flutter of fear seemed to increase the supernatural power that bore her on, while from her pale lips burst forth, in frequent ejaculations, the prayer to a Friend above—"Lord, help! Lord, save me!"

If it were *your* Harry, mother, or your Willie, that were going to be torn from you by a brutal trader, to-morrow morning,—if you had seen the man, and heard that the papers were signed and delivered, and you had only from twelve o'clock till morning to make good your escape,— how fast could *you* walk? How many miles could you make in those few brief hours, with the darling at your bosom,— the little sleepy head on your shoulder,—the small, soft arms trustingly holding on to your neck?

For the child slept. At first, the novelty and alarm kept him waking; but his mother so hurriedly repressed every breath or sound, and so assured him that if he were only still she would certainly save him, that he clung quietly round her neck, only asking, as he found himself sinking to sleep,

"Mother, I don't need to keep awake, do I?"

"No, my darling; sleep, if you want to."

"But, mother, if I do get asleep, you won't let him get me?"

"No! so may God help me!" said his mother, with a paler cheek, and a brighter light in her large dark eyes.

"You 're *sure*, an't you, mother?"

"Yes, *sure*!" said the mother, in a voice that startled herself; for it seemed to her to come from a spirit within, that was no part of her; and the boy dropped his little weary head on her shoulder, and was soon asleep. How the touch of those warm arms, the gentle breathings that came in her neck, seemed to add fire and spirit to her movements! It seemed to her as if strength poured into her in electric streams, from every gentle touch and movement of the sleeping, confiding child. Sublime is the dominion of the mind over the body, that, for a time, can make flesh and nerve impregnable, and string the sinews like steel, so that the weak become so mighty.

The boundaries of the farm, the grove, the wood-lot, passed by her dizzily, as she walked on; and still she went, leaving one familiar object after another, slacking not, pausing not, till reddening daylight found her many a long mile from all traces of any familiar objects upon the open highway.

She had often been, with her mistress, to visit some connections, in the little village of T——, not far from the Ohio river, and knew the road well. To go thither, to escape across the Ohio river, were the first hurried outlines of her plan of escape; beyond that, she could only hope in God.

When horses and vehicles began to move along the highway, with that alert perception peculiar to a state of excitement, and which seems to be a sort of inspiration, she became aware that her headlong pace and distracted air might bring on her remark and suspicion. She therefore put the boy on the ground, and, adjusting her dress and bonnet, she walked on at as rapid a pace as she thought consistent with the preservation of appearances. In her little bundle she had provided a store of cakes and apples, which she used as expedients for quickening the speed of the child, rolling the apple some yards before them, when the boy would run with all his might after it; and this ruse, often repeated, carried them over many a half-mile.

After a while, they came to a thick patch of woodland, through which murmured a clear brook. As the child complained of hunger and thirst, she climbed over the fence with him; and, sitting down behind a large rock which concealed them from the road, she gave him a breakfast out of her little package. The boy wondered and grieved that she could not eat; and when, putting his arms round her neck, he tried to wedge some of his cake into her mouth, it seemed to her that the rising in her throat would choke her.

"No, no, Harry darling! mother can't eat till you are safe! We must go on— on—till we come to the river!" And she hurried again into the road, and again constrained herself to walk regularly and composedly forward.

She was many miles past any neighborhood where she was personally known. If she should chance to meet any who knew her, she reflected that the well-known kindness of the family would be of itself a blind to suspicion, as making it an unlikely supposition that she could be a fugitive. As she was also so white as not to be known as of colored lineage, without a critical survey, and her child was white also, it was much easier for her to pass on unsuspected.

On this presumption, she stopped at noon at a neat farmhouse, to rest herself, and buy some dinner for her child and self; for, as the danger decreased with the distance, the supernatural tension of the nervous system lessened, and she found herself both weary and hungry.

The good woman, kindly and gossipping, seemed rather pleased than otherwise with having somebody come in to talk with; and accepted, without examination, Eliza's statement, that she "was going on a little piece, to spend a week with her friends,"—all which she hoped in her heart might prove strictly true.

An hour before sunset, she entered the village of T——, by the Ohio river, weary and foot-sore, but still strong in heart. Her first glance was at the river, which lay, like Jordan, between her and the Canaan of liberty on the other side.

It was now early spring, and the river was swollen and turbulent; great cakes of floating ice were swinging heavily to and fro in the turbid waters. Owing to the peculiar form of the shore on the Kentucky side, the land bending far out into the water, the ice had been lodged and detained in great quantities, and the narrow channel which swept round the bend was full of ice, piled one cake over another, thus forming a temporary barrier to the descending ice, which lodged, and formed a great, undulating raft, filling up the whole river, and extending almost to the Kentucky shore.

Eliza stood, for a moment, contemplating this unfavorable aspect of things, which she saw at once must prevent the usual ferry-boat from running, and then turned into a small public house on the bank, to make a few inquiries.

The hostess, who was busy in various fizzing and stewing operations over the fire, preparatory to the evening meal, stopped, with a fork in her hand, as Eliza's sweet and plaintive voice arrested her.

"What is it?" she said.

"Is n't there any ferry or boat, that takes people over to B——, now?" she said.

"No, indeed!" said the woman; "the boats has stopped running."

Eliza's look of dismay and disappointment struck the woman, and she said, inquiringly,

"May be you 're wanting to get over?—anybody sick? Ye seem mighty anxious?"

"I 've got a child that 's very dangerous," said Eliza. "I never heard of it till last night, and I 've walked quite a piece to-day, in hopes to get to the ferry."

"Well, now, that 's onlucky," said the woman, whose motherly sympathies were much aroused; "I 'm re'lly consarned for ye. Solomon!" she called, from the window, towards a small back building. A man, in leather apron and very dirty hands, appeared at the door.

"I say, Sol," said the woman, "is that ar man going to tote them bar'ls over to-night?"

"He said he should try, if 't was any way prudent," said the man.

"There 's a man a piece down here, that 's going over with some truck this evening, if he durs' to; he 'll be in here to supper to-night, so you 'd better set down and wait. That 's a sweet little fellow," added the woman, offering him a cake.

But the child, wholly exhausted, cried with weariness.

"Poor fellow! he is n't used to walking, and I 've hurried him on so," said Eliza.

"Well, take him into this room," said the woman, opening into a small bedroom, where stood a comfortable bed. Eliza laid the weary boy upon it, and held his hands in hers till he was fast asleep. For her there was no rest. As a fire in her bones, the thought of the pursuer urged her on; and she gazed with longing eyes on the sullen, surging waters that lay between her and liberty.

Here we must take our leave of her for the present, to follow the course of her pursuers.

---

Though Mrs. Shelby had promised that the dinner should be hurried on table, yet it was soon seen, as the thing has often been seen before, that it required more than one to make a bargain. So, although the order was fairly given out in Haley's hearing, and carried to Aunt Chloe by at least half a dozen juvenile messengers, that dignitary only gave certain very gruff snorts, and tosses of her head, and went on with every operation in an unusually leisurely and circumstantial manner.

For some singular reason, an impression seemed to reign among the servants generally that Missis would not be particularly disobliged by delay; and it was wonderful what a number of counter accidents occurred constantly, to retard the course of things. One luckless wight contrived to upset the gravy; and then gravy had to be got up *de novo*, with due care and formality, Aunt Chloe watching and stirring with dogged precision, answering shortly, to all suggestions of haste, that she "warn't a going to have raw gravy on the table, to help nobody's catchings." One tumbled down with the water, and had to go to the spring for more; and another precipitated the butter into the path of events; and there was from time to time giggling news brought into the kitchen that "Mas'r Haley was mighty oneasy, and that he could n't sit in his cheer no ways, but was a walkin' and stalkin' to the winders and through the porch."

"Sarves him right!" said Aunt Chloe, indignantly. "He 'll get wus nor oneasy, one of these days, if he don't mend his ways. *His* master 'll be sending for him, and then see how he 'll look!"

"He 'll go to torment, and no mistake," said little Jake.

"He desarves it!" said Aunt Chloe, grimly; "he 's broke a many, many, many hearts,—I tell ye all!" she said, stopping, with a fork uplifted in her hands; "it 's like what Mas'r George reads in Ravelations,—souls a callin' under the altar! and all a callin' on the Lord for vengeance on sich!—and by and by the Lord he 'll hear 'em—so he will!"

Aunt Chloe, who was much revered in the kitchen, was listened to with open mouth; and, the dinner being now fairly sent in, the whole kitchen was at leisure to gossip with her, and to listen to her remarks.

"Sich 'll be burnt up forever, and no mistake; won't ther?" said Andy.

"I 'd be glad to see it, I 'll be boun'," said little Jake.

"Chil'en!" said a voice, that made them all start. It was Uncle Tom, who had come in, and stood listening to the conversation at the door.

"Chil'en!" he said, "I 'm afeard you don't know what ye 're sayin'. Forever is a *dre'ful* word, chil'en; it 's awful to think on 't. You oughtenter wish that ar to any human crittur."

"We would n't to anybody but the soul-drivers," said Andy; "nobody can help wishing it to them, they 's so awful wicked."

"Don't natur herself kinder cry out on em?" said Aunt Chloe. "Don't dey tear der suckin' baby right off his mother's breast, and sell him, and der little children as is crying and holding on by her clothes,—don't dey pull 'em off and sells em? Don't dey tear wife and husband apart?" said Aunt Chloe, beginning to cry, "when it 's jest takin' the very life on 'em?—and all the while does they feel one bit,—don't dey drink and smoke, and take it oncommon easy? Lor, if the devil don't get them, what 's he good for?" And Aunt Chloe covered her face with her checked apron, and began to sob in good earnest.

"Pray for them that 'spitefully use you, the good book says," says Tom.

"Pray for 'em" said Aunt Chloe; "Lor, it 's too tough! I can't pray for 'em."

"It 's natur, Chloe, and natur 's strong," said Tom, "but the Lord's grace is stronger; besides, you oughter think what an awful state a poor crittur's soul 's in that 'll do them ar things,—you oughter thank God that you an't *like* him, Chloe. I 'm sure I 'd rather be sold, ten thousand times over, than to have all that ar poor crittur 's got to answer for."

"So 'd I, a heap," said Jake. "Lor, *should n't* we cotch it, Andy?"

Andy shrugged his shoulders, and gave an acquiescent whistle.

"I 'm glad Mas'r did n't go off this morning, as he looked to," said Tom; "that ar hurt me more than sellin', it did. Mebbe it might have been natural for him, but 't would have come desp't hard on me, as has known him from a baby; but I 've seen Mas'r, and I begin ter feel sort o' reconciled to the Lord's will now. Mas'r could n't help hisself; he did right, but I'm feared things will be kinder goin' to rack, when I 'm gone. Mas'r can't be spected to be a pryin' around everywhar, as I 've done, a keepin' up all the ends. The boys all means well, but they 's powerful car'less. That ar troubles me."

The bell here rang, and Tom was summoned to the parlor.

"Tom," said his master, kindly, "I want you to notice that I give this gentleman bonds to forfeit a thousand dollars if you are not on the spot when he wants you; he 's going to-day to look after his other business, and you can have the day to yourself. Go anywhere you like, boy."

"Thank you, Mas'r," said Tom.

"And mind yerself," said the trader, "and don't come it over your master with any o' yer nigger tricks; for I 'll take every cent out of him, if you an't thar. If he 'd hear to me, he would n't trust any on ye—slippery as eels!"

"Mas'r," said Tom,—and he stood very straight,—"I was jist eight years old when ole Missis put you into my arms, and you was n't a year old. 'Thar,' says she, 'Tom, that 's to be *your* young Mas'r; take good care on him,' says she. And now I jist ask you, Mas'r, have I ever broke word to you, or gone contrary to you, 'specially since I was a Christian?"

Mr. Shelby was fairly overcome, and the tears rose to his eyes.

"My good boy," said he, "the Lord knows you say but the truth; and if I was able to help it, all the world should n't buy you."

"And sure as I am a Christian woman," said Mrs. Shelby, "you shall be redeemed as soon as I can any way bring together means. Sir," she said to Haley, "take good account of who you sell him to, and let me know."

"Lor, yes, for that matter," said the trader, "I may bring him up in a year, not much the wuss for wear, and trade him back."

"I 'll trade with you then, and make it for your advantage," said Mrs. Shelby.

"Of course," said the trader, "all 's equal with me; li'ves trade 'em up as down, so I does a good business. All I want is a livin', you know, ma'am; that 's all any on us wants, I s'pose."

Mr. and Mrs. Shelby both felt annoyed and degraded by the familiar impudence of the trader, and yet both saw the absolute necessity of putting a constraint on their feelings. The more hopelessly sordid and insensible he appeared, the greater became Mrs. Shelby's dread of his succeeding in recapturing Eliza and her child, and of course the greater her motive for detaining him by every female artifice. She therefore graciously smiled, assented, chatted familiarly, and did all she could to make time pass imperceptibly.

At two o'clock Sam and Andy brought the horses up to the posts, apparently greatly refreshed and invigorated by the scamper of the morning.

Sam was there new oiled from dinner, with an abundance of zealous and ready officiousness. As Haley approached, he was boasting, in flourishing style, to Andy, of the evident and eminent success of the operation, now that he had "farly come to it."

"Your master, I s'pose, don't keep no dogs," said Haley, thoughtfully, as he prepared to mount.

"Heaps on 'em," said Sam, triumphantly; "thar 's Bruno—he 's a roarer! and, besides that, 'bout every nigger of us keeps a pup of some natur or uther."

"Poh!" said Haley,—and he said something else, too, with regard to the said dogs, at which Sam muttered,

"I don't see no use cussin' on 'em, no way."

"But your master don't keep no dogs (I pretty much know he don't) for trackin' out niggers."

Sam knew exactly what he meant, but he kept on a look of earnest and desperate simplicity.

"Our dogs all smells round considable sharp. I spect they 's the kind, though they han't never had no practice. They 's *far* dogs, though, at most anything, if you 'd get 'em started. Here, Bruno," he called, whistling to the lumbering Newfoundland, who came pitching tumultuously toward them.

"You go hang!" said Haley, getting up. "Come, tumble up now."

Sam tumbled up accordingly, dexterously contriving to tickle Andy as he did so, which occasioned Andy to split out into a laugh, greatly to Haley's indignation, who made a cut at him with his riding-whip.

"I 's 'stonished at yer, Andy," said Sam, with awful gravity. "This yer 's a seris bisness, Andy. Yer must n't be a makin' game. This yer an't no way to help Mas'r."

"I shall take the straight road to the river," said Haley, decidedly, after they had come to the boundaries of the estate. "I know the way of all of 'em—they makes tracks for the underground."

"Sartin," said Sam, "dat 's de idee. Mas'r Haley hits de thing right in de middle. Now, der 's two roads to de river,—de dirt road and der pike,—which Mas'r mean to take?"

Andy looked up innocently at Sam, surprised at hearing this new geographical fact, but instantly confirmed what he said, by a vehement reiteration.

"Cause," said Sam, "I 'd rather be 'clined to 'magine that Lizy 'd take de dirt road, bein' it 's the least travelled."

Haley, notwithstanding that he was a very old bird, and naturally inclined to be suspicious of chaff, was rather brought up by this view of the case.

"If yer warn't both on yer such cussed liars, now!" he said, contemplatively, as he pondered a moment.

The pensive, reflective tone in which this was spoken appeared to amuse Andy prodigiously, and he drew a little behind, and shook so as apparently to run a great risk of falling off his horse, while Sam's face was immovably composed into the most doleful gravity.

"Course," said Sam, "Mas'r can do as he 'd ruther; go de straight road, if Mas'r thinks best,—it 's all one to us. Now, when I study 'pon it, I think de straight road de best, *deridedly*."

"She would naturally go a lonesome way," said Haley, thinking aloud, and not minding Sam's remark.

"Dar an't no sayin'," said Sam; "gals is pecular; they never does nothin' ye thinks they will; mose gen'lly the contrar. Gals is nat'lly made contrary; and so, if you thinks they 've gone one road, it is sartin you 'd better go t' other, and then you 'll be sure to find 'em. Now, my private 'pinion is, Lizy took der dirt road; so I think we 'd better take de straight one."

This profound generic view of the female sex did not seem to dispose Haley particularly to the straight road; and he announced decidedly that he should go the other, and asked Sam when they should come to it.

"A little piece ahead," said Sam, giving a wink to Andy with the eye which was on Andy's side of the head; and he added, gravely, "but I 've studded on de matter, and I 'm quite clar we ought not to go dat ar way. I nebber been over it no way. It 's despit lonesome, and we might lose our way,—whar we 'd come to, de Lord only knows."

"Nevertheless," said Haley, "I shall go that way."

"Now I think on 't, I think I hearn 'em tell that dat ar road was all fenced up and down by der creek, and thar, an't it, Andy?"

Andy was n't certain; he 'd only "hearn tell" about that road, but never been over it. In short, he was strictly noncommittal.

Haley, accustomed to strike the balance of probabilities between lies of greater or lesser magnitude, thought that it lay in favor of the dirt road aforesaid. The mention of the thing he thought he perceived was involuntary on Sam's part at first, and his confused attempts to dissuade him he set down to a desperate lying on second thoughts, as being unwilling to implicate Eliza.

When, therefore, Sam indicated the road, Haley plunged briskly into it, followed by Sam and Andy.

Now, the road, in fact, was an old one, that had formerly been a thoroughfare to the river, but abandoned for many years after the laying of the new pike. It was open for about an hour's ride, and after that it was cut across by various farms and fences. Sam knew this fact perfectly well,—indeed, the road had been so long closed up, that Andy had never heard of it. He therefore rode along with an air of dutiful submission, only groaning and vociferating occasionally that 't was "desp't rough, and bad for Jerry's foot."

"Now, I jest give yer warning," said Haley, "I know yer; yer won't get me to turn off this yer road, with all yer fussin'—so you shet up!"

"Mas'r will go his own way!" said Sam, with rueful submission, at the same time winking most portentously to Andy, whose delight was now very near the explosive point.

Sam was in wonderful spirits,—professed to keep a very brisk look-out,—at one time exclaiming that he saw "a gal's bonnet" on the top of some distant eminence, or calling to Andy "if that thar was n't 'Lizy' down in the hollow;" always making these exclamations in some rough or craggy part of the road, where the sudden quickening of speed was a special inconvenience to all parties concerned, and thus keeping Haley in a state of constant commotion.

After riding about an hour in this way, the whole party made a precipitate and tumultuous descent into a barn-yard belonging to a large farming establishment. Not a soul was in sight, all the hands being employed in the fields; but, as the barn stood conspicuously and plainly square across the road, it was evident that their journey in that direction had reached a decided finale.

"Wan't dat ar what I tell Mas'r?" said Sam, with an air of injured innocence. "How does strange gentleman spect to know more about a country dan de natives born and raised?"

"You rascal!" said Haley, "you knew all about this."

"Did n't I tell yer I *know'd*, and yer would n't believe me? I telled Mas'r 't was all shet up, and fenced up, and I did n't spect we could get through,—Andy heard me."

It was all too true to be disputed, and the unlucky man had to pocket his wrath with the best grace he was able, and all three faced to the right about, and took up their line of march for the highway.

In consequence of all the various delays, it was about three-quarters of an hour after Eliza had laid her child to sleep in the village tavern that the party came riding into the same place. Eliza was standing by the window, looking out in another direction, when Sam's quick eye caught a glimpse of her. Haley and Andy were two yards behind. At this crisis, Sam contrived to have his hat blown off, and uttered a loud and characteristic ejaculation, which startled her at once; she drew suddenly back; the whole train swept by the window, round to the front door.

A thousand lives seemed to be concentrated in that one moment to Eliza. Her room opened by a side door to the river. She caught her child, and sprang down the steps towards it. The trader caught a full glimpse of her, just as she was disappearing down the bank; and throwing himself from his horse, and calling loudly on Sam and Andy, he was after her like a hound after a deer. In that dizzy moment her feet to her scarce seemed to touch the ground, and a moment brought her to the water's edge. Right on behind they came; and, nerved with strength such as God gives only to the desperate, with one wild cry and flying leap, she vaulted sheer over the turbid current by the shore, on to the raft of ice beyond. It was a desperate leap—impossible to anything but madness and despair; and Haley, Sam, and Andy, instinctively cried out, and lifted up their hands, as she did it.

The huge green fragment of ice on which she alighted pitched and creaked as her weight came on it, but she staid there not a moment. With wild cries and desperate energy she leaped to another and still another cake;—stumbling—leaping—slipping—springing upwards again! Her shoes are gone—her stockings cut from her feet—while blood marked every step; but she saw nothing, felt nothing, till dimly, as in a dream, she saw the Ohio side, and a man helping her up the bank.

"Yer a brave gal, now, whoever ye ar!" said the man, with an oath.

Eliza recognized the voice and face of a man who owned a farm not far from her old home.

"O, Mr. Symmes!—save me—do save me—do hide me!" said Eliza.

"Why, what 's this?" said the man. "Why, if 'tan't Shelby's gal!"

"My child!—this boy!—he 'd sold him! There is his Mas'r," said she, pointing to the Kentucky shore. "O, Mr. Symmes, you 've got a little boy!"

"So I have," said the man, as he roughly, but kindly, drew her up the steep bank. "Besides, you 're a right brave gal. I like grit, wherever I see it."

When they had gained the top of the bank, the man paused.

"I 'd be glad to do something for ye," said he; "but then there 's nowhar I could take ye. The best I can do is to tell ye to go *thar*," said he, pointing to a large white house which stood by itself, off the main street of the village. "Go thar; they 're kind folks. Thar 's no kind o' danger but they 'll help you,—they 're up to all that sort o' thing."

"The Lord bless you!" said Eliza, earnestly.

"No 'casion, no 'casion in the world," said the man. "What I 've done 's of no 'count."

"And, oh, surely, sir, you won't tell any one!"

"Go to thunder, gal! What do you take a feller for? In course not," said the man. "Come, now, go along like a likely, sensible gal, as you are. You 've arnt your liberty, and you shall have it, for all me."

The woman folded her child to her bosom, and walked firmly and swiftly away. The man stood and looked after her.

"Shelby, now, mebbe won't think this yer the most neighborly thing in the world; but what 's a feller to do? If he catches one of my gals in the same fix, he 's welcome to pay back. Somehow I never could see no kind o' critter a strivin' and pantin', and trying to clar theirselves, with the dogs arter 'em, and go agin 'em. Besides, I don't see no kind of 'casion for me to be hunter and catcher for other folks, neither."

So spoke this poor, heathenish Kentuckian, who had not been instructed in his constitutional relations, and consequently was betrayed into acting in a sort of Christianized manner, which, if he had been better situated and more enlightened, he would not have been left to do.

Haley had stood a perfectly amazed spectator of the scene, till Eliza had disappeared up the bank, when he turned a blank, inquiring look on Sam and Andy.

"That ar was a tolable fair stroke of business," said Sam.

"The gal 's got seven devils in her, I believe!" said Haley. "How like a wild-cat she jumped!"

"Wal, now," said Sam, scratching his head, "I hope Mas'r 'll 'scuse us tryin' dat ar road. Don't think I feel spry enough for dat ar, no way!" and Sam gave a hoarse chuckle.

"*You* laugh!" said the trader, with a growl.

"Lord bless you, Mas'r, I could n't help it, now," said Sam, giving way to the long pent-up delight of his soul. "She looked so curi's, a leapin' and springin'—ice a crackin'—and only to hear her,—plump! ker chunk! ker splash! Spring! Lord! how she goes it!" and Sam and Andy laughed till the tears rolled down their cheeks.

"I 'll make ye laugh t' other side yer mouths!" said the trader, laying about their heads with his riding-whip.

Both ducked, and ran shouting up the bank, and were on their horses before he was up.

"Good-evening, Mas'r!" said Sam, with much gravity. "I berry much spect Missis be anxious 'bout Jerry. Mas'r Haley won't want us no longer. Missis would n't hear of our ridin' the critters over Lizy's bridge to-night;" and, with a facetious poke into Andy's ribs, he started off, followed by the latter, at full speed,—their shouts of laughter coming faintly on the wind.

## VIII.
### Eliza's Escape

Eliza made her desperate retreat across the river just in the dusk of twilight. The gray mist of evening, rising slowly from the river, enveloped her as she disappeared up the bank, and the swollen current and floundering masses of ice presented a hopeless barrier between her and her pursuer. Haley therefore slowly and discontentedly returned to the little tavern, to ponder further what was to be done. The woman opened to him the door of a little parlor, covered with a rag carpet, where stood a table with a very shining black oil-cloth, sundry lank, high-backed wood chairs, with some plaster images in resplendent colors on the mantel-shelf, above a very dimly-smoking grate; a long hard-wood settle extended its uneasy length by the chimney, and here Haley sat him down to meditate on the instability of human hopes and happiness in general.

"What did I want with the little cuss, now," he said to himself, "that I should have got myself treed like a coon, as I am, this yer way?" and Haley relieved himself by repeating over a not very select litany of imprecations on himself, which, though there was the best possible reason to consider them as true, we shall, as a matter of taste, omit.

He was startled by the loud and dissonant voice of a man who was apparently dismounting at the door. He hurried to the window.

"By the land! if this yer an't the nearest, now, to what I 've heard folks call Providence," said Haley. "I do b'lieve that ar 's Tom Loker."

Haley hastened out. Standing by the bar, in the corner of the room, was a brawny, muscular man, full six feet in height, and broad in proportion. He was dressed in a coat of buffalo-skin, made with the hair outward, which gave him a shaggy and fierce appearance, perfectly in keeping with the whole air of his physiognomy. In the head and face every organ and lineament expressive of brutal and unhesitating violence was in a state of the highest possible development. Indeed, could our readers fancy a bull-dog come unto man's estate, and walking about in a hat and coat, they would have no unapt idea of the general style and effect of his physique. He was accompanied by a travelling companion, in many respects an exact contrast to himself. He was short and slender, lithe and cat-like in his motions, and had a peering, mousing expression about his keen black eyes, with which every feature of his face seemed sharpened into sympathy; his thin, long nose, ran out as if it was eager to bore into the nature of things in general; his sleek, thin, black hair was stuck eagerly forward, and all his motions and evolutions expressed a dry, cautious acuteness. The great big man poured out a big tumbler half full of raw spirits, and gulped it down without a word. The little man stood tip-toe, and putting his head first to one side and then to the other, and snuffing considerably in the directions of the various bottles, ordered at last a mint julep, in a thin and quivering voice, and with an air of great circumspection. When poured out, he took it and looked at it with a sharp, complacent air, like a man who thinks he has done about the right thing, and hit the nail on the head, and proceeded to dispose of it in short and well-advised sips.

"Wal, now, who 'd a thought this yer luck 'ad come to me? Why, Loker, how are ye?" said Haley, coming forward, and extending his hand to the big man.

"The devil!" was the civil reply. "What brought you here, Haley?"

The mousing man, who bore the name of Marks, instantly stopped his sipping, and, poking his head forward, looked shrewdly on the new acquaintance, as a cat sometimes looks at a moving dry leaf, or some other possible object of pursuit.

"I say, Tom, this yer 's the luckiest thing in the world. I 'm in a devil of a hobble, and you must help me out."

"Ugh? aw! like enough!" grunted his complacent acquaintance. "A body may be pretty sure of that, when *you 're* glad to see 'em; something to be made off of 'em. What 's the blow now?"

"You 've got a friend here?" said Haley, looking doubtfully at Marks; "partner, perhaps?"

"Yes, I have. Here, Marks! here 's that ar feller that I was in with in Natchez."

"Shall be pleased with his acquaintance," said Marks, thrusting out a long, thin hand, like a raven's claw. "Mr. Haley, I believe?"

"The same, sir," said Haley. "And now, gentlemen, seein' as we 've met so happily, I think I 'll stand up to a small matter of a treat in this here parlor. So, now, old coon," said he to the man at the bar, "get us hot water, and sugar, and cigars, and plenty of the *real stuff*, and we 'll have a blow-out."

Behold, then, the candles lighted, the fire stimulated to the burning point in the grate, and our three worthies seated round a table, well spread with all the accessories to good fellowship enumerated before.

Haley began a pathetic recital of his peculiar troubles. Loker shut up his mouth, and listened to him with gruff and surly attention. Marks, who was anxiously and with much fidgeting compounding a tumbler of punch to his own peculiar taste, occasionally looked up from his employment, and, poking his sharp nose and chin almost into Haley's face, gave the most earnest heed to the whole narrative. The conclusion of it appeared to amuse him extremely, for he shook his shoulders and sides in silence, and perked up his thin lips with an air of great internal enjoyment.

"So, then, ye 'r fairly sewed up, an't ye?" he said; "he! he! he! It 's neatly done, too."

"This yer young-un business makes lots of trouble in the trade," said Haley, dolefully.

"If we could get a breed of gals that did n't care, now, for their young uns," said Marks; "tell ye, I think 't would be 'bout the greatest mod'rn improvement I knows on,"—and Marks patronized his joke by a quiet introductory sniggle.

"Jes so," said Haley; "I never could n't see into it; young uns is heaps of trouble to 'em; one would think, now, they 'd be glad to get clar on 'em; but they arn't. And the more trouble a young un is, and the more good for nothing, as a gen'l thing, the tighter they sticks to 'em."

"Wal, Mr. Haley," said Marks, "jest pass the hot water. Yes, sir; you say jest what I feel and all'us have. Now, I bought a gal once, when I was in the trade,—a tight, likely wench she was, too, and quite considerable smart,—and she had a young un that was mis'able sickly; it had a crooked back, or something or other; and I jest gin 't away to a man that thought he 'd take his chance raising on 't, being it did n't cost nothin';—never thought, yer know, of the gal's takin' on about it,—but, Lord, yer oughter seen how she went on. Why, re'lly, she did seem to me to valley the child more 'cause 't *was* sickly and cross, and plagued her; and she warn't making b'lieve, neither,—cried about it, she did, and lopped round, as if she 'd lost every friend she had. It re'lly was droll to think on 't. Lord, there an't no end to women's notions."

"Wal, jest so with me," said Haley. "Last summer, down on Red river, I got a gal traded off on me, with a likely lookin' child enough, and his eyes looked as bright as yourn; but, come to look, I found him stone blind. Fact—he was stone blind. Wal, ye see, I thought there warn't no harm in my jest passing him along, and not sayin' nothin'; and I 'd got him nicely swapped off for a keg o' whiskey; but come to get him away from the gal, she was jest like a tiger. So 't was before we started, and I had n't got my gang chained up; so what should she do but ups on a cotton-bale, like a cat, ketches a knife from one of the deck hands, and, I tell ye, she made all fly for a minit, till she saw 'twan't no use; and she jest turns round, and pitches head first, young un and all, into the river,—went down plump, and never ris."

"Bah!" said Tom Loker, who had listened to these stories with ill-repressed disgust,—"shif'less, both on ye! *my* gals don't cut up no such shines, I tell ye!"

"Indeed! how do you help it?" said Marks, briskly.

"Help it? why, I buys a gal, and if she 's got a young un to be sold, I jest walks up and puts my fist to her face, and says, 'Look here, now, if you give me one word out of your head, I 'll smash yer face in. I won't hear one word—not the beginning of a word.' I says to 'em, 'This yer young un 's mine, and not yourn, and you 've no kind o' business with it. I 'm going to sell it, first chance; mind, you don't cut up none o' yer shines about it, or I 'll make ye wish ye 'd never been born.' I tell ye, they sees it an't no play, when I gets hold. I makes 'em as whist as fishes; and if one on 'em begins and gives a yelp, why,—" and Mr. Loker brought down his fist with a thump that fully explained the hiatus.

"That ar 's what ye may call *emphasis*," said Marks, poking Haley in the side, and going into another small giggle. "An't Tom peculiar? he! he! he! I say, Tom, I s'pect you make 'em *understand*, for all niggers' heads is woolly. They don't never have no doubt o' your meaning, Tom. If you an't the devil, Tom, you 's his twin brother, I 'll say that for ye!"

Tom received the compliment with becoming modesty, and began to look as affable as was consistent, as John Bunyan says, "with his doggish nature."

Haley, who had been imbibing very freely of the staple of the evening, began to feel a sensible elevation and enlargement of his moral faculties,—a phenomenon not unusual with gentlemen of a serious and reflective turn, under similar circumstances.

"Wal, now, Tom," he said, "ye re'lly is too bad, as I al'ays have told ye; ye know, Tom, you and I used to talk over these yer matters down in Natchez, and I used to prove to ye that we made full as much, and was as well off for this yer world, by treatin' on 'em well, besides keepin' a better chance for comin' in the kingdom at last, when wust comes to wust, and thar an't nothing else left to get, ye know."

"Boh!" said Tom, "*don't* I know?—don't make me too sick with any yer stuff,— my stomach is a leetle riled now;" and Tom drank half a glass of raw brandy.

"I say," said Haley, and leaning back in his chair and gesturing impressively, "I 'll say this now, I al'ays meant to drive my trade so as to make money on 't, *fust and foremost*, as much as any man; but, then, trade an't everything, and money an't everything, 'cause we 's all got souls. I don't care, now, who hears me say it,—and I think a cussed sight on it,—so I may as well come out with it. I b'lieve in religion, and one of these days, when I 've got matters tight and snug, I calculates to tend to my soul and them ar matters; and so what 's the use of doin' any more wickedness than 's re'lly necessary?—it don't seem to me it 's 't all prudent."

"Tend to yer soul!" repeated Tom, contemptuously; "take a bright look-out to find a soul in you,—save yourself any care on that score. If the devil sifts you through a hair sieve, he won't find one."

"Why, Tom, you 're cross," said Haley; "why can't ye take it pleasant, now, when a feller 's talking for your good?"

"Stop that ar jaw o' yourn, there," said Tom, gruffly. "I can stand most any talk o' yourn but your pious talk,—that kills me right up. After all, what 's the odds between me and you? 'Tan't that you care one bit more, or have a bit more feelin',—it 's clean, sheer, dog meanness, wanting to cheat the devil and save your own skin; don't I see through it? And your 'gettin' religion,' as you call it, arter all, is too p'isin mean for any crittur;—run up a bill with the devil all your life, and then sneak out when pay time comes! Boh!"

"Come, come, gentlemen, I say; this is n't business," said Marks. "There 's different ways, you know, of looking at all subjects. Mr. Haley is a very nice man, no doubt, and has his own conscience; and, Tom, you have your ways, and very good ones, too, Tom; but quarrelling, you know, won't answer no kind of purpose. Let 's go to business. Now, Mr. Haley, what is it?—you want us to undertake to catch this yer gal?"

"The gal 's no matter of mine,—she 's Shelby's; it 's only the boy. I was a fool for buying the monkey!"

"You 're generally a fool!" said Tom, gruffly.

"Come, now, Loker, none of your huffs," said Marks, licking his lips; "you see, Mr. Haley's a puttin' us in a way of a good job, I reckon; just hold still,—these yer arrangements is my forte. This yer gal, Mr. Haley, how is she? what is she?"

"Wal! white and handsome—well brought up. I 'd a gin Shelby eight hundred or a thousand, and then made well on her."

"White and handsome—well brought up!" said Marks, his sharp eyes, nose and mouth, all alive with enterprise. "Look here, now, Loker, a beautiful opening. We 'll do a business here on our own account;—we does the catchin'; the boy, of course, goes to Mr. Haley,—we takes the gal to Orleans to speculate on. An't it beautiful?"

Tom, whose great heavy mouth had stood ajar during this communication, now suddenly snapped it together, as a big dog closes on a piece of meat, and seemed to be digesting the idea at his leisure.

"Ye see," said Marks to Haley, stirring his punch as he did so, "ye see, we has justices convenient at all p'ints along shore, that does up any little jobs in our line quite reasonable. Tom, he does the knockin' down and that ar; and I come in all dressed up—shining boots—everything first chop, when the swearin' 's to be done. You oughter see, now." said Marks, in a glow of professional pride, "how I can tone it off. One day, I 'm Mr. Twickem, from New Orleans; 'nother day, I 'm just come from my plantation on Pearl river, where I works seven hundred niggers; then, again, I come out a distant relation of Henry Clay, or some old cock in Kentuck. Talents is different, you know. Now, Tom 's a roarer when there 's any thumping or fighting to be done; but at lying he an't good, Tom an't—ye see it don't come natural to him; but, Lord, if thar 's a feller in the country that can swear to anything and everything, and put in all the circumstances and flourishes with a longer face, and carry 't through better 'n I can, why, I 'd like to see him, that 's all! I b'lieve my heart, I could get along and snake through, even if justices were more particular than they is. Sometimes I rather wish they was more particular; 't would be a heap more relishin' if they was,—more fun, yer know."

Tom Loker, who, as we have made it appear, was a man of slow thoughts and movements, here interrupted Marks by bringing his heavy fist down on the table, so as to make all ring again. "*It 'll do!*" he said.

"Lord bless ye, Tom, ye need n't break all the glasses!" said Marks; "save your fist for time o' need."

"But, gentlemen, an't I to come in for a share of the profits?" said Haley.

"An't it enough we catch the boy for ye?" said Loker. "What do ye want?"

"Wal," said Haley, "if I gives you the job, it 's worth something,—say ten per cent. on the profits, expenses paid."

"Now," said Loker, with a tremendous oath, and striking the table with his heavy fist, "don't I know *you*, Dan Haley? Don't you think to come it over me! Suppose Marks and I have taken up the catchin' trade, jest to 'commodate gentlemen like you, and get nothin' for ourselves?—Not by a long chalk! we 'll have the gal out and out, and you keep quiet, or, ye see, we 'll have both,—what 's to hinder? Han't you show'd us the game? It 's as free to us as you, I hope. If you or Shelby wants to chase us, look where the partridges was last year; if you find them or us, you 're quite welcome."

"O, wal, certainly, jest let it go at that," said Haley, alarmed; "you catch the boy for the job;—you allers did trade *far* with me, Tom, and was up to yer word."

"Ye know that," said Tom; "I don't pretend none of your snivelling ways, but I won't lie in my 'counts with the devil himself. What I ses I 'll do, I will do,—you know *that*, Dan Haley."

"Jes so, jes so,—I said so, Tom," said Haley; "and if you 'd only promise to have the boy for me in a week, at any point you 'll name, that 's all I want."

"But it an't all I want, by a long jump," said Tom. "Ye don't think I did business with you, down in Natchez, for nothing, Haley; I 've learned to hold an eel, when I catch him. You 've got to fork over fifty dollars, flat down, or this child don't start a peg. I know yer."

"Why, when you have a job in hand that may bring a clean profit of somewhere about a thousand or sixteen hundred, why, Tom, you 're onreasonable," said Haley.

"Yes, and has n't we business booked for five weeks to come,—all we can do? And suppose we leaves all, and goes to bushwhacking round arter yer young un, and finally does n't catch the gal,—and gals allers is the devil *to* catch,—what 's then? would you pay us a cent—would you? I think I see you a doin' it—ugh!

No, no; flap down your fifty. If we get the job, and it pays, I 'll hand it back; if we don't, it 's for our trouble,— that 's *far*, an't it, Marks?"

"Certainly, certainly," said Marks, with a conciliatory tone; "it 's only a retaining fee, you see,—he! he! he!—we lawyers, you know. Wal, we must all keep good-natured,—keep easy, yer know. Tom 'll have the boy for yer, anywhere ye 'll name; won't ye, Tom?"

"If I find the young un, I 'll bring him on to Cincinnati, and leave him at Granny Belcher's, on the landing," said Loker.

Marks had got from his pocket a greasy pocket-book, and taking a long paper from thence, he sat down, and fixing his keen black eyes on it, began mumbling over its contents: "Barnes—Shelby County—boy Jim, three hundred dollars for him, dead or alive.

"Edwards—Dick and Lucy—man and wife, six hundred dollars; wench Polly and two children—six hundred for her or her head.

"I 'm jest a runnin' over our business, to see if we can take up this yer handily. Loker," he said, after a pause, "we must set Adams and Springer on the track of these yer; they 've been booked some time."

"They 'll charge too much," said Tom.

"I 'll manage that ar; they 's young in the business, and must spect to work cheap," said Marks, as he continued to read. "Ther 's three on 'em easy cases, 'cause all you've got to do is to shoot 'em, or swear they is shot; they could n't, of course, charge much for that. Them other cases," he said, folding the paper, "will bear puttin' off a spell. So now let 's come to the particulars. Now, Mr. Haley, you saw this yer gal when she landed?"

"To be sure,—plain as I see you."

"And a man helpin' on her up the bank?" said Loker.

"To be sure, I did."

"Most likely," said Marks, "she 's took in somewhere; but where, 's a question. Tom, what do you say?"

"We must cross the river to-night, no mistake," said Tom.

"But there 's no boat about," said Marks. "The ice is running awfully, Tom; an't it dangerous?"

"Don'no nothing 'bout that,—only it 's got to be done," said Tom, decidedly.

"Dear me," said Marks, fidgeting, "it 'll be—I say," he said, walking to the window, "it 's dark as a wolf's mouth, and, Tom—"

"The long and short is, you 're scared, Marks; but I can't help that,—you 've got to go. Suppose you want to lie by a day or two, till the gal 's been carried on the underground line up to Sandusky or so, before you start."

"O, no; I an't a grain afraid," said Marks, "only—"

"Only what?" said Tom.

"Well, about the boat. Yer see there an't any boat."

"I heard the woman say there was one coming along this evening, and that a man was going to cross over in it. Neck or nothing, we must go with him," said Tom.

"I s'pose you 've got good dogs," said Haley.

"First rate," said Marks. "But what 's the use? you han't got nothin' o' hers to smell on."

"Yes, I have," said Haley, triumphantly. "Here 's her shawl she left on the bed in her hurry; she left her bonnet, too."

"That ar 's lucky," said Loker; "fork over."

"Though the dogs might damage the gal, if they come on her unawars," said Haley.

"That ar 's a consideration," said Marks. "Our dogs tore a feller half to pieces, once, down in Mobile, 'fore we could get 'em off."

"Well, ye see, for this sort that 's to be sold for their looks, that ar won't answer, ye see," said Haley.

"I do see," said Marks. "Besides, if she 's got took in, 'tan't no go, neither. Dogs is no 'count in these yer up states where these critters gets carried; of course, ye can't get on their track. They only does down in plantations, where niggers, when they runs, has to do their own running, and don't get no help."

"Well," said Loker, who had just stepped out to the bar to make some inquiries, "they say the man 's come with the boat; so, Marks—"

That worthy cast a rueful look at the comfortable quarters he was leaving, but slowly rose to obey. After exchanging a few words of further arrangement, Haley, with visible reluctance, handed over the fifty dollars to Tom, and the worthy trio separated for the night.

If any of our refined and Christian readers object to the society into which this scene introduces them, let us beg them to begin and conquer their prejudices in time. The catching business, we beg to remind them, is rising to the dignity of a lawful and patriotic profession. If all the broad land between the Mississippi and the Pacific becomes one great market for bodies and souls, and human property retains the locomotive tendencies of this nineteenth century, the trader and catcher may yet be among our aristocracy.

---

While this scene was going on at the tavern, Sam and Andy, in a state of high felicitation, pursued their way home.

Sam was in the highest possible feather, and expressed his exultation by all sorts of supernatural howls and ejaculations, by divers odd motions and contortions of his whole system. Sometimes he would sit backward, with his face to the horse's tail and sides, and then, with a whoop and a somerset, come right side up in his place again, and, drawing on a grave face, begin to lecture Andy in high-sounding tones for laughing and playing the fool. Anon, slapping his sides with his arms, he would burst forth in peals of laughter, that made the old woods ring as they passed. With all these evolutions, he contrived to keep the horses up to the top of their speed, until, between ten and eleven, their heels resounded on the gravel at the end of the balcony. Mrs. Shelby flew to the railings.

"Is that you, Sam? Where are they?"

"Mas 'r Haley's a-restin' at the tavern; he 's drefful fatigued, Missis."

"And Eliza, Sam?"

"Wal, she 's clar 'cross Jordan. As a body may say, in the land o' Canaan."

"Why, Sam, what *do* you mean?" said Mrs. Shelby, breathless, and almost faint, as the possible meaning of these words came over her.

"Wal, Missis, de Lord he persarves his own. Lizy 's done gone over the river into 'Hio, as 'markably as if de Lord took her over in a charrit of fire and two hosses."

Sam's vein of piety was always uncommonly fervent in his mistress' presence; and he made great capital of scriptural figures and images.

"Come up here, Sam," said Mr. Shelby, who had followed on to the verandah, "and tell your mistress what she wants. Come, come, Emily," said he, passing his arm round her, "you are cold and all in a shiver; you allow yourself to feel too much."

"Feel too much! Am not I a woman,—a mother? Are we not both responsible to God for this poor girl? My God! lay not this sin to our charge."

"What sin, Emily? You see yourself that we have only done what we were obliged to."

"There 's an awful feeling of guilt about it, though," said Mrs. Shelby. "I can't reason it away."

"Here, Andy, you nigger, be alive!" called Sam, under the verandah; "take these yer hosses to der barn; don't ye hear Mas'r a callin'?" and Sam soon appeared, palm-leaf in hand, at the parlor door.

"Now, Sam, tell us distinctly how the matter was," said Mr. Shelby. "Where is Eliza, if you know?"

"Wal, Mas'r, I saw her, with my own eyes, a crossin' on the floatin' ice. She crossed most 'markably; it was n't no less nor a miracle; and I saw a man help her up the 'Hio side, and then she was lost in the dusk."

"Sam, I think this rather apocryphal,—this miracle. Crossing on floating ice is n't so easily done," said Mr. Shelby.

"Easy! could n't nobody a done it, widout de Lord. Why, now," said Sam, " 't was jist dis yer way. Mas'r Haley, and me, and Andy, we comes up to de little tavern by the river, and I rides a leetle ahead,—(I 's so zealous to be a cotchin' Lizy, that I could n't hold in, no way),—and when I comes by the tavern winder, sure enough there she was, right in plain sight, and dey diggin' on behind. Wal, I loses off my hat, and sings out nuff to raise the dead. Course Lizy she hars, and she dodges back, when Mas'r Haley he goes past the door; and then, I tell ye, she clared out de side door; she went down de river bank;—Mas'r Haley he seed her, and yelled out, and him, and me, and Andy, we took arter. Down she come to the river, and thar was the current running ten feet wide by the shore, and over t' other side ice a sawin' and a jiggling up and down, kinder as 't were a great island. We come right behind her, and I thought my soul he 'd got her sure enough,—when she gin sich a screech as I never hearn, and thar she was, clar over t' other side the current, on the ice, and then on she went, a screeching and a jumpin',—the ice went crack! c'wallop! cracking! chunk! and she a boundin' like a buck! Lord, the spring that ar gal 's got in her an't common, I 'm o' 'pinion."

Mrs. Shelby sat perfectly silent, pale with excitement, while Sam told his story.

"God be praised, she is n't dead!" she said; "but where is the poor child now?"

"De Lord will pervide," said Sam, rolling up his eyes piously. "As I 've been a sayin', dis yer's a providence and no mistake, as Missis has allers been a instructin' on us. Thar 's allers instruments ris up to do de Lord's will. Now, if 't had n't been for me to-day, she 'd a been took a dozen times. Warn't it I started off de hosses, dis yer mornin', and kept 'em chasin' till nigh dinner time? And did n't I car Mas'r Haley nigh five miles out of de road, dis evening, or else he 'd a come up with Lizy as easy as a dog arter a coon. These yer's all providences."

"They are a kind of providences that you 'll have to be pretty sparing of, Master Sam. I allow no such practices with gentlemen on my place," said Mr. Shelby, with as much sternness as he could command, under the circumstances.

Now, there is no more use in making believe be angry with a negro than with a child; both instinctively see the true state of the case, through all attempts to affect the contrary; and Sam was in no wise disheartened by this rebuke, though he assumed an air of doleful gravity, and stood with the corners of his mouth lowered in most penitential style.

"Mas'r 's quite right,—quite; it was ugly on me,—there 's no disputin' that ar; and of course Mas'r and Missis would n't encourage no such works. I 'm sensible of dat ar; but a poor nigger like me 's 'mazin' tempted to act ugly sometimes, when fellers will cut up such shines as dat ar Mas'r Haley; he an't no gen'l'man no way; anybody 's been raised as I 've been can't help a seein' dat ar."

"Well, Sam," said Mrs. Shelby, "as you appear to have a proper sense of your errors, you may go now and tell Aunt Chloe she may get you some of that cold ham that was left of dinner to-day. You and Andy must be hungry."

"Missis is a heap too good for us," said Sam, making his bow with alacrity, and departing.

It will be perceived, as has been before intimated, that Master Sam had a native talent that might, undoubtedly, have raised him to eminence in political life,— a talent of making capital out of everything that turned up, to be invested for his own especial praise and glory; and having done up his piety and humility, as he trusted, to the satisfaction of the parlor, he clapped his palm-leaf on his head, with a sort of rakish, free-and-easy air, and proceeded to the dominions of Aunt Chloe, with the intention of flourishing largely in the kitchen.

"I 'll speechify these yer niggers," said Sam to himself, "now I 've got a chance. Lord, I 'll reel it off to make 'em stare!"

It must be observed that one of Sam's especial delights had been to ride in attendance on his master to all kinds of political gatherings, where, roosted on some rail fence, or perched aloft in some tree, he would sit watching the orators, with the greatest apparent gusto, and then, descending among the various brethren of his own color, assembled on the same errand, he would edify and delight them with the most ludicrous burlesques and imitations, all delivered with the most imperturbable earnestness and solemnity; and though the auditors immediately about him were generally of his own color, it not unfrequently happened that they were fringed pretty deeply with those of a fairer complexion, who listened, laughing and winking, to Sam's great self-congratulation. In fact, Sam considered oratory as his vocation, and never let slip an opportunity of magnifying his office.

Now, between Sam and Aunt Chloe there had existed, from ancient times, a sort of chronic feud, or rather a decided coolness; but, as Sam was meditating something in the provision department, as the necessary and obvious foundation of his operations, he determined, on the present occasion, to be eminently conciliatory; for he well knew that although "Missis' orders" would undoubtedly be followed to the letter, yet he should gain a considerable deal by enlisting the spirit also. He therefore appeared before Aunt Chloe with a touchingly subdued, resigned expression, like one who has suffered immeasurable hardships in behalf of a persecuted fellow-creature,—enlarged upon the fact that Missis had directed him to come to Aunt Chloe for whatever might be wanting to make up the balance in his solids and fluids,—and thus unequivocally acknowledged her right and supremacy in the cooking department, and all thereto pertaining.

The thing took accordingly. No poor, simple, virtuous body was ever cajoled by the attentions of an electioneering politician with more ease than Aunt Chloe was won over by Master Sam's suavities; and if he had been the prodigal son himself, he could not have been overwhelmed with more maternal bountifulness; and he soon found himself seated, happy and glorious, over a large tin pan, containing a sort of *olla podrida* of all that had appeared on the table for two or three days past. Savory morsels of ham, golden blocks of corn-cake, fragments of pie of every conceivable mathematical figure, chicken wings, gizzards, and drumsticks, all appeared in picturesque confusion; and Sam, as monarch of all he surveyed, sat with his palm-leaf cocked rejoicingly to one side, and patronizing Andy at his right hand.

The kitchen was full of all his compeers, who had hurried and crowded in, from the various cabins, to hear the termination of the day's exploits. Now was Sam's hour of glory. The story of the day was rehearsed, with all kinds of ornament and varnishing which might be necessary to heighten its effect; for Sam, like some of our fashionable dilettanti, never allowed a story to lose any of its gilding by passing through his hands. Roars of laughter attended the narration, and were taken up and prolonged by all the smaller fry, who were lying, in any quantity, about on the floor, or perched in every corner. In the height of the uproar and laughter, Sam, however, preserved an immovable gravity, only from time to time rolling his eyes up, and giving his auditors divers inexpressibly droll glances, without departing from the sententious elevation of his oratory.

"Yer see, fellow-countrymen," said Sam, elevating a turkey's leg, with energy, "yer see, now, what dis yer chile 's up ter, for fendin' yer all,—yes, all on yer. For him as tries to get one o' our people, is as good as tryin' to get all; yer see the principle 's de same,—dat ar 's clar. And any one o' these yer drivers that comes smelling round arter any our people, why, he 's got *me* in his way; I 'm the feller he 's got to set in with,—I 'm the feller for yer all to come to, bredren,—I 'll stand up for yer rights,—I 'll fend 'em to the last breath!"

"Why, but Sam, yer told me, only this mornin', that you 'd help this yer Mas'r to cotch Lizy; seems to me yer talk don't hang together," said Andy.

"I tell you now, Andy," said Sam, with awful superiority, "don't yer be a talkin' 'bout what yer don't know nothin' on; boys like you, Andy, means well, but they can't be spected to collusitate the great principles of action."

Andy looked rebuked, particularly by the hard word collusitate, which most of the youngerly members of the company seemed to consider as a settler in the case, while Sam proceeded.

"Dat ar was *conscience*, Andy; when I thought of gwine arter Lizy, I railly spected Mas'r was sot dat way. When I found Missis was sot the contrar, dat ar was conscience *more yet*,—cause fellers allers gets more by stickin' to Missis' side,—so yer see I 's persistent either way, and sticks up to conscience, and holds on to principles. Yes, *principles*," said Sam, giving an enthusiastic toss to a chicken's neck,—"what 's principles good for, if we is n't persistent, I wanter know? Thar, Andy, you may have dat ar bone,—'tan't picked quite clean."

Sam's audience hanging on his words with open mouth, he could not but proceed.

"Dis yer matter 'bout persistence, feller-niggers," said Sam, with the air of one entering into an abstruse subject, "dis yer 'sistency 's a thing what an't seed into very clar, by most anybody. Now, yer see, when a feller stands up for a thing one day and night, de contrar de next, folks ses (and nat'rally enough dey ses), why he an't persistent,—hand me dat ar bit o' corn-cake, Andy. But let 's look inter it. I hope the gen'lmen and der fair sex will scuse my usin' an or'nary sort o' 'parison. Here! I 'm a tryin' to get top o' der hay. Wal, I puts up my larder dis yer side; 'tan't no go;—den, cause I don't try dere no more, but puts my larder right de contrar side, an't I persistent? I'm persistent in wantin' to get up which ary side my larder is; don't you see, all on yer?"

"It 's the only thing ye ever was persistent in, Lord knows!" muttered Aunt Chloe, who was getting rather restive; the merriment of the evening being to her somewhat after the Scripture comparison,—like "vinegar upon nitre."

"Yes, indeed!" said Sam, rising, full of supper and glory, for a closing effort. "Yes, my feller-citizens and ladies of de other sex in general, I has principles,— I 'm proud to 'oon 'em,—they 's perquisite to dese yer times, and ter *all* times. I has principles, and I sticks to 'em like forty,—jest anything that I thinks is principle, I goes in to 't;—I would n't mind if dey burnt me 'live,—I 'd walk right up to de stake, I would, and say, here I comes to shed my last blood fur my principles, fur my country, fur der gen'l interests of s'ciety."

"Well," said Aunt Chloe, "one o' yer principles will have to be to get to bed some time to-night, and not be a keepin' everybody up till mornin'; now, every one of you young uns that don't want to be cracked, had better be scase, mighty sudden."

"Niggers! all on yer," said Sam, waving his palm-leaf with benignity, "I give yer my blessin'; go to bed now, and be good boys."

And, with this pathetic benediction, the assembly dispersed.

## IX.
### In Which It Appears that a Senator Is but a Man

The light of the cheerful fire shone on the rug and carpet of a cosey parlor, and glittered on the sides of the teacups and well-brightened tea-pot, as Senator Bird was drawing off his boots, preparatory to inserting his feet in a pair of new handsome slippers, which his wife had been working for him while away on his senatorial tour. Mrs. Bird, looking the very picture of delight, was superintending the arrangements of the table, ever and anon mingling admonitory remarks to a number of frolicsome juveniles, who were effervescing in all those modes of untold gambol and mischief that have astonished mothers ever since the flood.

"Tom, let the door-knob alone,—there 's a man! Mary! Mary! don't pull the cat's tail,—poor pussy! Jim, you must n't climb on that table,—no, no!—You don't know, my dear, what a surprise it is to us all, to see you here to-night!" said she, at last, when she found a space to say something to her husband.

"Yes, yes, I thought I 'd just make a run down, spend the night, and have a little comfort at home. I 'm tired to death, and my head aches!"

Mrs. Bird cast a glance at a camphor-bottle, which stood in the half-open closet, and appeared to meditate an approach to it, but her husband interposed.

"No, no, Mary, no doctoring! a cup of your good hot tea, and some of our good home living, is what I want. It 's a tiresome business, this legislating!"

And the senator smiled, as if he rather liked the idea of considering himself a sacrifice to his country.

"Well," said his wife, after the business of the tea-table was getting rather slack, "and what have they been doing in the Senate?"

Now, it was a very unusual thing for gentle little Mrs. Bird ever to trouble her head with what was going on in the house of the state, very wisely considering that she had enough to do to mind her own. Mr. Bird, therefore, opened his eyes in surpirse, and said,

"Not very much of importance."

"Well; but is it true that they have been passing a law forbidding people to give meat and drink to those poor colored folks that come along? I heard they were talking of some such law, but I didn't think any Christian legislature would pass it!"

"Why, Mary, you are getting to be a politician, all at once."

"No, nonsense! I would n't give a fip for all your politics, generally, but I think this is something downright cruel and unchristian. I hope, my dear, no such law has been passed."

"There has been a law passed forbidding people to help off the slaves that come over from Kentucky, my dear; so much of that thing has been done by these reckless Abolitionists, that our brethren in Kentucky are very strongly excited, and it seems necessary, and no more than Christian and kind, that something should be done by our state to quiet the excitement."

"And what is the law? It don't forbid us to shelter these poor creatures a night, does it, and to give 'em something comfortable to eat, and a few old clothes, and send them quietly about their business?"

"Why, yes, my dear; that would be aiding and abetting, you know."

Mrs. Bird was a timid, blushing little woman, of about four feet in height, and with mild blue eyes, and a peach-blow complexion, and the gentlest, sweetest voice in the world;—as for courage, a moderate-sized cock-turkey had been known to put her to rout at the very first gobble, and a stout house-dog, of moderate capacity, would bring her into subjection merely by a show of his teeth. Her husband and children were her entire world, and in these she ruled more by entreaty and persuasion than by command or argument. There was only one thing that was capable of arousing her, and that provocation came in on the side of her unusually gentle and sympathetic nature;—anything in the shape of cruelty would throw her into a passion, which was the more alarming and inexplicable in proportion to the general softness of her nature. Generally the most indulgent and easy to be entreated of all mothers, still her boys had a very reverent remembrance of a most vehement chastisement she once bestowed on them, because she found them leagued with several graceless boys of the neighborhood, stoning a defenceless kitten.

"I'll tell you what," Master Bill used to say, "I was scared that time. Mother came at me so that I thought she was crazy, and I was whipped and tumbled off to bed, without any supper, before I could get over wondering what had come about; and, after that, I heard mother crying outside the door, which made me feel worse than all the rest. I'll tell you what," he'd say, "we boys never stoned another kitten!"

On the present occasion, Mrs. Bird rose quickly, with very red cheeks, which quite improved her general appearance, and walked up to her husband, with quite a resolute air, and said, in a determined tone,

"Now, John, I want to know if you think such a law as that is right and Christian?"

"You won't shoot me, now, Mary, if I say I do!"

"I never could have thought it of you, John; you did n't vote for it?"

"Even so, my fair politician."

"You ought to be ashamed, John! Poor, homeless, houseless creatures! It 's a shameful, wicked, abominal law, and I 'll break it, for one, the first time I get a chance; and I hope I *shall* have a chance, I do! Things have got to a pretty pass, if a woman can't give a warm supper and a bed to poor, starving creatures, just because they are slaves, and have been abused and oppressed all their lives, poor things!"

"But, Mary, just listen to me. Your feelings are all quite right, dear, and interesting, and I love you for them; but, then, dear, we must n't suffer our feelings to run away with our judgment; you must consider it 's not a matter of private feeling,—there are great public interests involved,—there is such a state of public agitation rising, that we must put aside our private feelings."

"Now, John, I don't know anything about politics, but I can read my Bible; and there I see that I must feed the hungry, clothe the naked, and comfort the desolate; and that Bible I mean to follow."

"But in cases where your doing so would involve a great public evil—"

"Obeying God never brings on public evils. I know it can't. It 's always safest, all round, to *do as He* bids us."

"Now, listen to me, Mary, and I can state to you a very clear argument, to show—"

"O, nonsense, John! you can talk all night, but you would n't do it. I put it to you, John,—would *you* now turn away a poor, shivering, hungry creature from your door, because he was a runaway? *Would* you, now?"

Now, if the truth must be told, our senator had the misfortune to be a man who had a particularly humane and accessible nature, and turning away anybody that was in trouble never had been his forte; and what was worse for him in this particular pinch of the argument was, that his wife knew it, and, of course, was making an assault on rather an indefensible point. So he had recourse to the usual means of gaining time for such cases made and provided; he said "ahem," and coughed several times, took out his pocket-handkerchief, and began to wipe his glasses. Mrs. Bird, seeing the defenceless condition of the enemy's territory, had no more conscience than to push her advantage.

"I should like to see you doing that, John—I really should! Turning a woman out of doors in a snow-storm, for instance; or, may be you 'd take her up and put her in jail, would n't you? You would make a great hand at that!"

"Of course, it would be a very painful duty," began Mr. Bird, in a moderate tone.

"Duty, John! don't use that word! You know it is n't a duty—it can't be a duty! If folks want to keep their slaves from running away, let 'em treat 'em well,— that 's my doctrine. If I had slaves (as I hope I never shall have), I 'd risk their wanting to run away from me, or you either, John. I tell you folks don't run away when they are happy; and when they do run, poor creatures! they suffer enough with cold and hunger and fear, without everybody's turning against them; and, law or no law, I never will, so help me God!"

"Mary! Mary! My dear, let me reason with you."

"I hate reasoning, John,—especially reasoning on such subjects. There 's a way you political folks have of coming round and round a plain right thing; and you don't believe in it yourselves, when it comes to practice. I know *you* well enough, John. You don't believe it 's right any more than I do; and you would n't do it any sooner than I."

At this critical juncture, old Cudjoe, the black man-of-all-work, put his head in at the door, and wished "Missis would come into the kitchen;" and our senator, tolerably relieved, looked after his little wife with a whimsical mixture of amusement and vexation, and, seating himself in the arm-chair, began to read the papers.

After a moment, his wife's voice was heard at the door, in a quick, earnest tone,—"John! John! I do wish you 'd come here, a moment."

He laid down his paper, and went into the kitchen, and started, quite amazed at the sight that presented itself:—A young and slender woman, with garments torn and frozen, with one shoe gone, and the stocking torn away from the cut and bleeding foot, was laid back in a deadly swoon upon two chairs. There was the impress of the despised race on her face, yet none could help feeling its mournful and pathetic beauty, while its stony sharpness, its cold, fixed, deathly aspect, struck a solemn chill over him. He drew his breath short, and stood in silence. His wife, and their only colored domestic, old Aunt Dinah, were busily engaged in restorative measures; while old Cudjoe had got the boy on his knee, and was busy pulling off his shoes and stockings, and chafing his little cold feet.

"Sure, now, if she an't a sight to behold!" said old Dinah, compassionately; " 'pears like 't was the heat that made her faint. She was tol'able peart when she cum in, and asked if she could n't warm herself here a spell; and I was just a askin' her where she cum from, and she fainted right down. Never done much hard work, guess, by the looks of her hands."

"Poor creature!" said Mrs. Bird, compassionately, as the woman slowly unclosed her large, dark eyes, and looked vacantly at her. Suddenly an expression of agony crossed her face, and she sprang up, saying, "O, my Harry! Have they got him?"

The boy, at this, jumped from Cudjoe's knee, and, running to her side, put up his arms. "O, he 's here! he 's here!" she exclaimed.

"O, ma'am!" said she, wildly, to Mrs. Bird, "do protect us! don't let them get him!"

"Nobody shall hurt you here, poor woman," said Mrs. Bird, encouragingly. "You are safe; don't be afraid."

"God bless you!" said the woman, covering her face and sobbing; while the little boy, seeing her crying, tried to get into her lap.

With many gently and womanly offices, which none knew better how to render than Mrs. Bird, the poor woman was, in time, rendered more calm. A temporary bed was provided for her on the settle, near the fire; and, after a short time, she fell into a heavy slumber, with the child, who seemed no less weary, soundly sleeping on her arm; for the mother resisted, with nervous anxiety, the kindest attempts to take him from her; and, even in sleep, her arm encircled him with an unrelaxing clasp, as if she could not even then be beguiled of her vigilant hold.

Mr. and Mrs. Bird had gone back to the parlor, where, strange as it may appear, no reference was made, on either side, to the preceding conversation; but Mrs. Bird busied herself with her knitting-work, and Mr. Bird pretended to be reading the paper.

"I wonder who and what she is!" said Mr. Bird, at last, as he laid it down.

"When she wakes up and feels a little rested, we will see," said Mrs. Bird.

"I say, wife!" said Mr. Bird, after musing in silence over his newspaper.

"Well, dear!"

"She could n't wear one of your gowns, could she, by any letting down, or such matter? She seems to be rather larger than you are."

A quite perceptible smile glimmered on Mrs. Bird's face, as she answered, "We 'll see."

Another pause, and Mr. Bird again broke out,

"I say, wife!"

"Well! What now?"

"Why, there 's that old bombazin cloak, that you keep on purpose to put over me when I take my afternoon's nap; you might as well give her that,—she needs clothes."

At this instant, Dinah looked in to say that the woman was awake, and wanted to see Missis.

Mr. and Mrs. Bird went into the kitchen, followed by the two eldest boys, the smaller fry having, by this time, been safely disposed of in bed.

The woman was now sitting up on the settle, by the fire. She was looking steadily into the blaze, with a calm, heartbroken expression, very different from her former agitated wildness.

"Did you want me?" said Mrs. Bird, in gentle tones. "I hope you feel better now, poor woman!"

A long-drawn, shivering sigh was the only answer; but she lifted her dark eyes, and fixed them on her with such a forlorn and imploring expression, that the tears came into the little woman's eyes.

"You need n't be afraid of anything; we are friends here, poor woman! Tell me where you came from, and what you want," said she.

"I came from Kentucky," said the woman.

"When?" said Mr. Bird, taking up the interrogatory.

"To-night."

"How did you come?"

"I crossed on the ice."

"Crossed on the ice!" said every one present.

"Yes," said the woman, slowly, "I did. God helping me, I crossed on the ice; for they were behind me—right behind—and there was no other way!"

"Law, Missis," said Cudjoe, "the ice is all in broken-up blocks, a swinging and a tetering up and down in the water!"

"I know it was—I know it!" said she, wildly; "but I did it! I would n't have thought I could,—I did n't think I should get over, but I did n't care! I could but die, if I did n't. The Lord helped me; nobody knows how much the Lord can help 'em, till they try," said the woman, with a flashing eye.

"Were you a slave?" said Mr. Bird.

"Yes, sir; I belonged to a man in Kentucky."

"Was he unkind to you?"

"No, sir; he was a good master."

"And was your mistress unkind to you?"

"No, sir—no! my mistress was always good to me."

"What could induce you to leave a good home, then, and run away, and go through such dangers?"

The woman looked up at Mrs. Bird, with a keen, scrutinizing glance, and it did not escape her that she was dressed in deep mourning.

"Ma'am," she said, suddenly, "have you ever lost a child?"

The question was unexpected, and it was a thrust on a new wound; for it was only a month since a darling child of the family had been laid in the grave.

Mr. Bird turned around and walked to the window, and Mrs. Bird burst into tears; but, recovering her voice, she said,

"Why do you ask that? I have lost a little one."

"Then you will feel for me. I have lost two, one after another,—left 'em buried there when I came away; and I had only this one left. I never slept a night without him; he was all I had. He was my comfort and pride, day and night; and, ma'am, they were going to take him away from me,— to *sell* him,—sell him down south, ma'am, to go all alone,—a baby that had never been away from his mother

in his life! I could n't stand it, ma'am. I knew I never should be good for anything, if they did; and when I knew the papers were signed, and he was sold, I
took him and came off in the night; and they chased me,—the man that bought
him, and some of Mas'r's folks,—and they were coming down right behind me,
and I heard 'em. I jumped right on to the ice; and how I got across, I don't know,—
but, first I knew, a man was helping me up the bank."

The woman did not sob nor weep. She had gone to a place where tears are
dry; but every one around her was, in some way characteristic of themselves,
showing signs of hearty sympathy.

The two little boys, after a desperate rummaging in their pockets, in search
of those pocket-handkerchiefs which mothers know are never to be found there,
had thrown themselves disconsolately into the skirts of their mother's gown,
where they were sobbing, and wiping their eyes and noses, to their hearts' content;—Mrs. Bird had her face fairly hidden in her pocket-handkerchief; and old
Dinah, with tears streaming down her black, honest face, was ejaculating, "Lord
have mercy on us!" with all the fervor of a camp-meeting;—while old Cudjoe,
rubbing his eyes very hard with his cuffs, and making a most uncommon variety
of wry faces, occasionally responded in the same key, with great fervor. Our senator was a statesman, and of course could not be expected to cry, like other mortals; and so he turned his back to the company, and looked out of the window,
and seemed particularly busy in clearing his throat and wiping his spectacle-
glasses, occasionally blowing his nose in a manner that was calculated to excite
suspicion, had any one been in a state to observe critically.

"How came you to tell me you had a kind master?" he suddenly exclaimed,
gulping down very resolutely some kind of rising in his throat, and turning suddenly round upon the woman.

"Because he *was* a kind master; I 'll say that of him, any way;—and my mistress was kind; but they could n't help themselves. They were owing money; and
there was some way, I can't tell how, that a man had a hold on them, and they
were obliged to give him his will. I listened, and heard him telling mistress that,
and she begging and pleading for me,—and he told her he could n't help himself, and that the papers were all drawn;—and then it was I took him and left my
home, and came away. I knew 't was no use of my trying to live, if they did it;
for 't 'pears like this child is all I have."

"Have you no husband?"

"Yes, but he belongs to another man. His master is real hard to him, and won't
let him come to see me, hardly ever; and he 's grown harder and harder upon us,
and he threatens to sell him down south;—it 's like I 'll never see *him* again!"

The quiet tone in which the woman pronounced these words might have led
a superficial observer to think that she was entirely apathetic; but there was a
calm, settled depth of anguish in her large, dark eye, that spoke of something far
otherwise.

"And where do you mean to go, my poor woman?" said Mrs. Bird.

"To Canada, if I only knew where that was. Is it very far off, is Canada?" said
she, looking up, with a simple, confiding air, to Mrs. Bird's face.

"Poor thing!" said Mrs. Bird, involuntarily.

"Is 't a very great way off, think?" said the woman, earnestly.

"Much further than you think, poor child!" said Mrs. Bird; "but we will try to think what can be done for you. Here, Dinah, make her up a bed in your own room, close by the kitchen, and I 'll think what to do for her in the morning. Meanwhile, never fear, poor woman; put your trust in God; he will protect you."

Mrs. Bird and her husband reëntered the parlor. She sat down in her little rocking-chair before the fire, swaying thoughtfully to and fro. Mr. Bird strode up and down the room, grumbling to himself, "Pish! pshaw! confounded awkward business!" At length, striding up to his wife, he said,

"I say, wife, she 'll have to get away from here, this very night. That fellow will be down on the scent bright and early to-morrow morning; if 't was only the woman, she could lie quiet till it was over; but that little chap can't be kept still by a troop of horse and foot, I 'll warrant me; he 'll bring it all out, popping his head out of some window or door. A pretty kettle of fish it would be for me, too, to be caught with them both here, just now! No; they 'll have to be got off to-night."

"To-night! How is it possible?—where to?"

"Well, I know pretty well where to," said the senator, beginning to put on his boots, with a reflective air; and, stopping when his leg was half in, he embraced his knee with both hands, and seemed to go off in deep meditation.

"It 's a confounded awkward, ugly business," said he, at last, beginning to tug at his boot-straps again, "and that 's a fact!" After one boot was fairly on, the senator sat with the other in his hand, profoundly studying the figure of the carpet. "It will have to be done, though, for aught I see,—hang it all!" and he drew the other boot anxiously on, and looked out of the window.

Now, little Mrs. Bird was a discreet woman,—a woman who never in her life said, "I told you so!" and, on the present occasion, though pretty well aware of the shape her husband's meditations were taking, she very prudently forbore to meddle with them, only sat very quietly in her chair, and looked quite ready to hear her liege lord's intentions, when he should think proper to utter them.

"You see," he said, "there 's my old client, Van Trompe, has come over from Kentucky, and set all his slaves free; and he has bought a place seven miles up the creek, here, back in the woods, where nobody goes, unless they go on purpose; and it 's a place that is n 't found in a hurry. There she 'd be safe enough; but the plague of the thing is, nobody could drive a carriage there to-night, but *me*."

"Why not? Cudjoe is an excellent driver."

"Ay, ay, but here it is. The creek has to be crossed twice; and the second crossing is quite dangerous, unless one knows it as I do. I have crossed it a hundred times on horseback, and know exactly the turns to take. And so, you see, there 's no help for it. Cudjoe must put in the the horses, as quietly as may be, about twelve o'clock, and I 'll take her over; and then, to give color to the matter, he must carry me on to the next tavern, to take the stage for Columbus, that comes by about three or four, and so it will look as if I had had the carriage only for that. I shall get into business bright and early in the morning. But I 'm thinking I shall feel rather cheap there, after all that 's been said and done; but, hang it, I can't help it!"

"Your heart is better than your head, in this case, John," said the wife, laying her little white hand on his. "Could I ever have loved you, had I not known you better than you know yourself?" And the little woman looked so handsome, with the tears sparkling in her eyes, that the senator thought he must be a decidedly clever fellow, to get such a pretty creature into such a passionate admiration of him; and so, what could he do but walk off soberly, to see about the carriage. At the door, however, he stopped a moment, and then coming back, he said, with some hesitation,

"Mary, I don't know how you 'd feel about it, but there 's that drawer full of things—of—of—poor little Henry's." So saying, he turned quickly on his heel, and shut the door after him.

His wife opened the little bed-room door adjoining her room, and, taking the candle, set it down on the top of a bureau there; then from a small recess she took a key, and put it thoughtfully in the lock of a drawer, and made a sudden pause, while two boys, who, boy like, had followed close on her heels, stood looking, with silent, significant glances, at their mother. And oh! mother that reads this, has there never been in your house a drawer, or a closet, the opening of which has been to you like the opening again of a little grave? Ah! happy mother that you are, if it has not been so.

Mrs. Bird slowly opened the drawer. There were little coats of many a form and pattern, piles of aprons, and rows of small stockings; and even a pair of little shoes, worn and rubbed at the toes, were peeping from the folds of a paper. There was a toy horse and wagon, a top, a ball,—memorials gathered with many a tear and many a heart-break! She sat down by the drawer, and, leaning her head on her hands over it, wept till the tears fell through her fingers into the drawer; then suddenly raising her head, she began, with nervous haste, selecting the plainest and most substantial articles, and gathering them into a bundle.

"Mamma," said one of the boys, gently touching her arm, "are you going to give away *those* things?"

"My dear boys," she said, softly and earnestly, "if our dear, loving little Henry looks down from heaven, he would be glad to have us do this. I could not find it in my heart to give them away to any common person—to anybody that was happy; but I give them to a mother more heart-broken and sorrowful than I am; and I hope God will send his blessings with them!"

There are in this world blessed souls, whose sorrows all spring up into joys for others; whose earthly hopes, laid in the grave with many tears, are the seed from which spring healing flowers and balm for the desolate and the distressed. Among such was the delicate woman who sits there by the lamp, dropping slow tears, while she prepares the memorials of her own lost one for the outcast wanderer.

After a while, Mrs. Bird opened a wardrobe, and, taking from thence a plain, serviceable dress or two, she sat down busily to her work-table, and, with needle, scissors, and thimble, at hand, quietly commenced the "letting down" process which her husband had recommended, and continued busily at it till the old clock in the corner struck twelve, and she heard the low rattling of wheels at the door.

"Mary," said her husband, coming in, with his overcoat in his hand, "you must wake her up now; we must be off."

Mrs. Bird hastily deposited the various articles she had collected in a small plain trunk, and locking it, desired her husband to see it in the carriage, and then proceeded to call the woman. Soon, arrayed in a cloak, bonnet, and shawl, that had belonged to her benefactress, she appeared at the door with her child in her arms. Mr. Bird hurried her into the carriage, and Mrs. Bird pressed on after her to the carriage steps. Eliza leaned out of the carriage, and put out her hand,—a hand as soft and beautiful as was given in return. She fixed her large, dark eyes, full of earnest meaning, on Mrs. Bird's face, and seemed going to speak. Her lips moved,—she tried once or twice, but there was no sound,—and pointing upward, with a look never to be forgotten, she fell back in the seat, and covered her face. The door was shut, and the carriage drove on.

What a situation, now, for a patriotic senator, that had been all the week before spurring up the legislature of his native state to pass more stringent resolutions against escaping fugitives, their harborers and abettors!

Our good senator in his native state had not been exceeded by any of his brethren at Washington, in the sort of eloquence which has won for them immortal renown! How sublimely he had sat with his hands in his pockets, and scouted all sentimental weakness of those who would put the welfare of a few miserable fugitives before great state interests!

He was as bold as a lion about it, and "mightily convinced" not only himself, but everybody that heard him;—but then his idea of a fugitive was only an idea of the letters that spell the word,—or, at the most, the image of a little newspaper picture of a man with a stick and bundle, with "Ran away from the subscriber" under it. The magic of the real presence of distress,—the imploring human eye, the frail, trembling human hand, the despairing appeal of helpless agony,—these he had never tried. He had never thought that a fugitive might be a hapless mother, a defenceless child,—like that one which was now wearing his lost boy's little well-known cap; and so, as our poor senator was not stone or steel,—as he was a man, and a downright noble-hearted one, too,—he was, as everybody must see, in a sad case for his patriotism. And you need not exult over him, good brother of the Southern States; for we have some inklings that many of you, under similar circumstances, would not do much better. We have reason to know, in Kentucky, as in Mississippi, are noble and generous hearts, to whom never was tale of suffering told in vain. Ah, good brother! is it fair for you to expect of us services which your own brave, honorable heart would not allow you to render, were you in our place?

Be that as it may, if our good senator was a political sinner, he was in a fair way to expiate it by his night's penance. There had been a long continuous period of rainy weather, and the soft, rich earth of Ohio, as every one knows, is admirably suited to the manufacture of mud,—and the road was an Ohio railroad of the good old times.

"Any pray, what sort of a road may that be?" says some eastern traveller, who has been accustomed to connect no ideas with a railroad, but those of smoothness or speed.

Know, then, innocent eastern friend, that in benighted regions of the west, where the mud is of unfathomable and sublime depth, roads are made of round rough logs, arranged transversely side by side, and coated over in their pristine freshness with earth, turf, and whatsoever may come to hand, and then the rejoicing native calleth it a road, and straightway essayeth to ride thereupon. In process of time, the rains wash off all the turf and grass aforesaid, move the logs hither and thither, in picturesque positions, up, down and crosswise, with divers chasms and ruts of black mud intervening.

Over such a road as this our senator went stumbling along, making moral reflections as continuously as under the circumstances could be expected,—the carriage proceeding along much as follows,—bump! bump! bump! slush! down in the mud!—the senator, woman and child, reversing their positions so suddenly as to come, without any very accurate adjustment, against the windows of the down-hill side. Carriage sticks fast, while Cudjoe on the outside is heard making a great muster among the horses. After various ineffectual pullings and twitchings, just as the senator is losing all patience, the carriage suddenly rights itself with a bounce,—two front wheels go down into another abyss, and senator, woman, and child, all tumble promiscuously on to the front seat,—senator's hat is jammed over his eyes and nose quite unceremoniously, and he considers himself fairly extinguished;—child cries, and Cudjoe on the outside delivers animated addresses to the horses, who are kicking, and floundering, and straining, under repeated cracks of the whip. Carriage springs up, with another bounce,—down go the hind wheels,—senator, woman, and child, fly over on to the back seat, his elbows encountering her bonnet, and both her feet being jammed into his hat, which flies off in the concussion. After a few moments the "slough" is passed, and the horses stop, panting;—the senator finds his hat, the woman straightens her bonnet and hushes her child, and they brace themselves firmly for what is yet to come.

For a while only the continuous bump! bump! intermingled, just by way of variety, with divers side plunges and compound shakes; and they begin to flatter themselves that they are not so badly off, after all. At last, with a square plunge, which puts all on to their feet and then down into their seats with incredible quickness, the carriage stops,—and, after much outside commotion, Cudjoe appears at the door.

"Please, sir, it 's powerful bad spot, this yer. I don't know how we 's to get clar out. I 'm a thinkin' we 'll have to be a gettin' rails."

The senator despairingly steps out, picking gingerly for some firm foothold; down goes one foot an immeasurable depth,—he tries to pull it up, loses his balance, and tumbles over into the mud, and is fished out, in a very despairing condition, by Cudjoe.

But we forbear, out of sympathy to our readers' bones. Western travellers, who have beguiled the midnight hour in the interesting process of pulling down rail fences, to pry their carriages out of mud holes, will have a respectful and mournful sympathy with our unfortunate hero. We beg them to drop a silent tear, and pass on.

It was full late in the night when the carriage emerged, dripping and bespattered, out of the creek, and stood at the door of a large farm-house.

It took no inconsiderable perseverance to arouse the inmates; but at last the respectable proprietor appeared, and undid the door. He was a great, tall, bristling

Orson of a fellow, full six feet and some inches in his stockings, and arrayed in a red flannel hunting-shirt. A very heavy *mat* of sandy hair, in a decidedly tousled condition, and a beard of some days' growth, gave the worthy man an appearance, to say the least, not particularly prepossessing. He stood for a few minutes holding the candle aloft, and blinking on our travellers with a dismal and mystified expression that was truly ludicrous. It cost some effort of our senator to induce him to comprehend the case fully; and while he is doing his best at that, we shall give him a little introduction to our readers.

Honest old John Van Trompe was once quite a considerable land-holder and slave-owner in the State of Kentucky. Having "nothing of the bear about him but the skin," and being gifted by nature with a great, honest, just heart, quite equal to his gigantic frame, he had been for some years witnessing with repressed uneasiness the workings of a system equally bad for oppressor and oppressed. At last, one day, John's great heart had swelled altogether too big to wear his bonds any longer; so he just took his pocket-book out of his desk, and went over into Ohio, and bought a quarter of a township of good, rich land, made out free papers for all his people,—men, women, and children—packed them up in wagons, and sent them off to settle down; and then honest John turned his face up the creek, and sat quietly down on a snug, retired farm, to enjoy his conscience and his reflections.

"Are you the man that will shelter a poor woman and child from slave-catchers?" said the senator, explicitly.

"I rather think I am," said honest John, with some considerable emphasis.

"I thought so," said the senator.

"If there 's anybody comes," said the good man, stretching his tall, muscular form upward, "why here I 'm ready for him: and I 've got seven sons, each six foot high, and they 'll be ready for 'em. Give our respects to 'em," said John; "tell 'em it 's no matter how soon they call,—make no kinder difference to us," said John, running his fingers through the shock of hair that thatched his head, and bursting out into a great laugh.

Weary, jaded, and spiritless, Eliza dragged herself up to the door, with her child lying in a heavy sleep on her arm. The rough man held the candle to her face, and uttering a kind of compassionate grunt, opened the door of a small bedroom adjoining to the large kitchen where they were standing, and motioned her to go in. He took down a candle, and lighting it, set it upon the table, and then addressed himself to Eliza.

"Now, I say, gal, you need n't be a bit afeard, let who will come here. I 'm up to all that sort o' thing," said he, pointing to two or three goodly rifles over the mantel-piece; "and most people that know me know that 't would n't be healthy to try to get anybody out o' my house when I 'm agin it. So *now* you jist go to sleep now, as quiet as if yer mother was a rockin' ye," said he, as he shut the door.

"Why, this is an uncommon handsome un," he said to the senator. "Ah, well; handsome uns has the greatest cause to run, sometimes, if they has any kind o' feelin, such as decent women should. I know all about that."

The senator, in a few words, briefly explained Eliza's history.

"O! ou! aw! now, I want to know?" said the good man, pitifully; "sho! now sho! That 's natur now, poor crittur! hunted down now like a deer,—hunted down, jest for havin' natural feelin's, and doin' what no kind o' mother could help a doin'! I tell ye what, these yer things make me come the nighest to swearin', now, o' most anything," said honest John, as he wiped his eyes with the back of a great, freckled, yellow hand. "I tell yer what, stranger, it was years and years before I'd jine the church, 'cause the ministers round in our parts used to preach that the Bible went in for these ere cuttings up,—and I could n't be up to 'em, with their Greek and Hebrew, and so I took up agin 'em, Bible and all. I never jined the church till I found a minister that was up to 'em all in Greek and all that, and he said right the contrary; and then I took right hold, and jined the church,—I did now, fact," said John, who had been all this time uncorking some very frisky bottled cider, which at this juncture he presented.

"Ye 'd better jest put up here, now, till daylight," said he, heartily, "and I 'll call up the old woman, and have a bed got ready for you in no time."

"Thank you, my good friend," said the senator, "I must be along, to take the night stage to Columbus."

"Ah! well, then, if you must, I 'll go a piece with you, and show you a cross road that will take you there better than the road you came on. That road 's mighty bad."

John equipped himself, and, with a lantern in hand, was soon seen guiding the senator's carriage towards a road that ran down in a hollow, back of his dwelling. When they parted, the senator put into his hand a ten-dollar bill.

"It 's for her," he said, briefly.

"Ay, ay," said John, with equal conciseness.

They shook hands, and parted.

## X.
### *The Property Is Carried Off*

The February morning looked gray and drizzling through the window of Uncle Tom's cabin. It looked on downcast faces, the images of mournful hearts. The little table stood out before the fire, covered with an ironing-cloth; a coarse but clean shirt or two, fresh from the iron, hung on the back of a chair by the fire, and Aunt Chloe had another spread out before her on the table. Carefully she rubbed and ironed every fold and every hem, with the most scrupulous exactness, every now and then raising her hand to her face to wipe off the tears that were coursing down her cheeks.

Tom sat by, with his Testament open on his knee, and his head leaning upon his hand;—but neither spoke. It was yet early, and the children lay all asleep together in their little rude trundle-bed.

Tom, who had, to the full, the gentle, domestic heart, which, woe for them! has been a peculiar characteristic of his unhappy race, got up and walked silently to look at his children.

"It 's the last time," he said.

Aunt Chloe did not answer, only rubbed away over and over on the coarse shirt, already as smooth as hands could make it; and finally setting her iron suddenly down with a despairing plunge, she sat down to the table, and "lifted up her voice and wept."

"S'pose we must be resigned; but oh Lord! how ken I? If I know'd anything whar you 's goin', or how they 'd sarve you! Missis says she 'll try and 'deem ye, in a year or two; but Lor! nobody never comes up that goes down thar! They kills 'em! I've hearn 'em tell how dey works 'em up on dem ar plantations."

"There 'll be the same God there, Chloe, that there is here."

"Well," said Aunt Chloe, "s'pose dere will; but de Lord lets drefful things happen, sometimes. I don't seem to get no comfort dat way."

"I 'm in the Lord's hands," said Tom; "nothin' can go no furder than he lets it;—and thar 's *one* thing I can thank him for. It 's *me* that 's sold and going down, and not you nur the chil'en. Here you 're safe;—what comes will come only on me; and the Lord, he 'll help me,—I know he will."

Ah, brave, manly heart,—smothering thine own sorrow, to comfort thy beloved ones! Tom spoke with a thick utterance, and with a bitter choking in his throat,—but he spoke brave and strong.

"Let 's think on our marcies!" he added, tremulously, as if he was quite sure he needed to think on them very hard indeed.

"Marcies!" said Aunt Chloe; "don't see no marcy in 't! 'tan't right! tan't right it should be so! Mas'r never ought ter left it so that ye *could* be took for his debts. Ye 've arnt him all he gets for ye, twice over. He owed ye yer freedom, and ought ter gin 't to yer years ago. Mebbe he can't help himself now, but I feel it 's wrong. Nothing can't beat that ar out o' me. Sich a faithful crittur as ye 've been,—and allers sot his business 'fore yer own every way,—and reckoned on him more than yer own wife and chil'en! Them as sells heart's love and heart's blood, to get out thar scrapes, de Lord 'll be up to 'em!"

"Chloe! now, if ye love me, ye won't talk so, when perhaps jest the last time we 'll ever have together! And I 'll tell ye, Chloe, it goes agin me to hear one word agin Mas'r. Wan't he put in my arms a baby?—it 's natur I should think a heap of him. And he could n't be spected to think so much of poor Tom. Mas'rs is used to havin' all these yer things done for 'em, and nat'lly they don't think so much on 't. They can't be spected to, no way. Set him 'longside of other Mas'rs— who 's had the treatment and the livin' I 've had? And he never would have let this yer come on me, if he could have seed it aforehand. I know he would n't."

"Wal, any way, thar 's wrong about it *somewhar*," said Aunt Chloe, in whom a stubborn sense of justice was a predominant trait; "I can't jest make out whar 't is, but thar 's wrong somewhar, I 'm *clar* o' that."

"Yer ought ter look up to the Lord above—he 's above all—thar don't a sparrow fall without him."

"It don't seem to comfort me, but I spect it orter," said Aunt Chloe. "But dar's no use talkin'; I 'll jes wet up de corn-cake, and get ye one good breakfast, 'cause nobody knows when you 'll get another."

In order to appreciate the sufferings of the negroes sold south, it must be remembered that all the instinctive affections of that race are peculiarly strong. Their local attachments are very abiding. They are not naturally daring and enterprising, but home-loving and affectionate. Add to this all the terrors with which ignorance invests the unknown, and add to this, again, that selling to the south is set before the negro from childhood as the last severity of punishment. The threat that terrifies more than whipping or torture of any kind is the threat of being sent down river. We have ourselves heard this feeling expressed by them, and seen the unaffected horror with which they will sit in their gossipping hours, and tell frightful stories of that "down river," which to them is

> "That undiscovered country, from whose bourn
> No traveller returns."

A missionary among the fugitives in Canada told us that many of the fugitives confessed themselves to have escaped from comparatively kind masters, and that they were induced to brave the perils of escape, in almost every case, by the desperate horror with which they regarded being sold south,—a doom which was hanging either over themselves or their husbands, their wives or children. This nerves the African, naturally patient, timid and unenterprising, with heroic courage, and leads him to suffer hunger, cold, pain, the perils of the wilderness, and the more dread penalties of re-capture.

The simple morning meal now smoked on the table, for Mrs. Shelby had excused Aunt Chloe's attendance at the great house that morning. The poor soul had expended all her little energies on this farewell feast,—had killed and dressed her choicest chicken, and prepared her corn-cake with scrupulous exactness, just to her husband's taste, and brought out certain mysterious jars on the mantelpiece, some preserves that were never produced except on extreme occasions.

"Lor, Pete," said Mose, triumphantly, "han't we got a buster of a breakfast!" at the same time catching at a fragment of the chicken.

Aunt Chloe gave him a sudden box on the ear. "Thar now! crowing over the last breakfast yer poor daddy 's gwine to have to home!"

"O, Chloe!" said Tom, gently.

"Wal, I can't help it," said Aunt Chloe, hiding her face in her apron; "I 's so tossed about, it makes me act ugly."

The boys stood quite still, looking first at their father and then at their mother, while the baby, climbing up her clothes, began an imperious, commanding cry.

"Thar!" said Aunt Chloe, wiping her eyes and taking up the baby; "now I 's done, I hope,—now do eat something. This yer 's my nicest chicken. Thar, boys, ye shall have some, poor critturs! Yer mammy 's been cross to yer."

The boys needed no second invitation, and went in with great zeal for the eatables; and it was well they did so, as otherwise there would have been very little performed to any purpose by the party.

"Now," said Aunt Chloe, bustling about after breakfast, "I must put up yer clothes. Jest like as not, he 'll take 'em all away. I know thar ways—mean as dirt, they is! Wal, now, yer flannels for rhumatis is in this corner; so be carful, 'cause there won't nobody make ye no more. Then here 's yer old shirts, and these yer is new ones. I toed off these yer stockings last night, and put de ball in 'em to mend with. But Lor! who 'll ever mend for ye?" and Aunt Chloe, again overcome, laid her head on the box side, and sobbed. "To think on 't! no crittur to do for ye, sick or well! I don't railly think I ought ter be good now!"

The boys, having eaten everything there was on the breakfast-table, began now to take some thought of the case; and, seeing their mother crying, and their father looking very sad, began to whimper and put their hands to their eyes. Uncle

Tom had the baby on his knee, and was letting her enjoy herself to the utmost extent, scratching his face and pulling his hair, and occasionally breaking out into clamorous explosions of delight, evidently arising out of her own internal reflections.

"Ay, crow away, poor crittur!" said Aunt Chloe; "ye 'll have to come to it, too! ye 'll live to see yer husband sold, or mebbe be sold yerself; and these yer boys, they 's to be sold, I s'pose, too, jest like as not, when dey gets good for somethin'; an't no use in niggers havin' nothin'!"

Here one of the boys called out, "Thar's Missis a-comin' in!"

"She can't do no good; what 's she coming for?" said Aunt Chloe.

Mrs. Shelby entered. Aunt Chloe set a chair for her in a manner decidedly gruff and crusty. She did not seem to notice either the action or the manner. She looked pale and anxious.

"Tom," she said, "I come to—" and stopping suddenly, and regarding the silent group, she sat down in the chair, and, covering her face with her handkerchief, began to sob.

"Lor, now, Missis, don't—don't!" said Aunt Chloe, bursting out in her turn; and for a few moments they all wept in company. And in those tears they all shed together, the high and the lowly, melted away all the heart-burnings and anger of the oppressed. O, ye who visit the distressed, do ye know that everything your money can buy, given with a cold, averted face, is not worth one honest tear shed in real sympathy?

"My good fellow," said Mrs. Shelby, "I can't give you anything to do you any good. If I give you money, it will only be taken from you. But I tell you solemnly, and before God, that I will keep trace of you, and bring you back as soon as I can command the money;—and, till then, trust in God!"

Here the boys called out that Mas'r Haley was coming, and then an unceremonious kick pushed open the door. Haley stood there in very ill humor, having ridden hard the night before, and being not at all pacified by his ill success in recapturing his prey.

"Come," said he, "ye nigger, ye 'r ready? Servant, ma'am!" said he, taking off his hat, as he saw Mrs. Shelby.

Aunt Chloe shut and corded the box, and, getting up, looked gruffly on the trader, her tears seeming suddenly turned to sparks of fire.

Tom rose up meekly, to follow his new master, and raised up his heavy box on his shoulder. His wife took the baby in her arms to go with him to the wagon, and the children, still crying, trailed on behind.

Mrs. Shelby, walking up to the trader, detained him for a few moments, talking with him in an earnest manner; and while she was thus talking, the whole family party proceeded to a wagon, that stood ready harnessed at the door. A crowd of all the old and young hands on the place stood gathered around it, to bid farewell to their old associate. Tom had been looked up to, both as a head servant and a Christian teacher, by all the place, and there was much honest sympathy and grief about him, particularly among the women.

"Why, Chloe, you bar it better 'n we do!" said one of the women, who had been weeping freely, noticing the gloomy calmness with which Aunt Chloe stood by the wagon.

"I 's done *my* tears!" she said, looking grimly at the trader, who was coming up. "I does not feel to cry 'fore dat ar old limb, no how!"

"Get in!" said Haley to Tom, as he strode through the crowd of servants, who looked at him with lowering brows.

Tom got in, and Haley, drawing out from under the wagon seat a heavy pair of shackles, made them fast around each ankle.

A smothered groan of indignation ran through the whole circle, and Mrs. Shelby spoke from the verandah,—

"Mr. Haley, I assure you that precaution is entirely unnecessary."

"Do'n know, ma'am; I 've lost one five hundred dollars from this yer place, and I can't afford to run no more risks."

"What else could she spect on him?" said Aunt Chloe, indignantly, while the two boys, who now seemed to comprehend at once their father's destiny, clung to her gown, sobbing and groaning vehemently.

"I 'm sorry," said Tom, "that Mas'r George happened to be away."

George had gone to spend two or three days with a companion on a neighboring estate, and having departed early in the morning, before Tom's misfortune had been made public, had left without hearing of it.

"Give my love to Mas'r George," he said, earnestly.

Haley whipped up the horse, and, with a steady, mournful look, fixed to the last on the old place, Tom was whirled away.

Mr. Shelby at this time was not at home. He had sold Tom under the spur of a driving necessity, to get out of the power of a man whom he dreaded,—and his first feeling, after the consummation of the bargain, had been that of relief. But his wife's expostulations awoke his half-slumbering regrets; and Tom's manly disinterestedness increased the unpleasantness of his feelings. It was in vain that he said to himself that he had a *right* to do it,—that everybody did it,—and that some did it without even the excuse of necessity;—he could not satisfy his own feelings; and that he might not witness the unpleasant scenes of the consummation, he had gone on a short business tour up the country, hoping that all would be over before he returned.

Tom and Haley rattled on along the dusty road, whirling past every old familiar spot, until the bounds of the estate were fairly passed, and they found themselves out on the open pike. After they had ridden about a mile, Haley suddenly drew up at the door of a blacksmith's shop, when, taking out with him a pair of handcuffs, he stepped into the shop, to have a little alteration in them.

"These yer 's a little too small for his build," said Haley, showing the fetters, and pointing out to Tom.

"Lor! now, if thar an't Shelby's Tom. He han't sold him, now?" said the smith.

"Yes, he has," said Haley.

"Now, ye don't! well, reely," said the smith, "who 'd a thought it! Why, ye need n't go to fetterin' him up this yer way. He's the faithfullest, best crittur—"

"Yes, yes," said Haley; "but your good fellers are just the critturs to want ter run off. Them stupid ones, as doesn't care whar they go, and shifless, drunken ones, as don't care for nothin', they 'll stick by, and like as not be rather pleased to be toted round; but these yer prime fellers, they hates it like sin. No way but to fetter 'em; got legs,—they 'll use 'em,—no mistake."

"Well," said the smith, feeling among his tools, "them plantations down thar, stranger, an't jest the place a Kentuck nigger wants to go to; they dies thar tol'able fast, don't they?"

"Wal, yes, tol'able fast, ther dying is; what with the 'climating and one thing and another, they dies so as to keep the market up pretty brisk," said Haley.

"Wal, now, a feller can't help thinkin' it 's a mighty pity to have a nice, quiet, likely feller, as good un as Tom is, go down to be fairly ground up on one of them ar sugar plantations."

"Wal, he 's got a fa'r chance. I promised to do well by him. I 'll get him in house-servant in some good old family, and then, if he stands the fever and 'climating, he 'll have a berth good as any nigger ought ter ask for."

"He leaves his wife and chil'en up here, s'pose?"

"Yes; but he 'll get another thar. Lord, thar 's women enough everywhar," said Haley.

Tom was sitting very mournfully on the outside of the shop while this conversation was going on. Suddenly he heard the quick, short click of a horse's hoof behind him; and, before he could fairly awake from his surprise, young Master George sprang into the wagon, threw his arms tumultuously round his neck, and was sobbing and scolding with energy.

"I declare, it 's real mean! I don't care what they say, any of 'em! It 's a nasty, mean shame! If I was a man, they should n't do it,—they should not, *so!*" said George, with a kind of subdued howl.

"O! Mas'r George! this does me good!" said Tom. "I could n't bar to go off without seein' ye! It does me real good, ye can't tell!" Here Tom made some movement of his feet, and George's eye fell on the fetters.

"What a shame!" he exclaimed, lifting his hands. "I 'll knock that old fellow down—I will!"

"No you won't, Mas'r George; and you must not talk so loud. It won't help me any, to anger him."

"Well, I won't then, for your sake; but only to think of it—is n't it a shame? They never sent for me, nor sent me any word, and, if it had n't been for Tom Lincoln, I should n't have heard it. I tell you, I blew 'em up well, all of 'em, at home!"

"That ar was n't right, I'm 'feard, Mas'r George."

"Can't help it! I say it 's a shame! Look here, Uncle Tom," said he, turning his back to the shop, and speaking in a mysterious tone, "*I 've brought you my dollar!*"

"O! I could n't think o' takin' on 't, Mas'r George, no ways in the world!" said Tom, quite moved.

"But you *shall* take it!" said George; "look here—I told Aunt Chloe I 'd do it, and she advised me just to make a hole in it, and put a string through, so you could hang it round your neck, and keep it out of sight; else this mean scamp would take it away. I tell ye, Tom, I want to blow him up! it would do me good!"

"No, don't, Mas'r George, for it won't do *me* any good."

"Well, I won't, for your sake," said George, busily tying his dollar round Tom's neck; "but there, now, button your coat tight over it, and keep it, and remember, every time you see it, that I 'll come down after you, and bring you back. Aunt Chloe and I have been talking about it. I told her not to fear; I 'll see to it, and I 'll tease father's life out, if he don't do it."

"O! Mas'r George, ye must n't talk so 'bout yer father!"

"Lor, Uncle Tom, I don't mean anything bad."

"And now, Mas'r George," said Tom, "ye must be a good boy; 'member how many hearts is sot on ye. Al'ays keep close to yer mother. Don't be gettin' into any of them foolish ways boys has of gettin' too big to mind their mothers. Tell ye what, Mas'r George, the Lord gives good many things twice over; but he don't give ye a mother but once. Ye 'll never see sich another woman, Mas'r George, if ye live to be a hundred years old. So, now, you hold on to her, and grow up, and be a comfort to her, thar 's my own good boy,—you will now, won't ye?"

"Yes, I will, Uncle Tom," said George, seriously.

"And be careful of yer speaking, Mas'r George. Young boys, when they comes to your age, is wilful, sometimes—it 's natur they should be. But real gentlemen, such as I hopes you 'll be, never lets fall no words that is n't 'spectful to thar parents. Ye an't 'fended, Mas'r George?"

"No, indeed, Uncle Tom; you always did give me good advice."

"I 's older, ye know," said Tom, stroking the boy's fine, curly head with his large, strong hand, but speaking in a voice as tender as a woman's, "and I sees all that 's bound up in you. O, Mas'r George, you has everything,—l'arnin', privileges, readin', writin',—and you 'll grow up to be a great, learned, good man, and all the people on the place and your mother and father 'll be so proud on ye! Be a good Mas'r, like yer father; and be a Christian, like yer mother. 'Member yer Creator in the days o' yer youth, Mas'r George."

"I 'll be *real* good, Uncle Tom, I tell you," said George. "I 'm going to be a *first-rater*; and don't you be discouraged. I 'll have you back to the place, yet. As I told Aunt Chloe this morning, I 'll build your house all over, and you shall have a room for a parlor with a carpet on it, when I 'm a man. O, you 'll have good times yet!"

Haley now came to the door, with the handcuffs in his hands.

"Look here, now, Mister," said George, with an air of great superiority, as he got out, "I shall let father and mother know how you treat Uncle Tom!"

"You 're welcome," said the trader.

"I should think you 'd be ashamed to spend all your life buying men and women, and chaining them, like cattle! I should think you 'd feel mean!" said George.

"So long as your grand folks wants to buy men and women, I 'm as good as they is," said Haley; "'tan't any meaner sellin' on 'em, than 't is buyin'!"

"I 'll never do either, when I 'm a man," said George; "I 'm ashamed, this day, that I 'm a Kentuckian. I always was proud of it before;" and George sat very straight on his horse, and looked round with an air, as if he expected the state would be impressed with his opinion.

"Well, good-by, Uncle Tom; keep a stiff upper lip," said George.

"Good-by, Mas'r George," said Tom, looking fondly and admiringly at him. "God Almighty bless you! Ah! Kentucky han't got many like you!" he said, in the fulness of his heart, as the frank, boyish face was lost to his view. Away he went, and Tom looked, till the clatter of his horse's heels died away, the last sound or sight of his home. But over his heart there seemed to be a warm spot, where those young hands had placed that precious dollar. Tom put up his hand, and held it close to his heart.

"Now, I tell ye what, Tom," said Haley, as he came up to the wagon, and threw in the hand-cuffs, "I mean to start fa'r with ye, as I gen'ally do with my niggers; and I 'll tell ye now, to begin with, you treat me fa'r, and I 'll treat you fa'r; I an't never hard on my niggers. Calculates to do the best for 'em I can. Now, ye see, you 'd better jest settle down comfortable, and not be tryin' no tricks; because nigger's tricks of all sorts I 'm up to, and it's no use. If niggers is quiet, and don't try to get off, they has good times with me; and if they don't, why, it 's thar fault, and not mine."

Tom assured Haley that he had no present intentions of running off. In fact, the exhortation seemed rather a superfluous one to a man with a great pair of iron fetters on his feet. But Mr. Haley had got in the habit of commencing his relations with his stock with little exhortations of this nature, calculated, as he deemed, to inspire cheerfulness and confidence, and prevent the necessity of any unpleasant scenes.

And here, for the present, we take our leave of Tom, to pursue the fortunes of other characters in our story.

## XI.
### In Which Property Gets into an Improper State of Mind

It was late in a drizzly afternoon that a traveller alighted at the door of a small country hotel, in the village of N——, in Kentucky. In the bar-room he found assembled quite a miscellaneous company, whom stress of weather had driven to harbor, and the place presented the usual scenery of such reunions. Great, tall, raw-boned Kentuckians, attired in hunting-shirts, and trailing their loose joints over a vast extent of territory, with the easy lounge peculiar to the race,—rifles stacked away in the corner, shot-pouches, game-bags, hunting-dogs, and little negroes, all rolled together in the corners,—were the characteristic features in the picture. At each end of the fireplace sat a long-legged gentleman, with his chair tipped back, his hat on his head, and the heels of his muddy boots reposing sublimely on the mantel-piece,—a position, we will inform our readers, decidedly favorable to the turn of reflection incident to western taverns, where travellers exhibit a decided preference for this particular mode of elevating their understandings.

Mine host, who stood behind the bar, like most of his countrymen, was great of stature, good-natured, and loose-jointed, with an enormous shock of hair on his head, and a great tall hat on the top of that.

In fact, everybody in the room bore on his head this characteristic emblem of man's sovereignty; whether it were felt hat, palm-leaf, greasy beaver, or fine new chapeau, there it reposed with true republican independence. In truth, it appeared to be the characteristic mark of every individual. Some wore them tipped rakishly to one side—these were your men of humor, jolly, free-and-easy dogs; some had them jammed independently down over their noses—these were your hard characters, thorough men, who, when they wore their hats, *wanted* to wear them, and to wear them just as they had a mind to; there were those who had them set far over back—wide-awake men, who wanted a clear prospect; while careless men, who did not know, or care, how their hats sat, had them shaking about in all directions. The various hats, in fact, were quite a Shakspearean study.

Divers negroes, in very free-and-easy pantaloons, and with no redundancy in the shirt line, were scuttling about, hither and thither, without bringing to pass any very particular results, except expressing a generic willingness to turn over everything in creation generally for the benefit of Mas'r and his guests. Add to this picture a jolly, crackling, rollicking fire, going rejoicingly up a great wide chimney,—the outer door and every window being set wide open, and the calico window-curtain flopping and snapping in a good stiff breeze of damp raw air,— and you have an idea of the jollities of a Kentucky tavern.

Your Kentuckian of the present day is a good illustration of the doctrine of transmitted instincts and peculiarities. His fathers were mighty hunters,—men who lived in the woods, and slept under the free, open heavens, with the stars to hold their candles; and their descendant to this day always acts as if the house were his camp,—wears his hat at all hours, tumbles himself about, and puts his heels on the tops of chairs or mantel-pieces, just as his father rolled on the green sward, and put his upon trees and logs,—keeps all the windows and doors open, winter and summer, that he may get air enough for his great lungs,—calls everybody "stranger," with nonchalant bonhommie, and is altogether the frankest, easiest, most jovial creature living.

Into such an assembly of the free and easy our traveller entered. He was a short, thick-set man, carefully dressed, with a round, good-natured countenance, and something rather fussy and particular in his appearance. He was very careful of his valise and umbrella, bringing them in with his own hands, and resisting, pertinaciously, all offers from the various servants to relieve him of them. He looked round the bar-room with rather an anxious air, and, retreating with his valuables to the warmest corner, disposed them under his chair, sat down, and looked rather apprehensively up at the worthy whose heels illustrated the end of the mantel-piece, who was spitting from right to left, with a courage and energy rather alarming to gentlemen of weak nerves and particular habits.

"I say, stranger, how are ye?" said the aforesaid gentleman, firing an honorary salute of tobacco-juice in the direction of the new arrival.

"Well, I reckon," was the reply of the other, as he dodged, with some alarm, the threatening honor.

"Any news?" said the respondent, taking out a strip of tobacco and a large hunting-knife from his pocket.

"Not that I know of," said the man.

"Chaw?" said the first speaker, handing the old gentleman a bit of his tobacco, with a decidedly brotherly air.

"No, thank ye—it don't agree with me," said the little man, edging off.

"Don't, eh?" said the other, easily, and stowing away the morsel in his own mouth, in order to keep up the supply of tobacco-juice, for the general benefit of society.

The old gentleman uniformly gave a little start whenever his long-sided brother fired in his direction; and this being observed by his companion, he very good-naturedly turned his artillary to another quarter, and proceeded to storm one of the fire-irons with a degree of military talent fully sufficient to take a city.

"What 's that?" said the old gentleman, observing some of the company formed in a group around a large handbill.

"Nigger advertised!" said one of the company, briefly.

Mr. Wilson, for that was the old gentleman's name, rose up, and, after carefully adjusting his valise and umbrella, proceeded deliberately to take out his spectacles and fix them on his nose; and, this operation being performed, read as follows:

> "Ran away from the subscriber, my mulatto boy, George. Said George six feet in height, a very light mulatto, brown curly hair; is very intelligent, speaks handsomely, can read and write; will probably try to pass for a white man; is deeply scarred on his back and shoulders; has been branded in his right hand with the letter H.
>
> "I will give four hundred dollars for him alive, and the same sum for satisfactory proof that he has been killed."

The old gentleman read this advertisement from end to end, in a low voice, as if he were studying it.

The long-legged veteran, who had been besieging the fire-iron, as before related, now took down his cumbrous length, and rearing aloft his tall form, walked up to the advertisement, and very deliberately spit a full discharge of tobacco-juice on it.

"There 's my mind upon that!" said he, briefly, and sat down again.

"Why, now, stranger, what 's that for?" said mine host.

"I 'd do it all the same to the writer of that ar paper, if he was here," said the long man, coolly resuming his old employment of cutting tobacco. "Any man that owns a boy like that, and can't find any better way o' treating on him, *deserves* to lose him. Such papers as these is a shame to Kentucky; that 's my mind right out, if anybody wants to know!"

"Well, now, that 's a fact," said mine host, as he made an entry in his book.

"I 've got a gang of boys, sir," said the long man, resuming his attack on the fire-irons, "and I jest tells 'em—'Boys,' says I,—'*run* now! dig! put! jest when ye want to! I never shall come to look after you!' That 's the way I keep mine. Let 'em know they are free to run any time, and it jest breaks up their wanting to. More 'n all, I 've got free papers for 'em all recorded, in case I gets keeled up any o' these times, and they knows it; and I tell ye, stranger, there an't a fellow in our parts gets more out of his niggers than I do. Why, my boys have been to Cincinnati, with five hundred dollars' worth of colts, and brought me back the money, all straight, time and agin. It stands to reason they should. Treat 'em like dogs, and you 'll have dogs' works and dogs' actions. Treat 'em like men, and you 'll have men's works." And the honest drover, in his warmth, endorsed this moral sentiment by firing a perfect *feu de joie* at the fireplace.

"I think you're altogether right, friend," said Mr. Wilson; "and this boy described here *is* a fine fellow—no mistake about that. He worked for me some half-dozen years in my bagging factory, and he was my best hand, sir. He is an ingenious fellow, too: he invented a machine for the cleaning of hemp—a really valuable affair; it 's gone into use in several factories. His master holds the patent of it."

"I 'll warrant ye," said the drover, "holds it and makes money out of it, and then turns round and brands the boy in his right hand. If I had a fair chance, I 'd mark him, I reckon, so that he 'd carry it *one* while."

"These yer knowin' boys is allers aggravatin' and sarcy," said a coarse-looking fellow, from the other side of the room; "that 's why they gets cut up and marked so. If they behaved themselves, they would n't."

"That is to say, the Lord made 'em men, and it 's a hard squeeze getting 'em down into beasts," said the drover, dryly.

"Bright niggers is n't no kind of 'vantage to their masters," continued the other, well intrenched, in a coarse, unconscious obtuseness, from the contempt of his opponent; "what 's the use o' talents and them things, if you can't get the use on 'em yourself? Why, all the use they make on 't is to get round you. I 've had one or two of these fellers, and I jest sold 'em down river. I knew I 'd got to lose 'em, first or last, if I did n't."

"Better send orders up to the Lord, to make you a set, and leave out their souls entirely," said the drover.

Here the conversation was interrupted by the approach of a small one-horse buggy to the inn. It had a genteel appearance, and a well-dressed, gentlemanly man sat on the seat, with a colored servant driving.

The whole part examined the new comer with the interest with which a set of loafers in a rainy day usually examine every new comer. He was very tall, with a dark, Spanish complexion, fine, expressive black eyes, and close-curling hair, also of a glossy blackness. His well-formed aquiline nose, straight thin lips, and the admirable contour of his finely-formed limbs, impressed the whole company instantly with the idea of something uncommon. He walked easily in among the company, and with a nod indicated to his waiter where to place his trunk, bowed to the company, and, with his hat in his hand, walked up leisurely to the bar, and gave in his name as Henry Butler, Oaklands, Shelby County. Turning, with an indifferent air, he sauntered up to the advertisement, and read it over.

"Jim," he said to his man, "seems to me we met a boy something like this, up at Bernan's, did n't we?"

"Yes, Mas'r," said Jim, "only I an't sure about the hand."

"Well, I did n't look, of course," said the stranger, with a careless yawn. Then, walking up to the landlord, he desired him to furnish him with a private apartment, as he had some writing to do immediately.

The landlord was all obsequious, and a relay of about seven negroes, old and young, male and female, little and big, were soon whizzing about, like a covey of partridges, bustling, hurrying, treading on each other's toes, and tumbling over each other, in their zeal to get Mas'r's room ready, while he seated himself easily on a chair in the middle of the room, and entered into conversation with the man who sat next to him.

The manufacturer, Mr. Wilson, from the time of the entrance of the stranger, had regarded him with an air of disturbed and uneasy curiosity. He seemed to himself to have met and been acquainted with him somewhere, but he could not recollect. Every few moments, when the man spoke, or moved, or smiled, he would start and fix his eyes on him, and then suddenly withdraw them, as the bright, dark eyes met his with such unconcerned coolness. At last, a sudden recollection seemed to flash upon him, for he stared at the stranger with such an air of blank amazement and alarm, that he walked up to him.

"Mr. Wilson, I think," said he, in a tone of recognition, and extending his hand. "I beg your pardon, I did n't recollect you before. I see you remember me,—Mr. Butler, of Oaklands, Shelby County."

"Ye—yes—yes, sir," said Mr. Wilson, like one speaking in a dream.

Just then a negro boy entered, and announced that Mas'r's room was ready.

"Jim, see to the trunks," said the gentleman, negligently; then addressing himself to Mr. Wilson, he added—"I should like to have a few moments' conversation with you on business, in my room, if you please."

Mr. Wilson followed him, as one who walks in his sleep; and they proceeded to a large upper chamber, where a newmade fire was crackling, and various servants flying about, putting finishing touches to the arrangements.

When all was done, and the servants departed, the young man deliberately locked the door, and putting the key in his pocket, faced about, and folding his arms on his bosom, looked Mr. Wilson full in the face.

"George!" said Mr. Wilson.

"Yes, George," said the young man.

"I could n't have thought it!"

"I am pretty well disguised, I fancy," said the young man, with a smile. "A little walnut bark has made my yellow skin a genteel brown, and I 've dyed my hair black; so you see I don't answer to the advertisement at all."

"O, George! but this is a dangerous game you are playing. I could not have advised you to it."

"I can do it on my own responsibility," said George, with the same proud smile.

We remark, *en passant*, that George was, by his father's side, of white descent. His mother was one of those unfortunates of her race, marked out by personal beauty to be the slave of the passions of her possessor, and the mother of children who may never know a father. From one of the proudest families in Kentucky he had inherited a set of fine European features, and a high, indomitable spirit. From his mother he had received only a slight mulatto tinge, amply compensated by its accompanying rich, dark eye. A slight change in the tint of the skin and the color of his hair had metamorphosed him into the Spanish-looking fellow he then appeared; and as gracefulness of movement and gentlemanly manners had always been perfectly natural to him, he found no difficulty in playing the bold part he had adopted—that of a gentleman travelling with his domestic.

Mr. Wilson, a good-natured but extemely fidgety and cautious old gentleman, ambled up and down the room, appearing, as John Bunyan hath it, "much tumbled up and down in his mind," and divided between his wish to help George, and a certain confused notion of maintaining law and order: so, as he shambled about, he delivered himself as follows:

"Well, George, I s'pose you 're running away—leaving your lawful master,

George—(I don't wonder at it)—at the same time, I 'm sorry, George,—yes, decidedly—I think I must say that, George—it 's my duty to tell you so."

"Why are you sorry, sir?" said George, calmly.

"Why, to see you, as it were, setting yourself in opposition to the laws of your country."

"*My* country!" said George, with a strong and bitter emphasis; "what country have I, but the grave,—and I wish to God that I was laid there!"

"Why, George, no—no—it won't do; this way of talking is wicked—unscriptural. George, you 've got a hard master—in fact, he is—well he conducts himself reprehensibly—I can't pretend to defend him. But you know how the angel commanded Hagar to return to her mistress, and submit herself under her hand; and the apostle sent back Onesimus to his master."

"Don't quote Bible at me that way, Mr. Wilson," said George, with a flashing eye, "don't! for my wife is a Christian, and I mean to be, if ever I get to where I can; but to quote Bible to a fellow in my circumstances, is enough to make him give it up altogether. I appeal to God Almighty;—I 'm willing to go with the case to Him, and ask Him if I do wrong to seek my freedom."

"These feelings are quite natural, George," said the good-natured man, blowing his nose. "Yes they 're natural, but it is my duty not to encourage 'em in you. Yes, my boy, I 'm sorry for you, now; it 's a bad case—very bad; but the apostle says, 'Let every one abide in the condition in which he is called.' We must all submit to the indications of Providence, George,—don't you see?"

George stood with his head drawn back, his arms folded tightly over his broad breast, and a bitter smile curling his lips.

"I wonder, Mr. Wilson, if the Indians should come and take you a prisoner away from your wife and children, and want to keep you all your life hoeing corn for them, if you 'd think it your duty to abide in the condition in which you were called. I rather think that you 'd think the first stray horse you could find an indication of Providence—should n't you?"

The little old gentleman stared with both eyes at this illustration of the case; but, though not much of a reasoner, he had the sense in which some logicians on this particular subject do not excel,—that of saying nothing, where nothing could be said. So, as he stood carefully stroking his umbrella, and folding and patting down all the creases in it, he proceeded on with his exhortations in a general way.

"You see, George, you know, now, I always have stood your friend; and whatever I 've said, I 've said for your good. Now, here, it seems to me, you 're running an awful risk. You can't hope to carry it out. If you 're taken, it will be worse with you than ever; they 'll only abuse you, and half kill you, and sell you down river."

"Mr. Wilson, I know all this," said George. "I *do* run a risk, but—" he threw open his overcoat, and showed two pistols and a bowie-knife. "There!" he said, "I'm ready for 'em! Down south I never *will* go. No! if it comes to that, I can earn myself at least six feet of free soil,—the first and last I shall ever own in Kentucky!"

"Why, George, this state of mind is awful; it 's getting really desperate, George. I 'm concerned. Going to break the laws of your country!"

"My country again! Mr. Wilson, *you* have a country; but what country have I, or any one like me, born of slave mothers? What laws are there for us? We don't make them,—we don't consent to them,—we have nothing to do with them; all they do for us is to crush us, and keep us down. Have n't I heard your Fourth-of-July speeches? Don't you tell us all, once a year, that governments derive their just power from the consent of the governed? Can't a fellow *think*, that hears such things? Can't he put this and that together, and see what it comes to?"

Mr. Wilson's mind was one of those that may not unaptly be represented by a bale of cotton,—downy, soft, benevolently fuzzy and confused. He really pitied George with all his heart, and had a sort of dim and cloudy perception of the style of feeling that agitated him; but he deemed it his duty to go on talking *good* to him, with infinite pertinacity.

"George, this is bad. I must tell you, you know, as a friend, you 'd better not be meddling with such notions; they are bad, George, very bad, for boys in your condition,—very;" and Mr. Wilson sat down to a table, and began nervously chewing the handle of his umbrella.

"See here, now, Mr. Wilson," said George, coming up and sitting himself determinately down in front of him; "look at me, now. Don't I sit before you, every way, just as much a man as you are? Look at my face,—look at my hands,—look at my body," and the young man drew himself up proudly; "why am I *not* a man, as much as anybody? Well, Mr. Wilson, hear what I can tell you. I had a father— one of your Kentucky gentlemen—who did n't think enough of me to keep me from being sold with his dogs and horses, to satisfy the estate, when he died. I saw my mother put up at sheriff's sale, with her seven children. They were sold before her eyes, one by one, all to different masters; and I was the youngest. She came and kneeled down before old Mas'r, and begged him to buy her with me, that she might have at least one child with her; and he kicked her away with his heavy boot. I saw him do it; and the last that I heard was her moans and screams, when I was tied to his horse's neck, to be carried off to his place."

"Well, then?"

"My master traded with one of the men, and bought my oldest sister. She was a pious, good girl,—a member of the Baptist church,—and as handsome as my poor mother had been. She was well brought up, and had good manners. At first, I was glad she was bought, for I had one friend near me. I was soon sorry for it. Sir, I have stood at the door and heard her whipped, when it seemed as if every blow cut into my naked heart, and I could n't do anything to help her; and she was whipped, sir, for wanting to live a decent Christian life, such as your laws give no slave girl a right to live; and at last I saw her chained with a trader's gang, to be sent to market in Orleans,—sent there for nothing else but that,—and that 's the last I know of her. Well, I grew up,—long years and years,—no father, no mother, no sister, not a living soul that cared for me more than a dog; nothing but whipping, scolding, starving. Why, sir, I 've been so hungry that I have been glad to take the bones they threw to their dogs; and yet, when I was a little fellow, and laid awake whole nights and cried, it was n't the hunger, it was n't the whipping, I cried for. No, sir; it was for *my mother* and *my sisters*,—it was because I had n't a friend to love me on earth. I never knew what peace or comfort was. I never had a kind word spoken to me till I came to work in your factory. Mr. Wilson, you treated me well; you encouraged me to do well, and to learn to read and write, and to try to make something of myself; and God knows how grateful I am for it. Then, sir, I found my wife; you 've seen her,—you know how beautiful she is. When I found she loved me, when I married her, I scarcely could believe I was alive, I was so happy; and, sir, she is as good as she is beautiful. But now what? Why, now comes my master, takes me right away from my work, and my friends, and all I like, and grinds me down into the very dirt! And why? Because, he says, I forgot who I was; he says, to teach me that I am only a nigger! After all, and last of all, he comes between me and my wife, and says I shall give her up, and live with another woman. And all this your laws give him power to do, in spite of God or man. Mr. Wilson, look at it! There is n't *one* of all these things, that have broken the hearts of my mother and my sister, and my wife and myself, but your laws allow, and give every man power to do, in Kentucky, and none can say to him nay! Do you call these the laws of *my* country? Sir, I have n't any country, any more than I have any father. But I 'm going to have one. I don't want anything of *your* country, except to be let alone,—to go peaceably out of it; and when I get to Canada, where the laws will own me and protect me, *that* shall be my country, and its laws I will obey. But if any man tries to stop me, let him take care, for I am desperate. I 'll fight for my liberty to the last breath I breathe. You say your fathers did it; if it was right for them, it is right for me!"

This speech, delivered partly while sitting at the table, and partly walking up and down the room,—delivered with tears, and flashing eyes, and despairing gestures,—was altogether too much for the good-natured old body to whom it was addressed, who had pulled out a great yellow silk pocket-handkerchief, and was mopping up his face with great energy.

"Blast 'em all!" he suddenly broke out. "Have n't I always said so—the infernal old cusses! I hope I an't swearing, now. Well! go ahead, George, go ahead; but be careful, my boy; don't shoot anybody, George, unless—well—you 'd *better* not shoot, I reckon; at least, I would n't *hit* anybody, you know. Where is your wife, George?" he added, as he nervously rose, and began walking the room.

"Gone, sir, gone, with her child in her arms, the Lord only knows where;— gone after the north star; and when we ever meet, or whether we meet at all in this world, no creature can tell."

"Is it possible! astonishing! from such a kind family?"

"Kind families get in debt, and the laws of *our* country allow them to sell the child out of its mother's bosom to pay its master's debts," said George, bitterly.

"Well, well," said the honest old man, fumbling in his pocket. "I s'pose, perhaps, I an't following my judgment,—hang it, I *won't* follow my judgment!" he added, suddenly; "so here, George," and, taking out a roll of bills from his pocketbook, he offered them to George.

"No, my kind, good sir!" said George, "you 've done a great deal for me, and this might get you into trouble. I have money enough, I hope, to take me as far as I need it."

"No; but you must, George. Money is a great help everywhere;—can't have too much, if you get it honestly. Take it,—*do* take it, *now,*—do, my boy!"

"On condition, sir, that I may repay it at some future time, I will," said George, taking up the money.

"And now, George, how long are you going to travel in this way?—not long or far, I hope. It 's well carried on, but too bold. And this black fellow,—who is he?"

"A true fellow, who went to Canada more than a year ago. He heard, after he got there, that his master was so angry at him for going off that he had whipped his poor old mother; and he has come all the way back to comfort her, and get a chance to get her away."

"Has he got her?"

"Not yet; he has been hanging about the place, and found no chance yet. Meanwhile, he is going with me as far as Ohio, to put me among friends that helped him, and then he will come back after her."

"Dangerous, very dangerous!" said the old man.

George drew himself up, and smiled disdainfully.

The old gentleman eyed him from head to foot, with a sort of innocent wonder.

"George, something has brought you out wonderfully. You hold up your head, and speak and move like another man," said Mr. Wilson.

"Because I'm a *freeman!*" said George, proudly. "Yes, sir; I 've said Mas'r for the last time to any man. *I'm free!*"

"Take care! You are not sure,—you may be taken."

"All men are free and equal *in the grave*, if it comes to that, Mr. Wilson," said George.

"I 'm perfectly dumb-foundered with your boldness!" said Mr. Wilson,—"to come right here to the nearest tavern!"

"Mr. Wilson, it is *so* bold, and this tavern is so near, that they will never think of it; they will fook for me on ahead, and you yourself would n't know me. Jim's master don't live in this county; he is n't known in these parts. Besides, he is given up; nobody is looking after him, and nobody will take me up from the advertisement, I think."

"But the mark in your hand?"

George drew off his glove, and showed a newly-healed scar in his hand.

"That is a parting proof of Mr. Harris' regard," he said, scornfully. "A fortnight ago, he took it into his head to give it to me, because he said he believed I should try to get away one of these days. Looks interesting, does n't it?" he said, drawing his glove on again.

"I declare, my very blood runs cold when I think of it,—your condition and your risks!" said Mr. Wilson.

"Mine has run cold a good many years, Mr. Wilson; at present, it 's about up to the boiling point," said George.

"Well, my good sir," continued George, after a few moments' silence, "I saw you knew me; I thought I 'd just have this talk with you, lest your surprised looks should bring me out. I leave early to-morrow morning, before daylight; by to-morrow night I hope to sleep safe in Ohio. I shall travel by daylight, stop at the best hotels, go to the dinner-tables with the lords of the land. So, good-by, sir; if you hear that I 'm taken, you may know that I 'm dead!"

George stood up like a rock, and put out his hand with the air of a prince. The friendly little old man shook it heartily, and after a little shower of caution, he took his umbrella, and fumbled his way out of the room.

George stood thoughtfully looking at the door, as the old man closed it. A thought seemed to flash across his mind. He hastily stepped to it, and opening it, said,

"Mr. Wilson, one word more."

The old gentleman entered again, and George, as before, locked the door, and then stood for a few moments looking on the floor, irresolutely. At last, raising his head with a sudden effort—

"Mr. Wilson, you have shown yourself a Christian in your treatment of me,—I want to ask one last deed of Christian kindness of you."

"Well, George."

"Well, sir,—what you said was true. I *am* running a dreadful risk. There isn't, on earth, a living soul to care if I die," he added, drawing his breath hard, and speaking with a great effort,—"I shall be kicked out and buried like a dog, and nobody 'll think of it a day after,—*only my poor wife!* Poor soul! she 'll mourn and grieve; and if you 'd only contrive, Mr. Wilson, to send this little pin to her. She gave it to me for a Christmas present, poor child! Give it to her, and tell her I loved her to the last. Will you? *Will* you?" he added, earnestly.

"Yes, certainly—poor fellow!" said the old gentleman, taking the pin, with watery eyes, and a melancholy quiver in his voice.

"Tell her one thing," said George; "it 's my last wish, if she *can* get to Canada, to go there. No matter how kind her mistress is,—no matter how much she loves her home; beg her not to go back,—for slavery always ends in misery. Tell her to bring up our boy a free man, and then he won't suffer as I have. Tell her this, Mr. Wilson, will you?"

"Yes, George, I 'll tell her; but I trust you won't die; take heart,—you 're a brave fellow. Trust in the Lord, George. I wish in my heart you were safe through, though,—that 's what I do."

"*Is* there a God to trust in?" said George, in such a tone of utter despair as arrested the old gentleman's words. "O, I 've seen things all my life that have made me feel that there can't be a God. You Christians don't know how these things look to us. There 's a God for you, but is there any for us?"

"O, now, don't—don't, my boy!" said the old man, almost sobbing as he spoke; "don't feel so! There is—there is; clouds and darkness are around about him, but righteousness and judgment are the habitation of his throne. There 's a *God*, George,—believe it; trust in Him, and I 'm sure He 'll help you. Everything will be set right,—if not in this life, in another."

The real piety and benevolence of the simple old man invested him with a temporary dignity and authority, as he spoke. George stopped his distracted walk up and down the room, stood thoughtfully a moment, and then said, quietly,

"Thank you for saying that, my good friend; I 'll *think of that*."

## XII.
### Select Incident of Lawful Trade

"In Ramah there was a voice heard,—weeping, and lamentation, and great mourning; Rachel weeping for her children, and would not be comforted."

Mr. Haley and Tom jogged onward in their wagon, each, for a time, absorbed in his own reflections. Now, the reflections of two men sitting side by side are a curious thing,—seated on the same seat, having the same eyes, ears, hands and organs of all sorts, and having pass before their eyes the same objects,—it is wonderful what a variety we shall find in these same reflections!

As, for example, Mr. Haley: he thought first of Tom's length, and breadth, and height, and what he would sell for, if he was kept fat and in good case till he got him into market. He thought of how he should make out his gang; he thought of the respective market value of certain supposititious men and women and children who were to compose it, and other kindred topics of the business; then he thought of himself, and how humane he was, that whereas other men chained their "niggers" hand and foot both, he only put fetters on the feet, and left Tom the use of his hands, as long as he behaved well; and he sighed to think how ungrateful human nature was, so that there was even room to doubt whether Tom appreciated his mercies. He had been taken in so by "niggers" whom he had favored; but still he was astonished to consider how good-natured he yet remained!

As to Tom, he was thinking over some words of an unfashionable old book, which kept running through his head, again and again, as follows: "We have here no continuing city, but we seek one to come; wherefore God himself is not ashamed to be called our God; for he hath prepared for us a city." These words of an ancient volume, got up principally by "ignorant and unlearned men," have, through all time, kept up, somehow, a strange sort of power over the minds of poor, simple fellows, like Tom. They stir up the soul from its depths, and rouse, as with trumpet call, courage, energy, and enthusiasm, where before was only the blackness of despair.

Mr. Haley pulled out of his pocket sundry newspapers, and began looking over their advertisements, with absorbed interest. He was not a remarkably fluent reader, and was in the habit of reading in a sort of recitative half-aloud, by way of calling in his ears to verify the deductions of his eyes. In this tone he slowly recited the following paragraph:

"EXECUTOR'S SALE,—NEGROES!—Agreeably to order of court, will be sold, on Tuesday, February 20, before the Court-house door, in the town of Washington, Kentucky, the following negroes: Hagar, aged 60; John, aged 30; Ben, aged 21; Saul, aged 25; Albert, aged 14. Sold for the benefit of the creditors and heirs of the estate of Jesse Blutchford, Esq.

SAMUEL MORRIS,
THOMAS FLINT,
*Executors.*"

"This yer I must look at," said he to Tom, for want of somebody else to talk to.

"Ye see, I 'm going to get up a prime gang to take down with ye, Tom; it 'll make it sociable and pleasant like,—good company will, ye know. We must drive right to Washington first and foremost, and then I 'll clap you into jail, while I does the business."

Tom received this agreeable intelligence quite meekly; simply wondering, in his own heart, how many of these doomed men had wives and children, and whether they would feel as he did about leaving them. It is to be confessed, too, that the naïve, off-hand information that he was to be thrown into jail by no means produced an agreeable impression on a poor fellow who had always prided himself on a strictly honest and upright course of life. Yes, Tom, we must confess it, was rather proud of his honesty, poor fellow,—not having very much else to be proud of;—if he had belonged to some of the higher walks of society, he, perhaps, would never have been reduced to such straits. However, the day wore on, and the evening saw Haley and Tom comfortably accommodated in Washington,— the one in a tavern, and the other in a jail.

About eleven o'clock the next day, a mixed throng was gathered around the court-house steps,—smoking, chewing, spitting, swearing, and conversing, according to their respective tastes and turns,—waiting for the auction to commence. The men and women to be sold sat in a group apart, talking in a low tone to each other. The woman who had been advertised by the name of Hagar was a regular African in feature and figure. She might have been sixty, but was older than that by hard work and disease, was partially blind, and somewhat crippled with rheumatism. By her side stood her only remaining son, Albert, a bright-looking little fellow of fourteen years. The boy was the only survivor of a large family, who had been successively sold away from her to a southern market. The mother held on to him with both her shaking hands, and eyed with intense trepidation every one who walked up to examine him.

"Don't be feard, Aunt Hagar," said the oldest of the men, "I spoke to Mas'r Thomas 'bout it, and he thought he might manage to sell you in a lot both together."

"Dey need n't call me worn out yet," said she, lifting her shaking hands. "I can cook yet, and scrub, and scour,—I 'm wuth a buying, if I do come cheap;— tell em dat ar,—you *tell* em," she added, earnestly.

Haley here forced his way into the group, walked up to the old man, pulled his mouth open and looked in, felt of his teeth, made him stand and straighten himself, bend his back, and perform various evolutions to show his muscles; and then passed on to the next, and put him through the same trial. Walking up last to the boy, he felt of his arms, straightened his hands, and looked at his fingers, and made him jump, to show his agility.

"He an't gwine to be sold widout me!" said the old woman, with passionate eagerness; "he and I goes in a lot together; I 's rail strong yet, Mas'r, and can do heaps o' work,—heaps on it, Mas'r."

"On plantation?" said Haley, with a contemptuous glance. "Likely story!" and, as if satisfied with his examination, he walked out and looked, and stood with his hands in his pocket, his cigar in his mouth, and his hat cocked on one side, ready for action.

"What think of 'em?" said a man who had been following Haley's examination, as if to make up his own mind from it.

"Wal," said Haley, spitting, "I shall put in, I think, for the youngerly ones and the boy."

"They want to sell the boy and the old woman together," said the man.

"Find it a tight pull;—why, she 's an old rack o' bones,—not worth her salt."

"You would n't, then?" said the man.

"Anybody 'd be a fool 't would. She 's half blind, crooked with rheumatis, and foolish to boot."

"Some buys up these yer old critturs, and ses there 's a sight more wear in 'em than a body 'd think," said the man, reflectively.

"No go, 't all," said Haley; "would n't take her for a present,—fact,—I 've *seen*, now."

"Wal, 't is kinder pity, now, not to buy her with her son,—her heart seems so sot on him,—s'pose they fling her in cheap,"

"Them that 's got money to spend that ar way, it 's all well enough. I shall bid off on that ar boy for a plantation-hand;—would n't be bothered with her, no way,—not if they 'd give her to me," said Haley.

"She 'll take on desp't," said the man.

"Nat'lly, she will," said the trader, coolly.

The conversation was here interrupted by a busy hum in the audience; and the auctioneer, a short, bustling, important fellow, elbowed his way into the crowd. The old woman drew in her breath, and caught instinctively at her son.

"Keep close to yer mammy, Albert,—close,—dey 'll put us up togedder," she said.

"O, mammy, I 'm feard they won't," said the boy.

"Dey must, child; I can't live, no ways, if they don't," said the old creature, vehemently.

The stentorian tones of the auctioneer, calling out to clear the way, now announced that the sale was about to commence. A place was cleared, and the bidding began. The different men on the list were soon knocked off at prices which showed a pretty brisk demand in the market; two of them fell to Haley.

"Come, now, young un," said the auctioneer, giving the boy a touch with his hammer, "be up and show your springs, now."

"Put us two up togedder, togedder,—do please, Mas'r," said the old woman, holding fast to her boy.

"Be off," said the man, gruffly, pushing her hands away; "you come last. Now, darkey, spring;" and, with the word, he pushed the boy toward the block, while a deep, heavy groan rose behind him. The boy paused, and looked back; but there was no time to stay, and, dashing the tears from his large, bright eyes, he was up in a moment.

His fine figure, alert limbs, and bright face, raised an instant competition, and half a dozen bids simultaneously met the ear of the auctioneer. Anxious, half-frightened, he looked from side to side, as he heard the clatter of contending bids,—now here, now there,—till the hammer fell. Haley had got him. He was pushed from the block toward his new master, but stopped one moment, and looked back, when his poor old mother, trembling in every limb, held out her shaking hands toward him.

"Buy me too, Mas'r, for de dear Lord's sake!—buy me,—I shall die if you don't!"

"You 'll die if I do, that 's the kink of it," said Haley,—"no!" And he turned on his heel.

The bidding for the poor old creature was summary. The man who had addressed Haley, and who seemed not destitute of compassion, bought her for a trifle, and the spectators began to disperse.

The poor victims of the sale, who had been brought up in one place together for years, gathered round the despairing old mother, whose agony was pitiful to see.

"Could n't dey leave me one? Mas'r allers said I should have one,—he did," she repeated over and over, in heart-broken tones.

"Trust in the Lord, Aunt Hagar," said the oldest of the men, sorrowfully.

"What good will it do?" said she sobbing passionately.

"Mother, mother,—don't! don't!" said the boy. "They say you 's got a good master."

"I don't care,—I don't care. O, Albert! oh, my boy! you 's my last baby. Lord, how ken I?"

"Come, take her off, can't some of ye?" said Haley, dryly; "don't do no good for her to go on that ar way."

The old men of the company, partly by persuasion and partly by force, loosed the poor creature's last despairing hold, and, as they led her off to her new master's wagon, strove to comfort her.

"Now!" said Haley, pushing his three purchases together, and producing a bundle of handcuffs, which he proceeded to put on their wrists; and fastening each handcuff to a long chain, he drove them before him to the jail.

A few days saw Haley, with his possessions, safely deposited on one of the Ohio boats. It was the commencement of his gang, to be augmented, as the boat moved on, by various other merchandise of the same kind, which he, or his agent, had stored for him in various points along shore.

The La Belle Rivière, as brave and beautiful a boat as ever walked the waters of her namesake river, was floating gayly down the stream, under a brilliant sky, the stripes and stars of free America waving and fluttering over head; the guards crowded with well-dressed ladies and gentlemen walking and enjoying the delightful day. All was full of life, buoyant and rejoicing;—all but Haley's gang, who were stored, with other freight, on the lower deck, and who, somehow, did not seem to appreciate their various privileges, as they sat in a knot, talking to each other in low tones.

"Boys," said Haley, coming up, briskly, "I hope you keep up good heart, and are cheerful. Now, no sulks, ye see; keep stiff upper lip, boys; do well by me, and I 'll do well by you."

The boys addressed responded the invariable "Yes, Mas'r," for ages the watch-word of poor Africa; but it 's to be owned they did not look particularly cheer-ful; they had their various little prejudices in favor of wives, mothers, sisters, and children, seen for the last time,—and though "they that wasted them required of them mirth," it was not instantly forthcoming.

"I 've got a wife," spoke out the article enumerated as "John, aged thirty," and he laid his chained hand on Tom's knee,—"and she don't know a word about this, poor girl!"

"Where does she live?" said Tom.

"In a tavern a piece down here," said John; "I wish, now, I *could* see her once more in this world," he added.

Poor John! It *was* rather natural; and the tears that fell, as he spoke, came as naturally as if he had been a white man. Tom drew a long breath from a sore heart, and tried, in his poor way, to comfort him.

And over head, in the cabin, sat fathers and mothers, husbands and wives; and merry, dancing children moved round among them, like so many little but-terflies, and everything was going on quite easy and comfortable.

"O, mamma," said a boy, who had just come up from below, "there 's a negro trader on board, and he 's brought four or five slaves down there."

"Poor creatures!" said the mother, in a tone between grief and indignation.

"What 's that?" said another lady.

"Some poor slaves below," said the mother.

"And they 've got chains on," said the boy.

"What a shame to our country that such sights are to be seen!" said another lady.

"O, there 's a great deal to be said on both sides of the subject," said a gen-teel woman, who sat at her state-room door sewing, while her little girl and boy were playing round her. "I 've been south, and I must say I think the negroes are better off than they would be to be free."

"In some respects, some of them are well off, I grant," said the lady to whose remark she had answered. "The most dreadful part of slavery, to my mind, is its outrages on the feelings and affections,—the separating of families, for example."

"That *is* a bad thing, certainly," said the other lady, holding up a baby's dress she had just completed, and looking intently on its trimmings; "but then, I fancy, it don't occur often."

"O, it does," said the first lady, eagerly; "I 've lived many years in Kentucky and Virginia both, and I 've seen enough to make any one's heart sick. Suppose, ma'am, your two children, there, should be taken from you, and sold?"

"We can't reason from our feelings to those of this class of persons," said the other lady, sorting out some worsteds on her lap.

"Indeed, ma'am, you can know nothing of them, if you say so," answered the first lady, warmly. "I was born and brought up among them. I know they *do* feel, just as keenly,—even more so, perhaps,—as we do."

The lady said "Indeed!" yawned, and looked out the cabin window, and fi-nally repeated, for a finale, the remark with which she had begun,—"After all, I think they are better off than they would be to be free."

"It 's undoubtedly the intentions of Providence that the African race should be servants,—kept in a low condition," said a grave-looking gentleman in black, a clergyman, seated by the cabin door. "'Cursed be Canaan; a servant of servants shall he be,' the scripture says."

"I say, stranger, is that ar what that text means?" said a tall man, standing by.

"Undoubtedly. It pleased Providence, for some inscrutable reason, to doom the race to bondage, ages ago; and we must not set up our opinion against that."

"Well, then, we 'll all go ahead and buy up niggers," said the man, "if that 's the way of Providence,—won't we, Squire?" said he, turning to Haley, who had been standing, with his hands in his pockets, by the stove, and intently listening to the conversation.

"Yes," continued the tall man, "we must all be resigned to the decrees of Providence. Niggers must be sold, and trucked round, and kept under; it 's what they 's made for. 'Pears like this yer view 's quite refreshing, an't it, stranger?" said he to Haley.

"I never thought on 't," said Haley. "I could n't have said as much, myself; I ha'nt no larning. I took up the trade just to make a living; if 't an't right, I calculated to 'pent on 't in time, ye know."

"And now you 'll save yerself the trouble, won't ye?" said the tall man. "See what 't is, now, to know scripture. If ye 'd only studied yer Bible, like this yer good man, ye might have know 'd it before, and saved ye a heap o' trouble. Ye could jist have said, 'Cussed be'—what 's his name?—'and 't would all have come right.'" And the stranger, who was no other than the honest drover whom we introduced to our readers in the Kentucky tavern, sat down, and began smoking, with a curious smile on his long, dry face.

A tall, slender young man, with a face expressive of great feeling and intelligence, here broke in, and repeated the words, "'All things whatsoever ye would that men should do unto you, do ye even so unto them.' I suppose," he added, "*that* is scripture, as much as 'Cursed be Canaan.'"

"Wal, it seems quite *as* plain a text, stranger," said John the drover, "to poor fellows like us, now;" and John smoked on like a volcano.

The young man paused, looked as if he was going to say more, when suddenly the boat stopped, and the company made the usual steamboat rush, to see where they were landing.

"Both them ar chaps parsons?" said John to one of the men, as they were going out.

The man nodded.

As the boat stopped, a black woman came running wildly up the plank, darted into the crowd, flew up to where the slave gang sat, and threw her arms round that unfortunate piece of merchandise before enumerated—"John, aged thirty," and with sobs and tears bemoaned him as her husband.

But what needs tell the story, told too oft,—every day told,—of heart-strings rent and broken,—the weak broken and torn for the profit and convenience of the strong! It needs not to be told;—every day is telling it,—telling it, too, in the ear of One who is not deaf, though he be long silent.

The young man who had spoken for the cause of humanity and God before stood with folded arms, looking on this scene. He turned, and Haley was standing at his side. "My friend," he said, speaking with thick utterance, "how can you, how dare you, carry on a trade like this? Look at those poor creatures! Here I am, rejoicing in my heart that I am going home to my wife and child; and the same bell which is a signal to carry me onward towards them will part this poor man and his wife forever. Depend upon it, God will bring you into judgment for this."

The trader turned away in silence.

"I say, now," said the drover, touching his elbow, "there 's differences in parsons, an't there? 'Cussed by Canaan' don't seem to go down with this 'un, does it?"

Haley gave an uneasy growl.

"And that ar an't the worst on 't," said John; "mabbe it won't go down with the Lord, neither, when ye come to settle with Him, one o' these days, as all on us must, I reckon."

Haley walked reflectively to the other end of the boat.

"If I make pretty handsomely on one or two next gangs," he thought, "I reckon I 'll stop off this yer; it 's really getting dangerous." And he took out his pocket-book, and began adding over his accounts—a process which many gentlemen besides Mr. Haley have found a specific for an uneasy conscience.

The boat swept proudly away from the shore, and all went on merrily, as before. Men talked, and loafed, and read, and smoked. Women sewed, and children played, and the boat passed on her way.

One day, when she lay to for a while at a small town in Kentucky, Haley went up into the place on a little matter of business.

Tom, whose fetters did not prevent his taking a moderate circuit, had drawn near the side of the boat, and stood listlessly gazing over the railings. After a time, he saw the trader returning, with an alert step, in company with a colored woman, bearing in her arms a young child. She was dressed quite respectably, and a colored man followed her, bringing along a small trunk. The woman came cheerfully onward, talking, as she came, with the man who bore her trunk, and so passed up the plank into the boat. The bell rung, the steamer whizzed, the engine groaned and coughed, and away swept the boat down the river.

The woman walked forward among the boxes and bales of the lower deck, and sitting down, busied herself with chirruping to her baby.

Haley made a turn or two about the boat, and then, coming up, seated himself near her, and began saying something to her in an indifferent undertone.

Tom soon noticed a heavy cloud passing over the woman's brow; and that she answered rapidly, and with great vehemence.

"I don't believe it,—I won't believe it!" he heard her say. "You 're jist a foolin with me."

"If you won't believe it, look here!" said the man, drawing out a paper; "this yer 's the bill of sale, and there 's your master's name to it; and I paid down good solid cash for it, too, I can tell you,—so, now!"

"I don't believe Mas'r would cheat me so; it can't be true!" said the woman, with increasing agitation.

"You can ask any of these men here, that can read writing. Here!" he said, to a man that was passing by, "jist read this yer, won't you! This yer gal won't believe me, when I tell her what 't is."

"Why, it 's a bill of sale, signed by John Fosdick," said the man, "making over to you the girl Lucy and her child. It 's all straight enough, for aught I see."

The woman's passionate exclamations collected a crowd around her, and the trader briefly explained to them the cause of the agitation.

"He told me that I was going down to Louisville, to hire out as cook to the same tavern where my husband works,—that 's what Mas'r told me, his own self; and I can't believe he 'd lie to me,' said the woman.

"But he has sold you, my poor woman, there 's no doubt about it," said a good-natured looking man, who had been examining the papers; "he has done it, and no mistake."

"Then it 's no account talking," said the woman, suddenly growing quite calm; and, clasping her child tighter in her arms, she sat down on her box, turned her back round, and gazed listlessly into the river.

"Going to take it easy, after all!" said the trader. "Gal's got grit, I see."

The woman looked calm, as the boat went on; and a beautiful soft summer breeze passed like a compassionate spirit over her head,—the gentle breeze, that never inquires whether the brow is dusky or fair that it fans. And she saw sunshine sparkling on the water, in golden ripples, and heard gay voices, full of ease and pleasure, talking around her everywhere; but her heart lay as if a great stone had fallen on it. Her baby raised himself up against her, and stroked her cheeks with his little hands; and, springing up and down, crowing and chatting, seemed determined to arouse her. She strained him suddenly and tightly in her arms, and slowly one tear after another fell on his wondering, unconscious face; and gradually she seemed, and little by little, to grow calmer, and busied herself with tending and nursing him.

The child, a boy of ten months, was uncommonly large and strong of his age, and very vigorous in his limbs. Never, for a moment, still, he kept his mother constantly busy in holding him, and guarding his springing activity.

"That 's a fine chap!" said a man, suddenly stopping opposite to him, with his hands in his pockets. "How old is he?"

"Ten months and a half," said the mother.

The man whistled to the boy, and offered him part of a stick of candy, which he eagerly grabbed at, and very soon had it in a baby's general depository, to wit, his mouth.

"Rum fellow!" said the man. "Knows what 's what!" and he whistled, and walked on. When he had got to the other side of the boat, he came across Haley, who was smoking on top of a pile of boxes.

The stranger produced a match, and lighted a cigar, saying, as he did so,

"Decentish kind o' wench you've got round there, stranger."

"Why, I reckon she *is* tol'able fair," said Haley, blowing the smoke out of his mouth.

"Taking her down south?" said the man.

Haley nodded, and smoked on.

"Plantation hand?" said the man.

"Wal," said Haley, "I'm fillin' out an order for a plantation, and I think I shall put her in. They told me she was a good cook; and they can use her for that, or set her at the cotton-picking. She 's got the right fingers for that; I looked at 'em. Sell well, either way;" and Haley resumed his cigar.

"They won't want the young'un on a plantation," said the man.

"I shall sell him, first chance I find," said Haley, lighting another cigar.

"S'pose you'd be selling him tol'able cheap," said the stranger, mounting the pile of boxes, and sitting down comfortably.

"Don't know 'bout that," said Haley; "he 's a pretty smart young 'un,— straight, fat, strong; flesh as hard as a brick!"

"Very true, but then there 's all the bother and expense of raisin'."

"Nonsense!" said Haley; "they is raised as easy as any kind of critter there is going; they an't a bit more trouble than pups. This yer chap will be running all round, in a month."

"I 've got a good place for raisin', and I thought of takin' in a little more stock," said the man. "One cook lost a young 'un last week,—got drownded in a wash-tub, while she was a hangin' out clothes,—and I reckon it would be well enough to set her to raisin' this yer."

Haley and the stranger smoked a while in silence, neither seeming willing to broach the test question of the interview. At last the man resumed:

"You would n't think of wantin' more than ten dollars for that ar chap, see-ing you *must* get him off yer hand, any how?"

Haley shook his head, and spit impressively.

"That won't do, no ways," he said, and began his smoking again.

"Well, stranger, what will you take?"

"Well, now," said Haley, "I *could* raise that ar chap myself, or get him raised; he 's oncommon likely and healthy, and he 'd fetch a hundred dollars, six months hence; and, in a year or two, he 'd bring two hundred, if I had him in the right spot;—so I shan't take a cent less nor fifty for him now."

"O, stranger! that 's rediculous, altogether," said the man.

"Fact!" said Haley, with a decisive nod of his head.

"I 'll give thirty for him," said the stranger, "but not a cent more."

"Now, I 'll tell ye what I will do," said Haley, spitting again, with renewed decision. "I 'll split the difference, and say forty-five; and that 's the most I will do."

"Well, agreed!" said the man, after an interval.

"Done!" said Haley. "Where do you land?"

"At Louisville," said the man.

"Louisville," said Haley. "Very fair, we get there about dusk. Chap will be alseep,—all fair,—get him off quietly, and no screaming,—happens beautiful,—I like to do everything quietly,—I hates all kind of agitation and fluster." And so, after a transfer of certain bills had passed from the man's pocket-book to the trader's, he resumed his cigar.

It was a bright, tranquil evening when the boat stopped at the wharf at Louisville. The woman had been sitting with her baby in her arms, now wrapped in a heavy sleep. When she heard the name of the place called out, she hastily laid the child down in a little cradle formed by the hollow among the boxes, first carefully spreading under it her cloak; and then she sprung to the side of the boat, in hopes that, among the various hotel-waiters who thronged the wharf, she might see her husband. In this hope, she pressed forward to the front rails, and, stretching far over them, strained her eyes intently on the moving heads on the shore, and the crowd pressed in between her and the child.

"Now 's your time," said Haley, taking the sleeping child up, and handing him to the stranger. "Don't wake him up, and set him to crying, now; it would make a devil of a fuss with the gal." The man took the bundle carefully, and was soon lost in the crowd that went up the wharf.

When the boat, creaking, and groaning, and puffing, had loosed from the wharf, and was beginning slowly to strain herself along, the woman returned to her old seat. The trader was sitting there,—the child was gone!

"Why, why,—where?" she began, in bewildered surprise.

"Lucy," said the trader, "your child 's gone; you may as well know it first as last. You see, I know 'd you could n't take him down south; and I got a chance to sell him to a first-rate family, that 'll raise him better than you can."

The trader had arrived at that stage of Christian and political perfection which has been recommended by some preachers and politicians of the north, lately, in which he had completely overcome every humane weakness and prejudice. His heart was exactly where yours, sir, and mine could be brought, with proper effort and cultivation. The wild look of anguish and utter despair that the woman cast on him might have disturbed one less practised; but he was used to it. He had seen that same look hundreds of times. You can get used to such things, too, my friend; and it is the great object of recent efforts to make our whole northern community used to them, for the glory of the Union. So the trader only regarded the mortal anguish which he saw working in those dark features, those clenched hands, and suffocating breathings, as necessary incidents of the trade, and merely calculated whether she was going to scream, and get up a commotion on the boat; for, like other supporters of our peculiar institution, he decidedly disliked agitation.

But the woman did not scream. The shot had passed too straight and direct through the heart, for cry or tear.

Dizzily she sat down. Her slack hands fell lifeless by her side. Her eyes looked straight forward, but she saw nothing. All the noise and hum of the boat, the groaning of the machinery, mingled dreamily to her bewildered ear; and the poor, dumb-stricken heart had neither cry nor tear to show for its utter misery. She was quite calm.

The trader, who, considering his advantages, was almost as humane as some of our politicians, seemed to feel called on to administer such consolation as the case admitted of.

"I know this yer comes kinder hard, at first, Lucy," said he; "but such a smart, sensible gal as you are, won't give way to it. You see it 's *necessary*, and can't be helped!"

"O! don't, Mas'r, don't!" said the woman, with a voice like one that is smothering.

"You 're a smart wench, Lucy," he persisted; "I mean to do well by ye, and get ye a nice place down river; and you 'll soon get another husband,—such a likely gal as you—"

"O! Mas'r, if you *only* won't talk to me now," said the woman, in a voice of such quick and living anguish that the trader felt that there was something at present in the case beyond his style of operation. He got up, and the woman turned away, and buried her head in her cloak.

The trader walked up and down for a time, and occasionally stopped and looked at her.

"Takes it hard, rather," he soliloquized, "but quiet, tho';—let her sweat a while; she 'll come right, by and by!"

Tom had watched the whole transaction from first to last, and had a perfect understanding of its results. To him, it looked like something unutterably horrible and cruel, because, poor, ignorant black soul! he had not learned to generalize, and to take enlarged views. If he had only been instructed by certain ministers of Christianity, he might have thought better of it, and seen in it an every-day incident of a lawful trade; a trade which is the vital support of an institution which an American divine* tells us has *"no evils but such as are inseparable from any other relations in social and domestic life."* But Tom, as we see, being a poor, ignorant fellow, whose reading had been confined entirely to the New Testament, could not comfort and solace himself with views like these. His very soul bled within him for what seemed to him the *wrongs* of the poor suffering thing that lay like a crushed reed on the boxes; the feeling, living, bleeding, yet immortal *thing*, which American state law coolly classes with the bundles, and bales, and boxes, among which she is lying.

Tom drew near, and tried to say something; but she only groaned. Honestly, and with tears running down his own cheeks, he spoke of a heart of love in the skies, of a pitying Jesus, and an eternal home; but the ear was deaf with anguish, and the palsied heart could not feel.

Night came on,—night calm, unmoved, and glorious, shining down with her innumerable and solemn angel eyes, twinkling, beautiful, but silent. There was no speech nor language, no pitying voice or helping hand, from that distant sky. One after another, the voices of business or pleasure died away; all on the boat were sleeping, and the ripples at the prow were plainly heard. Tom stretched himself out on a box, and there, as he lay, he heard, ever and anon, a smothered sob or cry from the prostrate creature,—"O! what shall I do? O Lord! O good Lord, do help me!" and so, ever and anon, until the murmur died away in silence.

At midnight, Tom waked, with a sudden start. Something black passed quickly by him to the side of the boat, and he heard a splash in the water. No one else saw or heard anything. He raised his head,—the woman's place was vacant! He got up, and sought about him in vain. The poor bleeding heart was still, at last, and the river rippled and dimpled just as brightly as if it had not closed above it.

*Dr. Joel Parker, of Philadelphia.

Patience! patience! ye whose hearts swell indignant at wrongs like these. Not one throb of anguish, not one tear of the oppressed, is forgotten by the Man of Sorrows, the Lord of Glory. In his patient, generous bosom he bears the anguish of a world. Bear thou, like him, in patience, and labor in love; for sure as he is God, "the year of his redeemed *shall* come."

The trader waked up bright and early, and came out to see to his live stock. It was now his turn to look about in perplexity.

"Where alive is that gal?" he said to Tom.

Tom, who had learned the wisdom of keeping counsel, did not feel called on to state his observations and suspicions, but said he did not know.

"She surely could n't have got off in the night at any of the landings, for I was awake, and on the look-out, whenever the boat stopped. I never trust these yer things to other folks."

This speech was addressed to Tom quite confidentially, as if it was something that would be specially interesting to him. Tom made no answer.

The trader searched the boat from stem to stern, among boxes, bales and barrels, around the machinery, by the chimneys, in vain.

"Now, I say, Tom, be fair about this yer," he said, when, after a fruitless search, he came where Tom was standing. "You know something about it, now. Don't tell me,—I know you do. I saw the gal stretched out here about ten o'clock, and ag'in at twelve, and ag'in between one and two; and then at four she was gone, and you was a sleeping right there all the time. Now, you know something,—you can't help it."

"Well, Mas'r," said Tom, "towards morning something brushed by me, and I kinder half woke; and then I hearn a great splash, and then I clare woke up, and the gal was gone. That 's all I know on 't."

The trader was not shocked nor amazed; because, as we said before, he was used to a great many things that you are not used to. Even the awful presence of Death struck no solemn chill upon him. He had seen Death many times,— met him in the way of trade, and got acquainted with him,—and he only thought of him as a hard customer, that embarrassed his property operations very unfairly; and so he only swore that the gal was a baggage, and that he was devilish unlucky, and that, if things went on in this way, he should not make a cent on the trip. In short, he seemed to consider himself an ill-used man, decidedly; but there was no help for it, as the woman had escaped into a state which *never will* give up a fugitive,—not even at the demand of the whole glorious Union. The trader, therefore, sat discontentedly down, with his little account-book, and put down the missing body and soul under the head of *losses*!

"He 's a shocking creature, is n't he,—this trader? so unfeeling! It 's dreadful, really!"

"O, but nobody thinks anything of these traders! They are universally despised,—never received into any decent society."

But who, sir, makes the trader? Who is most to blame? The enlightened, cultivated, intelligent man, who supports the system of which the trader is the inevitable result, or the poor trader himself? You make the public sentiment that calls for his trade, that debauches and depraves him, till he feels no shame in it; and in what are you better than he?

Are you educated and he ignorant, you high and he low, you refined and he coarse, you talented and he simple?

In the day of a future Judgment, these very considerations may make it more tolerable for him than for you.

In concluding these little incidents of lawful trade, we must beg the world not to think that American legislators are entirely destitute of humanity, as might, perhaps, be unfairly inferred from the great efforts made in our national body to protect and perpetuate this species of traffic.

Who does not know how our great men are outdoing themselves, in declaiming against the *foreign* slave-trade. There are a perfect host of Clarksons and Wilberforces risen up among us on that subject, most edifying to hear and behold. Trading negroes from Africa, dear reader, is so horrid! It is not to be thought of! But trading them from Kentucky,—that 's quite another thing!

## XIII.
## *The Quaker Settlement*

A quiet scene now rises before us. A large, roomy, neatly-painted kitchen, its yellow floor glossy and smooth, and without a particle of dust; a neat, well-blacked cooking-stove; rows of shining tin, suggestive of unmentionable good things to the appetite; glossy green wood chairs, old and firm; a small flag-bottomed rocking-chair, with a patch-work cushion in it, neatly contrived out of small pieces of different colored woollen goods, and a larger sized one, motherly and old, whose wide arms breathed hospitable invitation, seconded by the solicitation of its feather cushions,—a real comfortable, persuasive old chair, and worth, in the way of honest, homely enjoyment, a dozen of your plush or brochetelle drawing-room gentry; and in the chair, gently swaying back and forward, her eyes bent on some fine sewing, sat our old friend Eliza. Yes, there she is, paler and thinner than in her Kentucky home, with a world of quiet sorrow lying under the shadow of her long eyelashes, and marking the outine of her gentle mouth! It was plain to see how old and firm the girlish heart was grown under the discipline of heavy sorrow; and when, anon, her large dark eye was raised to follow the gambols of her little Harry, who was sporting, like some tropical butterfly, hither and thither over the floor, she showed a depth of firmness and steady resolve that was never there in her earlier and happier days.

By her side sat a woman with a bright tin pan in her lap, into which she was carefully sorting some dried peaches. She might be fifty-five or sixty; but hers was one of those faces that time seems to touch only to brighten and adorn. The snowy lisse crape cap, made after the strait Quaker pattern,—the plain white muslin handkerchief, lying in placid folds across her bosom,—the drab shawl and dress,— showed at once the community to which she belonged. Her face was round and rosy, with a healthful downy softness, suggestive of a ripe peach. Her hair, partially silvered by age, was parted smoothly back from a high placid forehead, on which time had written no inscription, except peace on earth, good will to men, and beneath shone a large pair of clear, honest, loving brown eyes; you only needed to look straight into them, to feel that you saw to the bottom of a heart as good and true as ever throbbed in woman's bosom. So much has been said and sung of beautiful young girls, why don't somebody wake up to the beauty of old women? If any want to get up an inspiration under this head, we refer them to our good friend Rachel Halliday, just as she sits there in her little rocking-chair. It had a turn for quacking and squeaking,—that chair had,—either from having taken cold in early life, or from some asthmatic affection, or perhaps from nervous derangement; but, as she gently swung backward and forward, the chair kept up a kind of subdued "creechy crawchy," that would have been intolerable in any other chair. But old Simeon Halliday often declared it was as good as any music to him, and the children all avowed that they would n't miss of hearing mother's chair for anything in the world. For why? for twenty years or more, nothing but loving words, and gentle moralities, and motherly loving kindness, had come from that chair;—head-aches and heart-aches innumerable had been cured there,—difficulties spiritual and temporal solved there,—all by one good, loving woman, God bless her!

"And so thee still thinks of going to Canada, Eliza?" she said, as she was quietly looking over her peaches.

"Yes, ma'am," said Eliza, firmly. "I must go onward. I dare not stop."

"And what 'll thee do, when thee gets there? Thee must think about that, my daughter."

"My daughter" came naturally from the lips of Rachel Halliday; for hers was just the face and form that made "mother" seem the most natural word in the world.

Eliza's hands trembled, and some tears fell on her fine work; but she answered, firmly,

"I shall do—anything I can find. I hope I can find something."

"Thee knows thee can stay here, as long as thee pleases," said Rachel.

"O, thank you," said Eliza, "but"—she pointed to Harry—"I can't sleep nights; I can't rest. Last night I dreamed I saw that man coming into the yard," she said, shuddering.

"Poor child!" said Rachel, wiping her eyes; "but thee must n't feel so. The Lord hath ordered it so that never hath a fugitive been stolen from our village. I trust thine will not be the first."

The door here opened, and a little short, round, pincushiony woman stood at the door, with a cheery, blooming face, like a ripe apple. She was dressed, like Rachel, in sober gray, with the muslin folded neatly across her round, plump little chest.

"Ruth Stedman," said Rachel, coming joyfully forward; "how is thee, Ruth?" she said, heartily taking both her hands.

"Nicely," said Ruth, taking off her little drab bonnet, and dusting it with her handkerchief, displaying, as she did so, a round little head, on which the Quaker cap sat with a sort of jaunty air, despite all the stroking and patting of the small fat hands, which were busily applied to arranging it. Certain stray locks of decidedly curly hair, too, had escaped here and there, and had to be coaxed and cajoled into their place again; and then the new comer, who might have been five-and-twenty, turned from the small looking-glass, before which she had been making these arrangements, and looked well pleased,—as most people who looked at her might have been,—for she was decidedly a wholesome, whole-hearted, chirruping little woman, as ever gladdened man's heart withal.

"Ruth, this friend is Eliza Harris; and this is the little boy I told thee of."

"I am glad to see thee, Eliza,—very," said Ruth, shaking hands, as if Eliza were an old friend she had long been expecting; "and this is thy dear boy,—I brought a cake for him," she said, holding out a little heart to the boy, who came up, gazing through his curls, and accepted it shyly.

"Where 's thy baby, Ruth?" said Rachel.

"O, he 's coming; but thy Mary caught him as I came in, and ran off with him to the barn, to show him to the children."

At this moment, the door opened, and Mary, an honest, rosy-looking girl, with large brown eyes, like her mother's, came in with the baby.

"Ah! ha!" said Rachel, coming up, and taking the great, white, fat fellow in her arms; "how good he looks, and how he does grow!"

"To be sure, he does," said little bustling Ruth, as she took the child, and began taking off a little blue silk hood, and various layers and wrappers of outer garments; and having given a twitch here, and a pull there, and variously adjusted and arranged him, and kissed him heartily, she set him on the floor to collect his thoughts. Baby seemed quite used to this mode of proceeding, for he put this thumb in his mouth (as if it were quite a thing of course), and seemed soon absorbed in his own reflections, while the mother seated herself, and taking out a long stocking of mixed blue and white yarn, began to knit with briskness.

"Mary, thee 'd better fill the kettle, had n't thee?" gently suggested the mother.

Mary took the kettle to the well, and soon reäppearing, placed it over the stove, where it was soon purring and steaming, a sort of censer of hospitality and good cheer. The peaches, moreover, in obedience to a few gentle whispers from Rachel, were soon deposited, by the same hand, in a stew-pan over the fire.

Rachel now took down a snowy moulding-board, and, tying on an apron, proceeded quietly to making up some biscuits, first saying to Mary,—"Mary, had n't thee better tell John to get a chicken ready?" and Mary disappeared accordingly.

"And how is Abigail Peters?" said Rachel, as she went on with her biscuits.

"O, she 's better," said Ruth; "I was in, this morning; made the bed, tidied up the house. Leah Hills went in, this afternoon, and baked bread and pies enough to last some days; and I engaged to go back to get her up, this evening."

"I will go in to-morrow, and do any cleaning there may be, and look over the mending," said Rachel.

"Ah! that is well," said Ruth. "I 've heard," she added, "that Hannah Stanwood is sick. John was up there, last night,—I must go there to-morrow."

"John can come in here to his meals, if thee needs to stay all day," suggested Rachel.

"Thank thee, Rachel; will see, to-morrow; but, here comes Simeon."

Simeon Halliday, a tall, straight, muscular man, in drab coat and pantaloons, and broad-brimmed hat, now entered.

"How is thee, Ruth?" he said, warmly, as he spread his broad open hand for her little fat palm; "and how is John?"

"O! John is well, and all the rest of our folks," said Ruth, cheerily.

"Any news, father?" said Rachel, as she was putting her biscuits into the oven.

"Peter Stebbins told me that they should be along to-night, with *friends*," said Simeon, significantly, as he was washing his hands at a neat sink, in a little back porch.

"Indeed!" said Rachel, looking thoughtfully, and glancing at Eliza.

"Did thee say thy name was Harris?" said Simeon to Eliza, as he reëntered.

Rachel glanced quickly at her husband, as Eliza tremulously answered "yes;" her fears, ever uppermost, suggesting that possibly there might be advertisements out for her.

"Mother!" said Simeon, standing in the porch, and calling Rachel out.

"What does thee want, father?" said Rachel, rubbing her floury hands, as she went into the porch.

"This child's husband is in the settlement, and will be here to-night," said Simeon.

"Now, thee does n't say that, father?" said Rachel, all her face radiant with joy.

"It 's really true. Peter was down yesterday, with the wagon, to the other stand, and there he found an old woman and two men; and one said his name was George Harris; and, from what he told of his history, I am certain who he is. He is a bright, likely fellow, too."

"Shall we tell her now?" said Simeon.

"Let 's tell Ruth," said Rachel. "Here, Ruth,—come here."

Ruth laid down her knitting-work, and was in the back porch in a moment.

"Ruth, what does thee think?" said Rachel. "Father says Eliza's husband is in the last company, and will be here to-night."

A burst of joy from the little Quakeress interrupted the speech. She gave such a bound from the floor, as she clapped her little hands, that two stray curls fell from under her Quaker cap, and lay brightly on her white neckerchief.

"Hush thee, dear!" said Rachel, gently; "hush, Ruth! Tell us, shall we tell her now?"

"Now! to be sure,—this very minute. Why, now, suppose 't was my John, how should I feel? Do tell her, right off."

"Thee uses thyself only to learn how to love thy neighbor, Ruth," said Simeon, looking, with a beaming face, on Ruth.

"To be sure. Is n't it what we are made for? If I did n't love John and the baby, I should not know how to feel for her. Come, now, do tell her,—do!" and she laid her hands persuasively on Rachel's arm. "Take her into thy bed-room, there, and let me fry the chicken while thee does it."

Rachel came out into the kitchen, where Eliza was sewing, and opening the door of a small bed-room, said, gently, "Come in here with me, my daughter; I have news to tell thee."

The blood flushed in Eliza's pale face; she rose, trembling with nervous anxiety, and looked towards her boy.

"No, no," said little Ruth, darting up, and seizing her hands. "Never thee fear; it 's good news, Eliza,—go in, go in!" And she gently pushed her to the door, which closed after her; and then, turning round, she caught little Harry in her arms, and began kissing him.

"Thee 'll see thy father, little one. Does thee know it? Thy father is coming," she said, over and over again, as the boy looked wonderingly at her.

Meanwhile, within the door, another scene was going on. Rachel Halliday drew Eliza toward her, and said, "The Lord hath had mercy on thee, daughter; thy husband hath escaped from the house of bondage."

The blood flushed to Eliza's cheek in a sudden glow, and went back to her heart with as sudden a rush. She sat down, pale and faint.

"Have courage, child," said Rachel, laying her hand on her head. "He is among friends, who will bring him here to-night."

"To-night!" Eliza repeated, "to-night!" The words lost all meaing to her; her head was dreamy and confused; all was mist for a moment.

———————

When she awoke, she found herself snugly tucked up on the bed, with a blanket over her, and little Ruth rubbing her hands with camphor. She opened her eyes in a state of dreamy, delicious languor, such as one has who has long been bearing a heavy load, and now feels it gone, and would rest. The tension of the nerves, which had never ceased a moment since the first hour of her flight, had given way, and a strange feeling of security and rest came over her; and, as she lay, with her large, dark eyes open, she followed, as in a quiet dream, the motions of those about her. She saw the door open into the other room; saw the supper-table, with its snowy cloth; heard the dreamy murmur of the singing tea-kettle; saw Ruth tripping backward and forward, with plates of cake and sauces of preserves, and ever and anon stopping to put a cake into Harry's hand, or pat his head, or twine his long curls round her snowy fingers. She saw the ample, motherly form of Rachel, as she ever and anon came to the bedside, and smoothed and arranged something about the bedclothes, and gave a tuck here and there, by way of expressing her good-will; and was conscious of a kind of sunshine beaming down upon her from her large, clear, brown eyes. She saw Ruth's husband come in,—saw her fly up to him, and commence whispering very earnestly, ever and anon, with impressive gesture, pointing her little finger toward the room. She saw her, with the baby in her arms, sitting down to tea; she saw them all at table, and little Harry in a high chair, under the shadow of Rachel's ample wing; there were low murmurs of talk, gentle tinkling of tea-spoons, and muscial clatter of cups and saucers, and all mingled in a delightful dream of rest; and Eliza slept, as she had not slept before, since the fearful midnight hour when she had taken her child and fled through the frosty star-light.

She dreamed of a beautiful country,—a land, it seemed to her, of rest,—green shores, pleasant islands, and beautifully glittering water; and there, in a house which kind voices told her was a home, she saw her boy playing, a free and happy child. She heard her husband's footsteps; she felt him coming nearer; his arms were around her, his tears falling on her face, and she awoke! It was no dream. The daylight had long faded; her child lay calmly sleeping by her side;

a candle was burning dimly on the stand, and her husband was sobbing by her pillow.

———————

The next morning was a cheerful one at the Quaker house. "Mother" was up betimes, and surrounded by busy girls and boys, whom we had scarce time to introduce to our readers yesterday, and who all moved obediently to Rachel's gentle "Thee had better," or more gentle "Had n't thee better?" in the work of getting breakfast; for a breakfast in the luxurious valleys of Indiana is a thing complicated and multiform, and, like picking up the rose-leaves and trimming the bushes in Paradise, asking other hands than those of the original mother. While, therefore, John ran to the spring for fresh water, and Simeon the second sifted meal for corn-cakes, and Mary ground coffee, Rachel moved gently and quietly about, making biscuits, cutting up chicken, and diffusing a sort of sunny radiance over the whole proceeding generally. If there was any danger of friction or collision from the ill-regulated zeal of so many operators, her gentle "Come! come!" or "I would n't, now," was quite sufficient to allay the difficulty. Bards have written of the cestus of Venus, that turned the heads of all the world in successive generations. We had rather, for our part, have the cestus of Rachel Halliday, that kept heads from being turned, and made everything go on harmoniously. We think it is more suited to our modern days, decidedly.

While all other preparations were going on, Simeon the elder stood in his shirt-sleeves before a little looking-glass in the corner, engaged in the anti-patriarchal operation of shaving. Everything went on so sociably, so quietly, so harmoniously, in the great kitchen,—it seemed so pleasant to every one to do just what they were doing, there was such an atmosphere of mutual confidence and good fellowship everywhere,—even the knives and forks had a social clatter as they went on to the table; and the chicken and ham had a cheerful and joyous fizzle in the pan, as if they rather enjoyed being cooked than otherwise;—and when George and Eliza and little Harry came out, they met such a hearty, rejoicing welcome, no wonder it seemed to them like a dream.

At last, they were all seated at breakfast, while Mary stood at the stove, baking griddle-cakes, which, as they gained the true exact golden-brown tint of perfection, were transferred quite handily to the table.

Rachel never looked so truly and benignly happy as at the head of her table. There was so much motherliness and fullheartedness even in the way she passed a plate of cakes or poured a cup of coffee, that it seemed to put a spirit into the food and drink she offered.

It was the first time that ever George had sat down on equal terms at any white man's table; and he sat down, at first, with some constraint and awkwardness; but they all exhaled and went off like fog, in the genial morning rays of this simple, overflowing kindness.

This, indeed, was a home,—*home*,—a word that George had never yet known a meaning for; and a belief in God, and trust in his providence, began to encircle his heart, as, with a golden cloud of protection and confidence, dark, misanthropic, pining, atheistic doubts, and fierce despair, melted away before the light of a living Gospel, breathed in living faces, preached by a thousand unconscious acts of love and good will, which, like the cup of cold water given in the name of a disciple, shall never lose their reward.

"Father, what if thee should get found out again?" said Simeon second, as he buttered his cake.

"I should pay my fine," said Simeon, quietly.

"But what if they put thee in prison?"

"Could n't thee and mother manage the farm?" said Simeon, smiling.

"Mother can do almost everything," said the boy. "But is n't it a shame to make such laws?"

"Thee must n't speak evil of thy rulers, Simeon," said his father, gravely. "The Lord only gives us our worldly goods that we may do justice and mercy; if our rulers require a price of us for it, we must deliver it up."

"Well, I hate those old slaveholders!" said the boy, who felt as unchristian as became any modern reformer.

"I am surprised at thee, son," said Simeon; "thy mother never taught thee so. I would do even the same for the slaveholder as for the slave, if the Lord brought him to my door in affliction."

Simeon second blushed scarlet; but his mother only smiled, and said, "Simeon is my good boy; he will grow older, by and by, and then he will be like his father."

"I hope, my good sir, that you are not exposed to any difficulty on our account," said George, anxiously.

"Fear nothing, George, for therefore are we sent into the world. If we would not meet trouble for a good cause, we were not worthy of our name."

"But, for *me*," said George, "I could not bear it."

"Fear not, then, friend George; it is not for thee, but for God and man, we do it," said Simeon. "And now thou must lie by quietly this day, and to-night, at ten o'clock, Phineas Fletcher will carry thee onward to the next stand,—thee and the rest of thy company. The pursuers are hard after thee; we must not delay."

"If that is the case, why wait till evening?" said George.

"Thou art safe here by daylight, for every one in the settlement is a Friend, and all are watching. It has been found safer to travel by night."

## XIV.
### *Evangeline*

"A young star! which shone
O'er life—too sweet an image for such glass!
A lovely being, scarcely formed or moulded;
A rose with all its sweetest leaves yet folded."

The Mississippi! How, as by an enchanted wand, have its scenes been changed, since Chateaubriand wrote his prose-poetic description of it, as a river of mighty, unbroken solitudes, rolling amid undreamed wonders of vegetable and animal existence.

But, as in an hour, this river of dreams and wild romance has emerged to a reality scarcely less visionary and splendid. What other river of the world bears on its bosom to the ocean the wealth and enterprise of such another country?— a country whose products embrace all between the tropics and the poles! Those turbid waters, hurrying, foaming, tearing along, an apt resemblance of that head- long tide of business which is poured along its wave by a race more vehement and energetic than any the old world ever saw. Ah! would that they did not also bear along a more fearful freight,—the tears of the oppressed, the sighs of the helpless, the bitter prayers of poor, ignorant hearts to an unknown God—un- known, unseen and silent, but who will yet "come out of his place to save all the poor of the earth!"

The slanting light of the setting sun quivers on the sea–like expanse of the river; the shivery canes, and the tall, dark cypress, hung with wreaths of dark, fu- nereal moss, glow in the golden ray, as the heavily laden steamboat marches on- ward.

Piled with cotton–bales, from many a plantation, up over deck and sides, till she seems in the distance a square, massive block of gray, she moves heavily on- ward to the nearing mart. We must look some time among its crowded decks be- fore we shall find again our humble friend Tom. High on the upper deck, in a little nook among the everywhere predominant cotton–bales, at last we may find him.

Partly from confidence inspired by Mr. Shelby's representations, and partly from the remarkably inoffensive and quiet character of the man, Tom had insen- sibly won his way far into the confidence even of such a man as Haley.

At first he had watched him narrowly through the day, and never allowed him to sleep at night unfettered; but the uncomplaining patience and apparent contentment of Tom's manner led him gradually to discontinue these restraints, and for some time Tom had enjoyed a sort of parole of honor, being permitted to come and go freely where he pleased on the boat.

Ever quiet and obliging, and more than ready to lend a hand in every emer- gency which occurred among the workmen below, he had won the good opinion of all the hands, and spent many hours in helping them with as hearty a good will as ever he worked on a Kentucky farm.

When there seemed to be nothing for him to do, he would climb to a nook among the cotton–bales of the upper deck, and busy himself in studying over his Bible,—and it is there we see him now.

For a hundred or more miles above New Orleans, the river is higher than the surrounding country, and rolls its tremendous volume between massive levees twenty feet in height. The traveller from the deck of the steamer, as from some floating castle top, overlooks the whole country for miles and miles around. Tom, therefore, had spread out full before him, in plantation after plantation, a map of the life to which he was approaching.

He saw the distant slaves at their toil; he saw afar their villages of huts gleam- ing out in long rows on many a plantation, distant from the stately mansions and pleasure–grounds of the master;—and as the moving picture passed on, his poor, foolish heart would be turning backward to the Kentucky farm, with its old shadowy beeches,—to the master's house, with its wide, cool halls, and, near by, the little cabin, overgrown with the multiflora and bignonia. There he seemed to see familiar faces of comrades, who had grown up with him from infancy; he saw his busy wife, bustling in her preparations for his evening meals; he heard the merry laugh of his boys at their play, and the chirrup of the baby at his knee; and then, with a start, all faded, and he saw again the cane–brakes and cypresses and gliding plantations, and heard again the creaking and groaning of the machinery, all telling him too plainly that all that phase of life had gone by forever.

In such a case, you write to your wife, and send messages to your children; but Tom could not write,—the mail for him had no existence, and the gulf of separation was unbridged by even a friendly word or signal.

Is it strange, then, that some tears fall on the pages of his Bible, as he lays it on the cotton–bale, and, with patient finger, threading his slow way from word to word, traces out its promises? Having learned late in life, Tom was but a slow reader, and passed on laboriously from verse to verse. Fortunate for him was it that the book he was intent on was one which slow reading cannot injure,—nay, one whose words, like ingots of gold, seem often to need to be weighed separately, that the mind may take in their priceless value. Let us follow him a moment, as, pointing to each word, and pronouncing each half aloud, he reads,

"Let—not—your—heart—be—troubled.   In—my—Father's—house—are— many—mansions. I—go—to—prepare—a—place—for—you."

Cicero, when he buried his darling and only daughter, had a heart as full of honest grief as poor Tom's,—perhaps no fuller, for both were only men;—but Cicero could pause over no such sublime words of hope, and look to no such future reünion; and if he *had* seen them, ten to one he would not have believed,— he must fill his head first with a thousand questions of authenticity of manuscript, and correctness of translation. But, to poor Tom, there it lay, just what he needed, so evidently true and divine that the possibility of a question never entered his simple head. It must be true; for, if not true, how could he live?

As for Tom's Bible, though it had no annotations and helps in margin from learned commentators, still it had been embellished with certain way–marks and guide–boards of Tom's own invention, and which helped him more than the most learned expositions could have done. It had been his custom to get the Bible read to him by his master's children, in particular by young Master George; and, as they read, he would designate, by bold, strong marks and dashes, with pen and ink, the passages which more particularly gratified his ear or affected his heart. His Bible was thus marked through, from one end to the other, with a variety of styles and designations; so he could in a moment seize upon his favorite passages, without the labor of spelling out what lay between them;—and while it lay there before him, every passage breathing of some old home scene, and recalling some past enjoyment, his Bible seemed to him all of this life that remained, as well as the promise of a future one.

Among the passengers on the boat was a young gentleman of fortune and family, resident in New Orleans, who bore the name of St. Clare. He had with him a daughter between five and six years of age, together with a lady who seemed to claim relationship to both, and to have the little one especially under her charge.

Tom had often caught glimpses of this little girl,—for she was one of those busy, tripping creatures, that can be no more contained in one place than a sunbeam or a summer breeze,—nor was she one that, once seen, could be easily forgotten.

Her form was the perfection of childish beauty, without its usual chubbiness and squareness of outline. There was about it an undulating and aërial grace, such as one might dream of for some mythic and allegorical being. Her face was remarkable less for its perfect beauty of feature than for a singular and dreamy earnestness of expression, which made the ideal start when they looked at her, and by which the dullest and most literal were impressed, without exactly knowing why. The shape of her head and the turn of her neck and bust was peculiarly noble, and the long golden–brown hair that floated like a cloud around it, the deep spiritual gravity of her violet blue eyes, shaded by heavy fringes of golden brown,—all marked her out from other children, and made every one turn and look after her, as she glided hither and thither on the boat. Nevertheless, the little one was not what you would have called either a grave child or a sad one. On the contrary, an airy and innocent playfulness seemed to flicker like the shadow of summer leaves over her childish face, and around her buoyant figure. She was always in motion, always with a half smile on her rosy mouth, flying hither and thither, with an undulating and cloud–like tread, singing to herself as she moved as in a happy dream. Her father and female guardian were incessantly busy in pursuit of her,—but, when caught, she melted from them again like a summer cloud; and as no word of chiding or reproof ever fell on her ear for whatever she chose to do, she pursued her own way all over the boat. Always dressed in white, she seemed to move like a shadow through all sorts of places, without contracting spot or stain; and there was not a corner or nook, above or below, where those fairy footsteps had not glided, and that visionary golden head, with its deep blue eyes, fleeted along.

The fireman, as he looked up from his sweaty toil, sometimes found those eyes looking wonderingly into the raging depths of the furnace, and fearfully and pityingly at him, as if she thought him in some dreadful danger. Anon the steersman at the wheel paused and smiled, as the picture–like head gleamed through the window of the round house, and in a moment was gone again. A thousand times a day rough voices blessed her, and smiles of unwonted softness stole over hard faces, as she passed; and when she tripped fearlessly over dangerous places, rough, sooty hands were stretched involuntarily out to save her, and smooth her path.

Tom, who had the soft, impressible nature of his kindly race, ever yearning toward the simple and childlike, watched the little creature with daily increasing interest. To him she seemed something almost divine; and whenever her golden head and deep blue eyes peered out upon him from behind some dusky cotton–bale, or looked down upon him over some ridge of packages, he half believed that he saw one of the angels stepped out of his New Testament.

Often and often she walked mournfully round the place where Haley's gang of men and women sat in their chains. She would glide in among them, and look at them with an air of perplexed and sorrowful earnestness; and sometimes she would lift their chains with her slender hands, and then sigh wofully, as she glided away. Several times she appeared suddenly among them, with her hands full of candy, nuts, and oranges, which she would distribute joyfully to them, and then be gone again.

Tom watched the little lady a great deal, before he ventured on any overtures towards acquaintanceship. He knew an abundance of simple acts to propitiate and invite the approaches of the little people, and he resolved to play his part right skilfully. He could cut cunning little baskets out of cherry–stones, could make grotesque faces on hickory–nuts, or odd–jumping figures out of elder–pith, and he was a very Pan in the manufacture of whistles of all sizes and sorts. His pockets were full of miscellaneous articles of attraction, which he had hoarded in days of old for his master's children, and which he now produced, with commendable prudence and economy, one by one, as overtures for acquaintance and friendship.

The little one was shy, for all her busy interest in everything going on, and it was not easy to tame her. For a while, she would perch like a canary–bird on some box or package near Tom, while busy in the little arts afore–named, and take from him, with a kind of grave bashfulness, the little articles he offered. But at last they got on quite confidential terms.

"What 's little missy's name?" said Tom, at last, when he thought matters were ripe to push such an inquiry.

"Evangeline St. Clare," said the little one, "though papa and everybody else call me Eva. Now, what 's your name?"

"My name 's Tom; the little chil'en used to call me Uncle Tom, way back thar in Kentucky."

"Then I mean to call you Uncle Tom, because, you see, I like you," said Eva. "So, Uncle Tom, where are you going?"

"I don't know, Miss Eva."

"Don't know?" said Eva.

"No. I am going to be sold to somebody. I don't know who."

"My papa can buy you," said Eva, quickly; "and if he buys you, you will have good times. I mean to ask him to, this very day."

"Thank you, my little lady," said Tom.

The boat here stopped at a small landing to take in wood, and Eva, hearing her father's voice, bounded nimbly away. Tom rose up, and went forward to offer his service in wooding, and soon was busy among the hands.

Eva and her father were standing together by the railings to see the boat start from the landing–place, the wheel had made two or three revolutions in the water, when, by some sudden movement, the little one suddenly lost her balance, and fell sheer over the side of the boat into the water. Her father, scarce knowing what he did, was plunging in after her, but was held back by some behind him, who saw that more efficient aid had followed his child.

Tom was standing just under her on the lower deck, as she fell. He saw her strike the water, and sink, and was after her in a moment. A broad–chested, strong–armed fellow, it was nothing for him to keep afloat in the water, till, in a moment or two, the child rose to the surface, and he caught her in his arms, and, swimming with her to the boat–side, handed her up, all dripping, to the grasp of hundreds of hands, which, as if they had all belonged to one man, were stretched eagerly out to receive her. A few moments more, and her father bore her, dripping and senseless, to the ladies' cabin, where, as is usual in cases of the kind, there ensued a very well–meaning and kind–hearted strife among the female occupants generally, as to who should do the most things to make a disturbance, and to hinder her recovery in every way possible.

---

It was a sultry, close day, the next day, as the steamer drew near to New Orleans. A general bustle of expectation and preparation was spread through the boat; in the cabin, one and another were gathering their things together, and arranging them, preparatory to going ashore. The steward and chambermaid, and all, were busily engaged in cleaning, furbishing, and arranging the splendid boat, preparatory to a grand entree.

On the lower deck sat our friend Tom, with his arms folded, and anxiously, from time to time, turning his eyes towards a group on the other side of the boat.

There stood the fair Evangeline, a little paler than the day before, but otherwise exhibiting no traces of the accident which had befallen her. A graceful, elegantly–formed young man stood by her, carlessly leaning one elbow on a bale of cotton, while a large pocket–book lay open before him. It was quite evident, at a glance, that the gentleman was Eva's father. There was the same noble cast of head, the same large blue eyes, the same golden–brown hair; yet the expression was wholly different. In the large, clear blue eyes, though in form and color exactly similar, there was wanting that misty, dreamy depth of expression; all was clear, bold, and bright, but with a light wholly of this world: the beautifully cut mouth had a proud and somewhat sarcastic expression, while an air of free–and–easy superiority sat not ungracefully in every turn and movement of his fine form. He was listening, with a good–humored, negligent air, half comic, half contemptuous, to Haley, who was very volubly expatiating on the quality of the article for which they were bargaining.

"All the moral and Christian virtues bound in black morocco, complete!" he said, when Haley had finished. "Well, now, my good fellow, what 's the damage, as they say in Kentucky; in short, what 's to be paid out for this business? How much are you going to cheat me, now? Out with it!"

"Wal," said Haley, "if I should say thirteen hundred dollars for that ar fellow, I should n't but just save myself; I should n't, now, re'ly."

"Poor fellow!" said the young man, fixing his keen, mocking blue eye on him; "but I suppose you 'd let me have him for that, out of a particular regard for me."

"Well, the young lady here seems to be sot on him, and nat'lly enough."

"O! certainly, there 's a call on your benevolence, my friend. Now, as a matter of Christian charity, how cheap could you afford to let him go, to oblige a young lady that 's particular sot on him?"

"Wal, now, just think on 't," said the trader; "just look at them limbs,— broad–chested, strong as a horse. Look at his head; them high forrads allays shows calculatin niggers, that 'll do any kind o' thing. I 've marked that ar. Now, a nigger of that ar heft and build is worth considerable, just, as you may say, for his body, supposin he 's stupid; but come to put in his calculatin faculties, and them which I can show he has oncommon, why, of course, it makes him come higher. Why, that ar fellow managed his master's whole farm. He has a strornary talent for business."

"Bad, bad, very bad; knows altogether too much!" said the young man, with the same mocking smile playing about his mouth. "Never will do, in the world. Your smart fellows are always running off, stealing horses, and raising the devil generally. I think you 'll have to take off a couple of hundred for his smartness."

"Wal, there might be something in that ar, if it warnt for his character; but I can show recommends from his master and others, to prove he is one of your real pious,—the most humble, prayin, pious crittur ye ever did see. Why, he 's been called a preacher in them parts he came from."

"And I might use him for a family chaplain, possibly," added the young man, dryly. "That 's quite an idea. Religion is a remarkably scarce article at our house."

"You 're joking, now."

"How do you know I am? Did n't you just warrant him for a preacher? Has he been examined by any synod or council? Come, hand over your papers."

If the trader had not been sure, by a certain good–humored twinkle in the large blue eye, that all this banter was sure, in the long run, to turn out a cash concern, he might have been somewhat out of patience; as it was, he laid down a greasy pocket–book on the cotton–bales, and began anxiously studying over certain papers in it, the young man standing by, the while, looking down on him with an air of careless, easy drollery.

"Papa, do buy him! it 's no matter what you pay," whispered Eva, softly, getting up on a package, and putting her arm around her father's neck. "You have money enough, I know. I want him."

"What for, pussy? Are you going to use him for a rattlebox, or a rocking–horse, or what?"

"I want to make him happy."

"An original reason, certainly."

Here the trader handed up a certificate, signed by Mr. Shelby, which the young man took with the tips of his long fingers, and glanced over carelessly.

"A gentlemanly hand," he said, "and well spelt, too. Well, now, but I 'm not sure, after all, about this religion," said he, the old wicked expression returning to his eye; "the country is almost ruined with pious white people: such pious politicians as we have just before elections,—such pious goings on in all departments of church and state, that a fellow does not know who 'll cheat him next. I don't know, either, about religion's being up in the market, just now. I have not looked in the papers lately, to see how it sells. How many hundred dollars, now, do you put on for this religion?"

"You like to be a jokin, now," said the trader; "but, then, there 's *sense* under all that ar. I know there 's differences in religion. Some kinds is mis'rable: there 's your meetin pious; there 's your singin, roarin pious; them ar an't no account, in black or white;—but these rayly is; and I 've seen it in niggers as often as any, your rail softly, quiet, stiddy, honest, pious, that the hull world could n't tempt 'em to do nothing that they thinks is wrong; and ye see in this letter what Tom's old master says about him."

"Now," said the young man, stooping gravely over his book of bills, "if you can assure me that I really can buy *this* kind of pious, and that it will be set down to my account in the book up above, as something belonging to me, I would n't care if I did go a little extra for it. How d' ye say?"

"Wal, raily, I can't do that," said the trader. "I 'm a thinkin that every man 'll have to hang on his own hook, in them ar quarters."

"Rather hard on a fellow that pays extra on religion, and can't trade with it in the state where he wants it most, an't it, now?" said the young man, who had been making out a roll of bills while he was speaking. "There, count your money, old boy!" he added, as he handed the roll to the trader.

"All right," said Haley, his face beaming with delight; and pulling out an old inkhorn, he proceeded to fill out a bill of sale, which, in a few moments, he handed to the young man.

"I wonder, now, if I was divided up and inventoried," said the latter, as he ran over the paper, "how much I might bring. Say so much for the shape of my head, so much for a high forehead, so much for arms, and hands, and legs, and then so much for education, learning, talent, honesty, religion! Bless me! there would be small charge on that last, I 'm thinking. But come, Eva," he said; and taking the hand of his daughter, he stepped across the boat, and carelessly putting the tip of his finger under Tom's chin, said, good–humoredly, "Look up, Tom, and see how you like your new master."

Tom looked up. It was not in nature to look into that gay, young, handsome face, without a feeling of pleasure; and Tom felt the tears start in his eyes as he said, heartily, "God bless you, Mas'r!"

"Well, I hope he will. What 's your name? Tom? Quite as likely to do it for your asking as mine, from all accounts. Can you drive horses, Tom?"

"I 've been allays used to horses," said Tom. "Mas'r Shelby raised heaps on 'em."

"Well, I think I shall put you in coachy, on condition that you won't be drunk more than once a week, unless in cases of emergency, Tom."

Tom looked surprised, and rather hurt, and said, "I never drink, Mas'r."

"I 've heard that story before, Tom; but then we 'll see. It will be a special accommodation to all concerned, if you don't. Never mind, my boy," he added, good–humoredly, seeing Tom still looked grave; "I don't doubt you mean to do well."

"I sartin do, Mas'r," said Tom.

"And you shall have good times," said Eva. "Papa is very good to everybody, only he always will laugh at them."

"Papa is much obliged to you for his recommendation," said St. Clare, laughing, as he turned on his heel and walked away.

## XV.
### Of Tom's New Master, and Various Other Matters

Since the thread of our humble hero's life has now become interwoven with that of higher ones, it is necessary to give some brief introduction to them.

Augustine St. Clare was the son of a wealthy planter of Louisiana. The family had its origin in Canada. Of two brothers, very similar in temperament and character, one had settled on a flourishing farm in Vermont, and the other became an opulent planter in Louisiana. The mother of Augustine was a Huguenot French lady, whose family had emigrated to Louisiana during the days of its early settlement. Augustine and another brother were the only children of their parents. Having inherited from his mother an exceeding delicacy of constitution, he was, at the instance of physicians, during many years of his boyhood, sent to the care of his uncle in Vermont, in order that his constitution might be strengthened by the cold of a more bracing climate.

In childhood, he was remarkable for an extreme and marked sensitiveness of character, more akin to the softness of woman than the ordinary hardness of his own sex. Time, however, overgrew this softness with the rough bark of manhood, and but few knew how living and fresh it still lay at the core. His talents were of the very first order, although his mind showed a preference always for the ideal and the aesthetic, and there was about him that repugnance to the actual business of life which is the common result of this balance of the faculties. Soon after the completion of his college course, his whole nature was kindled into one intense and passionate effervescence of romantic passion. His hour came,—the hour that comes only once; his star rose in the horizon,—that star that rises so often in vain, to be remembered only as a thing of dreams; and it rose for him in vain. To drop the figure,—he saw and won the love of a high minded and beautiful woman, in one of the northern states, and they were affianced. He returned south to make arrangements for their marriage, when, most unexpectedly, his letters were returned to him by mail, with a short note from her guardian, stating to him that ere this reached him the lady would be the wife of another. Stung to madness, he vainly hoped, as many another has done, to fling the whole thing from his heart by one desperate effort. Too proud to supplicate or seek explanation, he threw himself at once into a whirl of fashionable society, and in a fortnight from the time of the fatal letter was the accepted lover of the reigning belle of the season; and as soon as arrangements could be made, he became the husband of a fine figure, a pair of bright dark eyes, and a hundred thousand dollars; and, of course, everybody thought him a happy fellow.

The married couple were enjoying their honeymoon, and entertaining a brilliant circle of friends in their splendid villa, near Lake Pontchartrain, when, one day, a letter was brought to him in *that* well–remembered writing. It was handed to him while he was in full tide of gay and successful conversation, in a whole room–full of company. He turned deadly pale when he saw the writing, but still preserved his composure, and finished the playful warfare of badinage which he was at the moment carrying on with a lady opposite; and, a short time after, was missed from the circle. In his room, alone, he opened and read the letter, now worse than idle and useless to be read. It was from her, giving a long account of a persecution to which she had been exposed by her guardian's family, to lead her to unite herself with their son: and she related how, for a long time, his letters had ceased to arrive; how she had written time and again, till she became weary and doubtful; how her health had failed under her anxieties, and how, at last, she had discovered the whole fraud which had been practised on them both.

The letter ended with expressions of hope and thankfulness, and professions of undying affection, which were more bitter than death to the unhappy young man. He wrote to her immediately:

"I have received yours,—but too late. I believed all I heard. I was desperate. *I am married*, and all is over. Only forget,—it is all that remains for either of us."

And thus ended the whole romance and ideal of life for Augustine St. Clare. But the *real* remained,—the *real*, like the flat, bare, oozy tide–mud, when the blue sparkling wave, with all its company of gliding boats and white–winged ships, its music of oars and chiming waters, has gone down, and there it lies, flat, slimy, bare,–exceedingly real.

Of course, in a novel, people's hearts break, and they die, and that is the end of it; and in a story this is very convenient. But in real life we do not die when all that makes life bright dies to us. There is a most busy and important round of eating, drinking, dressing, walking, visiting, buying, selling, talking, reading, and all that makes up what is commonly called *living*, yet to be gone through; and this yet remained to Augustine. Had his wife been a whole woman, she might yet have done something—as woman can—to mend the broken threads of life, and weave again into a tissue of brightness. But Marie St. Clare could not even see that they had been broken. As before stated, she consisted of a fine figure, a pair of splendid eyes, and a hundred thousand dollars; and none of these items were precisely the ones to minister to a mind diseased.

When Augustine, pale as death, was found lying on the sofa, and pleaded sudden sick–headache as the cause of his distress, she recommended to him to smell of hartshorn; and when the paleness and headache came on week after week, she only said that she never thought Mr. St. Clare was sickly; but it seems he was very liable to sick–headaches, and that it was a very unfortunate thing for her, because he did n't enjoy going into company with her, and it seemed odd to go so much alone, when they were just married. Augustine was glad in his heart that he had married so undiscerning a woman; but as the glosses and civilities of the honeymoon wore away, he discovered that a beautiful young woman, who has lived all her life to be caressed and waited on, might prove quite a hard mistress in domestic life. Marie never had possessed much capability of affection, or much sensibility, and the little that she had, had been merged into a most intense and unconscious selfishness; a selfishness the more hopeless, from its quiet obtuse-ness, its utter ignorance of any claims but her own. From her infancy, she had been surrounded with servants, who lived only to study her caprices; the idea that they had either feelings or rights had never dawned upon her, even in dis-tant perspective. Her father, whose only child she had been, had never denied her anything that lay within the compass of human possibility; and when she entered life, beautiful, accomplished, and an heiress, she had, of course, all the eligibles and non–eligibles of the other sex sighing at her feet, and she had no doubt that Augustine was a most fortunate man in having obtained her. It is a great mistake to suppose that a woman with no heart will be an easy creditor in the exchange of affection. There is not on earth a more merciless exactor of love from others than a thoroughly selfish woman; and the more unlovely she grows, the more jealously and scrupulously she exacts love, to the uttermost farthing. When, therefore, St. Clare began to drop off those gallantries and small attentions which flowed at first through the habitude of courtship, he found his sultana no way ready to resign her slave; there were abundance of tears, poutings, and small tempests, there were discontents, pinings, upbraidings. St. Clare was good–natured and self–indulgent, and sought to buy off with presents and flatteries; and when Marie became mother to a beautiful daughter, he really felt awakened, for a time, to something like tenderness.

St. Clare's mother had been a woman of uncommon elevation and purity of character, and he gave to this child his mother's name, fondly fancying that she would prove a reproduction of her image. The thing had been remarked with petulant jealously by his wife, and she regarded her husband's absorbing devotion to the child with suspicion and dislike; all that was given to her seemed so much taken from herself. From the time of the birth of this child, her health gradually sunk. A life of constant inaction, bodily and mental,—the friction of ceaseless ennui and discontent, united to the ordinary weakness which attended the period of maternity,—in course of a few years changed the blooming young belle into a yellow, faded, sickly woman, whose time was divided among a variety of fanciful diseases, and who considered herself, in every sense, the most ill–used and suffering person in existence.

There was no end of her various complaints; but her principal forte appeared to lie in sick–headache, which sometimes would confine her to her room three days out of six. As, of course, all family arrangements fell into the hands of servants, St. Clare found his menage anything but comfortable. His only daughter was exceedingly delicate, and he feared that, with no one to look after her and attend to her, her health and life might yet fall a sacrifice to her mother's inefficiency. He had taken her with him on a tour to Vermont, and had persuaded his cousin, Miss Ophelia St. Clare, to return with him to his southern residence; and they are now returning on this boat, where we have introduced them to our readers.

And now, while the distant domes and spires of New Orleans rise to our view, there is yet time for an introduction to Miss Ophelia.

Whoever has travelled in the New England States will remember, in some cool village, the large farm–house, with its clean–swept grassy yard, shaded by the dense and massive foliage of the sugar maple; and remember the air of order and stillness, of perpetuity and unchanging repose, that seemed to breathe over the whole place. Nothing lost, or out of order; not a picket loose in the fence, not a particle of litter in the turfy yard, with its clumps of lilac–bushes growing up under the windows. Within, he will remember wide, clean rooms, where nothing ever seems to be doing or going to be done, where everything is once and forever rigidly in place, and where all household arrangements move with the punctual exactness of the old clock in the corner. In the family "keeping–room," as it is termed, he will remember the staid, respectable old book–case, with its glass doors, where Rollin's History, Milton's Paradise Lost, Bunyan's Pilgrim's Progress, and Scott's Family Bible, stand side by side in decorous order, with multitudes of other books, equally solemn and respectable. There are no servants in the house, but the lady in the snowy cap, with the spectacles, who sits sewing every after-

noon among her daughters, as if nothing ever had been done, or were to be done,—
she and her girls, in some long–forgotten fore part of the day, *"did up the work,"*
and for the rest of the time, probably, at all hours when you would see them, it
is *"done up."* The old kitchen floor never seems stained or spotted; the tables, the
chairs, and the various cooking utensils, never seem deranged or disordered;
though three and sometimes four meals a day are got there, though the family
washing and ironing is there performed, and though pounds of butter and cheese
are in some silent and mysterious manner there brought into existence.

On such a farm, in such a house and family, Miss Ophelia had spent a quiet
existence of some forty–five years, when her cousin invited her to visit his southern mansion. The eldest of a large family, she was still considered by her father
and mother as one of "the children," and the proposal that she should go to *Orleans*
was a most momentous one to the family circle. The old gray–headed father took
down Morse's Atlas out of the book–case, and looked out the exact latitude and
longitude; and read Flint's Travels in the South and West, to make up his own
mind as to the nature of the country.

The good mother inquired, anxiously, "if Orleans was n't an awful wicked
place," saying, "that it seemed to her most equal to going to the Sandwich Islands,
or anywhere among the heathen."

It was known at the minister's, and at the doctor's, and at Miss Peabody's
milliner shop, that Ophelia St. Clare was "talking about" going away down to
Orleans with her cousin; and of course the whole village could do no less than
help this very important process of *talking about* the matter. The minister, who inclined strongly to abolitionist views, was quite doubtful whether such a step might
not tend somewhat to encourage the southerners in holding on to their slaves;
while the doctor, who was a stanch colonizationist, inclined to the opinion that
Miss Ophelia ought to go, to show the Orleans people that we don't think hardly
of them, after all. He was of opinion, in fact, that southern people needed encouraging. When, however, the fact that she had resolved to go was fully before
the public mind, she was solemnly invited out to tea by all her friends and neighbors for the space of a fortnight, and her prospects and plans duly canvassed and
inquired into. Miss Moseley, who came into the house to help to do the dress–making, acquired daily accessions of importance from the developments with regard
to Miss Ophelia's wardrobe which she had been enabled to make. It was credi-
bly ascertained that Squire Sinclare, as his name was commonly contracted in the
neighborhood, had counted out fifty dollars, and given them to Miss Ophelia, and
told her to buy any clothes she thought best; and that two new silk dresses, and
a bonnet, had been sent for from Boston. As to the propriety of this extraordinary
outlay, the public mind was divided,—some affirming that it was well enough,
all things considered, for once in one's life, and others stoutly affirming that the
money had better have been sent to the missionaries; but all parties agreed that
there had been no such parasol seen in those parts as had been sent on from New
York; and that she had one silk dress that might fairly be trusted to stand alone,
whatever might be said of its mistress. There were credible rumors, also, of a hem-
stitched pocket–handkerchief; and report even went so far as to state that Miss
Ophelia had one pocket–handkerchief with lace all around it,—it was even added

that it was worked in the corners; but this latter point was never satisfactorily as-certained, and remains, in fact, unsettled to this day.

Miss Ophelia, as you now behold her, stands before you, in a very shining brown linen travelling–dress, tall, square–formed, and angular. Her face was thin, and rather sharp in its outlines; the lips compressed, like those of a person who is in the habit of making up her mind definitely on all subjects; while the keen, dark eyes had a peculiarly searching, advised movement, and travelled over everything, as if they were looking for something to take care of.

All her movements were sharp, decided, and energetic; and, though she was never much of a talker, her words were remarkably direct, and to the purpose, when she did speak.

In her habits, she was a living impersonation of order, method, and exactness. In punctuality, she was as inevitable as a clock, and as inexorable as a railroad engine; and she held in most decided contempt and abomination anything of a contrary character.

The great sin of sins, in her eyes,—the sum of all evils,—was expressed by one very common and important word in her vocabulary—"shiftlessness." Her finale and ultimatum of contempt consisted in a very emphatic pronunciation of the word "shiftless;" and by this she characterized all modes of procedure which had not a direct and inevitable relation to accomplishment of some purpose then definitely had in mind. People who did nothing, or who did not know exactly what they were going to do, or who did not take the most direct way to accom-plish what they set their hands to, were objects of her entire contempt,—a con-tempt shown less frequently by anything she said, than by a kind of stony grimness, as if she scorned to say anything about the matter.

As to mental cultivation,—she had a clear, strong, active mind, was well and thoroughly read in history and the older English classics, and thought with great strength within certain narrow limits. Her theological tenets were all made up, labelled in most positive and distinct forms, and put by, like the bundles in her patch trunk; there were just so many of them, and there were never to be any more. So, also, were her ideas with regard to most matters of practical life,—such as housekeeping in all its branches, and the various political relations of her na-tive village. And, underlaying all, deeper than anything else, higher and broader, lay the strongest principle of her being—conscientiousness. Nowhere is conscience so dominant and all–absorbing as with New England women. It is the granite for-mation, which lies deepest, and rises out, even to the tops of the highest moun-tains.

Miss Ophelia was the absolute bond–slave of the *"ought."* Once make her cer-tain that the "path of duty," as she commonly phrased it, lay in any given direc-tion, and fire and water could not keep her from it. She would walk straight down into a well, or up to a loaded cannon's mouth, if she were only quite sure that there the path lay. Her standard of right was so high, so all–embracing, so minute, and making so few concessions to human frailty, that, though she strove with heroic ardor to reach it, she never actually did so, and of course was burdened with a constant and often harassing sense of deficiency;—this gave a severe and somewhat gloomy cast to her religious character.

But, how in the world can Miss Ophelia get along with Augustine St. Clare,—gay, easy, unpunctual, unpractical, sceptical,—in short, walking with impudent and nonchalant freedom over every one of her most cherished habits and opinions?

To tell the truth, then, Miss Ophelia loved him. When a boy, it had been hers to teach him his catechism, mend his clothes, comb his hair, and bring him up generally in the way he should go; and her heart having a warm side to it, Augustine had, as he usually did with most people, monopolized a large share of it for himself, and therefore it was that he succeeded very easily in persuading her that the "path of duty" lay in the direction of New Orleans, and that she must go with him to take care of Eva, and keep everything from going to wreck and ruin during the frequent illnesses of his wife. The idea of a house without anybody to take care of it went to her heart; then she loved the lovely little girl, as few could help doing; and though she regarded Augustine as very much of a heathen, yet she loved him, laughed at his jokes, and forbore with his failings, to an extent which those who knew him thought perfectly incredible. But what more or other is to be known of Miss Ophelia our reader must discover by a personal acquaintance.

There she is, sitting now in her state–room, surrounded by a mixed multitude of little and big carpet–bags, boxes, baskets, each containing some separate responsibility which she is tying, binding up, packing, or fastening, with a face of great earnestness.

"Now, Eva, have you kept count of your things? Of course you have n't,—children never do: there 's the spotted carpet–bag and the little blue band–box with your best bonnet,—that 's two; then the India rubber satchel is three; and my tape and needle box is four; and my band–box, five; and my collar–box, six; and that little hair trunk, seven. What have you done with your sunshade? Give it to me, and let me put a paper round it, and tie it to my umbrella with my shade;—there, now."

"Why, aunty, we are only going up home;—what is the use?"

"To keep it nice, child; people must take care of their things, if they ever mean to have anything; and now, Eva, is your thimble put up?"

"Really, aunty, I don't know."

"Well, never mind; I 'll look your box over;—thimble, wax, two spools, scissors, knife, tape–needle; all right,—put it in here. What did you ever do, child, when you were coming on with only your papa. I should have thought you 'd a lost everything you had."

"Well, aunty, I did lose a great many; and then, when we stopped anywhere, papa would buy some more of whatever it was."

"Mercy on us, child,—what a way!"

"It was a very easy way, aunty," said Eva.

"It 's a dreadful shiftless one," said aunty.

"Why, aunty, what 'll you do now?" said Eva; "that trunk is too full to be shut down."

"It *must* shut down," said aunty, with the air of a general, as she squeezed the things in, and sprung upon the lid;—still a little gap remained about the mouth of the trunk.

"Get up here, Eva!" said Miss Ophelia, courageously; "what has been done can be done again. This trunk has *got to be* shut and locked—there are no two ways about it."

And the trunk, intimidated, doubtless, by this resolute statement, gave in. The hasp snapped sharply in its hole, and Miss Ophelia turned the key, and pocketed it in triumph.

"Now we 're ready. Where 's your papa? I think it time this baggage was set out. Do look out, Eva, and see if you see your papa."

"O, yes, he 's down the other end of the gentlemen's cabin, eating an orange."

"He can't know how near we are coming," said aunty; "had n't you better run and speak to him?"

"Papa never is in a hurry about anything," said Eva, "and we have n't come to the landing. Do step on the guards, aunty. Look! there 's our house, up that street!"

The boat now began, with heavy groans, like some vast, tired monster, to prepare to push up among the multiplied steamers at the levee. Eva joyously pointed out the various spires, domes, and way–marks, by which she recognized her native city.

"Yes, yes, dear; very fine," said Miss Ophelia. "But mercy on us! the boat has stopped! where is your father?"

And now ensued the usual turmoil of landing—waiters running twenty ways at once—men tugging trunks, carpet–bags, boxes—women anxiously calling to their children, and everybody crowding in a dense mass to the plank towards the landing.

Miss Ophelia seated herself resolutely on the lately vanquished trunk, and marshalling all her goods and chattels in fine military order, seemed resolved to defend them to the last.

"Shall I take your trunk, ma'am?" "Shall I take your baggage?" "Let me 'tend to your baggage, Missis?" "Shan't I carry out these yer, Missis?" rained down upon her unheeded. She sat with grim determination, upright as a darning–needle stuck in a board, holding on her bundle of umbrella and parasols, and replying with a determination that was enough to strike dismay even into a hackman, wondering to Eva, in each interval, "what upon earth her papa could be thinking of; he could n't have fallen over, now,—but something must have happened;"—and just as she had begun to work herself into a real distress, he came up, with his usually careless motion, and giving Eva a quarter of the orange he was eating, said,

"Well, Cousin Vermont, I suppose you are all ready."

"I 've been ready, waiting, nearly an hour," said Miss Ophelia; "I began to be really concerned about you."

"That 's a clever fellow, now," said he. "Well, the carriage is waiting, and the crowd are now off, so that one can walk out in a decent and Christian manner, and not be pushed and shoved. Here," he added to a driver who stood behind him, "take these things."

"I 'll go and see to his putting them in," said Miss Ophelia.

"O, pshaw, cousin, what 's the use?" said St. Clare.

"Well, at any rate, I 'll carry this, and this, and this," said Miss Ophelia, singling out three boxes and a small carpet–bag.

"My dear Miss Vermont, positively, you must n't come the Green Mountains over us that way. You must adopt at least a piece of a southern principle, and not walk out under all that load. They 'll take you for a waiting–maid; give them to this fellow; he 'll put them down as if they were eggs, now."

Miss Ophelia looked despairingly, as her cousin took all her treasures from her, and rejoiced to find herself once more in the carriage with them, in a state of preservation.

"Where 's Tom?" said Eva.

"O, he 's on the outside, Pussy. I 'm going to take Tom up to mother for a peace–offering, to make up for that drunken fellow that upset the carriage."

"O, Tom will make a splendid driver, I know," said Eva; "he 'll never get drunk."

The carriage stopped in front of an ancient mansion, built in that odd mixture of Spanish and French style, of which there are specimens in some parts of New Orleans. It was built in the Moorish fashion,—a square building enclosing a court–yard, into which the carriage drove through an arched gateway. The court, in the inside, had evidently been arranged to gratify a picturesque and voluptuous ideality. Wide galleries ran all around the four sides, whose Moorish arches, slender pillars, and arabesque ornaments, carried the mind back, as in a dream, to the reign of oriental romance in Spain. In the middle of the court, a fountain threw high its silvery water, falling in a never–ceasing spray into a marble basin, fringed with a deep border of fragrant violets. The water in the fountain, pellucid as crystal, was alive with myriads of gold and silver fishes, twinkling and darting through it like so many living jewels. Around the fountain ran a walk, paved with a mosaic of pebbles, laid in various fanciful patterns; and this, again, was surrounded by turf, smooth as green velvet, while a carriage–drive enclosed the whole. Two large orange–trees, now fragrant with blossoms, threw a delicious shade; and, ranged in a circle round upon the turf, were marble vases of arabesque sculpture, containing the choicest flowering plants of the tropics. Huge pomegranate trees, with their glossy leaves and flame–colored flowers, dark–leaved Arabian jessamines, with their silvery stars, geraniums, luxuriant roses bending beneath their heavy abundance of flowers, golden jessamines, lemon–scented verbenum, all united their bloom and fragrance, while here and there a mystic old aloe, with its strange, massive leaves, sat looking like some hoary old enchanter, sitting in weird grandeur among the more perishable bloom and fragrance around it.

The galleries that surrounded the court were festooned with a curtain of some kind of Moorish stuff, and could be drawn down at pleasure, to exclude the beams of the sun. On the whole, the appearance of the place was luxurious and romantic.

As the carriage drove in, Eva seemed like a bird ready to burst from a cage, with the wild eagerness of her delight.

"O, is n't it beautiful, lovely! my own dear, darling home!" she said to Miss Ophelia. "Is n't it beautiful?"

"'T is a pretty place," said Miss Ophelia, as she alighted; "though it looks rather old and heathenish to me."

Tom got down from the carriage, and looked about with an air of calm, still enjoyment. The negro, it must be remembered, is an exotic of the most gorgeous and superb countries of the world, and he has, deep in his heart, a passion for all that is splendid, rich and fanciful; a passion which, rudely indulged by an untrained taste, draws on them the ridicule of the colder and more correct white race.

St. Clare, who was in his heart a poetical voluptuary, smiled as Miss Ophelia made her remark on his premises, and, turning to Tom, who was standing looking round, his beaming black face perfectly radiant with admiration, he said,

"Tom, my boy, this seems to suit you."

"Yes, Mas'r, it looks about the right thing," said Tom.

All this passed in a moment, while trunks were being hustled off, hackman paid, and while a crowd, of all ages and sizes,—men, women, and children,— came running through the galleries, both above and below, to see Mas'r come in. Foremost among them was a highly–dressed young mulatto man, evidently a very *distingue* personage, attired in the ultra extreme of the mode, and gracefully waving a scented cambric handkerchief in his hand.

This personage had been exerting himself, with great alacrity, in driving all the flock of domestics to the other end of the verandah.

"Back! all of you. I am ashamed of you," he said, in a tone of authority. "Would you intrude on Master's domestic relations, in the first hour of his return?"

All looked abashed at this elegant speech, delivered with quite an air, and stood huddled together at a respectful distance, except two stout porters, who came up and began conveying away the baggage.

Owing to Mr. Adolph's systematic arrangements, when St. Clare turned round from paying the hackman, there was nobody in view but Mr. Adolph himself, conspicuous in satin vest, gold guard–chain, and white pants, and bowing with inexpressible grace and suavity.

"Ah, Adolph, is it you?" said his master, offering his hand to him; how are you, boy?" while Adolph poured forth, with great fluency, an extemporary speech, which he had been preparing, with great care, for a fortnight before.

"Well, well," said St. Clare, passing on, with his usual air of negligent drollery, "that 's very well got up, Adolph. See that the baggage is well bestowed. I 'll come to the people in a minute;" and, so saying, he led Miss Ophelia to a large parlor that opened on to the verandah.

While this had been passing, Eva had flown like a bird, through the porch and parlor, to a little boudoir opening likewise on the verandah.

A tall, dark–eyed, sallow woman, half rose from a couch on which she was reclining.

"Mamma!" said Eva, in a sort of a rapture, throwing herself on her neck, and embracing her over and over again.

"That 'll do,—take care, child,—don't, you make my head ache,' said the mother, after she had languidly kissed her.

St. Clare came in, embraced his wife in true, orthodox, husbandly fashion, and then presented to her his cousin. Marie lifted her large eyes on her cousin with an air of some curiosity, and received her with languid politeness. A crowd of servants now pressed to the entry door, and among them a middle–aged mulatto woman, of very respectable appearance, stood foremost, in a tremor of expectation and joy, at the door.

"O, there 's Mammy!" said Eva, as she flew across the room; and, throwing herself into her arms, she kissed her repeatedly.

This woman did not tell her that she made her head ache, but, on the contrary, she hugged her, and laughed, and cried, till her sanity was a thing to be doubted of; and when released from her, Eva flew from one to another, shaking hands and kissing, in a way that Miss Ophelia afterwards declared fairly turned her stomach.

"Well!" said Miss Ophelia, "you southern children can do something that I cound n't."

"What, now pray?" said St. Clare.

"Well, I want to be kind to everybody, and I would n't have anything hurt; but as to kissing—"

"Niggers," said St. Clare, "that you 're not up to,—hey?"

"Yes, that 's it. How can she?"

St. Clare laughed, as he went into the passage. "Halloa, here, what 's to pay out here? Here, you all—Mammy, Jimmy, Polly, Sukey—glad to see Mas'r?" he said, as he went shaking hands from one to another. "Look out for the babies!" he added, as he stumbled over a sooty little urchin, who was crawling upon all fours. "If I step upon anybody, let 'em mention it."

There was an abundance of laughing and blessing Mas'r, as St. Clare distributed small pieces of change among them.

"Come, now, take yourselves off, like good boys and girls," he said; and the whole assemblage, dark and light, disappeared through a door into a large verandah, followed by Eva, who carried a large satchel, which she had been filling with apples, nuts, candy, ribbons, laces, and toys of every description, during her whole homeward journey.

As St. Clare turned to go back, his eye fell upon Tom, who was standing uneasily, shifting from one foot to the other, while Adolph stood negligently leaning against the banisters, examining Tom through an opera–glass, with an air that would have done credit to any dandy living.

"Puh! you puppy," said his master, striking down the opera glass; "is that the way you treat your company? Seems to me, Dolph," he added, laying his finger on the elegant figured satin vest that Adolph was sporting, "seems to me that 's *my* vest."

"O! Master, this vest all stained with wine; of course, a gentleman in Master's standing never wears a vest like this. I understood I was to take it. It does for a poor nigger–fellow, like me."

And, Adolph tossed his head, and passed his fingers through his scented hair, with a grace.

"So, that 's it, is it?" said St. Clare, carelessly. "Well, here, I 'm going to show this Tom to his mistress, and then you take him to the kitchen; and mind you don't put on any of your airs to him. He 's worth two such puppies as you."

"Master always will have his joke," said Adolph, laughing. "I 'm delighted to see Master in such spirits."

"Here, Tom," said St. Clare, beckoning.

Tom entered the room. He looked wistfully on the velvet carpets, and the before unimagined splendors of mirrors, pictures, statues, and curtains, and, like the Queen of Sheba before Solomon, there was no more spirit in him. He looked afraid even to set his feet down.

"See here, Marie," said St. Clare to his wife, "I 've bought you a coachman, at last, to order. I tell you, he 's a regular hearse for blackness and sobriety, and will drive you like a funeral, if you want. Open your eyes, now, and look at him. Now, don't say I never think about you when I 'm gone."

Marie opened her eyes, and fixed them on Tom, without rising.

"I know he 'll get drunk," she said.

"No, he 's warranted a pious and sober article."

"Well, I hope he may turn out well," said the lady; "it 's more than I expect, though."

"Dolph," said St. Clare, "show Tom down stairs; and, mind yourself," he added; "remember what I told you."

Adolph tripped gracefully forward, and Tom, with lumbering tread, went after.

"He 's a perfect behemoth!" said Marie.

"Come, now, Marie," said St. Clare, seating himself on a stool beside her sofa, "be gracious, and say something pretty to a fellow."

"You 've been gone a fortnight beyond the time," said the lady, pouting.

"Well, you know I wrote you the reason."

"Such a short, cold letter!" said the lady.

"Dear me! the mail was just going, and it had to be that or nothing."

"That 's just the way, always," said the lady; "always something to make your journeys long, and letters short."

"See here, now," he added, drawing an elegant velvet case out of his pocket, and opening it, "here 's a present I got for you in New York."

It was a daguerreotype, clear and soft as an engraving, representing Eva and her father sitting hand in hand.

Marie looked at it with a dissatisfied air.

"What made you sit in such an awkward position?" she said.

"Well, the position may be a matter of opinion; but what do you think of the likeness?"

"If you don't think anything of my opinion in one case, I suppose you would n't in another," said the lady, shutting the daguerreotype.

"Hang the woman!" said St. Clare, mentally; but aloud he added, "Come, now, Marie, what do you think of the likeness? Don't be nonsensical, now."

"It 's very inconsiderate of you, St. Clare," said the lady, "to insist on my talking and looking at things. You know I 've been lying all day with the sick–headache; and there 's been such a tumult made ever since you came, I 'm half dead."

"You're subject to the sick–headache, ma'am?" said Miss Ophelia, suddenly rising from the depths of the large armchair, where she had sat quietly, taking an inventory of the furniture, and calculating its expense.

"Yes, I 'm a perfect martyr to it," said the lady.

"Juniper–berry tea is good for sick–headache," said Miss Ophelia; "at least, Auguste, Deacon Abraham Perry's wife, used to say so; and she was a great nurse."

"I 'll have the first juniper–berries that get ripe in our garden by the lake brought in for that especial purpose," said St. Clare, gravely pulling the bell as he did so; "meanwhile, cousin, you must be wanting to retire to your apartment, and refresh yourself a little, after your journey. Dolph," he added, "tell Mammy to come here." The decent mulatto woman whom Eva had caressed so rapturously soon entered; she was dressed neatly, with a high red and yellow turban on her head, the recent gift of Eva, and which the child had been arranging on her head. "Mammy," said St. Clare, "I put this lady under your care; she is tired, and wants rest; take her to her chamber, and be sure she is made comfortable;" and Miss Ophelia disappeared in the rear of Mammy.

## XVI.
### Tom's Mistress and Her Opinions

"And now, Marie," said St. Clare, "your golden days are dawning. Here is our practical, business–like New England cousin, who will take the whole budget of cares off your shoulders, and give you time to refresh yourself, and grow young and handsome. The ceremony of delivering the keys had better come off forthwith."

This remark was made at the breakfast–table, a few mornings after Miss Ophelia had arrived.

"I 'm sure she 's welcome," said Marie, leaning her head languidly on her hand. "I think she 'll find one thing, if she does, and that is, that it 's we mistresses that are the slaves, down here."

"O, certainly, she will discover that, and a world of wholesome truths besides, no doubt," said St. Clare.

"Talk about our keeping slaves, as if we did it for our *convenience*," said Marie. "I 'm sure, if we consulted *that*, we might let them all go at once."

Evangeline fixed her large, serious eyes on her mother's face, with an earnest and perplexed expression, and said, simply, "What do you keep them for, mamma?"

"I don't know, I 'm sure, except for a plague; they are the plague of my life. I believe that more of my ill health is caused by them than by any one thing; and ours, I know, are the very worst that ever anybody was plagued with."

"O, come, Marie, you 've got the blues, this morning," said St. Clare. "You know 't is n't so. There 's Mammy, the best creature living,—what could you do without her?"

"Mammy is the best I ever knew," said Marie; "and yet Mammy, now, is selfish—dreadfully selfish; it 's the fault of the whole race."

"Selfishness *is* a dreadful fault," said St. Clare, gravely.

"Well, now, there 's Mammy," said Marie, "I think it 's selfish of her to sleep so sound nights; she knows I need little attentions almost every hour, when my worst turns are on, and yet she 's so hard to wake. I absolutely am worse, this very morning, for the efforts I had to make to wake her last night."

"Has n't she sat up with you a good many nights, lately, mamma?" said Eva.

"How should you know that?" said Marie, sharply; "she 's been complaining, I suppose."

"She did n't complain; she only told me what bad nights you 'd had,—so many in succession."

"Why don't you let Jane or Rosa take her place, a night or two," said St. Clare, "and let her rest?"

"How can you propose it?" said Marie. "St. Clare, you really are inconsiderate. So nervous as I am, the least breath disturbs me; and a strange hand about me would drive me absolutely frantic. If Mammy felt the interest in me she ought to, she 'd wake easier,—of course, she would. I 've heard of people who had such devoted servants, but it never was *my* luck;" and Marie sighed.

Miss Ophelia had listened to this conversation with an air of shrewd, observant gravity; and she still kept her lips tightly compressed, as if determined fully to ascertain her longitude and position, before she committed herself.

"Now, Mammy has a *sort* of goodness," said Marie; "she 's smooth and respectful, but she 's selfish at heart. Now, she never will be done fidgeting and worrying about that husband of hers. You see, when I was married and came to live here, of course, I had to bring her with me, and her husband my father could n't spare. He was a blacksmith, and, of course, very necessary; and I thought and said, at the time, that Mammy and he had better give each other up, as it was n't likely to be convenient for them ever to live together again. I wish, now, I 'd insisted on it, and married Mammy to somebody else; but I was foolish and indulgent, and did n't want to insist. I told Mammy, at the time, that she must n't ever expect to see him more than once or twice in her life again, for the air of father's place does n't agree with my health, and I can't go there; and I advised her to take up with somebody else; but no—she would n't. Mammy has a kind of obstinacy about her, in spots, that everybody don't see as I do."

"Has she children?" said Miss Ophelia.

"Yes; she has two."

"I suppose she feels the separation from them?"

"Well, of course, I could n't bring them. They were little dirty things—I could n't have them about; and, besides, they took up too much of her time; but I believe that Mammy has always kept up a sort of sulkiness about this. She won't marry anybody else; and I do believe, now, though she knows how necessary she is to me, and how feeble my health is, she would go back to her husband to-morrow, if she only could. I *do*, indeed," said Marie; "they are just so selfish, now, the best of them."

"It 's distressing to reflect upon," said St. Clare, dryly.

Miss Ophelia looked keenly at him, and saw the flush of mortification and repressed vexation, and the sarcastic curl of the lip, as he spoke.

"Now, Mammy has always been a pet with me," said Marie. "I wish some of your northern servants could look at her closets of dresses,—silks and muslins, and one real linen cambric, she has hanging there. I 've worked sometimes whole afternoons, trimming her caps, and getting her ready to go to a party. As to abuse, she don't know what it is. She never was whipped more than once or twice in her whole life. She has her strong coffee or her tea every day, with white sugar in it. It 's abominable, to be sure; but St. Clare will have high life below–stairs, and they every one of them live just as they please. The fact is, our servants are overindulged. I suppose it is partly our fault that they are selfish, and act like spoiled children; but I 've talked to St. Clare till I am tired."

"And I, too," said St. Clare, taking up the morning paper.

Eva, the beautiful Eva, had stood listening to her mother, with that expression of deep and mystic earnestness which was peculiar to her. She walked softly round to her mother's chair, and put her arms round her neck.

"Well, Eva, what now?" said Marie.

"Mamma, could n't I take care of you one night—just one? I know I should n't make you nervous, and I should n't sleep. I often lie awake nights, thinking—"

"O, nonsense, child—nonsense!" said Marie; "you are such a strange child!"

"But may I, mamma? I think," she said, timidly, "that Mammy is n't well. She told me her head ached all the time, lately."

"O, that 's just one of Mammy's fidgets! Mammy is just like all the rest of them—makes such a fuss about every little head–ache or finger–ache; it 'll never do to encourage it—never! I 'm principled about this matter," said she, turning to Miss Ophelia; "you 'll find the necessity of it. If you encourage servants in giving way to every little disagreeable feeling, and complaining of every little ailment, you 'll have your hands full. I never complain myself—nobody knows what I endure. I feel it a duty to bear it quietly, and I do."

Miss Ophelia's round eyes expressed an undisguised amazement at this peroration, which struck St. Clare as so supremely ludicrous, that he burst into a loud laugh.

"St. Clare always laughs when I make the least allusion to my ill health," said Marie, with the voice of a suffering martyr. "I only hope the day won't come when he 'll remember it!" and Marie put her handkerchief to her eyes.

Of course, there was rather a foolish silence. Finally, St. Clare got up, looked at his watch, and said he had an engagement down street. Eva tripped away after him, and Miss Ophelia and Marie remained at the table alone.

"Now, that 's just like St. Clare!" said the latter, withdrawing her handkerchief with somewhat of a spirited flourish when the criminal to be affected by it was no longer in sight. "He never realizes, never can, never will, what I suffer, and have, for years. If I was one of the complaining sort, or ever made any fuss about my ailments, there would be some reason for it. Men do get tired, naturally, of a complaining wife. But I 've kept things to myself, and borne, and borne, till St. Clare has got in the way of thinking I can bear anything."

Miss Ophelia did not exactly know what she was expected to answer to this.

While she was thinking what to say, Marie gradually wiped away her tears, and smoothed her plumage in a general sort of way, as a dove might be supposed to make toilet after a shower, and began a housewifely chat with Miss Ophelia, concerning cupboards, closets, linen–presses, store–rooms, and other matters, of which the latter was, by common understanding, to assume the direction,—giving her so many cautious directions and charges, that a head less systematic and business–like than Miss Ophelia's would have been utterly dizzied and confounded.

"And now," said Marie, "I believe I 've told you everything; so that, when my next sick turn comes on, you 'll be able to go forward entirely, without consulting me;—only about Eva,—she requires watching."

"She seems to be a good child, very," said Miss Ophelia; "I never saw a better child."

"Eva 's peculiar," said her mother, "very. There are things about her so singular; she is n't like me, now, a particle;" and Marie sighed, as if this was a truly melancholy consideration.

Miss Ophelia in her own heart said, "I hope she is n't," but had prudence enough to keep it down.

"Eva always was disposed to be with servants; and I think that well enough with some children. Now, I always played with father's little negroes—it never did me any harm. But Eva somehow always seems to put herself on an equality with every creature that comes near her. It 's a strange thing about the child. I never have been able to break her of it. St. Clare, I believe, encourages her in it. The fact is, St. Clare indulges every creature under this roof but his own wife."

Again Miss Ophelia sat in blank silence.

"Now, there 's no way with servants," said Marie, "but to *put them down*, and keep them down. It was always natural to me, from a child. Eva is enough to spoil a whole house–full. What she will do when she comes to keep house herself, I 'm sure I don't know. I hold to being *kind* to servants—I always am; but you must make 'em *know their place*. Eva never does; there 's no getting into the child's head the first beginning of an idea what a servant's place is! You heard her offering to take care of me nights, to let Mammy sleep! That 's just a specimen of the way the child would be doing all the time, if she was left to herself."

"Why," said Miss Ophelia, bluntly, "I suppose you think your servants are human creatures, and ought to have some rest when they are tired."

"Certainly, of course. I 'm very particular in letting them have everything that comes convenient,—anything that does n't put one at all out of the way, you know. Mammy can make up her sleep, some time or other; there 's no difficulty about that. She 's the sleepiest concern that ever I saw; sewing, standing, or sitting, that creature will go to sleep, and sleep anywhere and everywhere. No danger but Mammy gets sleep enough. But this treating servants as if they were exotic flowers, or china vases, is really ridiculous," said Marie, as she plunged languidly into the depths of a voluminous and pillowy lounge, and drew towards her an elegant cut–glass vinaigrette.

"You see," she continued, in a faint and lady–like voice, like the last dying breath of an Arabian jessamine, or something equally ethereal, "you see, Cousin Ophelia, I don't often speak of myself. It is n't my *habit*; 't is n't agreeable to me. In fact, I have n't strength to do it. But there are points where St. Clare and I differ. St. Clare never understood me, never appreciated me. I think it lies at the root of all my ill health. St. Clare means well, I am bound to believe; but men are constitutionally selfish and inconsiderate to woman. That, at least, is my impression."

Miss Ophelia, who had not a small share of the genuine New England caution, and a very particular horror of being drawn into family difficulties, now
began to foresee something of this kind impending; so, composing her face into
a grim neutrality, and drawing out of her pocket about a yard and a quarter of
stocking, which she kept as a specific against what Dr. Watts asserts to be a personal habit of Satan when people have idle hands, she proceeded to knit most energetically, shutting her lips together in a way that said, as plain as words could,
"You need n't try to make me speak. I don't want anything to do with your affairs,"—in fact, she looked about as sympathizing as a stone lion. But Marie
did n't care for that. She had got somebody to talk to, and she felt it her duty to
talk, and that was enough; and reinforcing herself by smelling again at her vinaigrette, she went on.

"You see, I brought my own property and servants into the connection, when
I married St. Clare, and I am legally entitled to manage them my own way. St.
Clare had his fortune and his servants, and I 'm well enough content he should
manage them his way; but St. Clare will be interfering. He has wild, extravagant
notions about things, prticularly about the treatment of servants. He really does
act as if he set his servants before me, and before himself, too; for he lets them
make him all sorts of trouble, and never lifts a finger. Now, about some things,
St. Clare is really frightful—he frightens me—good–natured as he looks, in general. Now, he has set down his foot that, come what will, there shall not be a blow
struck in this house, except what he or I strike; and he does it in a way that I
really dare not cross him. Well, you may see what that leads to; for St. Clare
would n't raise his hand, if every one of them walked over him, and I—you see
how cruel it would be to require me to make the exertion. Now, you know these
servants are nothing but grown–up children."

"I don't know anything about it, and I thank the Lord that I don't!" said Miss
Ophelia, shortly.

"Well, but you will have to know something, and know it to your cost, if you
stay here. You don't know what a provoking, stupid, careless, unreasonable, childish, ungrateful set of wretches they are."

Marie seemed wonderfully supported, always, when she got upon this topic;
and she now opened her eyes, and seemed quite to forget her languor.

"You don't know, and you can't, the daily, hourly trials that beset a housekeeper from them, everywhere and every way. But it 's no use to complain to St.
Clare. He talks the strangest stuff. He says we have made them what they are,
and ought to bear with them. He says their faults are all owing to us, and that it
would be cruel to make the fault and punish it too. He says we should n't do any
better, in their place; just as if one could reason from them to us, you know."

"Don't you believe that the Lord made them of one blood with us?" said Miss
Ophelia, shortly.

"No, indeed, not I! A pretty story, truly! They are a degraded race."

"Don't you think they 've got immortal souls?" said Miss Ophelia, with increasing indignation.

"O, well," said Marie, yawning, "that, of course—nobody doubts that. But as
to putting them on any sort of equality with us, you know, as if we could be com-

pared, why, it 's impossible! Now, St. Clare really has talked to me as if keeping Mammy from her husband was like keeping me from mine. There 's no comparing in this way. Mammy could n't have the feelings that I should. It 's a different thing altogether,—of course, it is,—and yet St. Clare pretends not to see it. And just as if Mammy could love her little dirty babies as I love Eva! Yet St. Clare once really and soberly tried to persuade me that it was my duty, with my weak health, and all I suffer, to let Mammy go back, and take somebody else in her place. That was a little too much even for *me* to bear. I don't often show my feelings. I make it a principle to endure everything in silence; it 's a wife's hard lot, and I bear it. But I did break out, that time; so that he has never alluded to the subject since. But I know by his looks, and little things that he says, that he thinks so as much as ever; and it 's so trying, so provoking!"

Miss Ophelia looked very much as if she was afraid she should say something; but she rattled away with her needles in a way that had volumes of meaning in it, if Marie could only have understood it.

"So, you just see," she continued, "what you 've got to manage. A household without any rule; where servants have it all their own way, do what they please, and have what they please, except so far as I, with my feeble health, have kept up government. I keep my cowhide about, and sometimes I do lay it on; but the exertion is always too much for me. If St. Clare would only have this thing done as others do—"

"And how 's that?"

"Why, send them to the calaboose, or some of the other places to be flogged. That 's the only way. If I was n't such a poor, feeble piece, I believe I should manage with twice the energy that St. Clare does."

"And how does St. Clare contrive to manage?" said Miss Ophelia. "You say he never strikes a blow."

"Well, men have a more commanding way, you know; it is easier for them; besides, if you ever looked full in his eye, it 's peculiar,—that eye,—and if he speaks decidedly, there 's a kind of flash. I 'm afraid of it, myself; and the servants know they must mind. I could n't do as much by a regular storm and scolding as St. Clare can by one turn of his eye, if once he is in earnest. O, there 's no trouble about St. Clare; that 's the reason he 's no more feeling for me. But you 'll find, when you come to manage, that there 's no getting along without severity,— they are so bad, so deceitful, so lazy."

"The old tune," said St. Clare, sauntering in. "What an awful account these wicked creatures will have to settle, at last, especially for being lazy! You see, cousin," said he, as he stretched himself at full length on a lounge opposite to Marie, "it 's wholly inexcusable in them, in the light of the example that Marie and I set them,—this laziness."

"Come, now, St. Clare, you are too bad!" said Marie.

"Am I, now? Why, I thought I was talking good, quite remarkably for me. I try to enforce your remarks, Marie, always."

"You know you meant no such thing, St. Clare," said Marie.

"O, I must have been mistaken, then. Thank you, my dear, for setting me right."

"You do really try to be provoking," said Marie.

"O, come, Marie, the day is growing warm, and I have just had a long quarrel with Dolph, which has fatigued me excessively; so, pray be agreeable, now, and let a fellow repose in the light of your smile."

"What 's the matter about Dolph?" said Marie. "That fellow's impudence has been growing to a point that is perfectly intolerable to me. I only wish I had the undisputed management of him a while. I 'd bring him down!"

"What you say, my dear, is marked with your usual acuteness and good sense," said St. Clare. "As to Dolph, the case is this: that he has so long been engaged in imitating my graces and perfections, that he has, at last, really mistaken himself for his master; and I have been obliged to give him a little insight into his mistake."

"How?" said Marie.

"Why, I was obliged to let him understand explicitly that I preferred to keep *some* of my clothes for my own personal wearing; also, I put his magnificence upon an allowance of cologne–water, and actually was so cruel as to restrict him to one dozen of my cambric handkerchiefs. Dolph was particularly huffy about it, and I had to talk to him like a father, to bring him round."

"O! St. Clare, when will you learn how to treat your servants? It 's abominable, the way you indulge them!" said Marie.

"Why, after all, what 's the harm of the poor dog's wanting to be like his master; and if I have n't brought him up any better than to find his chief good in cologne and cambric handkerchiefs, why should n't I give them to him?"

"And why have n't you brought him up better?" said Miss Ophelia, with blunt determination.

"Too much trouble,—laziness, cousin, laziness,—which ruins more souls than you can shake a stick at. If it were n't for laziness, I should have been a perfect angel, myself. I 'm inclined to think that laziness is what your old Dr. Botherem, up in Vermont, used to call the 'essence of moral evil.' It 's an awful consideration, certainly."

"I think you slaveholders have an awful responsibility upon you," said Miss Ophelia. "I would n't have it, for a thousand worlds. You ought to educate your slaves, and treat them like reasonable creatures,—like immortal creatures, that you 've got to stand before the bar of God with. That 's my mind," said the good lady, breaking suddenly out with a tide of zeal that had been gaining strength in her mind all the morning.

"O! come, come," said St. Clare, getting up quickly; "what do you know about us?" And he sat down to the piano, and rattled a lively piece of music. St. Clare had a decided genius for music. His touch was brilliant and firm, and his fingers flew over the keys with a rapid and bird–like motion, airy, and yet decided. He played piece after piece, like a man who is trying to play himself into a good humor. After pushing the music aside, he rose up, and said, gayly, "Well, now, cousin, you 've given us a good talk, and done your duty; on the whole, I think the better of you for it. I make no manner of doubt that you threw a very diamond of truth at me, though you see it hit me so directly in the face that it was n't exactly appreciated, at first."

"For my part, I don't see any use in such sort of talk," said Marie. "I 'm sure, if anybody does more for servants than we do, I 'd like to know who; and it don't do 'em a bit good,—not a particle,—they get worse and worse. As to talking to them, or anything like that, I 'm sure I have talked till I was tired and hoarse, telling them their duty, and all that; and I 'm sure they can go to church when they like, though they don't understand a word of the sermon, more than so many pigs,—so it is n't of any great use for them to go, as I see; but they do go, and so they have every chance; but, as I said before, they are a degraded race, and always will be, and there is n't any help for them; you can't make anything of them, if you try. You see, Cousin Ophelia, I 've tried, and you have n't; I was born and bred among them, and I know."

Miss Ophelia thought she had said enough, and therefore sat silent. St. Clare whistled a tune.

"St. Clare, I wish you would n't whistle," said Marie; "it makes my head worse."

"I won't," said St. Clare. "Is there anything else you would n't wish me to do?"

"I wish you *would* have some kind of sympathy for my trials; you never have any feeling for me."

"My dear accusing angel!" said St. Clare.

"It 's provoking to be talked to in that way."

"Then, how will you be talked to? I 'll talk to order,—any way you 'll mention,—only to give satisfaction."

A gay laugh from the court rang through the silken curtains of the verandah. St. Clare stepped out, and lifting up the curtain, laughed too.

"What is it?" said Miss Ophelia, coming to the railing.

There sat Tom, on a little mossy seat in the court, every one of his button–holes stuck full of cape jessamines, and Eva, gayly laughing, was hanging a wreath of roses round his neck; and then she sat down on his knee, like a chip–sparrow, still laughing.

"O, Tom, you look so funny!"

Tom had a sober, benevolent smile, and seemed, in his quiet way, to be enjoying the fun quite as much as his little mistress. He lifted his eyes, when he saw his master, with a half–deprecating, apologetic air.

"How can you let her?" said Miss Ophelia.

"Why not?" said St. Clare.

"Why, I don't know, it seems so dreadful!"

"You would think no harm in a child's caressing a large dog, even if he was black; but a creature that can think, and reason, and feel, and is immortal, you shudder at; confess it, cousin. I know the feeling among some of you northerners well enough. Not that there is a particle of virtue in our not having it; but custom with us does what Christianity ought to do,—obliterates the feeling of personal prejudice. I have often noticed, in my travels north, how much stronger this was with you than with us. You loathe them as you would a snake or a toad, yet you are indignant at their wrongs. You would not have them abused; but you don't want to have anything to do with them yourselves. You would send them to Africa, out of your sight and smell, and then send a missionary or two to do up all the self–denial of elevating them compendiously. Is n't that it?"

"Well, cousin," said Miss Ophelia, thoughtfully, "there may be some truth in this."

"What would the poor and lowly do, without children?" said St. Clare, leaning on the railing, and watching Eva, as she tripped off, leading Tom with her. "Your little child is your only true democrat. Tom, now, is a hero to Eva; his stories are wonders in her eyes, his songs and Methodist hymns are better than an opera, and the traps and little bits of trash in his pocket a mine of jewels, and he the most wonderful Tom that ever wore a black skin. This is one of the roses of Eden that the Lord has dropped down expressly for the poor and lowly, who get few enough of any other kind."

"It 's strange, cousin," said Miss Ophelia; "one might almost think you were a *professor*, to hear you talk."

"A professor?" said St. Clare.

"Yes; a professor of religion."

"Not at all; not a professor, as your town–folks have it; and, what is worse, I 'm afraid, not a *practiser*, either."

"What makes you talk so, then?"

"Nothing is easier than talking," said St. Clare. "I believe Shakspeare makes somebody say, 'I could sooner show twenty what were good to be done, than be one of the twenty to follow my own showing.' Nothing like division of labor. My forte lies in talking, and yours, cousin, lies in doing."

---

In Tom's external situation, at this time, there was, as the world says, nothing to complain of. Little Eva's fancy for him—the instinctive gratitude and loveliness of a noble nature—had led her to petition her father that he might be her especial attendant, whenever she needed the escort of a servant, in her walks or rides; and Tom had general orders to let everything else go, and attend to Miss Eva whenever she wanted him,—orders which our readers may fancy were far from disagreeable to him. He was kept well dressed, for St. Clare was fastidiously particular on this point. His stable services were merely a sinecure, and consisted simply in a daily care and inspection, and directing an under–servant in his duties; for Marie St. Clare declared that she could not have any smell of the horses about him when he came near her, and that he must positively not be put to any service that would make him unpleasant to her, as her nervous system was entirely inadequate to any trial of that nature; one snuff of anything disagreeable being, according to her account, quite sufficient to close the scene, and put an end to all her earthly trials at once. Tom, therefore, in his well–brushed broadcloth suit, smooth beaver, glossy boots, faultless wristbands and collar, with his grave, good–natured black face, looked respectable enough to be a Bishop of Carthage, as men of his color were, in other ages.

Then, too, he was in a beautiful place, a consideration to which his sensitive race are never indifferent; and he did enjoy with a quiet joy the birds, the flowers, the fountains, the perfume, and light and beauty of the court, the silken hangings, and pictures, and lustres, and statuettes, and gilding, that made the parlors within a kind of Aladdin's palace to him.

If ever Africa shall show an elevated and cultivated race,—and come it must, some time, her turn to figure in the great drama of human improvement,—life will awake there with a gorgeousness and splendor of which our cold western tribes faintly have conceived. In that far–off mystic land of gold, and gems, and spices, and waving palms, and wondrous flowers, and miraculous fertility, will awake new forms of art, new styles of splendor; and the negro race, no longer despised and trodden down, will, perhaps, show forth some of the latest and most magnificent revelations of human life. Certainly they will, in their gentleness, their lowly docility of heart, their aptitude to repose on a superior mind and rest on a higher power, their childlike simplicity of affection, and facility of forgiveness. In all these they will exhibit the highest form of the peculiarly *Christian life*, and, perhaps, as God chasteneth whom he loveth, he hath chosen poor Africa in the furnace of affliction, to make her the highest and noblest in that kingdom which he will set up, when every other kingdom has been tried, and failed; for the first shall be last, and the last first.

Was this what Marie St. Clare was thinking of, as she stood, gorgeously dressed, on the verandah, on Sunday morning, clasping a diamond bracelet on her slender wrist? Most likely it was. Or, if it was n't that, it was something else, for Marie patronized good things, and she was going now, in full force,— diamonds, silk, and lace, and jewels, and all,—to a fashionable church, to be very religious. Marie always made a point to be very pious on Sundays. There she stood, so slender, so elegant, so airy and undulating in all her motions, her lace scarf enveloping her like a mist. She looked a graceful creature, and she felt very good and very elegant indeed. Miss Ophelia stood at her side, a perfect contrast. It was not that she had not as handsome a silk dress and shawl, and as fine a pocket–handkerchief; but stiffness and squareness, and bolt–uprightness, enveloped her with as indefinite yet appreciable a presence as did grace her elegant neighbor; not the grace of God, however,—that is quite another thing!

"Where 's Eva?" said Marie.

"The child stopped on the stairs, to say something to Mammy."

And what was Eva saying to Mammy on the stairs? Listen, reader, and you will hear, though Marie does not.

"Dear Mammy, I know your head is aching dreadfully."

"Lord bless you, Miss Eva! my head allers aches lately. You don't need to worry."

"Well, I 'm glad you 're going out; and here,"—and the little girl threw her arms around her,—"Mammy, you shall take my vinaigrette."

"What! your beautiful gold thing, thar, with them diamonds! Lor, Miss, 't would n't be proper, no ways."

"Why not? You need it, and I don't. Mamma always uses it for headache, and it 'll make you feel better. No, you shall take it, to please me, now."

"Do hear the darlin talk!" said Mammy, as Eva thrust it into her bosom, and, kissing her, ran down stairs to her mother.

"What were you stopping for?"

"I was just stopping to give Mammy my vinaigrette, to take to church with her."

"Eva!" said Marie, stamping impatiently,—"your gold vinaigrette to *Mammy*! When will you learn what 's *proper*? Go right and take it back, this moment!"

Eva looked downcast and aggrieved, and turned slowly.

"I say, Marie, let the child alone; she shall do as she pleases," said St. Clare.

"St. Clare, how will she ever get along in the world?" said Marie.

"The Lord knows," said St. Clare; "but she 'll get along in heaven better than you or I."

"O, papa, don't," said Eva, softly touching his elbow; "it troubles mother."

"Well, cousin, are you ready to go to meeting?" said Miss Ophelia, turning square about on St. Clare.

"I 'm not going, thank you."

"I do wish St. Clare ever would go to church," said Marie; "but he has n't a particle of religion about him. It really is n't respectable."

"I know it," said St. Clare. "You ladies go to church to learn how to get along in the world, I suppose, and your piety sheds respectability on us. If I did go at all, I would go where Mammy goes; there 's something to keep a fellow awake there, at least."

"What! those shouting Methodists? Horrible!" said Marie.

"Anything but the dead sea of your respectable churches, Marie. Positively, it 's too much to ask of a man. Eva, do you like to go? Come, stay at home and play with me."

"Thank you, papa; but I 'd rather go to church."

"Is n't it dreadful tiresome?" said St. Clare.

"I think it is tiresome, some," said Eva; "and I am sleepy, too, but I try to keep awake."

"What do you go for, then?"

"Why, you know, papa," she said, in a whisper, "cousin told me that God wants to have us; and he gives us everything, you know; and it is n't much to do it, if he wants us to. It is n't so very tiresome, after all."

"You sweet, little obliging soul!" said St. Clare, kissing her; "go along, that 's a good girl, and pray for me."

"Certainly, I always do," said the child, as she sprang after her mother into the carriage.

St. Clare stood on the steps and kissed his hand to her, as the carriage drove away; large tears were in his eyes.

"O, Evangeline! rightly named," he said; "hath not God made thee an evangel to me?"

So he felt a moment; and then he smoked a cigar, and read the Picayune, and forgot his little gospel. Was he much unlike other folks?

"You see, Evangeline," said her mother, "it 's always right and proper to be kind to servants, but it is n't proper to treat them *just* as we would our relations, or people in our own class of life. Now, if Mammy was sick, you would n't want to put her in your own bed."

"I should feel just like it, mamma," said Eva, "because then it would be handier to take care of her, and because, you know, my bed is better than hers."

Marie was in utter despair at the entire want of moral perception evinced in this reply.

"What can I do to make this child understand me?" she said.

"Nothing," said Miss Ophelia, significantly.

Eva looked sorry and disconcerted for a moment; but children, luckily, do not keep to one impression long, and in a few moments she was merrily laughing at various things which she saw from the coach–windows, as it rattled along.

————————

"Well, ladies," said St. Clare, as they were comfortably seated at the dinner–table, "and what was the bill of fare at church to–day?"

"O, Dr. G——preached a splendid sermon," said Marie. "It was just such a sermon as you ought to hear; it expressed all my views exactly."

"It must have been very improving," said St. Clare. "The subject must have been an extensive one."

"Well, I mean all my views about society, and such things," said Marie. "The text was, 'He hath made everything beautiful in its season;' and he showed how all the orders and distinctions in society came from God; and that it was so appropriate, you know, and beautiful, that some should be high and some low, and that some were born to rule and some to serve, and all that, you know; and he applied it so well to all this ridiculous fuss that is made about slavery, and he proved distinctly that the Bible was on our side, and supported all of our institutions so convincingly. I only wish you 'd heard him."

"O, I did n't need it," said St. Clare. "I can learn what does me as much good as that from the Picayune, any time, and smoke a cigar besides; which I can't do, you know, in a church."

"Why," said Miss Ophelia, "don't you believe in these views?"

"Who,—I? You know I'm such a graceless dog that these religious aspects of such subjects don't edify me much. If I was to say anything on this slavery matter, I would say out, fair and square, 'We 're in for it; we 've got 'em, and mean to keep 'em,—it 's for our convenience and our interest;' for that 's the long and short of it,—that 's just the whole of what all this sanctified stuff amounts to, after all; and I think that will be intelligible to everybody, everywhere."

"I do think, Augustine, you are so irreverent!" said Marie. "I think it 's shocking to hear you talk."

"Shocking! it 's the truth. This religious talk on such matters,—why don't they carry it a little further, and show the beauty, in its season, of a fellow's taking a glass too much, and sitting a little too late over his cards, and various providential arrangements of that sort, which are pretty frequent among us young men;— we 'd like to hear that those are right and godly, too."

"Well," said Miss Ophelia, "do you think slavery right or wrong?"

"I 'm not going to have any of your horrid New England directness, cousin," said St. Clare, gayly. "If I answer that question, I know you 'll be at me with half a dozen others, each one harder than the last; and I 'm not a going to define my position. I am one of the sort that lives by throwing stones at other people's glass houses, but I never mean to put up one for them to stone."

"That 's just the way he 's always talking," said Marie; "you can't get any satisfaction out of him. I believe it 's just because he don't like religion, that he 's always running out in this way he 's been doing."

"Religion!" said St. Clare, in a tone that made both ladies look at him. "Religion! Is what you hear at church religion? Is that which can bend and turn, and descend and ascend, to fit every crooked phase of selfish, worldly society, religion? Is that religion which is less scrupulous, less generous, less just, less considerate for man, than even my own ungodly, worldly, blinded nature? No! When I look for a religion, I must look for something above me, and not something beneath."

"Then you don't believe that the Bible justifies slavery," said Miss Ophelia.

"The Bible was my *mother's* book," said St. Clare. "By it she lived and died, and I would be very sorry to think it did. I 'd as soon desire to have it proved that my mother could drink brandy, chew tobacco, and swear, by way of satisfying me that I did right in doing the same. It would n't make me at all more satisfied with these things in my self, and it would take from me the comfort of respecting her; and it really is a comfort, in this world, to have anything one can respect. In short, you see," said he, suddenly resuming his gay tone, "all I want is that different things be kept in different boxes. The whole frame–work of society, both in Europe and America, is made up of various things which will not stand the scrutiny of any very ideal standard of morality. It 's pretty generally understood that men don't aspire after the absolute right, but only to do about as well as the rest of the world. Now, when any one speaks up, like a man, and says slavery is necessary to us, we can't get along without it, we should be beggared if we give it up, and, of course, we mean to hold on to it,—this is strong, clear, well–defined language; it has the respectability of truth to it; and, if we may judge by their practice, the majority of the world will bear us out in it. But when he begins to put on a long face, and snuffle, and quote Scripture, I incline to think he is n't much better than he should be."

"You are very uncharitable," said Marie.

"Well," said St. Clare, "suppose that something should bring down the price of cotton once and forever, and make the whole slave property a drug in the market, don't you think we should soon have another version of the Scripture doctrine? What a flood of light would pour into the church, all at once, and how immediately it would be discovered that everything in the Bible and reason went the other way!"

"Well, at any rate," said Marie, as she reclined herself on a lounge, "I 'm thankful I 'm born where slavery exists; and I believe it 's right,—indeed, I feel it must be; and, at any rate, I 'm sure I could n't get along without it."

"I say, what do you think, Pussy?" said her father to Eva, who came in at this moment, with a flower in her hand.

"What about, papa?"

"Why, which do you like the best,—to live as they do at your uncle's, up in Vermont, or to have a house–full of servants, as we do?"

"O, of course, our way is the pleasantest," said Eva.

"Why so?" said St. Clare, stroking her head.

"Why, it makes so many more round you to love, you know," said Eva, look-ing up earnestly.

"Now, that 's just like Eva," said Marie; "just one of her odd speeches."

"Is it an odd speech, papa?" said Eva, whisperingly, as she got upon his knee.

"Rather, as this world goes, Pussy," said St. Clare. "But where has my little Eva been, all dinner–time?"

"O, I 've been up in Tom's room, hearing him sing, and Aunt Dinah gave me my dinner."

"Hearing Tom sing, hey?"

"O, yes! he sings such beautiful things about the New Jerusalem, and bright angels, and the land of Canaan."

"I dare say; it 's better than the opera, is n't it?"

"Yes, and he 's going to teach them to me."

"Singing lessons, hey?—you *are* coming on."

"Yes, he sings for me, and I read to him in my Bible; and he explains what it means, you know."

"On my word," said Marie, laughing, "that is the latest joke of the season."

"Tom is n't a bad hand, now, at explaining Scripture, I 'll dare swear," said St. Clare. "Tom has a natural genius for religion. I wanted the horses out early, this morning, and I stole up to Tom's cubiculum there, over the stables, and there I heard him holding a meeting by himself; and, in fact, I have n't heard anything quite so savory as Tom's prayer, this some time. He put in for me, with a zeal that was quite apostolic."

"Perhaps he guessed you were listening. I 've heard of that trick before."

"If he did, he was n't very politic; for he gave the Lord his opinion of me, pretty freely. Tom seemed to think there was decidedly room for improvement in me, and seemed very earnest that I should be converted."

"I hope you 'll lay it to heart," said Miss Ophelia.

"I suppose you are much of the same opinion," said St. Clare. "Well, we shall see,—shan't we, Eva?"

## XVII.
### The Freeman's Defence

There was a gentle bustle at the Quaker house, as the afternoon drew to a close. Rachel Halliday moved quitely to and fro, collecting from her household stores such needments as could be arranged in the smallest compass, for the wanderers who were to go forth that night. The afternoon shadows stretched eastward, and the round red sun stood thoughtfully on the horizon, and his beams shone yel-low and calm into the little bed–room where George and his wife were sitting. He was sitting with his child on his knee, and his wife's hand in his. Both looked thoughtful and serious, and traces of tears were on their cheeks.

"Yes, Eliza," said George, "I know all you say is true. You are a good child,— a great deal better than I am; and I will try to do as you say. I 'll try to act wor-thy of a free man. I 'll try to feel like a Christian. God Almighty knows that I 've meant to do well,—tried hard to do well,—when everything has been against me;

and now I 'll forget all the past, and put away every hard and bitter feeling, and read my Bible, and learn to be a good man."

"And when we get to Canada," said Eliza, "I can help you. I can do dress–making very well; and I understand fine washing and ironing; and between us we can find something to live on."

"Yes, Eliza, so long as we have each other and our boy. O! Eliza, if these peo-ple only knew what a blessing it is for a man to feel that his wife and child be-long to *him*! I 've often wondered to see men that could call their wives and children *their own* fretting and worrying about anything else. Why, I feel rich and strong, though we have nothing but our bare hands. I feel as if I could scarcely ask God for any more. Yes, though I 've worked hard every day, till I am twenty–five years old, and have not a cent of money, not a roof to cover me, nor a spot of land to call my own, yet, if they will only let me alone now, I will be satisfied—thankful; I will work, and send back the money for you and my boy. As to my old master, he has been paid five times over for all he ever spent for me. I don't owe him anything."

"But yet we are not quite out of danger," said Eliza; "we are not yet in Canada."

"True," said George, "but it seems as if I smelt the free air, and it makes me strong."

At this moment, voices were heard in the outer apartment, in earnest con-versation, and very soon a rap was heard on the door. Eliza started and opened it.

Simeon Halliday was there, and with him a Quaker brother, whom he intro-duced as Phineas Fletcher. Phineas was tall and lathy, red–haired, with an ex-pression of great acuteness and shrewdness in his face. He had not the placid, quiet, unworldly air of Simeon Halliday; on the contrary, a particularly wide–awake and *au fait* appearance, like a man who rather prides himself on knowing what he is about, and keeping a bright look–out ahead; peculiarities which sorted rather oddly with his broad brim and formal phraseology.

"Our friend Phineas hath discovered something of importance to the inter-ests of thee and thy party, George," said Simeon; "it were well for thee to hear it."

"That I have," said Phineas, "and it shows the use of a man's always sleep-ing with one ear open, in certain places, as I 've always said. Last night I stopped at a little lone tavern, back on the road. Thee remembers the place, Simeon, where we sold some apples, last year, to that fat woman, with the great ear–rings. Well, I was tired with hard driving; and, after my supper, I stretched myself down on a pile of bags in the corner, and pulled a buffalo over me, to wait till my bed was ready; and what does I do, but get fast asleep."

"With one ear open, Phineas?" said Simeon, quietly.

"No; I slept, ears and all, for an hour or two, for I was pretty well tired; but when I came to myself a little, I found that there were some men in the room, sit-ting round a table, drinking and talking; and I thought, before I made much muster, I 'd just see what they were up to, especially as I heard them say some-thing about the Quakers. 'So,' says one, 'they are up in the Quaker settlement, no doubt,' says he. Then I listened with both ears, and I found that they were talking about this very party. So I lay and heard them lay off all their plans. This young man, they said, was to be sent back to Kentucky, to his master, who was going to make an example of him, to keep all niggers from running away; and his wife two of them were going to run down to New Orleans to sell, on their own account, and they calculated to get sixteen or eighteen hundred dollars for her; and the child, they said, was going to a trader, who had bought him; and then there was the boy, Jim, and his mother, they were to go back to their masters in Kentucky. They said that there were two constables, in a town a little piece ahead, who would go in with 'em to get 'em taken up, and the young woman was to be taken before a judge; and one of the fellows, who is small and smooth–spoken, was to swear to her for his property, and get her delivered over to him to take south. They've got a right notion of the track we are going to–night; and they'll be down after us, six or eight strong. So, now, what's to be done?"

The group that stood in various attitudes, after this communication, were worthy of a painter. Rachel Halliday, who had taken her hands out of a batch of biscuit, to hear the news, stood with them upraised and floury, and with a face of the deepest concern. Simeon looked profoundly thoughtful; Eliza had thrown her arms around her husband, and was looking up to him. George stood with clenched hands and glowing eyes, and looking as any other man might look, whose wife was to be sold at auction, and son sent to a trader, all under the shelter of a Christian nation's laws.

"What *shall* we do, George?" said Eliza, faintly.

"I know what *I* shall do," said George, as he stepped into the little room, and began examining his pistols.

"Ay, ay," said Phineas, nodding his head to Simeon; "thou seest, Simeon, how it will work."

"I see," said Simeon, sighing; "I pray it come not to that."

"I don't want to involve any one with or for me," said George. "If you will lend me your vehicle and direct me, I will drive alone to the next stand. Jim is a giant in strength, and brave as death and despair, and so am I."

"Ah, well, friend," said Phineas, "but thee'll need a driver, for all that. Thee's quite welcome to do all the fighting, thee knows; but I know a thing or two about the road, that thee does n't."

"But I don't want to involve you," said George.

"Involve," said Phineas, with a curious and keen expression of face. "When thee does involve me, please to let me know."

"Phineas is a wise and skilful man," said Simeon. "Thee does well, George, to abide by his judgment; and," he added, laying his hand kindly on George's shoulder, and pointing to the pistols, "be not over hasty with these,—young blood is hot."

"I will attack no man," said George. "All I ask of this country is to be let alone, and I will go out peaceably; but,"—he paused, and his brow darkened and his face worked,—"I've had a sister sold in that New Orleans market. I know what they are sold for; and am I going to stand by and see them take my wife and sell her, when God has given me a pair of strong arms to defend her? No; God help me! I 'll fight to the last breath, before they shall take my wife and son. Can you blame me?"

"Mortal man cannot blame thee, George. Flesh and blood could not do otherwise," said Simeon. "Woe unto the world because of offences, but woe unto them through whom the offence cometh."

"Would not even you, sir, do the same, in my place?"

"I pray that I be not tried," said Simeon; "the flesh is weak."

"I think my flesh would be pretty tolerable strong, in such a case," said Phineas, stretching out a pair of arms like the sails of a windmill. "I an't sure, friend George, that I should n't hold a fellow for thee, if thee had any accounts to settle with him."

"If man should *ever* resist evil," said Simeon, "then George should feel free to do it now: but the leaders of our people taught a more excellent way; for the wrath of man worketh not the righteousness of God; but it goes sorely against the corrupt will of man, and none can receive it save they to whom it is given. Let us pray the Lord that we be not tempted."

"And so *I* do," said Phineas; "but if we are tempted too much—why, let them look out, that's all."

"It 's quite plain thee was n't born a Friend," said Simeon, smiling. "The old nature hath its way in thee pretty strong as yet."

To tell the truth, Phineas had been a hearty, two–fisted backwoodsman, a vigorous hunter, and a dead shot at a buck; but, having wooed a pretty Quakeress, had been moved by the power of her charms to join the society in his neighborhood; and though he was an honest, sober, and efficient member, and nothing particular could be alleged against him, yet the more spiritual among them could not but discern an exceeding lack of savor in his developments.

"Friend Phineas will ever have ways of his own," said Rachel Halliday, smiling; "but we all think that his heart is in the right place, after all."

"Well," said George, "is n't it best that we hasten our flight?"

"I got up at four o'clock, and came on with all speed, full two or three hours ahead of them, if they start at the time they planned. It is n't safe to start till dark, at any rate; for there are some evil persons in the villages ahead, that might be disposed to meddle with us, if they saw our wagon, and that would delay us more than the waiting; but in two hours I think we may venture. I will go over to Michael Cross, and engage him to come behind on his swift nag, and keep a bright look–out on the road, and warn us if any company of men come on. Michael keeps a horse that can soon get ahead of most other horses; and he could shoot ahead and let us know, if there were any danger. I am going out now to warn Jim and the old woman to be in readiness, and to see about the horse. We have a pretty fair start, and stand a good chance to get to the stand before they can come up with us. So, have good courage, friend George; this is n't the first ugly scrape that I 've been in with thy people," said Phineas, as he closed the door.

"Phineas is pretty shrewd," said Simeon. "He will do the best that can be done for thee, George."

"All I am sorry for," said George, "is the risk to you."

"Thee 'll much oblige us, friend George, to say no more about that. What we do we are conscience bound to do; we can do no other way. And now, mother," said he, turning to Rachel, "hurry thy preparations for these friends, for we must not send them away fasting."

And while Rachel and her children were busy making corn-cake, and cooking ham and chicken, and hurrying on the *et ceteras* of the evening meal, George and his wife sat in their little room, with their arms folded about each other, in such talk as husband and wife have when they know that a few hours may part them forever.

"Eliza," said George, "people that have friends, and houses, and lands, and money, and all those things, *can't* love as we do, who have nothing but each other. Till I knew you, Eliza, no creature ever had loved me, but my poor, heart–broken mother and sister. I saw poor Emily that morning the trader carried her off. She came to the corner where I was lying asleep, and said, 'Poor George, your last friend is going. What will become of you, poor boy?' And I got up and threw my arms round her, and cried and sobbed, and she cried too; and those were the last kind words I got for ten long years; and my heart all withered up, and felt as dry as ashes, till I met you. And your loving me,—why, it was almost like raising one from the dead! I 've been a new man ever since! And now, Eliza, I 'll give my last drop of blood, but they *shall not* take you from me. Whoever gets you must walk over my dead body."

"O, Lord, have mercy!" said Eliza, sobbing. "If he will only let us get out of this country together, that is all we ask."

"Is God on their side?" said George, speaking less to his wife than pouring out his own bitter thoughts. "Does he see all they do? Why does he let such things happen? And they tell us that the Bible is on their side; certainly all the power is. They are rich, and healthy, and happy; they are members of churches, expecting to go to heaven; and they get along so easy in the world, and have it all their own way; and poor, honest, faithful Christians,—Christians as good or better than they,— are lying in the very dust under their feet. They buy 'em and sell 'em, and make trade of their heart's blood, and groans and tears,—and God *lets* them."

"Friend George," said Simeon, from the kitchen, "listen to this Psalm; it may do thee good."

George drew his seat near the door, and Eliza, wiping her tears, came forward also to listen, while Simeon read as follows:

"But as for me, my feet were almost gone; my steps had well–nigh slipped. For I was envious of the foolish, when I saw the prosperity of the wicked. They are not in trouble like other men, neither are they plagued like other men. Therefore, pride compasseth them as a chain; violence covereth them as a garment. Their eyes stand out with fatness; they have more than heart could wish. They are corrupt, and speak wickedly concerning oppression; they speak loftily. Therefore his people return, and the waters of a full cup are wrung out to them, and they say, How doth God know? and is there knowledge in the Most High?"

"Is not that the way thee feels, George?"

"It is so, indeed," said George,—"as well as I could have written it myself."

"Then, hear," said Simeon: "When I thought to know this, it was too painful for me until I went unto the sanctuary of God. Then understood I their end. Surely thou didst set them in slippery places, thou castedst them down to destruction. As a dream when one awaketh, so, oh Lord, when thou awakest, thou shalt despise their image. Nevertheless, I am continually with thee; thou hast holden me by my right hand. Thou shalt guide me by thy counsel, and afterwards receive me to glory. It is good for me to draw near unto God. I have put my trust in the Lord God."

The words of holy trust, breathed by the friendly old man, stole like sacred music over the harassed and chafed spirit of George; and after he ceased, he sat with a gentle and subdued expression on his fine features.

"If this world were all, George," said Simeon, "thee might, indeed, ask, where is the Lord? But it is often those who have least of all in this life whom he chooseth for the kingdom. Put thy trust in him, and, no matter what befalls thee here, he will make all right hereafter."

If these words had been spoken by some easy, self–indulgent exhorter, from whose mouth they might have come merely as pious and rhetorical flourish, proper to be used to people in distress, perhaps they might not have had much effect; but coming from one who daily and calmly risked fine and imprisonment for the cause of God and man, they had a weight that could not but be felt, and both the poor, desolate fugitives found calmness and strength breathing into them from it.

And now Rachel took Eliza's hand kindly, and led the way to the supper–table. As they were sitting down, a light tap sounded at the door, and Ruth entered. "I just ran in," she said, "with these little stockings for the boy,—three pair, nice, warm woollen ones. It will be so cold, thee knows, in Canada. Does thee keep up good courage, Eliza?" she added, tripping round to Eliza's side of the table, and shaking her warmly by the hand, and slipping a seed–cake into Harry's hand. "I brought a little parcel of these for him," she said, tugging at her pocket to get out the package. "Children, thee knows, will always be eating."

"O, thank you; you are too kind," said Eliza.

"Come, Ruth, sit down to supper," said Rachel.

"I could n't, any way. I left John with the baby, and some biscuits in the oven; and I can't stay a moment, else John will burn up all the biscuits, and give the baby all the sugar in the bowl. That 's the way he does," said the little Quakeress, laughing. "So, good–by, Eliza; good–by, George; the Lord grant thee a safe journey;" and, with a few tripping steps, Ruth was out of the apartment.

A little while after supper, a large covered–wagon drew up before the door; the night was clear starlight; and Phineas jumped briskly down from his seat to arrange his passengers. George walked out of the door, with his child on one arm and his wife on the other. His step was firm, his face settled and resolute. Rachel and Simeon came out after them.

"You get out, a moment," said Phineas to those inside, "and let me fix the back of the wagon, there, for the women–folks and the boy."

"Here are the two buffaloes," said Rachel. "Make the seats as comfortable as may be; it's hard riding all night."

Jim came out first, and carefully assisted out his old mother, who clung to his arm, and looked anxiously about, as if she expected the pursuer every moment.

"Jim, are your pistols all in order?" said George, in a low, firm voice.

"Yes, indeed," said Jim.

"And you 've no doubt what you shall do, if they come?"

"I rather think I have n't," said Jim, throwing open his broad chest, and taking a deep breath. "Do you think I 'll let them get mother again?"

During this brief colloquy, Eliza had been taking her leave of her kind friend, Rachel, and was handed into the carriage by Simeon, and, creeping into the back part with her boy, sat down among the buffalo–skins. The old woman was next handed in and seated, and George and Jim placed on a rough board seat front of them, and Phineas mounted in front.

"Farewell, my friends," said Simeon, from without.

"God bless you!" answered all from within.

And the wagon drove off, rattling and jolting over the frozen road.

There was no opportunity for conversation, on account of the roughness of the way and the noise of the wheels. The vehicle, therefore, rumbled on, through long, dark stretches of woodland,—over wide, dreary plains,—up hills, and down valleys,—and on, on, on they jogged, hour after hour. The child soon fell asleep, and lay heavily in his mother's lap. The poor, frightened old woman at last forgot her fears; and, even Eliza, as the night waned, found all her anxieties insufficient to keep her eyes from closing. Phineas seemed, on the whole, the briskest of the company, and beguiled his long drive with whistling certain very un-quaker–like songs, as he went on.

But about three o'clock George's ear caught the hasty and decided click of a horse's hoof coming behind them at some distance, and jogged Phineas by the elbow. Phineas pulled up his horses, and listened.

"That must be Michael," he said; "I think I know the sound of his gallop;" and he rose up and stretched his head anxiously back over the road.

A man riding in hot haste was now dimly descried at the top of a distant hill.

"There he is, I do believe!" said Phineas. George and Jim both sprang out of the wagon, before they knew what they were doing. All stood intensely silent, with their faces turned towards the expected messenger. On he came. Now he went down into a valley, where they could not see him; but they heard the sharp, hasty tramp, rising nearer and nearer; at last they saw him emerge on the top of an eminence, within hail.

"Yes, that 's Michael!" said Phineas; and, raising his voice, "Halloa, there, Michael!"

"Phineas! is that thee?"

"Yes; what news—they coming?"

"Right on behind, eight or ten of them, hot with brandy, swearing and foaming like so many wolves."

And, just as he spoke, a breeze brought the faint sound of galloping horsemen towards them.

"In with you,—quick, boys, *in!*" said Phineas. "If you must fight, wait till I get you a piece ahead." And, with the word, both jumped in, and Phineas lashed the horses to a run, the horseman keeping close beside them. The wagon rattled, jumped, almost flew, over the frozen ground; but plainer, and still plainer, came the noise of pursuing horsemen behind. The women heard it, and, looking anxiously out, saw, far in the rear, on the brow of a distant hill, a party of men looming up against the red–streaked sky of early dawn. Another hill, and their pursuers had evidently caught sight of their wagon, whose white cloth–covered top made it conspicuous at some distance, and a loud yell of brutal triumph came forward on the wind. Eliza sickened, and strained her child closer to her bosom; the old woman prayed and groaned, and George and Jim clenched their pistols with the grasp of despair. The pursuers gained on them fast; the carriage made a sudden turn, and brought them near a ledge of a steep over–hanging rock, that rose in an isolated ridge or clump in a large lot, which was, all around it, quite clear and smooth. This isolated pile, or range of rocks, rose up black and heavy against the brightening sky, and seemed to promise shelter and concealment. It was a place well known to Phineas, who had been familiar with the spot in his hunting days; and it was to gain this point he had been racing his horses.

"Now for it!" said he, suddenly checking his horses, and springing from his seat to the ground. "Out with you, in a twinkling, every one, and up into these rocks with me. Michael, thee tie thy horse to the wagon, and drive ahead to Amariah's, and get him and his boys to come back and talk to these fellows."

In a twinkling they were all out of the carriage.

"There," said Phineas, catching up Harry, "you, each of you, see to the women; and run, *now*, if you ever *did* run!"

There needed no exhortation. Quicker than we can say it, the whole party were over the fence, making with all speed for the rocks, while Michael, throwing himself from his horse, and fastening the bridle to the wagon, began driving it rapidly away.

"Come ahead," said Phineas, as they reached the rocks, and saw, in the mingled starlight and dawn, the traces of a rude but plainly marked foot–path leading up among them; "this is one of our old hunting–dens. Come up!"

Phineas went before, springing up the rocks like a goat, with the boy in his arms. Jim came second, bearing his trembling old mother over his shoulder, and George and Eliza brought up the rear. The party of horsemen came up to the fence, and, with mingled shouts and oaths, were dismounting, to prepare to follow them. A few moments' scrambling brought them to the top of the ledge; the path then passed between a narrow defile, where only one could walk at a time, till suddenly they came to a rift or chasm more than a yard in breadth, and beyond which lay a pile of rocks, separate from the rest of the ledge, standing full thirty feet high, with its sides steep and perpendicular as those of a castle. Phineas easily leaped the chasm, and sat down the boy on a smooth, flat platform of crisp white moss, that covered the top of the rock.

"Over with you!" he called; "spring, now, once, for your lives!" said he, as one after another sprang across. Several fragments of loose stone formed a kind of breast–work, which sheltered their position from the observation of those below.

"Well, here we all are," said Phineas, peeping over the stone breast–work to watch the assailants, who were coming tumultuously up under the rocks. "Let 'em get us, if they can. Whoever comes here has to walk single file between those two rocks, in fair range of your pistols, boys, d' ye see?"

"I do see," said George; "and now, as this matter is ours, let us take all the risk, and do all the fighting."

"Thee 's quite welcome to do the fighting, George," said Phineas, chewing some checkerberry–leaves as he spoke; "but I may have the fun of looking on, I suppose. But see, these fellows are kinder debating down there, and looking up, like hens when they are going to fly up on to the roost. Had n't thee better give 'em a word of advice, before they come up, just to tell 'em handsomely they 'll be shot if they do?"

The party beneath, now more apparent in the light of the dawn, consisted of our old acquaintances, Tom Loker and Marks, with two constables, and a posse consisting of such rowdies at the last tavern as could be engaged by a little brandy to go and help the fun of trapping a set of niggers.

"Well, Tom, yer coons are farly treed," said one.

"Yes, I see 'em go up right here," said Tom; "and here 's a path. I 'm for going right up. They can't jump down in a hurry, and it won't take long to ferret 'em out."

"But, Tom, they might fire at us from behind the rocks," said Marks. "That would be ugly, you know."

"Ugh!" said Tom, with a sneer. "Always for saving your skin, Marks! No danger! niggers are too plaguy scared!"

"I don't know why I *should n't* save my skin," said Marks. "It 's the best I 've got; and niggers *do* fight like the devil, sometimes."

At this moment, George appeared on the top of a rock above them, and, speaking in a calm, clear voice, said,

"Gentlemen, who are you, down there, and what do you want?"

"We want a party of runaway niggers," said Tom Loker. "One George Harris, and Eliza Harris, and their son, and Jim Selden, and an old woman. We 've got the officers, here, and a warrant to take 'em; and we 're going to have 'em, too. D 'ye hear? An't you George Harris, that belongs to Mr. Harris, of Shelby county, Kentucky?"

"I am George Harris. A Mr. Harris, of Kentucky, did call me his property. But now I 'm a free man, standing on God's free soil; and my wife and my child I claim as mine. Jim and his mother are here. We have arms to defend ourselves, and we mean to do it. You can come up, if you like; but the first one of you that comes within the range of our bullets is a dead man, and the next, and the next; and so on till the last."

"O, come! come!" said a short, puffy man, stepping forward, and blowing his nose as he did so. "Young man, this an't no kind of talk at all for you. You see, we 're officers of justice. We 've got the law on our side, and the power, and so forth; so you 'd better give up peaceably, you see; for you 'll certainly have to give up, at last."

"I know very well that you 've got the law on your side, and the power," said George, bitterly. "You mean to take my wife to sell in New Orleans, and put my boy like a calf in a trader's pen, and send Jim's old mother to the brute that whipped and abused her before, because he could n't abuse her son. You want to send Jim and me back to be whipped and tortured, and ground down under the heels of them that you call masters; and your laws *will* bear you out in it,—more shame for you and them! But you have n't got us. We don't own your laws; we don't own your country; we stand here as free, under God's sky, as you are; and, by the great God that made us, we 'll fight for our liberty till we die."

George stood out in fair sight, on the top of the rock, as he made his declaration of independence; the glow of dawn gave a flush to his swarthy cheek, and bitter indignation and despair gave fire to his dark eye; and, as if appealing from man to the justice of God, he raised his hand to heaven as he spoke.

If it had been only a Hungarian youth, now bravely defending in some mountain fastness the retreat of fugitives escaping from Austria into America, this would have been sublime heroism; but as it was a youth of African descent, defending the retreat of fugitives through America into Canada, of course we are too well instructed and patriotic to see any heroism in it; and if any of our readers do, they must do it on their own private responsibility. When despairing Hungarian fugitives make their way, against all the search–warrants and authorities of their lawful government, to America, press and political cabinet ring with applause and welcome. When despairing African fugitives do the same thing,—it is—what *is* it?

Be it as it may, it is certain that the attitude, eye, voice, manner, of the speaker, for a moment struck the party below to silence. There is something in boldness and determination that for a time hushes even the rudest nature. Marks was the only one who remained wholly untouched. He was deliberately cocking his pistol, and, in the momentary silence that followed George's speech, he fired at him.

"Ye see ye get jist as much for him dead as alive in Kentucky," he said, coolly, as he wiped his pistol on his coatsleeve.

George sprang backward,—Eliza uttered a shriek,—the ball had passed close to his hair, had nearly grazed the cheek of his wife, and struck in the tree above.

"It 's nothing, Eliza," said George, quickly.

"Thee 'd better keep out of sight, with thy speechifying," said Phineas; "they 're mean scamps."

"Now, Jim," said George, "look that your pistols are all right, and watch that pass with me. The first man that shows himself I fire at; you take the second, and so on. It won't do, you know, to waste two shots on one."

"But what if you don't hit?"

"I *shall* hit," said George, coolly.

"Good! now, there 's stuff in that fellow," muttered Phineas, between his teeth.

The party below, after Marks had fired, stood, for a moment, rather undecided.

"I think you must have hit some on 'em," said one of the men. "I heard a squeal!"

"I 'm going right up for one," said Tom. "I never was afraid of niggers, and I an't going to be now. Who goes after?" he said, springing up the rocks.

George heard the words distinctly. He drew up his pistol, examined it, pointed it towards that point in the defile where the first man would appear.

One of the most courageous of the party followed Tom, and, the way being thus made, the whole party began pushing up the rock,—the hindermost pushing the front ones faster than they would have gone of themselves. On they came, and in a moment the burly form of Tom appeared in sight, almost at the verge of the chasm.

George fired,—the shot entered his side,—but, though wounded, he would not retreat, but, with a yell like that of a mad bull, he was leaping right across the chasm into the party.

"Friend," said Phineas, suddenly stepping to the front, and meeting him with a push from his long arms, "thee is n't wanted here."

Down he fell into the chasm, crackling down among trees, bushes, logs, loose stones, till he lay, bruised and groaning, thirty feet below. The fall might have killed him, had it not been broken and moderated by his clothes catching in the branches of a large tree; but he came down with some force, however,—more than was at all agreeable or convenient.

"Lord, help us, they are perfect devils!" said Marks, heading the retreat down the rocks with much more of a will than he had joined the ascent, while all the party came tumbling precipitately after him,—the fat constable, in particular, blowing and puffing in a very energetic manner.

"I say, fellers," said Marks, "you jist go round and pick up Tom, there, while I run and get on to my horse, to go back for help,—that 's you;" and, without minding the hootings and jeers of his company, Marks was as good as his word, and was soon seen galloping away.

"Was ever such a sneaking varmint?" said one of the men; "to come on his business, and he clear out and leave us this yer way!"

"Well, we must pick up that feller," said another. "Cuss me if I much care whether he is dead or alive."

The men, led by the groans of Tom, scrambled and crackled through stumps, logs and bushes, to where that hero lay groaning and swearing, with alternate vehemence.

"Ye keep it agoing pretty loud, Tom," said one. "Ye much hurt?"

"Don't know. Get me up, can't ye? Blast that infernal Quaker! If it had n't been for him, I 'd a pitched some on 'em down here, to see how they liked it."

With much labor and groaning, the fallen hero was assisted to rise; and, with one holding him up under each shoulder, they got him as far as the horses.

"If you could only get me a mile back to that ar tavern. Give me a handkerchief or something, to stuff into this place, and stop this infernal bleeding."

George looked over the rocks, and saw them trying to lift the burly form of Tom into the saddle. After two or three ineffectual attempts, he reeled, and fell heavily to the ground.

"O, I hope he is n't killed!" said Eliza, who, with all the party, stood watching the proceeding.

"Why not?" said Phineas; "serves him right."

"Because, after death comes the judgment," said Eliza.

"Yes," said the old woman, who had been groaning and praying, in her Methodist fashion, during all the encounter, "it 's an awful case for the poor crittur's soul."

"On my word, they 're leaving him, I do believe," said Phineas.

It was true; for after some appearance of irresolution and consultation, the whole party got on their horses and rode away. When they were quite out of sight, Phineas began to bestir himself.

"Well, we must go down and walk a piece," he said. "I told Michael to go forward and bring help, and be along back here with the wagon; but we shall have to walk a piece along the road, I reckon, to meet them. The Lord grant he be along soon! It 's early in the day; there won't be much travel afoot yet a while; we an't much more than two miles from our stopping–place. If the road had n't been so rough last night, we could have outrun 'em entirely."

As the party neared the fence, they discovered in the distance, along the road, their own wagon coming back, accompanied by some men on horseback.

"Well, now, there 's Michael, and Stephen, and Amariah," exclaimed Phineas, joyfully. "Now we *are* made,—as safe as if we 'd got there."

"Well, do stop, then," said Eliza, "and do something for that poor man; he 's groaning dreadfully."

"It would be no more than Christian," said George; "let 's take him up and carry him on."

"And doctor him up among the Quakers!" said Phineas; "pretty well, that! Well, I don't care if we do. Here, let 's have a look at him;" and Phineas, who in the course of his hunting and backwoods life, had acquired some rude experience of surgery, kneeled down by the wounded man, and began a careful examination of his condition.

"Marks," said Tom, feebly, "is that you, Marks?"

"No; I reckon 't an't, friend," said Phineas. "Much Marks cares for thee, if his own skin 's safe. He 's off, long ago."

"I believe I'm done for," said Tom. "The cussed sneaking dog, to leave me to die alone! My poor old mother always told me 't would be so."

"La sakes! jist hear the poor crittur. He 's got a mammy, now," said the old negress. "I can't help kinder pityin' on him."

"Softly, softly; don't thee snap and snarl, friend," said Phineas, as Tom winced and pushed his hand away. "Thee has no chance, unless I stop the bleeding." And Phineas busied himself with making some off–hand surgical arrangements with his own pocket–handkerchief, and such as could be mustered in the company.

"You pushed me down there," said Tom, faintly.

"Well, if I had n't, thee would have pushed us down, thee sees," said Phineas, as he stooped to apply his bandage. "There, there,—let me fix this bandage. We mean well to thee; we bear no malice. Thee shall be taken to a house where they 'll nurse thee first rate,—as well as thy own mother could."

Tom groaned, and shut his eyes. In men of his class, vigor and resolution are entirely a physical matter, and ooze out with the flowing of the blood; and the gigantic fellow really looked piteous in his helplessness.

The other party now came up. The seats were taken out of the wagon. The buffalo–skins, doubled in fours, were spread all along one side, and four men, with great difficulty, lifted the heavy form of Tom into it. Before he was gotten in, he fainted entirely. The old negress, in the abundance of her compassion, sat down on the bottom, and took his head in her lap. Eliza, George and Jim, bestowed themselves, as well as they could, in the remaining space, and the whole party set forward.

"What do you think of him?" said George, who sat by Phineas in front.

"Well, it 's only a pretty deep flesh–wound; but, then, tumbling and scratching down that place did n't help him much. It has bled pretty freely,—pretty much dreaned him out, courage and all,—but he'll get over it, and may be learn a thing or two by it."

"I 'm glad to hear you say so," said George. "It would always be a heavy thought to me, if I 'd caused his death, even in a just cause."

"Yes," said Phineas, "killing is an ugly operation, any way they 'll fix it,—man or beast. I 've been a great hunter, in my day, and I tell thee I 've seen a buck that was shot down, and a dying, look that way on a feller with his eye, that it reely most made a feller feel wicked for killing on him; and human creatures is a more serious consideration yet, bein', as thy wife says, that the judgment comes to 'em after death. So I don't know as our people's notions on these matters is too strict; and, considerin' how I was raised, I fell in with them pretty considerably."

"What shall you do with this poor fellow?" said George.

"O, carry him along to Amariah's. There 's old Grandman Stephens there,—Dorcas, they call her,—she 's most an amazin' nurse. She takes to nursing real natural, and an't never better suited than when she gets a sick body to tend. We may reckon on turning him over to her for a fortnight or so."

A ride of about an hour more brought the party to a neat farm–house, where the weary travellers were received to an abundant breakfast. Tom Loker was soon carefully deposited in a much cleaner and softer bed than he had ever been in the habit of occupying. His wound was carefully dressed and bandaged, and he lay languidly opening and shutting his eyes on the white window–curtains and gently–gliding figures of his sick room, like a weary child. And here, for the present, we shall take our leave of one party.

# XVIII.
## Miss Ophelia's Experiences and Opinions

Our friend Tom, in his own simple musings, often compared his more fortunate lot, in the bondage into which he was cast, with that of Joseph in Egypt; and, in fact, as time went on, and he developed more and more under the eye of his master, the strength of the parallel increased.

St. Clare was indolent and careless of money. Hitherto the providing and marketing had been principally done by Adolph, who was, to the full, as careless and extravagant as his master; and, between them both, they had carried on the dispersing process with great alacrity. Accustomed, for many years, to regard his master's property as his own care, Tom saw, with an uneasiness he could scarcely repress, the wasteful expenditure of the establishment; and, in the quiet, indirect way which his class often acquire, would sometimes make his own suggestions.

St. Clare at first employed him occasionally; but, struck with his soundness of mind and good business capacity, he confided in him more and more, till gradually all the marketing and providing for the family were intrusted to him.

"No, no, Adolph," he said, one day, as Adolph was deprecating the passing of power out of his hands; "let Tom alone. You only understand what you want; Tom understands cost and come to; and there may be some end to money, bye and bye if we don't let somebody do that."

Trusted to an unlimited extent by a careless master, who handed him a bill without looking at it, and pocketed the change without counting it, Tom had every facility and temptation to dishonesty; and nothing but an impregnable simplicity of nature, strengthened by Christian faith, could have kept him from it. But, to that nature, the very unbounded trust reposed in him was bond and seal for the most scrupulous accuracy.

With Adolph the case had been different. Thoughtless and self-indulgent, and unrestrained by a master who found it easier to indulge than to regulate, he had fallen into an absolute confusion as to *meum tuum* with regard to himself and his master, which sometimes troubled even St. Clare. His own good sense taught him that such a training of his servants was unjust and dangerous. A sort of chronic remorse went with him everywhere, although not strong enough to make any decided change in his course; and this very remorse reäcted again into indulgence. He passed lightly over the most serious faults, because he told himself that, if he had done his part, his dependents had not fallen into them.

Tom regarded his gay, airy, handsome young master with an odd mixture of fealty, reverence, and fatherly solicitude. That he never read the Bible; never went to church; that he jested and made free with any and every thing that came in the way of his wit; that he spent his Sunday evenings at the opera or theatre; that he went to wine parties, and clubs, and suppers, oftener than was at all expedient,— were all things that Tom could see as plainly as anybody, and on which he based a conviction that "Mas'r was n't a Christian;"—a conviction, however, which he would have been very slow to express to any one else, but on which he founded many prayers, in his own simple fashion, when he was by himself in his little dormitory. Not that Tom had not his own way of speaking his mind occasionally, with something of the tact often observable in his class; as, for example, the very day after the Sabbath we have described, St. Clare was invited out to a convivial party of choice spirits, and was helped home, between one and two o'clock at night, in a condition when the physical had decidedly attained the upper hand of the intellectual. Tom and Adolph assisted to get him composed for the night, the latter in high spirits, evidently regarding the matter as a good joke, and laughing heartily at the rusticity of Tom's horror, who really was simple enough to lie awake most of the rest of the night, praying for his young master.

"Well, Tom, what are you waiting for?" said St. Clare, the next day, as he sat in his library, in dressing-gown and slippers. St. Clare had just been intrusting Tom with some money, and various commissions. "Is n't all right there, Tom?" he added, as Tom still stood waiting.

"I 'm 'fraid not, Mas'r," said Tom, with a grave face.

St. Clare laid down his paper, and set down his coffee-cup, and looked at Tom.

"Why, Tom, what 's the case? You look as solemn as a coffin."

"I feel very bad, Mas'r. I allays have thought that Mas'r would be good to everybody."

"Well, Tom, have n't I been? Come, now, what do you want? There 's something you have n't got, I suppose, and this is the preface."

"Mas'r allays been good to me. I have n't nothing to complain of, on that head. But there is one that Mas'r is n't good to."

"Why, Tom, what 's got into you? Speak out; what do you mean?"

"Last night, between one and two, I thought so. I studied upon the matter then. Mas'r isn't good to *himself*."

Tom said this with his back to his master, and his hand on the door-knob. St. Clare felt his face flush crimson, but he laughed.

"O, that's all, is it?" he said, gayly.

"All!" said Tom, turning suddenly round and falling on his knees. "O, my dear young Mas'r! I'm 'fraid it will be *loss of all—all*—body and soul. The good Book says, 'it biteth like a serpent and stingeth like an adder!' my dear Mas'r!"

Tom's voice choked, and the tears ran down his cheeks.

"You poor, silly fool!" said St. Clare, with tears in his own eyes. "Get up, Tom. I'm not worth crying over."

But Tom wouldn't rise, and looked imploring.

"Well, I won't go to any more of their cursed nonsense, Tom," said St. Clare; "on my honor, I won't. I don't know why I have n't stopped long ago. I 've always despised *it*, and myself for it,—so now, Tom, wipe up your eyes, and go about your errands. Come, come," he added, "no blessings. I 'm not so wonderfully good, now," he said, as he gently pushed Tom to the door. "There, I 'll pledge my honor to you, Tom, you don't see me so again," he said; and Tom went off, wiping his eyes, with great satisfaction.

"I 'll keep my faith with him, too," said St. Clare, as he closed the door.

And St. Clare did so,—for gross sensualism, in any form, was not the peculiar temptation of his nature.

But, all this time, who shall detail the tribulations manifold of our friend Miss Ophelia, who had begun the labors of a Southern housekeeper?

There is all the difference in the world in the servants of Southern establishments, according to the character and capacity of the mistresses who have brought them up.

South as well as north, there are women who have an extraordinary talent for command, and tact in educating. Such are enabled, with apparent ease, and without severity, to subject to their will, and bring into harmonious and systematic order, the various members of their small estate,—to regulate their peculiarities, and so balance and compensate the deficiencies of one by the excess of another, as to produce a harmonious and orderly system.

Such a housekeeper was Mrs. Shelby, whom we have already described; and such our readers may remember to have met with. If they are not common at the South, it is because they are not common in the world. They are to be found there as often as anywhere; and, when existing, find in that peculiar state of society a brilliant opportunity to exhibit their domestic talent.

Such a housekeeper Marie St. Clare was not, nor her mother before her. Indolent and childish, unsystematic and improvident, it was not to be expected that servants trained under her care should not be so likewise; and she had very justly described to Miss Ophelia the state of confusion she would find in the family, though she had not ascribed it to the proper cause.

The first morning of her regency, Miss Ophelia was up at four o'clock; and having attended to all the adjustments of her own chamber, as she had done ever since she came there, to the great amazement of the chamber-maid, she prepared for a vigorous onslaught on the cupboards and closets of the establishment of which she had the keys.

The store-room, the linen-presses, the china-closet, and kitchen and cellar, that day, all went under an awful review. Hidden things of darkness were brought to light to an extent that alarmed all the principalities and powers of kitchen and chamber, and caused many wonderings and murmurings about "dese yer northern ladies" from the domestic cabinet.

Old Dinah, the head cook, and principal of all rule and authority in the kitchen department, was filled with wrath at what she considered an invasion of privilege. No feudal baron in *Magna Charta* times could have more thoroughly resented some incursion of the crown.

Dinah was a character in her own way, and it would be injustice to her memory not to give the reader a little idea of her. She was a native and essential cook, as much as Aunt Chloe,—cooking being an indigenous talent of the African race; but Chloe was a trained and methodical one, who moved in an orderly domestic harness, while Dinah was a self-taught genius, and, like geniuses in general, was positive, opinionated and erratic, to the last degree.

Like a certain class of modern philosophers, Dinah perfectly scorned logic and reason in every shape, and always took refuge in intuitive certainty; and here she was perfectly impregnable. No possible amount of talent, or authority, or explanation, could ever make her believe that any other way was better than her own, or that the course she had pursued in the smallest matter could be in the least modified. This had been a conceded point with her old mistress, Marie's mother; and "Miss Marie," as Dinah always called her young mistress, even after her marriage, found it easier to submit than contend; and so Dinah had ruled supreme. This was the easier, in that she was perfect mistress of that diplomatic art which unites the utmost subservience of manner with the utmost inflexibility as to measure.

Dinah was mistress of the whole art and mystery of excuse-making, in all its branches. Indeed, it was an axiom with her that the cook can do no wrong; and a cook in a Southern kitchen finds abundance of heads and shoulders on which to lay off every sin and frailty, so as to maintain her own immaculateness entire. If any part of the dinner was a failure, there were fifty indisputably good reasons for it; and it was the fault undeniably of fifty other people, whom Dinah berated with unsparing zeal.

But it was very seldom that there was any failure in Dinah's last results. Though her mode of doing everything was peculiarly meandering and circuitous, and without any sort of calculation as to time and place,—though her kitchen generally looked as if it had been arranged by a hurricane blowing through it, and she had about as many places for each cooking utensil as there were days in the year,—yet, if one would have patience to wait her own good time, up would come her dinner in perfect order, and in a style of preparation with which an epicure could find no fault.

It was now the season of incipient preparation for dinner. Dinah, who required large intervals of reflection and repose, and was studious of ease in all her arrangements, was seated on the kitchen floor, smoking a short, stumpy pipe, to which she was much addicted, and which she always kindled up, as a sort of censer, whenever she felt the need of an inspiration in her arrangements. It was Dinah's mode of invoking the domestic Muses.

Seated around her were various members of that rising race with which a Southern household abounds, engaged in shelling peas, peeling potatoes, picking pin–feathers out of fowls, and other preparatory arrangements,—Dinah every once in a while interrupting her meditations to give a poke, or a rap on the head, to some of the young operators, with the pudding–stick that lay by her side. In fact, Dinah ruled over the woolly heads of the younger members with a rod of iron, and seemed to consider them born for no earthly purpose but to "save her steps," as she phrased it. It was the spirit of the system under which she had grown up, and she carried it out to its full extent.

Miss Ophelia, after passing on her reformatory tour through all the other parts of the establishment, now entered the kitchen. Dinah had heard, from various sources, what was going on, and resolved to stand on defensive and conservative ground,—mentally determined to oppose and ignore every new measure, without any actual and observable contest.

The kitchen was a large brick-floored apartment, with a great old-fashioned fireplace stretching along one side of it,—an arrangement which St. Clare had vainly tried to persuade Dinah to exchange for the convenience of a modern cookstove. Not she. No Puseyite, or conservative of any school, was ever more inflexibly attached to time-honored inconveniencies than Dinah.

When St. Clare had first returned from the north, impressed with the system and order of his uncle's kitchen arrangements, he had largely provided his own with an array of cupboards, drawers, and various apparatus, to induce systematic regulation, under the sanguine illusion that it would be of any possible assistance to Dinah in her arrangements. He might as well have provided them for a squirrel or a magpie. The more drawers and closets there were, the more hiding-holes could Dinah make for the accommodation of old rags, hair-combs, old shoes, ribbons, cast-off artificial flowers, and other articles of *vertu*, wherein her soul delighted.

When Miss Ophelia entered the kitchen, Dinah did not rise, but smoked on in sublime tranquillity, regarding her movements obliquely out of the corner of her eye, but apparently intent only on the operations around her.

Miss Ophelia commenced opening a set of drawers.

"What is this drawer for, Dinah?" she said.

"It 's handy for most anything, Missis," said Dinah. So it appeared to be. From the variety it contained, Miss Ophelia pulled out first a fine damask table-cloth stained with blood, having evidently been used to envelop some raw meat.

"What 's this, Dinah? You don't wrap up meat in your mistress' best table-cloths?"

"O Lor, Missis, no; the towels was all a missin',—so I jest did it. I laid out to wash that ar,—that 's why I put it thar."

"Shif'less!" said Miss Ophelia to herself, proceeding to tumble over the drawer, where she found a nutmeg-grater and two or three nutmegs, a Methodist hymn-book, a couple of soiled Madras handkerchiefs, some yarn and knitting-work, a paper of tobacco and a pipe, a few crackers, one or two gilded china-saucers with some pomade in them, one or two thin old shoes, a piece of flannel carefully pinned up enclosing some small white onions, several damask table-napkins, some coarse crash towels, some twine and darning-needles, and several broken papers, from which sundry sweet herbs were sifting into the drawer.

"Where do you keep your nutmegs, Dinah?" said Miss Ophelia, with the air of one who prayed for patience.

"Most anywhar, Missis; there 's some in that cracked teacup, up there, and there 's some over in that ar cupboard."

"Here are some in the grater," said Miss Ophelia, holding them up.

"Laws, yes, I put 'em there this morning,—I likes to keep my things handy," said Dinah. "You, Jake! what are you stopping for! You 'll cotch it! Be still, thar!" she added, with a dive of her stick at the criminal.

"What 's this?" said Miss Ophelia, holding up the saucer of pomade.

"Laws, it 's my har *grease*;—I put it thar to have it handy."

"Do you use your mistress' best saucers for that?"

"Law! it was cause I was driv, and in sich a hurry;—I was gwine to change it this very day."

"Here are two damask table-napkins."

"Them table-napkins I put thar, to get 'em washed out, some day."

"Don't you have some place here on purpose for things to be washed?"

"Well, Mas'r St. Clare got dat ar chest, he said, for dat; but I likes to mix up biscuit and hev my things on it some days, and then it an't handy a liftin' up the lid."

"Why don't you mix your biscuits on the pastry-table, there?"

"Law, Missis, it gets sot so full of dishes, and one thing and another, der an't no room, noways—"

"But you should *wash* your dishes, and clear them away."

"Wash my dishes!" said Dinah, in a high key, as her wrath began to rise over her habitual respect of manner; "what does ladies know 'bout work, I want to know? When 'd Mas'r ever get his dinner, if I was to spend all my time a washin' and a puttin' up dishes? Miss Marie never told me so, nohow."

"Well, here are these onions."

"Laws, yes!" said Dinah; "thar *is* whar I put 'em, now. I could n't 'member. Them 's particular onions I was a savin' for dis yer very stew. I 'd forgot they was in dat ar old flannel."

Miss Ophelia lifted out the sifting papers of sweet herbs.

"I wish Missis would n't touch dem ar. I likes to keep my things where I knows whar to go to 'em," said Dinah, rather decidedly.

"But you don't want these holes in the papers."

"Them 's handy for siftin' on 't out," said Dinah.

"But you see it spills all over the drawer."

"Laws, yes! if Missis will go a tumblin' things all up so, it will. Missis has spilt lots dat ar way," said Dinah, coming uneasily to the drawers. "If Missis only will go up stars till my clarin' up time comes, I 'll have everything right; but I can't do nothin' when ladies is round, a henderin'. You, Sam, don't you gib the baby dat ar sugar-bowl! I 'll crack ye over, if ye don't mind!"

"I 'm going through the kitchen, and going to put everything in order, *once*, Dinah; and then I 'll expect you to *keep* it so."

"Lor, now! Miss Phelia; dat ar an't no way for ladies to do. I never did see ladies doin' no sich; my old Missis nor Miss Marie never did, and I don't see no kinder need on 't;" and Dinah stalked indignantly about, while Miss Ophelia piled and sorted dishes, emptied dozens of scattering bowls of sugar into one receptacle, sorted napkins, table-cloths, and towels, for washing; washing, wiping, and arranging with her own hands, and with a speed and alacrity which perfectly amazed Dinah.

"Lor, now! if dat ar de way dem northern ladies do, dey an't ladies, nohow," she said to some of her satellites, when at a safe hearing distance. "I has things as straight as anybody, when my clarin' up time comes; but I don't want ladies round, a henderin', and getting my things all where I can't find 'em."

To do Dinah justice, she had, at irregular periods, paroxysms of reformation and arrangement, which she called "clarin' up times," when she would begin with great zeal, and turn every drawer and closet wrong side outward, on to the floor or tables, and make the ordinary confusion seven-fold more confounded. Then she would light her pipe, and leisurely go over her arrangements, looking things over, and discoursing upon them; making all the young fry scour most vigorously on the tin things, and keeping up for several hours a most energetic state of confusion, which she would explain to the satisfaction of all inquirers, by the remark that she was a "clarin' up." "She could n't hev things a gwine on so as they had been, and she was gwine to make these yer young ones keep better order;" for Dinah herself, somehow, indulged the illusion that she, herself, was the soul of order, and it was only the *young uns*, and the everybody else in the house, that were the cause of anything that fell short of perfection in this respect. When all the tins were scoured, and the tables scrubbed snowy white, and everything that could offend tucked out of sight in holes and corners, Dinah would dress herself up in a smart dress, clean apron, and high, brilliant Madras turban, and tell all marauding "young uns" to keep out of the kitchen, for she was gwine to have things kept nice. Indeed, these periodic seasons were often an inconvenience to the whole household; for Dinah would contract such an immoderate attachment to her scoured tin, as to insist upon it that it should n't be used again for any possible purpose,—at least, till the ardor of the "clarin' up" period abated.

Miss Ophelia, in a few days, thoroughly reformed every department of the house to a systematic pattern; but her labors in all departments that depended on the coöperation of servants were like those of Sisyphus or the Danaides. In despair, she one day appealed to St. Clare.

"There is no such thing as getting anything like system in this family!"

"To be sure, there is n't," said St. Clare.

"Such shiftless management, such waste, such confusion, I never saw!"

"I dare say you did n't."

"You would not take it so coolly, if you were housekeeper."

"My dear cousin, you may as well understand, once for all, that we masters are divided into two classes, oppressors and oppressed. We who are good-natured and hate severity make up our minds to a good deal of inconvenience. If we *will keep* a shambling, loose, untaught set in the community, for our convenience, why, we must take the consequence. Some rare cases I have seen, of persons, who, by a peculiar tact, can produce order and system without severity; but I 'm not one of them,—and so I made up my mind, long ago, to let things go just as they do. I will not have the poor devils thrashed and cut to pieces, and they know it,—and, of course, they know the staff is in their own hands."

"But to have no time, no place, no order,—all going on in this shiftless way!"

"My dear Vermont, you natives up by the North Pole set an extravagant value on time! What on earth is the use of time to a fellow who has twice as much of it as he knows what to do with? As to order and system, where there is nothing to be done but to lounge on the sofa and read, an hour sooner or later in breakfast or dinner is n't of much account. Now, there 's Dinah gets you a capital dinner,—soup, ragout, roast fowl, dessert, ice-creams and all,—and she creates it all out of chaos and old night down there, in that kitchen. I think it really sublime, the way she manages. But, Heaven bless us! if we are to go down there, and view all the smoking and squatting about, and hurryscurryation of the preparatory process, we should never eat more! My good cousin, absolve yourself from that! It 's more than a Catholic penance, and does no more good. You 'll only lose your own temper, and utterly confound Dinah. Let her go her own way."

"But, Augustine, you don't know how I found things."

"Don't I? Don't I know that the rolling-pin is under her bed, and the nutmeg-grater in her pocket with her tobacco,—that there are sixty-five different sugar-bowls, one in every hole in the house,—that she washes dishes with a dinner-napkin one day, and with a fragment of an old petticoat the next? But the upshot is, she gets up glorious dinners, makes superb coffee; and you must judge her as warriors and statesmen are judged, by *her success.*"

"But the waste,—the expense!"

"O, well! Lock everything you can, and keep the key. Give out by driblets, and never inquire for odds and ends,—it is n't best."

"That troubles me, Augustine. I can't help feeling as if these servants were not *strictly honest.* Are you sure they can be relied on?"

Augustine laughed immoderately at the grave and anxious face with which Miss Ophelia propounded the question.

"O, cousin, that 's too good,—*honest!*—as if that 's a thing to be expected! Honest!—why, of course, they arn't. Why should they be? What upon earth is to make them so?"

"Why don't you instruct?"

"Instruct! O, fiddlestick! What instructing do you think I should do? I look like it! As to Marie, she has spirit enough, to be sure, to kill off a whole plantation, if I 'd let her manage; but she would n't get the cheatery out of them."

"Are there no honest ones?"

"Well, now and then one, whom Nature makes so impracticably simple, truthful and faithful, that the worst possible influence can't destroy it. But, you see, from the mother's breast the colored child feels and sees that there are none but underhand ways open to it. It can get along no other way with its parents, its mistress, its young master and missie playfellows. Cunning and deception become necessary, inevitable habits. It is n't fair to expect anything else of him. He ought not to be punished for it. As to honesty, the slave is kept in that dependent, semi-childish state, that there is no making him realize the rights of property, or feel that his master's goods are not his own, if he can get them. For my part, I don't see how they *can* be honest. Such a fellow as Tom, here, is—is a moral miracle!"

"And what becomes of their souls?" said Miss Ophelia.

"That is n't my affair, as I know of," said St. Clare; "I am only dealing in facts of the present life. The fact is, that the whole race are pretty generally understood to be turned over to the devil, for our benefit, in this world, however it may turn out in another!"

"This is perfectly horrible!" said Miss Ophelia; "you ought to be ashamed of yourselves!"

"I don't know as I am. We are in pretty good company, for all that," said St. Clare, "as people in the broad road generally are. Look at the high and the low, all the world over, and it 's the same story,—the lower class used up, body, soul and spirit, for the good of the upper. It is so in England; it is so everywhere; and yet all Christendom stands aghast, with virtuous indignation, because we do the thing in a little different shape from what they do it."

"It is n't so in Vermont."

"Ah, well, in New England, and in the free States, you have the better of us, I grant. But there 's the bell; so, Cousin, let us for a while lay aside our sectional prejudices, and come out to dinner."

As Miss Ophelia was in the kitchen in the latter part of the afternoon, some of the sable children called out, "La, sakes! thar 's Prue a coming, grunting along like she allers does."

A tall, bony colored woman now entered the kitchen, bearing on her head a basket of rusks and hot rolls.

"Ho, Prue! you 've come," said Dinah.

Prue had a peculiar scowling expression of countenance, and a sullen, grumbling voice. She set down her basket, squatted herself down, and resting her elbows on her knees, said,

"O Lord! I wish 't I 's dead!"

"Why do you wish you were dead?" said Miss Ophelia.

"I 'd be out o' my misery," said the woman, gruffly, without taking her eyes from the floor.

"What need you getting drunk, then, and cutting up, Prue?" said a spruce quadroon chambermaid, dangling, as she spoke, a pair of coral ear-drops.

The woman looked at her with a sour, surly glance.

"Maybe you 'll come to it, one of these yer days. I 'd be glad to see you, I would; then you 'll be glad of a drop, like me, to forget your misery."

"Come, Prue," said Dinah, "let 's look at your rusks. Here 's Missis will pay for them."

Miss Ophelia took out a couple of dozen.

"Thar 's some tickets in that ar old cracked jug on the top shelf," said Dinah. "You, Jake, climb up and get it down."

"Tickets,—what are they for?" said Miss Ophelia.

"We buys tickets of her Mas'r, and she gives us bread for 'em."

"And they counts my money and tickets, when I gets home, to see if I 's got the change; and if I han't, they half kills me."

"And serves you right," said Jane, the pert chambermaid, "if you will take their money to get drunk on. That 's what she does, Missis."

"And that 's what I *will* do,—I can't live no other ways,—drink and forget my misery."

"You are very wicked and very foolish," said Miss Ophelia, "to steal your master's money to make yourself a brute with."

"It 's mighty likely, Missis; but I will do it,—yes, I will. O Lord! I wish I 's dead, I do,—I wish I 's dead, and out of my misery!" and slowly and stiffly the old creature rose, and got her basket on her head again; but before she went out, she looked at the quadroon girl, who still stood playing with her ear-drops.

"Ye think ye 're mighty fine with them ar, a frolickin' and a tossin' your head, and a lookin' down on everybody. Well, never mind,—you may live to be a poor, old, cut-up crittur, like me. Hope to the Lord ye will, I do; then see if ye won't drink,—drink,—drink,—yerself into torment; and sarve ye right, too—ugh!" and, with a malignant howl, the woman left the room.

"Disgusting old beast!" said Adolph, who was getting his master's shaving-water. "If I was her master, I 'd cut her up worse than she is."

"Ye could n't do that ar, no ways," said Dinah. "Her back 's a far sight now,— she can't never get a dress together over it."

"I think such low creatures ought not to be allowed to go round to genteel families," said Miss Jane. "What do you think, Mr. St. Clare?" she said, coquettishly tossing her head at Adolph.

It must be observed that, among other appropriations from his master's stock, Adolph was in the habit of adopting his name and address; and that the style under which he moved, among the colored circles of New Orleans, was that of *Mr. St. Clare.*

"I 'm certainly of your opinion, Miss Benoir," said Adolph.

Benoir was the name of Marie St. Clare's family, and Jane was one of her servants.

"Pray, Miss Benoir, may I be allowed to ask if those drops are for the ball, to-morrow night? They are certainly bewitching!"

"I wonder, now, Mr. St. Clare, what the impudence of you men will come to!" said Jane, tossing her pretty head till the ear-drops twinkled again. "I shan't dance with you for a whole evening, if you go to asking me any more questions."

"O, you could n't be so cruel, now! I was just dying to know whether you would appear in your pink tarletane," said Adolph.

"What is it?" said Rosa, a bright, piquant little quadroon, who came skipping down stairs at this moment.

"Why, Mr. St. Clare's so impudent!"

"On my honor," said Adolph, "I'll leave it to Miss Rosa, now."

"I know he 's always a saucy creature," said Rosa, poising herself on one of her little feet, and looking maliciously at Adolph. "He 's always getting me so angry with him."

"O! ladies, ladies, you will certainly break my heart, between you," said Adolph. "I shall be found dead in my bed, some morning, and you 'll have it to answer for."

"Do hear the horrid creature talk!" said both ladies, laughing immoderately.

"Come,—clar out, you! I can't have you cluttering up the kitchen," said Dinah; "in my way, foolin' round here."

"Aunt Dinah's glum, because she can't go to the ball," said Rosa.

"Don't want none o' your light-colored balls," said Dinah; "cuttin' round, makin' b'lieve you 's white folks. Arter all, you 's niggers, much as I am."

"Aunt Dinah greases her wool stiff, every day, to make it lie straight," said Jane.

"And it will be wool, after all," said Rosa, maliciously shaking down her long, silky curls.

"Well, in the Lord's sight, an't wool as good as har, any time?" said Dinah. "I 'd like to have Missis say which is worth the most,—a couple such as you, or one like me. Get out wid ye, ye trumpery,—I won't have ye round!"

Here the conversation was interrupted in a two-fold manner. St. Clare's voice was heard at the head of the stairs, asking Adolph if he meant to stay all night with his shaving-water; and Miss Ophelia, coming out of the dining–room, said,

"Jane and Rosa, what are you wasting your time for, here? Go in and attend to your muslins."

Our friend Tom, who had been in the kitchen during the conversation with the old rusk-woman, had followed her out into the street. He saw her go on, giving every once in a while a suppressed groan. At last she set her basket down on a door-step, and began arranging the old, faded shawl which covered her shoulders.

"I 'll carry your basket a piece," said Tom, compassionately.

"Why should ye?" said the woman. "I don't want no help."

"You seem to be sick, or in trouble, or somethin'," said Tom.

"I an't sick," said the woman, shortly.

"I wish," said Tom, looking at her earnestly,—"I wish I could persuade you to leave off drinking. Don't you know it will be the ruin of ye, body and soul?"

"I knows I 'm gwine to torment," said the woman, sullenly. "Ye don't need to tell me that ar. I 's ugly,—I 's wicked,—I 's gwine straight to torment. O, Lord! I wish I 's thar!"

Tom shuddered at these frightful words, spoken with a sullen, impassioned earnestness.

"O, Lord have mercy on ye! poor crittur. Han't ye never heard of Jesus Christ?"

"Jesus Christ,—who 's he?"

"Why, he 's *the Lord*," said Tom.

"I think I 've hearn tell o' the Lord, and the judgment and torment. I 've heard o' that."

"But did n't anybody ever tell you of the Lord Jesus, that loved us poor sinners, and died for us?"

"Don't know nothin' 'bout that," said the woman; "nobody han't never loved me, since my old man died."

"Where was you raised?" said Tom.

"Up in Kentuck. A man kept me to breed chil'en for market, and sold 'em as fast as they got big enough; last of all, he sold me to a speculator, and my Mas'r got me o' him."

"What set you into this bad way of drinkin'?"

"To get shet o' my misery. I had one child after I come here; and I thought then I 'd have one to raise, cause Mas'r was n't a speculator. It was de peartest little thing! and Missis she seemed to think a heap on 't, at first; it never cried,— it was likely and fat. But Missis tuck sick, and I tended her; and I tuck the fever, and my milk all left me, and the child it pined to skin and bone, and Missis would n't buy milk for it. She would n't hear to me, when I told her I had n't milk. She said she knowed I could feed it on what other folks eat; and the child kinder pined, and cried, and cried, and cried, day and night, and got all gone to skin and bones, and Missis got sot agin it, and she said 't wan't nothin' but crossness. She wished it was dead, she said; and she would n't let me have it o' nights, cause, she said, it kept me awake, and made me good for nothing. She made me sleep in her room; and I had to put it away off in a little kind o' garret, and thar it cried itself to death, one night. It did; and I tuck to drinkin', to keep its crying out of my ears! I did,—and I will drink! I will, if I do go to torment for it! Mas'r says I shall go to torment, and I tell him I 've got thar now!"

"O, ye poor crittur!" said Tom, "han't nobody never told ye how the Lord Jesus loved ye, and died for ye? Han't they told ye that he 'll help ye, and ye can go to heaven, and have rest, at last?"

"I looks like gwine to heaven," said the woman; "an't thar where white folks is gwine? S'pose they 'd have me thar? I 'd rather go to torment, and get away from Mas'r and Missis. I had *so*," she said, as, with her usual groan, she got her basket on her head, and walked sullenly away.

Tom turned, and walked sorrowfully back to the house. In the court he met little Eva,—a crown of tuberoses on her head, and her eyes radiant with delight.

"O, Tom! here you are. I 'm glad I 've found you. Papa says you may get out the ponies, and take me in my little new carriage," she said, catching his hand. "But what 's the matter, Tom?—you look sober."

"I feel bad, Miss Eva," said Tom, sorrowfully. "But I 'll get the horses for you."

"But do tell me, Tom, what is the matter. I saw you talking to cross old Prue."

Tom, in simple, earnest phrase, told Eva the woman's history. She did not exclaim, or wonder, or weep, as other children do. Her cheeks grew pale, and a deep, earnest shadow passed over her eyes. She laid both hands on her bosom, and sighed heavily.

## VOLUME II

### XIX.
### *Miss Ophelia's Experiences and Opinions, Continued*

"Tom, you need n't get me the horses. I don't want to go," she said.

"Why not, Miss Eva?"

"These things sink into my heart, Tom," said Eva,—"they sink into my heart," she repeated, earnestly. "I don't want to go;" and she turned from Tom, and went into the house.

A few days after, another woman came, in old Prue's place, to bring the rusks; Miss Ophelia was in the kitchen.

"Lor!" said Dinah, "what 's got Prue?"

"Prue isn't coming any more," said the woman, mysteriously.

"Why not?" said Dinah. "She an't dead, is she?"

"We does n't exactly know. She 's down cellar," said the woman, glancing at Miss Ophelia.

After Miss Ophelia had taken the rusks, Dinah followed the woman to the door.

"What *has* got Prue, any how?" she said.

The woman seemed desirous, yet reluctant, to speak, and answered, in a low, mysterious tone.

"Well, you must n't tell nobody. Prue, she got drunk agin,—and they had her down cellar,—and thar they left her all day,—and I hearn 'em saying that the *flies had got to her,—and she 's dead!*"

Dinah held up her hands, and, turning, saw close by her side the spirit–like form of Evangeline, her large, mystic eyes dilated with horror, and every drop of blood driven from her lips and cheeks.

"Lor bless us! Miss Eva 's gwine to faint away! What got us all, to let her har such talk? Her pa 'll be rail mad."

"I shan't faint, Dinah," said the child, firmly; "and why should n't I hear it? It an't so much for me to hear it, as for poor Prue to suffer it."

"*Lor sakes*! it is n't for sweet, delicate young ladies like you,—these yer stories is n't; it 's enough to kill 'em!"

Eva sighed again, and walked up stairs with a slow and melancholy step.

Miss Ophelia anxiously inquired the woman's story. Dinah gave a very garrulous version of it, to which Tom added the particulars which he had drawn from her that morning.

"An abominable business,—perfectly horrible!" she exclaimed, as she entered the room where St. Clare lay reading his paper.

"Pray, what iniquity has turned up now?" said he.

"What now? why, those folks have whipped Prue to death!" said Miss Ophelia, going on, with great strength of detail, into the story, and enlarging on its most shocking particulars.

"I thought it would come to that, some time," said St. Clare, going on with his paper.

"Thought so!—an't you going to *do* anything about it?" said Miss Ophelia. "Have n't you got any *selectmen*, or anybody, to interfere and look after such matters?"

"It 's commonly supposed that the *property* interest is a sufficient guard in these cases. If people choose to ruin their own possessions, I don't know what 's to be done. It seems the poor creature was a thief and a drunkard; and so there won't be much hope to get up sympathy for her."

"It is perfectly outrageous,—it is horrid, Augustine! It will certainly bring down vengeance upon you."

"My dear cousin, I did n't do it, and I can't help it; I would, if I could. If low-minded, brutal people will act like themselves, what am I to do? They have absolute control; they are irresponsible despots. There would be no use in interfering; there is no law that amounts to anything practically, for such a case. The best we can do is to shut our eyes and ears, and let it alone. It 's the only resource left us."

"How can you shut your eyes and ears? How can you let such things alone?"

"My dear child, what do you expect? Here is a whole class,—debased, uneducated, indolent, provoking,—put, without any sort of terms or conditions, entirely into the hands of such people as the majority in our world are; people who have neither consideration nor self-control, who have n't even an enlightened regard to their own interest,—for that 's the case with the largest half of mankind. Of course, in a community so organized, what can a man of honorable and humane feelings do, but shut his eyes all he can, and harden his heart? I can't buy every poor wretch I see. I can't turn knight-errant, and undertake to redress every individual case of wrong in such a city as this. The most I can do is to try and keep out of the way of it."

St. Clare's fine countenance was for a moment overcast; he looked annoyed, but suddenly calling up a gay smile, he said,

"Come, cousin, don't stand there looking like one of the Fates; you 've only seen a peep through the curtain,—a specimen of what is going on, the world over, in some shape or other. If we are to be prying and spying into all the dismals of life, we should have no heart to anything. 'T is like looking too close into the details of Dinah's kitchen;" and St. Clare lay back on the sofa, and busied himself with his paper.

Miss Ophelia sat down, and pulled out her knitting-work, and sat there grim with indignation. She knit and knit, but while she mused the fire burned; at last she broke out—

"I tell you, Augustine, I can't get over things so, if you can. It 's a perfect abomination for you to defend such a system,—that 's *my* mind!"

"What now?" said St. Clare, looking up. "At it again, hey?"

"I say it 's perfectly abominable for you to defend such a system!" said Miss Ophelia, with increasing warmth.

"*I* defend it, my dear lady? Who ever said I did defend it?" said St. Clare.

"Of course, you defend it,—you all do,—all you Southerners. What do you have slaves for, if you don't?"

"Are you such a sweet innocent as to suppose nobody in this world ever does what they don't think is right? Don't you, or did n't you ever, do anything that you did not think quite right?"

"If I do, I repent of it, I hope," said Miss Ophelia, rattling her needles with energy.

"So, do I," said St. Clare, peeling his orange; "I 'm repenting of it all the time."

"What do you keep on doing it for?"

"Did n't you ever keep on doing wrong, after you 'd repented, my good cousin?"

"Well, only when I 've been very much tempted," said Miss Ophelia.

"Well, I 'm very much tempted," said St. Clare; "that 's just my difficulty."

"But I always resolve I won't, and I try to break off."

"Well, I have been resolving I won't, off and on, these ten years," said St. Clare; "but I have n't, some how, got clear. Have you got clear of all your sins, cousin?"

"Cousin Augustine," said Miss Ophelia, seriously, and laying down her knitting-work. "I suppose I deserve that you should reprove my short-comings. I know all you say is true enough; nobody else feels them more than I do; but it does seem to me, after all, there is some difference between me and you. It seems to me I would cut off my right hand sooner than keep on, from day to day, doing what I thought was wrong. But, then, my conduct is so inconsistent with my profession, I don't wonder you reprove me."

"O, now, cousin," said Augustine, sitting down on the floor, and laying his head back in her lap, "don't take on so awfully serious! You know what a good-for-nothing, saucy boy I always was. I love to poke you up,—that 's all,—just to see you get earnest. I do think you are desperately, distressingly good; it tires me to death to think of it."

"But this is a serious subject, my boy, Auguste," said Miss Ophelia, laying her hand on his forehead.

"Dismally so," said he; "and I—well, I never want to talk seriously in hot weather. What with mosquitos and all, a fellow can't get himself up to any very sublime moral flights; and I believe," said St. Clare, suddenly rousing himself up, "there 's a theory, now! I understand now why northern nations are always more virtuous than southern ones,—I see into that whole subject."

"O, Auguste, you are a sad rattle-brain!"

"Am I? Well, so I am, I suppose; but for once I will be serious, now; but you must hand me that basket of oranges;—you see, you 'll have to 'stay me with flagons and comfort me with apples,' if I 'm going to make this effort. Now," said Augustine, drawing the basket up, "I 'll begin: When, in the course of human events, it becomes necessary for a fellow to hold two or three dozen of his fellow-worms in captivity, a decent regard to the opinions of society requires—"

"I don't see that you are growing more serious," said Miss Ophelia.

"Wait,—I 'm coming on,—you 'll hear. The short of the matter is, cousin," said he, his handsome face suddenly settling into an earnest and serious expression, "on this abstract question of slavery there can, as I think, be but one opinion. Planters, who have money to make by it,—clergymen, who have planters to please,—politicians, who want to rule by it,—may warp and bend language and ethics to a degree that shall astonish the world at their ingenuity; they can press nature and the Bible, and nobody knows what else, into the service; but, after all, neither they nor the world believe in it one particle the more. It comes from the devil, that's the short of it;—and, to my mind, it's a pretty respectable specimen of what he can do in his own line."

Miss Ophelia stopped her knitting, and looked surprised; and St. Clare, apparently enjoying her astonishment, went on.

"You seem to wonder; but if you will get me fairly at it, I'll make a clean breast of it. This cursed business, accursed of God and man, what is it? Strip it of all its ornament, run it down to the root and nucleus of the whole, and what is it? Why, because my brother Quashy is ignorant and weak, and I am intelligent and strong,—because I know how, and *can* do it,—therefore, I may steal all he has, keep it, and give him only such and so much as suits my fancy. Whatever is too hard, too dirty, too disagreeable, for me, I may set Quashy to doing. Because I don't like work, Quashy shall work. Because the sun burns me, Quashy shall stay in the sun. Quashy shall earn the money, and I will spend it. Quashy shall lie down in every puddle, that I may walk over dry-shod. Quashy shall do my will, and not his, all the days of his mortal life, and have such chance of getting to heaven, at last, as I find convenient. This I take to be about what slavery *is*. I defy anybody on earth to read our slave-code, as it stands in our lawbooks, and make anything else of it. Talk of the *abuses* of slavery! Humbug! The *thing itself* is the essence of all abuse! And the only reason why the land don't sink under it, like Sodom and Gomorrah, is because it is *used* in a way infinitely better than it is. For pity's sake, for shame's sake, because we are men born of women, and not savage beasts, many of us do not, and dare not,—we would *scorn* to use the full power which our savage laws put into our hands. And he who goes the furthest, and does the worst, only uses within limits the power that the law gives him."

St. Clare had started up, and, as his manner was when excited, was walking, with hurried steps, up and down the floor. His fine face, classic as that of a Greek statue, seemed actually to burn with the fervor of his feelings. His large blue eyes flashed, and he gestured with an unconscious eagerness. Miss Ophelia had never seen him in this mood before, and she sat perfectly silent.

"I declare to you," said he, suddenly stopping before his cousin "(it's no sort of use to talk or to feel on this subject), but I declare to you, there have been times when I have thought, if the whole country would sink, and hide all this injustice and misery from the light, I would willingly sink with it. When I have been travelling up and down on our boats, or about on my collecting tours, and reflected that every brutal, disgusting, mean, low-lived fellow I met, was allowed by our laws to become absolute despot of as many men, women and children, as he could cheat, steal, or gamble money enough to buy,—when I have seen such men in actual ownership of helpless children, of young girls and women,—I have been ready to curse my country, to curse the human race!"

"Augustine! Augustine!" said Miss Ophelia, "I'm sure you've said enough. I never, in my life, heard anything like this, even at the North."

"At the North!" said St. Clare, with a sudden change of expression, and resuming something of his habitual careless tone. "Pooh! your northern folks are cold-blooded; you are cool in everything! You can't begin to curse up hill and down as we can, when we get fairly at it."

"Well, but the question is," said Miss Ophelia.

"O, yes, to be sure, the *question is,*—and a deuce of a question it is! How came *you* in this state of sin and misery? Well, I shall answer in the good old words you used to teach me, Sundays. I came so by ordinary generation. My servants were my father's, and, what is more, my mother's; and now they are mine, they and their increase, which bids fair to be a pretty considerable item. My father, you know, came first from New England; and he was just such another man as your father,—a regular old Roman,—upright, energetic, noble-minded, with an iron will. Your father settled down in New England, to rule over rocks and stones, and to force an existence out of Nature; and mine settled in Louisiana, to rule over men and women, and force existence out of them. My mother," said St. Clare, getting up and walking to a picture at the end of the room, and gazing upward with a face fervent with veneration, "*she* was *divine!* Don't look at me so!—you know what I mean! She probably was of mortal birth; but, as far as ever I could observe, there was no trace of any human weakness or error about her; and everybody that lives to remember her, whether bond or free, servant, acquaintance, relation, all say the same. Why, cousin, that mother has been all that has stood between me and utter unbelief for years. She was a direct embodiment and personification of the New Testament,—a living fact, to be accounted for, and to be accounted for in no other way than by its truth. O, mother! mother!" said St. Clare, clasping his hands, in a sort of transport; and then suddenly checking himself, he came back, and seating himself on an ottoman, he went on:

"My brother and I were twins; and they say, you know, that twins ought to resemble each other; but we were in all points a contrast. He had black, fiery eyes, coal-black hair, a strong, fine Roman profile, and a rich brown complexion. I had blue eyes, golden hair, a Greek outline, and fair complexion. He was active and observing, I dreamy and inactive. He was generous to his friends and equals, but proud, dominant, overbearing, to inferiors, and utterly unmerciful to whatever set itself up against him. Truthful we both were; he from pride and courage, I from a sort of abstract ideality. We loved each other about as boys generally do,— off and on, and in general;—he was my father's pet, and I my mother's.

"There was a morbid sensitiveness and acuteness of feeling in me on all possible subjects, of which he and my father had no kind of understanding, and with which they could have no possible sympathy. But mother did; and so, when I had quarrelled with Alfred, and father looked sternly on me, I used to go off to mother's room, and sit by her. I remember just how she used to look, with her pale cheeks, her deep, soft, serious eyes, her white dress,—she always wore white; and I used to think of her whenever I read in Revelations about the saints that were arrayed in fine linen, clean and white. She had a great deal of genius of one sort and another, particularly in music; and she used to sit at her organ, playing fine old majestic music of the Catholic church, and singing with a voice more like an angel than a mortal woman; and I would lay my head down on her lap, and cry, and dream, and feel,—oh, immeasurably!—things that I had no language to say!

"In those days, this matter of slavery had never been canvassed as it has now; nobody dreamed of any harm in it.

"My father was a born aristocrat. I think, in some preëxistent state, he must have been in the higher circles of spirits, and brought all his old court pride along with him; for it was ingrain, bred in the bone, though he was originally of poor and not in any way of noble family. My brother was begotten in his image.

"Now, an aristocrat, you know, the world over, has no human sympathies, beyond a certain line in society. In England the line is in one place, in Burmah in another, and in America in another; but the aristocrat of all these countries never goes over it. What would be hardship and distress and injustice in his own class, is a cool matter of course in another one. My father's dividing line was that of color. *Among his equals*, never was a man more just and generous; but he considered the negro, through all possible gradations of color, as an intermediate link between man and animals, and graded all his ideas of justice or generosity on this hypothesis. I suppose, to be sure, if anybody had asked him, plump and fair, whether they had human immortal souls, he might have hemmed and hawed, and said yes. But my father was not a man much troubled with spiritualism; religious sentiment he had none, beyond a veneration for God, as decidedly the head of the upper classes.

"Well, my father worked some five hundred negroes; he was an inflexible, driving, punctilious business man; everything was to move by system,—to be sustained with unfailing accuracy and precision. Now, if you take into account that all this was to be worked out by a set of lazy, twaddling, shiftless laborers, who had grown up, all their lives, in the absence of every possible motive to learn how to do anything but 'shirk,' as you Vermonters say, and you'll see that there might naturally be, on his plantation, a great many things that looked horrible and distressing to a sensitive child, like me.

"Besides all, he had an overseer,—a great, tall, slab-sided, two-fisted renegade son of Vermont—(begging your pardon),—who had gone through a regular apprenticeship in hardness and brutality, and taken his degree to be admitted to practice. My mother never could endure him, nor I; but he obtained an entire ascendency over my father; and this man was the absolute despot of the estate.

"I was a little fellow then, but I had the same love that I have now for all kinds of human things,—a kind of passion for the study of humanity, come in what shape it would. I was found in the cabins and among the field-hands a great deal, and, of course, was a great favorite; and all sorts of complaints and grievances were breathed in my ear; and I told them to mother, and we, between us, formed a sort of committee for a redress of grievances. We hindered and repressed a great deal of cruelty, and congratulated ourselves on doing a vast deal of good, till, as often happens, my zeal overacted. Stubbs complained to my father that he could n't manage the hands, and must resign his position. Father was a fond, indulgent husband, but a man that never flinched from anything that he thought necessary; and so he put down his foot, like a rock, between us and the field-hands. He told my mother, in language perfectly respectful and deferential, but quite explicit, that over the house-servants she should be entire mistress, but that with the field-hands he could allow no interference. He revered and respected her above all living beings; but he would have said it all the same to the virgin Mary herself, if she had come in the way of his system.

"I used sometimes to hear my mother reasoning cases with him,—endeavoring to excite his sympathies. He would listen to the most pathetic appeals with the most discouraging politeness and equanimity. 'It all resolves itself into this,' he would say; 'must I part with Stubbs, or keep him? Stubbs is the soul of punctuality, honesty, and efficiency,—a thorough business hand, and as humane as the general run. We can't have perfection; and if I keep him, I must sustain his administration as a *whole*, even if there are, now and then, things that are exceptionable. All government includes some necessary hardness. General rules will bear hard on particular cases.' This last maxim my father seemed to consider a settler in most alleged cases of cruelty. After he had said *that*, he commonly drew up his feet on the sofa, like a man that has disposed of a business, and betook himself to a nap, or the newspaper, as the case might be.

"The fact is, my father showed the exact sort of talent for a statesman. He could have divided Poland as easily as an orange, or trod on Ireland as quietly and systematically as any man living. At last my mother gave up, in despair. It never will be known, till the last account, what noble and sensitive natures like hers have felt, cast, utterly helpless, into what seems to them an abyss of injustice and cruelty, and which seems so to nobody about them. It has been an age of long sorrow of such natures, in such a hell-begotten sort of world as ours. What remained for her, but to train her children in her own views and sentiments? Well, after all you say about training, children will grow up substantially what they *are* by nature, and only that. From the cradle, Alfred was an aristocrat; and as he grew up, instinctively, all his sympathies and all his reasonings were in that line, and all mother's exhortations went to the winds. As to me, they sunk deep into me. She never contradicted, in form, anything that my father said, or seemed directly to differ from him; but she impressed, burnt into my very soul, with all the force of her deep, earnest nature, an idea of the dignity and worth of the meanest human soul. I have looked in her face with solemn awe, when she would point up to the stars in the evening, and say to me, 'See there, Auguste! the poorest, meanest soul on our place will be living, when all these stars are gone forever,—will live as long as God lives!'

"She had some fine old paintings; one, in particular, of Jesus healing a blind man. They were very fine, and used to impress me strongly. 'See there, Auguste, she would say; 'the blind man was a beggar, poor and loathsome; therefore, he would not heal him *afar off*! He called him to him, and put *his hands on him*! Remember this, my boy.' If I had lived to grow up under her care, she might have stimulated me to I know not what of enthusiasm. I might have been a saint, reformer, martyr,—but, alas! alas! I went from her when I was only thirteen, and I never saw her again!"

St. Clare rested his head on his hands, and did not speak for some minutes. After a while, he looked up, and went on:

"What poor, mean trash this whole business of human virtue is! A mere matter, for the most part, of latitude and longitude, and geographical position, acting with natural temperament. The greater part is nothing but an accident! Your father, for example, settles in Vermont, in a town where all are, in fact, free and equal; becomes a regular church member and deacon, and in due time joins an Abolition society, and thinks us all little better than heathens. Yet he is, for all the world, in constitution and habit, a duplicate of my father. I can see it leaking out in fifty different ways,—just that same strong, overbearing, dominant spirit. You know very well how impossible it is to persuade some of the folks in your village that Squire Sinclair does not feel above them. The fact is, though he has fallen on democratic times, and embraced a democratic theory, he is to the heart an aristocrat, as much as my father, who ruled over five or six hundred slaves."

Miss Ophelia felt rather disposed to cavil at this picture, and was laying down her knitting to begin, but St. Clare stopped her.

"Now, I know every word you are going to say. I do not say they *were* alike, in fact. One fell into a condition where everything acted against the natural tendency, and the other where everything acted for it; and so one turned out a pretty wilful, stout, overbearing old democrat, and the other a wilful, stout old despot. If both had owned plantations in Louisiana, they would have been as like as two old bullets cast in the same mould."

"What an undutiful boy you are!" said Miss Ophelia.

"I don't mean them any disrespect," said St. Clare. "You know reverence is not my forte. But, to go back to my history:

"When father died, he left the whole property to us twin boys, to be divided as we should agree. There does not breathe on God's earth a nobler-souled, more generous fellow, than Alfred, in all that concerns his equals; and we got on admirably with this property question, without a single unbrotherly word or feeling. We undertook to work the plantation together; and Alfred, whose outward life and capabilities had double the strength of mine, became an enthusiastic planter, and a wonderfully successful one.

"But two years' trial satisfied me that I could not be a partner in that matter. To have a great gang of seven hundred, whom I could not know personally, or feel any individual interest in, bought and driven, housed, fed, worked like so many horned cattle, strained up to military precision,—the question of how little of life's commonest enjoyments would keep them in working order being a constantly recurring problem,—the *necessity* of drivers and overseers,—the ever-necessary whip, first, last, and only argument,—the whole thing was insufferably disgusting and loathsome to me; and when I thought of my mother's estimate of one poor human soul, it became even frightful!

"It 's all nonsense to talk to me about slaves *enjoying* all this! To this day, I have no patience with the unutterable trash that some of your patronizing Northerners have made up, as in their zeal to apologize for our sins. We all know better. Tell me that any man living wants to work all his days, from day-dawn till dark, under the constant eye of a master, without the power of putting forth one irresponsible volition, on the same dreary, monotonous, unchanging toil, and all for two pairs of pantaloons and a pair of shoes a year, with enough food and shelter to keep him in working order! Any man who thinks that human beings can, as a general thing, be made about as comfortable that way as any other, I wish he might try it. I 'd buy the dog, and work him, with a clear conscience!"

"I always have supposed," said Miss Ophelia, "that you, all of you, approved of these things, and thought them *right*,—according to Scripture."

"Humbug! We are not quite reduced to that yet. Alfred, who is as determined a despot as ever walked, does not pretend to this kind of defence;—no, he stands, high and haughty, on that good old respectable ground, *the right of the strongest*; and he says, and I think quite sensibly, that the American planter is 'only doing, in another form, what the English aristocracy and capitalists are doing by the lower classes;' that is, I take it, *appropriating* them, body and bone, soul and spirit, to their use and convenience. He defends both,—and I think, at least, *consistently*. He says that there can be no high civilization without enslavement of the masses, either nominal or real. There must, he says, be a lower class, given up to physical toil and confined to an animal nature; and a higher one thereby acquires leisure and wealth for a more expanded intelligence and improvement, and becomes the directing soul of the lower. So he reasons, because, as I said, he is born an aristocrat;—so I don't believe, because I was born a democrat."

"How in the world can the two things be compared?" said Miss Ophelia. "The English laborer is not sold, traded, parted from his family, whipped."

"He is as much at the will of his employer as if he were sold to him. The slave-owner can whip his refractory slave to death,—the capitalist can starve him to death. As to family security, it is hard to say which is the worst,—to have one's children sold, or see them starve to death at home."

"But it 's no kind of apology for slavery, to prove that it is n't worse than some other bad thing."

"I did n't give it for one,—nay, I 'll say, besides, that ours is the more bold and palpable infringement of human rights; actually buying a man up, like a horse,—looking at his teeth, cracking his joints, and trying his paces, and then paying down for him,—having speculators, breeders, traders, and brokers in human bodies and souls,—sets the thing before the eyes of the civilized world in a more tangible form, though the thing done be, after all, in its nature, the same; that is, appropriating one set of human beings to the use and improvement of another, without any regard to their own."

"I never thought of the matter in this light," said Miss Ophelia.

"Well, I 've travelled in England some, and I 've looked over a good many documents as to the state of their lower classes; and I really think there is no denying Alfred, when he says that his slaves are better off than a large class of the population of England. You see, you must not infer, from what I have told you, that Alfred is what is called a hard master; for he is n't. He is despotic, and unmerciful to insubordination; he would shoot a fellow down with as little remorse as he would shoot a buck, if he opposed him. But, in general, he takes a sort of pride in having his slaves comfortably fed and accommodated.

"When I was with him, I insisted that he should do something for their instruction; and, to please me, he did get a chaplain, and used to have them catechized Sunday, though, I believe, in his heart, that he thought it would do about as much good to set a chaplain over his dogs and horses. And the fact is, that a mind stupefied and animalized by every bad influence from the hour of birth, spending the whole of every week-day in unreflecting toil, cannot be done much with by a few hours on Sunday. The teachers of Sunday-schools among the manufacturing population of England, and among plantation-hands in our country, could perhaps testify to the same result, *there and here.* Yet some striking exceptions there are among us, from the fact that the negro is naturally more impressible to religious sentiment than the white."

"Well," said Miss Ophelia, "how came you to give up your plantation life?"

"Well, we jogged on together some time, till Alfred saw plainly that I was no planter. He thought it absurd, after he had reformed, and altered, and improved everywhere, to suit my notions, that I still remained unsatisfied. The fact was, it was, after all, the THING that I hated,—the using these men and women, the perpetuation of all this ignorance, brutality and vice,—just to make money for me!

"Besides, I was always interfering in the details. Being myself one of the laziest of mortals, I had altogether too much fellow-feeling for the lazy; and when poor, shiftless dogs put stones at the bottom of their cotton-baskets to make them weigh heavier, filled their sacks with dirt, with cotton at the top, it seemed so exactly like what I should do if I were they, I could n't and would n't have them flogged for it. Well, of course, there was an end of plantation discipline; and Alf and I came to about the same point that I and my respected father did, years before. So he told me that I was a womanish sentimentalist, and would never do for business life; and advised me to take the bank-stock and the New Orleans family mansion, and go to writing poetry, and let him manage the plantation. So we parted, and I came here."

"But why did n't you free your slaves?"

"Well, I was n't up to that. To hold them as tools for money-making, I could not;—have them to help spend money, you know, did n't look quite so ugly to me. Some of them were old house-servants, to whom I was much attached; and the younger ones were children to the old. All were well satisfied to be as they were." He paused, and walked reflectively up and down the room.

"There was," said St. Clare, "a time in my life when I had plans and hopes of doing something in this world, more than to float and drift. I had vague, indistinct yearnings to be a sort of emancipator,—to free my native land from this spot and stain. All young men have had such fever-fits, I suppose, some time,—but then—"

"Why did n't you?" said Miss Ophelia;—"you ought not to put your hand to the plough, and look back."

"O, well, things did n't go with me as I expected, and I got the despair of living that Solomon did. I suppose it was a necessary incident to wisdom in us both; but, some how or other, instead of being actor and regenerator in society, I became a piece of drift-wood, and have been floating and eddying about, ever since. Alfred scolds me, every time we meet; and he has the better of me, I grant,—for he really does something; his life is a logical result of his opinions, and mine is a contemptible *non sequitur.*"

"My dear cousin, can you be satisfied with such a way of spending your probation?"

"Satisfied! Was I not just telling you I despised it? But, then, to come back to this point,—we were on this liberation business. I don't think my feelings about slavery are peculiar. I find many men who, in their hearts, think of it just as I do. The land groans under it; and, bad as it is for the slave, it is worse, if anything, for the master. It takes no spectacles to see that a great class of vicious, improvident, degraded people, among us, are an evil to us, as well as to themselves. The capitalist and aristocrat of England cannot feel that as we do, because they do not mingle with the class they degrade as we do. They are in our houses; they are the associates of our children, and they form their minds faster than we can; for they are a race that children always will cling to and assimilate with. If Eva, now, was not more angel than ordinary, she would be ruined. We might as well allow the small-pox to run among them, and think our children would not take it, as to let them be uninstructed and vicious, and think our children will not be affected by that. Yet our laws positively and utterly forbid any efficient general educational system, and they do it wisely, too; for, just begin and thoroughly educate one generation, and the whole thing would be blown sky high. If we did not give them liberty, they would take it."

"And what do you think will be the end of this?" said Miss Ophelia.

"I don't know. One thing is certain,—that there is a mustering among the masses, the world over; and there is a *dies iræ* coming on, sooner or later. The same thing is working in Europe, in England, and in this country. My mother used to tell me of a millennium that was coming, when Christ should reign, and all men should be free and happy. And she taught me, when I was a boy, to pray, 'Thy kingdom come.' Sometimes I think all this sighing, and groaning, and stirring among the dry bones foretells what she used to tell me was coming. But who may abide the day of His appearing?"

"Augustine, sometimes I think you are not far from the kingdom," said Miss Ophelia, laying down her knitting, and looking anxiously at her cousin.

"Thank you for your good opinion; but it 's up and down with me,—up to heaven's gate in theory, down in earth's dust in practice. But there 's the tea-bell,—do let 's go,—and don't say, now, I have n't had one downright serious talk, for once in my life."

At table, Marie alluded to the incident of Prue. "I suppose you 'll think, cousin," she said, "that we are all barbarians."

"I think that 's a barbarous thing," said Miss Ophelia, "but I don't think you are all barbarians."

"Well, now," said Marie, "I know it 's impossible to get along with some of these creatures. They are so bad they ought not to live. I don't feel a particle of sympathy for such cases. If they 'd only behave themselves, it would not happen."

"But, mamma," said Eva, "the poor creature was unhappy; that 's what made her drink."

"O, fiddlestick! as if that were any excuse! I 'm unhappy, very often. I presume," she said, pensively, "that I 've had greater trials than ever she had. It 's just because they are so bad. There 's some of them that you cannot break in by any kind of severity. I remember father had a man that was so lazy he would run away just to get rid of work, and lie round in the swamps, stealing and doing all sorts of horrid things. That man was caught and whipped, time and again, and it never did him any good; and the last time he crawled off, though he couldn't but just go, and died in the swamp. There was no sort of reason for it, for father's hands were always treated kindly."

"I broke a fellow in, once," said St. Clare, "that all the overseers and masters had tried their hands on in vain."

"You!" said Marie; "well, I 'd be glad to know when *you* ever did anything of the sort."

"Well, he was a powerful, gigantic fellow,—a native-born African; and he appeared to have the rude instinct of freedom in him to an uncommon degree. He was a regular African lion. They called him Scipio. Nobody could do anything with him; and he was sold round from overseer to overseer, till at last Alfred bought him, because he thought he could manage him. Well, one day he knocked down the overseer, and was fairly off into the swamps. I was on a visit to Alf's plantation, for it was after we had dissolved partnership. Alfred was greatly exasperated; but I told him that it was his own fault, and laid him any wager that I could break the man; and finally it was agreed that, if I caught him, I should have him to experiment on. So they mustered out a party of some six or seven, with guns and dogs, for the hunt. People, you know, can get up just as much enthusiasm in hunting a man as a deer, if it is only customary; in fact, I got a little excited myself, though I had only put in as a sort of mediator, in case he was caught.

"Well, the dogs bayed and howled, and we rode and scampered, and finally we started him. He ran and bounded like a buck, and kept us well in the rear for some time; but at last he got caught in an impenetrable thicket of cane; then he turned to bay, and I tell you he fought the dogs right gallantly. He dashed them to right and left, and actually killed three of them with only his naked fists, when a shot from a gun brought him down, and he fell, wounded and bleeding, almost at my feet. The poor fellow looked up at me with manhood and despair both in his eye. I kept back the dogs and the party, as they came pressing up, and claimed him as my prisoner. It was all I could do to keep them from shooting him, in the flush of success; but I persisted in my bargain, and Alfred sold him to me. Well, I took him in hand, and in one fortnight I had him tamed down as submissive and tractable as heart could desire."

"What in the world did you do to him?" said Marie.

"Well, it was quite a simple process. I took him to my own room, had a good bed made for him, dressed his wounds, and tended him myself, until he got fairly on his feet again. And, in process of time, I had free papers made out for him, and told him he might go where he liked."

"And did he go?" said Miss Ophelia.

"No. The foolish fellow tore the paper in two, and absolutely refused to leave me. I never had a braver, better fellow,—trusty and true as steel. He embraced Christianity afterwards, and became as gentle as a child. He used to oversee my place on the lake, and did it capitally, too. I lost him the first cholera season. In fact, he laid down his life for me. For I was sick, almost to death; and when, through the panic, everybody else fled, Scipio worked for me like a giant, and actually brought me back into life again. But, poor fellow! he was taken, right after, and there was no saving him. I never felt anybody's loss more."

Eva had come gradually nearer and nearer to her father, as he told the story,— her small lips apart, her eyes wide and earnest with absorbing interest.

As he finished, she suddenly threw her arms around his neck, burst into tears, and sobbed convulsively.

"Eva, dear child! what is the matter?" said St. Clare, as the child's small frame trembled and shook with the violence of her feelings. "This child," he added, "ought not to hear any of this kind of thing,—she 's nervous."

"No, papa, I 'm not nervous," said Eva, controlling herself, suddenly, with a strength of resolution singular in such a child. "I 'm not nervous, but these things *sink into my heart*."

"What do you mean, Eva?"

"I can't tell you, papa. I think a great many thoughts. Perhaps some day I shall tell you."

"Well, think away, dear,—only don't cry and worry your papa," said St. Clare. "Look here,—see what a beautiful peach I have got for you!"

Eva took it, and smiled, though there was still a nervous twitching about the corners of her mouth.

"Come, look at the gold-fish," said St. Clare, taking her hand and stepping on to the verandah. A few moments, and merry laughs were heard through the silken curtains, as Eva and St. Clare were pelting each other with roses, and chasing each other among the alleys of the court.

---

There is a danger that our humble friend Tom be neglected amid the adventures of the higher born; but, if our readers will accompany us up to a little loft over the stable, they may, perhaps, learn a little of his affairs. It was a decent room, containing a bed, a chair, and a small, rough stand, where lay Tom's Bible and hymn-book; and where he sits, at present, with his slate before him, intent on something that seems to cost him a great deal of anxious thought.

The fact was, that Tom's home-yearnings had become so strong, that he had begged a sheet of writing-paper of Eva, and, mustering up all his small stock of literary attainment acquired by Mas'r George's instructions, he conceived the bold idea of writing a letter; and he was busy now, on his slate, getting out his first draft. Tom was in a good deal of trouble, for the forms of some of the letters he had forgotten entirely; and of what he did remember, he did not know exactly which to use. And while he was working, and breathing very hard, in his earnestness, Eva alighted, like a bird, on the round of his chair behind him, and peeped over his shoulder.

"O, Uncle Tom! what funny things you *are* making, there!"

"I 'm trying to write to my poor old woman, Miss Eva, and my little chil'en," said Tom, drawing the back of his hand over his eyes; "but, some how, I 'm feard I shan't make it out."

"I wish I could help you, Tom! I 've learnt to write some. Last year I could make all the letters, but I 'm afraid I 've forgotten."

So Eva put her little golden head close to his, and the two commenced a grave and anxious discussion, each one equally earnest, and about equally ignorant; and, with a deal of consulting and advising over every word, the composition began, as they both felt very sanguine, to look quite like writing.

"Yes, Uncle Tom, it really begins to look beautiful," said Eva, gazing delightedly on it. "How pleased your wife 'll be, and the poor little children! O, it 's a shame you ever had to go away from them! I mean to ask papa to let you go back, some time."

"Missis said that she would send down money for me, as soon as they could get it together," said Tom. "I 'm 'spectin' she will. Young Mas'r George, he said he 'd come for me; and he gave me this yer dollar as a sign;" and Tom drew from under his clothes the precious dollar.

"O, he 'll certainly come, then!" said Eva. "I 'm so glad!"

"And I wanted to send a letter, you know, to let 'em know whar I was, and tell poor Chloe that I was well off,—cause she felt so drefful, poor soul!"

"I say, Tom!" said St. Clare's voice, coming in the door at this moment.

Tom and Eva both started.

"What 's here?" said St. Clare, coming up and looking at the slate.

"O, it 's Tom's letter. I 'm helping him to write it," said Eva; "is n't it nice?"

"I would n't discourage either of you," said St. Clare, "but I rather think, Tom, you 'd better get me to write your letter for you. I 'll do it, when I come home from my ride."

"It 's very imporant he should write," said Eva, "because his mistress is going to send down money to redeem him, you know, papa; he told me they told him so."

St. Clare thought, in his heart, that this was probably only one of those things which good-natured owners say to their servants, to alleviate their horror of being sold, without any intention of fulfilling the expectation thus excited. But he did not make any audible comment upon it,—only ordered Tom to get the horses out for a ride.

Tom's letter was written in due form for him that evening, and safely lodged in the post-office.

Miss Ophelia still persevered in her labors in the housekeeping line. It was universally agreed, among all the household, from Dinah down to the youngest urchin, that Miss Ophelia was decidedly "curis,"—a term by which a southern servant implies that his or her betters don't exactly suit them.

The higher circle in the family—to wit, Adolph, Jane and Rosa—agreed that she was no lady; ladies never kept working about as she did;—that she had no *air* at all; and they were surprised that she should be any relation of the St. Clares. Even Marie declared that it was absolutely fatiguing to see Cousin Ophelia always so busy. And, in fact, Miss Ophelia's industry was so incessant as to lay some foundation for the complaint. She sewed and stitched away, from daylight till dark, with the energy of one who is pressed on by some immediate urgency; and then, when the light faded, and the work was folded away, with one turn out came the ever-ready knitting-work, and there she was again, going on as briskly as ever. It really was a labor to see her.

## XX.
### *Topsy*

One morning, while Miss Ophelia was busy in some of her domestic cares, St. Clare's voice was heard, calling her at the foot of the stairs.

"Come down here, Cousin; I 've something to show you."

"What is it?" said Miss Ophelia, coming down, with her sewing in her hand.

"I 've made a purchase for your department,—see here," said St. Clare; and, with the word, he pulled along a little negro girl, about eight or nine years of age.

She was one of the blackest of her race; and her round, shining eyes, glittering as glass beads, moved with quick and restless glances over everything in the room. Her mouth, half open with astonishment at the wonders of the new Mas'r's parlor, displayed a white and brilliant set of teeth. Her woolly hair was braided in sundry little tails, which stuck out in every direction. The expression of her face was an odd mixture of shrewdness and cunning, over which was oddly drawn, like a kind of veil, an expression of the most doleful gravity and solemnity. She was dressed in a single filthy, ragged garment, made of bagging; and stood with her hands demurely folded before her. Altogether, there was something odd and goblin-like about her appearance,—something, as Miss Ophelia afterwards said, "so heathenish," as to inspire that good lady with utter dismay; and, turning to St. Clare, she said,

"Augustine, what in the world have you brought that thing here for?"

"For you to educate, to be sure, and train in the way she should go. I thought she was rather a funny specimen in the Jim Crow line. Here, Topsy," he added, giving a whistle, as a man would to call the attention of a dog, "give us a song, now, and show us some of your dancing."

The black, glassy eyes glittered with a kind of wicked drollery, and the thing struck up, in a clear shrill voice, an odd negro melody, to which she kept time with her hands and feet, spinning round, clapping her hands, knocking her knees together, in a wild, fantastic sort of time, and producing in her throat all those odd guttural sounds which distinguish the native music of her race; and finally, turning a summerset or two, and giving a prolonged closing note, as odd and unearthly as that of a steam-whistle, she came suddenly down on the carpet, and stood with her hands folded, and a most sanctimonious expression of meekness and solemnity over her face, only broken by the cunning glances which she shot askance from the corners of her eyes.

Miss Ophelia stood silent, perfectly paralyzed with amazement.

St. Clare, like a mischievous fellow as he was, appeared to enjoy her astonishment; and, addressing the child again, said,

"Topsy, this is your new mistress. I 'm going to give you up to her; see now that you behave yourself."

"Yes, Mas'r," said Topsy, with sanctimonious gravity, her wicked eyes twinkling as she spoke.

"You 're going to be good, Topsy, you understand," said St. Clare.

"O yes, Mas'r," said Topsy, with another twinkle, her hands still devoutly folded.

"Now, Augustine, what upon earth is this for?" said Miss Ophelia. "Your house is so full of these little plagues, now, that a body can't set down their foot without treading on 'em. I get up in the morning, and find one asleep behind the door, and see one black head poking out from under the table, one lying on the door-mat,—and they are mopping and mowing and grinning between all the railings, and tumbling over the kitchen floor! What on earth did you want to bring this one for?"

"For you to educate—did n't I tell you? You 're always preaching about educating. I thought I would make you a present of a fresh-caught specimen, and let you try your hand on her, and bring her up in the way she should go."

"*I* don't want her, I am sure;—I have more to do with 'em now than I want to."

"That 's you Christians, all over!—you 'll get up a society, and get some poor missionary to spend all his days among just such heathen. But let me see one of you that would take one into your house with you, and take the labor of their conversion on yourselves! No; when it comes to that, they are dirty and disagreeable, and it 's too much care, and so on."

"Augustine, you know I did n't think of it in that light," said Miss Ophelia, evidently softening. "Well, it might be a real missionary work," said she, looking rather more favorably on the child.

St. Clare had touched the right string. Miss Ophelia's conscientiousness was ever on the alert. "But," she added, "I really did n't see the need of buying this one;—there are enough now, in your house, to take all my time and skill."

"Well, then, Cousin," said St. Clare, drawing her aside, "I ought to beg your pardon for my good-for-nothing speeches. You are so good, after all, that there 's no sense in them. Why, the fact is, this concern belonged to a couple of drunken creatures that keep a low restaurant that I have to pass by every day, and I was tired of hearing her screaming, and them beating and swearing at her. She looked bright and funny, too, as if something might be made of her;—so I bought her, and I 'll give her to you. Try, now, and give her a good orthodox New England bringing up, and see what it 'll make of her. You know I have n't any gift that way; but I 'd like you to try."

"Well, I 'll do what I can," said Miss Ophelia; and she approached her new subject very much as a person might be supposed to approach a black spider, supposing them to have benevolent designs toward it.

"She 's dreadfully dirty, and half naked," she said.

"Well, take her down stairs, and make some of them clean and clothe her up."

Miss Ophelia carried her to the kitchen regions.

"Don't see what Mas'r St. Clare wants of 'nother nigger!" said Dinah, surveying the new arrival with no friendly air. "Won't have her round under *my* feet, *I* know!"

"Pah!" said Rosa and Jane, with supreme disgust; "let her keep out of our way! What in the world Mas'r wanted another of these low niggers for, I can't see!"

"You go long! No more nigger dan you be, Miss Rosa," said Dinah, who felt this last remark a reflection on herself. "You seem to tink yourself white folks. You an't nerry one, black *nor* white. I 'd like to be one or turrer."

Miss Ophelia saw that there was nobody in the camp that would undertake to oversee the cleansing and dressing of the new arrival; and so she was forced to do it herself, with some very ungracious and reluctant assistance from Jane.

It is not for ears polite to hear the particulars of the first toilet of a neglected, abused child. In fact, in this world, multitudes must live and die in a state that it would be too great a shock to the nerves of their fellow-mortals even to hear described. Miss Ophelia had a good, strong, practical deal of resolution; and she went through all the disgusting details with heroic thoroughness, though, it must be confessed, with no very gracious air,—for endurance was the utmost to which her principles could bring her. When she saw, on the back and shoulders of the child, great welts and calloused spots, ineffaceable marks of the system under which she had grown up thus far, her heart became pitiful within her.

"See there!" said Jane, pointing to the marks, "don't that show she 's a limb? We 'll have fine works with her, I reckon. I hate these nigger young uns! so disgusting! I wonder that Mas'r would buy her!"

The "young un" alluded to heard all these comments with the subdued and doleful air which seemed habitual to her, only scanning, with a keen and furtive glance of her flickering eyes, the ornaments which Jane wore in her ears. When arrayed at last in a suit of decent and whole clothing, her hair cropped short to her head, Miss Ophelia, with some satisfaction, said she looked more Christian-like than she did, and in her own mind began to mature some plans for her instruction.

Sitting down before her, she began to question her.

"How old are you, Topsy?"

"Dun no, Missis," said the image, with a grin that showed all her teeth.

"Don't know how old you are? Did n't anybody ever tell you? Who was your mother?"

"Never had none!" said the child, with another grin.

"Never had any mother? What do you mean? Where were you born?"

"Never was born!" persisted Topsy, with another grin, that looked so goblin-like, that, if Miss Ophelia had been at all nervous, she might have fancied that she had got hold of some sooty gnome from the land of Diablerie; but Miss Ophelia was not nervous, but plain and business-like, and she said, with some sternness,

"You must n't answer me in that way, child; I 'm not playing with you. Tell me where you were born, and who your father and mother were."

"Never was born," reiterated the creature, more emphatically; "never had no father nor mother, nor nothin'. I was raised by a speculator, with lots of others. Old Aunt Sue used to take car on us."

The child was evidently sincere; and Jane, breaking into a short laugh, said,

"Laws, Missis, there 's heaps of 'em. Speculators buys 'em up cheap, when they 's little, and gets 'em raised for market."

"How long have you lived with your master and mistress?"

"Dun no, Missis."

"Is it a year, or more, or less?"

"Dun no, Missis."

"Laws, Missis, those low negroes,—they can't tell; they don't know anything about time," said Jane; "they don't know what a year is; they don't know their own ages."

"Have you ever heard anything about God, Topsy?"

The child looked bewildered, but grinned as usual.

"Do you know who made you?"

"Nobody, as I knows on," said the child, with a short laugh.

The idea appeared to amuse her considerably; for her eyes twinkled, and she added,

"I spect I grow'd. Don't think nobody never made me."

"Do you know how to sew?" said Miss Ophelia, who thought she would turn her inquiries to something more tangible.

"No, Missis."

"What can you do?—what did you do for your master and mistress?"

"Fetch water, and wash dishes, and rub knives, and wait on folks."

"Were they good to you?"

"Spect they was," said the child, scanning Miss Ophelia cunningly.

Miss Ophelia rose from this encouraging colloquy; St. Clare was leaning over the back of her chair.

"You find virgin soil there, Cousin; put in your own ideas,—you won't find many to pull up."

Miss Ophelia's ideas of education, like all her other ideas, were very set and definite; and of the kind that prevailed in New England a century ago, and which are still preserved in some very retired and unsophisticated parts, where there are no railroads. As nearly as could be expressed, they could be comprised in a very few words: to teach them to mind when they were spoken to; to teach them the catechism, sewing, and reading; and to whip them if they told lies. And though, of course, in the flood of light that is now poured on education, these are left far away in the rear, yet it is an undisputed fact that our grandmothers raised some tolerably fair men and women under this régime, as many of us can remember and testify. At all events, Miss Ophelia knew of nothing else to do; and, therefore, applied her mind to her heathen with the best diligence she could command.

The child was announced and considered in the family as Miss Ophelia's girl; and, as she was looked upon with no gracious eye in the kitchen, Miss Ophelia resolved to confine her sphere of operation and instruction chiefly to her own chamber. With a self-sacrifice which some of our readers will appreciate, she resolved, instead of comfortably making her own bed, sweeping and dusting her own chamber,—which she had hitherto done, in utter scorn of all offers of help from the chambermaid of the establishment,—to condemn herself to the martyrdom of instructing Topsy to perform these operations,—ah, woe the day! Did any of our readers ever do the same, they will appreciate the amount of her self-sacrifice.

Miss Ophelia began with Topsy by taking her into her chamber, the first morning, and solemnly commencing a course of instruction in the art and mystery of bed-making.

Behold, then, Topsy, washed and shorn of all the little braided tails wherein her heart had delighted, arrayed in a clean gown, with well-starched apron, standing reverently before Miss Ophelia, with an expression of solemnity well befitting a funeral.

"Now, Topsy, I 'm going to show you just how my bed is to be made. I am very particular about my bed. You must learn exactly how to do it."

"Yes, ma'am," says Topsy, with a deep sigh, and a face of woful earnestness.

"Now, Topsy, look here;—this is the hem of the sheet,—this is the right side of the sheet, and this is the wrong;—will you remember?"

"Yes, ma'am," says Topsy, with another sigh.

"Well, now, the under sheet you must bring over the bolster,—so,—and tuck it clear down under the mattress nice and smooth,—so,—do you see?"

"Yes, ma'am," said Topsy, with profound attention.

"But the upper sheet," said Miss Ophelia, "must be brought down in this way, and tucked under firm and smooth at the foot,—so,—the narrow hem at the foot."

"Yes, ma'am," said Topsy, as before;—but we will add, what Miss Ophelia did not see, that, during the time when the good lady's back was turned, in the zeal of her manipulations, the young disciple had contrived to snatch a pair of gloves and a ribbon, which she had adroitly slipped into her sleeves, and stood with her hands dutifully folded, as before.

"Now, Topsy, let 's see *you* do this," said Miss Ophelia, pulling off the clothes, and seating herself.

Topsy, with great gravity and adroitness, went through the exercise completely to Miss Ophelia's satisfaction; smoothing the sheets, patting out every wrinkle, and exhibiting, through the whole process, a gravity and seriousness with which her instructress was greatly edified. By an unlucky slip, however, a fluttering fragment of the ribbon hung out of one of her sleeves, just as she was finishing, and caught Miss Ophelia's attention. Instantly she pounced upon it. "What 's this? You naughty, wicked child,—you 've been stealing this?"

The ribbon was pulled out of Topsy's own sleeve, yet was she not in the least disconcerted; she only looked at it with an air of the most surprised and unconscious innocence.

"Laws! why, that ar 's Miss Feely's ribbon, an't it? How could it a got caught in my sleeve?"

"Topsy, you naughty girl, don't you tell me a lie,—you stole that ribbon!"

"Missis, I declar for't, I did n't;—never seed it till dis yer blessed minnit."

"Topsy," said Miss Ophelia, "don't you know it's wicked to tell lies?"

"I never tells no lies, Miss Feely," said Topsy, with virtuous gravity; "it 's jist the truth I 've been a tellin now, and an't nothin else."

"Topsy, I shall have to whip you, if you tell lies so."

"Laws, Missis, if you 's to whip all day, could n't say no other way," said Topsy, beginning to blubber. "I never seed dat ar,—it must a got caught in my sleeve. Miss Feely must have left it on the bed, and it got caught in the clothes, and so got in my sleeve."

Miss Ophelia was so indignant at the barefaced lie, that she caught the child and shook her.

"Don't you tell me that again!"

The shake brought the gloves on to the floor, from the other sleeve.

"There, you!" said Miss Ophelia, "will you tell me now, you did n't steal the ribbon?"

Topsy now confessed to the gloves, but still persisted in denying the ribbon.

"Now, Topsy," said Miss Ophelia, "if you 'll confess all about it, I won't whip you this time." Thus adjured, Topsy confessed to the ribbon and gloves, with woful protestations of penitence.

"Well, now, tell me. I know you must have taken other things since you have been in the house, for I let you run about all day yesterday. Now, tell me if you took anything, and I shan't whip you."

"Laws, Missis! I took Miss Eva's red thing she wars on her neck."

"You did, you naughty child!—Well, what else?"

"I took Rosa's yer-rings,—them red ones."

"Go bring them to me this minute, both of 'em."

"Laws, Missis! I can't,—they's burnt up!"

"Burnt up!—what a story! Go get 'em, or I 'll whip you."

Topsy, with loud protestations, and tears, and groans, declared that she *could* not. "they 's burnt up,—they was."

"What did you burn 'em up for?" said Miss Ophelia.

"'Cause I 's wicked,—I is. I 's mighty wicked, any how. I can't help it."

Just at this moment, Eva came innocently into the room, with the identical coral necklace on her neck.

"Why, Eva, where did you get your necklace?" said Miss Ophelia.

"Get it? Why, I 've had it on all day," said Eva.

"Did you have it on yesterday?"

"Yes; and what is funny, Aunty, I had it on all night. I forgot to take it off when I went to bed."

Miss Ophelia looked perfectly bewildered; the more so, as Rosa, at that instant, came into the room, with a basket of newly-ironed linen poised on her head, and the coral ear-drops shaking in her ears!

"I 'm sure I can't tell anything what to do with such a child!" she said, in despair. "What in the world did you tell me you took those things for, Topsy?"

"Why, Missis said I must 'fess; and I could n't think of nothin' else to 'fess," said Topsy, rubbing her eyes.

"But, of course, I did n't want you to confess things you did n't do," said Miss Ophelia; "that 's telling a lie, just as much as the other."

"Laws, now, is it?" said Topsy, with an air of innocent wonder.

"La, there an't any such thing as truth in that limb," said Rosa, looking indignantly at Topsy. "If I was Mas'r St. Clare, I 'd whip her till the blood run. I would,—I 'd let her catch it!"

"No, no, Rosa," said Eva, with an air of command, which the child could assume at times; "you must n't talk so, Rosa. I can't bear to hear it."

"La sakes! Miss Eva, you 's so good, you don't know nothing how to get along with niggers. There 's no way but to cut 'em well up, I tell ye."

"Rosa!" said Eva, "hush! Don't you say another word of that sort!" and the eye of the child flashed, and her cheek deepened its color.

Rosa was cowed in a moment.

"Miss Eva has got the St. Clare blood in her, that 's plain. She can speak, for all the world, just like her papa," she said, as she passed out of the room.

Eva stood looking at Topsy.

There stood the two children, representatives of the two extremes of society. The fair, high-bred child, with her golden head, her deep eyes, her spiritual, noble brow, and prince-like movements; and her black, keen, subtle, cringing, yet acute neighbor. They stood the representatives of their races. The Saxon, born of ages of cultivation, command, education, physical and moral eminence; the Afric, born of ages of oppression, submission, ignorance, toil, and vice!

Something, perhaps, of such thoughts struggled through Eva's mind. But a child's thoughts are rather dim, undefined instincts; and in Eva's noble nature many such were yearning and working, for which she had no power of utterance. When Miss Ophelia expatiated on Topsy's naughty, wicked conduct, the child looked perplexed and sorrowful, but said, sweetly,

"Poor Topsy, why need you steal? You 're going to be taken good care of, now. I 'm sure I 'd rather give you anything of mine, than have you steal it"

It was the first word of kindness the child had ever heard in her life; and the sweet tone and manner struck strangely on the wild, rude heart, and a sparkle of something like a tear shone in the keen, round, glittering eye; but it was followed by the short laugh and habitual grin. No! the ear that has never heard anything but abuse is strangely incredulous of anything so heavenly as kindness; and Topsy only thought Eva's speech something funny and inexplicable,—she did not believe it.

But what was to be done with Topsy? Miss Ophelia found the case a puzzler; her rules for bringing up did n't seem to apply. She thought she would take time to think of it; and, by the way of gaining time, and in hopes of some indefinite moral virtues supposed to be inherent in dark closets, Miss Ophelia shut Topsy up in one till she had arranged her ideas further on the subject.

"I don't see," said Miss Ophelia to St. Clare, "how I 'm going to manage that child, without whipping her."

"Well, whip her, then, to your heart's content; I 'll give you full power to do what you like."

"Children always have to be whipped," said Miss Ophelia; "I never heard of bringing them up without."

"O, well, certainly," said St. Clare; "do as you think best. Only I 'll make one suggestion: I 've seen this child whipped with a poker, knocked down with the shovel or tongs, whichever came handiest, &c.; and, seeing that she is used to that style of operation, I think your whippings will have to be pretty energetic, to make much impression."

"What is to be done with her, then?" said Miss Ophelia.

"You have started a serious question," said St. Clare; "I wish you 'd answer it. What is to be done with a human being that can be governed only by the lash,— *that* fails,—it 's a very common state of things down here!"

"I 'm sure I don't know; I never saw such a child as this."

"Such children are very common among us, and such men and women, too. How are they to be governed?" said St. Clare.

"I 'm sure it 's more than I can say," said Miss Ophelia.

"Or I either," said St. Clare. "The horrid cruelties and outrages that once and a while find their way into the papers,—such cases as Prue's, for example,—what do they come from? In many cases, it is a gradual hardening process on both sides,—the owner growing more and more cruel, as the servant more and more callous. Whipping and abuse are like laudanum; you have to double the dose as the sensibilities decline. I saw this very early when I became an owner; and I resolved never to begin, because I did not know when I should stop,—and I resolved, at least, to protect my own moral nature. The consequence is, that my servants act like spoiled children; but I think that better than for us both to be brutalized together. You have talked a great deal about our responsibilities in educating, Cousin. I really wanted you to *try* with one child, who is a specimen of thousands among us."

"It is your system makes such children," said Miss Ophelia.

"I know it; but they are *made*,—they exist,— and what is to be done with them?"

"Well, I can't say I thank you for the experiment. But, then, as it appears to be a duty, I shall persevere and try, and do the best I can," said Miss Ophelia; and Miss Ophelia, after this, did labor, with a commendable degree of zeal and energy, on her new subject. She instituted regular hours and employments for her, and undertook to teach her to read and to sew.

In the former art, the child was quick enough. She learned her letters as if by magic, and was very soon able to read plain reading; but the sewing was a more difficult matter. The creature was as lithe as a cat, and as active as a monkey, and the confinement of sewing was her abomination; so she broke her needles, threw them slyly out of windows, or down in chinks of the walls; she tangled, broke, and dirtied her thread, or, with a sly movement, would throw a spool away altogether. Her motions were almost as quick as those of a practised conjurer, and her command of her face quite as great; and though Miss Ophelia could not help feeling that so many accidents could not possibly happen in succession, yet she could not, without a watchfulness which would leave her no time for anything else, detect her.

Topsy was soon a noted character in the establishment. Her talent for every species of drollery, grimace, and mimicry,—for dancing, tumbling, climbing, singing, whistling, imitating every sound that hit her fancy,—seemed inexhaustible. In her play-hours, she invariably had every child in the establishment at her heels, open-mouthed with admiration and wonder,—not excepting Miss Eva, who appeared to be fascinated by her wild diablerie, as a dove is sometimes charmed by a glittering serpent. Miss Ophelia was uneasy that Eva should fancy Topsy's society so much, and implored St. Clare to forbid it.

"Poh! let the child alone," said St. Clare. "Topsy will do her good."

"But so depraved a child,—are you not afraid she will teach her some mischief?"

"She can't teach her mischief; she might teach it to some children, but evil rolls off Eva's mind like dew off a cabbage-leaf,—not a drop sinks in."

"Don't be too sure," said Miss Ophelia. "I know I'd never let a child of mine play with Topsy."

"Well, your children need n't," said St. Clare, "but mine may; if Eva could have been spoiled, it would have been done years ago."

Topsy was at first despised and contemned by the upper servants. They soon found reason to alter their opinion. It was very soon discovered that whoever cast an indignity on Topsy was sure to meet with some inconvenient accident shortly after;—either a pair of ear-rings or some cherished trinket would be missing, or an article of dress would be suddenly found utterly ruined, or the person would stumble accidentally into a pail of hot water, or a libation of dirty slop would unaccountably deluge them from above when in full gala dress;—and on all these occasions, when investigation was made, there was nobody found to stand sponsor for the indignity. Topsy was cited, and had up before all the domestic judicatories, time and again; but always sustained her examinations with most edifying innocence and gravity of appearance. Nobody in the world ever doubted who did the things; but not a scrap of any direct evidence could be found to establish the suppositions, and Miss Ophelia was too just to feel at liberty to proceed to any lengths without it.

The mischiefs done were always so nicely timed, also, as further to shelter the aggressor. Thus, the times for revenge on Rosa and Jane, the two chambermaids, were always chosen in those seasons when (as not unfrequently happened) they were in disgrace with their mistress, when any complaint from them would of course meet with no sympathy. In short, Topsy soon made the household understand the propriety of letting her alone; and she was let alone, accordingly.

Topsy was smart and energetic in all manual operations, learning everything that was taught her with surprising quickness. With a few lessons, she had learned to do the proprieties of Miss Ophelia's chamber in a way with which even that particular lady could find no fault. Mortal hands could not lay spread smoother, adjust pillows more accurately, sweep and dust and arrange more perfectly, than Topsy, when she chose,—but she didn't very often choose. If Miss Ophelia, after three or four days of careful and patient supervision, was so sanguine as to suppose that Topsy had at last fallen into her way, could do without overlooking, and so go off and busy herself about something else, Topsy would hold a perfect carnival of confusion, for some one or two hours. Instead of making the bed, she would amuse herself with pulling off the pillow-cases, butting her woolly head among the pillows, till it would sometimes be grotesquely ornamented with feathers sticking out in various directions; she would climb the posts, and hang head downward from the tops; flourish the sheets and spreads all over the apartment; dress the bolster up in Miss Ophelia's night-clothes, and enact various scenic performances with that,—singing and whistling, and making grimaces at herself in the looking-glass; in short, as Miss Ophelia phrased it, "raising Cain" generally.

One one occasion, Miss Ophelia found Topsy with her very best scarlet India Canton crape shawl wound round her head for a turban, going on with her rehearsals before the glass in great style,—Miss Ophelia having, with carelessness most unheard-of in her, left the key for once in her drawer.

"Topsy!" she would say, when at the end of all patience, "what does make you act so?"

"Dunno, Missis,—I spects cause I 's so wicked!"

"I don't know anything what I shall do with you, Topsy."

"Law, Missis, you must whip me; my old Missis allers whipped me. I an't used to workin' unless I gets whipped."

"Why, Topsy, I don't want to whip you. You can do well, if you 've a mind to; what is the reason you won't?"

"Laws, Missis, I 's used to whippin'; I spects it 's good for me."

Miss Ophelia tried the recipe, and Topsy invariably made a terrible commotion, screaming, groaning and imploring, though half an hour afterwards, when roosted on some projection of the balcony, and surrounded by a flock of admiring "young uns," she would express the utmost contempt of the whole affair.

"Law, Miss Feely whip!—would n't kill a skeeter, her whippins. Oughter see how old Mas'r made the flesh fly; old Mas'r know'd how!"

Topsy always made great capital of her own sins and enormities, evidently considering them as something peculiarly distinguishing.

"Law, you niggers," she would say to some of her auditors, "does you know you 's all sinners? Well, you is—everybody is. White folks is sinners too,—Miss Feely says so; but I spects niggers is the biggest ones; but lor! ye an't any on ye up to me. I 's so awful wicked there can't nobody do nothin' with me. I used to keep old Missis a swarin' at me half de time. I spects I 's the wickedest critter in the world;" and Topsy would cut a summerset, and come up brisk and shining on to a higher perch, and evidently plume herself on the distinction.

Miss Ophelia busied herself very earnestly on Sundays, teaching Topsy the catechism. Topsy had an uncommon verbal memory, and committed with a fluency that greatly encouraged her instructress.

"What good do you expect it is going to do her?" said St. Clare.

"Why, it always has done children good. It 's what children always have to learn, you know," said Miss Ophelia.

"Understand it or not," said St. Clare.

"O, children never understand it at the time; but, after they are grown up, it 'll come to them."

"Mine hasn't come to me yet," said St. Clare, "though I 'll bear testimony that you put it into me pretty thoroughly when I was a boy."

"Ah, you were always good at learning, Augustine. I used to have great hopes of you," said Miss Ophelia.

"Well, have n't you now?" said St. Clare.

"I wish you were as good as you were when you were a boy, Augustine."

"So do I, that 's a fact, Cousin," said St. Clare. "Well, go ahead and catechize Topsy; may be you 'll make out something yet."

Topsy, who had stood like a black statue during this discussion, with hands decently folded, now, at a signal from Miss Ophelia, went on:

"Our first parents, being left to the freedom of their own will, fell from the state wherein they were created."

Topsy's eyes twinkled, and she looked inquiringly.

"What is it, Topsy?" said Miss Ophelia.

"Please, Missis, was dat ar state Kintuck?"

"What state, Topsy?"

"Dat state dey fell out of. I used to hear Mas'r tell how we came down from Kintuck."

St. Clare laughed.

"You 'll have to give her a meaning, or she 'll make one," said he. "There seems to be a theory of emigration suggested there."

"O! Augustine, be still," said Miss Ophelia; "how can I do anything, if you will be laughing?"

"Well, I won't disturb the exercises again, on my honor;" and St. Clare took his paper into the parlor, and sat down, till Topsy had finished her recitations. They were all very well, only that now and then she would oddly transpose some important words, and persist in the mistake, in spite of every effort to the contrary; and St. Clare, after all his promises of goodness, took a wicked pleasure in these mistakes, calling Topsy to him whenever he had a mind to amuse himself, and getting her to repeat the offending passages, in spite of Miss Ophelia's remonstrances.

"How do you think I can do anything with the child, if you will go on so, Augustine?" she would say.

"Well, it is too bad,—I won't again; but I do like to hear the droll little image stumble over those big words!"

"But you confirm her in the wrong way."

"What 's the odds? One word is as good as another to her."

"You wanted me to bring her up right; and you ought to remember she is a reasonable creature, and be careful of your influence over her."

"O, dismal! so I ought; but, as Topsy herself says, 'I 's so wicked!'"

In very much this way Topsy's training proceeded, for a year or two,—Miss Ophelia worrying herself, from day to day, with her, as a kind of chronic plague, to whose inflictions she became, in time, as accustomed, as persons somtimes do to the neuralgia or sick head-ache.

St. Clare took the same kind of amusement in the child that a man might in the tricks of a parrot or a pointer. Topsy, whenever her sins brought her into disgrace in other quarters, always took refuge behind his chair; and St. Clare, in one way or other, would make peace for her. From him she got many a stray picayune, which she laid out in nuts and candies, and distributed, with careless generosity, to all the children in the family; for Topsy, to do her justice, was good-natured and liberal, and only spiteful in self-defence. She is fairly introduced into our *corps de ballet*, and will figure, from time to time, in her turn, with other performers.

## XXI.
### Kentuck

Our readers may not be unwilling to glance back, for a brief interval, at Uncle Tom's Cabin, on the Kentucky farm, and see what has been transpiring among those whom he had left behind.

It was late in the summer afternoon, and the doors and windows of the large parlor all stood open, to invite any stray breeze, that might feel in a good humor, to enter. Mr. Shelby sat in a large hall opening into the room, and running through the whole length of the house, to a balcony on either end. Leisurely tipped back in one chair, with his heels in another, he was enjoying his after-dinner cigar. Mrs. Shelby sat in the door, busy about some fine sewing; she seemed like one who had something on her mind, which she was seeking an opportunity to introduce.

"Do you know," she said, "that Chloe has had a letter from Tom?"

"Ah! has she? Tom 's got some friend there, it seems. How is the old boy?"

"He has been bought by a very fine family, I should think," said Mrs. Shelby,—"is kindly treated, and has not much to do."

"Ah! well, I 'm glad of it,—very glad," said Mr. Shelby, heartily. "Tom, I suppose, will get reconciled to a Southern residence;—hardly want to come up here again."

"On the contrary, he inquires very anxiously," said Mrs. Shelby, "when the money for his redemption is to be raised."

"I 'm sure *I* don't know," said Mr. Shelby. "Once get business running wrong, there does seem to be no end to it. It 's like jumping from one bog to another, all through a swamp; borrow of one to pay another, and then borrow of another to pay one,—and these confounded notes falling due before a man has time to smoke a cigar and turn round,—dunning letters and dunning messages,—all scamper and hurry-scurry."

"It does seem to me, my dear, that something might be done to straighten matters. Suppose we sell off all the horses, and sell one of your farms, and pay up square?"

"O, ridiculous, Emily! You are the finest woman in Kentucky; but still you have n't sense to know that you don't understand business;—women never do, and never can."

"But, at least," said Mrs. Shelby, "could not you give me some little insight into yours; a list of all your debts, at least, and of all that is owed to you, and let me try and see if I can't help you to economize."

"O, bother! don't plague me, Emily!—I can't tell exactly. I know somewhere about what things are likely to be; but there's no trimming and squaring my affairs, as Chloe trims crust off her pies. You don't know anything about business, I tell you."

And Mr. Shelby, not knowing any other way of enforcing his ideas, raised his voice,—a mode of arguing very convenient and convincing, when a gentleman is discussing matters of business with his wife.

Mrs. Shelby ceased talking, with something of a sigh. The fact was, that though her husband had stated she was a woman, she had a clear, energetic, practical mind, and a force of character every way superior to that of her husband; so that it would not have been so very absurd a supposition, to have allowed her capable of managing, as Mr. Shelby supposed. Her heart was set on performing her promise to Tom and Aunt Chloe, and she sighed as discouragements thickened around her.

"Don't you think we might in some way contrive to raise that money? Poor Aunt Chloe! her heart is so set on it!"

"I 'm sorry, if it is. I think I was premature in promising. I 'm not sure, now, but it 's the best way to tell Chloe, and let her make up her mind to it. Tom 'll have another wife, in a year or two; and she had better take up with somebody else."

"Mr. Shelby, I have taught my people that their marriages are as sacred as ours. I never could think of giving Chloe such advice."

"It 's a pity, wife, that you have burdened them with a morality above their condition and prospects. I always thought so."

"It 's only the morality of the Bible, Mr. Shelby."

"Well, well, Emily, I don't pretend to interfere with your religious notions; only they seem extremely unfitted for people in that condition."

"They are, indeed," said Mrs. Shelby, "and that is why, from my soul, I hate the whole thing. I tell you, my dear, *I* cannot absolve myself from the promises I make to these helpless creatures. If I can get the money no other way, I will take music-scholars;—I could get enough, I know, and earn the money myself."

"You would n't degrade yourself that way, Emily? I never could consent to it."

"Degrade! would it degrade me as much as to break my faith with the helpless? No, indeed!"

"Well, you are always heroic and transcendental," said Mr. Shelby, "but I think you had better think before you undertake such a piece of Quixotism."

Here the conversation was interrupted by the appearance of Aunt Chloe, at the end of the verandah.

"If you please, Missis," said she.

"Well, Chloe, what is it?" said her mistress, rising, and going to the end of the balcony.

"If Missis would come and look at dis yer lot o' poetry."

Chloe had a particular fancy for calling poultry poetry,—an application of language in which she always persisted, notwithstanding frequent corrections and advisings from the young members of the family.

"La sakes!" she would say, "I can't see; one jis good as turry,—poetry suthin good, any how;" and so poetry Chloe continued to call it.

Mrs. Shelby smiled as she saw a prostrate lot of chickens and ducks, over which Chloe stood, with a very grave face of consideration.

"I 'm a thinkin whether Missis would be a havin a chicken pie o' dese yer."

"Really, Aunt Chloe, I don't much care;—serve them any way you like."

Chloe stood handling them over abstractedly; it was quite evident that the chickens were not what she was thinking of. At last, with the short laugh with which her tribe often introduced a doubtful proposal, she said,

"Laws me, Missis! what should Mas'r and Missis be a troublin theirselves' bout de money, and not a usin what's right in der hands?" and Chloe laughed again.

"I don't understand you, Chloe," said Mrs. Shelby, nothing doubting, from her knowledge of Chloe's manner, that she had heard every word of the conversation that had passed between her and her husband.

"Why, laws me, Missis!" said Chloe, laughing again, "other folks hires out der niggers and makes money on 'em! Don't keep sich a tribe eatin 'em out of house and home."

"Well, Chloe, who do you propose that we should hire out?"

"Laws! I an't a proposin nothin; only Sam he said der was one of dese yer *perfectioners*, dey calls 'em in Louisville, said he wanted a good hand at cake and pastry; and said he 'd give four dollars a week to one, he did."

"Well, Chloe."

"Well, laws, I 's a thinkin, Missis, it 's time Sally was put along to be doin' something. Sally 's been under my care now, dis some time, and she does most as well as me, considerin; and if Missis would only let me go, I would help fetch up de money. I an't afraid to put my cake, nor pies nother, 'long side no *perfectioner's*."

"Confectioner's, Chloe."

"Law sakes, Missis! 't an't no odds;—words is so curis, can't never get 'em right!"

"But, Chloe, do you want to leave your children?"

"Laws, Missis! de boys is big enough to do day's works; dey does well enough; and Sally, she 'll take de baby,—She 's such a peart young un, she won't take no lookin arter."

"Louisville is a good way off."

"Law sakes! who 's afeard?—it 's down river, somer near my old man, perhaps?" said Chloe, speaking the last in the tone of a question, and looking at Mrs. Shelby.

"No, Chloe; it 's many a hundred miles off," said Mrs. Shelby.

Chloe's countenance fell.

"Never mind; your going there shall bring you nearer, Chloe. Yes, you may go; and your wages shall every cent of them be laid aside for your husband's redemption."

As when a bright sunbeam turns a dark cloud to silver, so Chloe's dark face brightened immediately,—it really shone.

"Laws! if Missis is n't too good! I was thinking of dat ar very thing; cause I should n't need no clothes, nor shoes, nor nothin,—I could save every cent. How many weeks is der in a year, Missis?"

"Fifty-two," said Mrs. Shelby.

"Laws! now, dere is? and four dollars for each on 'em. Why, how much 'd dat ar be?"

"Two hundred and eight dollars," said Mrs. Shelby.

"Why-e!" said Chloe, with an accent of surprise and delight; "and how long would it take me to work it out, Missis?"

"Some four or five years, Chloe; but, then, you need n't do it all,—I shall add something to it."

"I would n't hear to Missis' givin lessons nor nothin. Mas'r's quite right in dat ar;—'t would n't do, no ways. I hope none our family ever be brought to dat ar, while I 's got hands."

"Don't fear, Chloe; I 'll take care of the honor of the family," said Mrs. Shelby, smiling. "But when do you expect to go?"

"Well, I want spectin nothin; only Sam, he 's a gwine to de river with some colts, and he said I could go long with him; so I jes put my things together. If Missis was willin, I 'd go with Sam to-morrow morning, if Missis would write my pass, and write me a commendation."

"Well, Chloe, I 'll attend to it, if Mr. Shelby has no objections. I must speak to him."

Mrs. Shelby went up stairs, and Aunt Chloe, delighted, went out to her cabin, to make her preparation.

"Law sakes, Mas'r George! ye did n't know I 's a gwine to Louisville to-morrow!" she said to George, as, entering her cabin, he found her busy in sorting over her baby's clothes. "I thought I 'd jis look over sis's things, and get 'em straightened up. But I 'm gwine, Mas'r George,—gwine to have four dollars a week; and Missis is gwine to lay it all up, to buy back my old man agin!"

"Whew!" said George, "here 's a stroke of business, to be sure! How are you going?"

"To-morrow, wid Sam. And now, Mas'r George, I knows you 'll jis sit down and write to my old man, and tell him all about it,—won't ye?"

"To be sure," said George; "Uncle Tom 'll be right glad to hear from us. I 'll go right in the house, for paper and ink; and then, you know, Aunt Chloe, I can tell about the new colts and all."

"Sartin, sartin, Mas'r George; you go 'long, and I 'll get ye up a bit o' chicken, or some sich; ye won't have many more suppers wid yer poor old aunty."

## XXII.
### "The Grass Withereth—the Flower Fadeth"

Life passes, with us all, a day at a time; so it passed with our friend Tom, till two years were gone. Though parted from all his soul held dear, and though often yearning for what lay beyond, still was he never positively and consciously miserable; for, so well is the harp of human feeling strung, that nothing but a crash that breaks every string can wholly mar its harmony; and, on looking back to seasons which in review appear to us as those of deprivation and trial, we can remember that each hour, as it glided, brought its diversions and alleviations, so that, though not happy wholly, we were not, either, wholly miserable.

Tom read, in his only literary cabinet, of one who had "learned in whatsoever state he was, therewith to be content." It seemed to him good and reasonable doctrine, and accorded well with the settled and thoughtful habit which he had acquired from the reading of that same book.

His letter homeward, as we related in the last chapter, was in due time answered by Master George, in a good, round, school-boy hand, that Tom said might be read "most acrost the room." It contained various refreshing items of home intelligence, with which our reader is fully acquainted: stated how Aunt Chloe had been hired out to a confectioner in Louisville, where her skill in the pastry line was gaining wonderful sums of money, all of which, Tom was informed, was to be laid up to go to make up the sum of his redemption money; Mose and Pete were thriving, and the baby was trotting all about the house, under the care of Sally and the family generally.

Tom's cabin was shut up for the present; but George expatiated brilliantly on ornaments and additions to be made to it when Tom came back.

The rest of this letter gave a list of George's school studies, each one headed by a flourishing capital; and also told the names of four new colts that appeared on the premises since Tom left; and stated, in the same connection, that father and mother were well. The style of the letter was decidedly concise and terse; but Tom thought it the most wonderful specimen of composition that had appeared in modern times. He was never tired of looking at it, and even held a council with Eva on the expediency of getting it framed, to hang up in his room. Nothing but the difficulty of arranging it so that both sides of the page would show at once stood in the way of this undertaking.

The friendship between Tom and Eva had grown with the child's growth. It would be hard to say what place she held in the soft, impressible heart of her faithful attendant. He loved her as something frail and earthly, yet almost worshipped her as something heavenly and divine. He gazed on her as the Italian sailor gazes on his image of the child Jesus,—with a mixture of reverence and tenderness; and to humor her graceful fancies, and meet those thousand simple wants which invest childhood like a many-colored rainbow, was Tom's chief delight. In the market, at morning, his eyes were always on the flower-stalls for rare bouquets for her, and the choicest peach or orange was slipped into his pocket to give to her when he came back; and the sight that pleased him most was her sunny head looking out the gate for his distant approach, and her childish question,— "Well, Uncle Tom, what have you got for me to-day?"

Nor was Eva less zealous in kind offices, in return. Though a child, she was a beautiful reader;—a fine musical ear, a quick poetic fancy, and an instinctive sympathy with what is grand and noble, made her such a reader of the Bible as Tom had never before heard. At first, she read to please her humble friend; but soon her own earnest nature threw out its tendrils, and wound itself around the majestic book; and Eva loved it, because it woke in her strange yearnings, and strong, dim emotions, such as impassioned, imaginative children love to feel.

The parts that pleased her most were the Revelations and the Prophecies,— parts whose dim and wondrous imagery, the fervent language, impressed her the more, that she questioned vainly of their meaning;—and she and her simple friend, the old child and the young one, felt just alike about it. All that they knew was, that they spoke of a glory to be revealed,—a wondrous something yet to come, wherein their soul rejoiced, yet knew not why; and though it be not so in the physical, yet in moral science that which cannot be understood is not always profitless. For the soul awakes, a trembling stranger, between two dim eternities,—the eternal past, the eternal future. The light shines only on a small space around her; therefore, she needs must yearn towards the unknown; and the voices and shadowy movings which come to her from out the cloudy pillar of inspiration have each one echoes and answers in her own expecting nature. Its mystic imagery are so many talismans and gems inscribed with unknown hieroglyphics; she folds them in her bosom, and expects to read them when she passes beyond the veil.

At this time in our story, the whole St. Clare establishment is, for the time being, removed to their villa on Lake Pontchartrain. The heats of summer had driven all who were able to leave the sultry and unhealthy city, to seek the shores of the lake, and its cool sea-breezes.

St. Clare's villa was an East Indian cottage, surrounded by light verandahs of bamboo-work, and opening on all sides into gardens and pleasure-grounds. The common sitting-room opened on to a large garden, fragrant with every picturesque plant and flower of the tropics, where winding paths ran down to the very shores of the lake, whose silvery sheet of water lay there, rising and falling in the sunbeams,—a picture never for an hour the same, yet every hour more beautiful.

It is now one of those intensely golden sunsets which kindles the whole horizon into one blaze of glory, and makes the water another sky. The lake lay in rosy or golden streaks, save where white-winged vessels glided hither and thither, like so many spirits, and little golden stars twinkled through the glow, and looked down at themselves as they trembled in the water.

Tom and Eva were seated on a little mossy seat, in an arbor, at the foot of the garden. It was Sunday evening, and Eva's Bible lay open on her knee. She read,— "And I saw a sea of glass, mingled with fire."

"Tom," said Eva, suddenly stopping, and pointing to the lake, "There 't is."

"What, Miss Eva?"

"Don't you see,—there?" said the child, pointing to the glassy water, which, as it rose and fell, reflected the golden glow of the sky. "There 's a 'sea of glass, mingled with fire.'"

"True enough, Miss Eva," said Tom; and Tom sang—

> "O, had I the wings of the morning,
> I'd fly away to Canaan's shore;
> Bright angels should convey me home,
> To the new Jerusalem."

"Where do you suppose new Jerusalem is, Uncle Tom?" said Eva.

"O, up in the clouds, Miss Eva."

"Then I think I see it," said Eva. "Look in those clouds!—they look like great gates of pearl; and you can see beyond them—far, far off—it 's all gold. Tom, sing about 'spirits bright.'"

Tom sung the words of a well-known Methodist hymn,

> "I see a band of spirits bright,
> That taste the glories there;
> They all are robed in spotless white,
> And conquering palms they bear."

"Uncle Tom, I 've seen *them*," said Eva.

Tom had no doubt of it at all; it did not surprise him in the least. If Eva had told him she had been to heaven, he would have thought it entirely probable.

"They come to me sometimes in my sleep, those spirits;" and Eva's eyes grew dreamy, and she hummed, in a low voice,

"They are all robed in spotless white,
And conquering palms they bear."

"Uncle Tom," said Eva, "I 'm going there."

"Where, Miss Eva?"

The child rose, and pointed her little hand to the sky; the glow of the evening lit her golden hair and flushed cheek with a kind of unearthly radiance, and her eyes were bent earnestly on the skies.

"I 'm going *there*," she said, "to the spirits bright, Tom; *I 'm going, before long*."

The faithful old heart felt a sudden thrust; and Tom thought how often he had noticed, within six months, that Eva's little hands had grown thinner, and her skin more transparent, and her breath shorter; and how, when she ran or played in the garden, as she once could for hours, she became soon so tired and languid. He had heard Miss Ophelia speak often of a cough, that all her medicaments could not cure; and even now that fervent cheek and little hand were burning with hectic fever; and yet the thought that Eva's words suggested had never come to him till now.

Has there ever been a child like Eva? Yes, there have been; but their names are always on grave-stones, and their sweet smiles, their heavenly eyes, their singular words and ways, are among the buried treasures of yearning hearts. In how many families do you hear the legend that all the goodness and graces of the living are nothing to the peculiar charms of one who *is not*. It is as if heaven had an especial band of angels, whose office it was to sojourn for a season here, and endear to them the wayward human heart, that they might bear it upward with them in their homeward flight. When you see that deep, spiritual light in the eye,—when the little soul reveals itself in words sweeter and wiser than the ordinary words of children,—hope not to retain that child; for the seal of heaven is on it, and the light of immortality looks out from its eyes.

Even so, beloved Eva! fair star of thy dwelling! Thou art passing away; but they that love thee dearest know it not.

The colloquy between Tom and Eva was interrupted by a hasty call from Miss Ophelia.

"Eva—Eva!—why, child, the dew is falling; you must n't be out there!"

Eva and Tom hastened in.

Miss Ophelia was old, and skilled in the tactics of nursing. She was from New England, and knew well the first guileful footsteps of that soft, insidious disease, which sweeps away so many of the fairest and loveliest, and, before one fibre of life seems broken, seals them irrevocably for death.

She had noted the slight, dry cough, the daily brightening cheek; nor could the lustre of the eye, and the airy buoyancy born of fever, deceive her.

She tried to communicate her fears to St. Clare; but he threw back her suggestions with a restless petulance, unlike his usual careless good-humor.

"Don't be croaking, Cousin,—I hate it!" he would say; "don't you see that the child is only growing. Children always lose strength when they grow fast."

"But she has that cough!"

"O! nonsense of that cough!—it is not anything. She has taken a little cold, perhaps."

"Well, that was just the way Eliza Jane was taken, and Ellen and Maria Sanders."

"O! stop these hobgoblin' nurse legends. You old hands got so wise, that a child cannot cough, or sneeze, but you see desperation and ruin at hand. Only take care of the child, keep her from the night air, and don't let her play too hard, and she 'll do well enough."

So St. Clare said; but he grew nervous and restless. He watched Eva fever-ishly day by day, as might be told by the frequency with which he repeated over that "the child was quite well"—that there wasn't anything in that cough,—it was only some little stomach affection, such as children often had. But he kept by her more than before, took her oftener to ride with him, brought home every few days some receipt or strengthening mixture,—"not," he said, "that the child *needed* it, but then it would not do her any harm."

If it must be told, the thing that struck a deeper pang to his heart than any-thing else was the daily increasing maturity of the child's mind and feelings. While still retaining all a child's fanciful graces, yet she often dropped, unconsciously, words of such a reach of thought, and strange unworldly wisdom, that they seemed to be an inspiration. At such times, St. Clare would feel a sudden thrill, and clasp her in his arms, as if that fond clasp could save her; and his heart rose up with wild determination to keep her, never to let her go.

The child's whole heart and soul seemed absorbed in works of love and kind-ness. Impulsively generous she had always been; but there was a touching and womanly thoughtfulness about her now, that every one noticed. She still loved to play with Topsy, and the various colored children; but she now seemed rather a spectator than an actor of their plays, and she would sit for half an hour at a time, laughing at the odd tricks of Topsy,—and then a shadow would seem to pass across her face, her eyes grew misty, and her thoughts were afar.

"Mamma," she said, suddenly, to her mother, one day, "why don't we teach our servants to read?"

"What a question, child! People never do."

"Why don't they?" said Eva.

"Because it is no use for them to read. It don't help them to work any better, and they are not made for anything else."

"But they ought to read the Bible, mamma, to learn God's will."

"O! they can get that read to them all *they* need."

"It seems to me, mamma, the Bible is for every one to read themselves. They need it a great many times when there is nobody to read it."

"Eva, you are an odd child," said her mother.

"Miss Ophelia has taught Topsy to read," continued Eva.

"Yes, and you see how much good it does. Topsy is the worst creature I ever saw!"

"Here 's poor Mammy!" said Eva. "She does love the Bible so much, and wishes so she could read! And what will she do when I can't read to her?"

Marie was busy, turning over the contents of a drawer, as she answered,

"Well, of course, by and by, Eva, you will have other things to think of, besides reading the Bible round to servants. Not but that is very proper; I 've done it myself, when I had health. But when you come to be dressing and going into company, you won't have time. See here!" she added, "these jewels I'm going to give you when you come out. I wore them to my first ball. I can tell you, Eva, I made a sensation."

Eva took the jewel-case, and lifted from it a diamond necklace. Her large, thoughtful eyes rested on them, but it was plain her thoughts were elsewhere.

"How sober you look, child!" said Marie.

"Are these worth a great deal of money, mamma?"

"To be sure, they are. Father sent to France for them. They are worth a small fortune."

"I wish I had them," said Eva, "to do what I pleased with!"

"What would you do with them?"

"I 'd sell them, and buy a place in the free states, and take all our people there, and hire teachers, to teach them to read and write."

Eva was cut short by her mother's laughing.

"Set up a boarding-school! Would n't you teach them to play on the piano, and paint on velvet?"

"I 'd teach them to read their own Bible, and write their own letters, and read letters that are written to them," said Eva, steadily. "I know, mamma, it does come very hard on them, that they can't do these things. Tom feels it,—Mammy does,— a great many of them do. I think it 's wrong."

"Come, come, Eva; you are only a child! You don't know anything about these things," said Marie; "besides, your talking makes my head ache."

Marie always had a head-ache on hand for any conversation that did not exactly suit her.

Eva stole away; but after that, she assiduously gave Mammy reading lessons.

## XXIII.
### Henrique

About this time, St. Clare's brother Alfred, with his eldest son, a boy of twelve, spent a day or two with the family at the lake.

No sight could be more singular and beautiful than that of these twin brothers. Nature, instead of instituting resemblances between them, had made them opposites on every point; yet a mysterious tie seemed to unite them in a closer friendship than ordinary.

They used to saunter, arm in arm, up and down the alleys and walks of the garden. Augustine, with his blue eyes and golden hair, his ethereally flexible form and vivacious features; and Alfred, dark-eyed, with haughty Roman profile, firmly-knit limbs, and decided bearing. They were always abusing each other's opinions and practices, and yet never a whit the less absorbed in each other's society; in fact, the very contrariety seemed to unite them, like the attraction between opposite poles of the magnet.

Henrique, the eldest son of Alfred, was a noble, dark-eyed, princely boy, full of vivacity and spirit; and, from the first moment of introduction, seemed to be perfectly fascinated by the spirituelle graces of his cousin Evangeline.

Eva had a little pet pony, of a snowy whiteness. It was easy as a cradle, and as gentle as its little mistress; and this pony was now brought up to the back verandah by Tom, while a little mulatto boy of about thirteen led along a small black Arabian, which had just been imported, at a great expense, for Henrique.

Henrique had a boy's pride in his new possession; and, as he advanced and took the reins out of the hands of his little groom, he looked carefully over him, and his brow darkened.

"What 's this, Dodo, you little lazy dog! you have n't rubbed my horse down, this morning."

"Yes, Mas'r," said Dodo, submissively; "he got that dust on his own self."

"You rascal, shut your mouth!" said Henrique, violently raising his riding-whip. "How dare you speak?"

The boy was a handsome, bright-eyed mulatto, of just Henrique's size, and his curling hair hung round a high, bold forehead. He had white blood in his veins, as could be seen by the quick flush in his cheek, and the sparkle of his eye, as he eagerly tried to speak.

"Mas'r Henrique!—" he began.

Henrique struck him across the face with his riding-whip, and, seizing one of his arms, forced him on to his knees, and beat him till he was out of breath.

"There, you impudent dog! Now will you learn not to answer back when I speak to you? Take the horse back, and clean him properly. I 'll teach you your place!"

"Young Mas'r," said Tom, "I specs what he was gwine to say was, that the horse would roll when he was bringing him up from the stable; he 's so full of spirits,—that 's the way he got that dirt on him; I looked to his cleaning."

"You hold your tongue till you 're asked to speak!" said Henrique, turning on his heel, and walking up the steps to speak to Eva, who stood in her riding-dress.

"Dear Cousin, I 'm sorry this stupid fellow has kept you waiting," he said, "Let 's sit down here, on this seat, till they come. What 's the matter, Cousin?—you look sober."

"How could you be so cruel and wicked to poor Dodo?" said Eva.

"Cruel,—wicked!" said the boy, with unaffected surprise. "What do you mean, dear Eva?"

"I don't want you to call me dear Eva, when you do so," said Eva.

"Dear Cousin, you don't know Dodo; it 's the only way to manage him, he 's so full of lies and excuses. The only way is to put him down at once,—not let him open his mouth; that 's the way papa manages."

"But Uncle Tom said it was an accident, and he never tells what is n't true."

"He 's an uncommon old nigger, then!" said Henrique. "Dodo will lie as fast as he can speak."

"You frighten him into deceiving, if you treat him so."

"Why, Eva, you 've really taken such a fancy to Dodo, that I shall be jealous."

"But you beat him,—and he did n't deserve it."

"O, well, it may go for some time when he does, and don't get it. A few cuts never come amiss with Dodo,—he 's a regular spirit, I can tell you; but I won't beat him again before you, if it troubles you."

Eva was not satisfied, but found it in vain to try to make her handsome cousin understand her feelings.

Dodo soon appeared, with the horses.

"Well, Dodo, you 've done pretty well, this time," said his young master, with a more gracious air. "Come, now, and hold Miss Eva's horse, while I put her on to the saddle."

Dodo came and stood by Eva's pony. His face was troubled; his eyes looked as if he had been crying.

Henrique, who valued himself on his gentlemanly adroitness in all matters of gallantry, soon had his fair cousin in the saddle, and, gathering the reins, placed them in her hands.

But Eva bent to the other side of the horse, where Dodo was standing, and said, as he relinquished the reins,—"that 's a good boy, Dodo;—thank you!"

Dodo looked up in amazement into the sweet young face; the blood rushed to his cheeks, and the tears to his eyes.

"Here, Dodo," said his master, imperiously.

Dodo sprang and held the horse, while his master mounted.

"There 's a picayune for you to buy candy with, Dodo," said Henrique; "go get some."

And Henrique cantered down the walk after Eva. Dodo stood looking after the two children. One had given him money; and one had given him what he wanted far more,—a kind word, kindly spoken. Dodo had been only a few months away from his mother. His master had bought him at a slave warehouse, for his handsome face, to be a match to the handsome pony; and he was now getting his breaking in, at the hands of his young master.

The scene of the beating had been witnessed by the two brothers St. Clare, from another part of the garden.

Augustine's cheek flushed; but he only observed, with his usual sarcastic carelessness,

"I suppose that 's what we may call republican education, Alfred?"

"Henrique is a devil of a fellow, when his blood 's up," said Alfred, carelessly.

"I suppose you consider this an instructive practice for him," said Augustine, drily.

"I could n't help it, if I did n't. Henrique is a regular little tempest;—his mother and I have given him up, long ago. But, then, that Dodo is a perfect sprite,—no amount of whipping can hurt him."

"And this by way of teaching Henrique the first verse of a republican's catechism, 'All men are born free and equal!'"

"Poh!" said Alfred; "one of Tom Jefferson's pieces of French sentiment and humbug. It 's perfectly ridiculous to have that going the rounds among us, to this day."

"I think it is," said St. Clare, significantly.

"Because," said Alfred, "we can see plainly enough that all men are *not* born free, nor born equal; they are born anything else. For my part, I think half this republican talk sheer humbug. It is the educated, the intelligent, the wealthy, the refined, who ought to have equal rights, and not the canaille."

"If you can keep the canaille of that opinion," said Augustine. "They took *their* turn once, in France."

"Of course, they must be *kept down*, consistently, steadily, as I *should*," said Alfred, setting his foot hard down, as if he were standing on somebody.

"It makes a terrible slip when they get up," said Augustine,—"In St. Domingo, for instance."

"Poh!" said Alfred, "we 'll take care of that, in this country. We must set our face against all this educating, elevating talk, that is getting about now; the lower class must not be educated."

"That is past praying for," said Augustine; "educated they will be, and we have only to say how. Our system is educating them in barbarism and brutality. We are breaking all humanizing ties, and making them brute beasts; and, if they get the upper hand, such we shall find them."

"They never shall get the upper hand!" said Alfred.

"That 's right," said St. Clare; "put on the steam, fasten down the escape-valve, and sit on it, and see where you 'll land."

"Well," said Alfred, "we *will* see. I 'm not afraid to sit on the escape-valve, as long as the boilers are strong, and the machinery works well."

"The nobles in Louis XVI.'s time thought just so; and Austria and Pius IX. think so now; and, some pleasant morning, you may all be caught up to meet each other in the air, *when the boilers burst*."

"*Dies declarabit*," said Alfred, laughing.

"I tell you," said Augustine, "if there is anything that is revealed with the strength of a divine law in our times, it is that the masses are to rise, and the under class become the upper one."

"That 's one of your red republican humbugs, Augustine! Why did n't you ever take to the stump;—you 'd make a famous stump orator! Well, I hope I shall be dead before this millennium of your greasy masses comes on."

"Greasy or not greasy, they will govern *you*, when their time comes," said Augustine; "and they will be just such rulers as you make them. The French noblesse chose to have the people 'sans culottes,' and they had 'sans culotte' governors to their hearts' content. The people of Hayti—"

"O, come, Augustine! as if we had n't had enough of that abominable, contemptible Hayti! the Haytiens were not Anglo Saxons; if they had been, there would have been another story. The Anglo Saxon is the dominant race of the world, and *is to be so*."

"Well, there is a pretty fair infusion of Anglo Saxon blood among our slaves, now," said Augustine. "There are plenty among them who have only enough of the African to give a sort of tropical warmth and fervor to our calculating firmness and foresight. If ever the San Domingo hour comes, Anglo Saxon blood will lead on the day. Sons of white fathers, with all our haughty feelings burning in their veins, will not always be bought and sold and traded. They will rise, and raise with them their mother's race."

"Stuff!—nonsense!"

"Well," said Augustine, "there goes an old saying to this effect, 'As it was in the days of Noah, so shall it be;—they ate, they drank, they planted, they builded, and knew not till the flood came and took them.' "

"On the whole, Augustine, I think your talents might do for a circuit rider," said Alfred, laughing. "Never you fear for us; possession is our nine points. We 've got the power. This subject race," said he, stamping firmly, "is down, and shall *stay* down! We have energy enough to manage our own powder."

"Sons trained like your Henrique will be grand guardians of your powder-magazines," said Augustine,—"so cool and self-possessed! The proverb says, 'they that cannot govern themselves cannot govern others.' "

"There is a trouble there," said Alfred, thoughtfully; "there 's no doubt that our system is a difficult one to train children under. It gives too free scope to the passions, altogether, which, in our climate, are hot enough. I find trouble with Henrique. The boy is generous and warm-hearted, but a perfect fire-cracker when excited. I believe I shall send him North for his education, where obedience is more fashionable, and where he will associate more with equals, and less with dependants."

"Since training children is the staple work of the human race," said Augustine, "I should think it something of a consideration that our system does not work well there."

"It does not for some things," said Alfred; "for others, again, it does. It makes boys manly and courageous; and the very vices of an abject race tend to strengthen in them the opposite virtues. I think Henrique, now, has a keener sense of the beauty of truth, from seeing lying and deception the universal badge of slavery."

"A Christian-like view of the subject, certainly!" said Augustine.

"It 's true, Christian-like or not; and is about as Christian-like as most other things in the world," said Alfred.

"That may be," said St. Clare.

"Well, there 's no use in talking, Augustine. I believe we 've been round and round this old track five hundred times, more or less. What do you say to a game of backgammon?"

The two brothers ran up the verandah steps, and were soon seated at a light bamboo stand, with the backgammon-board between them. As they were setting their men, Alfred said,

"I tell you, Augustine, if I thought as you do, I should do something."

"I dare say you would,—you are one of the doing sort,—but what?"

"Why, elevate your own servants, for a specimen," said Alfred, with a half-scornful smile.

"You might as well set Mount Aetna on them flat, and tell them to stand up under it, as tell me to elevate my servants under all the superincumbent mass of society upon them. One man can do nothing, against the whole action of a community. Education, to do anything, must be a state education; or there must be enough agreed in it to make a current."

"You take the first throw," said Alfred; and the brothers were soon lost in the game, and heard no more till the scraping of horses' feet was heard under the verandah.

"There come the children," said Augustine, rising. "Look here, Alf! Did you ever see anything so beautiful?" And, in truth, it *was* a beautiful sight. Henrique, with his bold brow, and dark, glossy curls, and glowing cheek, was laughing gayly, as he bent towards his fair cousin, as they came on. She was dressed in a blue riding-dress, with a cap of the same color. Exercise had given a brilliant hue to her cheeks, and heightened the effect of her singularly transparent skin, and golden hair.

"Good heavens! what perfectly dazzling beauty!" said Alfred. "I tell you, Auguste, won't she make some hearts ache, one of these days?"

"She will, too truly,—God knows I 'm afraid so!" said St. Clare, in a tone of sudden bitterness, as he hurried down to take her off her horse.

"Eva, darling! you 're not much tired?" he said, as he clasped her in his arms.

"No, papa," said the child; but her short, hard breathing alarmed her father.

"How could you ride so fast, dear?—you know it 's bad for you."

"I felt so well, papa, and liked it so much, I forgot."

St. Clare carried her in his arms into the parlor, and laid her on the sofa.

"Henrique, you must be careful of Eva," said he; "you must n't ride fast with her."

"I 'll take her under my care," said Henrique, seating himself by the sofa, and taking Eva's hand.

Eva soon found herself much better. Her father and uncle resumed their game, and the children were left together.

"Do you know, Eva, I 'm so sorry papa is only going to stay two days here, and then I shan't see you again for ever so long! If I stay with you, I 'd try to be good, and not be cross to Dodo, and so on. I don't mean to treat Dodo ill; but, you know, I 've got such a quick temper. I 'm not really bad to him, though. I give him a picayune, now and then; and you see he dresses well. I think, on the whole, Dodo 's pretty well off."

"Would you think you were well off, if there were not one creature in the world near you to love you?"

"I?—Well, of course not."

"And you have taken Dodo away from all the friends he ever had, and now he has not a creature to love him;—nobody can be good that way."

"Well, I can't help it, as I know of. I can't get his mother, and I can't love him myself, nor anybody else, as I know of."

"Why can't you?" said Eva.

"*Love* Dodo! Why, Eva, you wouldn't have me! I may *like* him well enough; but you don't *love* your servants."

"I do, indeed."

"How odd!"

"Don't the Bible say we must love everybody?"

"O, the Bible! To be sure, it says a great many such things; but, then, nobody ever thinks of doing them,—you know, Eva, nobody does."

Eva did not speak; her eyes were fixed and thoughtful, for a few moments.

"At any rate," she said, "dear Cousin, do love poor Dodo, and be kind to him, for my sake!"

"I could love anything, for your sake, dear Cousin; for I really think you are the loveliest creature that I ever saw!" And Henrique spoke with an earnestness that flushed his handsome face. Eva received it with perfect simplicity, without even a change of feature; merely saying, "I 'm glad you feel so, dear Henrique! I hope you will remember."

The dinner-bell put an end to the interview.

## XXIV.
### Foreshadowings

Two days after this, Alfred St. Clare and Augustine parted; and Eva, who had been stimulated, by the society of her young cousin, to exertions beyond her strength, began to fail rapidly. St. Clare was at last willing to call in medical advice,—a thing from which he had always shrunk, because it was the admission of an unwelcome truth.

But, for a day or two, Eva was so unwell as to be confined to the house; and the doctor was called.

Marie St. Clare had taken no notice of the child's gradually decaying health and strength, because she was completely absorbed in studying out two or three new forms of disease to which she believed she herself was a victim. It was the first principle of Marie's belief that nobody ever was or could be so great a sufferer as *herself*; and, therefore, she always repelled quite indignantly any suggestion that any one around her could be sick. She was always sure, in such a case, that it was nothing but laziness, or want of energy; and that, if they had had the suffering *she* had, they would soon know the difference.

Miss Ophelia had several times tried to awaken her maternal fears about Eva; but to no avail.

"I don't see as anything ails the child," she would say; "she runs about, and plays."

"But she has a cough."

"Cough! you don't need to tell *me* about a cough. I 've always been subject to a cough, all my days. When I was of Eva's age, they thought I was in a consumption. Night after night, Mammy used to sit up with me. O! Eva's cough is not anything."

"But she gets weak, and is short-breathed."

"Law! I 've had that, years and years; it 's only a nervous affection."

"But she sweats so, nights!"

"Well, I have, these ten years. Very often, night after night, my clothes will be wringing wet. There won't be a dry thread in my night-clothes, and the sheets will be so that Mammy has to hang them up to dry! Eva does n't sweat anything like that!"

Miss Ophelia shut her mouth for a season. But, now that Eva was fairly and visibly prostrated, and a doctor called, Marie, all on a sudden, took a new turn.

"She knew it," she said; "she always felt it, that she was destined to be the most miserable of mothers. Here she was, with her wretched health, and her only darling child going down to the grave before her eyes;"—and Marie routed up Mammy nights, and rumpussed and scolded, with more energy than ever, all day, on the strength of this new misery.

"My dear Marie, don't talk so!" said St. Clare. "You ought not to give up the case so, at once."

"You have not a mother's feelings, St. Clare! You never could understand me!—you don't now."

"But don't talk so, as if it were a gone case!"

"I can't take it as indifferently as you can, St. Clare. If *you* don't feel when your only child is in this alarming state, *I* do. It 's a blow too much for me, with all I was bearing before."

"It 's true," said St. Clare, "that Eva is very delicate, *that* I always knew; and that she has grown so rapidly as to exhaust her strength; and that her situation is critical. But just now she is only prostrated by the heat of the weather, and by the excitement of her cousin's visit, and the exertions she made. The physician says there is room for hope."

"Well, of course, if you can look on the bright side, pray do; it 's a mercy if people have n't sensitive feelings, in this world. I am sure I wish I did n't feel as I do; it only makes me completely wretched! I wish I *could* be as easy as the rest of you!"

And the "rest of them" had good reason to breathe the same prayer, for Marie paraded her new misery as the reason and apology for all sorts of inflictions on every one about her. Every word that was spoken by anybody, everything that was done or was not done everywhere, was only a new proof that she was surrounded by hard-hearted, insensible beings, who were unmindful of her peculiar sorrows. Poor Eva heard some of these speeches; and nearly cried her little eyes out, in pity for her mamma, and in sorrow that she should make her so much distress.

In a week or two, there was a great improvement of symptoms,—one of those deceitful lulls, by which her inexorable disease so often beguiles the anxious heart, even on the verge of the grave. Eva's step was again in the garden,—in the balconies; she played and laughed again,—and her father, in a transport, declared that they should soon have her as hearty as anybody. Miss Ophelia and the physician alone felt no encouragement from this illusive truce. There was one other heart, too, that felt the same certainty, and that was the little heart of Eva. What is it that sometimes speaks in the soul so calmly, so clearly, that its earthly time is short? Is it the secret instinct of decaying nature, or the soul's impulsive throb, as immortality draws on? Be it what it may, it rested in the heart of Eva, a calm, sweet, prophetic certainty that Heaven was near; calm as the light of sunset, sweet as the bright stillness of autumn, there her little heart reposed, only troubled by sorrow for those who loved her so dearly.

For the child, though nursed so tenderly, and though life was unfolding before her with every brightness that love and wealth could give, had no regret for herself in dying.

In that book which she and her simple old friend had read so much together, she had seen and taken to her young heart the image of one who loved the little child; and, as she gazed and mused, He had ceased to be an image and a picture of the distant past, and come to be a living, all-surrounding reality. His love enfolded her childish heart with more than mortal tenderness; and it was to Him, she said, she was going, and to his home.

But her heart yearned with sad tenderness for all that she was to leave behind. Her father most,—for Eva, though she never distinctly thought so, had an instinctive perception that she was more in his heart than any other. She loved her mother because she was so loving a creature, and all the selfishness that she had seen in her only saddened and perplexed her; for she had a child's implicit trust that her mother could not do wrong. There was something about her that Eva never could make out; and she always smoothed it over with thinking that, after all, it was mamma, and she loved her very dearly indeed.

She felt, too, for those fond, faithful servants, to whom she was as daylight and sunshine. Children do not usually generalize; but Eva was an uncommonly mature child, and the things that she had witnessed of the evils of the system under which they were living had fallen, one by one, into the depths of her thoughtful, pondering heart. She had vague longings to do something for them,—to bless and save not only them, but all in their condition,—longings that contrasted sadly with the feebleness of her little frame.

"Uncle Tom," she said, one day, when she was reading to her friend, "I can understand why Jesus *wanted* to die for us."

"Why, Miss Eva?"

"Because I 've felt so, too."

"What is it, Miss Eva?—I don't understand."

"I can't tell you; but, when I saw those poor creatures on the boat, you know, when you came up and I,—some had lost their mothers, and some their husbands, and some mothers cried for their little children,—and when I heard about poor Prue,—oh, was n't that dreadful!—and a great many other times, I 've felt that I would be glad to die, if my dying could stop all this misery. I *would die* for them, Tom, if I could," said the child, earnestly, laying her little thin hand on his.

Tom looked at the child with awe; and when she, hearing her father's voice, glided away, he wiped his eyes many times, as he looked after her.

"It 's jest no use tryin' to keep Miss Eva here," he said to Mammy, whom he met a moment after. "She 's got the Lord's mark in her forehead."

"Ah, yes, yes," said Mammy, raising her hands, "I 've allers said so. She was n't never like a child that 's to live—there was allers something deep in her eyes. I 've told Missis so, many the time; it 's a comin' true,—we all sees it,—dear, little, blessed lamb!"

Eva came tripping up the verandah steps to her father. It was late in the afternoon, and the rays of the sun formed a kind of glory behind her, as she came forward in her white dress, with her golden hair and glowing cheeks, her eyes unnaturally bright with the slow fever that burned in her veins.

St. Clare had called her to show a statuette that he had been buying for her; but her appearance, as she came on, impressed him suddenly and painfully. There is a kind of beauty so intense, yet so fragile, that we cannot bear to look at it. Her father folded her suddenly in his arms, and almost forgot what he was going to tell her.

"Eva, dear, you are better now-a-days,—are you not?"

"Papa," said Eva, with sudden firmness, "I 've had things I wanted to say to you, a great while. I want to say them now, before I get weaker."

St. Clare trembled as Eva seated herself in his lap. She laid her head on his bosom, and said,

"It 's all no use, papa, to keep it to myself any longer. The time is coming that I am going to leave you. I am going, and never to come back!" and Eva sobbed.

"O, now, my dear little Eva!" said St. Clare, trembling as he spoke, but speaking cheerfully, "you 've got nervous and low-spirited; and must n't indulge such gloomy thoughts. See here, I 've bought a statuette for you!"

"No, papa," said Eva, putting it gently away, "don't deceive yourself!—I am *not* any better, I know it perfectly well,—and I am going, before long. I am not nervous,—I am not low-spirited. If it were not for you, papa, and my friends, I should be perfectly happy. I want to go,—I long to go!"

"Why, dear child, what has made your poor little heart so sad? You have had everything, to make you happy, that could be given you."

"I had rather be in heaven; though, only for my friends' sake, I would be willing to live. There are a great many things here that make me sad, that seem dreadful to me; I had rather be there; but I don't want to leave you,—it almost breaks my heart!"

"What makes you sad, and seems dreadful, Eva?"

"O, things that are done, and done all the time. I feel sad for our poor people; they love me dearly, and they are all good and kind to me. I wish, papa, they were all *free*."

"Why, Eva, child, don't you think they are well enough off now?"

"O, but, papa, if anything should happen to you, what would become of them? There are very few men like you, papa. Uncle Alfred isn't like you, and mamma isn't; and then, think of poor old Prue's owners! What horrid things people do, and can do!" and Eva shuddered.

"My dear child, you are too sensitive. I 'm sorry I ever let you hear such stories."

"O, that 's what troubles me, papa. You want me to live so happy, and never to have any pain,—never suffer anything,—not even hear a sad story, when other poor creatures have nothing but pain and sorrow, all their lives;—it seems selfish. I ought to know such things, I ought to feel about them! Such things always sunk into my heart; they went down deep; I 've thought and thought about them. Papa, is n't there any way to have all slaves made free?"

"That 's a difficult question, dearest. There 's no doubt that this way is a very bad one; a great many people think so; I do myself. I heartily wish that there were not a slave in the land; but, then, I don't know what is to be done about it!"

"Papa, you are such a good man, and so noble, and kind, and you always have a way of saying things that is so pleasant, could n't you go all round and try to persuade people to do right about this? When I am dead, papa, then you will think of me, and do it for my sake. I would do it, if I could."

"When you are dead, Eva," said St. Clare, passionately. "O, child, don't talk to me so! You are all I have on earth."

"Poor old Prue's child was all that she had,—and yet she had to hear it crying, and she could n't help it! Papa, these poor creatures love their children as much as you do me. O! do something for them! There 's poor Mammy loves her children; I 've seen her cry when she talked about them. And Tom loves his children; and it 's dreadful, papa, that such things are happening, all the time!"

"There, there, darling," said St. Clare, soothingly; "only don't distress yourself, and don't talk of dying, and I will do anything you wish."

"And promise me, dear father, that Tom shall have his freedom as soon as"— she stopped, and said, in a hesitating tone—"I am gone!"

"Yes, dear, I will do anything in the world,—anything you could ask me to."

"Dear papa," said the child, laying her burning cheek against his, "how I wish we could go together!"

"Where, dearest?" said St. Clare.

"To our Saviour's home; it 's so sweet and peaceful there—it is all so loving there!" The child spoke unconsciously, as of a place where she had often been. "Don't you want to go, papa?" she said.

St. Clare drew her closer to him, but was silent.

"You will come to me," said the child, speaking in a voice of calm certainty which she often used unconsciously.

"I shall come after you. I shall not forget you."

The shadows of the solemn evening closed round them deeper and deeper, as St. Clare sat silently holding the little frail form to his bosom. He saw no more the deep eyes, but the voice came over him as a spirit voice, and, as in a sort of judgment vision, his whole past life rose in a moment before his eyes: his mother's prayers and hymns; his own early yearnings and aspirings for good; and, between them and this hour, years of worldliness and scepticism, and what man calls respectable living. We can think *much*, very much, in a moment. St. Clare saw and felt many things, but spoke nothing; and, as it grew darker, he took his child to her bed-room; and, when she was prepared for rest, he sent away the attendants, and rocked her in his arms, and sung to her till she was asleep.

## XXV.
### The Little Evangelist

It was Sunday afternoon. St. Clare was stretched on a bamboo lounge in the verandah, solacing himself with a cigar. Marie lay reclined on a sofa, opposite the window opening on the verandah, closely secluded, under an awning of transparent gauze, from the outrages of the mosquitos, and languidly holding in her hand an elegantly bound prayer-book. She was holding it because it was Sunday, and she imagined she had been reading it,—though, in fact, she had been only taking a succession of short naps, with it open in her hand.

Miss Ophelia, who, after some rummaging, had hunted up a small Methodist meeting within riding distance, had gone out, with Tom as driver, to attend it; and Eva had accompanied them.

"I say, Augustine," said Marie after dozing a while, "I must send to the city after my old Doctor Posey; I'm sure I've got the complaint of the heart."

"Well; why need you send for him? This doctor that attends Eva seems skilful."

"I would not trust him in a critical case," said Marie; "and I think I may say mine is becoming so! I've been thinking of it, these two or three nights past; I have such distressing pains, and such strange feelings."

"O, Marie, you are blue; I don't believe it's heart complaint."

"I dare say *you* don't," said Marie; "I was prepared to expect *that*. You can be alarmed enough, if Eva coughs, or has the least thing the matter with her; but you never think of me."

"If it's particularly agreeable to you to have heart disease, why, I'll try and maintain you have it," said St. Clare; "I did n't know it was."

"Well, I only hope you won't be sorry for this, when it's too late!" said Marie; "but, believe it or not, my distress about Eva, and the exertions I have made with that dear child, have developed what I have long suspected."

What the *exertions* were which Marie referred to, it would have been difficult to state. St. Clare quietly made this commentary to himself, and went on smoking, like a hard-hearted wretch of a man as he was, till a carriage drove up before the verandah, and Eva and Miss Ophelia alighted.

Miss Ophelia marched straight to her own chamber, to put away her bonnet and shawl, as was always her manner, before she spoke a word on any subject; while Eva came, at St. Clare's call, and was sitting on his knee, giving him an account of the services they had heard.

They soon heard loud exclamations from Miss Ophelia's room, which, like the one in which they were sitting, opened on to the verandah, and violent reproof addressed to somebody.

"What new witchcraft has Tops been brewing!" asked St. Clare. "That commotion is of her raising, I'll be bound!"

And, in a moment after, Miss Ophelia, in high indignation, came dragging the culprit along.

"Come out here, now!" she said, "I *will* tell your master!"

"What's the case now?" asked Augustine.

"The case is, that I cannot be plagued with this child, any longer! It's past all bearing; flesh and blood cannot endure it! Here, I locked her up, and gave her a hymn to study; and what does she do, but spy out where I put my key, and has gone to my bureau, and got a bonnet-trimming, and cut it all to pieces, to make dolls' jackets! I never saw anything like it, in my life!"

"I told you, Cousin," said Marie, "that you'd find out that these creatures can't be brought up, without severity. If I had *my* way, now," she said, looking reproachfully at St. Clare, "I'd send that child out, and have her thoroughly whipped; I'd have her whipped till she could n't stand!"

"I don't doubt it," said St. Clare. "Tell me of the lovely rule of woman! I never saw above a dozen women that wouldn't half kill a horse, or a servant, either, if they had their own way with them!—let alone a man.

"There is no use in this shilly-shally way of yours, St. Clare!" said Marie. "Cousin is a woman of sense, and she sees it now, as plain as I do."

Miss Ophelia had just the capability of indignation that belongs to the thorough-paced housekeeper, and this had been pretty actively roused by the artifice and wastefulness of the child; in fact, many of my lady readers must own that they should have felt just so in her circumstances; but Marie's words went beyond her, and she felt less heat.

"I would n't have the child treated so, for the world," she said; "but, I am sure, Augustine, I don't know what to do. I 've taught and taught; I 've talked till I 'm tired; I 've whipped her; I 've punished her in every way I can think of, and still she 's just what she was at first."

"Come here, Tops, you monkey!" said St. Clare, calling the child up to him.

Topsy came up; her round, hard eyes glittering and blinking with a mixture of apprehensiveness and their usual odd drollery.

"What makes you behave so?" said St. Clare, who could not help being amused with the child's expression.

"Spects it 's my wicked heart," said Topsy, demurely; "Miss Feely says so."

"Don't you see how much Miss Ophelia has done for you? She says she has done everything she can think of."

"Lor, yes, Mas'r! old Missis used to say so, too. She whipped me a heap harder, and used to pull my har, and knock my head agin the door; but it did n't do me no good! I spects, if they 's to pull every spire o' har out o' my head, it would n't do no good, neither,—I 's so wicked! Laws! I 's nothing but a nigger, no ways!"

"Well, I shall have to give her up," said Miss Ophelia; "I can't have that trouble any longer."

"Well, I 'd just like to ask one question," said St. Clare.

"What is it?"

"Why, if your Gospel is not strong enough to save one heathen child, that you can have at home here, all to yourself, what 's the use of sending one or two poor missionaries off with it among thousands of just such? I suppose this child is about a fair sample of what thousands of your heathen are."

Miss Ophelia did not make an immediate answer; and Eva, who had stood a silent spectator of the scene thus far, made a silent sign to Topsy to follow her. There was a little glass-room at the corner of the verandah, which St. Clare used as a sort of reading-room; and Eva and Topsy disappeared into this place.

"What 's Eva going about, now?" said St. Clare, "I mean to see."

And, advancing on tiptoe, he lifted up a curtain that covered the glass-door, and looked in. In a moment, laying his finger on his lips, he made a silent gesture to Miss Ophelia to come and look. There sat the two children on the floor, with their side faces towards them. Topsy, with her usual air of careless drollery and unconcern; but, opposite to her, Eva, her whole face fervent with feeling, and tears in her large eyes.

"What does make you so bad, Topsy? Why won't you try and be good? Don't you love *anybody*, Topsy?"

"Donno nothing 'bout love; I loves candy and sich, that's all," said Topsy.

"But you love your father and mother?"

"Never had none, ye know. I telled ye that, Miss Eva."

"O, I know," said Eva, sadly; "but had n't you any brother, or sister, or aunt, or—"

"No, none on 'em,—never had nothing nor nobody."

"But, Topsy, if you 'd only try to be good, you might—"

"Could n't never be nothin' but a nigger, if I was ever so good," said Topsy. "If I could be skinned, and come white, I 'd try then."

"But people can love you, if you are black, Topsy. Miss Ophelia would love you, if you were good."

Topsy gave a short, blunt laugh that was her common mode of expressing incredulity.

"Don't you think so?" said Eva.

"No; she can't bar me, 'cause I'm a nigger!—she 'd 's soon have a toad touch her! There can't nobody lover niggers, and niggers can't do nothin'! I don't care," said Topsy, beginning to whistle.

"O, Topsy, poor child, I love you!" said Eva, with a sudden burst of feeling, and laying her little thin, white hand on Topsy's shoulder; "I love you, because you have n't had any father, or mother, or friends;—because you 've been a poor, abused child! I love you, and I want you to be good. I am very unwell, Topsy, and I think I shan't live a great while; and it really grieves me, to have you be so naughty. I wish you would try to be good, for my sake;—it 's only a little while I shall be with you."

The round, keen eyes of the black child were overcast with tears;—large, bright drops rolled heavily down, one by one, and fell on the little white hand. Yes, in that moment, a ray of real belief, a ray of heavenly love, had penetrated the darkness of her heathen soul! She laid her head down between her knees, and wept and sobbed,—while the beautiful child, bending over her, looked like the picture of some bright angel stopping to reclaim a sinner.

"Poor Topsy!" said Eva, "don't you know that Jesus loves all alike? He is just as willing to love you, as me. He loves you just as I do,—only more, because he is better. He will help you to be good; and you can go to Heaven at last, and be an angel forever, just as much as if you were white. Only think of it, Topsy!—*you* can be one of those spirits bright, Uncle Tom sings about."

"O, dear Miss Eva, dear Miss Eva!" said the child; "I will try, I will try; I never did care nothin' about it before."

St. Clare, at this instant, dropped the curtain. "It puts me in mind of mother," he said to Miss Ophelia. "It is true what she told me; if we want to give sight to the blind, we must be willing to do as Christ did,—call them to us, and *put our hands on them.*"

"I 've always had a prejudice against negroes," said Miss Ophelia, "and it 's a fact, I never could bear to have that child touch me; but, I don't think she knew it."

"Trust any child to find that out," said St. Clare; "there 's no keeping it from them. But I believe that all the trying in the world to benefit a child, and all the substantial favors you can do them, will never excite one emotion of gratitude, while that feeling of repugnance remains in the heart;—it 's a queer kind of a fact,—but so it is."

"I don't know how I can help it," said Miss Ophelia; "they *are* disagreeable to me,—this child in particular,—how can I help feeling so?"

"Eva does, it seems."

"Well, she so loving! After all, though, she 's no more than Christ-like," said Miss Ophelia; "I wish I were like her. She might teach me a lesson."

"It would n't be the first time a little child had been used to instruct an old disciple, if it *were* so," said St. Clare.

## XXVI.
## Death

Weep not for those whom the veil of the tomb,
In life's early morning, hath hid from our eyes.

Eva's bed-room was a spacious apartment, which, like all the other rooms in the house, opened on to the broad verandah. The room communicated, on one side, with her father and mother's apartment; on the other, with that appropriated to Miss Ophelia. St. Clare had gratified his own eye and taste, in furnishing this room in a style that had a peculiar keeping with the character of her for whom it was intended. The windows were hung with curtains of rose-colored and white muslin, the floor was spread with a matting which had been ordered in Paris, to a pattern of his own device, having round it a border of rose-buds and leaves, and a centre-piece with full-blown roses. The bedstead, chairs, and lounges, were of bamboo, wrought in peculiarly graceful and fanciful patterns. Over the head of the bed was an alabaster bracket, on which a beautiful sculptured angel stood, with drooping wings, holding out a crown of myrtle-leaves. From this depended, over the bed, light curtains of rose-colored gauze, striped with silver, supplying that protection from mosquitos which is an indispensable addition to all sleeping accommodation in that climate. The graceful bamboo lounges were amply supplied with cusions of rose-colored damask, while over them, depending from the hands of sculptured figures, were gauze curtains similar to those of the bed. A light, fanciful bamboo table stood in the middle of the room, where a Parian vase, wrought in the shape of a white lily, with its buds, stood, ever filled with flowers. On this table lay Eva's books and little trinkets, with an elegantly wrought alabaster writing-stand, which her father had supplied to her when he saw her trying to improve herself in writing. There was a fireplace in the room, and on the marble mantle above stood a beautifully wrought statuette of Jesus receiving little children, and on either side marble vases, for which it was Tom's pride and delight to offer bouquets every morning. Two or three exquisite paintings of children, in various attitudes, embellished the wall. In short, the eye could turn nowhere without meeting images of childhood, of beauty, and of peace. Those little eyes never opened, in the morning light, without falling on something which suggested to the heart soothing and beautiful thoughts.

The deceitful strength which had buoyed Eva up for a little while was fast passing away; seldom and more seldom her light footstep was heard in the verandah, and oftener and oftener she was found reclined on a little lounge by the open window, her large, deep eyes fixed on the rising and falling waters of the lake.

It was towards the middle of the afternoon, as she was so reclining,—her Bible half open, her little transparent fingers lying listlessly between the leaves,—suddenly she heard her mother's voice, in sharp tones, in the verandah.

"What now, you baggage!—what new piece of mischief! You 've been picking the flowers, hey?" and Eva heard the sound of a smart slap.

"Law, Missis!—they 's for Miss Eva," she heard a voice say, which she knew belonged to Topsy.

"Miss Eva! A pretty excuse!—you suppose she wants *your* flowers, you good-for-nothing nigger! Get along off with you!"

In a moment, Eva was off from her lounge, and in the verandah.

"O, don't, mother! I should like the flowers; do give them to me; I want them!"

"Why, Eva, your room is full now."

"I can't have too many," said Eva. "Topsy, do bring them here."

Topsy, who had stood sullenly, holding down her head, now came up and offered her flowers. She did it with a look of hesitation and bashfulness, quite unlike the eldrich boldness and brightness which was usual with her.

"It 's a beautiful bouquet!" said Eva, looking at it.

It was rather a singular one,—a brilliant scarlet geranium, and one single white japonica, with its glossy leaves. It was tied up with an evident eye to the contrast of color, and the arrangement of every leaf had carefully been studied.

Topsy looked pleased, as Eva said,—"Topsy, you arrange flowers very prettily. Here," she said, "is this vase I have n't any flowers for. I wish you 'd arrange something every day for it."

"Well, that 's odd!" said Marie. "What in the world do you want that for?"

"Never mind, mamma; you 'd as lief as not Topsy should do it,—had you not?"

"Of course, anything you please, dear! Topsy, you hear your young mistress;—see that you mind."

Topsy made a short courtesy, and looked down; and, as she turned away, Eva saw a tear roll down her dark cheek.

"You see, mamma, I knew poor Topsy wanted to do something for me," said Eva to her mother.

"O, nonsense! it 's only because she likes to do mischief. She knows she must n't pick flowers,—so she does it; that 's all there is to it. But, if you fancy to have her pluck them, so be it."

"Mamma, I think Topsy is different from what she used to be; she 's trying to be a good girl."

"She 'll have to try a good while before *she* gets to be good," said Marie, with a careless laugh.

"Well, you know, mamma, poor Topsy! everything has always been against her."

"Not since she 's been here, I 'm sure. If she has n't been talked to, and preached to, and every earthly thing done that anybody could do;—and she 's just so ugly, and always will be; you can't make anything of the creature!"

"But, mamma, it 's so different to be brought up as I 've been, with so many friends, so many things to make me good and happy; and to be brought up as she 's been, all the time, till she came here!"

"Most likely," said Marie, yawning,—"dear me, how hot it is!"

"Mamma, you believe, don't you, that Topsy could become an angel, as well as any of us, if she were a Christian?"

"Topsy! what a ridiculous idea! Nobody but you would ever think of it. I suppose she could, though."

"But, mamma, is n't God her father, as much as ours? Is n't Jesus her Saviour?"

"Well, that may be. I suppose God made everybody," said Marie. "Where is my smelling-bottle?"

"It 's such a pity,—oh! *such* a pity!" said Eva, looking out on the distant lake, and speaking half to herself.

"What 's a pity?" said Marie.

"Why, that any one, who could be a bright angel, and live with angels, should go all down, down, down, and nobody help them!—oh, dear!"

"Well, we can't help it; it 's no use worrying, Eva! I don't know what 's to be done; we ought to be thankful for our own advantages."

"I hardly can be," said Eva, "I 'm so sorry to think of poor folks that have n't any."

"That 's odd enough," said Marie;—"I 'm sure my religion makes me thankful for my advantages."

"Mamma," said Eva, "I want to have some of my hair cut off,—a good deal of it."

"What for?" said Marie.

"Mamma, I want to give some away to my friends, while I am able to give it to them myself. Won't you ask aunty to come and cut it for me?"

Marie raised her voice, and called Miss Ophelia, from the other room.

The child half rose from her pillow as she came in, and, shaking down her long golden-brown curls, said, rather playfully, "Come, aunty, shear the sheep!"

"What 's that?" said St. Clare, who just then entered with some fruit he had been out to get for her.

"Papa, I just want aunty to cut off some of my hair;—there 's too much of it, and it makes my head hot. Besides, I want to give some of it away."

Miss Ophelia came, with her scissors.

"Take care,—don't spoil the looks of it!" said her father; "cut underneath, where it won't show. Eva's curls are my pride."

"O, papa!" said Eva, sadly.

"Yes, and I want them kept handsome against the time I take you up to your uncle's plantation, to see Cousin Henrique," said St. Clare, in a gay tone.

"I shall never go there, papa;—I am going to a better country. O, do believe me! Don't you see, papa, that I get weaker, every day?"

"Why do you insist that I shall believe such a cruel thing, Eva?" said her father.

"Only because it is *true*, papa: and, if you will believe it now, perhaps you will get to feel about it as I do."

St. Clare closed his lips, and stood gloomily eying the long, beautiful curls, which, as they were separated from the child's head, were laid, one by one, in her lap. She raised them up, looked earnestly at them, twined them around her thin fingers, and looked, from time to time, anxiously at her father.

"It 's just what I 've been foreboding!" said Marie; "it 's just what has been preying on my health, from day to day, bringing me downward to the grave, though nobody regards it. I have seen this, long. St. Clare, you will see, after a while, that I was right."

"Which will afford you great consolation, no doubt!" said St. Clare, in a dry, bitter tone.

Marie lay back on a lounge, and covered her face with her cambric handkerchief.

Eva's clear blue eye looked earnestly from one to the other. It was the calm, comprehending gaze of a soul half loosed from its earthly bonds; it was evident she saw, felt, and appreciated, the difference between the two.

She beckoned with her hand to her father. He came, and sat down by her.

"Papa, my strength fades away every day, and I know I must go. There are some things I want to say and do,—that I ought to do; and you are so unwilling to have me speak a word on this subject. But it must come; there 's no putting it off. Do be willing I should speak now!"

"My child, I *am* willing!" said St. Clare, covering his eyes with one hand, and holding up Eva's hand with the other.

"Then, I want to see all our people together. I have some things I *must* say to them," said Eva.

"*Well,*" said St. Clare, in a tone of dry endurance.

Miss Ophelia despatched a messenger, and soon the whole of the servants were convened in the room.

Eva lay back on her pillows; her hair hanging loosely about her face, her crimson cheeks contrasting painfully with the intense whiteness of her complexion and the thin contour of her limbs and features, and her large, soul-like eyes fixed earnestly on every one.

The servants were struck with a sudden emotion. The spiritual face, the long locks of hair cut off and lying by her, her father's averted face, and Marie's sobs, struck at once upon the feelings of a sensitive and impressible race; and, as they came in, they looked one on another, sighed, and shook their heads. There was a deep silence, like that of a funeral.

Eva raised herself, and looked long and earnestly round at every one. All looked sad and apprehensive. Many of the women hid their faces in their aprons.

"I sent for you all, my dear friends," said Eva, "because I love you. I love you all; and I have something to say to you, which I want you always to remember . . . . . . . I am going to leave you. In a few more weeks, you will see me no more—"

Here the child was interrupted by bursts of groans, sobs, and lamentations, which broke from all present, and in which her slender voice was lost entirely. She waited a moment, and then, speaking in a tone that checked the sobs of all, she said,

"If you love me, you must not interrupt me so. Listen to what I say. I want to speak to you about your souls. . . . . . Many of you, I am afraid, are very careless. You are thinking only about this world. I want you to remember that there is a beautiful world, where Jesus is. I am going there, and you can go there. It is for you, as much as me. But, if you want to go there, you must not live idle, careless, thoughtless lives. You must be Christians. You must remember that each one of you can become angels, and be angels forever. . . . . If you want to be Christians, Jesus will help you. You must pray to him; you must read—"

The child checked herself, looked piteously at them, and said sorrowfully,

"O, dear! you *can't* read,—poor souls!" and she hid her face in the pillow and sobbed, while many a smothered sob from those she was addressing, who were kneeling on the floor, aroused her.

"Never mind," she said, raising her face and smiling brightly through her tears, "I have prayed for you; and I know Jesus will help you, even if you can't read. Try all to do the best you can; pray every day; ask Him to help you, and get the Bible read to you whenever you can; and I think I shall see you all in heaven."

"Amen," was the murmured response from the lips of Tom and Mammy, and some of the elder ones, who belonged to the Methodist church. The younger and more thoughtless ones, for the time completely overcome, were sobbing, with their heads bowed upon their knees.

"I know," said Eva, "you all love me."

"Yes; oh, yes! indeed we do! Lord bless her!" was the involuntary answer of all.

"Yes, I know you do! There is n't one of you that has n't always been very kind to me; and I want to give you something that, when you look at, you shall always remember me. I 'm going to give all of you a curl of my hair; and, when you look at it, think that I loved you and am gone to heaven, and that I want to see you all there."

It is impossible to describe the scene, as, with tears and sobs, they gathered round the little creature, and took from her hands what seemed to them a last mark of her love. They fell on their knees; they sobbed, and prayed, and kissed the hem of her garment; and the elder ones poured forth words of endearment, mingled in prayers and blessings, after the manner of their susceptible race.

As each one took their gift, Miss Ophelia, who was apprehensive for the effect of all this excitement on her little patient, signed to each one to pass out of the apartment.

At last, all were gone but Tom and Mammy.

"Here, Uncle Tom," said Eva, "is a beautiful one for you. O, I am so happy, Uncle Tom, to think I shall see you in heaven,—for I 'm sure I shall; and Mammy,— dear, good, kind Mammy!" she said, fondly throwing her arms round her old nurse,—"I know you 'll be there, too."

"O, Miss Eva, don't see how I can live without ye, no how!" said the faithful creature. "'Pears like it 's just taking everything off the place to oncet!" and Mammy gave way to a passion of grief.

Miss Ophelia pushed her and Tom gently from the apartment, and thought they were all gone; but, as she turned, Topsy was standing there.

"Where did you start up from?" she said, suddenly.

"I was here," said Topsy, wiping the tears from her eyes. "O, Miss Eva, I 've been a bad girl; but won't you give *me* one, too?"

"Yes, poor Topsy! to be sure, I will. There—every time you look at that, think that I love you, and wanted you to be a good girl!"

"O, Miss Eva, I *is* tryin'!" said Topsy, earnestly; "but, Lor, it 's so hard to be good! 'Pears like I an't used to it, no ways!"

"Jesus knows it, Topsy; he is sorry for you; he will help you."

Topsy, with her eyes hid in her apron, was silently passed from the apartment by Miss Ophelia; but, as she went, she hid the precious curl in her bosom.

All being gone, Miss Ophelia shut the door. That worthy lady had wiped away many tears of her own, during the scene; but concern for the consequence of such an excitement to her young charge was uppermost in her mind.

St. Clare had been sitting, during the whole time, with his hand shading his eyes, in the same attitude. When they were all gone, he sat so still.

"Papa!" said Eva, gently, laying her hand on his.

He gave a sudden start and shiver; but made no answer.

"Dear papa!" said Eva.

"I *cannot*," said St. Clare, rising, "I *cannot* have it so! the Almighty hath dealt *very bitterly* with me!" and St. Clare pronounced these words with a bitter emphasis, indeed.

"Augustine! has not God a right to do what he will with his own?" said Miss Ophelia.

"Perhaps so; but that does n't make it any easier to bear," said he, with a dry, hard, tearless manner, as he turned away.

"Papa, you break my heart!" said Eva, rising and throwing herself into his arms; "you must not feel so!" and the child sobbed and wept with a violence which alarmed them all, and turned her father's thoughts at once to another channel.

"There, Eva,—there, dearest! Hush! hush! I was wrong; I was wicked. I will feel any way, do any way,—only don't distress yourself; don't sob so. I will be resigned; I was wicked to speak as I did."

Eva soon lay like a wearied dove in her father's arms; and he, bending over her, soothed her by every tender word he could think of.

Marie rose and threw herself out of the apartment into her own, when she fell into violent hysterics.

"You did n't give me a curl, Eva," said her father, smiling sadly.

"They are all yours, papa," said she, smiling,—"yours and mamma's; and you must give dear aunty as many as she wants. I only gave them to our poor people myself, because you know, papa, they might be forgotten when I am gone, and because I hoped it might help them remember. . . . . You are a Christian, are you not, papa?" said Eva, doubtfully.

"Why do you ask me?"

"I don't know. You are so good, I don't see how you can help it."

"What is being a Christian, Eva?"

"Loving Christ most of all," said Eva.

"Do you, Eva?"

"Certainly I do."

"You never saw him," said St. Clare.

"That makes no difference," said Eva. "I believe him, and in a few days I shall *see* him;" and the young face grew fervent, radiant with joy.

St. Clare said no more. It was a feeling which he had seen before in his mother; but no chord within vibrated to it.

Eva, after this, declined rapidly; there was no more any doubt of the event; the fondest hope could not be blinded. Her beautiful room was avowedly a sick room; and Miss Ophelia day and night performed the duties of a nurse,—and never did her friends appreciate her value more than in that capacity. With so well-trained a hand and eye, such perfect adroitness and practice in every art which could promote neatness and comfort, and keep out of sight every disagreeable incident of sickness,—with such a perfect sense of time, such a clear, untroubled head, such exact accuracy in remembering every prescription and direction of the doctors,—she was everything to him. They who had shrugged their shoulders at her little peculiarities and setnesses, so unlike the careless freedom of southern manners, acknowledged that now she was the exact person that was wanted.

Uncle Tom was much in Eva's room. The child suffered much from nervous restlessness, and it was a relief to her to be carried; and it was Tom's greatest delight to carry her little frail form in his arms, resting on a pillow, now up and down her room, now out into the verandah; and when the fresh sea-breezes blew from the lake,—and the child felt freshest in the morning,—he would sometimes walk with her under the orange-trees in the garden, or, sitting down in some of their old seats, sing to her their favorite old hymns.

Her father often did the same thing; but his frame was slighter, and when he was weary, Eva would say to him,

"O, papa, let Tom take me. Poor fellow! it pleases him; and you know it 's all he can do now, and he wants to do something!"

"So do I, Eva!" said her father.

"Well, papa, you can do everything, and are everything to me. You read to me,—you sit up nights,—and Tom has only this one thing, and his singing; and I know, too, he does it easier than you can. He carries me so strong!"

The desire to do something was not confined to Tom. Every servant in the establishment showed the same feeling, and in their way did what they could.

Poor Mammy's heart yearned towards her darling; but she found no opportunity, night or day, as Marie declared that the state of her mind was such, it was impossible for her to rest; and, of course, it was against her principles to let any one else rest. Twenty times in a night, Mammy would be roused to rub her feet, to bathe her head, to find her pocket-handkerchief, to see what the noise was in Eva's room, to let down a curtain because it was too light, or to put it up because it was too dark; and, in the day-time, when she longed to have some share in the nursing of her pet, Marie seemed unusually ingenious in keeping her busy anywhere and everywhere all over the house, or about her own person; so that stolen interviews and momentary glimpses were all she could obtain.

"I feel it my duty to be particularly careful of myself, now," she would say, "feeble as I am, and with the whole care and nursing of that dear child upon me."

"Indeed, my dear," said St. Clare, "I thought our cousin relieved you of that."

"You talk like a man, St. Clare,—just as if a mother *could* be relieved of the care of a child in that state; but, then, it 's all alike,—no one ever knows what I feel! I can't throw things off, as you do."

St. Clare smiled. You must excuse him, he couldn't help it,—for St. Clare could smile yet. For so bright and placid was the farewell voyage of the little spirit,—by such sweet and fragrant breezes was the small bark borne towards the heavenly shores,—that it was impossible to realize that it was death that was approaching. The child felt no pain,—only a tranquil, soft weakness, daily and almost insensibly increasing; and she was so beautiful, so loving, so trustful, so happy, that one could not resist the soothing influence of that air of innocence and peace which seemed to breathe around her. St. Clare found a strange calm coming over him. It was not hope,—that was impossible; it was not resignation; it was only a calm resting in the present, which seemed so beautiful that he wished to think of no future. It was like that hush of spirit which we feel amid the bright, mild woods of autumn, when the bright hectic flush is on the trees, and the last lingering flowers by the brook; and we joy in it all the more, because we know that soon it will all pass away.

The friend who knew most of Eva's own imaginings and foreshadowings was her faithful bearer, Tom. To him she said what she would not disturb her father by saying. To him she imparted those mysterious intimations which the soul feels, as the cords begin to unbind, ere it leaves its clay forever.

Tom, at last, would not sleep in his room, but lay all night in the outer verandah, ready to rouse at every call.

"Uncle Tom, what alive have you taken to sleeping anywhere and everywhere, like a dog, for?" said Miss Ophelia. "I thought you was one of the orderly sort, that liked to lie in bed in a Christian way."

"I do, Miss Feely," said Tom, mysteriously. "I do, but now—"

"Well, what now?"

"We must n't speak loud; Mas'r St. Clare won't hear on 't; but Miss Feely, you know there must be somebody watchin' for the bridegroom."

"What do you mean, Tom?"

"You know it says in Scripture, 'At midnight there was a great cry made. Behold, the bridegroom cometh.' That 's what I 'm spectin now, every night, Miss Feely,—and I couldn't sleep out o' hearin, no ways."

"Why, Uncle Tom, what makes you think so?"

"Miss Eva, she talks to me. The Lord, he sends his messenger in the soul. I must be thar, Miss Feely; for when that ar blessed child goes into the kingdom, they 'll open the door so wide, we 'll all get a look in at the glory, Miss Feely."

"Uncle Tom, did Miss Eva say she felt more unwell than usual to-night?"

"No; but she told me, this morning, she was coming nearer,—thar 's them that tells it to the child, Miss Feely. It 's the angels,—'it 's the trumpet sound afore the break o' day,'" said Tom, quoting from a favorite hymn.

This dialogue passed between Miss Ophelia and Tom, between ten and eleven, one evening, after her arrangements had all been made for the night, when, on going to bolt her outer door, she found Tom stretched along by it, in the outer verandah.

She was not nervous or impressible; but the solemn, heart-felt manner struck her. Eva had been unusually bright and cheerful, that afternoon, and had sat raised in her bed, and looked over all her little trinkets and precious things, and designated the friends to whom she would have them given; and her manner was more animated, and her voice more natural, than they had known it for weeks. Her father had been in, in the evening, and had said that Eva appeared more like her former self than ever she had done since her sickness; and when he kissed her for the night, he said to Miss Ophelia,—"Cousin, we may keep her with us, after all; she is certainly better;" and he had retired with a lighter heart in his bosom than he had had there for weeks.

But at midnight,—strange, mystic hour!—when the veil between the frail present and the eternal future grows thin,— then came the messenger!

There was a sound in that chamber, first of one who stepped quickly. It was Miss Ophelia, who had resolved to sit up all night with her little charge, and who, at the turn of the night, had discerned what experienced nurses significantly call "a change." The outer door was quickly opened, and Tom, who was watching outside, was on the alert, in a moment.

"Go for the doctor, Tom! lose not a moment," said Miss Ophelia; and stepping across the room, she rapped at St. Clare's door.

"Cousin," she said, "I wish you would come."

Those words fell on his heart like clods upon a coffin. Why did they? He was up and in the room in an instant, and bending over Eva, who still slept.

What was it he saw that made his heart stand still? Why was no word spoken between the two? Thou canst say, who hast seen that same expression on the face dearest to thee;—that look indescribable, hopeless, unmistakable, that says to thee that thy beloved is no longer thine.

On the face of the child, however, there was no ghastly imprint,—only a high and almost sublime expression,—the overshadowing presence of spiritual natures, the dawning of immortal life in that childish soul.

They stood there so still, gazing upon her, that even the ticking of the watch seemed too loud. In a few moments, Tom returned, with the doctor. He entered, gave one look, and stood silent as the rest.

"When did this change take place?" said he, in a low whisper, to Miss Ophelia.

"About the turn of the night," said the reply.

Marie, roused by the entrance of the doctor, appeared, hurriedly, from the next room.

"Augustine! Cousin!—O!—what!" she hurriedly began.

"Hush!" said St. Clare, hoarsely; "she is dying!"

Mammy heard the words, and flew to awaken the servants. The house was soon roused,—lights were seen, footsteps heard, anxious faces thronged the verandah, and looked tearfully through the glass doors; but St. Clare heard and said nothing,—he saw only that look on the face of the little sleeper.

"O, if she would only wake, and speak once more!" he said; and, stooping over her, he spoke in her ear,—"Eva, darling!"

The large blue eyes unclosed,—a smile passed over her face;—she tried to raise her head, and to speak.

"Do you know me, Eva?"

"Dear papa," said the child, with a last effort, throwing her arms about his neck. In a moment they dropped again; and, as St. Clare raised his head, he saw a spasm of mortal agony pass over the face,—she struggled for breath, and threw up her little hands.

"O, God, this is dreadful!" he said, turning away in agony, and wringing Tom's hand, scarce conscious what he was doing. "O, Tom, my boy, it is killing me!"

Tom had his master's hands between his own; and, with tears streaming down his dark cheeks, looked up for help where he had always been used to look.

"Pray that this may be cut short!" said St. Clare,—"this wrings my heart."

"O, bless the Lord! it 's over,—it 's over, dear Master!" said Tom; "look at her."

The child lay panting on her pillows, as one exhausted,—the large clear eyes rolled up and fixed. Ah, what said those eyes, that spoke so much of heaven? Earth was past, and earthly pain; but so solemn, so mysterious, was the triumphant brightness of that face, that it checked even the sobs of sorrow. They pressed around her, in breathless stillness.

"Eva," said St. Clare, gently.

She did not hear.

"O, Eva, tell us what you see! What is it?" said her father.

A bright, a glorious smile passed over her face, and she said, brokenly,—"O! love,—joy,—peace!" gave one sigh, and passed from death unto life!

"Farewell, beloved child! the bright, eternal doors have closed after thee; we shall see thy sweet face no more. O, woe for them who watched thy entrance into heaven, when they shall wake and find only the cold gray sky of daily life, and thou gone forever!"

## XXVII.
### "This is the Last of Earth."
#### —John Q. Adams

The statuettes and pictures in Eva's room were shrouded in white napkins, and only hushed breathings and muffled foot-falls were heard there, and the light stole in solemnly through windows partially darkened by closed blinds.

The bed was draped in white; and there, beneath the drooping angel-figure, lay a little sleeping form,—sleeping never to waken!

There she lay, robed in one of the simple white dresses she had been wont to wear when living; the rose-colored light through the curtains cast over the icy coldness of death a warm glow. The heavy eyelashes drooped softly on the pure cheek; the head was turned a little to one side, as if in natural sleep, but there was diffused over every lineament of the face that high celestial expression, that mingling of rapture and repose, which showed it was no earthly or temporary sleep, but the long, sacred rest which "He giveth to his beloved."

There is no death to such as thou, dear Eva! neither darkness nor shadow of death; only such a bright fading as when the morning star fades in the golden dawn. Thine is the victory without the battle,—the crown without the conflict.

So did St. Clare think, as, with folded arms, he stood there gazing. Ah! who shall say what he did think? for, from the hour that voices had said, in the dying chamber, "she is gone," it had been all a dreary mist, a heavy "dimness of anguish." He had heard voices around him; he had had questions asked, and answered them; they had asked him when he would have the funeral, and where they should lay her; and he had answered, impatiently, that he cared not.

Adolph and Rosa had arranged the chamber; volatile, fickle and childish, as they generally were, they were soft-hearted and full of feeling; and, while Miss Ophelia presided over the general details of order and neatness, it was their hands that added those soft, poetic touches to the arrangements, that took from the death-room the grim and ghastly air which too often marks a New England funeral.

There were still flowers on the shelves,—all white, delicate and fragrant, with graceful, drooping leaves. Eva's little table, covered with white, bore on it her favorite vase, with a single white moss rose-bud in it. The folds of the drapery, the fall of the curtains, had been arranged and rearranged, by Adolph and Rosa, with that nicety of eye which characterizes their race. Even now, while St. Clare stood there thinking, little Rosa tripped softly into the chamber with a basket of white flowers. She stepped back when she saw St. Clare, and stopped respectfully; but, seeing that he did not observe her, she came forward to place them around the dead. St. Clare saw her as in a dream, while she placed in the small hands a fair cape jessamine, and, with admirable taste, disposed other flowers around the couch.

The door opened again, and Topsy, her eyes swelled with crying, appeared, holding something under her apron. Rosa made a quick, forbidding gesture; but she took a step into the room.

"You must go out," said Rosa, in a sharp, positive whisper; "*you* have n't any business here!"

"O, do let me! I brought a flower,—such a pretty one!" said Topsy, holding up a half-blown tea rose-bud. "Do let me put just one there."

"Get along!" said Rosa, more decidedly.

"Let her stay!" said St. Clare, suddenly stamping his foot. "She shall come."

Rosa suddenly retreated, and Topsy came forward and laid her offering at the feet of the corpse; then suddenly, with a wild and bitter cry, she threw herself on the floor alongside the bed, and wept, and moaned aloud.

Miss Ophelia hastened into the room, and tried to raise and silence her; but in vain.

"O, Miss Eva! oh, Miss Eva! I wish I 's dead, too,—I do!"

There was a piercing wildness in the cry; the blood flushed into St. Clare's white, marble-like face, and the first tears he had shed since Eva died stood in his eyes.

"Get up, child," said Miss Ophelia, in a softened voice; "don't cry so. Miss Eva is gone to heaven; she is an angel."

"But I can't see her!" said Topsy. "I never shall see her!" and she sobbed again. They all stood a moment in silence.

"*She* said she *loved* me," said Topsy,—"she did! O, dear! oh, dear! there an't *nobody* left now,—there an't!"

"That 's true enough," said St. Clare; "but do," he said to Miss Ophelia, "see if you can't comfort the poor creature."

"I jist wish I had n't never been born," said Topsy. "I did n't want to be born, no ways; and I don't see no use on't."

Miss Ophelia raised her gently, but firmly, and took her from the room; but, as she did so, some tears fell from her eyes.

"Topsy, you poor child," she said, as she led her into her room, "don't give up! *I* can love you, though I am not like that dear little child. I hope I 've learnt something of the love of Christ from her. I can love you; I do, and I 'll try to help you to grow up a good Christian girl."

Miss Ophelia's voice was more than her words, and more than that were the honest tears that fell down her face. From that hour, she acquired an influence over the mind of the destitute child that she never lost.

"O, my Eva, whose little hour on earch did so much of good," thought St. Clare, "what account have I to give for my long years?"

There were, for a while, soft whisperings and foot-falls in the chamber, as one after another stole in, to look at the dead; and then came the little coffin; and then there was a funeral, and carriages drove to the door, and strangers came and were seated; and there were white scarfs and ribbons, and crape bands, and mourners dressed in black crape; and there were words read from the Bible, and prayers offered; and St. Clare lived, and walked, and moved, as one who has shed every tear;—to the last he saw only one thing, that golden head in the coffin; but then he saw the cloth spread over it, the lid of the coffin closed; and he walked, when he was put beside the others, down to a little place at the bottom of the garden, and there, by the mossy seat where she and Tom had talked, and sung, and read so often, was the little grave. St. Clare stood beside it,—looked vacantly down; he saw them lower the little coffin; he heard, dimly, the solemn words, "I am the resurrection and the Life; he that believeth in me, though he were dead, yet shall he live;" and, as the earth was cast in and filled up the little grave, he could not realize that it was his Eva that they were hiding from his sight.

Nor was it!—not Eva, but only the frail seed of that bright, immortal form with which she shall yet come forth, in the day of the Lord Jesus!

And then all were gone, and the mourners went back to the place which should know her no more; and Marie's room was darkened, and she lay on the bed, sobbing and moaning in uncontrollable grief, and calling every moment for the attentions of all her servants. Of course, they had no time to cry,—why should they? the grief was *her* grief, and she was fully convinced that nobody on earth did, could, or would feel it as she did.

"St. Clare did not shed a tear," she said; "he did n't sympathize with her; it was perfectly wonderful to think how hard-hearted and unfeeling he was, when he must know how she suffered."

So much are people the slave of their eye and ear, that many of the servants really thought that Missis was the principal sufferer in the case, especially as Marie began to have hysterical spasms, and sent for the doctor, and at last declared herself dying; and, in the running and scampering, and bringing up hot bottles, and heating of flannels, and chafing, and fussing, that ensued, there was quite a diversion.

Tom, however, had a feeling at his own heart, that drew him to his master. He followed him wherever he walked, wistfully and sadly; and when he saw him sitting, so pale and quiet, in Eva's room, holding before his eyes her little open Bible, though seeing no letter or word of what was in it, there was more sorrow to Tom in that still, fixed, tearless eye, than in all Marie's moans and lamentations.

In a few days the St. Clare family were back again in the city; Augustine, with the restlessness of grief, longing for another scene, to change the current of his thoughts. So they left the house and garden, with its little grave, and came back to New Orleans; and St. Clare walked the streets busily, and strove to fill up the chasm in his heart with hurry and bustle, and change of place; and people who saw him in the street, or met him at the café, knew of his loss only by the weed on his hat; for there he was, smiling and talking, and reading the newspaper, and speculating on politics, and attending to business matters; and who could see that all this smiling outside was but a hollowed shell over a heart that was a dark and silent sepulchre?

"Mr. St. Clare is a singular man," said Marie to Miss Ophelia, in a complaining tone. "I used to think, if there was anything in the world he did love, it was our dear little Eva; but he seems to be forgetting her very easily. I cannot ever get him to talk about her. I really did think he would show more feeling!"

"Still waters run deepest, they used to tell me," said Miss Ophelia oracularly.

"O, I don't believe in such things; it 's all talk. If people have feeling, they will show it,—they can't help it; but, then, it 's a great misfortune to have feeling. I 'd rather have been made like St. Clare. My feelings prey upon me so!"

"Sure, Missis, Mas'r St. Clare is gettin' thin as a shader. They say, he don't never eat nothin'," said Mammy. "I know he don't forget Miss Eva; I know there couldn't nobody,—dear, little, blessed cretur!" she added, wiping her eyes.

"Well, at all events, he has no consideration for me," said Marie; "he has n't spoken one word of sympathy, and he must know how much more a mother feels than any man can."

"The heart knoweth its own bitterness," said Miss Ophelia, gravely.

"That 's just what I think. I know just what I feel,—nobody else seems to. Eva used to, but she is gone!" and Marie lay back on her lounge, and began to sob disconsolately.

Marie was one of those unfortunately constituted mortals, in whose eyes whatever is lost and gone assumes a value which it never had in possession. Whatever she had, she seemed to survey only to pick flaws in it; but, once fairly away, there was no end to her valuation of it.

While this conversation was taking place in the parlor, another was going on in St. Clare's library.

Tom, who was always uneasily following his master about, had seen him go to his library, some hours before; and, after vainly waiting for him to come out, determined, at last, to make an errand in. He entered softly. St. Clare lay on his lounge, at the further end of the room. He was lying on his face, with Eva's Bible open before him, at a little distance. Tom walked up, and stood by the sofa. He hesitated; and, while he was hesitating, St. Clare suddenly raised himself up. The honest face, so full of grief, and with such an imploring expression of affection and sympathy, struck his master. He laid his hand on Tom's, and bowed down his forehead on it.

"O, Tom, my boy, the whole world is as empty as an eggshell."

"I know it, Mas'r,—I know it," said Tom; "but, oh, if Mas'r could only look up,—up where our dear Miss Eva is,—up to the dear Lord Jesus!"

"Ah, Tom! I do look up; but the trouble is, I don't see anything, when I do. I wish I could."

Tom sighed heavily.

"It seems to be given to children, and poor, honest fellows, like you, to see what we can't," said St. Clare. "How comes it?"

"Thou hast 'hid from the wise and prudent, and revealed unto babes,'" murmured Tom; "'even so, Father, for so it seemed good in thy sight.'"

"Tom, I don't believe,—I can't believe,—I've got the habit of doubting," said St. Clare. "I want to believe this Bible,—and I can't."

"Dear Mas'r, pray to the good Lord,—'Lord, I believe; help thou my unbelief.'"

"Who knows anything about anything?" said St. Clare, his eyes wandering dreamily, and speaking to himself. "Was all that beautiful love and faith only one of the ever-shifting phases of human feeling, having nothing real to rest on, passing away with the little breath? And is there no more Eva,—no heaven,—no Christ,—nothing?"

"O, dear Mas'r, there is! I know it; I'm sure of it," said Tom, falling on his knees. "Do, do, dear Mas'r, believe it!"

"How do you know there's any Christ, Tom? You never saw the Lord."

"Felt Him in my soul, Mas'r,—feel Him now! O, Mas'r, when I was sold away from my old woman and the children, I was jest a'most broke up. I felt as if there warn't nothin' left; and then the good Lord, he stood by me, and he says, 'Fear not, Tom;' and he brings light and joy into a poor feller's soul,—makes all peace; and I 's so happy, and loves everybody, and feels willin' jest to be the Lord's, and have the Lord's will done, and be put jest where the Lord wants to put me. I know it couldn't come from me, cause I 's a poor, complainin' cretur; it comes from the Lord; and I know He 's willin' to do for Mas'r."

Tom spoke with fast-running tears and choking voice. St. Clare leaned his head on his shoulder, and wrung the hard, faithful, black hand.

"Tom, you love me," he said.

"I 's willin' to lay down my life, this blessed day, to see Mas'r a Christian."

"Poor, foolish boy!" said St. Clare, half-raising himself. "I 'm not worth the love of one good, honest heart, like yours."

"O, Mas'r, dere 's more than me loves you,—the blessed Lord Jesus loves you."

"How do you know that, Tom?" said St. Clare.

"Feels it in my soul. O, Mas'r! 'the love of Christ, that passeth knowledge.'"

"Singular!" said St. Clare, turning away, "that the story of a man that lived and died eighteen hundred years ago can affect people so yet. But he was no man," he added, suddenly. "No man ever had such long and living power! O, that I could believe what my mother taught me, and pray as I did when I was a boy!"

"If Mas'r pleases," said Tom, "Miss Eva used to read this so beautifully. I wish Mas'r'd be so good as read it. Don't get no readin', hardly, now Miss Eva 's gone."

The chapter was the eleventh of John,—the touching account of the raising of Lazarus. St. Clare read it aloud, often pausing to wrestle down feelings which were roused by the pathos of the story. Tom knelt before him, with clasped hands, and with an absorbed expression of love, trust, adoration, on his quiet face.

"Tom," said his Master, "this is all *real* to you!"

"I can jest fairly *see* it, Mas'r," said Tom.

"I wish I had your eyes, Tom."

"I wish, to the dear Lord, Mas'r had!"

"But, Tom, you know that I have a great deal more knowledge than you; what if I should tell you that I don't believe this Bible?"

"O, Mas'r!" said Tom, holding up his hands, with a deprecating gesture.

"Wouldn't it shake your faith some, Tom?"

"Not a grain," said Tom.

"Why, Tom, you must know I know the most."

"O, Mas'r, have n't you jest read how he hides from the wise and prudent, and reveals unto babes? But Mas'r was n't in earnest, for sartin, now?" said Tom, anxiously.

"No, Tom, I was not. I don't disbelieve, and I think there is reason to believe; and still I don't. It 's a troublesome bad habit I 've got, Tom."

"If Mas'r would only pray!"

"How do you know I don't, Tom?"

"Does Mas'r?"

"I would, Tom, if there was anybody there when I pray; but it 's all speaking unto nothing, when I do. But come, Tom, you pray, now, and show me how."

Tom's heart was full; he poured it out in prayer, like waters that have been long suppressed. One thing was plain enough; Tom thought there was somebody to hear, whether there were or not. In fact, St. Clare felt himself borne, on the tide of his faith and feeling, almost to the gates of that heaven he seemed so vividly to conceive. It seemed to bring him nearer to Eva.

"Thank you, my boy," said St. Clare, when Tom rose. "I like to hear you, Tom; but go, now, and leave me alone; some other time, I 'll talk more."

Tom silently left the room.

## XXVIII.
## Reunion

Week after week glided away in the St. Clare mansion, and the waves of life settled back to their usual flow, where that little bark had gone down. For how imperiously, how coolly, in disregard of all one's feeling, does the hard, cold, uninteresting course of daily realities move on! Still must we eat, and drink, and sleep, and wake again,—still bargain, buy, sell, ask and answer questions,—pursue, in short, a thousand shadows, though all interest in them be over; the cold mechanical habit of living remaining, after all vital interest in it has fled.

All the interests and hopes of St. Clare's life had unconsciously wound themselves around this child. It was for Eva that he had managed his property; and, to do this and that for Eva,—to buy, improve, alter, and arrange, or dispose something for her,—had been so long his habit, that now she was gone, there seemed nothing to be thought of, and nothing to be done.

True, there was another life,—a life which, once believed in, stands as a solemn, significant figure before the otherwise unmeaning ciphers of time, changing them to orders of mysterious, untold value. St. Clare knew this well; and often, in many a weary hour, he heard that slender, childish voice calling him to the skies, and saw that little hand pointing to him the way of life; but a heavy lethargy of sorrow lay on him,—he could not rise. He had one of those natures which could better and more clearly conceive of religious things from its own perceptions and instincts, than many a matter-of-fact and practical Christian. The gift to appreciate and the sense to feel the finer shades and relations of moral things, often seems an attribute of those whose whole life shows a careless disregard of them. Hence Moore, Byron, Goethe, often speak words more wisely descriptive of the true religious sentiment, than another man, whose life is governed by it. In such minds, disregard of religion is a more fearful treason,—a more deadly sin.

St. Clare had never pretended to govern himself by any religious obligation; and a certain fineness of nature gave him such an instinctive view of the extent of the requirements of Christianity, that he shrank, by anticipation, from what he felt would be the exactions of his own conscience, if he once did resolve to assume them. For, so inconsistent is human nature, especially in the ideal, that not to undertake a thing at all seems better than to undertake and come short.

Still St. Clare was, in many respects, another man. He read his little Eva's Bible seriously and honestly; he thought more soberly and practically of his relations to his servants,—enough to make him extremely dissatisfied with both his past and present course; and one thing he did, soon after his return to New Orleans, and that was to commence the legal steps necessary to Tom's emancipation, which was to be perfected as soon as he could get through the necessary formalities. Meantime, he attached himself to Tom more and more, every day. In all the wide world, there was nothing that seemed to remind him so much of Eva; and he would insist on keeping him constantly about him, and, fastidious and unapproachable as he was with regard to his deeper feelings, he almost thought aloud to Tom. Nor would any one have wondered at it, who had seen the expression of affection and devotion with which Tom continually followed his young master.

"Well, Tom," said St. Clare, the day after he had commenced the legal formalities for his enfranchisement, "I 'm going to make a free man of you;—so, have your trunk packed, and get ready to set out for Kentuck."

The sudden light of joy that shone in Tom's face as he raised his hands to heaven, his emphatic "Bless the Lord!" rather discomposed St. Clare; he did not like it that Tom should be so ready to leave him.

"You have n't had such very bad times here, that you need be in such a rapture, Tom," he said, drily.

"No, no, Mas'r! 'tan't that,—it 's bein' a *free man!* That 's what I 'm joyin' for."

"Why, Tom, don't you think, for your own part, you 've been better off than to be free?"

"No, *indeed*, Mas'r St. Clare," said Tom, with a flash of energy. "No, indeed!"

"Why, Tom, you could n't possibly have earned, by your work, such clothes and such living as I have given you."

"Knows all that, Mas'r St. Clare; Mas'r 's been too good; but, Mas'r, I 'd rather have poor clothes, poor house, poor everything, and have 'em *mine*, than have the best, and have 'em any man's else,—I had *so*, Mas'r; I think it 's natur, Mas'r."

"I suppose so, Tom, and you 'll be going off and leaving me, in a month or so," he added, rather discontentedly. "Though why you should n't, no mortal knows," he said, in a gayer tone; and, getting up, he began to walk the floor.

"Not while Mas'r is in trouble," said Tom. "I 'll stay with Mas'r as long as he wants me,—so as I can be any use."

"Not while I 'm in trouble, Tom?" said St. Clare, looking sadly out of the window. . . . . "And when will *my* trouble be over?"

"When Mas'r St. Clare 's a Christian," said Tom.

"And you really mean to stay by till that day comes?" said St. Clare, half smiling, as he turned from the window, and laid his hand on Tom's shoulder. "Ah, Tom, you soft, silly boy! I won't keep you till that day. Go home to your wife and children, and give my love to all."

"I 's faith to believe that day will come," said Tom, earnestly, and with tears in his eyes; "the Lord has a work for Mas'r."

"A work, hey?" said St. Clare; "well, now, Tom, give me your views on what sort of work it is;—let 's hear."

"Why, even a poor fellow like me has a work from the Lord; and Mas'r St. Clare, that has larnin, and riches, and friends,—how much he might do for the Lord!"

"Tom, you seem to think the Lord needs a great deal done for him," said St. Clare, smiling.

"We does for the Lord when we does for his critturs," said Tom.

"Good theology, Tom; better than Dr. B. preaches, I dare swear," said St. Clare.

The conversation was here interrupted by the announcement of some visitors.

Marie St. Clare felt the loss of Eva as deeply as she could feel anything; and, as she was a woman that had a great faculty of making everybody unhappy when she was, her immediate attendants had still stronger reason to regret the loss of their young mistress, whose winning ways and gentle intercessions had so often been a shield to them from the tyrannical and selfish exactions of her mother. Poor old Mammy, in particular, whose heart, severed from all natural domestic ties, had consoled itself with this one beautiful being, was almost heart–broken. She cried day and night, and was, from excess of sorrow, less skilful and alert in her ministrations on her mistress than usual, which drew down a constant storm of invectives on her defenceless head.

Miss Ophelia felt the loss; but, in her good and honest heart, it bore fruit unto everlasting life. She was more softened, more gentle; and, though equally assiduous in every duty, it was with a chastened and quiet air, as one who communed with her own heart not in vain. She was more diligent in teaching Topsy,—taught her mainly from the Bible,—did not any longer shrink from her touch, or manifest in ill-repressed disgust, because she felt none. She viewed her now through the softened medium that Eva's hand had first held before her eyes, and saw in her only an immortal creature, whom God had sent to be led by her to glory and virtue. Topsy did not become at once a saint; but the life and death of Eva did work a marked change in her. The callous indifference was gone; there was now sensibility, hope, desire, and the striving for good,—a strife irregular, interrupted, suspended oft, but yet renewed again.

One day, when Topsy had been sent for by Miss Ophelia, she came, hastily thrusting something into her bosom.

"What are you doing there, you limb? You 've been stealing something, I 'll be bound," said the imperious little Rosa, who had been sent to call her, seizing her, at the same time, roughly by the arm.

"You go 'long, Miss Rosa!" said Topsy, pulling from her; "'tan't none o' your business!"

"None o' your sa'ce!" said Rosa. "I saw you hiding something,—I know yer tricks," and Rosa seized her arm, and tried to force her hand into her bosom, while Topsy, enraged, kicked and fought valiantly for what she considered her rights. The clamor and confusion of the battle drew Miss Ophelia and St. Clare both to the spot.

"She 's been stealing!" said Rosa.

"I han't, neither!" vociferated Topsy, sobbing with passion.

"Give me that, whatever it is!" said Miss Ophelia, firmly.

Topsy hesitated; but, on a second order, pulled out of her bosom a little parcel done up in the foot of one of her own old stockings.

Miss Ophelia turned it out. There was a small book, which had been given to Topsy by Eva, containing a single verse of Scripture, arranged for every day in the year, and in a paper the curl of hair that she had given her on that memorable day when she had taken her last farewell.

St. Clare was a good deal affected at the sight of it; the little book had been rolled in a long strip of black crape, torn from the funeral weeds.

"What did you wrap *this* round the book for?" said St. Clare, holding up the crape.

"Cause,—cause,—cause 't was Miss Eva. O, don't take 'em away, please!" she said; and, sitting flat down on the floor, and putting her apron over her head, she began to sob vehemently.

It was a curious mixture of the pathetic and the ludicrous,—the little old stocking,—black crape,—text–book,—fair, soft curl,—and Topsy's utter distress.

St. Clare smiled; but there were tears in his eyes, as he said,

"Come, come,—don't cry; you shall have them!" and, putting them together, he threw them into her lap, and drew Miss Ophelia with him into the parlor.

"I really think you can make something of that concern," he said, pointing with his thumb backward over his shoulder. "Any mind that is capable of a *real sorrow* is capable of good. You must try and do something with her."

"The child has improved greatly," said Miss Ophelia. "I have great hopes of her; but, Augustine," she said, laying her hand on his arm, "one thing I want to ask; whose is this child to be?—yours or mine?"

"Why, I gave her to *you*," said Augustine.

"But not legally;—I want her to be mine legally," said Miss Ophelia.

"Whew! cousin," said Augustine. "What will the Abolition Society think? They 'll have a day of fasting appointed for this backsliding, if you become a slave-holder!"

"O, nonsense! I want her mine, that I may have a right to take her to the free States, and give her her liberty, that all I am trying to do be not undone."

"O, cousin, what an awful 'doing evil that good may come'! I can't encourage it."

"I don't want you to joke, but to reason," said Miss Ophelia. "There is no use in my trying to make this child a Christian child, unless I save her from all the chances and reverses of slavery; and, if you really are willing I should have her, I want you to give me a deed of gift, or some legal paper."

"Well, well," said St. Clare, "I will;" and he sat down, and unfolded a newspaper to read.

"But I want it done now," said Miss Ophelia.

"What 's your hurry?"

"Because now is the only time there ever is to do a thing in," said Miss Ophelia. "Come, now, here 's paper, pen, and ink; just write a paper."

St. Clare, like most men of his class of mind, cordially hated the present tense of action, generally; and, therefore, he was considerably annoyed by Miss Ophelia's downrightness.

"Why, what 's the matter?" said he. "Can't you take my word? One would think you had taken lessons of the Jews, coming at a fellow so!"

"I want to make sure of it," said Miss Ophelia. "You may die, or fail, and then Topsy be hustled off to auction, spite of all I can do."

"Really, you are quite provident. Well, seeing I 'm in the hands of a Yankee, there is nothing for it but to concede;" and St. Clare rapidly wrote off a deed of gift, which, as he was well versed in the forms of law, he could easily do, and signed his name to it in sprawling capitals, concluding by a tremendous flourish.

"There, is n 't that black and white, now, Miss Vermont?" he said, as he handed it to her.

"Good boy," said Miss Ophelia, smiling. "But must it not be witnessed?"

"O, bother!—yes. Here," he said, opening the door into Marie's apartment, "Marie, Cousin wants your autograph; just put your name down here."

"What 's this?" said Marie, as she ran over the paper. "Ridiculous! I thought Cousin was too pious for such horrid things," she added, as she carelessly wrote her name; "but, if she has a fancy for that article, I am sure she 's welcome."

"There, now, she 's yours, body and soul," said St. Clare, handing the paper.

"No more mine now than she was before," said Miss Ophelia. "Nobody but God has a right to give her to me; but I can protect her now."

"Well, she 's yours by a fiction of law, then," said St. Clare, as he turned back into the parlor, and sat down to this paper.

Miss Ophelia, who seldom sat much in Marie's company, followed him into the parlor, having first carefully laid away the paper.

"Augustine," she said, suddenly, as she sat knitting, "have you ever made any provision for your servants, in case of your death?"

"No," said St. Clare, as he read on.

"Then all your indulgence to them may prove a great cruelty, by and by."

St. Clare had often thought the same think himself; but he answered, negligently,

"Well, I mean to make a provision, by and by."

"When?" said Miss Ophelia.

"O, one of these days."

"What if you should die first?"

"Cousin, what 's the matter?" said St. Clare, laying down his paper and looking at her. "Do you think I show symptoms of yellow fever or cholera, that you are making post mortem arrangements with such zeal?"

" 'In the midst of life we are in death,'" said Miss Ophelia.

St. Clare rose up, and laying the paper down, carelessly, walked to the door that stood open on the verandah, to put an end to a conversation that was not agreeable to him. Mechanically, he repeated the last word again,—"*Death!*"—and, as he leaned against the railings, and watched the sparkling water as it rose and fell in the fountain; and, as in a dim and dizzy haze, saw flowers and trees and vases of the courts, he repeated again the mystic word so common in every mouth, yet of such fearful power,—"DEATH!" "Strange that there should be such a word," he said, "and such a thing, and we ever forget it; that one should be living, warm and beautiful, full of hopes, desires and wants, one day, and the next be gone, utterly gone, and forever!"

It was a warm, golden evening; and, as he walked to the other end of the verandah, he saw Tom busily intent on his Bible, pointing, as he did so, with his finger to each successive word, and whispering them to himself with an earnest air.

"Want me to read to you, Tom?" said St. Clare, seating himself carelessly by him.

"If Mas'r pleases," said Tom, gratefully, "Mas'r makes it so much plainer."

St. Clare took the book and glanced at the place, and began reading one of the passages which Tom had designated by the heavy marks around it. It ran as follows:

"When the Son of man shall come in his glory, and all his holy angels with him, then shall he sit upon the throne of his glory: and before him shall be gathered all nations; and he shall separate them one from another, as a shepherd divideth his sheep from the goats." St. Clare read on in an animated voice, till he came to the last of the verses.

"Then shall the king say unto them on his left hand, Depart from me, ye cursed, into everlasting fire: for I was an hungered, and ye gave me no meat: I was thirsty, and ye gave me no drink: I was a stranger, and ye took me not in: naked, and ye clothed me not: I was sick, and in prison, and ye visited me not. Then shall they answer unto Him, Lord when saw we thee an hungered, or athirst, or a stranger, or naked, or sick, or in prison, and did not minister unto thee? Then shall he say unto them, Inasmuch as ye did it not to one of the least of these my brethren, ye did it not to me."

St. Clare seemed struck with this last passage, for he read it twice,—the second time slowly, and as if he were revolving the words in his mind.

"Tom," he said, "these folks that get such hard measure seem to have been doing just what I have,—living good, easy, respectable lives; and not troubling themselves to inquire how many of their brethren were hungry or athirst, or sick, or in prison."

Tom did not answer.

St. Clare rose up and walked thoughtfully up and down the verandah, seeming to forget everything in his own thoughts; so absorbed was he, that Tom had to remind him twice that the tea-bell had run, before he could get his attention.

St. Clare was absent and thoughtful, all tea-time. After tea, he and Marie and Miss Ophelia took possession of the parlor, almost in silence.

Marie disposed herself on a lounge, under a silken mosquito curtain, and was soon sound asleep. Miss Ophelia silently busied herself with her knitting. St. Clare sat down to the piano, and began playing a soft and melancholy movement with the Æolian accompaniment. He seemed in a deep reverie, and to be soliloquizing to himself by music. After a little, he opened one of the drawers, took out an old music book whose leaves were yellow with age, and began turning it over.

"There," he said to Miss Ophelia, "this was one of my mother's books,—and here is her handwriting,—come and look at it. She copied and arranged this from Mozart's Requiem." Miss Ophelia came accordingly.

"It was something she used to sing often," said St. Clare. "I think I can hear her now."

He struck a few majestic chords, and began singing that grand old Latin piece, the "Dies Iræ."

Tom, who was listening in the outer verandah, was drawn by the sound to the very door, where he stood earnestly. He did not understand the words, of course; but the music and manner of singing appeared to affect him strongly, especially when St. Clare sang the more pathetic parts. Tom would have sympathized more heartily, if he had known the meaning of the beautiful words:

> Recordare Jesu pie
> Quod sum causa tuæ viæ
> No me perdas, illa die
> Querens me sedisti lassus
> Redemisti crucem passus
> Tantus labor non sit cassus.*

St. Clare threw a deep and pathetic expression into the words; for the shadowy veil of years seemed drawn away, and he seemed to hear his mother's voice leading his. Voice and instrument seemed both living, and threw out with vivid sympathy those strains which the ethereal Mozart first conceived as his own dying requiem.

When St. Clare had done singing, he sat leaning his head upon his hand a few moments, and then began walking up and down the floor.

"What a sublime conception is that of a last judgment!" said he,—"a righting of all the wrongs of ages!—a solving of all moral problems, by an unanswerable wisdom! It is, indeed, a wonderful image."

"It is a fearful one to us," said Miss Ophelia.

"It ought to be to me, I suppose," said St. Clare, stopping, thoughtfully. "I was reading to Tom, this afternoon, that chapter in Matthew that gives an account of it, and I have been quite struck with it. One should have expected some terrible enormities charged to those who are excluded from Heaven, as the reason; but no,—they are condemned for *not* doing positive good, as if that included every possible harm."

"Perhaps," said Miss Ophelia, "it is impossible for a person who does no good not to do harm."

"And what," said St. Clare, speaking abstractedly, but with deep feeling, "what shall be said of one whose own heart, whose education, and the wants of society, have called in vain to some noble purpose; who has floated on, a dreamy, neutral spectator of the struggles, agonies, and wrongs of man, when he should have been a worker?"

"I should say," said Miss Ophelia, "that he ought to repent, and begin now."

"Always practical and to the point!" said St. Clare, his face breaking out into a smile. "You never leave me any time for general reflections, Cousin; you always

*These lines have been thus rather inadequately translated:

> Think, O Jesus, for what reason
> Thou endured'st earth's spite and treason,
> Nor me lose, in that dread season;
> Seeking me, thy worn feet hasted,
> On the cross thy soul death tasted,
> Let not all these toils be wasted.

bring me short up against the actual present; you have a kind of eternal *now*, always in your mind."

"*Now* is all the time I have anything to do with," said Miss Ophelia.

"Dear little Eva,—poor child!" said St. Clare, "she had set her little simple soul on a good work for me."

It was the first time since Eva's death that he had ever said as many words as these of her, and he spoke now evidently repressing very strong feelings.

"My view of Christianity is such," he added, "that I think no man can consistently profess it without throwing the whole weight of his being against this monstrous system of injustice that lies at the foundation of all our society; and, if need be, sacrificing himself in the battle. That is, I mean that *I* could not be a Christian otherwise, though I have certainly had intercourse with a great many enlightened and Christian people who did no such thing; and I confess that the apathy of religious people on this subject, their want of perception of wrongs that filled me with horror, have engendered in me more skepticism than any other thing."

"If you knew all this," said Miss Ophelia, "why did n't you do it?"

"O, because I have had only that kind of benevolence which consists in lying on a sofa, and cursing the church and clergy for not being martyrs and confessors. One can see, you know, very easily, how others ought to be martyrs."

"Well, are you going to do differently now?" said Miss Ophelia.

"God only knows the future," said St. Clare. "I am braver than I was, because I have lost all; and he who has nothing to lose can afford all risks."

"And what are you going to do?"

"My duty, I hope, to the poor and lowly, as fast as I find it out," said St. Clare, "beginning with my own servants, for whom I have yet done nothing; and, perhaps, at some future day, it may appear that I can do something for a whole class; something to save my country from the disgrace of that false position in which she now stands before all civilized nations."

"Do you suppose it possible that a nation ever will voluntarily emancipate?" said Miss Ophelia.

"I don't know," said St. Clare. "This is a day of great deeds. Heroism and disinterestedness are rising up, here and there, in the earth. The Hungarian nobles set free millions of serfs, at an immense pecuniary loss; and, perhaps, among us may be found generous spirits, who do not estimate honor and justice by dollars and cents."

"I hardly think so," said Miss Ophelia.

"But, suppose we should rise up to-morrow and emancipate, who would educate these millions, and teach them how to use their freedom? They never would rise to do much among us. The fact is, we are too lazy and unpractical, ourselves, ever to give them much of an idea of that industry and energy which is necessary to form them into men. They will have to go north, where labor is the fashion,—the universal custom; and tell me, now, is there enough Christian philanthropy, among your northern states, to bear with the process of their education and elevation? You send thousands of dollars to foreign missions; but could you endure to have the heathen sent into your towns and villages, and give your time, and thoughts, and money, to raise them to the Christian standard? That 's what I want to know. If we emancipate, are you willing to educate? How many families, in your town, would take in a negro man and woman, teach them, bear with them, and seek to make them Christians? How many merchants would take Adolph, if I wanted to make him a clerk; or mechanics, if I wanted him taught a trade? If I wanted to put Jane and Rosa to a school, how many schools are there in the northern states that would take them in? how many families that would board them? and yet they are as white as many a woman, north or south. You see, Cousin, I want justice done us. We are in a bad position. We are the more *obvious* oppressors of the negro; but the unchristian prejudice of the north is an oppressor almost equally severe."

"Well, Cousin, I know it is so," said Miss Ophelia,—"I know it was so with me, till I saw that it was my duty to overcome it; but, I trust I have overcome it; and I know there are many good people at the north, who in this matter need only to be *taught* what their duty is, to do it. It would certainly be a greater self–denial to receive heathen among us, than to send missionaries to them; but I think we would do it."

"*You* would, I know," said St. Clare. "I 'd like to see anything you would n't do, if you thought it your duty!"

"Well, I 'm not uncommonly good," said Miss Ophelia. "Others would, if they saw things as I do. I intend to take Topsy home, when I go. I suppose our folks will wonder, at first; but I think they will be brought to see as I do. Besides, I know there are many people at the north who do exactly what you said."

"Yes, but they are a minority; and, if we should begin to emancipate to any extent, we should soon hear from you."

Miss Ophelia did not reply. There was a pause of some moments; and St. Clare's countenance was overcast by a sad, dreamy expression.

"I don't know what makes me think of my mother so much, to-night," he said. "I have a strange kind of feeling, as if she were near me. I keep thinking of things she used to say. Strange, what brings these past things so vividly back to us, sometimes!"

St. Clare walked up and down the room for some minutes more, and then said,

"I believe I 'll go down street, a few moments, and hear the news, to-night."

He took his hat, and passed out.

Tom followed him to the passage, out of the court, and asked if he should attend him.

"No, my boy," said St. Clare. "I shall be back in an hour."

Tom sat down in the verandah. It was a beautiful moonlight evening, and he sat watching the rising and falling spray of the fountain, and listening to its murmur. Tom thought of his home, and that he should soon be a free man, and able to return to it at will. He thought how he should work to buy his wife and boys. He felt the muscles of his brawny arms with a sort of joy, as he thought they would soon belong to himself, and how much they could do to work out the freedom of his family. Then he thought of his noble young master, and, ever second to that, came the habitual prayer that he had always offered for him; and then his thoughts passed on to the beautiful Eva, whom he now thought of among the angels; and he thought till he almost fancied that that bright face and golden hair were looking upon him, out of the spray of the fountain. And, so musing, he fell asleep, and dreamed he saw her coming bounding towards him, just as she used to come, with a wreath of jessamine in her hair, her cheeks bright, and her eyes radiant with delight; but, as he looked, she seemed to rise from the ground; her cheeks wore a paler hue,—her eyes had a deep, divine radiance, a golden halo seemed around her head,—and she vanished from his sight; and Tom was awakened by a loud knocking, and a sound of many voices at the gate.

He hastened to undo it; and, with smothered voices and heavy tread, came several men, bringing a body, wrapped in a cloak, and lying on a shutter. The light of the lamp fell full on the face; and Tom gave a wild cry of amazement and despair, that rung through all the galleries, as the men advanced, with their burden, to the open parlor door, where Miss Ophelia still sat knitting.

St. Clare had turned into a café, to look over an evening paper. As he was reading, an affray arose between two gentlemen in the room, who were both partially intoxicated. St. Clare and one or two others made an effort to separate them, and St. Clare received a fatal stab in the side with a bowie-knife, which he was attempting to wrest from one of them.

The house was full of cries and lamentations, shrieks and screams; servants frantically tearing their hair, throwing themselves on the ground, or running distractedly about, lamenting. Tom and Miss Ophelia alone seemed to have any presence of mind; for Marie was in strong hysteric convulsions. At Miss Ophelia's direction, one of the lounges in the parlor was hastily prepared, and the bleeding form laid upon it. St. Clare had fainted, through pain and loss of blood; but, as Miss Ophelia applied restoratives, he revived, opened his eyes, looked fixedly on them, looked earnestly around the room, his eyes travelling wistfully over every object, and finally they rested on his mother's picture.

The physician now arrived, and made his examination. It was evident, from the expression of his face, that there was no hope; but he applied himself to dressing the wound, and he and Miss Ophelia and Tom proceeded composedly with this work, amid the lamentations and sobs and cries of the affrighted servants, who had clustered about the doors and windows of the verandah.

"Now," said the physician, "we must turn all these creatures out; all depends on his being kept quiet."

St. Clare opened his eyes, and looked fixedly on the distressed beings, whom Miss Ophelia and the doctor were trying to urge from the apartment. "Poor creatures!" he said, and an expression of bitter self-reproach passed over his face. Adolph absolutely refused to go. Terror had deprived him of all presence of mind; he threw himself along on the floor, and nothing could persuade him to rise. The rest yielded to Miss Ophelia's urgent representations, that their master's safety depended on their stillness and obedience.

St. Clare could say but little; he lay with his eyes shut, but it was evident that he wrestled with bitter thoughts. After a while, he laid his hand on Tom's, who was kneeling beside him, and said, "Tom! poor fellow!"

"What, Mas'r?" said Tom, earnestly.

"I am dying!" said St. Clare, pressing his hand; "pray!"

"If you would like a clergyman—" said the physician.

St. Clare hastily shook his head, and said again to Tom, more earnestly, "Pray!"

And Tom did pray, with all his mind and strength, for the soul that was passing,—the soul that seemed looking so steadily and mournfully from those large, melancholy blue eyes. It was literally prayer offered with strong crying and tears.

When Tom ceased to speak, St. Clare reached out and took his hand, looking earnestly at him, but saying nothing. He closed his eyes, but still retained his hold; for, in the gates of eternity, the black hand and the white hold each other with an equal clasp. He murmured softly to himself, at broken intervals,

"Recordare Jesu pie—

\* \* \*

Ne me perdas—ille die
Querens me—sedisti lassus."

It was evident that the words he had been singing that evening were passing through his mind,—words of entreaty addressed to Infinite Pity. His lips moved at intervals, as parts of the hymn fell brokenly from them.

"His mind is wandering," said the doctor

"No! it is coming HOME, at last!" said St. Clare, energetically; "at last! at last!"

The effort of speaking exhausted him. The sinking paleness of death fell on him; but with it there fell, as if shed from the wings of some pitying spirit, a beautiful expression of peace, like that of a wearied child who sleeps.

So he lay for a few moments. They saw that the mighty hand was on him. Just before the spirit parted, he opened his eyes, with a sudden light, as of joy and recognition, and said *"Mother!"* and then he was gone!

# XXIX.
## *The Unprotected*

We hear often of the distress of the negro servants, on the loss of a kind master; and with good reason, for no creature on God's earth is left more utterly unprotected and desolate than the slave in these circumstances.

The child who has lost a father has still the protection of friends, and of the law; he is something, and can do something,—has acknowledged rights and position; the slave has none. The law regards him, in every respect, as devoid of rights as a bale of merchandise. The only possible acknowledgement of any of the longings and wants of a human and immortal creature, which are given to him, comes to him through the sovereign and irresponsible will of his master; and when that master is stricken down, nothing remains.

The number of those men who know how to use wholly irresponsible power humanely and generously is small. Everybody knows this, and the slave knows it best of all; so that he feels that there are ten chances of his finding an abusive and tyrannical master, to one of his finding a considerate and kind one. Therefore is it that the wail over a kind master is loud and long, as well it may be.

When St. Clare breathed his last, terror and consternation took hold of all his household. He had been stricken down so in a moment, in the flower and strength of his youth! Every room and gallery of the house resounded with sobs and shrieks of despair.

Marie, whose nervous system had been enervated by a constant course of self-indulgence, had nothing to support the terror of the shock, and, at the time her husband breathed his last, was passing from one fainting fit to another; and he to whom she had been joined in the mysterious tie of marriage passed from her forever, without the possibility of even a parting word.

Miss Ophelia, with characteristic strength and self-control, had remained with her kinsman to the last,—all eye, all ear, all attention; doing everything of the little that could be done, and joining with her whole soul in the tender and impassioned prayers which the poor slave had poured forth for the soul of his dying master.

When they were arranging him for his last rest, they found upon his bosom a small, plain miniature case, opening with a spring. It was the miniature of a noble and beautiful female face; and on the reverse, under a crystal, a lock of dark hair. They laid them back on the lifeless breast,—dust to dust,—poor mournful relics of early dreams, which once made that cold heart beat so warmly!

Tom's whole soul was filled with thoughts of eternity; and while he ministered around the lifeless clay, he did not once think that the sudden stroke had left him in hopeless slavery. He felt at peace about his master; for in that hour, when he had poured forth his prayer into the bosom of his Father, he had found an answer of quietness and assurance springing up within himself. In the depths of his own affectionate nature, he felt able to perceive something of the fulness of Divine love; for an old oracle hath thus written,—"He that dwelleth in love dwelleth in God, and God in him." Tom hoped and trusted, and was at peace.

But the funeral passed, with all its pageant of black crape, and prayers, and solemn faces; and back rolled the cool, muddy waves of every-day life; and up came the everlasting hard inquiry of "What is to be done next?"

It rose to the mind of Marie, as dressed in loose morning-robes, and surrounded by anxious servants, she sat up in a great easy-chair, and inspected samples of crape and bombazine. It rose to Miss Ophelia, who began to turn her thoughts towards her northern home. It rose, in silent terrors, to the minds of the servants, who well knew the unfeeling, tyrannical character of the mistress in whose hands they were left. All knew, very well, that the indulgences which had been accorded to them were not from their mistress, but from their master; and that, now he was gone, there would be no screen between them and every tyrannous infliction which a temper soured by affliction might devise.

It was about a fortnight after the funeral, that Miss Ophelia, busied one day in her apartment, heard a gentle tap at the door. She opened it, and there stood

Rosa, the pretty young quadroon, whom we have before often noticed, her hair in disorder, and her eyes swelled with crying.

"O, Miss Feely," she said, falling on her knees, and catching the skirt of her dress, "*do, do go* to Miss Marie for me! do plead for me! She 's goin' to send me out to be whipped,—look there!" And she handed to Miss Ophelia a paper.

It was an order, written in Marie's delicate Italian hand, to the master of a whipping-establishment, to give the bearer fifteen lashes.

"What have you been doing?" said Miss Ophelia.

"You know, Miss Feely, I 've got such a bad temper; it 's very bad of me. I was trying on Miss Marie's dress, and she slapped my face; and I spoke out before I thought, and was saucy; and she said that she 'd bring me down, and have me know, once for all, that I was n't going to be so topping as I had been; and she wrote this, and says I shall carry it. I 'd rather she 'd kill me, right out."

Miss Ophelia stood considering, with the paper in her hand.

"You see, Miss Feely," said Rosa, "I don't mind the whipping so much, if Miss Marie or you was to do it; but, to be sent to a *man*! and such a horrid man,—the shame of it, Miss Feely!"

Miss Ophelia well knew that it was the universal custom to send women and young girls to whipping-houses, to the hands of the lowest of men,—men vile enough to make this their profession,—there to be subjected to brutal exposure and shameful correction. She had *known* it before; but hitherto she had never realized it, till she saw the slender form of Rosa almost convulsed with distress. All the honest blood of womanhood, the strong New England blood of liberty, flushed to her cheeks, and throbbed bitterly in her indignant heart; but, with habitual prudence and self-control, she mastered herself, and crushing the paper firmly in her hand, she merely said to Rosa,

"Sit down, child, while I go to your mistress."

"Shameful! monstrous! outrageous!" she said to herself, as she was crossing the parlor.

She found Marie sitting up in her easy–chair, with Mammy standing by her, combing her hair; Jane sat on the ground before her, busy in chafing her feet.

"How do you find yourself, to-day?" said Miss Ophelia.

A deep sigh, and a closing of the eyes, was the only reply, for a moment; and then Marie answered, "O, I don't know, Cousin; I suppose I 'm as well as I ever shall be!" and Marie wiped her eyes with a cambric handkerchief, bordered with an inch deep of black.

"I came," said Miss Ophelia, with a short, dry cough, such as commonly introduces a difficult subject,—"I came to speak with you about poor Rosa."

Marie's eyes were open wide enough now, and a flush rose to her sallow cheeks, as she answered, sharply,

"Well, what about her?"

"She is very sorry for her fault."

"She is, is she? She 'll be sorrier, before I 've done with her! I 've endured that child's impudence long enough; and now I 'll bring her down,—I 'll make her lie in the dust!"

"But could not you punish her some other way,—some way that would be less shameful?"

"I mean to shame her; that 's just what I want. She has all her life presumed on her delicacy, and her good looks, and her lady-like airs, till she forgets who she is;—and I 'll give her one lesson that will bring her down, I fancy!"

"But, cousin, consider that, if you destroy delicacy and a sense of shame in a young girl, you deprave her very fast."

"Delicacy!" said Marie, with a scornful laugh,—"a fine word for such as she! I 'll teach her, with all her airs, that she 's no better than the raggedest black wench that walks the streets! She 'll take no more airs with me!"

"You will answer to God for such cruelty!" said Miss Ophelia, with energy.

"Cruelty,—I 'd like to know what the cruelty is! I wrote orders for only fifteen lashes, and told him to put them on lightly. I 'm sure there 's no cruelty there!"

"No cruelty!" said Miss Ophelia. "I 'm sure any girl might rather be killed outright!"

"It may seem so to anybody with your feeling; but all these creatures get used to it; it 's the only way they can be kept in order. Once let them feel that they are to take any airs about delicacy, and all that, and they 'll run all over you, just as my servants always have. I 've begun now to bring them under; and I 'll have them all to know that I 'll send one out to be whipped, as soon as another, if they don't mind themselves!" said Marie, looking around her decidedly.

Jane hung her head and cowered at this, for she felt as if it was particularly directed to her. Miss Ophelia sat for a moment, as if she had swallowed some explosive mixture, and were ready to burst. Then, recollecting the utter uselessness of contention with such a nature, she shut her lips resolutely, gathered herself up, and walked out of the room.

It was hard to go back and tell Rosa that she could do nothing for her; and, shortly after, one of the man-servants came to say that her mistress had ordered him to take Rosa with him to the whipping-house, whither she was hurried, in spite of her tears and entreaties.

A few days after, Tom was standing musing by the balconies, when he was joined by Adolph, who, since the death of his master, had been entirely crest–fallen and disconsolate. Adolph knew that he had always been an object of dislike to Marie; but while his master lived he had paid but little attention to it. Now that he was gone, he had moved about in daily dread and trembling, not knowing what might befall him next. Marie had held several consultations with her lawyer; after communicating with St. Clare's brother, it was determined to sell the place, and all the servants, except her own personal property, and these she intended to take with her, and go back to her father's plantation.

"Do ye know, Tom, that we 've all got to be sold?" said Adolph.

"How did you hear that?" said Tom.

"I hid myself behind the curtains when Missis was talking with the lawyer. In a few days we shall all be sent off to auction, Tom."

"The Lord's will be done!" said Tom, folding his arms and sighing heavily.

"We 'll never get another such a master," said Adolph, apprehensively; "but I 'd rather be sold than take my chance under Missis."

Tom turned away; his heart was full. The hope of liberty, the thought of distant wife and children, rose up before his patient soul, as to the mariner shipwrecked almost in port rises the vision of the church-spire and loving roofs of his native village, seen over the top of some black wave only for one last farewell. He drew his arms tightly over his bosom, and choked back the bitter tears, and tried to pray. The poor old soul had such a singular, unaccountable prejudice in favor of liberty, that it was a hard wrench for him; and the more he said, "Thy will be done," the worse it felt.

He sought Miss Ophelia, who, ever since Eva's death, had treated him with marked and respectful kindness.

"Miss Feely," he said, "Mas'r St. Clare promised me my freedom. He told me that he had begun to take it out for me; and now, perhaps, if Miss Feely would be good enough to speak about it to Missis, she would feel like goin' on with it, as it was Mas'r St. Clare's wish."

"I'll speak for you, Tom, and do my best," said Miss Ophelia; "but, if it depends on Mrs. St. Clare, I can't hope much for you;—nevertheless, I will try."

This incident occurred a few days after that of Rosa, while Miss Ophelia was busied in preparations to return north.

Seriously reflecting within herself, she considered that perhaps she had shown too hasty a warmth of language in her former interview with Marie; and she resolved that she would now endeavor to moderate her zeal, and to be as conciliatory as possible. So the good soul gathered herself up, and, taking her knitting, resolved to go into Marie's room, be as agreeable as possible, and negotiate Tom's case with all the diplomatic skill of which she was mistress.

She found Marie reclining at length upon a lounge, supporting herself on one elbow by pillows, while Jane, who had been out shopping, was displaying before her certain samples of thin black stuffs.

"That will do," said Marie, selecting one; "only I 'm not sure about its being properly mourning."

"Laws, Missis," said Jane, volubly, "Mrs. General Derbenon wore just this very thing, after the General died, last summer; it makes up lovely!"

"What do you think?" said Marie to Miss Ophelia.

"It 's matter of custom, I suppose," said Miss Ophelia. "You can judge about it better than I."

"The fact is," said Marie, "that I have n't a dress in the world that I can wear; and, as I am going to break up the establishment, and go off, next week, I must decide upon something."

"Are you going so soon?"

"Yes. St. Clare's brother has written, and he and the lawyer think that the servants and furniture had better be put up at auction, and the place left with our lawyer."

"There 's one thing I wanted to speak with you about," said Miss Ophelia. "Augustine promised Tom his liberty, and began the legal forms necessary to it. I hope you will use your influence to have it perfected."

"Indeed, I shall do no such thing!" said Marie, sharply. "Tom is one of the most valuable servants on the place,—it could n't be afforded, any way. Besides, what does he want of liberty? He 's a great deal better off as he is."

"But he does desire it, very earnestly, and his master promised it," said Miss Ophelia.

"I dare say he does want it," said Marie; "they all want it, just because they are a discontented set,—always wanting what they have n't got. Now, I 'm principled against emancipating, in any case. Keep a negro under the care of a master, and he does well enough, and is respectable; but set them free, and they get lazy, and won't work, and take to drinking, and go all down to be mean, worthless fellows. I 've seen it tried, hundreds of times. It 's no favor to set them free."

"But Tom is so steady, industrious, and pious."

"O, you need n't tell me! I 've seen a hundred like him. He 'll do very well, as long as he 's taken care of,—that 's all."

"But, then, consider," said Miss Ophelia, "when you set him up for sale, the chances of his getting a bad master."

"O, that 's all humbug!" said Marie; "it is n't one time in a hundred that a good fellow gets a bad master; most masters are good, for all the talk that is made. I 've lived and grown up here, in the South, and I never yet was acquainted with a master that did n't treat his servants well,—quite as well as is worth while. I don't feel any fears on that head."

"Well," said Miss Ophelia, energetically, "I know it was one of the last wishes of your husband that Tom should have his liberty; it was one of the promises that he made to dear little Eva on her death-bed, and I should not think you would feel at liberty to disregard it."

Marie had her face covered with her handkerchief at this appeal, and began sobbing and using her smelling-bottle, with great vehemence.

"Everybody goes against me!" she said. "Everybody is so inconsiderate! I should n't have expected that *you* would bring up all these remembrances of my troubles to me,—it 's so inconsiderate! But nobody ever does consider,—my trials are so peculiar! It 's so hard, that when I had only one daughter, she should have been taken! —and when I had a husband that just exactly suited me,—and I 'm so hard to be suited!—he should be taken! And you seem to have so little feeling for me, and keep bringing it up to me so carelessly,—when you know how it overcomes me! I suppose you mean well; but it is very inconsiderate,—very!" And Marie sobbed, and gasped for breath, and called Mammy to open the window, and to bring her the camphor-bottle, and to bathe her head, and unhook her dress. And, in the general confusion that ensued, Miss Ophelia made her escape to her apartment.

She saw, at once, that it would do no good to say anything more; for Marie had an indefinite capacity for hysteric fits; and, after this, whenever her husband's or Eva's wishes with regard to the servants were alluded to, she always found it convenient to set one in operation. Miss Ophelia, therefore, did the next best thing she could for Tom,—she wrote a letter to Mrs. Shelby for him, stating his troubles, and urging them to send to his relief.

The next day, Tom and Adolph, and some half a dozen other servants, were marched down to a slave-warehouse, to await the convenience of the trader, who was going to make up a lot for auction.

## XXX.
## The Slave Warehouse

A slave warehouse! Perhaps some of my readers conjure up horrible visions of such a place. They fancy some foul, obscure den, some horrible *Tartarus "informis, ingens, cui lumen ademptum."* But no, innocent friend; in these days men have learned the art of sinning expertly and genteelly, so as not to shock the eyes and senses of respectable society. Human property is high in the market; and is, therefore, well fed, well cleaned, tended, and looked after, that it may come to sale sleek, and strong, and shining. A slave-warehouse in New Orleans is a house externally not much unlike many others, kept with neatness; and where every day you may see arranged, under a sort of shed along the outside, rows of men and women, who stand there as a sign of the property sold within.

Then you shall be courteously entreated to call and examine, and shall find an abundance of husbands, wives, brothers, sisters, fathers, mothers, and young children, to be "sold separately, or in lots to suit the convenience of the purchaser;" and that soul immortal, once bought with blood and anguish by the Son of God, when the earth shook, and the rocks rent, and the graves were opened, can be sold, leased, mortgaged, exchanged for groceries or dry goods, to suit the phases of trade, or the fancy of the purchaser.

It was a day or two after the conversation between Marie and Miss Ophelia, that Tom, Adolph, and about half a dozen others of the St. Clare estate, were turned over to the loving kindness of Mr. Skeggs, the keeper of a depot on—— street, to await the auction, next day.

Tom had with him quite a sizable trunk full of clothing, as had most others of them. They were ushered, for the night, into a long room, where many other men, of all ages, sizes, and shades of complexion, were assembled, and from which roars of laughter and unthinking merriment were proceeding.

"Ah, ha! that's right. Go it, boys,—go it!" said Mr. Skeggs, the keeper. "My people are always so merry! Sambo, I see!" he said, speaking approvingly to a burly negro who was performing tricks of low buffoonery, which occasioned the shouts which Tom had heard.

As might be imagined, Tom was in no humor to join these proceedings; and, therefore, setting his trunk as far as possible from the noisy group, he sat down on it, and leaned his face against the wall.

The dealers in the human article made scrupulous and systematic efforts to promote noisy mirth among them, as a means of drowning reflection, and rendering them insensible to their condition. The whole object of the training to which the negro is put, from the time he is sold in the northern market till he arrives south, is systematically directed towards making him callous, unthinking, and brutal. The slave-dealer collects his gang in Virginia or Kentucky, and drives them to some convenient, healthy place,—often a watering place,—to be fattened. Here they are fed full daily; and, because some incline to pine, a fiddle is kept commonly going among them, and they are made to dance daily; and he who refuses to be merry—in whose soul thoughts of wife, or child, or home, are too strong for him to be gay—is marked as sullen and dangerous, and subjected to all the evils which the ill will of an utterly irresponsible and hardened man can inflict upon him. Briskness, alertness, and cheerfulness of appearance, especially before observers, are constantly enforced upon them, both by the hope of thereby getting a good master, and the fear of all that the driver may bring upon them, if they prove unsalable.

"What dat ar nigger doin here?" said Sambo, coming up to Tom, after Mr. Skeggs had left the room. Sambo was a full black, of great size, very lively, voluble, and full of trick and grimace.

"What you doin here?" said Sambo, coming up to Tom, and poking him facetiously in the side. "Meditatin', eh?"

"I am to be sold at the auction, to-morrow!" said Tom, quietly.

"Sold at auction,—haw! haw! boys, an't this yer fun! I wish't I was gwine that ar way!—tell ye, would n't I make em laugh? But how is it,—dis yer whole lot gwine to-morrow?" said Sambo, laying his hand freely on Adolph's shoulder.

"Please to let me alone!" said Adolph, fiercely, straightening himself up, with extreme disgust.

"Law, now, boys! dis yer 's one o' yer white niggers,—kind o' cream color, ye know, scented!" said he, coming up to Adolph and snuffing. "O, Lor! he 'd do for a tobaccer-shop; they could keep him to scent snuff! Lor, he 'd keep a whole shop agwine,—he would!"

"I say, keep off, can't you?" said Adolph, enraged.

"Lor, now, how touchy we is,—we white niggers! Look at us, now!" and Sambo gave a ludicrous imitation of Adolph's manner; "here 's de airs and graces. We 's been in a good family, I specs."

"Yes," said Adolph; "I had a master that could have bought you all for old truck!"

"Laws, now, only think," said Sambo, "the gentlemens that we is!"

"I belonged to the St. Clare family," said Adolph, proudly.

"Lor, you did! Be hanged if they ar' n't lucky to get shet of ye. Spects they 's gwine to trade ye off with a lot o' cracked tea-pots and sich like!" said Sambo, with a provoking grin.

Adolph, enraged at this taunt, flew furiously at his adversary, swearing and striking on every side of him. The rest laughed and shouted, and the uproar brought the keeper to the door.

"What now, boys? Order,—order!" he said, coming in and flourishing a large whip.

All fled in different directions, except Sambo, who, presuming on the favor which the keeper had to him as a licensed wag, stood his ground, ducking his head with a facetious grin, whenever the master made a dive at him.

"Lor, Mas'r, 'tan't us,—we 's reglar stiddy,—it 's these yer new hands; they 's real aggravatin',—kinder pickin' at us, all time!"

The keeper, at this, turned upon Tom and Adolph, and distributing a few kicks and cuffs without much inquiry, and leaving general orders for all to be good boys and go to sleep, left the apartment.

While this scene was going on in the men's sleeping-room, the reader may be curious to take a peep at the corresponding apartment allotted to the women.

Stretched out in various attitudes over the floor, he may see numberless sleeping forms of every shade of complexion, from the purest ebony to white, and of all years, from childhood to old age, lying now asleep. Here is a fine bright girl, of ten years, whose mother was sold out yesterday, and who to-night cried herself to sleep when nobody was looking at her. Here, a worn old negress, whose thin arms and callous fingers tell of hard toil, waiting to be sold to-morrow, as a cast-off article, for what can be got for her; and some forty or fifty others, with heads variously enveloped in blankets or articles of clothing, lie stretched around them. But, in a corner, sitting apart from the rest, are two females of a more interesting appearance than common. One of these is a respectably-dressed mulatto woman between forty and fifty, with soft eyes and a gentle and pleasing physiognomy. She has on her head a high-raised turban, made of a gay red Madras handkerchief, of the first quality, and her dress is neatly fitted, and of good material, showing that she has been provided for with a careful hand. By her side, and nestling closely to her, is a young girl of fifteen,—her daughter. She is a quadroon, as may be seen from her fairer complexion, though her likeness to her mother is quite discernible. She has the same soft, dark eye, with longer lashes, and her curling hair is of a luxuriant brown. She also is dressed with great neatness, and her white, delicate hands betray very little acquaintance with servile toil. These two are to be sold to-morrow, in the same lot with the St. Clare servants; and the gentleman to whom they belong, and to whom the money for their sale is to be transmitted, is a member of a Christian church in New York, who will receive the money, and go thereafter to the sacrament of his Lord and theirs, and think no more of it.

These two, whom we shall call Susan and Emmeline, had been the personal attendants of an amiable and pious lady of New Orleans, by whom they had been carefully and piously instructed and trained. They had been taught to read and write, diligently instructed in the truths of religion, and their lot had been as happy an one as in their condition it was possible to be. But the only son of their protectress had the management of her property; and, by carelessness and extravagance involved it to a large amount, and at last failed. One of the largest creditors was the respectable firm of B. & Co., in New York. B. & Co. wrote to their lawyer in New Orleans, who attached the real estate (these two articles and a lot of plantation hands formed the most valuable part of it), and wrote word to that effect to New York. Brother B., being, as we have said, a Christian man, and a resident in a free State, felt some uneasiness on the subject. He did n't like trading in slaves and souls of men,—of course, he did n't; but, then, there were thirty thousand dollars in the case, and that was rather too much money to be lost for a principle; and so, after much considering, and asking advice from those that he knew would advise to suit him, Brother B. wrote to his lawyer to dispose of the business in the way that seemed to him that most suitable, and remit the proceeds.

The day after the letter arrived in New Orleans, Susan and Emmeline were attached, and sent to the depot to await a general auction on the following morning; and as they glimmer faintly upon us in the moonlight which steals through the grated window, we may listen to their conversation. Both are weeping, but each quietly, that the other may not hear.

"Mother, just lay your head on my lap, and see if you can't sleep a little," says the girl, trying to appear calm.

"I have n't any heart to sleep, Em; I can't; it 's the last night we may be together!"

"O, mother, don't say so! perhaps we shall get sold together,—who knows?"

"If 't was anybody's else case, I should say so, too, Em," said the woman; "but I 'm so feard of losin' you that I don't see anything but the danger."

"Why, mother, the man said we were both likely, and would sell well."

Susan remembered the man's looks and words. With a deadly sickness at her heart, she remembered how he had looked at Emmeline's hands, and lifted up her curly hair, and pronounced her a first-rate article. Susan had been trained as a Christian, brought up in the daily reading of the Bible, and had the same horror of her child's being sold to a life of shame that any other Christian mother might have; but she had no hope,—no protection.

"Mother, I think we might do first rate, if you could get a place as cook, and I as chamber-maid or seamstress, in some family. I dare say we shall. Let 's both look as bright and lively as we can, and tell all we can do, and perhaps we shall," said Emmeline.

"I want you to brush your hair all back straight, to-morrow," said Susan.

"What for, mother? I don't look near so well, that way."

"Yes, but you 'll sell better so,"

"I don't see why!" said the child.

"Respectable families would be more apt to buy you, if they saw you looked plain and decent, as if you was n't trying to look handsome. I know their ways better 'n you do," said Susan.

"Well, mother, then I will."

"And, Emmeline, if we should n't ever see each other again, after to-morrow, —if I 'm sold way up on a plantation somewhere, and you somewhere else,—always remember how you 've been brought up, and all Missis has told you; take your Bible with you, and your hymn-book; and if you 're faithful to the Lord, he 'll be faithful to you."

So speaks the poor soul, in sore discouragement; for she knows that to-morrow any man, however vile and brutal, however godless and merciless, if he only has money to pay for her, may become owner of her daughter, body and soul; and then, how is the child to be faithful? She thinks of all this, as she holds her daughter in her arms, and wishes that she were not handsome and attractive. It seems almost an aggravation to her to remember how purely and piously, how much above the ordinary lot, she has been brought up. But she has no resort but to *pray*; and many such prayers to God have gone up from those same trim, neatly-arranged, respectable slave-prisons,—prayers which God has not forgotten, as a coming day shall show; for it is written, "Who causeth one of these little ones to offend, it were better for him that a mill-stone were hanged about his neck, and that he were drowned in the depths of the sea."

The soft, earnest, quiet moonbeam looks in fixedly, marking the bars of the grated windows on the prostrate, sleeping forms. The mother and daughter are singing together a wild and melancholy dirge, common as a funeral hymn among the slaves:

"O, where is weeping Mary?
O, where is weeping Mary?
        'Rived in the goodly land.
She is dead and gone to Heaven;
She is dead and gone to Heaven;
        'Rived in the goodly land."

These words, sung by voices of a peculiar and melancholy sweetness, in an air which seemed like the sighing of earthly despair after heavenly hope, floated through the dark prison rooms with a pathetic cadence, as verse after verse was breathed out:

"O, where are Paul and Silas?
O, where are Paul and Silas?
        Gone to the goodly land.
They are dead and gone to Heaven;
They are dead and gone to Heaven;
        'Rived in the goodly land."

Sing on, poor souls! The night is short, and the morning will part you forever!

But now it is morning, and everybody is astir; and the worthy Mr. Skeggs is busy and bright, for a lot of goods is to be fitted out for auction. There is a brisk look-out on the toilet; injunctions passed around to every one to put on their best face and be spry; and now all are arranged in a circle for a last review, before they are marched up to the Bourse.

Mr. Skeggs, with his palmetto on and his cigar in his mouth, walks around to put farewell touches on his wares.

"How 's this?" he said, stepping in front of Susan and Emmeline. "Where 's your curls, gal?"

The girl looked timidly at her mother, who, with the smooth adroitness common among her class, answers,

"I was telling her, last night, to put up her hair smooth and neat, and not havin' it flying about in curls; looks more respectable so."

"Bother!" said the man, peremptorily, turning to the girl; "You go right along, and curl yourself real smart!" He added, giving a crack to a rattan he held in his hand, "And be back in quick time, too!"

"You go and help her," he added, to the mother. "Them curls may make a hundred dollars difference in the sale of her."

---

Beneath a splendid dome were men of all nations, moving to and fro, over the marble pave. On every side of the circular area were little tribunes, or stations, for the use of speakers and auctioneers. Two of these, on opposite sides of the area, were now occupied by brilliant and talented gentleman, enthusiastically forcing up, in English and French commingled, the bids of connoisseurs in their various wares. A third one, on the other side, still unoccupied, was surrounded by a group, waiting the moment of sale to begin. And here we may recognize the

St. Clare servants,—Tom, Adolph, and others; and there, too, Susan and Emmeline, awaiting their turn with anxious and dejected faces. Various spectators, intending to purchase, or not intending, as the case might be, gathered around the group, handling, examining, and commenting on their various points and faces with the same freedom that a set of jockeys discuss the merits of a horse.

"Hulloa, Alf! what brings you here?" said a young exquisite, slapping the shoulder of a sprucely-dressed young man, who was examining Adolph through an eye-glass.

"Well, I was wanting a valet, and I heard that St. Clare's lot was going. I thought I 'd just look at his—"

"Catch me ever buying any of St. Clare's people! Spoilt niggers, every one. Impudent as the devil!" said the other.

"Never fear that!" said the first. "If I get 'em, I 'll soon have their airs out of them; they 'll soon find that they 've another kind of master to deal with than Monsieur St. Clare. 'Pon my word, I 'll buy that fellow. I like the shape of him."

"You 'll find it 'll take all you 've got to keep him. He 's deucedly extravagant!"

"Yes, but my lord will find that he *can't* be extravagant with *me*. Just let him be sent to the calaboose a few times, and thoroughly dressed down! I 'll tell you if it don't bring him to a sense of his ways! O, I 'll reform him, up hill and down,— you 'll see. I buy him, that 's flat!"

Tom had been standing wistfully examining the multitude of faces thronging around him, for one whom he would wish to call master. And if you should ever be under the necessity, sir, of selecting, out of two hundred men, one who was to become your absolute owner and disposer, you would, perhaps, realize, just as Tom did, how few there were that you would feel at all comfortable in being made over to. Tom saw abundance of men,—great, burly, gruff men; little, chirping, dried men; long-favored, lank, hard men; and every variety of stubbed-looking, commonplace men, who pick up their fellow-men as one picks up chips, putting them into the fire or a basket with equal unconcern, according to their convenience; but he saw no St. Clare.

A little before the sale commenced, a short, broad, muscular man, in a checked shirt considerably open at the bosom, and pantaloons much the worse for dirt and wear, elbowed his way through the crowd, like one who is going actively into a business; and, coming up to the group, began to examine them systematically. From the moment that Tom saw him approaching, he felt an immediate and revolting horror at him, that increased as he came near. He was evidently, though short, of gigantic strength. His round, bullet head, large, light-gray eyes, with their shaggy, sandy eye-brows, and stiff, wiry, sun-burned hair, were rather unprepossessing items, it is to be confessed; his large, coarse mouth was distended with tobacco, the juice of which, from time to time, he ejected from him with great decision and explosive force; his hands were immensely large, hairy, sun-burned, freckled, and very dirty, and garnished with long nails, in a very foul condition. This man proceeded to a very free personal examination of the lot. He seized Tom by the jaw, and pulled open his mouth to inspect his teeth; made him strip up his sleeve, to show his muscle; turned him round, made him jump and spring, to show his paces.

"Where was you raised?" he added, briefly, to these investigations.

"In Kintuck, Mas'r" said Tom, looking about, as if for deliverance.

"What have you done?"

"Had care of Mas'r's farm," said Tom.

"Likely story!" said the other, shortly, as he passed on. He paused a moment before Dolph; then spitting a discharge of tobacco-juice on his well-blacked boots, and giving a contemptuous umph, he walked on. Again he stopped before Susan and Emmeline. He put out his heavy, dirty hand, and drew the girl towards him; passed it over her neck and bust, felt her arms, looked at her teeth, and then pushed her back against her mother, whose patient face showed the suffering she had been going through at every motion of the hideous stranger.

The girl was frightened, and began to cry.

"Stop that, you minx!" said the salesman; "no whimpering here,—the sale is going to begin." And accordingly the sale begun.

Adolph was knocked off, at a good sum, to the young gentleman who had previously stated his intention of buying him; and the other servants of the St. Clare lot went to various bidders.

"Now, up with you, boy! d 'ye hear?" said the auctioneer to Tom.

Tom stepped upon the block, gave a few anxious looks round; all seemed mingled in a common, indistinct noise,—the clatter of the salesman crying off his qualifications in French and English, the quick fire of French and English bids; and almost in a moment came the final thump of the hammer, and the clear ring on the last syllable of the word "*dollars*," as the auctioneer announced his price, and Tom was made over.—He had a master!

He was pushed from the block;—the short, bullet–headed man seizing him roughly by the shoulder, pushed him to one side, saying, in a harsh voice, "Stand there, *you*!"

Tom hardly realized anything; but still the bidding went on,—rattling, clattering, now French, now English. Down goes the hammer again,—Susan is sold! She goes down from the block, stops, looks wistfully back,—her daughter stretches her hands towards her. She looks with agony in the face of the man who has bought her,—a respectable middle–aged man, of benevolent countenance.

"O, Mas'r, please do buy my daughter!"

"I 'd like to, but I 'm afraid I can't afford it!" said the gentleman, looking, with painful interest, as the young girl mounted the block, and looked around her with a frightened and timid glance.

The blood flushes painfully in her otherwise colorless cheek, her eye has a feverish fire, and her mother groans to see that she looks more beautiful than she ever saw her before. The auctioneer sees his advantage, and expatiates volubly in mingled French and English, and bids rise in rapid succession.

"I 'll do anything in reason," said the benevolent-looking gentleman, pressing in and joining with the bids. In a few moments they have run beyond his purse. He is silent; the auctioneer grows warmer; but bids gradually drop off. It lies now between an aristocratic old citizen and our bullet-headed acquaintance. The citizen bids for a few turns, contemptuously measuring his opponent; but the bullet-head has the advantage over him, both in obstinacy and concealed length of purse, and the controversy lasts but a moment; the hammer falls,—he has got the girl, body and soul, unless God help her!

Her master is Mr. Legree, who owns a cotton plantation on the Red river. She is pushed along into the same lot with Tom and two other men, and goes off, weeping as she goes.

The benevolent gentleman is sorry; but, then, the thing happens every day! One sees girls and mothers crying, at these sales, *always*! it can't be helped, &c.; and he walks off, with his acquisition, in another direction.

Two days after, the lawyer of the Christian firm of B. & Co., New York, sent on their money to them. On the reverse of that draft, so obtained, let them write these words of the great Paymaster, to whom they shall make up their account in a future day: "*When he maketh inquisition for blood, he forgetteth not the cry of the humble!*"

## XXXI.
### The Middle Passage

"Thou art of purer eyes than to behold evil, and canst not look upon iniquity: wherefore lookest thou upon them that deal treacherously, and holdest thy tongue when the wicked devoureth the man that is more righteous than he?"—HAB. 1:13.

On the lower part of a small, mean boat, on the Red river, Tom sat,—chains on his wrists, chains on his feet, and a weight heavier than chains lay on his heart. All had faded from his sky,—moon and star; all had passed by him, as the trees and banks were now passing, to return no more. Kentucky home, with wife and children, and indulgent owners; St. Clare home, with all its refinements and splendors; the golden head of Eva, with its saint-like eyes; the proud, gay, handsome, seemingly careless, yet ever-kind St. Clare; hours of ease and indulgent leisure,— all gone! and in place thereof, *what* remains?

It is one of the bitterest apportionments of a lot of slavery, that the negro, sympathetic and assimilative, after acquiring, in a refined family, the tastes and feelings which form the atmosphere of such a place, is not the less liable to become the bond-slave of the coarsest and most brutal,—just as a chair or table, which once decorated the superb saloon, comes, at last, battered and defaced, to the bar-room of some filthy tavern, or some low haunt of vulgar debauchery. The great difference is, that the table and chair cannot feel, and the *man* can; for even a legal enactment that he shall be "taken, reputed, adjudged in law, to be a chattel personal," cannot blot out his soul, with its own private little world of memories, hopes, loves, fears, and desires.

Mr. Simon Legree, Tom's master, had purchased slaves at one place and another, in New Orleans, to the number of eight, and driven them, handcuffed, in couples of two and two, down to the good steamer Pirate, which lay at the levee, ready for a trip up the Red river.

Having got them fairly on board, and the boat being off, he came round, with that air of efficiency which ever characterized him, to take a review of them.

Stopping opposite to Tom, who has been attired for sale in his best broadcloth suit, with well-starched linen and shining boots, he briefly expressed himself as follows:

"Stand up."

Tom stood up.

"Take off that stock!" and, as Tom, encumbered by his fetters, proceeded to do it, he assisted him, by pulling it, with no gentle hand, from his neck, and putting it in his pocket.

Legree now turned to Tom's trunk, which, previous to this, he had been ransacking, and, taking from it a pair of old pantaloons and a dilapidated coat, which Tom had been wont to put on about his stable-work, he said, liberating Tom's hands from the handcuffs, and pointing to a recess in among the boxes.

"You go there, and put these on."

Tom obeyed, and in a few moments returned.

"Take off your boots," said Mr. Legree.

Tom did so.

"There," said the former, throwing him a pair of coarse, stout shoes, such as were common among the slaves, "put these on."

In Tom's hurried exchange, he had not forgotten to transfer his cherished Bible to his pocket. It was well he did so; for Mr. Legree, having refitted Tom's handcuffs, proceeded deliberately to investigate the contents of his pockets. He drew out a silk handkerchief, and put it into his own pocket. Several little trifles, which Tom had treasured, chiefly because they had amused Eva, he looked upon with a contemptuous grunt, and tossed them over his shoulder into the river.

Tom's Methodist hymn-book, which, in his hurry, he had forgotten, he now held up and turned over.

"Humph! pious, to be sure. So, what 's yer name,—you belong to the church, eh?"

"Yes, Mas'r," said Tom, firmly.

"Well, I 'll soon have *that* out of you. I have none o' yer bawling, praying, singing niggers on my place; so remember. Now, mind yourself," he said, with a stamp and a fierce glance of his gray eye, directed at Tom, "*I 'm* your church now! You understand,—you 've got to be as *I* say."

Something within the silent black man answered *No!* and, as if repeated by an invisible voice, came the words of an old prophetic scroll, as Eva had often read them to him,—"Fear not! for I have redeemed thee. I have called thee by my name. Thou art MINE!"

But Simon Legree heard no voice. That voice is one he never shall hear. He only glared for a moment on the down-cast face of Tom, and walked off. He took Tom's trunk, which contained a very neat and abundant wardrobe, to the forecastle, where it was soon surrounded by various hands of the boat. With much laughing, at the expense of niggers who tried to be gentlemen, the articles very readily were sold to one and another, and the empty trunk finally put up at auction. It was a good joke, they all thought, especially to see how Tom looked after his things, as they were going this way and that; and then the auction of the trunk, that was funnier than all, and occasioned abundant witticisms.

This little affair being over, Simon sauntered up again to his property.

"Now, Tom, I 've relieved you of any extra baggage, you see. Take mighty good care of them clothes. It 'll be long enough 'fore you get more. I go in for making niggers careful; one suit has to do for one year, on my place."

Simon next walked up to the place where Emmeline was sitting, chained to another woman.

"Well, my dear," he said, chucking her under the chin, "keep up your spirits."

The involuntary look of horror, fright and aversion, with which the girl regarded him, did not escape his eye. He frowned fiercely.

"None o' your shines, gal! you 's got to keep a pleasant face, when I speak to ye,—d' ye hear? And you, you old yellow poco moonshine!" he said, giving a shove to the mulatto woman to whom Emmeline was chained, "don't you carry that sort of face! You 's got to look chipper, I tell ye!"

"I say, all on ye," he said retreating a pace or two back, "look at me,—look at me,—look me right in the eye,—*straight*, now!" said he, stamping his foot at every pause.

As by a fascination, every eye was now directed to the glaring greenish-gray eye of Simon.

"Now," said he, doubling his great, heavy fist into something resembling a blacksmith's hammer, "d' ye see this fist? Heft it!" he said, bringing it down on Tom's hand. "Look at these yer bones! Well, I tell ye this yer fist has got as hard as iron *knocking down niggers*. I never see the nigger, yet, I could n't bring down with one crack," said he, bringing his fist down so near to the face of Tom that he winked and drew back. "I don't keep none o' yer cussed overseers; I does my own overseeing; and I tell you things *is* seen to. You 's every one on ye got to toe the mark, I tell ye; quick,—straight,—the moment I speak. That 's the way to keep in with me. Ye won't find no soft spot in me, nowhere. So, now, mind yerselves; for I don't show no mercy!"

The women involuntarily drew in their breath, and the whole gang sat with downcast, dejected faces. Meanwhile, Simon turned on his heel, and marched up to the bar of the boat for a dram.

"That 's the way I begin with my niggers," he said, to a gentlemanly man, who had stood by him during his speech. "It 's my system to begin strong,—just let 'em know what to expect."

"Indeed!" said the stranger, looking upon him with the curiosity of a naturalist studying some out-of-the-way specimen.

"Yes, indeed. I 'm none o' yer gentlemen planters, with lily fingers, to slop round and be cheated by some old cuss of an overseer! Just feel of my knuckles, now; look at my fist. Tell ye, sir, the flesh on 't has come jest like a stone, practising on niggers,—feel on it."

The stranger applied his fingers to the implement in question, and simply said,

"'T is hard enough; and, I suppose," he added, "practice has made your heart just like it."

"Why, yes, I may say so," said Simon, with a hearty laugh. "I reckon there 's as little soft in me as in any one going. Tell you, nobody comes it over me! Niggers never gets round me, neither with squalling nor soft soap,—that 's a fact."

"You have a fine lot there."

"Real," said Simon. "There 's that Tom, they told me he was suthin' uncommon. I paid a little high for him, tendin' him for a driver and a managing chap;
only get the notions out that he 's larnt by bein' treated as niggers never ought to
be, he 'll do prime! The yellow woman I got took in. I rayther think she 's sickly,
but I shall put her through for what she 's worth; she may last a year or two. I don't
go for savin' niggers. Use up, and buy more, 's my way;—makes you less trouble,
and I 'm quite sure it comes cheaper in the end;" and Simon sipped his glass.

"And how long to they generally last?" said the stranger.

"Well, donno; 'cordin' as their constitution is. Stout fellers last six or seven
years; trashy ones gets worked up in two or three. I used to, when I fust begun,
have considerable trouble fussin' with 'em and trying to make 'em hold out,—
doctorin' on 'em up when they 's sick, and givin' on 'em clothes and blankets,
and what not, tryin' to keep 'em all sort o' decent and comfortable. Law, 't was n't
no sort o' use; I lost money on 'em, and 't was heaps o' trouble. Now, you see, I
just put 'em straight through, sick or well. When one nigger 's dead, I buy another; and I find it comes cheaper and easier, every way."

The stranger turned away, and seated himself beside a gentleman, who had
been listening to the conversation with repressed uneasiness.

"You must not take that fellow to be any specimen of Southern planters," said
he.

"I should hope not," said the young gentleman, with emphasis.

"He is a mean, low, brutal fellow!" said the other.

"And yet your laws allow him to hold any number of human beings subject
to his absolute will, without even a shadow of protection; and, low as he is, you
cannot say that there are not many such."

"Well," said the other, "there are also many considerate and humane men
among planters."

"Granted," said the young man; "but, in my opinion, it is you considerate,
humane men, that are responsible for all the brutality and outrage wrought by
these wretches; because, if it were not for your sanction and influence, the whole
system could not keep foot-hold for an hour. If there were no planters except such
as that one," said he, pointing with his finger to Legree, who stood with his back
to them, "the whole thing would go down like a mill-stone. It is your respectability and humanity that licenses and protects his brutality."

"You certainly have a high opinion of my good nature," said the planter, smiling; "but I advise you not to talk quite so loud, as there are people on board the
boat who might not be quite so tolerant to opinion as I am. You had better wait
till I get up to my plantation, and there you may abuse us all, quite at your leisure."

The young gentleman colored and smiled, and the two were soon busy in a
game of backgammon. Meanwhile, another conversation was going on in the
lower part of the boat, between Emmeline and the mulatto woman with whom
she was confined. As was natural, they were exchanging with each other some
particulars of their history.

"Who did you belong to?" said Emmeline.

"Well, my Mas'r was Mr. Ellis,—lived on Levee-street. P'raps you 've seen the
house."

"Was he good to you? said Emmeline.

"Mostly, till he tuk sick. He 's lain sick, off and on, more than six months, and been orful oneasy. 'Pears like he warnt willin' to have nobody rest, day nor night; and got so curous, there could n't nobody suit him. 'Pears like he just grow crosser, every day; kep me up nights till I got farly beat out, and could n't keep awake no longer; and cause I got to sleep, one night, Lors, he talk so orful to me, and he tell me he 'd sell me to just the hardest master he could find; and he 'd promised me my freedom, too, when he died."

"Had you any friends?" said Emmeline.

"Yes, my husband,—he 's a blacksmith. Mas'r gen'ly hired him out. They took me off so quick, I did n't even have time to see him; and I 's got four children. O, dear me!" said the woman, covering her face with her hands.

It is a natural impulse, in every one, when they hear a tale of distress, to think of something to say by way of consolation. Emmeline wanted to say something, but she could not think of anything to say. What was there to be said? As by a common consent, they both avoided, with fear and dread, all mention of the horrible man who was now their master.

True, there is religious trust for even the darkest hour. The mulatto woman was a member of the Methodist church, and had an unenlightened but very sincere spirit of piety. Emmeline had been educated much more intelligently,—taught to read and write, and diligently instructed in the Bible, by the care of a faithful and pious mistress; yet, would it not try the faith of the firmest Christian, to find themselves abandoned, apparently, of God, in the grasp of ruthless violence? How much more must it shake the faith of Christ's poor little ones, weak in knowledge and tender in years!

The boat moved on,— freighted with its weight of sorrow,—up the red, muddy, turbid current, through the abrupt, tortuous windings of the Red river; and sad eyes gazed wearily on the steep red-clay banks, as they glided by in dreary sameness. At last the boat stopped at a small town, and Legree, with his party, disembarked.

## XXXII.
### Dark Places

"The dark places of the earth are full of the habitations of cruelty."


Trailing wearily behind a rude wagon, and over a ruder road, Tom and his associates faced onward.

In the wagon was seated Simon Legree; and the two women, still fettered together, were stowed away with some baggage in the back part of it, and the whole company were seeking Legree's plantation, which lay a good distance off.

It was a wild, forsaken road, now winding through dreary pine barrens, where the wind whispered mournfully, and now over log causeways, through long cypress swamps, the doleful trees rising out of the slimy, spongy ground, hung with long wreaths of funereal black moss, while ever and anon the loathsome form of the moccasin snake might be seen sliding among broken stumps and shattered branches that lay here and there, rotting in the water.

It is disconsolate enough, this riding, to the stranger, who, with well-filled pocket and well-appointed horse, threads the lonely way on some errand of business; but wilder, drearier, to the man enthralled, whom every weary step bears further from all that man loves and prays for.

So one should have thought, that witnessed the sunken and dejected expression on those dark faces; the wistful, patient weariness with which those sad eyes rested on object after object that passed them in their sad journey.

Simon rode on, however, apparently well pleased, occasionally pulling away at a flask of spirit, which he kept in his pocket.

"I say, *you!*" he said, as he turned back and caught a glance at the dispirited faces behind him! "Strike up a song, boys,—come!"

The men looked at each other, and the *"come"* was repeated, with a smart crack of the whip which the driver carried in his hands. Tom began a Methodist hymn,

> "Jerusalem, my happy home!
>    Name ever dear to me!
> When shall my sorrows have an end,
>    Thy joys when shall—"

"Shut up, you black cuss!" roared Legree; "did ye think I wanted any o' yer infernal old Methodism? I say, tune up, now, something real rowdy,—quick!"

One of the other men struck up one of those unmeaning songs, common among the slaves.

> "Mas'r see'd me cotch a coon,
>    High boys, high!
> He laughed to split,—d' ye see the moon,
>    Ho! ho! ho! boys, ho!
> Ho! yo! hi—e! oh!"

The singer appeared to make up the song to his own pleasure, generally hitting on rhyme, without much attempt at reason; and all the party took up the chorus, at intervals,

> "Ho! ho! ho! boys, ho!
> High—e—oh! high—e—oh!"

It was sung very boisterously, and with a forced attempt at merriment; but no wail of despair, no words of impassioned prayer, could have had such a depth of woe in them as the wild notes of the chorus. As if the poor, dumb heart, threatened,—prisoned,—took refuge in that inarticulate sanctuary of music, and found there a language in which to breathe its prayer to God! There was a prayer in it, which Simon could not hear. He only heard the boys singing noisily, and was well pleased; he was making them "keep up their spirits."

"Well, my little dear," said he, turning to Emmeline, and laying his hand on her shoulder, "we 're almost home!"

When Legree scolded and stormed, Emmeline was terrified; but when he laid his hand on her, and spoke as he now did, she felt as if she had rather he would strike her. The expression of his eyes made her soul sick, and her flesh creep. Involuntarily she clung closer to the mulatto woman by her side, as if she were her mother.

"You did n't ever wear ear-rings," he said, taking hold of her small ear with his coarse fingers.

"No, Mas'r!" said Emmeline, trembling and looking down.

"Well, I 'll give you a pair, when we get home, if you 're a good girl. You need n't be so frightened; I don't mean to make you work very hard. You 'll have fine times with me, and live like a lady,—only be a good girl."

Legree had been drinking to that degree that he was inclining to be very gracious; and it was about this time that the enclosures of the plantation rose to view. The estate had formerly belonged to a gentleman of opulence and taste, who had bestowed some considerable attention to the adornment of his grounds. Having died insolvent, it had been purchased, at a bargain, by Legree, who used it, as he did everything else, merely as an implement for money-making. The place had that ragged, forlorn appearance, which is always produced by the evidence that the care of the former owner has been left to go to utter decay.

What was once a smooth-shaven lawn before the house, dotted here and there with ornamental shrubs, was now covered with frowsy tangled grass, with horse-posts set up, here and there, in it, where the turf was stamped away, and the ground littered with broken pails, cobs of corn, and other slovenly remains. Here and there, a mildewed jessamine or honeysuckle hung raggedly from some ornamental support, which had been pushed to one side by being used as a horse-post. What once was a large garden was now all grown over with weeds, through which, here and there, some solitary exotic reared its forsaken head. What had been a conservatory had now no window-sashes, and on the mouldering shelves stood some dry, forsaken flower-pots, with sticks in them, whose dried leaves showed they had once been plants.

The wagon rolled up a weedy gravel walk, under a noble avenue of China trees, whose graceful forms and ever-springing foliage seemed to be the only things there that neglect could not daunt or alter,—like noble spirits, so deeply rooted in goodness, as to flourish and grow stronger amid discouragement and decay.

The house had been large and handsome. It was built in a manner common at the South; a wide verandah of two stories running round every part of the house, into which every outer door opened, the lower tier being supported by brick pillars.

But the place looked desolate and uncomfortable; some windows stopped up with boards, some with shattered panes, and shutters hanging by a single hinge,— all telling of coarse neglect and discomfort.

Bits of board, straw, old decayed barrels and boxes, garnished the ground in all directions; and three or four ferocious-looking dogs, roused by the sound of the wagon-wheels, came tearing out, and were with difficulty restrained from laying hold of Tom and his companions, by the effort of the ragged servants who came after them.

"Ye see what ye 'd get!" said Legree, caressing the dogs with grim satisfaction, and turning to Tom and his companions. "Ye see what ye 'd get, if ye try to run off. These yer dogs has been raised to track niggers; and they 'd jest as soon chaw one on ye up as eat their supper. So, mind yerself! How now, Sambo!" he said, to a ragged fellow, without any brim to his hat, who was officious in his attentions. "How have things been going?"

"Fust rate, Mas'r."

"Quimbo," said Legree to another, who was making zealous demonstrations to attract his attention, "ye minded what I telled ye?"

"Guess I did, did n't I?"

These two colored men were the two principal hands on the plantation. Legree had trained them in savageness and brutality as systematically as he had his bull-dogs; and, by long practice in hardness and cruelty, brought their whole nature to about the same range of capacities. It is a common remark, and one that is thought to militate strongly against the character of the race, that the negro overseer is always more tyrannical and cruel than the white one. This is simply saying that the negro mind has been more crushed and debased than the white. It is no more true of this race than of every oppressed race, the world over. The slave is always a tyrant, if he can get a chance to be one.

Legree, like some potentates we read of in history, governed his plantation by a sort of resolution of forces. Sambo and Quimbo cordially hated each other; the plantation hands, one and all, cordially hated them; and, by playing off one against another, he was pretty sure, through one or the other of the three parties, to get informed of whatever was on foot in the place.

Nobody can live entirely without social intercourse; and Legree encouraged his two black satellites to a kind of coarse familiarity with him,—a familiarity, however, at any moment liable to get one or the other of them into trouble; for, on the slightest provocation, one of them always stood ready, at a nod, to be a minister of his vengeance on the other.

As they stood there now by Legree, they seemed an apt illustration of the fact that brutal men are lower even than animals. Their coarse, dark, heavy features; their great eyes, rolling enviously on each other; their barbarous, guttural, half-brute intonation; their dilapidated garments fluttering in the wind,—were all in admirable keeping with the vile and unwholesome character of everything about the place.

"Here, you Sambo," said Legree, "take these yer boys down to the quarters; and here 's a gal I 've got for *you*," said he, as he separated the mulatto woman from Emmeline, and pushed her towards him;—"I promised to bring you one, you know."

The woman gave a sudden start, and, drawing back, said, suddenly,

"O, Mas'r! I left my old man in New Orleans."

"What of that, you———; won't you want one here? None o' your words,— go long!" said Legree, raising his whip.

"Come, mistress," he said to Emmeline, "you go in here with me."

A dark, wild face was seen, for a moment, to glance at the window of the house; and, as Legree opened the door, a female voice said something, in a quick, imperative tone. Tom, who was looking, with anxious interest, after Emmeline, as she went in, noticed this, and heard Legree answer, angrily, "You may hold your tongue! I 'll do as I please, for all you!"

Tom heard no more; for he was soon following Sambo to the quarters. The quarters was a little sort of street of rude shanties, in a row, in a part of the plantation, far off from the house. They had a forlorn, brutal, forsaken air. Tom's heart sunk when he saw them. He had been comforting himself with the thought of a cottage, rude, indeed, but one which he might make neat and quiet, and where he might have a shelf for his Bible, and a place to be alone out of his laboring hours. He looked into several; they were mere rude shells, destitute of any species of furniture, except a heap of straw, foul with dirt, spread confusedly over the floor, which was merely the bare ground, trodden hard by the tramping of innumerable feet.

"Which of these will be mine?" said he, to Sambo, submissively.

"Dunno; ken turn in here, I spose," said Sambo; "spects thar's room for another thar; thar's a pretty smart heap o' niggers to each on 'em, now; sure, I dunno what I 's to do with more."

---

It was late in the evening when the weary occupants of the shanties came flocking home,—men and women, in soiled and tattered garments, surly and uncomfortable, and in no mood to look pleasantly on new-comers. The small village was alive with no inviting sounds; hoarse, guttural voices contending at the hand-mills where their morsel of hard corn was yet to be ground into meal, to fit it for the cake that was to constitute their only supper. From the earliest dawn of the day, they had been in the fields, pressed to work under the driving lash of the overseers; for it was now in the very heat and hurry of the season, and no means was left untried to press every one up to the top of their capabilities. "True," says the negligent lounger; "picking cotton is n't hard work." Is n't it? And it is n't much inconvenience, either, to have one drop of water fall on your head; yet the worst torture of the inquisition is produced by drop after drop, drop after drop, falling moment after moment, with monotonous succession, on the same spot; and work, in itself not hard, becomes so, by being pressed, hour after hour, with unvarying, unrelenting sameness, with not even the consciousness of free-will to take from its tediousness. Tom looked in vain among the gang, as they poured along, for companionable faces. He saw only sullen, scowling, imbruted men, and feeble, discouraged women, or women that were not women,—the strong pushing away the weak,—the gross, unrestricted animal selfishness of human beings, of whom nothing good was expected and desired; and who, treated in every way like brutes, had sunk as nearly to their level as it was possible for human beings to do. To a late hour in the night the sound of the grinding was protracted; for the mills were few in number compared with the grinders, and the weary and feeble ones were driven back by the strong, and came on last in their turn.

"Ho yo!" said Sambo, coming to the mulatto woman, and throwing down a bag of corn before her; "what a cuss yo name?"

"Lucy," said the woman.

"Wal, Lucy, yo my woman now. Yo grind dis yer corn, and get *my* supper baked, ye har?"

"I an't your woman, and I won't be!" said the woman, with the sharp, sudden courage of despair; "you go long!"

"I 'll kick yo, then!" said Sambo, raising his foot threateningly.

"Ye may kill me, if ye choose,—the sooner the better! Wish't I was dead!" said she.

"I say, Sambo, you go to spilin' the hands, I 'll tell Mas'r o' you," said Quimbo, who was busy at the mill, from which he had viciously driven two or three tired women, who were waiting to grind corn.

"And I 'll tell him ye won't let the women come to the mills, yo old nigger!" said Sambo. "Yo jes keep to yo own row."

Tom was hungry with his day's journey, and almost faint for want of food.

"Thar, yo!" said Quimbo, throwing down a coarse bag, which contained a peck of corn; "thar, nigger, grab, take car on 't,—yo won't get no more, *dis* yer week."

Tom waited till a late hour, to get a place at the mills; and then, moved by the utter weariness of two women, whom he saw trying to grind their corn there, he ground for them, put together the decaying brands of the fire, where many had baked cakes before them, and then went about getting his own supper. It was a new kind of work there,—a deed of charity, small as it was; but it woke an answering touch in their hearts,—an expression of womanly kindness came over their hard faces; they mixed his cake for him, and tended its baking; and Tom sat down by the light of the fire, and drew out his Bible,—for he had need of comfort.

"What 's that?" said one of the women.

"A Bible," said Tom.

"Good Lord! han't seen un since I was in Kentuck."

"Was you raised in Kentuck?" said Tom, with interest.

"Yes, and well raised, too; never 'spected to come to dis yer!" said the woman, sighing.

"What 's dat ar book, any way?" said the other woman.

"Why, the Bible."

"Laws a me! what 's dat?" said the woman.

"Do tell! you never hearn on 't?" said the other woman, "I used to har Missis a readin' on 't, sometimes, in Kentuck; but, laws o' me! we don't har nothin' here but crackin' and swarin'."

"Read a piece, anyways!" said the first woman, curiously, seeing Tom attentively poring over it.

Tom read,—"Come unto ME, all ye that labor and are heavy laden, and I will give you rest."

"Them 's good words, enough," said the woman; "who says 'em?"

"The Lord," said Tom.

"I jest wish I know'd whar to find Him," said the woman. "I would go; 'pears like I never should get rested agin. My flesh is fairly sore, and I tremble all over, every day, and Sambo 's allers a jawin' at me, 'cause I does n't pick faster; and nights it 's most midnight 'fore I can get my supper; and den 'pears like I don't turn over and shut my eyes, 'fore I hear de horn blow to get up, and at it agin in de mornin'. If I know whar de Lor was, I 'd tell him."

"He 's here, he 's everywhere," said Tom.

"Lor, you an't gwine to make me believe dat ar! I know de Lord an't here," said the woman; "'t an't no use talking, though. I 's jest gwine to camp down, and sleep while I ken."

The women went off to their cabins, and Tom sat alone, by the smouldering fire, that flickered up redly in his face.

The silver, fair-browed moon rose in the purple sky, and looked down, calm and silent, as God looks on the scene of misery and oppression,—looked calmly on the lone black man, as he sat, with his arms folded, and his Bible on his knee.

"Is God HERE?" Ah, how is it possible for the untaught heart to keep its faith, unswerving, in the face of dire misrule, and palpable, unrebuked injustice? In that simple heart waged a fierce conflict: the crushing sense of wrong, the foreshadowing of a whole life of future misery, the wreck of all past hopes, mournfully tossing in the soul's sight, like dead corpses of wife, and child, and friend, rising from the dark wave, and surging in the face of the half-drowned mariner! Ah, was it easy *here* to believe and hold fast the great password of Christian faith, that "God IS, and is the REWARDER of them that diligently seek Him"?

Tom rose, disconsolate, and stumbled into the cabin that had been allotted to him. The floor was already strewn with weary sleepers, and the foul air of the place almost repelled him; but the heavy night-dews were chill, and his limbs weary, and, wrapping about him a tattered blanket, which formed his only bed-clothing, he stretched himself in the straw and fell asleep.

In dreams, a gentle voice came over his ear; he was sitting on the mossy seat in the garden by Lake Pontchartrain, and Eva, with her serious eyes bent downward, was reading to him from the Bible; and he heard her read,

"When thou passest through the waters, I will be with thee, and the rivers they shall not overflow thee; when thou walkest through the fire, thou shalt not be burned, neither shall the flame kindle upon thee; for I am the Lord thy God, the Holy One of Israel, thy Saviour."

Gradually the words seemed to melt and fade, as in a divine music; the child raised her deep eyes, and fixed them lovingly on him, and rays of warmth and comfort seemed to go from them to his heart; and, as if wafted on the music, she seemed to rise on shining wings, from which flakes and spangles of gold fell off like stars, and she was gone.

Tom woke. Was it a dream? Let it pass for one. But who shall say that that sweet young spirit, which in life so yearned to comfort and console the distressed, was forbidden of God to assume this ministry after death?

It is a beautiful belief,
That ever round our head

Are hovering, on angel wings,
The spirits of the dead.

## XXXIII.
### *Cassy*

"And behold, the tears of such as were oppressed, and they had no comforter; and on the side of their oppressors there was *power*, but they had no comforter."

—*Eccl. 4:1.*

It took but a short time to familiarize Tom with all that was to be hoped or feared in his new way of life. He was an expert and efficient workman in whatever he undertook; and was, both from habit and principle, prompt and faithful. Quiet and peaceable in his disposition, he hoped, by unremitting diligence, to avert from himself at least a portion of the evils of his condition. He saw enough of abuse and misery to make him sick and weary; but he determined to toil on, with religious patience, committing himself to Him that judgeth righteously, not without hope that some way of escape might yet be opened to him.

Legree took silent note of Tom's availability. He rated him as a first-class hand; and yet he felt a secret dislike to him,—the native antipathy of bad to good. He saw, plainly, that when, as was often the case, his violence and brutality fell on the helpless, Tom took notice of it; for, so subtle is the atmosphere of opinion, that it will make itself felt, without words; and the opinion even of a slave may annoy a master. Tom in various ways manifested a tenderness of feeling, a commiseration for his fellow-sufferers, strange and new to them, which was watched with a jealous eye by Legree. He had purchased Tom with a view of eventually making him a sort of overseer, with whom he might, at times, intrust his affairs, in short absences; and, in his view, the first, second, and third requisite for that place, was *hardness*. Legree made up his mind, that, as Tom was not hard to his hand, he would harden him forthwith; and some few weeks after Tom had been on the place, he determined to commence the process.

One morning, when the hands were mustered for the field, Tom noticed, with surprise, a new comer among them, whose appearance excited his attention. It was a woman, tall and slenderly formed, with remarkably delicate hands and feet, and dressed in neat and respectable garments. By the appearance of her face, she might have been between thirty-five and forty; and it was a face that, once seen, could never be forgotten,—one of those that, at a glance, seem to convey to us an idea of a wild, painful, and romantic history. Her forehead was high, and her eyebrows marked with beautiful clearness. Her straight, well-formed nose, her finely-cut mouth, and the graceful contour of her head and neck, showed that she must once have been beautiful; but her face was deeply wrinkled with lines of pain, and of proud and bitter endurance. Her complexion was sallow and unhealthy, her cheeks thin, her features sharp, and her whole form emaciated. But her eye was the most remarkable feature,—so large, so heavily black, overshadowed by long lashes of equal darkness, and so wildly, mournfully despairing. There was a fierce pride and defiance in every line of her face, in every curve of the flexible lip, in every motion of her body; but in her eye was a deep, settled night of anguish,—an expression so hopeless and unchanging as to contrast fearfully with the scorn and pride expressed by her whole demeanor.

Where she came from, or who she was, Tom did not know. The first he did know, she was walking by his side, erect and proud, in the dim gray of the dawn. To the gang, however, she was known; for there was much looking and turning of heads, and a smothered yet apparent exultation among the miserable, ragged, half-starved creatures by whom she was surrounded.

"Got to come to it, at last,—glad of it!" said one.

"He! he! he!" said another; "you 'll know how good it is, Misse!"

"We 'll see her work!"

"Wonder if she 'll get a cutting up, at night, like the rest of us!"

"I 'd be glad to see her down for a flogging, I 'll bound!" said another.

The woman took no notice of these taunts, but walked on, with the same expression of angry scorn, as if she heard nothing. Tom had always lived among refined and cultivated people, and he felt intuitively, from her air and bearing, that she belonged to that class; but how or why she could be fallen to those degrading circumstances, he could not tell. The woman neither looked at him nor spoke to him, though, all the way to the field, she kept close at his side.

Tom was soon busy at his work; but, as the woman was at no great distance from him, he often glanced an eye to her, at her work. He saw, at a glance, that a native adroitness and handiness made the task to her an easier one than it proved to many. She picked very fast and very clean, and with an air of scorn, as if she despised both the work and the disgrace and humiliation of the circumstances in which she was placed.

In the course of the day, Tom was working near the mulatto woman who had been bought in the same lot with himself. She was evidently in a condition of great suffering, and Tom often heard her praying, as she wavered and trembled, and seemed about to fall down. Tom silently, as he came near to her, transferred several handfuls of cotton from his own sack to hers.

"O, don't, don't!" said the woman, looking surprised; "it 'll get you into trouble."

Just then Sambo came up. He seemed to have a special spite against this woman; and, flourishing his whip, said, in brutal, guttural tones, "What dis yer, Luce,—foolin' a'?" and, with the word, kicking the woman with his heavy cowhide shoe, he struck Tom across the face with his whip.

Tom silently resumed his task; but the woman, before at the last point of exhaustion, fainted.

"I 'll bring her to!" said the driver, with a brutal grin. "I 'll give her something better than camphire!" and, taking a pin from his coat-sleeve, he buried it to the head in her flesh. The woman groaned, and half rose. "Get up, you beast, and work, will yer, or I 'll show yer a trick more!"

The woman seemed stimulated, for a few moments, to an unnatural strength, and worked with desperate eagerness.

"See that you keep to dat ar," said the man, "or yer 'll wish yer 's dead to-night, I reckin!"

"That I do now!" Tom heard her say; and again he heard her say, "O, Lord, how long! O, Lord, why don't you help us?"

At the risk of all that he might suffer, Tom came forward again, and put all the cotton in his sack into the woman's.

"O, you must n't! you donno what they 'll do to ye!" said the woman.

"I can bar it!" said Tom, "better 'n you;" and he was at his place again. It passed in a moment.

Suddenly, the stranger woman whom we have described, and who had, in the course of her work, come near enough to hear Tom's last words, raised her heavy black eyes, and fixed them, for a second, on him; then, taking a quantity of cotton from her basket, she placed it in his.

"You know nothing about this place," she said, "or you would n't have done that. When you 've been here a month, you 'll be done helping anybody; you 'll find it hard enough to take care of your own skin!"

"The Lord forbid, Missis!" said Tom, using instinctively to his field companion the respecful form proper to the high bred with whom he had lived.

"The Lord never visits these parts," said the woman, bitterly, as she went nimbly forward with her work; and again the scornful smile curled her lips.

But the action of the woman had been seen by the driver, across the field; and, flourishing his whip, he came up to her.

"What! what!" he said to the woman, with an air of triumph, "YOU a foolin'? Go along! yer under me now,—mind yourself, or yer 'll cotch it!"

A glance like sheet-lightning suddenly flashed from those black eyes; and, facing about, with quivering lip and dilated nostrils, she drew herself up, and fixed a glance, blazing with rage and scorn, on the driver.

"Dog!" she said, "touch *me*, if you dare! I 've power enough, yet, to have you torn by the dogs, burnt alive, cut to inches! I 've only to say the word!"

"What de devil you here for, den?" said the man, evidently cowed, and sullenly retreating a step or two. "Did n't mean no harm, Misse Cassy!"

"Keep your distance, then!" said the woman. And, in truth, the man seemed greatly inclined to attend to something at the other end of the field, and started off in quick time.

The woman suddenly turned to her work, and labored with a despatch that was perfectly astonishing to Tom. She seemed to work by magic. Before the day was through, her basket was filled, crowded down, and piled, and she had several times put largely into Tom's. Long after dusk, the whole weary train, with their baskets on their heads, defiled up to the building appropriated to the storing and weighing the cotton. Legree was there, busily conversing with the two drivers.

"Dat ar Tom 's gwine to make a powerful deal o' trouble; kept a puttin' into Lucy's basket.—One o' these yer dat will get all der niggers to feelin' 'bused, if Mas'r don't watch him!" said Sambo.

"Hey-dey! The black cuss!" said Legree. "He 'll have to get a breakin' in, won't he, boys?"

Both negroes grinned a horrid grin, at this intimation.

"Ay, ay! let Mas'r Legree alone, for breakin' in! De debil heself could n't beat Mas'r at dat!" said Quimbo.

"Wal, boys, the best way is to give him the flogging to do, till he gets over his notions. Break him in!"

"Lord, Mas'r 'll have hard work to get dat out o' him!"

"It 'll have to come out of him, though!" said Legree, as he rolled his tobacco in his mouth.

"Now, dar 's Lucy,—de aggravatinest, ugliest wench on de place!" pursued Sambo.

"Take care, Sam; I shall begin to think what 's the reason for your spite agin Lucy."

"Well, Mas'r knows she sot herself up agin Mas 'r, and would n't have me, when he telled her to."

"I 'd a flogged her into 't," said Legree, spitting, "only there 's such a press o' work, it don't seem wuth a while to upset her jist now. She 's slender; but these yer slender gals will bear half killin' to get their own way!"

"Wal, Lucy was real aggravatin' and lazy, sulkin' round; would n't do nothin',—and Tom he tuck up for her."

"He did, eh! Wal, then, Tom shall have the pleasure of flogging her. It 'll be a good practice for him, and he won't put it on to the gal like you devils, neither."

"Ho, ho! haw! haw! haw!" laughed both the sooty wretches; and the diabolical sounds seemed, in truth, a not unapt expression of the fiendish character which Legree gave them.

"Wal, but, Mas'r, Tom and Misse Cassy, and dey among 'em, filled Lucy's basket. I ruther guess der weight 's in it, Mas'r!"

"*I do the weighing!*" said Legree, emphatically.

Both the drivers again laughed their diabolical laugh.

"So!" he added, "Misse Cassy did her day's work."

"She picks like de debil and all his angels!"

"She 's got 'em all in her, I believe!" said Legree; and, growling a brutal oath, he proceeded to the weighing-room.

----

Slowly the weary, dispirited creatures, wound their way into the room, and, with crouching reluctance, presented their baskets to be weighed.

Legree noted on a slate, on the side of which was pasted a list of names, the amount.

Tom's basket was weighed and approved; and he looked, with an anxious glance, for the success of the woman he had befriended.

Tottering with weakness, she came forward, and delivered her basket. It was of full weight, as Legree well perceived; but, affecting anger, he said,

"What, you lazy beast! short again! stand aside, you 'll catch it, pretty soon!"

The woman gave a groan of utter despair, and sat down on a board.

The person who had been called Misse Cassy now came forward, and, with a haughty, negligent air, delivered her basket. As she delivered it, Legree looked in her eyes with a sneering yet inquiring glance.

She fixed her black eyes steadily on him, her lips moved slightly, and she said something in French. What it was, no one knew; but Legree's face became perfectly demoniacal in its expression, as she spoke; he half raised his hand, as if to strike,—a gesture which she regarded with fierce disdain, as she turned and walked away.

"And now," said Legree, "come here, you Tom. You see, I telled ye I did n't buy ye jest for the common work; I mean to promote ye, and make a driver of ye; and to-night ye may jest as well begin to get yer hand in. Now, ye jest take this yer gal and flog her; ye 've seen enough on 't to know how."

"I beg Mas'r's pardon," said Tom; "hopes Mas'r won't set me at that. It 's what I an't used to,—never did,—and can't do, no way possible."

"Ye 'll larn a pretty smart chance of things ye never did know, before I 've done with ye!" said Legree, taking up a cow-hide, and striking Tom a heavy blow across the cheek, and following up the infliction by a shower of blows.

"There!" he said, as he stopped to rest; "now, will ye tell me ye can't do it?"

"Yes, Mas'r," said Tom, putting up his hand, to wipe the blood, that trickled down his face. "I 'm willin' to work, night and day, and work while there 's life and breath in me; but this yer thing I can't feel it right to do;—and, Mas'r, I *never* shall do it,—*never!*"

Tom had a remarkably smooth, soft voice, and a habitually respectful manner, that had given Legree an idea that he would be cowardly, and easily subdued. When he spoke these last words, a thrill of amazement went through every one; the poor woman clasped her hands, and said, "O Lord!" and every one involuntarily looked at each other and drew in their breath, as if to prepare for the storm that was about to burst.

Legree looked stupefied and confounded; but at last burst forth,—

"What! ye blasted black beast! tell *me* ye don't think it *right* to do what I tell ye! What have any of you cussed cattle to do with thinking what 's right? I 'll put a stop to it! Why, what do ye think ye are? May be ye think ye 'r a gentleman master, Tom, to be a telling your master what 's right, and what an't! So you pretend it 's wrong to flog the gal!"

"I think so, Mas'r," said Tom; "the poor crittur 's sick and feeble; 't would be downright cruel, and it 's what I never will do, nor begin to. Mas'r, if you mean to kill me, kill me; but, as to my raising my hand agin any one here, I never shall,— I 'll die first!"

Tom spoke in a mild voice, but with a decision that could not be mistaken. Legree shook with anger; his greenish eyes glared fiercely, and his very whiskers seemed to curl with passion; but, like some ferocious beast, that plays with its victim before he devours it, he kept back his strong impulse to proceed to immediate violence, and broke out into bitter raillery.

"Well, here 's a pious dog, at last, let down among us sinners!—a saint, a gentleman, and no less, to talk to us sinners about our sins! Powerful holy critter, he must be! Here, you rascal, you make believe to be so pious,—did n't you never hear, out of yer Bible, 'Servants, obey yer masters'? An't I yer master? Did n't I pay down twelve hundred dollars, cash, for all there is inside yer old cussed black shell? An't yer mine, now, body and soul?" he said, giving Tom a violent kick with his heavy boot; "tell me!"

In the very depth of physical suffering, bowed by brutal oppression, this question shot a gleam of joy and triumph through Tom's soul. He suddenly stretched himself up, and, looking earnestly to heaven, while the tears and blood that flowed down his face mingled, he exclaimed,

"No! no! no! my soul an't yours, Mas'r! You have n't bought it,—ye can't buy it! It 's been bought and paid for, by one that is able to keep it;—no matter, no matter, you can't harm me!"

"I can't!" said Legree, with a sneer; "we 'll see,—we 'll see! Here, Sambo, Quimbo, give this dog such a breakin' in as he won't get over, this month!"

The two gigantic negroes that now laid hold of Tom, with fiendish exultation in their faces, might have formed no unapt personification of powers of darkness. The poor woman screamed with apprehension, and all rose, as by a general impulse, while they dragged him unresisting from the place.

## XXXIV.
## The Quadroon's Story

And behold the tears of such as are oppressed; and on the side of their oppressors there was power. Wherefore I parised the dead that are already dead more than the living that are yet alive.

—*Eccl. 4:1.*

It was late at night, and Tom lay groaning and bleeding alone, in an old forsaken room of the gin-house, among pieces of broken machinery, piles of damaged cotton, and other rubbish which had there accumulated.

The night was damp and close, and the thick air swarmed with myriads of mosquitos, which increased the restless torture of his wounds; whilst a burning thirst—a torture beyond all others—filled up the uttermost measure of physical anquish.

"O, good Lord! *Do* look down,—give me the victory!—give me the victory over all!" prayed poor Tom, in his anguish.

A footstep entered the room, behind him, and the light of a lantern flashed on his eyes.

"Who 's there? O, for the Lord's massy, please give me some water!"

The woman Cassy—for it was she—set down her lantern, and, pouring water from a bottle, raised his head, and gave him drink. Another and another cup were drained, with feverish eagerness.

"Drink all ye want," she said; "I knew how it would be. It is n't the first time I 've been out in the night, carrying water to such as you."

"Thank you, Missis," said Tom, when he had done drinking.

"Don't call me Missis! I 'm a miserable slave, like yourself,—a lower one than you can ever be!" said she, bitterly; "but now," said she, going to the door, and dragging in a small pallaise, over which she had spread linen cloths wet with cold water, "try, my poor fellow, to roll yourself on to this."

Stiff with wounds and bruises, Tom was a long time in accomplishing this movement; but, when done, he felt a sensible relief from the cooling application to his wounds.

The woman, whom long practice with the victims of brutality had made familiar with many healing arts, went on to make many applications to Tom's wounds, by means of which he was soon somewhat relieved.

"Now," said the woman, when she had raised his head on a roll of damaged cotton, which served for a pillow, "there 's the best I can do for you."

Tom thanked her; and the woman, sitting down on the floor, drew up her knees, and embracing them with her arms, looked fixedly before her, with a bitter and painful expression of countenance. Her bonnet fell back, and long wavy streams of black hair fell around her singular and melancholy face.

"It 's no use, my poor fellow!" she broke out, at last, "it 's of no use, this you 've been trying to do. You were a brave fellow,—you had the right on your side; but it 's all in vain, and out of the question, for you to struggle. You are in the devil's hands;—he is the strongest, and you must give up!"

Give up! and, had not human weakness and physical agony whispered that, before? Tom started; for the bitter woman, with her wild eyes and melancholy voice, seemed to him an embodiment of the temptation with which he had been wrestling.

"O Lord! O Lord!" he groaned, "how can I give up?"

"There 's no use calling on the Lord,—he never hears," said the woman, steadily; "there is n't any God, I believe; or, if there is, he 's taken sides against us. All goes against us, heaven and earth. Everything is pushing us into hell. Why should n't we go?"

Tom closed his eyes, and shuddered at the dark, atheistic words.

"You see," said the woman, "*you* don't know anything about it;—I do. I 've been on this place five years, body and soul, under this man's foot; and I hate him as I do the devil! Here you are, on a lone plantation, ten miles from any other, in the swamps; not a white person here, who could testify, if you were burned alive,—if you were scalded, cut into inch-pieces, set up for the dogs to tear, or hung up and whipped to death. There 's no law here, of God or man, that can do you, or any one of us, the least good; and, this man! there 's no earthly thing that he 's too good to do. I could make any one's hair rise, and their teeth chatter, if I should only tell what I 've seen and been knowing to, here,—and it 's no use resisting! Did I *want* to live with him? Was n't I a woman delicately bred; and he— God in heaven! what was he, and is he? And yet, I 've lived with him these five years, and cursed every moment of my life,—night and day! And now, he 's got a new one,—a young thing, only fifteen, and she brought up, she says, piously. Her good mistress taught her to read the Bible; and she 's brought her Bible here— to hell with her!"—and the woman laughed a wild and doleful laugh, that rung, with a strange, supernatural sound, through the old ruined shed.

Tom folded his hands; all was darkness and horror.

"O Jesus! Lord Jesus! have you quite forgot us poor critturs?" burst forth, at last;—"help, Lord, I perish!"

The woman sternly continued:

"And what are these miserable low dogs you work with, that you should suffer on their account? Every one of them would turn against you, the first time they got a chance. They are all of 'em as low and cruel to each other as they can be; there 's no use in your suffering to keep from hurting them."

"Poor critturs!" said Tom,—"what made 'em cruel?—and, if I give out, I shall get used to 't, and grow, little by little, just like 'em! No, no, Missis! I 've lost everything,—wife, and children, and home, and a kind Mas'r,—and he would have set me free, if he 'd only lived a week longer; I 've lost everything in *this* world, and it 's clean gone, forever,—and now I *can't* lose Heaven, too; no, I can't get to be wicked, besides all!"

"But it can't be that the Lord will lay sin to our account," said the woman; "he won't charge it to us, when we 're forced to it; he 'll charge it to them that drove us to it."

"Yes," said Tom; "but that won't keep us from growing wicked. If I get to be as hard-hearted as that ar' Sambo, and as wicked, it won't make much odds to me how I come so; it 's the *bein' so*,—that ar's what I 'm a dreadin'."

The woman fixed a wild and startled look on Tom, as if a new thought had struck her; and then heavily groaning, said,

"O God a' mercy! you speak the truth! O—O—O!"—and, with groans, she fell on the floor, like one crushed and writhing under the extremity of mental anguish.

There was a silence, a while, in which the breathing of both parties could be heard, when Tom faintly said, "O, please, Missis!"

The woman suddenly rose up, with her face composed to its usual stern, melancholy expression.

"Please, Missis, I saw 'em throw my coat in that ar' corner, and in my coat-pocket is my Bible;—if Missis would please get it for me."

Cassy went and got it. Tom opened, at once, to a heavily marked passage, much worn, of the last scenes in the life of Him by whose stripes we are healed.

"If Missis would only be so good as read that ar',—it 's better than water."

Cassy took the book, with a dry, proud air, and looked over the passage. She then read aloud, in a soft voice, and with a beauty of intonation that was peculiar, that touching account of anguish and of glory. Often, as she read, her voice faltered, and sometimes failed her altogether, when she would stop, with an air of frigid composure, till she had mastered herself. When she came to the touching words, "Father forgive them, for they know not what they do," she threw down the book, and, burying her face in the heavy masses of her hair, she sobbed aloud, with a convulsive violence.

Tom was weeping, also, and occasionally uttering a smothered ejaculation.

"If we only could keep up to that ar'!" said Tom;—"it seemed to come so natural to him, and we have to fight so hard for 't! O Lord, help us! O blessed Lord Jesus, do help us!"

"Missis," said Tom, after a while, "I can see that, some how, you 're quite 'bove me in everything; but there 's one thing Missis might learn even from poor Tom. Ye said the Lord took sides against us, because he lets us be 'bused and knocked round; but ye see what come on his own Son,—the blessed Lord of Glory,—wan't he allays poor? and have we, any on us, yet come so low as he come? The Lord han't forgot us,—I 'm sartin' o' that ar'. If we suffer with him, we shall also reign, Scripture says; but, if we deny Him, he also will deny us. Did n't they all suffer?—the Lord and all his? It tells how they was stoned and sawn asunder, and wandered about in sheep-skins and goat-skins and was destitute, afflicted, tormented. Sufferin' an't no reason to make us think the Lord 's turned agin us; but jest the contrary, if only we hold on to him, and does n't give up to sin."

"But why does he put us where we can't help but sin?" said the woman.

"I think we *can* help it," said Tom.

"You 'll see," said Cassy; "what 'll you do? To-morrow they 'll be at you again. I know 'em; I 've seen all their doings; I can't bear to think of all they 'll bring you to;—and they 'll make you give out, at last!"

"Lord Jesus!" said Tom, "you *will* take care of my soul? O Lord, do!—don't let me give out!"

"O dear!" said Cassy; "I 've heard all this crying and praying before; and yet, they 've been broken down, and brought under. There 's Emmeline, she 's trying to hold on, and you 're trying,—but what use? You must give up, or be killed by inches."

"Well, then, I *will* die!" said Tom. "Spin it out as long as they can, they can't help my dying, some time!—and, after that, they can't do no more. I 'm clar, I 'm set! I *know* the Lord 'll help me, and bring me through."

The woman did not answer; she sat with her black eyes intently fixed on the floor.

"May be it 's the way," she murmured to herself; "but those that *have* given up, there 's no hope for them!—none! We live in filth, and grow loathsome, till we loath ourselves! And we long to die, and we don't dare to kill ourselves!— No hope! no hope! no hope!—this girl now,—just as old as I was!

"You see me now," she said, speaking to Tom very rapidly; "see what I am! Well, I was brought up in luxury; the first I remember is, playing about, when I was a child, in splendid parlors;—when I was kept dressed up like a doll, and company and visiters used to praise me. There was a garden opening from the saloon windows; and there I used to play hide-and-go-seek, under the orange-trees, with my brothers and sisters. I went to a convent, and there I learned music, French and embroidery, and what not; and when I was fourteen, I came out to my father's funeral. He died very suddenly, and when the property came to be settled, they found that there was scarcely enough to cover the debts; and when the creditors took an inventory of the property, I was set down in it. My mother was a slave woman, and my father had always meant to set me free; but he had not done it, and so I was set down in the list. I 'd always known who I was, but never thought much about it. Nobody ever expects that a strong, healthy man is a going to die. My father was a well man only four hours before he died;—it was one of the first cholera cases in New Orleans. The day after the funeral, my father's wife took her children, and went up to her father's plantation. I thought they treated me strangely, but did n't know. There was a young lawyer who they left to settle the business; and he came every day, and was about the house, and spoke very politely to me. He brought with him, one day, a young man, whom I thought the handsomest I had ever seen. I shall never forget that evening. I walked with him in the garden. I was lonesome and full of sorrow, and he was so kind and gentle to me; and he told me that he had seen me before I went to the convent, and that he had loved me a great while, and that he would be my friend and protector;—in short, though he did n't tell me, he had paid two thousand dollars for me, and I was his property,—I became his willingly, for I loved him. Loved!" said the woman, stopping. "O, how I *did* love that man! How I love him now,—and always shall, while I breathe! He was so beautiful, so high, so noble! He put me into a beautiful house, with servants, horses, and carriages, and furniture, and dresses. Everything that money could buy, he gave me; but I did n't set any value on all that,—I only cared for him. I loved him better than my God and my own soul; and, if I tried, I could n't do any other way from what he wanted me to.

"I wanted only one thing—I did want him to *marry* me. I thought, if he loved me as he said he did, and if I was what he seemed to think I was, he would be willing to marry me and set me free. But he convinced me that it would be impossible; and he told me that, if we were only faithful to each other, it was marriage before God. If that is true, was n't I that man's wife? Was n't I faithful? For seven years, did n't I study every look and motion, and only live and breathe to please him? He had the yellow fever, and for twenty days and nights I watched with him. I alone,—and gave him all his medicine, and did everything for him; and then he called me his good angel, and said I 'd saved his life. We had two beautiful children. The first was a boy, and we called him Henry. He was the image of his father,—he had such beautiful eyes, such a forehead, and his hair hung all in curls around it; and he had all his father's spirit, and his talent, too. Little Elise, he said, looked like me. He used to tell me that I was the most beautiful woman in Louisiana, he was so proud of me and the children. He used to love to have me dress them up, and take them and me about in an open carriage, and hear the remarks that people would make on us; and he used to fill my ears constantly with the fine things that were said in praise of me and the children. O, those were happy days! I thought I was as happy as any one could be; but then there came evil times. He had a cousin come to New Orleans, who was his particular friend,—he thought all the world of him;—but, from the first time I saw him, I could n't tell why, I dreaded him; for I felt sure he was going to bring misery on us. He got Henry to going out with him, and often he would not come home nights till two or three o'clock. I did not dare say a word; for Henry was so high-spirited, I was afraid to. He got him to the gaming-houses; and he was one of the sort that, when he once got a going there, there was no holding back. And then he introduced him to another lady, and I saw soon that his heart was gone from me. He never told me, but I saw it,—I knew it, day after day,—I felt my heart breaking, but I could not say a word! At this, the wretch offered to buy me and the children of Henry, to clear off his gambling debts, which stood in the way of his marrying as he wished;—and *he sold us*. He told me, one day, that he had business in the country, and should be gone two or three weeks. He spoke kinder than usual, and said he should come back; but it did n't deceive me. I knew that the time had come; I was just like one turned into stone; I could n't speak, nor shed a tear. He kissed me and kissed the children, a good many times, and went out. I saw him get on his horse, and I watched him till he was quite out of sight; and then I fell down, and fainted.

"Then *he* came, the cursed wretch! he came to take possession. He told me that he had bought me and my children; and showed me the papers. I cursed him before God, and told him I 'd die sooner than live with him.

"'Just as you please,' said he; 'but, if you don't behave reasonably, I 'll sell both the children, where you shall never see them again.' He told me that he always had meant to have me, from the first time he saw me; and that he had drawn Henry on, and got him in debt, on purpose to make him willing to sell me. That he got him in love with another woman; and that I might know, after all that, that he should not give up for a few airs and tears, and things of that sort.

"I gave up, for my hands were tied. He had my children;—whenever I resisted his will anywhere, he would talk about selling them, and he made me as submissive as he desired. O, what a life it was! to live with my heart breaking, every day,—to keep on, on, on, loving, when it was only misery; and to be bound, body and soul, to one I hated. I used to love to read to Henry, to play to him, to waltz with him, and sing to him; but everything I did for this one was a perfect drag,—yet I was afraid to refuse anything. He was very imperious, and harsh to the children. Elise was a timid little thing; but Henry was bold and high-spirited, like his father, and he had never been brought under, in the least, by any one. He was always finding fault, and quarrelling with him; and I used to live in daily fear and dread. I tried to make the child respectful;—I tried to keep them apart, for I held on to those children like death; but it did no good. *He sold both those children.* He took me to ride, one day, and when I came home, they were nowhere to be found! He told me he had sold them; he showed me the money, the price of their blood. Then it seemed as if all good forsook me. I raved and cursed,—cursed God and man; and, for a while, I believe, he really was afraid of me. But he did n't give up so. He told me that my children were sold, but whether I ever saw their faces again, depended on him; and that, if I was n't quiet, they should smart for it. Well, you can do anything with a woman, when you 've got her children. He made me submit; he made me be peaceable; he flattered me with hopes that, perhaps, he would buy them back; and so things went on, a week or two. One day, I was out walking, and passed by the calaboose; I saw a crowd about the gate, and heard a child's voice,—and suddenly my Henry broke away from two or three men who were holding him, and ran, screaming, and caught my dress. They came up to him, swearing dreadfully; and one man, whose face I shall never forget, told him that he would n't get away so; that he was going with him into the calaboose, and he 'd get a lesson there he 'd never forget. I tried to beg and plead,—they only laughed; the poor boy screamed and looked into my face, and held on to me, until, in tearing him off, they tore the skirt of my dress half away; and they carried him in, screaming 'Mother! mother! mother!' There was one man stood there seemed to pity me. I offered him all the money I had, if he 'd only interfere. He shook his head, and said that the boy had been impudent and disobedient, ever since he bought him; that he was going to break him in, once for all. I turned and ran; and every step of the way, I thought that I heard him scream. I got into the house; ran, all out of breath, to the parlor, where I found Butler. I told him, and begged him to go and interfere. He only laughed, and told me the boy had got his deserts. He'd got to be broken in,—the sooner the better; 'what did I expect?' he asked.

"It seemed to me something in my head snapped, at that moment, I felt dizzy and furious. I remember seeing a great sharp bowie-knife on the table; I remember something about catching it, and flying upon him; and then all grew dark, and I did n't know any more—not for days and days.

"When I came to myself, I was in a nice room,—but not mine. An old black woman tended me; and a doctor came to see me, and there was a great deal of care taken of me. After a while, I found that he had gone away, and left me at this house to be sold; and that's why they took such pains with me.

"I did n't mean to get well, and hoped I should n't; but, in spite of me, the fever went off, and I grew healthy, and finally got up. Then, they made me dress up, every day; and gentlemen used to come in and stand and smoke their cigars, and look at me, and ask questions, and debate my price. I was so gloomy and silent, that none of them wanted me. They threatened to whip me, if I was n't gayer, and did n't take some pains to make myself agreeable. At length, one day, came a gentleman named Stuart. He seemed to have some feeling for me; he saw that something dreadful was on my heart, and he came to see me alone, a great many times, and finally persuaded me to tell him. He bought me, at last, and promised to do all he could to find and buy back my children. He went to the hotel where my Henry was; they told him he had been sold to a planter up on Pearl river; that was the last that I ever heard. Then he found where my daughter was; an old woman was keeping her. He offered an immense sum for her, but they would not sell her. Butler found out that it was for me he wanted her; and he sent me word that I should never have her. Captain Stuart was very kind to me; he had a splendid plantation, and took me to it. In the course of a year, I had a son born. O, that child!—how I loved it! How just like my poor Henry the little thing looked! But I had made up my mind,—yes, I had. I would never again let a child live to grow up! I took the little fellow in my arms, when he was two weeks old, and kissed him, and cried over him; and then I gave him laudanum, and held him close to my bosom, while he slept to death. How I mourned and cried over it! and who ever dreamed that it was anything but a mistake, that had made me give it the laudanum? but it's one of the few things that I'm glad of, now. I am not sorry, to this day; he, at least, is out of pain. What better than death could I give him, poor child! After a while, the cholera came, and Captain Stuart died; everybody died that wanted to live,—and I,—I, though I went down to death's door,—*I lived!* Then I was sold, and passed from hand to hand, till I grew faded and wrinkled, and I had a fever; and then this wretch bought me, and brought me here,—and here I am!"

The woman stopped. She had hurried on through her story, with a wild, passionate utterance; sometimes seeming to address it to Tom, and sometimes speaking as in a soliloquy. So vehement and overpowering was the force with which she spoke, that, for a season, Tom was beguiled even from the pain of his wounds, and, raising himself on one elbow, watched her as she paced restlessly up and down, her long black hair swaying heavily about her, as she moved.

"You tell me," she said, after a pause, "that there is a God,—a God that looks down and sees all these things. May be it 's so. The sisters in the convent used to tell me of a day of judgment, when everything is coming to light;—won't there be vengeance, then!

"They think it 's nothing, what we suffer,—nothing, what our children suffer! It 's all a small matter; yet I 've walked the streets when it seemed as if I had misery enough in my one heart to sink the city. I 've wished the houses would fall on me, or the stones sink under me. Yes! and, in the judgment day, I will stand up before God, a witness against those that have ruined me and my children, body and soul!

"When I was a girl, I thought I was religious; I used to love God and prayer. Now, I 'm a lost soul, pursued by devils that torment me day and night; they keep pushing me on and on—and I 'll do it, too, some of these days!" she said, clenching her hand, while an insane light glanced in her heavy black eyes. "I 'll send him where he belongs,—a short way, too,—one of these nights, if they burn me alive for it!" A wild, long laugh, rang through the deserted room, and ended in a hysteric sob; she threw herself on the floor, in convulsive sobbings and struggles.

In a few moments, the frenzy fit seemed to pass off; she rose slowly, and seemed to collect herself.

"Can I do anything more for you, my poor fellow?" she said, approaching where Tom lay; "shall I give you some more water?"

There was a graceful and compassionate sweetness in her voice and manner, as she said this, that formed a strange contrast with the former wildness.

Tom drank the water, and looked earnestly and pitifully into her face.

"O, Missis, I wish you 'd go to him that can give you living waters!"

"Go to him! Where is he? Who is he?" said Cassy.

"Him that you read of to me,—the Lord."

"I used to see the picture of him, over the altar, when I was a girl," said Cassy, her dark eyes fixing themselves in an expression of mournful reverie; "but, *he is n't here!* there's nothing here, but sin and long, long, long despair! O!" She laid her hand on her breast and drew in her breath, as if to lift a heavy weight.

Tom looked as if he would speak again; but she cut him short, with a decided gesture.

"Don't talk, my poor fellow. Try to sleep, if you can." And, placing water in his reach, and making whatever little arrangements for his comfort she could, Cassy left the shed.

## XXXV.
### The Tokens

"And slight, withal, may be the things that bring
Back on the heart the weight which it would fling
Aside forever; it may be a sound,
A flower, the wind, the ocean, which shall wound,—
Striking the electric chain wherewith we 're darkly bound."
*Childe Harold's Pilgrimage, Can. 4.*

The sitting-room of Legree's establishment was a large, long room, with a wide, ample fireplace. It had once been hung with a showy and expensive paper, which now hung mouldering, torn and discolored, from the damp walls. The place had that peculiar sickening, unwholesome smell, compounded of mingled damp, dirt and decay, which one often notices in close old houses. The wall-paper was defaced, in spots, by slops of beer and wine; or garnished with chalk memorandums, and long sums footed up, as if somebody had been practising arithmetic there. In the fireplace stood a brazier full of burning charcoal; for, though the weather was not cold, the evenings always seemed damp and chilly in that great room; and Legree, moreover, wanted a place to light his cigars, and heat his water for punch. The ruddy glare of the charcoal displayed the confused and unpromising aspect of the room,—saddles, bridles, several sorts of harness, riding-whips, overcoats, and various articles of clothing, scattered up and down the room in confused variety; and the dogs, of whom we have before spoken, had encamped themselves among them, to suit their own taste and convenience.

Legree was just mixing himself a tumbler of punch, pouring his hot water from a cracked and broken-nosed pitcher, grumbling, as he did so,

"Plague on that Sambo, to kick up this yer row between me and the new hands! The fellow won't be fit to work for a week, now,—right in the press of the season!"

"Yes, just like you," said a voice, behind his chair. It was the woman Cassy, who had stolen upon his soliloquy.

"Hah! you she-devil! you 've come back, have you?"

"Yes, I have," she said, coolly; "come to have my own way, too!"

"You lie, you jade! I 'll be up to my word. Either behave yourself, or stay down to the quarters, and fare and work with the rest."

"I 'd rather, ten thousand times," said the woman, "live in the dirtiest hole at the quarters, than be under your hoof!"

"But you *are* under my hoof, for all that," said he, turning upon her, with a savage grin; "that 's one comfort. So, sit down here on my knee, my dear, and hear to reason," said he, laying hold on her wrist.

"Simon Legree, take care!" said the woman, with a sharp flash of her eye, a glance so wild and insane in its light as to be almost appalling. "You 're afraid of me, Simon," she said, deliberately; "and you 've reason to be! But be careful, for I 've got the devil in me!"

The last words she whispered in a hissing tone, close to his ear.

"Get out! I believe, to my soul, you have!" said Legree, pushing her from him, and looking uncomfortably at her. "After all, Cassy," he said, "why can't you be friends with me, as you used to?"

"Used to!" said she, bitterly. She stopped short,—a world of choking feelings, rising in her heart, kept her silent.

Cassy had always kept over Legree the kind of influence that a strong, impassioned woman can ever keep over the most brutal man; but, of late, she had grown more and more irritable and restless, under the hideous yoke of her servitude, and her irritability, at times, broke out into raving insanity; and this liability made her a sort of object of dread to Legree, who had that superstitious horror of insane persons which is common to coarse and uninstructed minds. When Legree brought Emmeline to the house, all the smouldering embers of womanly feeling flashed up in the worn heart of Cassy, and she took part with the girl; and a fierce quarrel ensued between her and Legree. Legree, in a fury, swore she should be put to field service, if she would not be peaceable. Cassy, with proud scorn, declared she *would* go to the field. And she worked there one day, as we have described, to show how perfectly she scorned the threat.

Legree was secretly uneasy, all day; for Cassy had an influence over him from which he could not free himself. When she presented her basket at the scales, he had hoped for some concession, and addressed her in a sort of half conciliatory, half scornful tone; and she had answered with the bitterest contempt.

The outrageous treatment of poor Tom had roused her still more; and she had followed Legree to the house, with no particular intention, but to upbraid him for his brutality.

"I wish, Cassy," said Legree, "you 'd behave yourself decently."

"*You* talk about behaving decently! And what have you been doing?—you, who have n't even sense enough to keep from spoiling one of your best hands, right in the most pressing season, just for your devilish temper!"

"I was a fool, it 's a fact, to let any such brangle come up," said Legree; "but, when the boy set up his will, he had to be broke in."

"I reckon you won't break *him* in!"

"Won't I?" said Legree, rising, passionately. "I 'd like to know if I won't? He 'll be the first nigger that ever came it round me! I 'll break every bone in his body, but he *shall* give up!"

Just then the door opened, and Sambo entered. He came forward, bowing, and holding out something in a paper.

"What 's that, you dog?" said Legree.

"It 's a witch thing, Mas'r!"

"A what?"

"Something that niggers gets from witches. Keeps 'em from feelin' when they 's flogged. He had it tied round his neck, with a black string."

Legree, like most godless and cruel men, was superstitious. He took the paper, and opened it uneasily.

There dropped out of it a silver dollar, and a long, shining curl of fair hair,—hair which, like a living thing, twined itself round Legree's fingers.

"Damnation!" he screamed, in sudden passion, stamping on the floor, and pulling furiously at the hair, as if it burned him. "Where did this come from? Take it off!—burn it up!—burn it up!" he screamed, tearing it off, and throwing it into the charcoal. "What did you bring it to me for?"

Sambo stood, with his heavy mouth wide open, and aghast with wonder; and Cassy, who was preparing to leave the apartment, stopped, and looked at him in perfect amazement.

"Don't you bring me any more of your devilish things!" said he, shaking his fist at Sambo, who retreated hastily towards the door; and, picking up the silver dollar, he sent it smashing through the window-pane, out into the darkness.

Sambo was glad to make his escape. When he was gone, Legree seemed a little ashamed of his fit of alarm. He sat doggedly down in his chair, and began sullenly sipping his tumbler of punch.

Cassy prepared herself for going out, unobserved by him; and slipped away to minister to poor Tom, as we have already related.

And what was the matter with Legree? and what was there in a simple curl of fair hair to appall that brutal man, familiar with every form of cruelty? To answer this, we must carry the reader backward in his history. Hard and reprobate as the godless man seemed now, there had been a time when he had been rocked on the bosom of a mother,—cradled with prayers and pious hymns,—his now seared brow bedewed with the waters of holy baptism. In early childhood, a fair-haired woman had led him, at the sound of Sabbath bell, to worship and to pray. Far in New England that mother had trained her only son, with long, unwearied love, and patient prayers. Born of a hard-tempered sire, on whom that gentle woman had wasted a world of unvalued love, Legree had followed in the steps of his father. Boisterous, unruly, and tyrannical, he despised all her counsel, and would none of her reproof; and, at an early age, broke from her, to seek his fortunes at sea. He never came home but once, after; and then, his mother, with the yearning of a heart that must love something, and has nothing else to love, clung to him, and sought, with passionate prayers and entreaties, to win him from a life of sin, to his soul's eternal good.

That was Legree's day of grace; then good angels called him; then he was almost persuaded, and mercy held him by the hand. His heart inly relented,—there was a conflict,—but sin got the victory, and he set all the force of his rough nature against the conviction of his conscience. He drank and swore,—was wilder and more brutal than ever. And, one night, when his mother, in the last agony of her despair, knelt at his feet, he spurned her from him,—threw her senseless on the floor, and, with brutal curses, fled to his ship. The next Legree heard of his mother was, when, one night, as he was carousing among drunken companions, a letter was put into his hand. He opened it, and a lock of long, curling hair fell from it, and twined about his fingers. The letter told him his mother was dead, and that, dying, she blest and forgave him.

There is a dread, unhallowed necromancy of evil, that turns things sweetest and holiest to phantoms of horror and affright. That pale, loving mother,—her dying prayers, her forgiving love,—wrought in that demoniac heart of sin only as a damning sentence, bringing with it a fearful looking for of judgment and fiery indignation. Legree burned the hair, and burned the letter; and when he saw them hissing and crackling in the flame, inly shuddered as he thought of everlasting fires. He tried to drink, and revel, and swear away the memory; but often, in the deep night, whose solemn stillness arraigns the bad soul in forced communion with herself, he had seen that pale mother rising by his bedside, and felt the soft twining of that hair around his fingers, till the cold sweat would roll down his face, and he would spring from his bed in horror. Ye who have wondered to hear, in the same evangel, that God is love, and that God is a consuming fire, see ye not how, to the soul resolved in evil, perfect love is the most fearful torture, the seal and sentence of the direst despair?

"Blast it!" said Legree to himself, as he sipped his liquor; "where did he get that? If it did n't look just like—whoo! I thought I 'd forgot that. Curse me, if I think there 's any such thing as forgetting anything, any how,—hang it! I 'm lonesome! I mean to call Em. She hates me—the monkey! I don't care,—I 'll *make* her come!"

Legree stepped out into a large entry, which went upstairs, by what had formerly been a superb winding staircase; but the passage-way was dirty and dreary, encumbered with boxes and unsightly litter. The stairs, uncarpeted, seemed winding up, in the gloom, to nobody knew where! The pale moonlight streamed through a shattered fanlight over the door; the air was unwholesome and chilly, like that of a vault.

Legree stopped at the foot of the stairs, and heard a voice singing. It seemed strange and ghostlike in that dreary old house, perhaps because of the already tremulous state of his nerves. Hark! what is it?

A wild, pathetic voice, chants a hymn common among the slaves:

> "O there 'll be mourning, mourning, mourning,
> O there 'll be mourning, at the judgment-seat of Christ!"

"Blast the girl!" said Legree. "I 'll choke her.—Em! Em!" he called, harshly; but only a mocking echo from the walls answered him. The sweet voice still sung on:

> "Parents and children there shall part!
> Parents and children there shall part!
> Shall part to meet no more!"

And clear and loud swelled through the empty halls the refrain,

> "O there 'll be mourning, mourning, mourning,
> O there 'll be mourning, at the judgment-seat of Christ!"

Legree stopped. He would have been ashamed to tell of it, but large drops of sweat stood on his forehead, his heart beat heavy and thick with fear; he even thought he saw something white rising and glimmering in the gloom before him, and shuddered to think what if the form of his dead mother should suddenly appear to him.

"I know one thing," he said to himself, as he stumbled back in the sitting-room, and sat down; "I 'll let that fellow alone, after this! What did I want of his cussed paper? I b'lieve I am bewitched, sure enough! I 've been shivering and sweating, ever since! Where did he get that hair? It could n't have been *that*! I burnt *that* up, I know I did! It would be a joke, if hair could rise from the dead!"

Ah, Legree! that golden tress *was* charmed; each hair had in it a spell of terror and remorse for thee, and was used by a mightier power to bind thy cruel hands from inflicting uttermost evil on the helpless!

"I say," said Legree, stamping and whistling to the dogs, "wake up, some of you, and keep me company!" but the dogs only opened one eye at him, sleepily, and closed it again.

"I 'll have Sambo and Quimbo up here, to sing and dance one of their hell dances, and keep off these horrid notions," said Legree; and, putting on his hat, he went on to the verandah, and blew a horn, with which he commonly summoned his two sable drivers.

Legree was often wont, when in a gracious humor, to get these two worthies into his sitting-room, and, after warming them up with whiskey, amuse himself by setting them to singing, dancing or fighting, as the humor took him.

It was between one and two o'clock at night, as Cassy was returning from her ministrations to poor Tom, that she heard the sound of wild shrieking, whooping, halloing, and singing, from the sitting-room, mingled with the barking of dogs, and other symptoms of general uproar.

She came up on the verandah steps, and looked in. Legree and both the drivers, in a state of furious intoxication, were singing, whooping, upsetting chairs, and making all manner of ludicrous and horrid grimaces at each other.

She rested her small, slender hand on the window-blind, and looked fixedly at them;—there was a world of anguish, scorn, and fierce bitterness, in her black eyes, as she did so. "Would it be a sin to rid the world of such a wretch?" she said to herself.

She turned hurriedly away, and, passing round to a back door, glided up stairs, and tapped at Emmeline's door.

## XXXVI.
### Emmeline and Cassy

Cassy entered the room, and found Emmeline sitting, pale with fear, in the furthest corner of it. As she came in, the girl started up nervously; but, on seeing who it was, rushed forward, and catching her arm, said, "O, Cassy, is it you? I 'm so glad you 've come! I was afraid it was—. O, you don't know what a horrid noise there has been, down stairs, all this evening!"

"I ought to know," said Cassy, dryly. "I 've heard it often enough."

"O Cassy! do tell me,—could n't we get away from this place? I don't care where,—into the swamp among the snakes,—anywhere! Could n't we get somewhere away from here?"

"Nowhere, but into our graves," said Cassy.

"Did you ever try?"

"I 've seen enough of trying, and what comes of it," said Cassy.

"I 'd be willing to live in the swamps, and gnaw the bark from trees. I an't afraid of snakes! I 'd rather have one near me than him," said Emmeline, eagerly.

"There have been a good many here of your opinion," said Cassy; "but you could n't stay in the swamps,—you 'd be tracked by the dogs, and brought back, and then—then—"

"What would he do?" said the girl, looking, with breathless interest, into her face.

"What would n't he do, you 'd better ask," said Cassy. "He 's learned his trade well, among the pirates in the West Indies. You would n't sleep much, if I should tell you things I 've seen,—things that he tells of, sometimes, for good jokes. I 've heard screams here that I have n't been able to get out of my head for weeks and weeks. There 's a place way out down by the quarters, where you can see a black, blasted tree, and the ground all covered with black ashes. Ask any one what was done there, and see if they will dare to tell you."

"O! what do you mean?"

"I won't tell you. I hate to think of it. And I tell you, the Lord only knows what we may see to-morrow, if that poor fellow holds out as he 's begun."

"Horrid!" said Emmeline, every drop of blood receding from her cheeks. "O, Cassy, do tell me what I shall do!"

"What I 've done. Do the best you can,—do what you must,—and make it up in hating and cursing."

"He wanted to make me drink some of his hateful brandy," said Emmeline; "and I hate it so—"

"You 'd better drink," said Cassy. "I hated it, too; and now I can't live without it. One must have something;—things don't look so dreadful, when you take that."

"Mother used to tell me never to touch any such thing," said Emmeline.

"*Mother* told you!" said Cassy, with a thrilling and bitter emphasis on the word mother. "What use is it for mothers to say anything? You are all to be bought and paid for, and your souls belong to whoever gets you. That 's the way it goes. I say, *drink* brandy; drink all you can, and it 'll make things come easier."

"O, Cassy! do pity me!"

"Pity you!—don't I? Have n't I a daughter,—Lord knows where she is, and whose she is, now,—going the way her mother went, before her, I suppose, and that her children must go, after her! There 's no end to the curse—forever!"

"I wish I 'd never been born!" said Emmeline, wringing her hands.

"That 's an old wish with me," said Cassy. "I 've got used to wishing that. I 'd die, if I dared to," she said, looking out into the darkness, with that still, fixed despair which was the habitual expression of her face when at rest.

"It would be wicked to kill one's self," said Emmeline.

"I don't know why,— no wickeder than things we live and do, day after day. But the sisters told me things, when I was in the convent, that make me afraid to die. If it would only be the end of us, why, then—"

Emmeline turned away, and hid her face in her hands.

While this conversation was passing in the chamber, Legree, overcome with his carouse, had sank to sleep in the room below. Legree was not an habitual drunkard. His coarse, strong nature craved, and could endure, a continual stimulation, that would have utterly wrecked and crazed a finer one. But a deep, underlying spirit of cautiousness prevented his often yielding to appetite in such measure as to lose control of himself.

This night, however, in his feverish efforts to banish from his mind those fearful elements of woe and remorse which woke within him, he had indulged more than common; so that, when he had discharged his sable attendants, he fell heavily on a settle in the room, and was sound asleep.

O! how dares the bad soul to enter the shadowy world of sleep?—that land whose dim outlines lie so fearfully near to the mystic scene of retribution! Legree dreamed. In his heavy and feverish sleep, a veiled form stood beside him, and laid a cold, soft hand upon him. He thought he knew who it was; and shuddered, with creeping horror, though the face was veiled. Then he thought he felt *that hair* twining round his fingers; and then, that it slid smoothly round his neck, and tightened and tightened, and he could not draw his breath; and then he thought voices *whispered* to him,—whispers that chilled him with horror. Then it seemed to him he was on the edge of a frightful abyss, holding on and struggling in mortal fear, while dark hands stretched up, and were pulling him over; and Cassy came behind him laughing, and pushed him. And then rose up that solemn veiled figure, and drew aside the veil. It was his mother; and she turned away from him, and he fell down, down, down, amid a confused noise of shrieks, and groans, and shouts of demon laughter,—and Legree awoke.

Calmly the rosy hue of dawn was stealing into the room. The morning star stood, with its solemn, holy eye of light, looking down on the man of sin, from out the brightening sky. O, with what freshness, what solemnity and beauty, is each new day born; as if to say to insensate man, "Behold! thou hast one more chance! *Strive* for immortal glory!" There is no speech nor language where this voice is not heard; but the bold, bad man heard it not. He woke with an oath and a curse. What to him was the gold and purple, the daily miracle of morning! What to him the sanctity of that star which the Son of God has hallowed as his own emblem? Brute-like, he saw without perceiving; and, stumbling forward, poured out a tumbler of brandy, and drank half of it.

"I 've had a h—l of a night!" he said to Cassy, who just then entered from an opposite door.

"You 'll get plenty of the same sort, by and by," said she, dryly.

"What do you mean, you minx?"

"You 'll find out, one of these days," returned Cassy, in the same tone. "Now, Simon, I 've one piece of advice to give you."

"The devil, you have!"

"My advice is," said Cassy, steadily, as she began adjusting some things about the room, "that you let Tom alone."

"What business is 't of yours?"

"What? To be sure, I don't know what it should be. If you want to pay twelve hundred for a fellow, and use him right up in the press of the season, just to serve your own spite, it 's no business of mine. I 've done what I could for him."

"You have? What business have you meddling in my matters?"

"None, to be sure. I 've saved you some thousands of dollars, at different times, by taking care of your hands,—that 's all the thanks I get. If your crop comes shorter into market than any of theirs, you won't lose your bet, I suppose? Tompkins won't lord it over you, I suppose,—and you 'll pay down your money like a lady, won't you? I think I see you doing it!"

Legree, like many other planters, had but one form of ambition,—to have in the heaviest crop of the season,—and he had several bets on this very present season pending in the next town. Cassy, therefore, with woman's tact, touched the only string that could be made to vibrate.

"Well, I 'll let him off at what he 's got," said Legree; "but he shall beg my pardon, and promise better fashions."

"That he won't do," said Cassy.

"Won't,—eh?"

"No, he won't," said Cassy.

"I 'd like to know *why*, Mistress," said Legree, in the extreme of scorn.

"Because he 's done right, and he knows it, and won't say he 's done wrong."

"Who a cuss cares what he knows? The nigger shall say what I please, or—"

"Or, you 'll lose your bet on the cotton crop, by keeping him out of the field, just at this very press."

"But he *will* give up,—course, he will; don't I know what niggers is? He 'll beg like a dog, this morning."

"He won't, Simon; you don't know this kind. You may kill him by inches,—you won't get the first word of confession out of him."

"We 'll see;—where is he?" said Legree, going out.

"In the waste-room of the gin-house," said Cassy.

Legree, though he talked so stoutly to Cassy, still sallied forth from the house with a degree of misgiving which was not common with him. His dreams of the past night, mingled with Cassy's prudential suggestions, considerably affected his mind. He resolved that nobody should be witness of his encounter with Tom; and determined, if he could not subdue him by bullying, to defer his vengeance, to be wreaked in a more convenient season.

The solemn light of dawn—the angelic glory of the morning-star—had looked in through the rude window of the shed where Tom was lying; and, as if descending on that starbeam, came the solemn words, "I am the root and off-spring of David, and the bright and morning star." The mysterious warnings and intimations of Cassy, so far from discouraging his soul, in the end had roused it as with a heavenly call. He did not know but that the day of his death was dawning in the sky; and his heart throbbed with solemn throes of joy and desire, as he thought that the wondrous *all*, of which he had often pondered,—the great white throne, with its ever radiant rainbow; the white-robed multitude, with voices as many waters; the crowns, the palms, the harps,—might all break upon his vision before that sun should set again. And, therefore, without shuddering or trembling, he heard the voice of his persecutor, as he drew near.

"Well, my boy," said Legree, with a contemptuous kick, "how do you find yourself? Did n't I tell yer I could larn yer a thing or two? How do yer like it,—eh? How did yer whaling agree with yer, Tom? An't quite so crank as ye was last night. Ye could n't treat a poor sinner, now, to a bit of a sermon, could ye,—eh?"

Tom answered nothing.

"Get up, you beast!" said Legree, kicking him again.

This was a difficult matter for one so bruised and faint; and, as Tom made efforts to do so, Legree laughed brutally.

"What makes ye so spry, this morning, Tom? Cotched cold, may be, last night."

Tom by this time had gained his feet, and was confronting his master with a steady, unmoved front.

"The devil, you can!" said Legree, looking him over, "I believe you have n't got enough yet. Now, Tom, get right down on yer knees and beg my pardon, for yer shines last night."

Tom did not move.

"Down, you dog!" said Legree, striking him with his riding-whip.

"Mas'r Legree," said Tom, "I can't do it. I did only what I thought was right. I shall do just so again, if ever the time comes. I never will do a cruel thing, come what may."

"Yes, but ye don't know what may come, Master Tom. Ye think what you 've got is something. I tell you 't an't anything,—nothing 't all. How would ye like to be tied to a tree, and have a slow fire lit up around ye;—would n't that be pleasant,—eh, Tom?"

"Mas'r," said Tom, "I know ye can do dreadful things; but,"—he stretched himself upward and clasped his hands,—"but, after ye 've killed the body, there an't no more ye can do. And O, there 's all ETERNITY to come, after that!"

ETERNITY,—the word thrilled through the black man's soul with light and power, as he spoke; it thrilled through the sinner's soul, too, like the bite of a scorpion. Legree gnashed on him with his teeth, but rage kept him silent; and Tom, like a man disenthralled, spoke, in a clear and cheerful voice,

"Mas'r Legree, as ye bought me, I 'll be a true and faithful servant to ye. I 'll give ye all the work of my hands, all my time, all my strength; but my soul I won't give up to mortal man. I will hold on to the Lord, and put his commands before all,—die or live; you may be sure on 't. Mas'r Legree, I an't a grain afeard to die. I 'd as soon die as not. Ye may whip me, starve me, burn me,—it 'll only send me sooner where I want to go."

"I 'll make ye give out, though, 'fore I 've done!" said Legree, in a rage.

"I shall have *help*," said Tom; "you 'll never do it."

"Who the devil 's going to help you?" said Legree, scornfully.

"The Lord Almighty," said Tom.

"D—n you!" said Legree, as with one blow of his fist he felled Tom to the earth.

A cold soft hand fell on Legree's, at this moment. He turned,—it was Cassy's; but the cold soft touch recalled his dream of the night before, and, flashing through the chambers of his brain, came all the fearful images of the nightwatches, with a portion of the horror that accompanied them.

"Will you be a fool?" said Cassy, in French. "Let him go! Let me alone to get him fit to be in the field again. Is n't it just as I told you?"

They say the alligator, the rhinoceros, though enclosed in bullet-proof mail, have each a spot where they are vulnerable; and fierce, reckless, unbelieving reprobates, have commonly this point in superstitious dread.

Legree turned away, determined to let the point go for the time.

"Well, have it your own way," he said, doggedly, to Cassy.

"Hark, ye!" he said to Tom; "I won't deal with ye now, because the business is pressing, and I want all my hands; but I *never* forget. I 'll score it against ye, and sometime I 'll have my pay out o' yer old black hide,—mind ye!"

Legree turned, and went out.

"There you go," said Cassy, looking darkly after him; "your reckoning 's to come, yet!—My poor fellow, how are you?"

"The Lord God hath sent his angel, and shut the lion's mouth, for this time," said Tom.

"For this time, to be sure," said Cassy; "but now you 've got his ill will upon you, to follow you day in, day out, hanging like a dog on your throat,—sucking your blood, bleeding away your life, drop by drop. I know the man."

## XXXVII.
### Liberty

"No matter with what solemnities he may have been devoted upon the altar of slavery, the moment he touches the sacred soil of Britain, the altar and the God sink together in the dust, and he stands redeemed, regenerated, and disenthralled, by the irresistible genius of universal emancipation."

—*Curran.*

Awhile we must leave Tom in the hands of his persecutors, while we turn to pursue the fortunes of George and his wife, whom we left in friendly hands, in a farm-house on the road-side.

Tom Loker we left groaning and touzling in a most immaculately clean Quaker bed, under the motherly supervision of Aunt Dorcas, who found him to the full as tractable a patient as a sick bison.

Imagine a tall, dignified, spiritial woman, whose clear muslin cap shades waves of silvery hair, parted on a broad, clear forehead, which overarches thoughtful gray eyes. A snowy handkerchief of lisse crape is folded neatly across her bosom; her glossy brown silk dress rustles peacefully, as she glides up and down the chamber.

"The devil!" says Tom Loker, giving a great throw to the bed-clothes.

"I must request thee, Thomas, not to use such language," says Aunt Dorcas, as she quietly rearranged the bed.

"Well, I won't, granny, if I can help it," says Tom; "but it is enough to make a fellow swear,—so cursedly hot!"

Dorcas removed a comforter from the bed, straightened the clothes again, and tucked them in till Tom looked something like a chrysalis; remarking, as she did so,

"I wish, friend, thee would leave off cursing and swearing, and think upon thy ways."

"What the devil," said Tom, "should I think of *them* for? Last thing ever I want to think of—hang it all!" And Tom flounced over, untucking and disarranging everything, in a manner frightful to behold.

"That fellow and gal are here, I 'spose," said he, sullenly, after a pause.

"They are so," said Dorcas.

"They 'd better be off up to the lake," said Tom; "the quicker the better."

"Probably they will do so." said Aunt Dorcas, knitting peacefully.

"And hark ye," said Tom; "we 've got correspondents in Sandusky, that watch the boats for us. I don't care if I tell, now. I hope they *will* get away, just to spite Marks,—the cursed puppy!—d—n him!"

"Thomas!" said Dorcas.

"I tell you, granny, if you bottle a fellow up too tight, I shall split," said Tom. "But about the gal,—tell 'em to dress her up some way, so 's to alter her. Her description 's out in Sandusky."

"We will attend to that matter," said Dorcas, with characteristic composure.

As we at this place take leave of Tom Loker, we may as well say, that, having lain three weeks at the Quaker dwelling, sick with a rheumatic fever, which set in, in company with his other afflictions, Tom arose from his bed a somewhat sadder and wiser man; and, in place of slave-catching, betook himself to life in one of the new settlements, where his talents developed themselves more happily in trapping bears, wolves, and other inhabitants of the forest, in which he made himself quite a name in the land. Tom always spoke reverently of the Quakers. "Nice people," he would say; "wanted to convert me, but could n't come it, exactly. But, tell ye what, stranger, they do fix up a sick fellow first rate,—no mistake. Make jist the tallest kind o' broth and knicknacks."

As Tom had informed them that their party would be looked for in Sandusky, it was thought prudent to divide them. Jim, with his old mother, was forwarded separately; and a night or two after, George and Eliza, with their child, were driven privately into Sandusky, and lodged beneath a hospitable roof, preparatory to taking their last passage on the lake.

Their night was now far spent, and the morning star of liberty rose fair before them. Liberty!—electric word! What is it? Is there anything more in it than a name—a rhetorical flourish? Why, men and women of America, does your heart's blood thrill at that word, for which your fathers bled, and your braver mothers were willing that their noblest and best should die?

Is there anything in it glorious and dear for a nation, that is not also glorious and dear for a man? What is freedom to a nation, but freedom to the individuals in it? What is freedom to that young man, who sits there, with his arms folded over his broad chest, the tint of African blood in his cheek, its dark fires in his eye,—what is freedom to George Harris? To your fathers, freedom was the right of a nation to be a nation. To him, it is the right of a man to be a man, and not a brute; the right to call the wife of his bosom his wife, and to protect her from lawless violence; the right to protect and educate his child; the right to have a home of his own, a religion of his own, a character of his own, unsubject to the will of another. All these thoughts were rolling and seething in George's breast, as he was pensively leaning his head on his hand, watching his wife, as she was adapting to her slender and pretty form the articles of man's attire, in which it was deemed safest she should make her escape.

"Now for it," said she, as she stood before the glass, and shook down her silky abundance of black curly hair. "I say, George, it 's almost a pity, is n't it," she said, as she held up some of it, playfully,—"pity it 's all got to come off?"

George smiled sadly, and made no answer.

Eliza turned to the glass, and the scissors glittered as one long lock after another was detached from her head.

"There, now, that 'll do," she said, taking up a hair-brush; "now for a few fancy touches."

"There, an't I a pretty young fellow?" she said, turning around to her husband, laughing and blushing at the same time.

"You always will be pretty, do what you will," said George.

"What does make you so sober?" said Eliza, kneeling on one knee, and laying her hand on his. "We are only within twenty-four hours of Canada, they say. Only a day and a night on the lake, and then—oh, then!—"

"O, Eliza!" said George, drawing her towards him; "that is it! Now my fate is all narrowing down to a point. To come so near, to be almost in sight, and then lose all. I should never live under it, Eliza."

"Don't fear," said his wife, hopefully. "The good Lord would not have brought us so far, if he did n't mean to carry us through. I seem to feel him with us, George."

"You are a blessed woman, Eliza!" said George, clasping her with a convulsive grasp. "But,—oh, tell me! can this great mercy be for us? Will these years and years of misery come to an end?—shall we be free?"

"I am sure of it, George," said Eliza, looking upward, while tears of hope and enthusiasm shone on her long, dark lashes. "I feel it in me, that God is going to bring us out of bondage, this very day."

"I will believe you, Eliza," said George, rising suddenly up. "I will believe,— come, let 's be off. Well, indeed," said he, holding her off at arm's length, and looking admiringly at her, "you *are* a pretty little fellow. That crop of little, short curls, is quite becoming. Put on your cap. So—a little to one side. I never saw you look quite so pretty. But, it 's almost time for the carriage;—I wonder if Mrs. Smyth has got Harry rigged?"

The door opened, and a respectable, middle-aged woman entered, leading little Harry, dressed in girl's clothes.

"What a pretty girl he makes," said Eliza, turning him round. "We call him Harriet, you see;—don't the name come nicely?"

The child stood gravely regarding his mother in her new and strange attire, observing a profound silence, and occasionally drawing deep sighs, and peeping at her from under his dark curls.

"Does Harry know mamma?" said Eliza, stretching her hands toward him.

The child clung shyly to the woman.

"Come, Eliza, why do you try to coax him, when you know that he has got to be kept away from you?"

"I know it 's foolish," said Eliza; "yet, I can't bear to have him turn away from me. But come,—where 's my cloak? Here,—how is it men put on cloaks, George?"

"You must wear it so," said her husband, throwing it over his shoulders.

"So, then," said Eliza, imitating the motion,—"and I must stamp, and take long steps, and try to look saucy."

"Don't exert yourself," said George. "There is, now and then, a modest young man; and I think it would be easier for you to act that character."

"And these gloves! mercy upon us!" siad Eliza; "why, my hands are lost in them."

"I advise you to keep them on pretty strictly," said George. "Your little slender paw might bring us all out. Now, Mrs. Smyth, you are to go under our charge, and be our aunty,—you mind."

"I 've heard," said Mrs. Smyth, "that there have been men down, warning all the packet captains against a man and woman, with a little boy."

"They have!" said George. "Well, if we see any such people, we can tell them."

A hack now drove to the door, and the friendly family who had received the fugitives crowded around them with farewell greetings.

The disguises the party had assumed were in accordance with the hints of Tom Loker. Mrs. Smyth, a respectable woman from the settlement in Canada, whither they were fleeing, being fortunately about crossing the lake to return thither, had consented to appear as the aunt of little Harry; and, in order to attach him to her, he had been allowed to remain, the two last days, under her sole charge; and an extra amount of petting, joined to an indefinite amount of seed-cakes and candy, had cemented a very close attachment on the part of the young gentleman.

The hack drove to the wharf. The two young men, as they appeared, walked up the plank into the boat, Eliza gallantly giving her arm to Mrs. Smyth, and George attending to their baggage.

George was standing at the captain's office, settling for his party, when he overheard two men talking by his side.

"I 've watched every one that came on board," said one, "and I know they 're not on this boat."

The voice was that of the clerk of the boat. The speaker whom he addressed was our sometime friend Marks, who, with that valuable perseverance which characterized him, had come on to Sandusky, seeking whom he might devour.

"You would scarcely know the woman from a white one," said Marks. "The man is a very light mulatto; he has a brand in one of his hands."

The hand with which George was taking the tickets and change trembled a little; but he turned coolly aroung, fixed an unconcerned glance on the face of the speaker, and walked leisurely toward another part of the boat, where Eliza stood waiting for him.

Mrs. Smyth, with little Harry, sought the seclusion of the ladies' cabin, where the dark beauty of the supposed little girl drew many flattering comments from the passengers.

George had the satisfaction, as the bell rang out its farewell peal, to see Marks walk down the plank to the shore; and drew a long sigh of relief, when the boat had put a returnless distance between them.

It was a superb day. The blue waves of Lake Erie danced, rippling and sparkling, in the sun-light. A fresh breeze blew from the shore, and the lordly boat ploughed her way right gallantly onward.

O, what an untold world there is in one human heart! Who thought, as George walked calmly up and down the deck of the steamer, with his shy companion at his side, of all that was burning in his bosom? The mighty good that seemed approaching seemed too good, too fair, even to be a reality; and he felt a jealous dread, every moment of the day, that something would rise to snatch it from him.

But the boat swept on. Hours fleeted, and, at last, clear and full rose the blessed English shores; shores charmed by a mighty spell,—with one touch to dissolve every incantation of slavery, no matter in what language pronounced, or by what national power confirmed.

George and his wife stood arm in arm, as the boat neared the small town of Amherstberg, in Canada. His breath grew thick and short; a mist gathered before his eyes; he silently pressed the little hand that lay trembling on his arm. The bell rang; the boat stopped. Scarcely seeing what he did, he looked out his baggage, and gathered his little party. The little company were landed on the shore. They stood still till the boat had cleared; and then, with tears and embracings, the husband and wife, with their wondering child in their arms, knelt down and lifted up their hearts to God!

> "'T was something like the burst fom death to life;
>    From the grave's cerements to the robes of heaven;
> From sin's dominion, and from passion's strife,
>    To the pure freedom of a soul forgiven;
>    Where all the bonds of death and hell are riven,
> And mortal puts on immortality,
> When Mercy's hand hath turned the golden key,
> And Mercy's voice hath said, *Rejoice, thy soul is free.*"

The little party were soon guided, by Mrs. Smyth, to the hospitable abode of a good missionary, whom Christian charity has placed here as a shepherd to the out-cast and wandering, who are constantly finding an asylum on this shore.

Who can speak the blessedness of that first day of freedom? Is not the *sense* of liberty a higher and a finer one than any of the five? To move, speak and breathe,—go out and come in unwatched, and free from danger! Who can speak the blessings of that rest which comes down on the free man's pillow, under laws which insure to him the rights that God has given to man? How fair and precious to that mother was that sleeping child's face, endeared by the memory of a thousand dangers! How impossible was it to sleep, in the exuberant possession of such blessedness! And yet, these two had not one acre of ground,—not a roof that they could call their own,—they had spent their all, to the last dollar. They had nothing more than the birds of the air, or the flowers of the field,—yet they could not sleep for joy. "O, ye who take freedom from man, with what words shall ye answer it to God?"

## XXXVIII.
### The Victory

"Thanks be unto God, who giveth us the victory."

Have not many of us, in the weary way of life, felt, in some hours, how far easier it were to die than to live?

The martyr, when faced even by a death of bodily anguish and horror, finds in the very terror of his doom a strong stimulant and tonic. There is a vivid excitement, a thrill and fervor, which may carry through any crisis of suffering that is the birth-hour of eternal glory and rest.

But to live,—to wear on, day after day, of mean, bitter, low, harassing servitude, every nerve dampened and depressed, every power of feeling gradually smothered,—this long and wasting heart-martyrdom, this slow, daily bleeding away of the inward life, drop by drop, hour after hour,—this is the true searching test of what there may be in man or woman.

When Tom stood face to face with his persecutor, and heard his threats, and thought in his very soul that his hour was come, his heart swelled bravely in him, and he thought he could bear torture and fire, bear anything, with the vision of Jesus and heaven but just a step beyond; but, when he was gone, and the present excitement passed off, came back the pain of his bruised and weary limbs,—came back the sense of his utterly degraded, hopeless, forlorn estate; and the day passed wearily enough.

Long before his wounds were healed, Legree insisted that he should be put to the regular field-work; and then came day after day of pain and weariness, aggravated by every kind of injustice and indignity that the ill-will of a mean and malicious mind could devise. Whoever, in *our* circumstances, has made trial of pain, even with all the alleviations which, for us, usually attend it, must know the irritation that comes with it. Tom no longer wondered at the habitual surliness of his associates; nay, he found the placid, sunny temper, which had been the habitude of his life, broken in on, and sorely strained, by the inroads of the same thing. He had flattered himself on leisure to read his Bible; but there was no such thing as leisure there. In the height of the season, Legree did not hesitate to press all his hands through, Sundays and weekdays alike. Why should n't he?— he made more cotton by it, and gained his wager; and if it wore out a few more hands, he could buy better ones. At first, Tom used to read a verse or two of his Bible, by the flicker of the fire, after he had returned from his daily toil; but, after the cruel treatment he received, he used to come home so exhausted, that his head swam and his eyes failed when he tried to read; and he was fain to stretch himself down, with the others, in utter exhaustion.

Is it strange that the religious peace and trust, which had upborne him hitherto, should give way to tossings of soul and despondent darkness? The gloomiest problem of this mysterious life was constantly before his eyes,—souls crushed and ruined, evil triumphant, and God silent. It was weeks and months that Tom wrestled, in his own soul, in darkness and sorrow. He thought of Miss Ophelia's letter to his Kentucky friends, and would pray earnestly that God would send him deliverance. And then he would watch, day after day, in the vague hope of seeing somebody sent to redeem him; and, when nobody came, he would crush back to his soul bitter thoughts,—that it was vain to serve God, that God had forgotten him. He sometimes saw Cassy; and sometimes, when summoned to the house, caught a glimpse of the dejected form of Emmeline, but held very little communion with either; in fact, there was no time for him to commune with anybody.

One evening, he was sitting, in utter dejection and prostration, by a few decaying brands, where his coarse supper was baking. He put a few bits of brushwood on the fire, and strove to raise the light, and then drew his worn Bible from his pocket. There were all the marked passages, which had thrilled his soul so often,—words of patriarchs and seers, poets and sages, who from early time had spoken courage to man,—voices from the great cloud of witnesses who ever surround us in the race of life. Had the word lost its power, or could the failing eye and weary sense no longer answer to the touch of that mighty inspiration? Heavily sighing, he put it in his pocket. A coarse laugh roused him; he looked up,—Legree was standing opposite to him.

"Well, old boy," he said, "you find your religion don't work, it seems! I thought I should get that through your wool, at last!"

The cruel taunt was more than hunger and cold and nakedness. Tom was silent.

"You were a fool," said Legree; "for I meant to do well by you, when I bought you. You might have been better off than Sambo, or Quimbo either, and had easy times; and, instead of getting cut up and thrashed, every day or two, ye might have had liberty to lord it round, and cut up the other niggers; and ye might have had, now and then, a good warming of whiskey punch. Come, Tom, don't you think you 'd better be reasonable?—heave that ar old pack of trash in the fire, and join my church!"

"The Lord forbid!" said Tom, fervently.

"You see the Lord an't going to help you; if he had been, he would n't have let *me* get you! This yer religion is all a mess of lying trumpery, Tom. I know all about it. Ye 'd better hold to me; I 'm somebody, and can do something!"

"No, Mas'r," said Tom; "I 'll hold on. The Lord may help me, or not help; but I 'll hold to him, and believe him to the last!"

"The more fool you!" said Legree, spitting scornfully at him, and spurning him with his foot. "Never mind; I 'll chase you down, yet, and bring you under,— you 'll see!" and Legree turned away.

When a heavy weight presses the soul to the lowest level at which endurance is possible, there is an instant and desperate effort of every physical and moral nerve to throw off the weight; and hence the heaviest anguish often precedes a return tide of joy and courage. So was it now with Tom. The atheistic taunts of his cruel master sunk his before dejected soul to the lowest ebb; and, though the hand of faith still held to the eternal rock, it was with a numb, despairing grasp. Tom sat, like one stunned, at the fire. Suddenly everything around him seemed to fade, and a vision rose before him of one crowned with thorns, buffeted and bleeding. Tom gazed, in awe and wonder, at the majestic patience of the face; the deep, pathetic eyes thrilled him to his inmost heart; his soul woke, as, with floods of emotion, he stretched out his hands and fell upon his knees,—when, gradually, the vision changed: the sharp thorns became rays of glory; and, in splendor inconceivable, he saw that same face bending compassionately towards him, and a voice said, "He that overcometh shall sit down with me on my throne, even as I also overcame, and am set down with my Father on his throne."

How long Tom lay there, he knew not. When he came to himself, the fire was gone out, his clothes were wet with the chill and drenching dews; but the dread soul-crisis was past, and, in the joy that filled him, he no longer felt hunger, cold, degradation, disappointment, wretchedness. From his deepest soul, he that hour loosed and parted from every hope in the life that now is, and offered his own will an unquestioning sacrifice to the Infinite. Tom looked up to the silent, ever-living stars,—types of the angelic hosts who ever look down on man; and the solitude of the night rung with the triumphant words of a hymn, which he had sung often in happier days, but never with such feeling as now:

> "The earth shall be dissolved like snow,
>     The sun shall cease to shine;
> But God, who called me here below,
>     Shall be forever mine.
>
> "And when this mortal life shall fail,
>     And flesh and sense shall cease,
> I shall possess within the veil
>     A life of joy and peace.
>
> "When we 've been there ten thousand years,
>     Bright shining like the sun,
> We 've no less days to sing God's praise
>     Than when we first begun."

Those who have been familiar with the religious histories of the slave population know that relations like what we have narrated are very common among them. We have heard some from their own lips, of a very touching and affecting character. The psychologist tells us of a state, in which the affections and images of the mind become so dominant and overpowering, that they press into their service the outward senses, and make them give tangible shape to the inward imagining. Who shall measure what an all-pervading Spirit may do with these capabilities of our mortality, or the ways in which He may encourage the desponding souls of the desolate? If the poor forgotten slave believes that Jesus hath appeared and spoken to him, who shall contradict him? Did He not say that his mission, in all ages, was to bind up the broken-hearted, and set at liberty them that are bruised?

When the dim gray of dawn woke the slumberers to go forth to the field, there was among those tattered and shivering wretches one who walked with an exultant tread; for firmer than the ground he trod on was his strong faith in Almighty, eternal love. Ah, Legree, try all your forces now! Utmost agony, woe, degradation, want, and loss of all things, shall only hasten on the process by which he shall be made a king and a priest unto God!

From this time, an inviolable sphere of peace encompassed the lowly heart of the oppressed one,—an ever-present Saviour hallowed it as a temple. Past now the bleeding of earthly regrets; past its fluctuations of hope, and fear, and desire; the human will, bent, and bleeding, and struggling long, was now entirely merged in the Divine. So short now seemed the remaining voyage of life,—so near, so vivid, seemed eternal blessedness,—that life's uttermost woes fell from him un-harming.

All noticed the change in his appearance. Cheerfulness and alertness seemed to return to him, and a quietness which no insult or injury could ruffle seemed to possess him.

"What the devil 's got into Tom?" Legree said to Sambo. "A while ago he was all down in the mouth, and now he 's peart as a cricket."

"Dunno, Mas'r; gwine to run off, mebbe."

"Like to see him try that," said Legree, with a savage grin, "would n't we, Sambo?"

"Guess we would! Haw! haw! ho!" said the sooty gnome, laughing obse-quiously. "Lord, de fun! To see him stickin' in de mud,—chasin' and tarin' through de bushes, dogs a holdin' on to him! Lord, I laughed fit to split, dat ar time we cotched Molly. I thought they 'd a had her all stripped up afore I could get 'em off. She car's de marks o' dat ar spree yet."

"I reckon she will, to her grave," said Legree. "But now, Sambo, you look sharp. If the nigger 's got anything of this sort going, trip him up."

"Mas'r, let me lone for dat," said Sambo. "I 'll tree de coon. Ho, ho, ho!"

This was spoken as Legree was getting on to his horse, to go to the neigh-boring town. That night, as he was returning, he thought he would turn his horse and ride round the quarters, and see if all was safe.

It was a superb moonlight night, and the shadows of the graceful China trees lay minutely pencilled on the turf below, and there was that transparent stillness in the air which it seems almost unholy to disturb. Legree was at a lit-tle distance from the quarters, when he heard the voice of some one singing. It was not a usual sound there, and he paused to listen. A musical tenor voice sang,

"When I can read my title clear
To mansions in the skies,
I 'll bid farewell to every fear,
And wipe my weeping eyes.

"Should earth against my soul engage,
And hellish darts be hurled,
Then I can smile at Satan's rage,
And face a frowning world.

"Let cares like a wild deluge come,
And storms of sorrow fall,
May I but safely reach my home,
My God, my Heaven, my All."

"So ho!" said Legree to himself, "he thinks so, does he? How I hate these cursed Methodist hymns! Here, you nigger," said he, coming suddenly out upon Tom, and raising his riding-whip, "how dare you be gettin' up this yer row, when you ought to be in bed? Shut yer old black gash, and get along in with you!"

"Yes, Mas'r," said Tom, with ready cheerfulness, as he rose to go in.

Legree was provoked beyond measure by Tom's evident happiness; and, riding up to him, belabored him over his head and shoulders.

"There, you dog," he said, "see if you 'll feel so comfortable, after that!"

But the blows fell now only on the outer man, and not, as before, on the heart. Tom stood perfectly submissive; and yet Legree could not hide from himself that his power over his bond thrall was somehow gone. And, as Tom disappeared in his cabin, and he wheeled his horse suddenly round, there passed through his mind one of those vivid flashes that often send the lightning of conscience across the dark and wicked soul. He understood full well that it was GOD who was standing, between him and his victim, and he blasphemed him. That submissive and silent man, whom taunts, nor threats, nor stripes, nor cruelties, could disturb, roused a voice within him, such as of old his Master roused in the demoniac soul, saying, "What have we to do with thee, thou Jesus of Nazareth?—art thou come to torment us before the time?"

Tom's whole soul overflowed with compassion and sympathy for the poor wretches by whom he was surrounded. To him it seemed as if his life-sorrows were now over, and as if, out of that strange treasury of peace and joy, with which he had been endowed from above, he longed to pour out something for the relief of their woes. It is true, opportunities were scanty; but, on the way to the fields, and back again, and during the hours of labor, chances fell in his way of extending a helping-hand to the weary, the disheartened and discouraged. The poor, worn-down, brutalized creatures, at first, could scarce comprehend this; but, when it was continued week after week, and month after month, it began to awaken long-silent chords in their benumbed hearts. Gradually and imperceptibly the strange, silent, patient man, who was ready to bear every one's burden, and sought help from none,—who stood aside for all, and came last, and took least, yet was foremost to share his little all with any who needed,—the man who, in cold nights, would give up his tattered blanket to add to the comfort of some woman who shivered with sickness, and who filled the baskets of the weaker ones in the field, at the terrible risk of coming short in his own measure,—and who, though pursued with unrelenting cruelty by their common tyrant, never joined in uttering a word of reviling or cursing,—this man, at last, began to have a strange power over them; and, when the more pressing season was past, and they were allowed again their Sundays for their own use, many would gather together to hear from him of Jesus. They would gladly have met to hear, and pray, and sing, in some place, together; but Legree would not permit it, and more than once broke up such attempts, with oaths and brutal execrations,—so that the blessed news had to circulate from individual to individual. Yet who can speak the simple joy with which some of those poor outcasts, to whom life was a joyless journey to a dark unknown, heard of a compassionate Redeemer and a heavenly home? It is the statement of missionaries, that, of all races of the earth, none have received the Gospel with such eager docility as the African. The principle of reliance and unquestioning faith, which is its foundation, is more a native element in this race, than any other; and it has often been found among them, that a stray seed of truth, borne on some breeze of accident into hearts the most ignorant, has sprung up into fruit, whose abundance has shamed that of higher and more skilful culture.

The poor mulatto woman, whose simple faith had been well-nigh crushed and overwhelmed, by the avalanche of cruelty and wrong which had fallen upon her, felt her soul raised up by the hymns and passages of Holy Writ, which this lowly missionary breathed into her ear in intervals, as they were going to and returning from work; and even the half-crazed and wandering mind of Cassy was soothed and calmed by his simple and unobtrusive influences.

Stung to madness and despair by the crushing agonies of a life, Cassy had often resolved in her soul an hour of retribution, when her hand should avenge on her oppressor all the injustice and cruelty to which she had been witness, or which *she* had in her own person suffered.

One night, after all in Tom's cabin were sunk in sleep, he was suddenly aroused by seeing her face at the hole between the logs, that served for a window. She made a silent gesture for him to come out.

Tom came out the door. It was between one and two o'clock at night,—broad, calm, still moonlight. Tom remarked, as the light of the moon fell upon Cassy's large, black eyes, that there was a wild and peculiar glare in them, unlike their wonted fixed despair.

"Come here, Father Tom," she said, laying her small hand on his wrist, and drawing him forward with a force as if the hand were of steel; "come here,—I 've news for you."

"What, Misse Cassy?" said Tom, anxiously.

"Tom, would n't you like your liberty?"

"I shall have it, Misse, in God's time," said Tom.

"Ay, but you may have it to-night," said Cassy, with a flash of sudden energy. "Come on."

Tom hesitated.

"Come!" said she, in a whisper, fixing her black eyes on him. "Come along! He 's asleep—sound. I put enough into his brandy to keep him so. I wish I 'd had more,—I should n't have wanted you. But come, the back door is unlocked; there 's an axe there, I put it there,—his room door is open; I 'll show you the way. I 'd a done it myself, only my arms are so weak. Come along!"

"Not for ten thousand worlds, Misse!" said Tom, firmly, stopping and holding her back, as she was pressing forward.

"But think of all these poor creatures," said Cassy. "We might set them all free, and go somewhere in the swamps, and find an island, and live by ourselves; I 've heard of its being done. Any life is better than this."

"No!" said Tom, firmly. "No! good never comes of wickedness. I 'd sooner chop my right hand off!"

"Then *I* shall do it," said Cassy, turning.

"O, Misse Cassy!" said Tom, throwing himself before her, "for the dear Lord's sake that died for ye, don't sell your precious soul to the devil, that way! Nothing but evil will come of it. The Lord has n't called us to wrath. We must suffer, and wait his time."

"Wait!" said Cassy. "Have n't I waited?—waited till my head is dizzy and my heart sick? What has he made me suffer? What has he made hundreds of poor creatures suffer? Is n't he wringing the life-blood out of you? I 'm called on; they call me! His time 's come, and I 'll have his heart's blood!"

"No, no, no!" said Tom, holding her small hands, which were clenched with spasmodic violence. "No, ye poor, lost soul, that ye must n't do. The dear, blessed Lord never shed no blood but his own, and that he poured out for us when we was enemies. Lord, help us to follow his steps, and love our enemies."

"Love!" said Cassy, with a fierce glare; "love *such* enemies! It is n't in flesh and blood."

"No, Misse, it is n't" said Tom, looking up; "but He gives it to us, and that 's the *victory*. When we can love and pray over all and through all, the battle 's past, and the victory 's come,—glory be to God!" And, with streaming eyes and choking voice, the black man looked up to heaven.

And this, of Africa! latest called of nations,—called to the crown of thorns, the scourge, the bloody sweat, the cross of agony,—this is to be *thy* victory; by this shalt thou reign with Christ when his kingdom shall come on earth.

The deep fervor of Tom's feelings, the softness of his voice, his tears, fell like dew on the wild, unsettled spirit of the poor woman. A softness gathered over the lurid fires of her eye; she looked down, and Tom could feel the relaxing muscles of her hands, as she said,

"Did n't I tell you that evil spirits followed me? O! Father Tom, I can't pray,—I wish I could. I never have prayed since my children were sold! What you say must be right, I know it must; but when I try to pray, I can only hate and curse. I can't pray!"

"Poor soul!" said Tom, compassionately. "Satan desires to have ye, and sift ye as wheat. I pray the Lord for ye. O! Misse Cassy, turn to the dear Lord Jesus. He came to bind up the broken-hearted, and comfort all that mourn."

Cassy stood silent, while large, heavy tears dropped from her downcast eyes.

"Misse Cassy," said Tom, in a hesitating tone, after surveying her a moment in silence, "if ye only could get away from here,—if the thing was possible,—I 'd 'vise ye and Emmeline to do it; that is, if ye could go without blood-guiltiness,—not otherwise."

"Would you try it with us, Father Tom?"

"No," said Tom; "time was when I would; but the Lord 's given me a work among these yer poor souls, and I 'll stay with 'em and bear my cross with 'em till the end. It 's different with you; it 's a snare to you,—it 's more 'n you can stand,—and you 'd better go, if you can."

"I know no way but through the grave," said Cassy. "There 's no beast or bird but can find a home somewhere; even the snakes and the alligators have their places to lie down and be quiet; but there 's no place for us. Down in the darkest swamps, their dogs will hunt us out, and find us. Everybody and everything is against us; even the very beasts side against us,—and where shall we go?"

Tom stood silent; at length he said,

"Him that saved Daniel in the den of lions,—that saved the children in the fiery furnace,—Him that walked on the sea, and bade the winds be still,—He 's alive yet; and I 've faith to believe he can deliver you. Try it, and I 'll pray, with all my might, for you."

By what strange law of mind is it that an idea long overlooked, and trodden under foot as a useless stone, suddenly sparkles out in new light, as a discovered diamond?

Cassy had often revolved, for hours, all possible or probable schemes of escape, and dismissed them all, as hopeless and impracticable; but at this moment there flashed through her mind a plan, so simple and feasible in all its details, as to awaken an instant hope.

"Father Tom, I 'll try it!" she said, suddenly.

"Amen!" said Tom; "the Lord help ye!"

## XXXIX.
## The Stratagem

"The way of the wicked is as darkness; he knoweth not at what he stumbleth."

The garret of the house that Legree occupied, like most other garrets, was a great, desolate space, dusty, hung with cobwebs, and littered with cast-off lumber. The opulent family that had inhabited the house in the days of its splendor had imported a great deal of splendid furniture, some of which they had taken away with them, while some remained standing desolate in mouldering, unoccupied rooms, or stored away in this place. One or two immense packing-boxes, in which this furniture was brought, stood against the sides of the garret. There was a small window there, which let in, through its dingy, dusty panes, a scanty, uncertain light on the tall, high-backed chairs and dusty tables, that had once seen better days. Altogether, it was a weird and ghostly place; but, ghostly as it was, it wanted not in legends among the superstitious negroes, to increase its terrors. Some few years before, a negro woman, who had incurred Legree's displeasure, was confined there for several weeks. What passed there, we do not say; the negroes used to whisper darkly to each other; but it was known that the body of the unfortunate creature was one day taken down from there, and buried; and, after that, it was said that oaths and cursings, and the sound of violent blows, used to ring through that old garret, and mingled with wailings and groans of despair. Once, when Legree chanced to overhear something of this kind, he flew into a violent passion, and swore that the next one that told stories about that garret should have an opportunity of knowing what was there, for he would chain them up there for a week. This hint was enough to repress talking, though, of course, it did not disturb the credit of the story in the least.

Gradually, the staircase that led to the garret, and even the passage-way to the staircase, were avoided by every one in the house, from every one fearing to speak of it, and the legend was gradually falling into desuetude. It had suddenly occurred to Cassy to make use of the superstitious excitability, which was so great in Legree, for the purpose of her liberation, and that of her fellow-sufferer.

The sleeping-room of Cassy was directly under the garret. One day, without consulting Legree, she suddenly took it upon her, with some considerable ostentation, to change all the furniture and appurtenances of the room to one at some considerable distance. The under-servants, who were called on to effect this movement, were running and bustling about with great zeal and confusion, when Legree returned from a ride.

"Hallo! you Cass!" said Legree, "what 's in the wind now?"

"Nothing; only I choose to have another room," said Cassy doggedly.

"And what for, pray?" said Legree.

"I choose to," said Cassy.

"The devil you do! and what for?"

"I 'd like to get some sleep, now and then."

"Sleep! well, what hinders your sleeping?"

"I could tell, I suppose, if you want to hear," said Cassy, dryly.

"Speak out, you minx!" said Legree.

"O! nothing. I suppose it would n't disturb *you*! Only groans, and people scuffling, and rolling round on the garret floor, half the night, from twelve to morning!"

"People up garret!" said Legree, uneasily, but forcing a laugh; "who are they, Cassy?"

Cassy raised her sharp, black eyes, and looked in the face of Legree, with an expression that went through his bones, as she said, "To be sure, Simon, who are they? I 'd like to have *you* tell me. You don't know, I suppose!"

With an oath, Legree struck at her with his riding-whip; but she glided to one side, and passed through the door, and looking back, said, "If you 'll sleep in that room, you 'll know all about it. Perhaps you 'd better try it!" and then immediately she shut and locked the door.

Legree blustered and swore, and threatened to break down the door; but apparently thought better of it, and walked uneasily into the sitting-room. Cassy perceived that her shaft had struck home; and, from that hour, with the most exquisite address, she never ceased to continue the train of influences she had begun.

In a knot-hole of the garret, that had opened, she had inserted the neck of an old bottle, in such a manner that when there was the least wind, most doleful and lugubrious wailing sounds proceeded from it, which, in a high wind, increased to a perfect shriek, such as to credulous and superstitious ears might easily seem to be that of horror and despair.

These sounds were, from time to time, heard by the servants, and revived in full force the memory of the old ghost legend. A superstitious creeping horror seemed to fill the house; and though no one dared to breathe it to Legree, he found himself encompassed by it, as by an atomsphere.

No one is so thoroughly superstitious as the godless man. The Christian is composed by the belief of a wise, all-ruling Father, whose presence fills the void unknown with light and order; but to the man who has dethroned God, the spirit-land is, indeed, in the words of the Hebrew poet, "a land of darkness and the shadow of death," without any order, where the light is as darkness. Life and death to him are haunted grounds, filled with goblin forms of vague and shadowy dread.

Legree had had the slumbering moral element in him roused by his encounters with Tom,—roused, only to be resisted by the determinate force of evil; but still there was a thrill and commotion of the dark, inner world, produced by every word, or prayer, or hymn, that reäcted in superstitious dread.

The influence of Cassy over him was of a strange and singular kind. He was her owner, her tyrant and tormentor. She was, as he knew, wholly, and without any possibility of help or redress, in his hands; and yet so it is, that the most brutal man cannot live in constant association with a strong female influence, and not be greatly controlled by it. When he first bought her, she was, as she had said, a woman delicately bred; and then he crushed her, without scruple, beneath the foot of his brutality. But, as time, and debasing influences, and despair, hardened womanhood within her, and waked the fires of fiercer passions, she had become in a measure his mistress, and he alternately tyrannized over and dreaded her.

This influence had become more harassing and decided, since partial insanity had given a strange, weird, unsettled cast to all her words and language.

A night or two after this, Legree was sitting in the old sitting-room, by the side of a flickering wood fire, that threw uncertain glances round the room. It was a stormy, windy night, such as raises whole squadrons of nondescript noises in rickety old houses. Windows were rattling, shutters flapping, the wind carousing, rumbling, and tumbling down the chimney, and, every once in a while, puffing out smoke and ashes, as if a legion of spirits were coming after them. Legree had been casting up accounts and reading newspapers for some hours, while Cassy sat in the corner, sullenly looking into the fire. Legree laid down his paper, and seeing an old book lying on the table, which he had noticed Cassy reading, the first part of the evening, took it up, and began to turn it over. It was one of those collections of stories of bloody murders, ghostly legends, and supernatural visitations, which, coarsely got up and illustrated, have a strange fascination for one who once begins to read them.

Legree poohed and pished, but read, turning page after page, till, finally, after reading some way, he threw down the book, with an oath.

"You don't believe in ghosts, do you, Cass?" said he, taking the tongs and settling the fire. "I thought you 'd more sense than to let noises scare *you*."

"No matter what I believe," said Cassy, sullenly.

"Fellows used to try to frighten me with their yarns at sea," said Legree. "Never come it round me that way. I 'm too tough for any such trash, tell ye."

Cassy sat looking intensely at him in the shadow of the corner. There was that strange light in her eyes that always impressed Legree with uneasiness.

"Them noises was nothing but rats and the wind," said Legree. "Rats will make a devil of a noise. I used to hear 'em sometimes down in the hold of the ship; and wind,—Lord's sake! ye can make anything out o' wind."

Cassy knew Legree was uneasy under her eyes, and, therefore, she made no answer, but sat fixing them on him, with that strange, unearthly expression, as before.

"Come, speak out, woman,—don't you think so?" said Legree.

"Can rats walk down stairs, and come walking through the entry, and open a door when you 've locked it and set a chair against it?" said Cassy; "and come walk, walk, walking right up to your bed, and put out their hand, so?"

Cassy kept her glittering eyes fixed on Legree, as she spoke, and he stared at her like a man in the nightmare, till, when she finished by laying her hand, icy cold, on his, he sprung back, with an oath.

"Woman! what do you mean? Nobody did?"—

"O, no,—of course not,—did I say they did?" said Cassy, with a smile of chilling derision.

"But—did—have you really seen?—Come, Cass, what is it, now,—speak out!"

"You may sleep there, yourself," said Cassy, "if you want to know."

"Did it come from the garret, Cassy?"

"*It,*—what?" said Cassy.

"Why, what you told of—"

"I did n't tell you anything," said Cassy, with dogged sullenness.

Legree walked up and down the room, uneasily.

"I 'll have this yer thing examined. I 'll look into it, this very night. I 'll take my pistols—"

"Do," said Cassy; "sleep in that room. I 'd like to see you doing it. Fire your pistols,—do!"

Legree stamped his foot, and swore violently.

"Don't swear," said Cassy; "nobody knows who may be hearing you. Hark! What was that?"

"What?" said Legree, starting.

A heavy old Dutch clock, that stood in the corner of the room, began, and slowly struck twelve.

For some reason or other, Legree neither spoke nor moved; a vague horror fell on him; while Cassy, with a keen, sneering glitter in her eyes, stood looking at him, counting the strokes.

"Twelve o'clock; well, *now* we 'll see," said she, turning, and opening the door into the passage-way, and standing as if listening.

"Hark! What 's that?" said she, raising her finger.

"It 's only the wind," said Legree. "Don't you hear how cursedly it blows?"

"Simon, come here," said Cassy, in a whisper, laying her hand on his, and leading him to the foot of the stairs: "do you know what *that* is? Hark!"

A wild shriek came pealing down the stairway. It came from the garret. Legree's knees knocked together; his face grew white with fear.

"Had n't you better get your pistols?" said Cassy, with a sneer that froze Legree's blood. "It 's time this thing was looked into, you know. I 'd like to have you go up now; *they 're at it.*"

"I won't go!" said Legree, with an oath.

"Why not? There an't any such thing as ghosts, you know! Come!" and Cassy flitted up the winding stairway, laughing, and looking back after him. "Come on."

"I believe you *are* the devil!" said Legree. "Come back, you hag,—come back, Cass! You shan't go!"

But Cassy laughed wildly, and fled on. He heard her open the entry doors that led to the garret. A wild bust of wind swept down, extinguishing the candle he held in his hand, and with it the fearful, unearthly screams; they seemed to be shrieked in his very ear.

Legree fled frantically into the parlor, whither, in a few moments, he was followed by Cassy, pale, calm, cold as an avenging spirit, and with that same fearful light in her eye.

"I hope you are satisfied," said she.

"Blast you, Cass!" said Legree.

"What for?" said Cassy. "I only went up and shut the doors. *What 's the matter with the garret*, Simon, do you suppose?" said she.

"None of your business!" said Legree.

"O, it an't? Well," said Cassy, "at any rate, I 'm glad *I* don't sleep under it."

Anticipating the rising of the wind, that very evening, Cassy had been up and opened the garret window. Of course, the moment the doors were opened, the wind had drafted down, and extinguished the light.

This may serve as a specimen of the game that Cassy played with Legree, until he would sooner have put his head into a lion's mouth than to have explored that garret. Meanwhile, in the night, when everybody else was asleep, Cassy slowly and carefully accumulated there a stock of provisions sufficient to afford subsistence for some time; she transferred, article by article, a greater part of her own and Emmeline's wardrobe. All things being arranged, they only waited a fitting opportunity to put their plan in execution.

By cajoling Legree, and taking advantage of a good-natured interval, Cassy had got him to take her with him to the neighboring town, which was situated directly on the Red river. With a memory sharpened to almost preternatural clearness, she remarked every turn in the road, and formed a mental estimate of the time to be occupied in traversing it.

At the time when all was matured for action, our readers may, perhaps, like to look behind the scenes, and see the final *coup d'état*.

It was now near evening. Legree had been absent, on a ride to a neighboring farm. For many days Cassy had been unusually gracious and accommodating in her humors; and Legree and she had been, apparently, on the best of terms. At present, we may behold her and Emmeline in the room of the latter, busy in sorting and arranging two small bundles.

"There, these will be large enough," said Cassy. "Now put on your bonnet, and let 's start: it 's just about the right time."

"Why, they can see us yet," said Emmeline.

"I mean they shall," said Cassy, coolly. "Don't you know that they must have their chase after us, at any rate? The way of the thing is to be just this:—We will steal out of the back door, and run down by the quarters. Sambo or Quimbo will be sure to see us. They will give chase, and we will get into the swamp; then, they can't follow us any further till they go up and give the alarm, and turn out the dogs, and so on; and, while they are blundering round, and tumbling over each other, as they always do, you and I will just slip along to the creek, that runs back of the house, and wade along in it, till we get opposite the back door. That will put the dogs all at fault; for scent won't lie in the water. Every one will run out of the house to look after us, and then we 'll whip in at the back door, and up into the garret, where I 've got a nice bed made up in one of the great boxes. We must stay in that garret a good while; for, I tell you, he will raise heaven and earth after us. He 'll muster some of those old overseers on the other plantations, and have a great hunt; and they 'll go over every inch of ground in that swamp. He makes it his boast that nobody ever got away from him. So let him hunt at his leisure."

"Cassy, how well you have planned it!" said Emmeline. "Who ever would have thought of it, but you?"

There was neither pleasure nor exultation in Cassy's eyes,—only a despairing firmness.

"Come," she said, reaching her hand to Emmeline.

The two fugitives glided noiselessly from the house, and flitted, through the gathering shadows of evening, along by the quarters. The crescent moon, set like a silver signet in the western sky, delayed a little the approach of night. As Cassy expected, when quite near the verge of the swamps that encircled the plantation, they heard a voice calling to them to stop. It was not Sambo, however, but Legree, who was pursuing them with violent execrations. At the sound, the feebler spirit of Emmeline gave way; and, laying hold of Cassy's arm, she said, "O, Cassy, I 'm going to faint!"

"If you do, I 'll kill you!" said Cassy, drawing a small, glittering stiletto, and flashing it before the eyes of the girl.

The diversion accomplished the purpose. Emmeline did not faint, and succeeded in plunging, with Cassy, into a part of the labyrinth of swamp, so deep and dark that it was perfectly hopeless for Legree to think of following them, without assistance.

"Well," said he, chuckling brutally; "at any rate, they 've got themselves into a trap now—the baggages! They 're safe enough. They shall sweat for it!"

"Hulloa, there! Sambo! Quimbo! All hands!" called Legree, coming to the quarters, when the men and women were just returning from work. "There 's two runaways in the swamps. I 'll give five dollars to any nigger as catches 'em. Turn out the dogs! Turn out Tiger, and Fury, and the rest!"

The sensation produced by this news was immediate. Many of the men sprang forward, officiously, to offer their services, either from the hope of the reward, or from that cringing subserviency which is one of the most baleful effects of slavery. Some ran one way, and some another. Some were for getting flambeaux of pine-knots. Some were uncoupling the dogs, whose hoarse, savage bay added not a little to the animation of the scene.

"Mas'r, shall we shoot 'em, if we can't cotch 'em?" said Sambo, to whom his master brought out a rifle.

"You may fire on Cass, if you like; it 's time she was gone to the devil, where she belongs; but the gal, not," said Legree. "And now, boys, be spry and smart.

Five dollars for him that gets 'em; and a glass of spirits to every one of you, any-how."

The whole band, with the glare of blazing torches, and whoop, and shout, and savage yell, of man and beast, proceeded down the swamp, followed, at some distance, by every servant in the house. The establishment was, of a consequence, wholly deserted, when Cassy and Emmeline glided into it the back way. The whooping and shouts of their pursuers were still filling the air; and, looking from the sitting-room windows, Cassy and Emmeline could see the troop, with their flambeaux, just dispersing themselves along the edge of the swamp.

"See there!" said Emmeline, pointing to Cassy; "the hunt is begun! Look how those lights dance about! Hark! the dogs! Don't you hear? If we were only *there*, our chance would n't be worth a picayune. O, for pity's sake, do let 's hide our-selves. Quick!"

"There 's no occasion for hurry," said Cassy, coolly; "they are all out after the hunt,—that 's the amusement of the evening! We 'll go up stairs, by and by. Meanwhile," said she, deliberately taking a key from the pocket of a coat that Legree had thrown down in his hurry, "meanwhile I shall take something to pay our passage."

She unlocked the desk, took from it a roll of bills, which she counted over rapidly.

"O, don't let 's do that!" said Emmeline.

"Don't!" said Cassy; "why not? Would you have us starve in the swamps, or have that that will pay our way to the free states? Money will do anything, girl." And, as she spoke, she put the money in her bosom.

"It would be stealing," said Emmeline, in a distressed whisper.

"Stealing!" said Cassy, with a scornful laugh. "They who steal body and soul need n't talk to us. Every one of these bills is stolen,—stolen from poor, starving, sweating creatures, who must go to the devil at last, for his profit. Let *him* talk about stealing! But come, we may as well go up garret; I 've got a stock of can-dles there, and some books to pass away the time. You may be pretty sure they won't come *there* to inquire after us. If they do, I 'll play ghost for them."

When Emmeline reached the garret, she found an immense box, in which some heavy pieces of furniture had once been brought, turned on its side, so that the opening faced the wall, or rather the eaves. Cassy lit a small lamp, and, creeping round under the eaves, they established themselves in it. It was spread with a couple of small mattresses and some pillows; a box near by was plentifully stored with candles, provisions, and all the clothing necessary to their journey, which Cassy had arranged into bundles of an astonishingly small com-pass.

"There," said Cassy, as she fixed the lamp into a small hook, which she had driven into the side of the box for that purpose; "this is to be our home for the present. How do you like it?"

"Are you sure they won't come and search the garret?"

"I 'd like to see Simon Legree doing that," said Cassy. "No, indeed; he will be too glad to keep away. As to the servants, they would any of them stand and be shot, sooner than show their faces here."

Somewhat reässured, Emmeline settled herself back on her pillow.

"What did you mean, Cassy, by saying you would kill me?" she said, simply.

"I meant to stop your fainting," said Cassy, "and I did do it. And now I tell you, Emmeline, you must make up your mind *not* to faint, let what will come; there 's no sort of need of it. If I had not stopped you, that wretch might have had his hands on you now."

Emmeline shuddered.

The two remained some time in silence. Cassy busied herself with a French book; Emmeline, overcome with the exhaustion, fell into a doze, and slept some time. She was awakened by loud shouts and outcries, the tramp of horses' feet, and the baying of dogs. She started up, with a faint shriek.

"Only the hunt coming back," said Cassy, coolly; "never fear. Look out of this knot-hole. Don't you see 'em all down there? Simon has to give it up, for this night. Look, how muddy his horse is, flouncing about in the swamp; the dogs, too, look rather crest-fallen. Ah, my good sir, you 'll have to try the race again and again,—the game is n't there."

"O, don't speak a word!" said Emmeline; "what if they should hear you?"

"If they do hear anything, it will make them very particular to keep away," said Cassy. "No danger; we may make any noise we please, and it will only add to the effect."

At length the stillness of midnight settled down over the house. Legree, cursing his ill luck, and vowing dire vengeance on the morrow, went to bed.

## XL.
## The Martyr

> "Deem not the just by Heaven forgot!
>   Though life its common gifts deny,—
> Though, with a crushed and bleeding heart,
>   And spurned of man, he goes to die!
> For God hath marked each sorrowing day,
>   And numbered every bitter tear;
> And heaven's long years of bliss shall pay
>   For all his children suffer here."—*Bryant*

The longest way must have its close,—the gloomiest night will wear on to a morning. An eternal, inexorable lapse of moments is ever hurrying the day of the evil to an eternal night, and the night of the just to an eternal day. We have walked with our humble friend thus far in the valley of slavery; first through flowery fields of ease and indulgence, then through heart-breaking separations from all that man holds dear. Again, we have waited with him in a sunny island, where generous hands concealed his chains with flowers; and, lastly, we have followed him when the last ray of earthly hope went out in night, and seen how, in the blackness of earthly darkness, the firmament of the unseen has blazed with stars of new and significant lustre.

The morning-star now stands over the tops of the mountains, and gales and breezes, not of earth, show that the gates of day are unclosing.

The escape of Cassy and Emmeline irritated the before surly temper of Legree to the last degree; and his fury, as was to be expected, fell upon the defenceless head of Tom. When he hurriedly announced the tidings among his hands, there was a sudden light in Tom's eye, a sudden upraising of his hands, that did not escape him. He saw that he did not join the muster of the pursuers. He thought of forcing him to do it; but, having had, of old, experience of his inflexibility when commanded to take part in any deed of inhumanity, he would not, in his hurry, stop to enter into any conflict with him.

Tom, therefore, remained behind, with a few who had learned of him to pray, and offered up prayers for the escape of the fugitives.

When Legree returned, baffled and disappointed, all the long-working hatred of his soul towards his slave began to gather in a deadly and desperate form. Had not this man braved him,—steadily, powerfully, resistlessly,—ever since he bought him? Was there not a spirit in him which, silent as it was, burned on him like the fires of perdition?

"I *hate* him!" said Legree, that night, as he sat up in his bed; "I *hate* him! And is n't he MINE? Can't I do what I like with him? Who 's to hinder, I wonder?" And Legree clenched his fist, and shook it, as if he had something in his hands that he could rend in pieces.

But, then, Tom was a faithful, valuable servant; and, although Legree hated him the more for that, yet the consideration was still somewhat of a restraint to him.

The next morning, he determined to say nothing, as yet; to assemble a party, from some neighboring plantations, with dogs and guns; to surround the swamp, and go about the hunt systematically. If it succeeded, well and good; if not, he would summon Tom before him, and—his teeth clenched and his blood boiled— *then* he would break that fellow down, or—there was a dire inward whisper, to which his soul assented.

Ye say that the *interest* of the master is a sufficient safeguard for the slave. In the fury of man's mad will, he will wittingly, and with open eye, sell his own soul to the devil to gain his ends; and will he be more careful of his neighbor's body?

"Well," said Cassy, the next day, from the garret, as she reconnoitred through the knot-hole, "the hunt 's going to begin again, to-day!"

Three or four mounted horsemen were curvetting about, on the space front of the house; and one or two leashes of strange dogs were struggling with the negroes who held them, baying and barking at each other.

The men are, two of them, overseers of plantations in the vicinity; and others were some of Legree's associates at the tavern-bar of a neighboring city, who had come for the interest of the sport. A more hard-favored set, perhaps, could not be imagined. Legree was serving brandy, profusely, round among them, as also among the negroes, who had been detailed from the various plantations for this service; for it was an object to make every service of this kind, among the negroes, as much of a holiday as possible.

Cassy placed her ear at the knot-hole; and, as the morning air blew directly towards the house, she could overhear a good deal of the conversation. A grave sneer overcast the dark, severe gravity of her face, as she listened, and heard them divide out the ground, discuss the rival merits of the dogs, give orders about firing, and the treatment of each, in case of capture.

Cassy drew back; and, clasping her hands, looked upward, and said, "O, great Almighty God! we are *all* sinners; but what have *we* done, more than all the rest of the world, that we should be treated so?"

There was a terrible earnestness in her face and voice, as she spoke.

"If it was n't for *you*, child," she said, looking at Emmeline, "I 'd *go* out to them; and I 'd thank any one of them that *would* shoot me down; for what use will freedom be to me? Can it give me back my children, or make me what I used to be?"

Emmeline, in her child-like simplicity, was half afraid of the dark moods of Cassy. She looked perplexed, but made no answer. She only took her hand, with a gentle, caressing movement.

"Don't!" said Cassy, trying to draw it away; "you 'll get me to loving you; and I never mean to love anything, again!"

"Poor Cassy!" said Emmeline, "don't feel so! If the Lord gives us liberty, perhaps he 'll give you back your daughter; at any rate, I 'll be like a daughter to you. I know I 'll never see my poor old mother again! I shall love you, Cassy, whether you love me or not!"

The gentle, child-like spirit conquered. Cassy sat down by her, put her arm round her neck, stroked her soft, brown hair; and Emmeline then wondered at the beauty of her magnificent eyes, now soft with tears.

"O, Em!" said Cassy, "I 've hungered for my children, and thirsted for them, and my eyes fail with longing for them! Here! here!" she said, striking her breast, "it 's all desolate, all empty! If God would give me back my children, then I could pray."

"You must trust him, Cassy," said Emmeline; "he is our Father!"

"His wrath is upon us," said Cassy; "he has turned away in anger."

"No, Cassy! He will be good to us! Let us hope in Him," said Emmeline,—"I always have had hope."

———————

The hunt was long, animated, and thorough, but unsuccessful; and, with grave, ironic exultation, Cassy looked down on Legree, as, weary and dispirited, he alighted from his horse.

"Now, Quimbo," said Legree, as he stretched himself down in the sitting-room, "you jest go and walk that Tom up here, right away! The old cuss is at the bottom of this yer whole matter; and I 'll have it out of his old black hide, or I 'll know the reason why!"

Sambo and Quimbo, both, though hating each other, were joined in one mind by a no less cordial hatred of Tom. Legree had told them, at first, that he had bought him for a general overseer, in his absence; and this had begun an ill will, on their part, which had increased, in their debased and servile natures, as they saw him becoming obnoxious to their master's displeasure. Quimbo, therefore, departed, with a will, to execute his orders.

Tom heard the message with a forewarning heart; for he knew all the plan of the fugitives' escape, and the place of their present concealment;—he knew the deadly character of the man he had to deal with, and his despotic power. But he felt strong in God to meet death, rather than betray the helpless.

He sat his basket down by the row, and looking up, said, "Into thy hands I commend my spirit! Thou hast redeemed me, oh Lord God of truth!" and then quietly yielded himself to the rough, brutal grasp with which Quimbo seized him.

"Ay, ay!" said the giant, as he dragged him along; "ye 'll cotch it, now! I 'll boun' Mas'r's back 's up *high*! No sneaking out, now! Tell ye, ye 'll get it, and no mistake! See how ye 'll look, now, helpin' Mas'r's niggers to run away! See what ye 'll get!"

The savage words none of them reached that ear!—a higher voice there was saying, "Fear not them that kill the body, and, after that, have no more that they can do." Nerve and bone of that poor man's body vibrated to those words, as if touched by the finger of God; and he felt the strength of a thousand souls in one. As he passed along, the trees and bushes, the huts of his servitude, the whole scene of his degradation, seemed to whirl by him as the landscape by the rushing car. His soul throbbed,—his home was in sight,—and the hour of release seemed at hand.

"Well, Tom!" said Legree, walking up, and seizing him grimly by the collar of his coat, and speaking through his teeth, in a paroxysm of determined rage. "do you know I 've make up my mind to KILL you?"

"It 's very likely, Mas'r," said Tom, calmly.

"I *have*," said Legree, with grim, terrible calmness, "*done—just—that—thing*, Tom, unless you 'll tell me what you know about these yer gals!"

Tom stood silent.

"D' ye hear?" said Legree, stamping, with a roar like that of an incensed lion. "Speak!"

"*I han't got nothing to tell, Mas'r*," said Tom, with a slow, firm, deliberate utterance.

"Do you dare to tell me, ye old black Christian, ye don't *know*?" said Legree. Tom was silent.

"Speak!" thundered Legree, striking him furiously. "Do you know anything?"

"I know, Mas'r; but I can't tell anything. *I can die!*"

Legree drew in a long breath; and, suppressing his rage, took Tom by the arm, and, approaching his face almost to his, said, in a terrible voice, "Hark 'e, Tom!—ye think, 'cause I 've let you off before, I don't mean what I say; but, this time, I 've *made up my mind*, and counted the cost. You 've always stood it out agin' me: now, I 'll *conquer ye; or kill ye!*—one or t' other. I 'll count every drop of blood there is in you, and take 'em, one by one, till ye give up!"

Tom looked up to his master, and answered, "Mas'r, if you was sick, or in trouble, or dying, and I could save ye, I 'd *give* ye my heart's blood; and, if taking every drop of blood in this poor old body would save your precious soul, I 'd give 'em freely, as the Lord gave his for me. O, Mas'r! don't bring this great sin on your soul! It will hurt you more than 't will me! Do the worst you can, my troubles 'll be over soon; but, if ye don't repent, yours won't *never* end!"

Like a strange snatch of heavenly music, heard in the lull of a tempest, this burst of feeling made a moment's blank pause. Legree stood aghast, and looked at Tom; and there was such a silence, that the tick of the old clock could be heard, measuring, with silent touch, the last moments of mercy and probation to that hardened heart.

It was but a moment. There was one hesitating pause,—one irresolute, relenting thrill,—and the spirit of evil came back, with seven-fold vehemence; and Legree, foaming with rage, smote his victim to the ground.

———

Scenes of blood and cruelty are shocking to our ear and heart. What man has nerve to do, man has not nerve to hear. What brother-man and brother-Christian must suffer, cannot be told us, even in our secret chamber, it so harrows up the soul! And yet, oh my country! these things are done under the shadow of thy laws! O, Christ! thy church sees them, almost in silence!

But, of old, there was One whose suffering changed an instrument of torture, degradation and shame, into a symbol of glory, honor, and immortal life; and, where His spirit is, neither degrading stripes, nor blood, nor insults, can make the Christian's last struggle less than glorious.

Was he alone, that long night, whose brave, loving spirit was bearing up, in that old shed, against buffeting and brutal stripes?

Nay! There stood by him ONE,—seen by him alone,—"like unto the Son of God."

The tempter stood by him, too,—blinded by furious, despotic will,—every moment pressing him to shun that agony by the betrayal of the innocent. But the brave, true heart was firm on the Eternal Rock. Like his Master, he knew that, if he saved others, himself he could not save; nor could utmost extremity wring from him words, save of prayer and holy trust.

"He 's most gone, Mas'r," said Sambo, touched, in spite of himself, by the patience of his victim.

"Pay away, till he gives up! Give it to him!—give it to him!" shouted Legree. "I 'll take every drop of blood he has, unless he confesses!"

Tom opened his eyes, and looked upon his master. "Ye poor miserable critter!" he said, "there an't no more ye can do! I forgive ye, with all my soul!" and he fainted entirely away.

"I b'lieve, my soul, he 's done for, finally," said Legree, stepping forward, to look at him. "Yes, he is! Well, his mouth 's shut up, at last,—that 's one comfort!"

Yes, Legree; but who shall shut up that voice in thy soul? that soul, past repentance, past prayer, past hope, in whom the fire that never shall be quenched is already burning!

Yet Tom was not quite gone. His wondrous words and pious prayers had struck upon the hearts of the imbruted blacks, who had been the instruments of cruelty upon him; and, the instant Legree withdrew, they took him down, and, in their ignorance, sought to call him back to life,—as if *that* were any favor to him.

"Sartin, we 's been doin' a drefful wicked thing!" said Sambo; "hopes Mas'r 'll have to 'count for it, and not we."

They washed his wounds,—they provided a rude bed, of some refuse cotton, for him to lie down on; and one of them, stealing up to the house, begged a drink of brandy of Legree, pretending that he was tired, and wanted it for himself. He brought it back, and poured it down Tom's throat.

"O, Tom!" said Quimbo, "we 's been awful wicked to ye!"

"I forgive ye, with all my heart!" said Tom, faintly.

"O, Tom! do tell us who is *Jesus*, anyhow?" said Sambo;—"Jesus, that 's been a standin' by you so, all this night!—Who is he?"

The word roused the failing, fainting spirit. He poured forth a few energetic sentences of that wondrous One,—his life, his death, his everlasting presence, and power to save.

They wept,—both the two savage men.

"Why did n't I never hear this before?" said Sambo; "but I do believe!—I can't help it! Lord Jesus, have mercy on us!"

"Poor critters!" said Tom, "I 'd be willing to bar' all I have, if it 'll only bring ye to Christ! O, Lord! give me these two more souls, I pray!"

That prayer was answered!

## XLI.
### The Young Master

Two days after, a young man drove a light wagon up through the avenue of china-trees, and, throwing the reins hastily on the horses' neck, sprang out and inquired for the owner of the place.

It was George Shelby; and, to show how he came to be there, we must go back in our story.

The letter of Miss Ophelia to Mrs. Shelby had, by some unfortunate accident, been detained, for a month or two, at some remote post-office, before it reached its destination; and, of course, before it was received, Tom was already lost to view among the distant swamps of the Red river.

Mrs. Shelby read the intelligence with the deepest concern; but any immediate action upon it was an impossibility. She was then in attendance on the sick-bed of her husband who lay delirious in the crisis of a fever. Master George Shelby, who, in the interval, had changed from a boy to a tall young man, was her constant and faithful assistant, and her only reliance in superintending his father's affairs. Miss Ophelia had taken the precaution to send them the name of the lawyer who did business for the St. Clares; and the most that, in the emergency, could be done, was to address a letter of inquiry to him. The sudden death of Mr. Shelby, a few days after, brought, of course, an absorbing pressure of other interests, for a season.

Mr. Shelby showed his confidence in his wife's ability, by appointing her sole executrix upon his estates; and thus immediately a large and complicated amount of business was brought upon her hands.

Mrs. Shelby, with characteristic energy, applied herself to the work of straightening the entangled web of affairs; and she and George were for some time occupied with collecting and examining accounts, selling property and settling debts; for Mrs. Shelby was determined that everything should be brought into tangible and recognizable shape, let the consequences to her prove what they might. In the mean time, they received a letter from the lawyer to whom Miss Ophelia had referred them, saying that he knew nothing of the matter; that the man was sold at a public auction, and that, beyond receiving the money, he knew nothing of the affair.

Neither George nor Mrs. Shelby could be easy at this result; and, accordingly, some six months after, the latter, having business for his mother, down the river, resolved to visit New Orleans, in person, and push his inquiries, in hopes of discovering Tom's whereabouts, and restoring him.

After some months of unsuccessful search, by the merest accident, George fell in with a man, in New Orleans, who happened to be possessed of the desired information; and with his money in his pocket, our hero took steamboat for Red river, resolving to find out and re-purchase his old friend.

He was soon introduced into the house, where he found Legree in the sitting-room.

Legree received the stranger with a kind of surly hospitality.

"I understand," said the young man, "that you bought, in New Orleans, a boy, named Tom. He used to be on my father's place, and I came to see if I could n't buy him back."

Legree's brow grew dark, and he broke out, passionately; "Yes, I did buy such a fellow,—and a h—l of a bargain I had of it, too! The most rebellious, saucy, impudent dog! Set up my niggers to run away; got off two gals, worth eight hunderd or a thousand dollars apiece. He owned to that, and, when I bid him tell me where they was, he up and said he knew, but he would n't tell; and stood to it, though I gave him the cussedest flogging I ever gave nigger yet. I b'lieve he's trying to die; but I don't know as he 'll make it out."

"Where is he?" said George, impetuously. "Let me see him." The cheeks of the young man were crimson, and his eyes flashed fire; but he prudently said nothing, as yet.

"He 's in dat ar shed," said a little fellow, who stood holding George's horse.

Legree kicked the boy, and swore at him; but George, without saying another word, turned and strode to the spot.

Tom had been lying two days since the fatal night; not suffering, for every nerve of suffering was blunted and destroyed. He lay, for the most part, in a quiet stupor; for the laws of a powerful and well-knit frame would not at once release the imprisoned spirit. By stealth, there had been there, in the darkness of the night, poor desolated creatures, who stole from their scanty hours' rest, that they might repay to him some of those ministrations of love in which he had always been so abundant. Truly, those poor disciples had little to give,—only the cup of cold water; but it was given with full hearts.

Tears had fallen on that honest, insensible face,—tears of late repentance in the poor, ignorant heathen, whom his dying love and patience had awakened to repentance, and bitter prayers, breathed over him to a late-found Saviour, of whom they scarce knew more than the name, but whom the yearning ignorant heart of man never implores in vain.

Cassy, who had glided out of her place of concealment, and, by over-hearing, learned the sacrifice that had been made for her and Emmeline, had been there, the night before, defying the danger of detection; and, moved by the few last words which the affectionate soul had yet strength to breathe, the long winter of despair, the ice of years, had given way, and the dark, despairing woman had wept and prayed.

When George entered the shed, he felt his head giddy and his heart sick.

"Is it possible,—is it possible?" said he, kneeling down by him. "Uncle Tom, my poor, poor old friend!"

Something in the voice penetrated to the ear of the dying. He moved his head gently, smiled, and said,

> "Jesus can make a dying-bed
> Feel soft as downy pillows are."

Tears which did honor to his manly heart fell from the young man's eyes, as he bent over his poor friend.

"O, dear Uncle Tom! do wake,—do speak once more! Look up! Here 's Mas'r George,—your own little Mas'r George. Don't you know me?"

"Mas'r George!" said Tom, opening his eyes, and speaking in a feeble voice; "Mas'r George!" He looked bewildered.

Slowly the idea seemed to fill his soul; and the vacant eye became fixed and brightened, the whole face lighted up, the hard hands clasped, and tears ran down the cheeks.

"Bless the Lord! it is,—it is,—it 's all I wanted! They have n't forgot me. It warms my soul; it does my old heart good! Now I shall die content! Bless the Lord, oh my soul!"

"You shan't die! you *must n't* die, nor think of it! I 've come to buy you, and take you home," said George, with impetuous vehemence.

"O, Mas'r George, ye 're too late. The Lord 's bought me, and is going to take me home,—and I long to go. Heaven is better than Kintuck."

"O, don't die! It 'll kill me!—it 'll break my heart to think what you 've suffered,—and lying in this old shed, here! Poor, poor fellow!"

"Don't call me poor fellow!" said Tom, solemnly. "I *have* been poor fellow; but that 's all past and gone, now. I 'm right in the door, going into glory! O, Mas'r George! *Heaven has come!* I 've got the victory!—the Lord Jesus has given it to me! Glory be to His name!"

George was awe-struck at the force, the vehemence, the power, with which these broken sentences were uttered. He sat gazing in silence.

Tom grasped his hand, and continued,—"Ye must n't, now, tell Chloe, poor soul! how ye found me;—'t would be so dreful to her. Only tell her ye found me going into glory; and that I could n't stay for no one. And tell her the Lord 's stood by me everywhere and al'ays, and made everything light and easy. And oh, the poor chil'en, and the baby!—my old heart 's been most broke for 'em, time and agin! Tell 'em all to follow me—follow me! Give my love to Mas'r, and dear good Missis, and everybody in the place! Ye don't know! 'Pears like I loves 'em all! I loves every creatur', everywhar!—it 's nothing *but* love! O, Mas'r George! what a thing 't is to be a Christian!"

At this moment, Legree sauntered up to the door of the shed, looked in, with a dogged air of affected carelessness, and turned away.

"The old satan!" said George, in his indignation. "It 's a comfort to think the devil will pay *him* for this, some of these days!"

"O, don't!—oh, ye must n't!" said Tom, grasping his hand; "he 's a poor mis'able critter! it 's awful to think on 't! O, if he only could repent, the Lord would forgive him now; but I 'm 'feared he never will!"

"I hope he won't!" said George; "I never want to see *him* in heaven!"

"Hush, Mas'r George!—it worries me! Don't feel so! He an't done me no real harm,—only opened the gate of the kingdom for me; that 's all!"

At this moment, the sudden flush of strength which the joy of meeting his young master had infused into the dying man gave way. A sudden sinking fell upon him; he closed his eyes; and that mysterious and sublime change passed over his face, that told the approach of other worlds.

He began to draw his breath with long, deep inspirations; and his broad chest rose and fell, heavily. The expression of his face was that of a conqueror.

"Who,—who,—who shall separate us from the love of Christ?" he said, in a voice that contended with mortal weakness; and, with a smile, he fell asleep.

George sat fixed with solemn awe. It seemed to him that the place was holy; and, as he closed the lifeless eyes, and rose up from the dead, only one thought possessed him,—that expressed by his simple old friend,—"What a thing it is to be a Christian!"

He turned: Legree was standing, sullenly, behind him.

Something in that dying scene had checked the natural fierceness of youthful passion. The presence of the man was simply loathsome to George; and he felt only an impulse to get away from him, with as few words as possible.

Fixing his keen dark eyes on Legree, he simply said, pointing to the dead, "You have got all you ever can of him. What shall I pay you for the body? I will take it away, and bury it decently."

"I don't sell dead niggers," said Legree, doggedly. "You are welcome to bury him where and when you like."

"Boys," said George, in an authoritative tone, to two or three negroes, who were looking at the body, "help me lift him up, and carry him to my wagon; and get me a spade."

One of them ran for a spade; the other two assisted George to carry the body to the wagon.

George neither spoke to nor looked at Legree, who did not countermand his orders, but stood, whistling, with an air of forced unconcern. He sulkily followed them to where the wagon stood at the door.

George spread his cloak in the wagon, and had the body carefully disposed of in it,—moving the seat, so as to give it room. Then he turned, fixed his eyes on Legree, and said, with forced composure.

"I have not, as yet, said to you what I think of this most atrocious affair;—this is not the time and place. But, sir, this innocent blood shall have justice. I will proclaim this murder, I will go to the very first magistrate, and expose you."

"Do!" said Legree, snapping his fingers, scornfully. "I'd like to see you doing it. Where you going to get witnesses?—how you going to prove it?—Come, now!"

George saw, at once, the force of this defiance. There was not a white person on the place; and, in all southern courts, the testimony of colored blood is nothing. He felt, at that moment, as if he could have rent the heavens with his heart's indignant cry for justice; but in vain.

"After all, what a fuss, for a dead nigger!" said Legree.

The word was as a spark to a powder magazine. Prudence was never a cardinal virtue of the Kentucky boy. George turned, and, with one indignant blow, knocked Legree flat upon his face; and, as he stood over him, blazing with wrath and defiance, he would have formed no bad personification of his great namesake triumphing over the dragon.

Some men, however, are decidedly bettered by being knocked down. If a man lays them fairly flat in the dust, they seem immediately to conceive a respect for him; and Legree was one of this sort. As he rose, therefore, and brushed the dust from his clothes, he eyed the slowly-retreating wagon with some evident consideration; nor did he open his mouth till it was out of sight.

Beyond the boundaries of the plantation, George had noticed a dry, sandy knoll, shaded by a few trees: there they made the grave.

"Shall we take off the cloak, Mas'r?" said the negroes, when the grave was ready.

"No, no,—bury it with him! It's all I can give you, now, poor Tom, and you shall have it."

They laid him in; and the men shovelled away, silently. They banked it up, and laid green turf over it.

"You may go, boys," said George, slipping a quarter into the hand of each. They lingered about, however.

"If young Mas'r would please buy us—" said one.

"We'd serve him so faithful!" said the other.

"Hard times here, Mas'r!" said the first. "Do, Mas'r, buy us, please!"

"I can't!—I can't!" said George, with difficulty, motioning them off; "it's impossible!"

The poor fellows looked dejected, and walked off in silence.

"Witness, eternal God!" said George, kneeling on the grave of his poor friend; "oh, witness, that, from this hour, I will do *what one man can* to drive out this curse of slavery from my land!"

There is no monument to mark the last resting-place of our friend. He needs none! His Lord knows where he lies, and will raise him up, immortal, to appear with him when he shall appear in his glory.

Pity him not! Such a life and death is not for pity! Not in the riches of omnipotence is the chief glory of God; but in self-denying, suffering love! And blessed are the men whom he calls to fellowship with him, bearing their cross after him with patience. Of such it is written, "Blessed are they that mourn, for they shall be comforted."

## XLII.
### An Authentic Ghost Story

For some remarkable reason, ghostly legends were uncommonly rife, about this time, among the servants on Legree's place.

It was whisperingly asserted that footsteps, in the dead of night, had been heard descending the garret stairs, and patrolling the house. In vain the doors of the upper entry had been locked; the ghost either carried a duplicate key in its pocket, or availed itself of a ghost's immemorial privilege of coming through the keyhole, and promenaded as before, with a freedom that was alarming.

Authorities were somewhat divided, as to the outward form of the spirit, owing to a custom quite prevalent among negroes,—and, for aught we know, among whites, too,—of invariably shutting the eyes, and covering up heads under blankets, petticoats, or whatever else might come in use for a shelter, on these occasions. Of course, as everybody knows, when the bodily eyes are thus out of the lists, the spiritual eyes are uncommonly vivacious and perspicuous; and, therefore, there were abundance of full-length portraits of the ghost, abundantly sworn and testified to, which, as is often the case with portraits, agreed with each other in no particular, except the common family peculiarity of the ghost tribe,—the wearing of a *white sheet*. The poor souls were not versed in ancient history, and did not know that Shakspeare had authenticated this costume, by telling how

> "The *sheeted* dead
> Did squeak and gibber in the streets of Rome."

And, therefore, their all hitting upon this is a striking fact in pneumatology, which we recommend to the attention of spiritual media generally.

Be it as it may, we have private reasons for knowing that a tall figure in a white sheet did walk, at the most approved ghostly hours, around the Legree premises,—pass out the doors, glide about the house,—disappear at intervals, and, reäppearing, pass up the silent stair-way, into that fatal garret; and that, in the morning, the entry doors were all found shut and locked as firm as ever.

Legree could not help overhearing this whispering; and it was all the more exciting to him, from the pains that were taken to conceal it from him. He drank more brandy than usual; held up his head briskly, and swore louder than ever in the day-time; but he had bad dreams, and the visions of his head on his bed were anything but agreeable. The night after Tom's body had been carried away, he rode to the next town for a carouse, and had a high one. Got home late and tired; locked his door, took out the key and went to bed.

After all, let a man take what pains he may to hush it down, a human soul is an awful ghostly, unquiet possession, for a bad man to have. Who knows the metes and bounds of it? Who knows all its awful perhapses,—those shudderings and tremblings, which it can no more live down than it can outlive its own eternity! What a fool is he who locks his door to keep out spirits, who has in his own bosom a spirit he dares not meet alone,—whose voice, smothered far down, and piled over with mountains of earthliness, is yet like the forewarning trumpet of doom!

But Legree locked his door and set a chair against it; he set a night-lamp at the head of his bed; and he put his pistols there. He examined the catches and fastenings of the windows, and then swore he "did n't care for the devil and all his angels," and went to sleep.

Well, he slept, for he was tired,—slept soundly. But, finally, there came over his sleep a shadow, a horror, an apprehension of something dreadful hanging over him. It was his mother's shroud, he thought; but Cassy had it, holding it up, and showing it to him. He heard a confused noise of screams and groanings; and, with it all, he knew he was asleep, and he struggled to wake himself. He was half awake. He was sure something was coming into his room. He knew the door was opening, but he could not stir hand or foot. At last he turned, with a start; the door *was* open, and he saw a hand putting out his light.

It was a cloudy, misty moonlight, and there he saw it!—something white, gliding in! He heard the still rustle of its ghostly garments. It stood still by his bed;—a cold hand touched his; a voice said, three times, in a low, fearful whisper, "Come! come! come!" And, while he lay sweating with terror, he knew not when or how, the thing was gone. He sprang out of bed, and pulled at the door. It was shut and locked, and the man fell down in a swoon.

After this, Legree became a harder drinker than ever before. He no longer drank cautiously, prudently, but imprudently and recklessly.

There were reports around the country, soon after, that he was sick and dying. Excess had brought on that frightful disease that seems to throw the lurid shadows of a coming retribution back into the present life. None could bear the horrors of that sick room, when he raved and screamed, and spoke of sights which almost stopped the blood of those who heard him; and, at his dying bed, stood a stern, white, inexorable figure saying, "Come! come! come!"

By a singular coincidence, on the very night that this vision appeared to Legree, the house-door was found open in the morning, and some of the negroes had seen two white figures gliding down the avenue towards the high-road.

It was near sunrise when Cassy and Emmeline paused, for a moment, in a little knot of trees near the town.

Cassy was dressed after the manner of Creole Spanish ladies,—wholly in black. A small black bonnet on her head, covered by a veil thick with embroidery, concealed her face. It had been agreed that, in their escape, she was to personate the character of a Creole lady, and Emmeline that of her servant.

Brought up, from early life, in connection with the highest society, the language, movements and air of Cassy, were all in agreement with this idea; and she had still enough remaining with her, of a once splendid wardrobe, and sets of jewels, to enable her to personate the thing to advantage.

She stopped in the outskirts of the town, where she had noticed trunks for sale, and purchased a handsome one. This she requested the man to send along with her. And, accordingly, thus escorted by a boy wheeling her trunk, and Emmeline behind her, carrying her carpet-bag and sundry bundles, she made her appearance at the small tavern, like a lady of consideration.

The first person that struck her, after her arrival, was George Shelby, who was staying there, awaiting the next boat.

Cassy had remarked the young man from her loop-hole in the garret, and seen him bear away the body of Tom, and observed, with secret exultation, his rencontre with Legree. Subsequently, she had gathered, from the conversations she had overheard among the negroes, as she glided about in her ghostly disguise, after nightfall, who he was, and in what relation he stood to Tom. She, therefore, felt an immediate accession of confidence, when she found that he was, like herself, awaiting the next boat.

Cassy's air and manner, address, and evident command of money, prevented any rising disposition to suspicion in the hotel. People never inquire too closely into those who are fair on the main point, of paying well,—a thing which Cassy had foreseen when she provided herself with money.

In the edge of the evening, a boat was heard coming along, and George Shelby handed Cassy aboard, with the politeness which comes naturally to every Kentuckian, and exerted himself to provide her with a good state-room.

Cassy kept her room and bed, on pretext of illness, during the whole time they were on Red river; and was waited on, with obsequious devotion, by her attendant.

When they arrived at the Mississippi river, George, having learned that the course of the strange lady was upward, like his own, proposed to take a state-room for her on the same boat with himself,—good-naturedly compassionating her feeble health, and desirous to do what he could to assist her.

Behold, therefore, the whole party safely transferred to the good steamer Cincinnati, and sweeping up the river under a powerful head of steam.

Cassy's health was much better. She sat upon the guards, came to the table, and was remarked upon in the boat as a lady that must have been very handsome.

From the moment that George got the first glimpse of her face, he was troubled with one of those fleeting and indefinite likenesses, which almost everybody can remember, and has been, at times, perplexed with. He could not keep himself from looking at her, and watching her perpetually. At table, or sitting at her state-room door, still she would encounter the young man's eyes fixed on her, and politely withdrawn, when she showed, by her countenance, that she was sensible of the observation.

Cassy became uneasy. She began to think that he suspected something; and finally resolved to throw herself entirely on his generosity, and intrusted him with her whole history.

George was heartily disposed to sympathize with any one who had escaped from Legree's plantation,—a place that he could not remember or speak of with patience,—and, with the courageous disregard of consequences which is characteristic of his age and state, he assured her that he would do all in his power to protect and bring them through.

The next state-room to Cassy's was occupied by a French lady, named De Thoux, who was accompanied by a fine little daughter, a child of some twelve summers.

This lady, having gathered, from George's conversation, that he was from Kentucky, seemed evidently disposed to cultivate his acquaintance; in which design she was seconded by the graces of her little girl, who was about as pretty a plaything as ever diverted the weariness of a fortnight's trip on a steamboat.

George's chair was often placed at her state-room door; and Cassy, as she sat upon the guards, could hear their conversation.

Madame de Thoux was very minute in her inquiries as to Kentucky, where she said she had resided in a former period of her life. George discovered, to his surprise, that her former residence must have been in his own vicinity; and her inquiries showed a knowledge of people and things in his vicinity, that was perfectly surprising to him.

"Do you know," said Madame de Thoux to him, one day, "of any man, in your neighborhood, of the name of Harris?"

"There is an old fellow, of that name, lives not far from my father's place," said George. "We never have had much intercourse with him, though."

"He is a large slave-owner, I believe," said Madame de Thoux, with a manner which seemed to betray more interest than she was exactly willing to show.

"He is," said George, looking rather surprised at her manner.

"Did you ever know of his having—perhaps, you may have heard of his having a mulatto boy, named George?"

"O, certainly,—George Harris,—I know him well; he married a servant of my mother's, but has escaped, now, to Canada."

"He has?" said Madame de Thoux, quickly. "Thank God!"

George looked a surprised inquiry, but said nothing.

Madame de Thoux leaned her head on her hand, and burst into tears.

"He is my brother," she said.

"Madame!" said George, with a strong accent of surprise.

"Yes," said Madame de Thoux, lifting her head, proudly, and wiping her tears; "Mr. Shelby, George Harris is my brother!"

"I am perfectly astonished," said George, pushing back his chair a pace or two, and looking at Madame de Thoux.

"I was sold to the South when he was a boy," said she. "I was bought by a good and generous man. He took me with him to the West Indies, set me free, and married me. It is but lately that he died; and I was coming up to Kentucky, to see if I could find and redeem my brother."

"I have heard him speak of a sister Emily, that was sold South," said George.

"Yes, indeed! I am the one," said Madame de Thoux;—"tell me what sort of a—"

"A very fine young man," said George, "notwithstanding the curse of slavery that lay on him. He sustained a first rate character, both for intelligence and principle. I know, you see," he said; "because he married in our family."

"What sort of a girl?" said Madame de Thoux, eagerly.

"A treasure," said George; "a beautiful, intelligent, amiable girl. Very pious.

My mother had brought her up, and trained her as carefully, almost, as a daughter. She could read and write, embroider and sew, beautifully; and was a beautiful singer."

"Was she born in your house?" said Madame de Thoux.

"No. Father bought her once, in one of his trips to New Orleans, and brought her up as a present to mother. She was about eight or nine years old, then. Father would never tell mother what he gave for her; but, the other day, in looking over his old papers, we came across the bill of sale. He paid an extravagant sum for her, to be sure. I suppose, on account of her extraordinary beauty."

George sat with his back to Cassy, and did not see the absorbed expression of her countenance, as he was giving these details.

At this point in the story, she touched his arm, and, with a face perfectly white with interest, said, "Do you know the names of the people he bought her of?"

"A man of the name of Simmons, I think, was the principal in the transaction. At least, I think that was the name on the bill of sale."

"O, my God!" said Cassy, and fell insensible on the floor of the cabin.

George was wide awake now, and so was Madame de Thoux. Though neither of them could conjecture what was the cause of Cassy's fainting, still they made all the tumult which is proper in such cases;—George upsetting a wash-pitcher, and breaking two tumblers, in the warmth of his humanity; and various ladies in the cabin, hearing that somebody had fainted, crowded the state-room door, and kept out all the air they possibly could, so that, on the whole, everything was done that could be expected.

Poor Cassy! when she recovered, turned her face to the wall, and wept and sobbed like a child,—perhaps, mother, you can tell what she was thinking of! Perhaps you cannot,—but she felt as sure, in that hour, that God had had mercy on her, and that she should see her daughter,—as she did, months afterwards,—when—but we anticipate.

## XLIII.
### Results

The rest of our story is soon told. George Shelby, interested, as any other young man might be, by the romance of the incident, no less than by feelings of humanity, was at the pains to send to Cassy the bill of sale of Eliza; whose date and name all corresponded with her own knowledge of facts, and left no doubt upon her mind as to the identity of her child. It remained now only for her to trace out the path of the fugitives.

Madame de Thoux and she, thus drawn together by the singular coincidence of their fortunes, proceeded immediately to Canada, and began a tour of inquiry among the stations, where the numerous fugitives from slavery are located. At Amherstberg they found the missionary with whom George and Eliza had taken shelter, on their first arrival in Canada; and through him were enabled to trace the family to Montreal.

George and Eliza had now been five years free. George had found constant occupation in the shop of a worthy machinist, where he had been earning a competent support for his family, which, in the mean time, had been increased by the addition of another daughter.

Little Harry—a fine bright boy—had been put to a good school, and was making rapid proficiency in knowledge.

The worthy pastor of the station, in Amherstberg, where George had first landed, was so much interested in the statements of Madame de Thoux and Cassy, that he yielded to the solicitations of the former, to accompany them to Montreal, in their search,—she bearing all the expense of the expedition.

The scene now changes to a small, neat tenement, in the outskirts of Montreal; the time, evening. A cheerful fire blazes on the hearth; a tea-table, covered with a snowy cloth, stands prepared for the evening meal. In one corner of the room was a table covered with a green cloth, where was an open writing-desk, pens, paper, and over it a shelf of well-selected books.

This was George's study. The same zeal for self-improvement, which led him to steal the much coveted arts of reading and writing, amid all the toils and discouragements of his early life, still led him to devote all his leisure time to self-cultivation.

At this present time, he is seated at the table, making notes from a volume of the family library he has been reading.

"Come, George," says Eliza, "you 've been gone all day. Do put down that book, and let 's talk, while I 'm getting tea,—do."

And little Eliza seconds the effort, by toddling up to her father, and trying to pull the book out of his hand, and install herself on his knee as a substitute.

"O, you little witch!" says George, yielding, as, in such circumstances, man always must.

"That 's right," says Eliza, as she begins to cut a loaf of bread. A little older she looks; her form a little fuller; her air more matronly than of yore; but evidently contented and happy as woman need be.

"Harry, my boy, how did you come on in that sum, today?" says George, as he laid his hand on his son's head.

Harry has lost his long curls; but he can never lose those eyes and eyelashes, and that fine, bold brow, that flushes with triumph, as he answers, "I did it, every bit of it, *myself*, father; and *nobody* helped me!"

"That 's right," says his father; "depend on yourself, my son. You have a better chance than ever your poor father had."

At this moment, there is a rap at the door; and Eliza goes and opens it. The delighted—"Why!—this you?"—calls up her husband; and the good pastor of Amherstberg is welcomed. There are two more women with him, and Eliza asks them to sit down.

Now, if the truth must be told, the honest pastor had arranged a little programme, according to which this affair was to develop itself; and, on the way up, all had very cautiously and prudently exhorted each other not to let things out, except according to previous arrangement.

What was the good man's consternation, therefore, just as he had motioned to the ladies to be seated, and was taking out his pocket-handkerchief to wipe his mouth, so as to proceed to his introductory speech in good order, when Madame de Thoux upset the whole plan, by throwing her arms around George's neck, and letting all out at once, by saying, "O, George! don't you know me? I'm your sister Emily."

Cassy had seated herself more composedly, and would have carried on her part very well, had not little Eliza suddenly appeared before her in exact shape and form, every outline and curl, just as her daughter was when she saw her last. The little thing peered up in her face; and Cassy caught her up in her arms, pressed her to her bosom, saying, what, at the moment she really believed, "Darling, I'm your mother!"

In fact, it was a troublesome matter to do up exactly in proper order; but the good pastor, at last, succeeded in getting everybody quiet, and delivering the speech with which he had intended to open the exercises; and in which, at last, he succeeded so well, that his whole audience were sobbing about him in a manner that ought to satisfy any orator, ancient or modern.

They knelt together, and the good man prayed,—for there are some feelings so agitated and tumultuous, that they can find rest only by being poured into the bosom of Almighty love,—and then, rising up, the new-found family embraced each other, with a holy trust in Him, who from such peril and dangers, and by such unknown ways, had brought them together.

The note-book of a missionary, among the Canadian fugitives, contains truth stranger than fiction. How can it be otherwise, when a system prevails which whirls families and scatters their members, as the wind whirls and scatters the leaves of autumn? These shores of refuge, like the eternal shore, often unite again, in glad communion, hearts that for long years have mourned each other as lost. And affecting beyond expression is the earnestness with which every new arrival among them is met, if, perchance, it may bring tidings of mother, sister, child or wife, still lost to view in the shadows of slavery.

Deeds of heroism are wrought here more than those of romance, when, defying torture, and braving death itself, the fugitive voluntarily threads his way back to the terrors and perils of that dark land, that he may bring out his sister, or mother, or wife.

One young man, of whom a missionary has told us, twice re-captured, and suffering shameful stripes for his heroism, had escaped again; and, in a letter which we heard read, tells his friends that he is going back a third time, that he may, at last, bring away his sister. My good sir, is this man a hero, or a criminal? Would not you do as much for your sister? And can you blame him?

But, to return to our friends, whom we left wiping their eyes, and recovering themselves from too great and sudden a joy. They are now seated around the social board, and are getting decidedly companionable; only that Cassy, who keeps little Eliza on her lap, occasionally squeezes the little thing, in a manner that rather astonishes her, and obstinately refuses to have her mouth stuffed with cake to the extent the little one desires,—alleging, what the child rather wonders at, that she has got something better than cake, and does n't want it.

And, indeed, in two or three days, such a change has passed over Cassy, that our readers would scarcely know her. The despairing, haggard expression of her face had given way to one of gentle trust. She seemed to sink, at once, into the bosom of the family, and take the little ones into her heart, as something for which it long had waited. Indeed, her love seemed to flow more naturally to the little Eliza than to her own daughter; for she was the exact image and body of the child whom she had lost. The little one was a flowery bond between mother and daughter, through whom grew up acquaintanceship and affection. Eliza's steady, consistent piety, regulated by the constant reading of the sacred word, made her a proper guide for the shattered and wearied mind of her mother. Cassy yielded at once, and with her whole soul, to every good influence, and became a devout and tender Christian.

After a day or two, Madame de Thoux told her brother more particularly of her affairs. The death of her husband had left her an ample fortune, which she generously offered to share with the family. When she asked George what way she could best apply it for him, he answered, "Give me an education, Emily; that has always been my heart's desire. Then, I can do all the rest."

On mature deliberation, it was decided that the whole family should go, for some years, to France; whither they sailed, carrying Emmeline with them.

The good looks of the latter won the affection of the first mate of the vessel; and, shortly after entering the port, she became his wife.

George remained four years at a French university, and applying himself with an unintermitted zeal, obtained a very thorough education.

Political troubles in France, at last, led the family again to seek an asylum in this country.

George's feelings and views, as an educated man, may be best expressed in a letter to one of his friends.

"I feel somewhat at a loss, as to my future course. True, as you have said to me, I might mingle in the circles of the whites, in this country, my shade of color is so slight, and that of my wife and family scarce perceptible. Well, perhaps, on sufferance, I might. But, to tell you the truth, I have no wish to.

"My sympathies are not for my father's race, but for my mother's. To him I was no more than a fine dog or horse; to my poor heart-broken mother I was a *child*; and, though I never saw her, after the cruel sale that separated us, till she died, yet I *know* she always loved me dearly. I know it by my own heart. When I think of all she suffered, of my own early sufferings, of the distresses and struggles of my heroic wife, of my sister, sold in the New Orleans slave-market,— though I hope to have no unchristian sentiments, yet I may be excused for saying, I have no wish to pass for an American, or to identify myself with them.

"It is with the oppressed, enslaved African race that I cast in my lot; and, if I wished anything, I would wish myself two shades darker, rather than one lighter.

"The desire and yearning of my soul is for an African *nationality*. I want a people that shall have a tangible, separate existence of its own; and where am I to look for it? Not in Hayti; for in Hayti they had nothing to start with. A stream cannot rise above its fountain. The race that formed the character of the Haytiens was a worn-out, effeminate one; and, of course, the subject race will be centuries in rising to anything.

"Where, then, shall I look? On the shores of Africa I see a republic,—a republic formed of picked men, who, by energy and self-educating force, have, in many cases, individually, raised themselves above a condition of slavery. Having gone through a preparatory stage of feebleness, this republic has, at last, become an acknowledged nation on the face of the earth,—acknowledged by both France and England. There it is my wish to go, and find myself a people.

"I am aware, now, that I shall have you all against me; but, before you strike, hear me. During my stay in France, I have followed up, with intense interest, the history of my people in America. I have noted the struggle between abolitionist and colonizationist, and have received some impressions, as a distant spectator, which could never have occurred to me as a participator.

"I grant that this Liberia may have subserved all sorts of purposes, by being played off, in the hands of our oppressors, against us. Doubtless the scheme may have been used, in unjustifiable ways, as a means of retarding our emancipation. But the question to me is, Is there not a God above all man's schemes? May He not have overruled their designs, and founded for us a nation by them?

"In these days, a nation is born in a day. A nation starts, now, with all the great problems of republican life and civilization wrought out to its hand;—it has not to discover, but only to apply. Let us, then, all take hold together, with all our might, and see what we can do with this new enterprise, and the whole splendid continent of Africa opens before us and our children. *Our nation* shall roll the tide of civilization and Christianity along its shores, and plant there mighty republics, that, growing with the rapidity of tropical vegetation, shall be for all coming ages.

"Do you say that I am deserting my enslaved brethren? I think not. If I forget them one hour, one moment of my life, so may God forget me! But, what can I do for them, here? Can I break their chains? No, not as an individual; but, let me go and form part of a nation, which shall have a voice in the councils of nations, and then we can speak. A nation has a right to argue, remonstrate, implore, and present the cause of its race,—which an individual has not.

"If Europe ever becomes a grand council of free nations,—as I trust in God it will,—if, there, serfdom, and all unjust and oppressive social inequalities, are done away; and if they, as France and England have done, acknowledge our position,—then, in the great congress of nations, we will make our appeal, and present the cause of our enslaved and suffering race; and it cannot be that free, enlightened America will not then desire to wipe from her escutcheon that bar sinister which disgraces her among nations, and is as truly a curse to her as to the enslaved.

"But, you will tell me, our race have equal rights to mingle in the American republic as the Irishman, the German, the Swede. Granted, they have. We *ought* to be free to meet and mingle,—to rise by our individual worth, without any consideration of caste or color; and they who deny us this right are false to their own professed principles of human equality. We ought, in particular, to be allowed *here*. We have *more* than the rights of common men;—we have the claim of an injured race for reparation. But, then, *I do not want it*; I want a country, a nation, of my own. I think that the African race has peculiarities, yet to be unfolded in the light of civilization and Christianity, which, if not the same with those of the Anglo-Saxon, may prove to be, morally, of even a higher type.

"To the Anglo-Saxon race has been intrusted the destinies of the world, during its pioneer period of struggle and conflict. To that mission its stern, inflexible, energetic elements, were well adapted; but, as a Christian, I look for another era to arise. On its borders I trust we stand; and the throes that now convulse the nations are, to my hope, but the birth-pangs of an hour of universal peace and brotherhood.

"I trust that the development of Africa is to be essentially a Christian one. If not a dominant and commanding race, they are, at least, an affectionate, magnanimous, and forgiving one. Having been called in the furnace of injustice and oppression, they have need to bind closer to their hearts that sublime doctrine of love and forgiveness, through which alone they are to conquer, which it is to be their mission to spread over the continent of Africa.

"In myself, I confess, I am feeble for this,—full half the blood in my veins is the hot and hasty Saxon; but I have an eloquent preacher of the Gospel ever by my side, in the person of my beautiful wife. When I wander, her gentler spirit ever restores me, and keeps before my eyes the Christian calling and mission of our race. As a Christian patriot, as a teacher of Christianity, I go to *my country,*— my chosen, my glorious Africa!—and to her, in my heart, I sometimes apply those splendid words of prophecy: 'Whereas thou hast been forsaken and hated, so that no man went through thee; *I* will make thee an eternal excellence, a joy of many generations!'

"You will call me an enthusiast: you will tell me that I have not well considered what I am undertaking. But I have considered, and counted the cost. I go to *Liberia,* not as to an Elysium of romance, but as to *a field of work.* I expect to work with both hands,—to work *hard;* to work against all sorts of difficulties and discouragements; and to work till I die. This is what I go for; and in this I am quite sure I shall not be disappointed.

"Whatever you may think of my determination, do not divorce me from your confidence; and think that, in whatever I do, I act with a heart wholly given to my people.

"GEORGE HARRIS."

George, with his wife, children, sister and mother, embarked for Africa, some few weeks after. If we are not mistaken, the world will yet hear from him there.

Of our other characters we have nothing very particular to write, except a word relating to Miss Ophelia and Topsy, and a farewell chapter, which we shall dedicate to George Shelby.

Miss Ophelia took Topsy home to Vermont with her, much to the surprise of that grave deliberative body whom a New Englander recognizes under the term *"Our folks."* "Our folks," at first, thought it an odd and unnecessary addition to their well-trained domestic establishment; but, so thoroughly efficient was Miss Ophelia in her conscientious endeavor to do her duty by her elève, that the child rapidly grew in grace and in favor with the family and neighborhood. At the age of womanhood, she was, by her own request baptized, and became a member of the Christian church in the place; and showed so much intelligence, activity and zeal, and desire to do good in the world, that she was at last recommended, and approved, as a missionary to one of the stations in Africa; and we have heard that the same activity and ingenuity which, when a child, made her so multiform and restless in her developments, is now employed, in a safer and wholesomer manner, in teaching the children of her own country.

P. S.—It will be a satisfaction to some mother, also, to state, that some inquiries, which were set on foot by Madame de Thoux, have resulted recently in the discovery of Cassy's son. Being a young man of energy, he had escaped, some years before his mother, and been received and educated by friends of the oppressed in the north. He will soon follow his family to Africa.

## XLIV.
### The Liberator

George Shelby had written to his mother merely a line, stating the day that she might expect him home. Of the death scene of his old friend he had not the heart to write. He had tried several times, and only succeeded in half choking himself; and invariably finished by tearing up the paper, wiping his eyes, and rushing somewhere to get quiet.

There was a pleased bustle all through the Shelby mansion, that day, in expectation of the arrival of young Mas'r George.

Mrs. Shelby was seated in her comfortable parlor, where a cheerful hickory fire was dispelling the chill of the late autumn evening. A supper-table, glittering with plate and cut glass, was set out, on whose arrangements our former friend, old Chloe, was presiding.

Arrayed in a new calico dress, with clean, white apron, and high, well-starched turban, her black polished face glowing with satisfaction, she lingered, with needless punctiliousness, around the arrangements of the table, merely as an excuse for talking a little to her mistress.

"Laws, now! won't it look natural to him?" she said. "Thar,—I set his plate just whar he likes it,—round by the fire. Mas'r George allers wants de warm seat. O, go way!—why did n't Sally get out de *best* tea-pot,—de little new one, Mas'r George got for Missis, Christmas? I 'll have it out! And Missis has heard from Mas'r George?" she said, inquiringly.

"Yes, Chloe; but only a line, just to say he would be home to-night, if he could,—that 's all."

"Did n't say nothin' 'bout my old man, s'pose?" said Chloe, still fidgeting with the tea-cups.

"No, he did n't. He did not speak of anything, Chloe. He said he would tell all, when he got home."

"Jes like Mas'r George,—he 's allers so ferce for tellin' everything hisself. I allers minded dat ar in Mas'r George. Don't see, for my part, how white people gen'lly can bar to hev to write things much as they do, writin' 's such slow, oneasy kind o' work."

Mrs. Shelby smiled.

"I 'm a thinkin' my old man won't know de boys and de baby. Lor'! she 's de biggest gal, now,—good she is, too, and peart, Polly is. She 's out to the house, now, watchin' de hoecake. I 's got just de very pattern my old man liked so much, a bakin'. Jist sich as I gin him the mornin' he was took off. Lord bless us! how I felt, dat ar mornin'!"

Mrs. Shelby sighed, and felt a heavy weight on her heart, at this allusion. She had felt uneasy, ever since she received her son's letter, lest something should prove to be hidden behind the veil of silence which he had drawn.

"Missis has got dem bills?" said Chloe, anxiously.

"Yes, Chloe."

" 'Cause I wants to show my old man dem very bills de *perfectioner* gave me. 'And,' says he, 'Chloe, I wish you 'd stay longer.' 'Thank you, Mas'r,' says I, 'I would, only my old man 's coming home, and Missis,—she can't do without me no longer.' There 's jist what I told him. Berry nice man, dat Mas'r Jones was."

Chloe had pertinaciously insisted that the very bills in which her wages had been paid should be preserved, to show to her husband, in memorial of her capability. And Mrs. Shelby had readily consented to humor her in the request.

"He won't know Polly,—my old man won't. Laws, it 's five year since they tuck him! She was a baby den,—could n't but jist stand. Remember how tickled he used to be, cause she would keep a fallin' over, when she sot out to walk. Laws a me!"

The rattling of wheels now was heard.

"Mas'r George!" said Aunt Chloe, starting to the window.

Mrs. Shelby ran to the entry door, and was folded in the arms of her son. Aunt Chloe stood anxiously straining her eyes out into the darkness.

"O, *poor* Aunt Chloe!" said George, stopping compassionately, and taking her hard, black hand between both his; "I 'd have given all my fortune to have brought him with me, but he 's gone to a better country."

There was a passionate exclamation from Mrs. Shelby, but Aunt Chloe said nothing.

The party entered the supper-room. The money, of which Chloe was so proud, was still lying on the table.

"Thar," said she, gathering it up, and holding it, with a trembling hand, to her mistress, "don't never want to see nor hear on 't again. Jist as I knew 't would be,—sold, and murdered on dem ar' old plantations!"

Chloe turned, and was walking proudly out of the room. Mrs. Shelby followed her softly, and took one of her hands, drew her down into a chair, and sat down by her.

"My poor, good Chloe!" said she.

Chloe leaned her head on her mistress' shoulder, and sobbed out, "O Missis! 'scuse me, my heart 's broke,—dat 's all!"

"I know it is," said Mrs. Shelby, as her tears fell fast; "and I cannot heal it, but Jesus can. He healeth the broken hearted, and bindeth up their wounds."

There was a silence for some time, and all wept together. At last, George, sitting down beside the mourner, took her hand, and, with simple pathos, repeated the triumphant scene of her husband's death, and his last messages of love.

About a month after this, one morning, all the servants of the Shelby estate were convened together in the great hall that ran through the house, to hear a few words from their young master.

To the surprise of all, he appeared among them with a bundle of papers in his hand, containing a certificate of freedom to every one on the place, which he read successively, and presented, amid the sobs and tears and shouts of all present.

Many, however, pressed around him, earnestly begging him not to send them away; and, with anxious faces, tendering back their free papers.

"We don't want to be no freer than we are. We 's allers had all we wanted. We don't want to leave de ole place, and Mas'r and Missis, and de rest!"

"My good friends," said George, as soon as he could get a silence, "there 'll be no need for you to leave me. The place wants as many hands to work it as it did before. We need the same about the house that we did before. But, you are now free men and free women. I shall pay you wages for your work, such as we shall agree on. The advantage is, that in case of my getting in debt, or dying,—things that might happen,—you cannot now be taken up and sold. I expect to carry on the estate, and to teach you what, perhaps, it will take you some time to learn,—how to use the rights I give you as free men and women. I expect you to be good, and willing to learn; and I trust in God that I shall be faithful, and willing to teach. And now, my friends, look up, and thank God for the blessing of freedom."

An aged, patriarchal negro, who had grown gray and blind on the estate, now rose, and, lifting his trembling hand said, "Let us give thanks unto the Lord!" As all kneeled by one consent, a more touching and hearty Te Deum never ascended to heaven, though borne on the peal of organ, bell and cannon, than came from that honest old heart.

On rising, another struck up a Methodist hymn, of which the burden was,

> "The year of Jubilee is come,—
> Return, ye ransomed sinners, home."

"One thing more," said George, as he stopped the congratulations of the throng; "you all remember our good old Uncle Tom?"

George here gave a short narration of the scene of his death, and of his loving farewell to all on the place, and added,

"It was on his grave, my friends, that I resolved, before God, that I would never own another slave, while it was possible to free him; that nobody, through me, should ever run the risk of being parted from home and friends, and dying on a lonely plantation, as he died. So, when you rejoice in your freedom, think that you owe it to that good old soul, and pay it back in kindness to his wife and children. Think of your freedom, every time you see UNCLE TOM'S CABIN; and let it be a memorial to put you all in mind to follow in his steps, and be as honest and faithful and Christian as he was."

## XLV.
### Concluding Remarks

The writer has often been inquired of, by correspondents from different parts of the country, whether this narrative is a true one; and to these inquiries she will give one general answer.

The separate incidents that compose the narrative are, to a very great extent, authentic, occurring, many of them, either under her own observation, or that of her personal friends. She or her friends have observed characters the counterpart of almost all that are here introduced; and many of the sayings are word for word as heard herself, or reported to her.

The personal appearance of Eliza, the character ascribed to her, are sketches drawn from life. The incorruptible fidelity, piety and honesty, of Uncle Tom, had more than one development, to her personal knowledge. Some of the most deeply tragic and romantic, some of the most terrible incidents, have also their parallel in reality. The incident of the mother's crossing the Ohio river on the ice is a well-known fact. The story of "old Prue," in the second volume, was an incident that fell under the personal observation of a brother of the writer, then collecting-clerk to a large mercantile house, in New Orleans. From the same source was derived the character of the planter Legree. Of him her brother thus wrote, speaking of visiting his plantation, on a collecting tour: "He actually made me feel of his fist, which was like a blacksmith's hammer, or a nodule of iron, telling me that it was 'calloused with knocking down niggers.' When I left the plantation, I drew a long breath, and felt as if I had escaped from an ogre's den."

That the tragical fate of Tom, also, has too many times had its parallel, there are living witnesses, all over our land, to testify. Let it be remembered that in all southern states it is a principle of jurisprudence that no person of colored lineage can testify in a suit against a white, and it will be easy to see that such a case may occur, wherever there is a man whose passions outweigh his interests, and a slave who has manhood or principle enough to resist his will. There is, actually, nothing to protect the slave's life, but the *character* of the master. Facts too shocking to be contemplated occasionally force their way to the public ear, and the comment that one often hears made on them is more shocking than the thing itself. It is said, "Very likely such cases may now and then occur, but they are no sample of general practice." If the laws of New England were so arranged that a master could *now and then* torture an apprentice to death, without a possibility of being brought to justice, would it be received with equal composure? Would it be said, "These cases are rare, and no samples of general practice"? This injustice is an *inherent* one in the slave system,—it cannot exist without it.

The public and shameless sale of beautiful mulatto and quadroon girls has acquired a notoriety, from the incidents following the capture of the Pearl. We extract the following from the speech of Hon. Horace Mann, one of the legal counsel for the defendants in that case. He says: "In that company of seventy-six persons, who attempted, in 1848, to escape from the District of Columbia in the schooner Pearl, and whose officers I assisted in defending, there were several young and healthy girls, who had those peculiar attractions of form and feature which connoisseurs prize so highly. Elizabeth Russel was one of them. She immediately fell into the slave-trader's fangs, and was doomed for the New Orleans market. The hearts of those that saw her were touched with pity for her fate. They offered eighteen hundred dollars to redeem her; and some there were who offered to give, that would not have much left after the gift; but the fiend of a slave-trader was inexorable. She was despatched to New Orleans; but, when about half way there, God had mercy on her, and smote her with death. There were two girls named Edmundson in the same company. When about to be sent to the same market, an older sister went to the shambles, to plead with the wretch who owned them, for the love of God, to spare his victims. He bantered her, telling what fine dresses and fine furniture they would have. 'Yes,' she said, 'that may do very well in this life, but what will become of them in the next?' They too were sent to New Orleans; but were afterwards redeemed, at an enormous ransom, and brought back." Is it not plain, from this, that the histories of Emmeline and Cassy may have many counterparts?

Justice, too, obliges the author to state that the fairness of mind and generosity attributed to St. Clare are not without a parallel, as the following anecdote will show. A few years since, a young southern gentleman was in Cincinnati, with a favorite servant, who had been his personal attendant from a boy. The young man took advantage of this opportunity to secure his own freedom, and fled to the protection of a Quaker, who was quite noted in affairs of this kind. The owner was exceedingly indignant. He had always treated the slave with such indulgence, and his confidence in his affection was such, that he believed he must have been practised upon to induce him to revolt from him. He visited the Quaker, in high anger; but, being possessed of uncommon candor and fairness, was soon quieted by his arguments and representations. It was a side of the subject which he never had heard,—never had thought on; and he immediately told the Quaker that, if his slave would, to his own face, say that it was his desire to be free, he would liberate him. An interview was forthwith procured, and Nathan was asked by his young master whether he had ever had any reason to complain of his treatment, in any respect.

"No, Mas'r," said Nathan; "you 've always been good to me."

"Well, then, why do you want to leave me?"

"Mas'r may die, and then who get me?—I 'd rather be a free man."

After some deliberation, the young master replied, "Nathan, in your place, I think I should feel very much so, myself. You are free."

He immediately made him out free papers; deposited a sum of money in the hands of the Quaker, to be judiciously used in assisting him to start in life, and left a very sensible and kind letter of advice to the young man. That letter was for some time in the writer's hands.

The author hopes she has done justice to that nobility, generosity, and humanity, which in many cases characterize individuals at the South. Such instances save us from utter despair of our kind. But, she asks any person, who knows the world, are such characters *common*, anywhere?

For many years of her life, the author avoided all reading upon or allusion to the subject of slavery, considering it as too painful to be inquired into, and one which advancing light and civilization would certainly live down. But, since the legislative act of 1850, when she heard, with perfect surprise and consternation, Christian and humane people actually recommending the remanding escaped fugitives into slavery, as a duty binding on good citizens,—when she heard, on all hands, from kind, compassionate and estimable people, in the free states of the North, deliberations and discussions as to what Christian duty could be on this head,—she could only think, These men and Christians cannot know what slavery is; if they did, such a question could never be open for discussion. And from this arose a desire to exhibit it in a *living dramatic reality*. She has endeavored to show it fairly, in its best and its worst phases. In its *best* aspect, she has, perhaps, been successful; but, oh! who shall say what yet remains untold in that valley and shadow of death, that lies the other side?

To you, generous, noble-minded men and women, of the South,—you, whose virtue, and magnanimity, and purity of character, are the greater for the severer trial it has encountered,—to you is her appeal. Have you not, in your own secret souls, in your own private conversings, felt that there are woes and evils, in this accursed system, far beyond what are here shadowed, or can be shadowed? Can it be otherwise? Is *man* ever a creature to be trusted with wholly irresponsible power? And does not the slave system, by denying the slave all legal right of testimony, make every individual owner an irresponsible despot? Can anybody fail to make the inference what the practical result will be? If there is, as we admit, a public sentiment among you, men of honor, justice and humanity, is there not also another kind of public sentiment among the ruffian, the brutal and debased? And cannot the ruffian, the brutal, the debased, by slave law, own just as many slaves as the best and purest? Are the honorable, the just, the high-minded and compassionate, the majority anywhere in this world?

The slave-trade is now, by American law, considered as piracy. But a slave-trade, as systematic as ever was carried on on the coast of Africa, is an inevitable attendant and result of American slavery. And its heart-break and its horrors, *can* they be told?

The writer has given only a faint shadow, a dim picture, of the anguish and despair that are, at this very moment, riving thousands of hearts, shattering thousands of families, and driving a helpless and sensitive race to frenzy and despair. There are those living who know the mothers whom this accursed traffic has driven to the murder of their children; and themselves seeking in death a shelter from woes more dreaded than death. Nothing of tragedy can be written, can be spoken, can be conceived, that equals the frightful reality of scenes daily and hourly acting on our shores, beneath the shadow of American law, and the shadow of the cross of Christ.

And now, men and women of America, is this a thing to be trifled with, apologized for, and passed over in silence? Farmers of Massachusetts, of New Hampshire, of Vermont, of Connecticut, who read this book by the blaze of your winter-evening fire,—strong-hearted, generous sailors and shipowners of Maine,—is this a thing for you to countenance and encourage? Brave and generous men of New York, farmers of rich and joyous Ohio, and ye of the wide prairie states,—answer, is this a thing for you to protect and countenance? And you, mothers of America,—you, who have learned, by the cradles of your own children, to love and feel for all mankind,—by the sacred love you bear your child; by your joy in his beautiful, spotless infancy; by the motherly pity and tenderness with which you guide his growing years; by the anxieties of his education; by the prayers you breathe for his soul's eternal good;—I beseech you, pity the mother who has all your affections, and not one legal right to protect, guide, or educate, the child of her bosom! By the sick hour of your child; by those dying eyes, which you can never forget; by those last cries, that wrung your heart when you could neither help nor save; by the desolation of that empty cradle, that silent nursery,—I beseech you, pity those mothers that are constantly made childless by the American slave-trade! And say, mothers of America, is this a thing to be defended, sympathized with, passed over in silence?

Do you say that the people of the free states have nothing to do with it, and can do nothing? Would to God this were true! But it is not true. The people of the free states have defended, encouraged, and participated; and are more guilty for it, before God, than the South, in that they have *not* the apology of education or custom.

If the mothers of the free states had all felt as they should, in times past, the sons of the free states would not have been the holders, and, proverbially, the hardest masters of slaves; the sons of the free states would not have connived at the extension of slavery, in our national body; the sons of the free states would not, as they do, trade the souls and bodies of men as an equivalent to money, in their mercantile dealings. There are multitudes of slaves temporarily owned, and sold again, by merchants in northern cities; and shall the whole guilt or obloquy of slavery fall only on the South?

Northern men, northern mothers, northern Christians, have something more to do than denounce their brethren at the South; they have to look to the evil among themselves.

But, what can any individual do? Of that, every individual can judge. There is one thing that every individual can do,—they can see to it that *they feel right.* An atmosphere of sympathetic influence encircles every human being; and the man or woman who *feels* strongly, healthily and justly, on the great interests of humanity, is a constant benefactor to the human race. See, then, to your sympathies in this matter! Are they in harmony with the sympathies of Christ? or are they swayed and perverted by the sophistries of worldly policy?

Christian men and women of the North! still further,—you have another power; you can *pray!* Do you believe in prayer? or has it become an indistinct apostolic tradition? You pray for the heathen abroad; pray also for the heathen at home. And pray for those distressed Christians whose whole chance of religious improvement is an accident of trade and sale; from whom any adherence to the morals of Christianity is, in many cases, an impossibility, unless they have given them, from above, the courage and grace of martyrdom.

But, still more. On the shores of our free states are emerging the poor, shattered, broken remnants of families,—men and women, escaped, by miraculous providences, from the surges of slavery,—feeble in knowledge, and, in many cases, infirm in moral constitution, from a system which confounds and confuses every principle of Christianity and morality. They come to seek a refuge among you; they come to seek education, knowledge, Christianity.

What do you owe to these poor unfortunates, oh Christians? Does not every American Christian owe to the African race some effort at reparation for the wrongs that the American nation has brought upon them? Shall the doors of churches and school-houses be shut upon them? Shall states arise and shake them out? Shall the church of Christ hear in silence the taunt that is thrown at them, and shrink away from the helpless hand that they stretch out; and, by her silence, encourage the cruelty that would chase them from our borders? If it must be so, it will be a mournful spectacle. If it must be so, the country will have reason to tremble, when it remembers that the fate of nations is in the hands of One who is very pitiful, and of tender compassion.

Do you say, "We don't want them here; let them go to Africa"?

That the providence of God has provided a refuge in Africa, is, indeed, a great and noticeable fact; but that is no reason why the church of Christ should throw off that responsibility to this outcast race which her profession demands of her.

To fill up Liberia with an ignorant, inexperienced, half-barbarized race, just escaped from the chains of slavery, would be only to prolong, for ages, the period of struggle and conflict which attends the inception of new enterprises. Let the church of the north receive these poor sufferers in the spirit of Christ; receive them to the educating advantages of Christian republican society and schools, until they have attained to somewhat of a moral and intellectual maturity, and then assist them in their passage to those shores, where they may put in practice the lessons they have learned in America.

There is a body of men at the north, comparatively small, who have been doing this; and, as the result, this country has already seen examples of men, formerly slaves, who have rapidly acquired property, reputation, and education. Talent has been developed, which, considering the circumstances, is certainly remarkable; and, for moral traits of honesty, kindness, tenderness of feeling,—for heroic efforts and self-denials, endured for the ransom of brethren and friends yet in slavery,—they have been remarkable to a degree that, considering the influence under which they were born, is surprising.

The writer has lived, for many years, on the frontier-line of slave states, and has had great opportunities of observation among those who formerly were slaves. They have been in her family as servants; and, in default of any other school to receive them, she has, in many cases, had them instructed in a family school, with her own children. She has also the testimony of missionaries, among the fugitives in Canada, in coincidence with her own experience; and her deductions, with regard to the capabilities of the race, are encouraging in the highest degree.

The first desire of the emancipated slave, generally, is for *education*. There is nothing that they are not willing to give or do to have their children instructed; and, so far as the writer has observed herself, or taken the testimony of teachers among them, they are remarkably intelligent and quick to learn. The results of schools, founded for them by benevolent individuals in Cincinnati, fully establish this.

The author gives the following statement of facts, on the authority of Professor C. E. Stowe, then of Lane Seminary, Ohio, with regard to emancipated slaves, now resident in Cincinnati; given to show the capability of the race, even without any very particular assistance or encouragement.

The intital letters alone are given. They are all residents of Cincinnati.

"B———. Furniture maker; twenty years in the city; worth ten thousand dollars, all his own earnings; a Baptist.

"C———. Full black; stolen from Africa; sold in New Orleans; been free fifteen years; paid for himself six hundred dollars; a farmer; owns several farms in Indiana; Presbyterian; probably worth fifteen or twenty thousand dollars, all earned by himself.

"K———. Full black; dealer in real estate; worth thirty thousand dollars; about forty years old; free six years; paid eighteen hundred dollars for his family; member of the Baptist church; received a legacy from his master, which he has taken good care of, and increased.

"G———. Full black; coal dealer; about thirty years old; worth eighteen thousand dollars; paid for himself twice, being once defrauded to the amount of sixteen hundred dollars; made all his money by his own efforts—much of it while a slave, hiring his time of his master, and doing business for himself; a fine, gentlemanly fellow.

"W———. Three-fourths black; barber and waiter; from Kentucky; nineteen years free; paid for self and family over three thousand dollars; deacon in the Baptist church.

"G. D———. Three-fourths black; white-washer; from Kentucky; nine years free; paid fifteen hundred dollars for self and family; recently died, aged sixty; worth six thousand dollars."

Professor Stowe says, "With all these, except G———, I have been, for some years, personally acquainted, and make my statements from my own knowledge."

The writer well remembers an aged colored woman, who was employed as a washerwoman in her father's family. The daughter of this woman married a slave. She was a remarkably active and capable young woman, and, by her industry and thrift, and the most persevering self-denial, raised nine hundred dollars for her husband's freedom, which she paid, as she raised it, into the hands of his master. She yet wanted a hundred dollars of the price, when he died. She never recovered any of the money.

These are but few facts, among multitudes which might be adduced, to show the self-denial, energy, patience, and honesty, which the slave has exhibited in a state of freedom.

And let it be remembered that these individuals have thus bravely succeeded in conquering for themselves comparative wealth and social position, in the face of every disadvantage and discouragement. The colored man, by the law of Ohio, cannot be a voter, and, till within a few years, was even denied the right of testimony in legal suits with the white. Nor are these instances confined to the State of Ohio. In all states of the Union we see men, but yesterday burst from the shackles of slavery, who, by a self-educating force, which cannot be too much admired, have risen to highly respectable stations in society. Pennington, among clergymen, Douglas and Ward, among editors, are well known instances.

If this persecuted race, with every discouragement and disadvantage, have done thus much, how much more they might do, if the Christian church would act towards them in the spirit of her Lord!

This is an age of the world when nations are trembling and convulsed. A mighty influence is abroad, surging and heaving the world, as with an earthquake.

And is America safe? Every nation that carries in its bosom great and unredressed injustice has in it the elements of this last convulsion.

For what is this mighty influence thus rousing in all nations and languages those groanings that cannot be uttered, for man's freedom and equality?

O, Church of Christ, read the signs of the times! Is not this power the spirit of HIM whose kingdom is yet to come, and whose will to be done on earth as it is in heaven?

But who may abide the day of his appearing? "for that day shall burn as an oven: and he shall appear as a swift witness against those that oppress the hireling in his wages, the widow and the fatherless, and that *turn aside the stranger in his right*: and he shall break in pieces the oppressor."

Are not these dread words for a nation bearing in her bosom so mighty an injustice? Christians! every time that you pray that the kingdom of Christ may come, can you forget that prophecy associates, in dread fellowship, the *day of vengeance* with the year of his redeemed?

A day of grace is yet held out to us. Both North and South have been guilty before God; and the *Christian church* has a heavy account to answer. Not by combining toegther, to protect injustice and cruelty, and making a common capital of sin, is this Union to be saved,—but by repentance, justice and mercy; for, not surer is the eternal law by which the millstone sinks in the ocean, than that stronger law, by which injustice and cruelty shall bring on nations the wrath of Almighty God!

# A Key to Uncle Tom's Cabin

In *A Key to Uncle Tom's Cabin*, published in 1853 by J. P. Jewett, Stowe defended the veracity of her account of slavery by providing voluminous documentation of characters and incidents. In some cases this material illuminates the actual sources she drew upon for her novel; in many more cases the material corroborates her portraits after the fact. Like Theodore Weld's *Slavery As It Is*, which may have been the model for her work, her *Key* uses the words of slaveholders themselves to indict the institution of slavery, making astute use of evidence from legal cases and newspaper ads for runaway slaves.

Thus Stowe's *Key* is more than a defense of *Uncle Tom's Cabin*, it is an antislavery polemic in its own right. Stowe uses the occasion to preach—taking her own novel as the text. She explains, interprets, expands, exhorts, and sometimes breaks into dialogue as if she were writing another chapter of her novel. The complexity and contradiction of her views on race are evident in her discussion of the sources for her hero, Tom. Miss Ophelia occasions well-honed remarks on the hypocrisy of Christians who sacrifice to bring the gospel to the heathen in foreign lands but do not raise a finger when a black family is deliberately burned out of their home in the North, or when Frederick Douglass is denied a berth in a steamer or Dr. Pennington a seat on the omnibus. Arguing that such northern prejudice allowed slaveowners to rationalize that their slaves were better off under their patriarchal protection, Stowe concludes, "They, then, who keep up this prejudice, may be said to be, in a certain sense, slaveholders."

Throughout her welter of examples, whether she is exploring sources for characters, investigating the legal status of the slave, or indicting American churches for their proslavery pronouncements, Stowe keeps her eye trained on the systemic nature of the oppression she describes. Just as Karl Marx explained the logic of capital, Stowe explains the logic of slavery. Satire is a natural ally here, as when she defends Legree's murder of Tom as essential to the maintenance of the sytem. Those who wept over his death in *Uncle Tom's Cabin* were confronted, in the *Key*, with an iron logic that had no room for the sentimental.

The index to the first edition of *A Key to Uncle Tom's Cabin* is reprinted in its entirety (with page references omitted) so that the reader may see the scope and structure of Stowe's undertaking.

# INDEX

## PART I

to commit crimes for which they are executed.—Is the negro a person in any sense?—Judge Clark's argument to prove that he is a human being.—Decision that a woman may be given to one person, and her unborn children to another.—Disproportioned punishment of the slave compared with the master.—Case of State *v.* Mann, showing that the owner or hirer of a slave cannot be punished for inflicting cruel, unwarrantable and disproportioned punishments.—Judge Ruffin's speech.

## PART III

# Part I

## *Chapter I*

At different times, doubt has been expressed whether the representations of "Uncle Tom's Cabin" are a fair representation of slavery as it at present exists. This work, more, perhaps, than any other work of fiction that ever was written, has been a collection and arrangement of real incidents,—of actions really performed, of words and expressions really uttered,—grouped together with reference to a general result, in the same manner that the mosaic artist groups his fragments of various stones into one general picture. His is a mosaic of gems,—this is a mosaic of facts.

Artistically considered, it might not be best to point out in which quarry and from which region each fragment of the mosaic picture had its origin; and it is equally unartistic to disentangle the glittering web of fiction, and show out of what real warp and woof it is woven, and with what real coloring dyed. But the book had a purpose entirely transcending the artistic one, and accordingly encounters, at the hands of the public, demands not usually made on fictitious works.

It is *treated* as a reality,—sifted, tried and tested, as a reality; and therefore as a reality it may be proper that it should be defended.

The writer acknowledges that the book is a very inadequate representation of slavery; and it is so, necessarily, for this reason,—that slavery, in some of its workings, is too dreadful for the purposes of art. A work which should represent it strictly as it is would be a work which could not be read. And all works which ever mean to give pleasure must draw a veil somewhere, or they cannot succeed.

The author will now proceed along the course of the story, from the first page onward, and develop, as far as possible, the incidents by which different parts were suggested.

## Chapter V

### Eliza

The writer stated in her book that Eliza was a portrait drawn from life. The incident which brought the original to her notice may be simply narrated.

While the writer was travelling in Kentucky, many years ago, she attended church in a small country town. While there, her attention was called to a beautiful quadroon girl, who sat in one of the slips of the church, and appeared to have charge of some young children. The description of Eliza may suffice for a description of her. When the author returned from church, she inquired about the girl, and was told that she was as good and amiable as she was beautiful; that she was a pious girl, and a member of the church; and, finally, that she was *owned* by Mr. So-and-so. The idea that this girl was a slave struck a chill to her heart, and she said, earnestly, "O, I hope they treat her kindly."

"O, certainly," was the reply; "they think as much of her as of their own children."

"I hope they will never sell her," said a person in the company.

"Certainly they will not; a Southern gentleman, not long ago, offered her master a thousand dollars for her; but he told him that she was too good to be his wife, and he certainly should not have her for a mistress."

This is all that the writer knows of that girl.

With regard to the incident of Eliza's crossing the river on the ice,—as the possibility of the thing has been disputed,—the writer gives the following circumstance in confirmation.

Last spring, while the author was in New York, a Presbyterian clergyman, of Ohio, came to her, and said, "I understand they dispute that fact about the woman's crossing the river. Now, I know all about that, for I got the story from the very man that helped her up the bank. I know it is true, for she is now living in Canada."

It has been objected that the representation of the scene in which the plan for kidnapping Eliza, concocted by Haley, Marks and Loker, at the tavern, is a gross caricature on the state of things in Ohio.

What knowledge the author has had of the facilities which some justices of the peace, under the old fugitive law of Ohio, were in the habit of giving to kidnapping, may be inferred by comparing the statement in her book with some in her personal knowledge.

"Ye see," said Marks to Haley, stirring his punch as he did so, "ye see, we has justices convenient at all p'ints along shore, that does up any little jobs in our line quite reasonable. Tom, he does the knockin' down, and that ar; and I come in all dressed up,—shining boots,—everything first chop,—when the swearin' 's to be done. You oughter see me, now!" said Marks, in a glow of professional pride, "how I can tone it off. One day I 'm Mr. Twickem, from New Orleans; 'nother day, I 'm just come from my plantation on Pearl river, where I works seven hundred niggers; then, again, I come out a distant relation to Henry Clay, or some old cock in Kentuck. Talents is different, you know. Now, Tom 's a roarer when there 's any thumping or fighting to be done; but at lying he an't good, Tom an't; ye see it don't come natural to him; but, Lord! if thar 's a feller in the country that can swear to anything and everything, and put in all the circumstances and flourishes with a longer face, and carry 't through better 'n I can, why, I 'd like to see him, that 's all! I b'lieve, my heart, I could get along, and make through, even if justices were more particular than they is. Sometimes I rather wish they was more particular; 't would be a heap more relishin' if they was,— more fun, yer know."

In the year 1839, the writer received into her family, as a servant, a girl from Kentucky. She had been the slave of one of the lowest and most brutal families, with whom she had been brought up, in a log-cabin, in a state of half-barbarism. In proceeding to give her religious instruction, the author heard, for the first time in her life; an inquiry which she had not supposed possible to be made in America:—"Who is Jesus Christ, now, anyhow?"

When the author told her the history of the love and life and death of Christ, the girl seemed wholly overcome; tears streamed down her cheeks; and she exclaimed, piteously, "Why did n't nobody never tell me this before?"

"But," said the writer to her, "have n't you ever seen the Bible?"

"Yes, I have seen missus a-readin' on 't sometimes; but, law sakes! she 's just a-readin' on 't 'cause she could; don't s'pose it did her no good, no way."

She said she had been to one or two camp-meetings in her life, but "did n't notice very particular."

At all events, the story certainly made great impression on her, and had such an effect in improving her conduct, that the writer had great hopes of her.

On inquiring into her history, it was discovered that, by the laws of Ohio, she was legally entitled to her freedom, from the fact of her having been brought into the state, and left there, temporarily, by the consent of her mistress. These facts being properly authenticated before the proper authorities, papers attesting her freedom were drawn up, and it was now supposed that all danger of pursuit was over. After she had remained in the family for some months, word was sent, from various sources, to Professor Stowe, that the girl's young master was over, looking for her, and that, if care were not taken, she would be conveyed back into slavery.

Professor Stowe called on the magistrate who had authenticated her papers, and inquired whether they were not sufficient to protect her. The reply was, "Certainly they are, in law, if she could have a fair hearing; but they will come to your house in the night, with an officer and a warrant; they will take her before Justice D—, and swear to her. He 's the man that does all this kind of business, and he 'll deliver her up, and there 'll be an end to it."

Mr. Stowe then inquired what could be done; and was recommended to carry her to some place of security till the inquiry for her was over. Accordingly, that night, a brother of the author, with Professor Stowe, performed for the fugitive that office which the senator is represented as performing for Eliza. They drove about ten miles on a solitary road, crossed the creek at a very dangerous fording, and presented themselves, at midnight, at the house of John Van Zandt, a noble-minded Kentuckian, who had performed the good deed which the author, in her story, ascribes to Van Tromp.

After some rapping at the door, the worthy owner of the mansion appeared, candle in hand, as has been narrated.

"Are you the man that would save a poor colored girl from kidnappers?" was the first question.

"Guess I am," was the prompt response; "where is she?"

"Why, she 's here."

"But how did you come?"

"I crossed the creek."

"Why, the Lord helped you!" said he; "I should n't dare cross it myself in the night. A man and his wife, and five children, were drowned there, a little while ago."

The reader may be interested to know that the poor girl never was re-taken; that she married well in Cincinnati, is a very respectable woman, and the mother of a large family of children.

## Chapter VI

### Uncle Tom

The character of Uncle Tom has been objected to as improbable; and yet the writer has received more confirmations of that character, and from a greater variety of sources, than of any other in the book.

Many people have said to her, "I knew an Uncle Tom in such and such a Southern State." All the histories of this kind which have thus been related to her would of themselves, if collected, make a small volume. The author will relate a few of them.

While visiting in an obscure town in Maine, in the family of a friend, the conversation happened to turn upon this subject, and the gentleman with whose family she was staying related the following. He said that, when on a visit to his brother, in New Orleans, some years before, he found in his possession a most valuable negro man, of such remarkable probity and honesty that his brother literally trusted him with all he had. He had frequently seen him take out a handful of bills, without looking at them, and hand them to this servant, bidding him go and provide what was necessary for the family, and bring him the change. He remonstrated with his brother on this imprudence; but the latter replied that he had had such proof of this servant's impregnable conscientiousness that he felt it save to trust him to any extent.

The history of the servant was this. He had belonged to a man in Baltimore, who, having a general prejudice against all the religious exercises of slaves, did all that he could to prevent his having any time for devotional duties, and strictly forbade him to read the Bible and pray, either by himself, or with the other servants; and because, like a certain man of old, named Daniel, he constantly disobeyed this unchristian edict, his master inflicted upon him that punishment which a master always has in his power to inflict,—he sold him into perpetual exile from his wife and children, down to New Orleans.

The gentleman who gave the writer this information says that, although not himself a religious man at the time, he was so struck with the man's piety that he said to his brother, "I hope you will never do anything to deprive this man of his religious privileges, for I think a judgment will come upon you if you do." To this his brother replied that he should be very foolish to do it, since he had made up his mind that the man's religion was the root of his extraordinary excellences.

Some time since, there was sent to the writer from the South, through the mail, a little book, entitled, "Sketches of Old Virginia Family Servants," with a preface by Bishop Meade. The book contains an account of the following servants: African Bella, Old Milly, Blind Lucy, Aunt Betty, Springfield Bob, Mammy Chris, Diana Washington, Aunt Margaret, Rachel Parker, Nelly Jackson, My Own Mammy, Aunt Beck.

The following extract from Bishop Meade's preface may not be uninteresting.

> The following sketches were placed in my hands with a request that I would examine them with a view to publication.
>
> After reading them I could not but think that they would be both pleasing and edifying.
>
> Very many such examples of fidelity and piety might be added from the old Virginia families. These will suffice as specimens, and will serve to show how interesting the relation between master and servant often is.
>
> Many will doubtless be surprised to find that there was so much intelligence, as well as piety, in some of the old servants of Virginia, and that they had learned to read the Sacred Scriptures, so as to be useful in this way among their fellow-servants. It is, and always has been true, in regard to the servants of the Southern States, that although public schools may have been prohibited, yet no interference has been attempted, where the owners have chosen to teach their servants, or permit them to learn in a private way, how to read God's word. Accordingly, there always have been some who were thus taught. In the more southern states the number of these has most abounded. Of this fact I became well assured, about thirty years since, when visiting the Atlantic states, with a view to the formation of auxiliary colonization societies, and the selection of the first colonists for Africa. In the city of Charleston, South Carolina, I found more intelligence and character among the free colored population than any-

where else. The same was true of some of those in bondage. A respectable number might be seen in certain parts of the Episcopal churches which I attended using their prayer-books, and joining in the responses of the church.

Many purposes of convenience and hospitality were subserved by this encouragement of cultivation in some of the servants, on the part of the owners.

When travelling many years since with a sick wife, and two female relatives, from Charleston to Virginia, at a period of the year when many of the families from the country resort to the town for health, we were kindly urged to call at the seat of one of the first families in South Carolina, and a letter from the mistress, then in the city, was given us, to her servant, who had charge of the house in the absence of the family. On reaching there and delivering the letter to a most respectable-looking female servant, who immediately read it, we were kindly welcomed, and entertained, during a part of two days, as sumptuously as though the owner had been present. We understood that it was no uncommon thing in South Carolina for travellers to be thus entertained by the servants in the absence of the owners, on receiving letters from the same.

Instances of confidential and affectionate relationship between servants and their masters and mistresses, such as are set forth in the following Sketches, are still to be found in all the slave-holding states. I mention one, which has come under my own observation. The late Judge Upshur, of Virginia, had a faithful house-servant (by his will now set free), with whom he used to correspond on matters of business, when he was absent on his circuit. I was dining at his house, some years since, with a number of persons, himself being absent, when the conversation turned on the subject of the presidential election, then going on through the United States, and about which there was an intense interest; when his servant informed us that he had that day received a letter from his master, then on the western shore, in which he stated that the friends of General Harrison might be relieved from all uneasiness, as the returns already received made his election quite certain.

Of course it is not to be supposed that we design to convey the impression that such instances are numerous, the nature of the relationship forbidding it; but we do mean emphatically to affirm that there is far more of kindly and Christian intercourse than many at a distance are apt to believe. That there is a great and sad want of Christian instruction, notwithstanding the more recent efforts put forth to impart it, we most sorrowfully acknowledge.

Bishop Meade adds that these sketches are published with the hope that they might have the effect of turning the attention of ministers and heads of families more seriously to the duty of caring for the souls of their servants.

With regard to the servant of Judge Upshur, spoken of in this communication of Bishop Meade, his master has left, in his last will, the following remarkable tribute to his worth and excellence of character:

> I emancipate and set free my servant, David Rice, and direct my executors to give him *one hundred dollars.* I recommend him in the strongest manner to the respect, esteem and confidence, of any community in which he may happen to live. He has been my slave for twenty-four years, during all which time he has been trusted to every extent, and in every respect; my confidence in him has been unbounded; his relation to myself and family has always been such as to afford him daily opportunities to deceive and injure us, yet he has never been detected in any serious fault, nor even in an unintentional breach of the decorum of his station. His intelligence is of a high

order, his integrity above all suspicion, and his sense of right and propriety correct, and even refined. I feel that he is justly entitled to carry this certificate from me in the new relations which he must now form; it is due to his long and most faithful services, and to the sincere and steady friendship which I bear to him. In the uninterrupted confidential intercourse of twenty-four years, I have never given him, nor had occasion to give him, one unpleasant word. I know no man who has fewer faults or more excellences than he.

In the free states there have been a few instances of such extraordinary piety among negroes, that their biography and sayings have been collected in religious tracts, and published for the instruction of the community.

One of these was, before his conversion, a convict in a state-prison in New York, and there received what was, perhaps, the first religious instruction that had ever been imparted to him. He became so eminent an example of humility, faith, and, above all, fervent love, that his presence in the neighborhood was esteemed a blessing to the church. A lady has described to the writer the manner in which he would stand up and exhort in the church-meetings for prayer, when, with streaming eyes and the deepest abasement, humbly addressing them as his masters and misses, he would nevertheless pour forth religious exhortations which were edifying to the most cultivated and refined.

In the town of Brunswick, Maine, where the writer lived when writing "Uncle Tom's Cabin," may now be seen the grave of an aged colored woman, named Phebe, who was so eminent for her piety and loveliness of character, that the writer has never heard her name mentioned except with that degree of awe and respect which one would imagine due to a saint. The small cottage where she resided is still visited and looked upon as a sort of shrine, as the spot where old Phebe lived and prayed. Her prayers and pious exhortations were supposed to have been the cause of the conversion of many young people in the place. Notwithstanding that the unchristian feeling of caste prevails as strongly in Maine as anywhere else in New England, and the negro, commonly speaking, is an object of aversion and contempt, yet, so great was the influence of her piety and loveliness of character, that she was uniformly treated with the utmost respect and attention by all classes of people. The most cultivated and intelligent ladies of the place esteemed it a privilege to visit her cottage; and when she was old and helpless, her wants were most tenderly provided for. When the news of her death was spread abroad in the place, it excited a general and very tender sensation of regret. "We have lost Phebe's prayers," was the remark frequently made afterwards by members of the church, as they met one another. At her funeral the ex-governor of the state and the professors of the college officiated as pall-bearers, and a sermon was preached in which the many excellences of her Christian character were held up as an example to the community. A small religious tract, containing an account of her life, was published by the American Tract Society, prepared by a lady of Brunswick. The writer recollects that on reading the tract, when she first went to Brunswick, a doubt arose in her mind whether it was not somewhat exaggerated. Some time afterwards she overheard some young persons conversing together about the tract, and saying that they did not think it gave exactly the right idea of Phebe. "Why, is it too highly colored?" was the inquiry of the author. "O, no, no, indeed," was the earnest response; "it does n't begin to give an idea of how good she was."

Such instances as these serve to illustrate the words of the apostle, "God hath chosen the foolish things of the world to confound the wise; and God hath chosen the weak things of the world to confound the things which are mighty."

John Bunyan says that although the valley of humiliation be unattractive in the eyes of the men of this world, yet the very sweetest flowers grow there. So it is with the condition of the lowly and poor in this world. God has often, indeed always, shown a particular regard for it, in selecting from that class the recipients of his grace. It is to be remembered that Jesus Christ, when he came to found the Christian dispensation, did not choose his apostles from the chief priests and the scribes, learned in the law, and high in the church; nor did he choose them from philosophers and poets, whose educated and comprehensive minds might be supposed best able to appreciate his great designs; but he chose twelve plain, poor fishermen, who were ignorant, and felt that they were ignorant, and who, therefore, were willing to give themselves up with all simplicity to his guidance. What God asks of the soul more than anything else is faith and simplicity, the affection and reliance of the little child. Even these twelve fancied too much that they were wise, and Jesus was obliged to set a little child in the midst of them, as a more perfect teacher.

The negro race is confessedly more simple, docile, child-like and affectionate, than other races; and hence the divine graces of love and faith, when in-breathed by the Holy Spirit, find in their natural temperament a more congenial atmosphere.

A last instance parallel with that of Uncle Tom is to be found in the published memoirs of the venerable Josiah Henson,[1] now, as we have said, a clergyman in Canada. He was "raised" in the State of Maryland. His first recollections were of seeing his father mutilated and covered with blood, suffering the penalty of the law for the crime of raising his hand against a white man,—that white man being the overseer, who had attempted a brutal assault upon his mother. This punishment made his father surly and dangerous, and he was subsequently sold south, and thus parted forever from his wife and children. Henson grew up in a state of heathenism, without any religious instruction, till, in a camp-meeting, he first heard of Jesus Christ, and was electrified by the great and thrilling news that He had tasted death for every man, the bond as well as the free. This story produced an immediate conversion, such as we read of in the Acts of the Apostles, where the Ethiopian eunuch, from one interview, hearing the story of the cross, at once believes and is baptized. Henson forthwith not only became a Christian, but began to declare the news to those about him; and, being a man of great natural force of mind and strength of character, his earnest endeavors to enlighten his fellow-heathen were so successful that he was gradually led to assume the station of a negro preacher; and though he could not read a word of the Bible or hymn-book, his labors in this line were much prospered. He became immediately a very valu-

[1]*The Life of Josiah Henson, Formerly a Slave, Now an Inhabitant of Canada, As Narrated by Himself* (Boston: Arthur D. Phelps, 1849).

able slave to his master, and was intrusted by the latter with the oversight of his whole estate, which he managed with great judgment and prudence. His master appears to have been a very ordinary man in every respect,—to have been entirely incapable of estimating him in any other light than as exceedingly valuable property, and to have had no other feeling excited by his extraordinary faithfulness than the desire to make the most of him. When his affairs became embarrassed, he formed the design of removing all his negroes into Kentucky, and intrusted the operation entirely to his overseer. Henson was to take them alone, without any other attendant, from Maryland to Kentucky, a distance of some thousands of miles, giving only his promise as a Christian that he would faithfully perform this undertaking. On the way thither they passed through a portion of Ohio, and there Henson was informed that he could now secure his own freedom and that of all his fellows, and he was strongly urged to do it. He was exceedingly tempted and tried, but his Christian principle was invulnerable. No inducements could lead him to feel that it was right for a Christian to violate a pledge solemnly given, and his influence over the whole band was so great that he took them all with him into Kentucky. Those casuists among us who lately seem to think and teach that it is right for us to violate the plain commands of God whenever some great national good can be secured by it, would do well to contemplate the inflexible principle of this poor slave, who, without being able to read a letter of the Bible, was yet enabled to perform this most sublime act of self-renunciation in obedience to its commands. Subsequently to this, his master, in a relenting moment, was induced by a friend to sell him his freedom for four hundred dollars; but, when the excitement of the importunity had passed off, he regretted that he had suffered so valuable a piece of property to leave his hands for so slight a remuneration. By an unworthy artifice, therefore, he got possession of his servant's free papers, and condemned him still to hopeless slavery. Subsequently, his affairs becoming still more involved, he sent his son down the river with a flat-boat loaded with cattle and produce for the New Orleans market, directing him to take Henson along, and sell him after they had sold the cattle and the boat. All the depths of the negro's soul were torn up and thrown into convulsion by this horrible piece of ingratitude, cruelty and injustice; and, while outwardly calm, he was struggling with most bitter temptations from within, which, as he could not read the Bible, he could repel only by a recollection of its sacred truths, and by earnest prayer. As he neared the New Orleans market, he says that these convulsions of soul increased, especially when he met some of his old companions from Kentucky, whose despairing countenances and emaciated forms told of hard work and insufficient food, and confirmed all his worst fears of the lower country. In the transports of his despair, the temptation was more urgently presented to him to murder his young master and the other hand on the flat-boat in their sleep, to seize upon the boat and make his escape. He thus relates the scene where he was almost brought to the perpetration of this deed:

> One dark, rainy night, within a few days of New Orleans, my hour seemed to have come. I was alone on the deck; Mr. Amos and the hands were all asleep below, and I crept down noiselessly, got hold of an axe, entered the cabin, and looking by the aid of the dim light there for my victims, my eye fell upon Master Amos, who was near-

est to me; my hand slid along the axe-handle, I raised it to strike the fatal blow,—when suddenly the thought came to me, "What! commit *murder!* and you a Christian?" I had not called it murder before. It was self-defence,—it was preventing others from murdering me,—it was justifiable, it was even praiseworthy. But now, all at once, the truth burst upon me that it was a crime. I was going to kill a young man, who had done nothing to injure me, but obey commands which he could not resist; I was about to lose the fruit of all my efforts at self-improvement, the character I had acquired, and the peace of mind which had never deserted me. All this came upon me instantly, and with a distinctness which made me almost think I heard it whispered in my ear; and I believe I even turned my head to listen. I shrunk back, laid down the axe, crept up on deck again, and thanked God, as I have done every day since, that I had not committed murder.

My feelings were still agitated, but they were changed. I was filled with shame and remorse for the design I had entertained, and with the fear that my companions would detect it in my face, or that a careless word would betray my guilty thoughts. I remained on deck all night, instead of rousing one of the men to relieve me; and nothing brought composure to my mind, but the solemn resolution I then made to resign myself to the will of God, and take with thankfulness, if I could, but with submission, at all events, whatever he might decide should be my lot. I reflected that if my life were reduced to a brief term I should have less to suffer, and that it was better to die with a Christian's hope, and a quiet conscience, than to live with the incessant recollection of a crime that would destroy the value of life, and under the weight of a secret that would crush out the satisfaction that might be expected from freedom, and every other blessing.

Subsequently to this, his young master was taken violently down with the river fever, and became as helpless as a child. He passionately entreated Henson not to desert him, but to attend to the selling of the boat and produce, and put him on board the steamboat, and not to leave him, dead or alive, till he had carried him back to his father.

The young master was borne in the arms of his faithful servant to the steamboat, and there nursed by him with unremitting attention during the journey up the river; nor did he leave him till he had placed him in his father's arms.

Our love for human nature would lead us to add, with sorrow, that all this disinterestedness and kindness was rewarded only by empty praises, such as would be bestowed upon a very fine dog; and Henson indignantly resolved no longer to submit to the injustice. With a degree of prudence, courage and address, which can scarcely find a parallel in any history, he managed, with his wife and two children, to escape into Canada. Here he learned to read, and, by his superior talent and capacity for management, laid the foundation for the fugitive settlement of Dawn, which is understood to be one of the most flourishing in Canada.

It would be well for the most cultivated of us to ask, whether our ten talents in the way of religious knowledge have enabled us to bring forth as much fruit to the glory of God, to withstand temptation as patiently, to return good for evil as disinterestedly, as this poor, ignorant slave. A writer in England has sneeringly remarked that such a man as Uncle Tom might be imported as a missionary to teach the most cultivated in England or America the true nature of religion. These instances show that what has been said with a sneer is in truth a sober verity; and it should never be forgotten that out of this race whom man despiseth have often been chosen of God true messengers of his grace, and temples for the indwelling of his Spirit.

*"For thus saith the high and lofty One that inhabiteth eternity, whose name is Holy, I dwell in the high and holy place, with him also that is of a contrite and humble spirit, to revive the spirit of the humble, and to revive the heart of the contrite ones."*

The vision attributed to Uncle Tom introduces quite a curious chapter of psychology with regard to the negro race, and indicates a peculiarity which goes far to show how very different they are from the white race. They are possessed of a nervous organization peculiarly susceptible and impressible. Their sensations and impressions are very vivid, and their fancy and imagination lively. In this respect the race has an oriental character, and betrays its tropical origin. Like the Hebrews of old and the oriental nations of the present, they give vent to their emotions with the utmost vivacity of expression, and their whole bodily system sympathizes with the movements of their minds. When in distress, they actually life up their voices to weep, and "cry with an exceeding bitter cry." When alarmed, they are often paralyzed, and rendered entirely helpless. Their religious exercises are all colored by this sensitive and exceedingly vivacious temperament. Like oriental nations, they incline much to outward expressions, violent gesticulations, and agitating movements of the body. Sometimes, in their religious meetings, they will spring from the floor many times in succession, with a violence and rapidity which is perfectly astonishing. They will laugh, weep, embrace each other convulsively, and sometimes become entirely paralyzed and cataleptic. A clergyman from the North once remonstrated with a Southern clergyman for permitting such extravagances among his flock. The reply of the Southern minister was, in effect, this: "Sir, I am satisfied that the races are so essentially different that they cannot be regulated by the same rules. I, at first, felt as you do; and, though I saw that genuine conversions did take place, with all this outward manifestation, I was still so much annoyed by it as to forbid it among my negroes, till I was satisfied that the repression of it was a serious hindrance to real religious feeling; and then I became certain that all men cannot be regulated in their religious exercises by one model. I am assured that conversions produced with these accessories are quite as apt to be genuine, and to be as influential over the heart and life, as those produced in any other way." The fact is, that the Anglo-Saxon race—cool, logical and practical—have yet to learn the doctrine of toleration for the peculiarities of other races; and perhaps it was with a foresight of their peculiar character, and dominant position in the earth, that God gave the Bible to them in the fervent language and with the glowing imagery of the more susceptible and passionate oriental races.

Mesmerists have found that the negroes are singularly susceptible to all that class of influences which produce catalepsy, mesmeric sleep, and partial clairvoyant phenomena.

The African race, in their own climate, are believers in spells, in "fetish and obi," in "the evil eye," and other singular influences, for which, probably, there is an origin in this peculiarity of constitution. The magicians in scriptural history were Africans; and the so-called magical arts are still practised in Egypt, and other parts of Africa, with a degree of skill and success which can only be accounted for by supposing peculiarities of nervous constitution quite different from those of the whites. Considering those distinctive traits of the race, it is no matter of surprise to find in their religious histories, when acted upon by the powerful stimulant of the Christian religion, very peculiar features. We are not surprised to find almost constantly, in the narrations of their religious histories, accounts of visions, of heavenly voices, of mysterious sympathies and transmissions of knowledge from heart to heart without the intervention of the senses, or what the Quakers call being "baptized into the spirit" of those who are distant.

Cases of this kind are constantly recurring in their histories. The young man whose story was related to the Boston lady and introduced above in the chapter on George Harris, stated this incident concerning the recovery of his liberty: That, after the departure of his wife and sister, he, for a long time, and very earnestly, sought some opportunity of escape, but that every avenue appeared to be closed to him. At length, in despair, he retreated to his room, and threw himself upon his bed, resolving to give up the undertaking, when, just as he was sinking to sleep, he was roused by a voice saying in his ear, "Why do you sleep now? Rise up, if you ever mean to be free!" He sprang up, went immediately out, and, in the course of two hours, discovered the means of escape which he used.

A lady whose history is known to the writer resided for some time on a Southern plantation, and was in the habit of imparting religious instruction to the slaves. One day, a woman from a distant plantation called at her residence, and inquired for her. The lady asked, in surprise, "How did you know about me?" The old woman's reply was, that she had long been distressed about her soul; but that, several nights before, some one had appeared to her in a dream, told her to go to this plantation and inquire for the strange lady there, and that she would teach her the way to heaven.

Another specimen of the same kind was related to the writer by a slave-woman who had been through the whole painful experience of a slave's life. She was originally a young girl of pleasing exterior and gentle nature, carefully reared as a seamstress and nurse to the children of a family in Virginia, and attached, with all the warmth of her susceptible nature, to these children. Although one of the tenderest of mothers when the writer knew her, yet she assured the writer that she had never loved a child of her own as she loved the dear little young mistress who was her particular charge. Owing, probably, to some pecuniary difficulty in the family, this girl, whom we will call Louisa, was sold, to go on to a Southern plantation. She has often described the scene when she was forced into a carriage and saw her dear young mistress leaning from the window, stretching her arms towards her, screaming and calling her name, with all the vehemence of childish grief. She was carried in a coffle, and sold as cook on a Southern plantation. With the utmost earnestness of language she has described to the writer her utter loneliness, and the distress and despair of her heart, in this situation, parted forever from all she held dear on earth, without even the possibility of writing letters or sending messages, surrounded by those who felt no kind of interest in her, and forced to a toil for which her more delicate education had entirely unfitted her. Under these circumstances, she began to believe that it was for some dreadful sin she had thus been afflicted. The course of her mind after this may be best told in her own simple words:

"After that, I began to feel awful wicked,—O, so wicked, you 've no idea! I felt so wicked that my sins seemed like a load on me, and I went so heavy all the day! I felt so wicked that I did n't feel worthy to pray in the house, and I used to go way off in the lot and pray. At last, one day, when I was praying, the Lord he came and spoke to me."

"The Lord spoke to you?" said the writer; "what do you mean, Louisa?"

With a face of the utmost earnestness, she answered, "Why, ma'am, the Lord Jesus he came and spoke to me, you know; and I never, till the last day of my life, shall forget what he said to me."

"What was it?" said the writer.

"He said, 'Fear not, my little one; thy sins are forgiven thee;' " and she added to this some verses, which the writer recognized as those of a Methodist hymn.

Being curious to examine more closely this phenomenon, the author said,

"You mean that you dreamed this, Louisa."

With an air of wounded feeling, and much earnestness, she answered,

"O no, Mrs. Stowe; that never was a dream; you 'll never make me believe that."

The thought at once arose in the writer's mind, If the Lord Jesus is indeed everywhere present, and if he is as tender-hearted and compassionate as he was on earth,—and we know he is,—must he not sometimes long to speak to the poor, desolate slave, when he knows that no voice but His can carry comfort and healing to his soul?

This instance of Louisa is so exactly parallel to another case, which the author received from an authentic source, that she is tempted to place the two side by side.

Among the slaves who were brought into the New England States, at the time when slavery was prevalent, was one woman, who, immediately on being told the history of the love of Jesus Christ, exclaimed, "He is the one; that is what I wanted."

This language causing surprise, her history was inquired into. It was briefly this: While living in her simple hut in Africa, the kidnappers one day rushed upon her family, and carried her husband and children off to the slave-ship, she escaping into the woods. On returning to her desolate home, she mourned with the bitterness of "Rachel weeping for her children." For many days her heart was oppressed with a heavy weight of sorrow; and, refusing all sustenance, she wandered up and down the desolate forest.

At last, she says, a strong impulse came over her to kneel down and pour out her sorrows into the ear of some unknown Being whom she fancied to be above her, in the sky.

She did so; and, to her surprise, found an inexpressible sensation of relief. After this, it was her custom daily to go out to this same spot, and supplicate this unknown Friend. Subsequently, she was herself taken, and brought over to America; and, when the story of Jesus and his love was related to her, she immediately felt in her soul that this Jesus was the very friend who had spoken comfort to her yearning spirit in the distant forest of Africa.

Compare now these experiences with the earnest and beautiful language of Paul: "He hath made of one blood all nations of men, for to dwell on all the face of the earth; and hath determined the times before appointed *and the bounds* of their habitation, *that* THEY SHOULD *seek the Lord, if haply they might* FEEL AFTER HIM AND FIND HIM *though he be not far from every one of us.*"

Is not this truly *"feeling after God and finding Him"*? And may we not hope that the yearning, troubled, helpless heart of man, pressed by the insufferable anguish of this short life, or wearied by its utter vanity, never extends its ignorant, pleading hand to God in vain? Is not the veil which divides us from an almighty and most merciful Father much thinner than we, in the pride of our philosophy, are apt to imagine? and is it not the most worthy conception of Him to suppose that the more utterly helpless and ignorant the human being is that seeks His aid, the more tender and the more condescending will be His communication with that soul?

If a mother has among her children one whom sickness has made blind, or deaf, or dumb, incapable of acquiring knowledge through the usual channels of communication, does she not seek to reach its darkened mind by modes of communication tenderer and more intimate than those which she uses with the stronger and more favored ones? But can the love of any mother be compared with the infinite love of Jesus? Has He not described himself as that good Shepherd who leaves the whole flock of secure and well-instructed ones, to follow over the mountains of sin and ignorance the one lost sheep; and, when He hath found it, rejoicing more over that one than over the ninety and nine that went not astray? Has He not told us that each of these little ones has a guardian angel that doth always behold the face of his Father which is in heaven? And is it not comforting to us to think that His love and care will be in proportion to the ignorance and the wants of His chosen ones?

Since the above was prepared for the press the author has received the following extract from a letter written by a gentleman in Missouri to the editor of the *Oberlin* (Ohio) *Evangelist*:

> I really thought, while reading "Uncle Tom's Cabin," that the authoress, when describing the character of Tom, had in her mind's eye a slave whose acquaintance I made some years since, in the State of Mississippi, called "Uncle Jacob." I was staying a day or two with a planter, and in the evening, when out in the yard, I heard a well-known hymn and tune sung in one of the "quarters," and then the voice of prayer; and O, *such* a prayer! what fervor, what unction,—nay, the man "prayed right up;" and when I read of Uncle Tom, how "nothing could exceed the touching simplicity, the childlike earnestness, of his prayer, enriched with the language of Scripture, which seemed so entirely to have wrought itself into his being as to have become a part of himself," the recollections of that evening prayer were strangely vivid. On entering the house and referring to what I had heard, his master replied, "Ah, sir, if I covet anything in this world, it is Uncle Jacob's religion. If there is a good man on earth, he certainly is one." He said Uncle Jacob was a regulator on the plantation; that a *word*

or a *look* from him, addressed to younger slaves, had more efficacy than a *blow* from the overseer.

The next morning Uncle Jacob informed me he was from Kentucky, opposite Cincinnati; that his opportunities for attending religious worship had been frequent; that at about the age of forty he was sold south, was set to picking cotton; could not, when doing his best, pick the task assigned him; was whipped and whipped, he could not possibly tell how often; was of the opinion that the overseer came to the conclusion that whipping could not bring one more pound out of him, for he set him to driving a team. At this and other work he could "make a *hand;*" had changed owners three or four times. He expressed himself as well pleased with his present situation as he expected to be in the South, but was yearning to return to his former associations in Kentucky.

## Chapter VII

### Miss Ophelia

MISS OPHELIA stands as the representative of a numerous class of the very best of Northern people; to whom, perhaps, if our Lord should again address his churches a letter, as he did those of old time, he would use the same words as then: "I know thy works, and thy labor, and thy patience, and how thou canst not bear them which are evil; and thou hast tried them which are apostles and are not, and hast found them liars: and hast borne, and hast patience, and for my name's sake hast labored and hast not fainted. Nevertheless, I have somewhat against thee, because thou hast left thy first love."

There are in this class of people activity, zeal, unflinching conscientiousness, clear intellectual discriminations between truth and error, and great logical and doctrinal correctness; but there is a want of that spirit of love, without which, in the eye of Christ, the most perfect character is as deficient as a wax flower—wanting in life and perfume.

Yet this blessed principle is not dead in their hearts, but only sleepeth; and so great is the real and genuine goodness, that, when the true magnet of divine love is applied, they always answer to its touch.

So when the gentle Eva, who is an impersonation in childish form of the love of Christ, solves at once, by a blessed instinct, the problem which Ophelia has long been unable to solve by dint of utmost hammering and vehement effort, she at once, with a good and honest heart, perceives and acknowledges her mistake, and is willing to learn even of a little child.

Miss Ophelia, again, represents one great sin, of which, unconsciously, American Christians have allowed themselves to be guilty. Unconsciously it must be, for nowhere is conscience so predominant as among this class, and nowhere is there a more honest strife to bring every thought into captivity to the obedience of Christ.

One of the first and most declared objects of the gospel has been to break down all those irrational barriers and prejudices which separate the human brotherhood into diverse and contending clans. Paul says, "In Christ Jesus there is neither Jew nor Greek, barbarian, Scythian, bond nor free." The Jews at that time were separated from the Gentiles by an insuperable wall of prejudice. They could not eat and drink together, nor pray together. But the apostles most earnestly labored to show them the sin of this prejudice. St. Paul says to the Ephesians, speaking of this former division, "He is our peace, who hath made both one, and hath broken down the middle wall of partition between us."

It is very easy to see that although slavery has been abolished in the New England States, it has left behind it the most baneful feature of the system—that which makes American worse than Roman slavery—the prejudice of caste and color. In the New England States the negro has been treated as belonging to an inferior race of beings;—forced to sit apart by himself in the place of worship; his children excluded from the schools; himself excluded from the railroad-car and the omnibus, and the peculiarities of his race made the subject of bitter contempt and ridicule.

This course of conduct has been justified by saying that they are a degraded race. But how came they degraded? Take any class of men, and shut them from the means of education, deprive them of hope and self-respect, close to them all avenues of honorable ambition, and you will make just such a race of them as the negroes have been among us.

So singular and so melancholy is the dominion of prejudice over the human mind, that professors of Christianity in our New England States have often, with very serious self-denial to themselves, sent the gospel to heathen as dark-complexioned as the Africans, when in their very neighborhood were persons of dark complexion, who, on that account, were forbidden to send their children to the schools, and discouraged from entering the churches. The effect of this has been directly to degrade and depress the race, and then this very degradation and depression has been pleaded as the reason for continuing this course.

Not long since the writer called upon a benevolent lady, and during the course of the call the conversation turned upon the incidents of a fire which had occurred the night before in the neighborhood. A deserted house had been burned to the ground. The lady said it was supposed it had been set on fire. "What could be any one's motive for setting it on fire?" said the writer.

"Well," replied the lady, "it was supposed that a colored family was about to move into it, and it was thought that the neighborhood would n't consent to that. So it was supposed that was the reason."

This was said with an air of innocence and much unconcern.

The writer inquired, "Was it a family of bad character?"

"No, not particularly, that I know of," said the lady; "but then they are negroes, you know."

Now, this lady is a very pious lady. She probably would deny herself to send the gospel to the heathen, and if she had ever thought of considering this family a heathen family, would have felt the deepest interest in their welfare; because on the subject of duty to the heathen she had been frequently instructed from the pulpit, and had all her religious and conscientious sensibilities awake. Probably she had never listened from the pulpit to a sermon which should exhibit the great truth, that "in Christ Jesus there is neither Jew nor Greek, barbarian, Scythian, bond nor free."

Supposing our Lord was now on earth, as he was once, what course is it probable that he would pursue with regard to this unchristian prejudice of color?

There was a class of men in those days as much despised by the Jews as the negroes are by us; and it was a complaint made of Christ that he was a friend of publicans and sinners. And if Christ should enter, on some communion season, into a place of worship, and see the colored man sitting afar off by himself, would it not be just in his spirit to go there and sit with him, rather than to take the seats of his richer and more prosperous brethren?

It is, however, but just to our Northern Christians to say that this sin has been committed ignorantly and in unbelief, and that within a few years signs of a much better spirit have begun to manifest themselves. In some places, recently, the doors of school-houses have been thrown open to the children, and many a good Miss Ophelia has opened her eyes in astonishment to find that, while she has been devouring the *Missionary Herald*, and going without butter on her bread and sugar in her tea to send the gospel to the Sandwich Islands, there is a very thriving colony of heathen in her own neighborhood at home; and, true to her own good and honest heart, she has resolved, *not* to give up her prayers and efforts for the heathen abroad, but to add thereunto labors for the heathen at home.

Our safety and hope in this matter is this: that there are multitudes in all our churches who do most truly and sincerely love Christ above all things, and who, just so soon as a little reflection shall have made them sensible of their duty in this respect, will most earnestly perform it.

It is true that, if they do so, they may be called Abolitionists; but the true Miss Ophelia is not afraid of a hard name in a good cause, and has rather learned to consider "the reproach of Christ a greater treasure than the riches of Egypt."

That there is much already for Christians to do in enlightening the moral sense of the community on this subject, will appear if we consider that even so well-educated and gentlemanly a man as Frederick Douglass was recently obliged to pass the night on the deck of a steamer, when in delicate health, because this senseless prejudice deprived him of a place in the cabin; and that that very laborious and useful minister, Dr. Pennington,[2] of New York, has, during the last season, been often obliged seriously to endanger his health, by walking to his pastoral labors, over his very extended parish, under a burning sun, because he could not be allowed the common privilege of the omnibus, which conveys every class of white men, from the most refined to the lowest and most disgusting.

Let us consider now the number of professors of the religion of Christ in New York, and consider also that, by the very fact of their profession, they consider Dr. Pennington the brother of their Lord, and a member with them of the body of Christ.

Now, these Christians are influential, rich and powerful; they can control public sentiment on any subject that they think of any particular importance, and they profess, by their religion, that "if one member suffers, all the members suffer with it."

[2]James W. C. Pennington, an escaped slave and author of *The Fugitive Blacksmith* (London, 1849), achieved fame for his eloquence as a Congregational and Presbyterian minister.

It is a serious question, whether such a marked indignity offered to Christ and his ministry, in the person of a colored brother, without any remonstrance on their part, will not lead to a general feeling that all that the Bible says about the union of Christians is a mere hollow sound, and means nothing.

Those who are anxious to do something directly to improve the condition of the slave, can do it in no way so directly as by elevating the condition of the free colored people around them, and taking every pain to give them equal rights and privileges.

This unchristian prejudice has doubtless stood in the way of the emancipation of hundreds of slaves. The slave-holder, feeling and acknowledging the evils of slavery, has come to the North, and seen evidences of this unkindly and unchristian state of feeling towards the slave, and has thus reflected within himself:

"If I keep my slave at the South, he is, it is true, under the dominion of a very severe law; but then he enjoys the advantage of my friendship and assistance, and derives, through his connection with me and my family, some kind of a position in the community. As my servant he is allowed a seat in the car and a place at the table. But if I emancipate and send him North, he will encounter substantially all the disadvantages of slavery, with no master to protect him."

This mode of reasoning has proved an apology to many a man for keeping his slaves in a position which he confesses to be a bad one; and it will be at once perceived that, should the position of the negro be conspicuously reversed in our northern states, the effect upon the emancipation of the slave would be very great. They, then, who keep up this prejudice, may be said to be, in a certain sense, slave-holders.

It is not meant by this that all distinctions of society should be broken over, and that people should be obliged to choose their intimate associates from a class unfitted by education and habits to sympathize with them.

The negro should not be lifted out of his sphere of life because he is a negro, but he should be treated with Christian courtesy *in* his sphere. In the railroad car, in the omnibus and steamboat, all ranks and degrees of white persons move with unquestioned freedom side by side; and Christianity requires that the negro have the same privilege.

That the dirtiest and most uneducated foreigner or American, with breath redolent of whiskey and clothes foul and disordered, should have an unquestioned right to take a seat next to any person in a railroad car or steamboat, and that the respectable, decent and gentlemanly negro should be excluded simply because he is a negro, cannot be considered otherwise than as an irrational and unchristian thing: and any Christian who allows such things done in his presence without remonstrance, and the use of his Christian influence, will certainly be made deeply sensible of his error when he comes at last to direct and personal interview with his Lord.

There is no hope for this matter, if the love of Christ is not strong enough, and if it cannot be said, with regard to the two races, "He is our peace who hath made both one, and hath broken down the middle wall of partition between us."

The time is coming rapidly when the upper classes in society must learn that their education, wealth and refinement, are not their own; that they have no right to use them for their own selfish benefit; but that they should hold them rather, as Fenelon expresses it, as "a ministry," a stewardship, which they hold in trust for the benefit of their poorer brethren.

In some of the very highest circles in England and America we begin to see illustrious examples of the commencement of such a condition of things.

One of the merchant princes of Boston, whose funeral has lately been celebrated in our city, afforded in his life a beautiful example of this truth. His wealth was the wealth of thousands. He was the steward of the widow and the orphan. His funds were a savings bank, wherein were laid up the resources of the poor; and the mourners at his funeral were the scholars of the schools which he had founded, the officers of literary institutions which his munificence had endowed, the widows and orphans whom he had counselled and supported, and the men, in all ranks and conditions of life, who had been made by his benevolence to feel that his wealth was their wealth. May God raise up many men in Boston to enter into the spirit and labors of Amos Lawrence!

This is the *true* socialism, which comes from the spirit of Christ, and, without breaking down existing orders of society, *by love* makes the property and possessions of the higher class the property of the lower.

Men are always seeking to begin their reforms with the *outward* and *physical*. Christ begins his reforms in the heart. Men would break up all ranks of society, and throw all property into a common stock; but Christ would inspire the higher class with that Divine Spirit by which all the wealth and means and advantages of their position are used for the good of the lower.

We see, also, in the highest aristocracy of England, instances of the same tendency.

Among her oldest nobility there begin to arise lecturers to mechanics and patrons of ragged schools; and it is said that even on the throne of England is a woman who weekly instructs her class of Sunday-school scholars from the children in the vicinity of her country residence.

In this way, and not by an outward and physical division of property, shall all things be had in common. And when the white race shall regard their superiority over the colored one only as a talent intrusted for the advantage of their weaker brother, *then* will the prejudice of caste melt away in the light of Christianity.

# Part II

## Chapter III

### Souther v. The Commonwealth—The Ne Plus Ultra of Legal Humanity

"Yet in the face of *such* laws and decisions as *these*! Mrs. Stowe, &c."
—*Courier & Enquirer.*

The case of Souther *v.* the Commonwealth has been cited by the *Courier & Enquirer* as a particularly favorable specimen of judicial proceedings under the slave-code, with the following remark:

And yet, in the face of such laws and decisions as these, Mrs. Stowe winds up a long series of cruelties upon her other black personages, by causing her faultless hero, Tom, to be literally whipped to death in Louisiana, by his master, Legree; and these acts, which the laws make criminal, and punish as such, she sets forth in the most repulsive colors, to illustrate the institution of slavery!

By the above language the author was led into the supposition that this case had been conducted in a manner so creditable to the feelings of our common humanity as to present a fairer side of criminal jurisprudence in this respect. She accordingly took the pains to procure a report of the case, designing to publish it as an offset to the many barbarities which research into this branch of the subject obliges one to unfold. A legal gentleman has copied the case from Grattan's Reports, and it is here given. If the reader is astounded at it, he cannot be more so than was the writer.

*Souther v. The Commonwealth. 7 Grattan, 673,* 1851.

The killing of a slave by his master and owner, by wilful and excessive whipping, is murder in the first degree: though it may not have been the purpose and intention of the master and owner to kill the slave.

Simeon Souther was indicted at the October Term, 1850, of the Circuit Court for the County of Hanover, for the murder of his own slave. The indictment contained fifteen counts, in which the various modes of punishment and torture by which the homicide was charged to have been committed were stated singly, and in various combinations. The fifteenth count unites them all: and, as the court certifies that the *indictment was sustained by the evidence*, the giving the facts stated in that count will show what was the charge against the prisoner, and what was the proof to sustain it.

The count charged that on the 1st day of September, 1849, the prisoner tied his negro slave, Sam, with ropes about his wrists, neck, body, legs and ankles, to a tree. That whilst so tied, the prisoner first whipped the slave with switches. That he next beat and cobbed the slave with a shingle, and compelled two of his slaves, a man and a woman, also to cob the deceased with the shingle. That whilst the deceased was so tied to the tree, the prisoner did strike, knock, kick, stamp and beat him upon various parts of his head, face and body; that he applied fire to his body; . . . that he then washed his body with warm water, in which pods of red pepper had been put and steeped; and he compelled his two slaves aforesaid also to wash him with this same preparation of warm water and red pepper. That after the tying, whipping, cobbing, striking, beating, knocking, kicking, stamping, wounding, bruising, lacerating, burning, washing and torturing, as aforesaid, the prisoner untied the deceased from the tree in such way as to throw him with violence to the ground; and he then and there did knock, kick, stamp and beat the deceased upon his head, temples, and various parts of his body. That the prisoner then had the deceased carried into a shed-room of his house, and there he compelled one of his slaves, in his presence, to confine the deceased's feet in stocks, by making his legs fast to a piece of timber, and to tie a rope about the neck of the deceased, and fasten it to a bed-post in the room, thereby strangling, choking and suffocating the deceased. And that whilst the deceased was thus made fast in stocks as aforesaid, the prisoner did kick, knock, stamp and beat him upon his head, face, breast, belly, sides, back and body; and he again compelled his two slaves to apply fire to the body of the deceased, whilst he was so made fast as aforesaid. And the count charged that from these various modes of punishment and torture the slave Sam then and there died. It appeared that the prisoner commenced the punishment of the deceased in the morning, and that it was continued throughout the day: and that the deceased died in the presence of the prisoner, and one of his slaves, and one of the witnesses, whilst the punishment was still progressing.

Field J. delivered the opinion of the court.

The prisoner was indicted and convicted of *murder in the second degree,* in the Circuit Court of Hanover, at its April term last past, and was sentenced to the *penitentiary for five years,* the period of time ascertained by the jury. The murder consisted in the killing of a negro man-slave by the name of Sam, the property of the prisoner, by cruel and excessive whipping and torture, inflicted by Souther, aided by two of his other slaves, on the 1st day of September, 1849. The prisoner moved for a new trial, upon the ground that the offence, *if any,* amounted only to manslaughter. The motion for a new trial was overruled, and a bill of exceptions taken to the opinion of the court, setting forth the facts proved, or as many of them as were deemed material for the consideration of the application for a new trial. The bill of exception states: That the slave Sam, in the indictment mentioned, was the slave and property of the prisoner. That for the purpose of chastising the slave for the offence of getting drunk, and dealing as the slave confessed and alleged with Henry and Stone, two of the witnesses for the Commonwealth, he caused him to be tied and punished in the presence of the said witnesses, with the exception of slight whipping with peach or apple-tree switches, before the said witnesses arrived at the scene after they were sent for by the prisoner (who were present by request from the defendant), and of several slaves of the prisoner, in the manner and by the means charged in the indictment; and the said slave died under and from the infliction of the said punishment, in the presence of the prisoner, one of his slaves, and of one of the witnesses for the Commonwealth. But it did not appear that it was the design of the prisoner to kill the said slave, unless such design be properly inferable from the manner, means and duration, of the punishment. And, on the contrary, it did appear that the prisoner frequently declared, while the said slave was undergoing the punishment, that he believed the said slave was feigning, and pretending to be suffering and injured when he was not. The judge certifies that the slave was punished in the *manner and by the means charged in the indictment.* The indictment contains fifteen counts, and sets forth a case of the most cruel and excessive whipping and torture.[*]

It is believed that the records of criminal jurisprudence do not contain a case of more atrocious and wicked cruelty than was presented upon the trial of Souther; and yet it has been gravely and earnestly contended here by his counsel that his offence amounts to manslaughter only.

---

[*] The following is Judge Field's statement of the punishment:

The negro was tied to a tree and whipped with switches. When Souther became fatigued with the labor of whipping, he called upon a negro man of his, and made him cob Sam with a shingle. He also made a negro woman of his help to cob him. And, after cobbing and whipping, he applied fire to the body of the slave. . . . He then caused him to be washed down with hot water, in which pods of red pepper had been steeped. The negro was also tied to a log and to the bed-post with ropes, which choked him, and he was kicked and stamped by Souther. This sort of punishment was continued and repeated until the negro died under its infliction.

It has been contended by the counsel of the prisoner that a man cannot be indicted and prosecuted for the cruel and excessive whipping of his own slave. That it is lawful for the master to chastise his slave, and that if death ensues from such chastisement, unless it was intended to produce death, it is like the case of homicide which is committed by a man in the performance of a lawful act, which is manslaughter only. It has been decided by this court in Turner's case, 5 Rand, that the owner of a slave, for the malicious, cruel and excessive beating of his own slave, cannot be indicted; yet it by no means follows, when such malicious, cruel and excessive beating results in death, though not intended and premeditated, that the beating is to be regarded as lawful for the purpose of reducing the crime to manslaughter, when the whipping is inflicted for the sole purpose of chastisement. *It is the policy of the law, in respect to the relation of master and slave, and for the sake of securing proper subordination and obedience on the part of the slave, to protect the master from prosecution in all such cases, even if the whipping and punishment be malicious, cruel and excessive.* But in so inflicting punishment for the sake of punishment, the owner of the slave acts at his peril; and if death ensues in consequence of such punishment, the relation of master and slave affords no ground of excuse or palliation. The principles of the common law, in relation to homicide, apply to his case without qualification or exception; and according to those principles, the act of the prisoner, in the case under consideration, amounted to murder. . . . The crime of the prisoner is not manslaughter, but murder in the first degree.

On the case now presented there are some remarks to be made.

This scene of torture, it seems, occupied about twelve hours. It occurred in the State of Virginia, in the County of Hanover. Two white men were witnesses to nearly the whole proceeding, and, so far as we can see, made no effort to arouse the neighborhood, and bring in help to stop the outrage. What sort of an education, what habits of thought, does this presuppose in these men?

The case was brought to trial. It requires no ordinary nerve to read over the counts of this indictment. Nobody, one would suppose, could willingly read them twice. One would think that it would have laid a cold hand of horror on every heart;—that the community would have risen, by an universal sentiment, to shake out the man, as Paul shook the viper from his hand. It seems, however, that they were quite self-possessed; that lawyers calmly sat, and examined, and cross-examined, on particulars known before only in the records of the Inquisition; that it was "ably and earnestly argued" by educated, intelligent, American men, that this catalogue of horrors did not amount to a murder! and, in the cool language of legal precision, that "the offence, IF ANY, amounted to manslaughter;" and that an American jury found that the offence was murder *in the second degree.* Any one who reads the indictment will certainly think that, if this be murder in the *second degree,* in Virginia, one might earnestly pray to be murdered in the first degree, to begin with. Had Souther walked up to the man, and shot him through the head with a pistol, before white witnesses, *that* would have been murder in the *first* degree. As he preferred to spend *twelve hours* in killing him by torture, under the name of *"chastisement,"* that, says the verdict, is murder in the second degree; *"because,"* says the bill of exceptions, with admirable coolness, *"it did not appear that it was the design of the prisoner to kill the slave,* UNLESS SUCH DESIGN BE PROPERLY INFERABLE FROM THE MANNER, MEANS AND DURATION, OF THE PUNISHMENT."

The bill evidently seems to have a leaning to the idea that twelve hours spent in beating, stamping, scalding, burning and mutilating a human being, might possibly be considered as presumption of something beyond the limits of lawful chastisement. So startling an opinion, however, is expressed cautiously, and with a becoming diffidence, and is balanced by the very striking fact, which is also quoted in this remarkable paper, that the prisoner frequently declared, while the slave was undergoing the punishment, that he believed the slave was feigning and pretending to be suffering, when he was not. This view appears to have struck the court as eminently probable,—as going a long way to prove the propriety of Souther's intentions, making it at least extremely probable that only *correction* was intended.

It seems, also, that Souther, so far from being crushed by the united opinion of the community, found those to back him who considered five years in the penitentiary an unjust severity for his crime, and hence the bill of exceptions from which we have quoted, and the appeal to the Superior Court; and hence the form in which the case stands in law-books, *"Souther v. the Commonwealth."* Souther evidently considers himself an ill-used man, and it is in this character that he appears before the Superior Court.

As yet there has been no particular overflow of humanity in the treatment of the case. The manner in which it has been discussed so far reminds one of nothing so much as of some discussions which the reader may have seen quoted from the records of the Inquisition, with regard to the propriety of roasting the feet of children who have not arrived at the age of thirteen years, with a view of eliciting evidence.

Let us now come to the decision of the Superior Court, which the editor of the *Courier & Enquirer* thinks so particularly enlightened and humane. Judge Field thinks that the case is a very atrocious one, and in this respect he seems to differ materially from judge, jury and lawyers, of the court below. Furthermore, he doubts whether the annals of jurisprudence furnish a case of equal atrocity, wherein certainly he appears to be not far wrong; and he also states unequivocally the principle that killing a slave by torture under the name of correction is murder in the first degree; and here too, certainly, everybody will think that he is also right; the only wonder being that any man could ever have been called to express such an opinion, judicially. But he states, quite as unequivocally as Judge Ruffin, that awful principle of slave-laws, that the law cannot interfere with the master for any amount of torture inflicted on his slave which does not result in death. The decision, if it establishes anything, establishes this principle quite as strongly as it does the other. Let us hear the words of the decision:

> It has been decided by this court, in Turner's case, that *the owner of a slave, for the malicious, cruel and excessive beating of his own slave, cannot be indicted.*
> *It is the policy of the law, in respect to the relation of master and slave, and for the sake of securing proper subordination and obedience on the part of the slave, to protect the master from prosecution in all such cases, even if the whipping and punishment be malicious, cruel and excessive.*

What follows as a corollary from this remarkable declaration is this,—that if the victim of this twelve hours' torture had only possessed a little stronger constitution, and had not actually died under it, there is no law in Virginia by which Souther could even have been indicted for misdemeanor.

If this is not filling out the measure of the language of St. Clare, that "he who goes the furthest and does the worst only uses within limits the power which the law gives him," how could this language be verified? Which is *"the worst,"* death outright, or torture indefinitely prolonged? This decision, in so many words, gives every master the power of indefinite torture, and takes from him only the power of terminating the agony by merciful death. And this is the judicial decision which the *Courier & Enquirer* cites as a perfectly convincing specimen of legal humanity. It must be hoped that the editor never read the decision, else he never would have cited it. Of all who knock at the charnel-house of legal precedents, with the hope of disinterring any evidence of humanity in the slave system, it may be said, in the awful words of the Hebrew poet:

> "He knoweth not that the dead are there,
> And that her guests are in the depths of hell."

The upshot of this case was, that Souther, instead of getting off from his five years' imprisonment, got simply a judicial *opinion* from the Superior Court that he ought to be hung; but he could not be tried over again, and, as we may infer from all the facts in the case that he was a man of tolerably resolute nerves and not very exquisite sensibility, it is not likely that the *opinion* gave him any very serious uneasiness. He has probably made up his mind to get over his five years with what grace he may. When he comes out, there is no law in Virginia to prevent his buying as many more negroes as he chooses, and going over the same scene with any one of them at a future time, if only he profit by the information which has been so explicitly conveyed to him in this decision, that he must take care and stop his tortures short of the point of death,—a matter about which, as the history of the Inquisition shows, men, by careful practice, can be able to judge with considerable precision. Probably, also, the next time, he will not be so foolish as to send out and request the attendance of two white witnesses, even though they may be so complacently interested in the proceedings as to spend the whole day in witnessing them without effort at prevention.

Slavery, as defined in American law, is no more capable of being regulated in its administration by principles of humanity, than the torture system of the Inquisition. Every act of humanity of every individual owner is an illogical result from the legal definition; and the reason why the slave-code of America is more atrocious than any ever before exhibited under the sun, is that the Anglo-Saxon race are a more coldly and strictly logical race, and have an unflinching courage to meet the consequences of every premise which they lay down, and to work out an accursed principle, with mathematical accuracy, to its most accursed results. The decisions in American law-books show nothing so much as this severe, unflinching accuracy of logic. It is often and evidently, not because judges are inhuman or partial, but because they are logical and truthful, that they announce from the bench, in the calmest manner, decisions which one would think might make the earth shudder, and the sun turn pale.

The French and the Spanish nations are, by constitution, more impulsive, passionate and poetic, than logical; hence it will be found that while there may be more instances of individual barbarity, as might be expected among impulsive and passionate people, there is in their slave-code more exhibition of humanity. The code of the State of Louisiana contains more really humane provisions, were there any means of enforcing them, than that of any other state in the Union.

It is believed that there is no code of laws in the world which contains such a perfect cabinet crystallization of every tear and every drop of blood which can be wrung from humanity, so accurately, elegantly and scientifically arranged, as the slave-code of America. It is a case of elegant surgical instruments for the work of dissecting the living human heart;—every instrument wrought with exactest temper and polish, and adapted with exquisite care, and labelled with the name of the nerve or artery or muscle which it is designed to sever. The instruments of the anatomist are instruments of earthly steel and wood, designed to operate at most on perishable and corruptible matter; but these are instruments of keener temper, and more ethereal workmanship, designed in the most precise and scientific manner to DESTROY THE IMMORTAL SOUL, and carefully and gradually to reduce man from the high position of a free agent, a social, religious, accountable being, down to the condition of the brute, or of inanimate matter.

## Chapter X

### *Principles Established.—State* v. *Legree; A case not in the Books.*

From a review of all the legal cases which have hitherto been presented, and of the principles established in the judicial decisions upon them, the following facts must be apparent to the reader:

*First,* That masters do, now and then, kill slaves by the torture.

*Second,* That the fact of so killing a slave is not of itself held presumption of murder, in slave jurisprudence.

*Third,* That the slave in the act of resistance to his master may always be killed.

From these things it will be seen to follow, that, if the facts of the death of Tom had been fully proved by two white witnesses, in open court, Legree could not have been held by any *consistent* interpreter of slave-law to be a murderer; for Tom was in the act of resistance to the will of his master. His master had laid a command on him, in the presence of other slaves. Tom had deliberately refused to obey the command. The master commenced chastisement, to reduce him to obedience. And it is evident, at the first glance, to every one, that, if the law does not sustain him in enforcing obedience in such a case, there is an end of the whole slave power. No Southern court would dare to decide that Legree did wrong to continue the punishment, as long as Tom continued the insubordination. Legree stood by him every moment of the time, pressing him to yield, and offering to let him go as soon as he did yield. Tom's resistance was *insurrection*. It was an example which could not be allowed, for a moment, on any Southern plantation. By the express words of the constitution of Georgia, and by the understanding and usage of all slave-law, the power of life and death is always left in the hands of the master, in exigencies like this. This is not a case like that of Souther *v*. The Commonwealth. The victim of Souther was not in a state of resistance or insurrection. The punishment, in his case, was a simple vengeance for a past offence, and not an attempt to reduce him to subordination.

There is no principle of slave jurisprudence by which a man could be pronounced a murderer, for acting as Legree did, in his circumstances. Everybody must see that such an admission would strike at the foundations of the slave system. To be sure, Tom was in a state of insurrection for conscience' sake. But the law does not, and cannot, contemplate that the negro shall have a conscience independent of his master's. To allow that the negro may refuse to obey his master whenever he thinks that obedience would be wrong, would be to produce universal anarchy. If Tom had been allowed to disobey his master in this case, for conscience' sake, the next day Sambo would have had a case of conscience, and Quimbo the next. Several of them might very justly have thought that it was a sin to work as they did. The mulatto woman would have remembered that the command of God forbade her to take another husband. Mothers might have considered that it was more their duty to stay at home and take care of their children, when they were young and feeble, than to work for Mr. Legree in the cotton-field. There would be no end to the havoc made upon cotton-growing operations, were the negro allowed the right of maintaining his own conscience on moral subjects. If the slave system is a right system, and ought to be maintained, Mr. Legree ought not to be blamed for his conduct in this case; for he did only what was absolutely essential to maintain the system; and Tom died in fanatical and fool-hardy resistance to "the powers that be, which are ordained of God." He followed a sentimental impulse of his desperately depraved heart, and neglected those "solid teachings of the written word," which, as recently elucidated, have proved so refreshing to eminent political men.

# Part III

## Chapter VIII

### Kidnapping

The principle which declares that one human being may lawfully hold another as property leads directly to the trade in human beings; and that trade has, among its other horrible results, the temptation to the crime of kidnapping.

The trader is generally a man of coarse nature and low associations, hardhearted, and reckless of right or honor. He who is not so is an exception, rather than a specimen. If he has anything good about him when he begins the business, it may well be seen that he is in a fair way to lose it.

Around the trader are continually passing and repassing men and women who would be worth to him thousands of dollars in the way of trade,—who belong to a class whose rights nobody respects, and who, if reduced to slavery, could not easily make their word good against him. The probability is that hundreds of free men and women and children are all the time being precipitated into slavery in this way.

The recent case of *Northrop*, tried in Washington, D.C., throws light on this fearful subject. The following account is abridged from the *New York Times*:

> Solomon Northrop is a free colored citizen of the United States; he was born in Essex county, New York, about the year 1808; became early a resident of Washington county, and married there in 1829. His father and mother resided in the county of Washington about fifty years, till their decease, and were both free. With his wife and children he resided at Saratoga Springs in the winter of 1841, and while there was employed by two gentlemen to drive a team South, at the rate of a dollar a day. In fulfilment of his employment, he proceeded to New York, and, having taken out free papers, to show that he was a citizen, he went on to Washington city, where he arrived the second day of April, the same year, and put up at Gadsby's Hotel. Soon after he arrived he felt unwell, and went to bed.
>
> While suffering with severe pain, some persons came in, and, seeing the condition he was in, proposed to give him some medicine, and did so. This is the last thing of which he had any recollection, until he found himself chained to the floor of Williams' slave-pen in this city, and handcuffed. In the course of a few hours, James H. Burch, a slave-dealer, came in, and the colored man asked him to take the irons off from him, and wanted to know why they were put on. Burch told him it was none of his business. The colored man said he was free, and told where he was born. Burch called in a man by the name of Ebenezer Rodbury, and they two stripped the man and laid him across a bench, Rodbury holding him down by his wrists. Burch whipped him with a paddle until he broke that, and then with a cat-o'-nine-tails, giving him a hundred lashes; and he swore he would kill him if he ever stated to any one that he was a free man. From that time forward the man says he did not communicate the fact from fear, either that he was a free man, or what his name was, until the last summer. He was kept in the slave-pen about ten days, when he, with others, was taken out of the pen in the night by Burch, handcuffed and shackled, and taken down the river by a steamboat, and then to Richmond, where he, with forty-eight others, was put on board the brig *Orleans*. There Burch left them. The brig sailed for New Orleans, and on arriving there, before she was fastened to the wharf, Theophilus Freeman, another slave-dealer, belonging in the city of New Orleans, and who in 1833 had been a partner with Burch in the slave-trade, came to the wharf, and received the slaves as they were landed, under his direction. This man was immediately taken by Freeman and shut up in his pen in that city. He was taken sick with the small-pox immediately after getting there, and was sent to a hospital, where he lay two or three weeks. When he had sufficiently recovered to leave the hospital, Freeman declined to sell him to any person in that vicinity, and sold him to a Mr. Ford, who resided in Rapides Parish, Louisiana, where he was taken and lived more than a year, and worked as a carpenter, working with Ford at that business.
>
> Ford became involved, and had to sell him. A Mr. Tibaut became the purchaser. He, in a short time, sold him to Edwin Eppes, in Bayou Beouf, about one hundred and thirty miles from the mouth of Red river, where Eppes has retained him on a cotton plantation since the year 1843. . . .

It is a singular coincidence that this man was carried to a plantation in the Red river country, that same region where the scene of Tom's captivity was laid; and his account of this plantation, his mode of life there, and some incidents which he describes, form a striking parallel to that history. We extract them from the article of the *Times*:

> The condition of this colored man during the nine years that he was in the hands of Eppes was of a character nearly approaching that described by Mrs. Stowe as the condition of "Uncle Tom" while in that region. During that whole period his hut contained neither a floor, nor a chair, nor a bed, nor a mattress, nor anything for him to lie upon, except a board about twelve inches wide, with a block of wood for his pillow, and with a single blanket to cover him, while the walls of his hut did not by any means protect him from the inclemency of the weather. He was sometimes compelled to perform acts revolting to humanity, and outrageous in the highest degree. On one occasion, a colored girl belonging to Eppes, about seventeen years of age, went one Sunday, without the permission of her master, to the nearest plantation, about half a mile distant, to visit another colored girl of her acquaintance. She returned in the course of two or three hours, and for that offence she was called up for punishment, which Solomon was required to inflict. Eppes compelled him to drive four stakes into the ground at such distances that the hands and ankles of the girl might be tied to them, as she lay with her face upon the ground; and, having thus fastened her down, he compelled him, while standing by himself, to inflict one hundred lashes upon her bare flesh, she being stripped naked. Having inflicted the hundred blows, Solomon refused to proceed any further. Eppes tried to compel him to go on, but he absolutely set him at defiance, and refused to murder the girl. Eppes then seized the whip, and applied it until he was too weary to continue it. Blood flowed from her neck to her feet, and in this condition she was compelled the next day to go into the field to work as a field-hand. She bears the marks still upon her body, although the punishment was inflicted four years ago.
>
> When Solomon was about to leave, under the care of Mr. Northrop, this girl came from behind her hut, unseen by her master, and, throwing her arms around the neck of Solomon, congratulated him on his escape from slavery, and his return to his family; at the same time, in language of despair, exclaiming, "But, O God! what will become of me?"
>
> These statements regarding the condition of Solomon while with Eppes, and the punishment and brutal treatment of the colored girls, are taken from Solomon himself. It has been stated that the nearest plantation was distant from that of Eppes a half-mile, and of course there could be no interference on the part of neighbors in any punishment, however cruel, or however well disposed to interfere they might be.

Had not Northrop been able to write, as few of the free blacks in the slave states are, his doom might have been sealed for life in this den of misery. . . .

## Chapter IX

### *Slaves As They Are, On Testimony Of Owners*

The investigation into the actual condition of the slave population at the South is beset with many difficulties. So many things are said *pro* and *con*,—so many said in one connection and denied in another,—that the effect is very confusing.

Thus, we are told that the state of the slaves is one of blissful contentment; that they would not take freedom as a gift; that their family relations are only now and then invaded; that they are a stupid race, almost sunk to the condition of animals; that generally they are kindly treated, &c. &c. &c.

In reading over some two hundred Southern newspapers this fall, the author has been struck with the very graphic and circumstantial pictures, which occur in all of them, describing fugitive slaves. From these descriptions one may learn a vast many things. The author will here give an assortment of them, taken at random. It is a commentary on the contented state of the slave population that the writer finds two or three always, and often many more, in every one of the hundreds of Southern papers examined.

In reading the following little sketches of "slaves as they are," let the reader notice:

1. The color and complexion of the majority of them.
2. That it is customary either to describe slaves by some *scar*, or to say *"No scars recollected."*
3. The *intelligence* of the parties advertised.
4. The number that *say they are free* that are to be *sold to pay jail-fees.*

Every one of these slaves has a history,—a history of woe and crime, degradation, endurance, and wrong. Let us open the chapter:

*South-side Democrat*, October 28, 1852. Petersburgh, Virginia:

### REWARD

Twenty-five dollars, with the payment of all necessary expenses, will be given for the apprehension and delivery of my man CHARLES, if taken on the Appomattox river, or within the precincts of Petersburgh. He ran off about a week ago, and, if he leaves the neighborhood, will no doubt make for Farmville and Petersburgh. He is a *mulatto*, rather below the medium height and size, but well proportioned, and very active and sensible. He is aged about 27 years, has a mild, submissive look, *and will, no doubt, show the marks of a recent whipping, if taken.* He must be delivered to the care of Peebles, White, Davis & Co.

R. H. DeJarnett,
Oct. 25                                                                                                    Lunenburgh.

Poor Charles!—*mulatto!*—has a mild, submissive look, and will probably show marks of a recent whipping! . . .

*American Baptist*, Dec. 20, 1852:

### TWENTY DOLLARS REWARD FOR A PREACHER

The following paragraph, headed "Twenty Dollars Reward," appeared in a recent number of the *New Orleans Picayune*:

"Run away from the plantation of the undersigned the negro man Shedrick, a preacher, 5 feet 9 inches high, about 40 years old, but looking not over 23, *stamped N. E. on the breast, and having both small toes cut off.* He is of a very dark complexion, with eyes small but bright, *and a look quite insolent.* He dresses good, and was arrested as a runaway at Donaldsonville, some three years ago. The above reward will be paid for his arrest, by addressing Messrs. Armant Brothers, St. James parish, or A. Miltenberger & Co., 30 Carondelet-street."

Here is a preacher who is branded on the breast and has both toes cut off,— and *will* look insolent yet! There's depravity for you! . . .

*The Alabama Standard* has for its motto:
"RESISTANCE TO TYRANTS IS OBEDIENCE TO GOD."

Date of Nov. 29th, this advertisement:

### COMMITTED
To the Jail of Choctaw County, by Judge Young, of Marengo County, a RUNAWAY SLAVE, who calls his name BILLY, and says he belongs to the late William Johnson, and was in the employment of John Jones, near Alexandria, La. He is about 5 feet 10 inches high, black, about 40 years old, *much scarred on the face and head*, and *quite intelligent.*

The owner is requested to come forward, prove his property, and take him from Jail, or he will be disposed of according to law.

S. S. HOUSTON, Jailer C. C.

December 1, 1852.

Query: Whether this "quite intelligent" Billy had n't been corrupted by hearing this incendiary motto of the *Standard*? . . .

*The Alexandria Gazette*, November 29, 1852, under the device of Liberty trampling on a tyrant, motto "*Sic semper tyrannis*," has the following:

### TWENTY-FIVE DOLLARS REWARD
Ranaway from the subscriber, living in the County of Rappahannock, on Tuesday last, DANIEL, *a bright mulatto*, about 5 feet 8 inches high, about 35 years old, *very intelligent*, has been a wagoner for several years, and is pretty well acquainted from Richmond to Alexandria. He calls himself DANIEL TURNER; *his hair curls, without showing black blood, or wool; he has a scar on one cheek, and his left hand has been seriously injured by a pistol-shot*, and he was shabbily dressed when last seen. I will give the above reward if taken out of the county, and secured in jail, so that I get him again, or $10 if taken in the county.

A. M. WILLIS.

Rappahannock Co., Va., Nov. 29.

Another "very intelligent," straight-haired man. Who was his father?

*The New Orleans Daily Crescent*, office No. 93 St. Charles-street; Tuesday morning, December 13, 1852:

### BROUGHT TO THE FIRST DISTRICT POLICE PRISON
NANCY, a griffe, about 34 years old, 5 feet $1\frac{3}{4}$ inch high, a *scar on left wrist*; says she belongs to Madame Wolf.

CHARLES HALL, a black, about 13 years old, 5 feet 6 inches high; *says he is free*, but supposed to be a slave.

PHILOMONIA, a mulattress, about 10 years old, 4 feet 3 inches high; *says she is free*, but supposed to be a slave.

COLUMBUS, a griffe, about 21 years old, 5 feet $5\frac{3}{4}$ inches high; *says he is free*, but supposed to be a slave.

SEYMOUR, a black, about 21 years old, 5 feet $1\frac{3}{4}$ inch high; *says he is free*, but supposed to be a slave.

The owners will please comply with the law respecting them.

J. WORRALL, Warden.

New Orleans, Dec. 14, 1852.

What chance for any of these poor fellows who *say they are free*?

### $50 REWARD

RANAWAY from the subscriber, living in Unionville, Frederick County, Md., on Sunday morning, the 17th instant, a DARK MULATTO GIRL, about 18 years of age, 5 feet 4 or 5 inches high, *looks pleasant generally*, talks very quick, *converses tolerably well*, and can *read*. It is supposed she had on, when she left, a red Merino dress, black Visette or plaid Shawl, and a purple calico Bonnet, as those articles are missing.

A reward of Twenty-five Dollars will be given for her, if taken in the State, or Fifty Dollars if taken out of the State, and lodged in jail, so that I get her again.

G. R. SAPPINGTON.

Oct. 13.

*Southern Standard*, Oct. 16, 1852:

### $50 REWARD!!!

RANAWAY, or stolen, from the subscriber, living near Aberdeen, Miss., a light mulatto woman, of small size, and about 23 years old. She has *long, black, straight hair, and she usually keeps it in good order*. When she left she had on either a white dress, or a brown calico one with white spots or figures, and took with her a red handkerchief, and a red or pink sun-bonnet. *She generally dresses very neatly*. She generally calls herself Mary Ann Paine,—can *read print*,—has some freckles on her face and hands,—shoes No. 4,—had a ring or two on her fingers. She is very intelligent, and converses well. The above reward will be given for her, if taken out of the State, and $25 if taken within the State.

U. MCALLISTER.

*Memphis* (weekly) *Appeal* will insert to the amount of $5, and send account to this office.

October 6th, 1853.

Much can be seen of this Mary Ann in this picture. The black, straight hair, usually kept in order,—the general neatness of dress,—the ring or two on the fingers,—the ability to read,—the fact of being intelligent and conversing well, are all to be noticed. . . .

*Richmond Semi-weekly Examiner*, October 29, 1852:

### FIFTY DOLLARS REWARD

Ranaway from the subscriber, residing in the County of Halifax, about the middle of last August, a Negro Man, Ned, aged some thirty or forty years, of medium height, *copper color*, full forehead, and cheek bones a little prominent. *No scars recollected*, except one of his fingers—the little one, probably—is stiff and crooked. The man Ned was purchased in Richmond, of Mr. Robert Goodwin, who resides near Frederick-Hall, in Louisa County, *and has a wife in that vicinity*. He has been seen in the neighborhood, and is supposed to have gone over the Mountains, and to be now at work as a free man at some of the Iron Works; some one having given him free papers. The above reward will be given for the apprehension of the slave Ned, and his delivery to R. H. Dickinson & Bro., in Richmond, or to the undersigned, in Halifax, Virginia, or twenty-five if confined in any jail in the Commonwealth, so that I get him.

Jas. M. Chappell,

[Firm of Chappell & Tucker.]
Aug. 10.

This unfortunate copper-colored article is supposed to have gone after his *wife*.

*Kentucky Whig*, Oct. 22, '52:

$200 REWARD

Ranaway from the subscriber, near Mount Sterling, Ky., on the night of the 20th of October, a negro man named PORTER. Said boy is black, about 22 years old, very stout and active, weighs about 165 or 170 pounds. *He is a smart fellow, converses well, without the negro accent; no particular scars recollected.* He had on a pair of coarse boots about half worn, no other clothing recollected. He was raised near Sharpsburg, in Bath county, by Harrison Caldwell, and may be lurking in that neighborhood, but will probably endeavor to reach Ohio.

I will pay the above-mentioned reward for him, if taken out of the State; $50, if taken in any county bordering on the Ohio river; or $25, if taken in this or any adjoining county, and secured so that I can get him.

He is supposed to have ridden a yellow Horse, 15 hands and one inch high, mane and tail both yellow, five years old, and paces well.

October 21st, 1852.                                            G. W. Proctor.

"No particular scars recollected"! . . .

*Frankfort Commonwealth*, October 21, 1852:

COMMITTED TO JAIL

A negro boy, who calls his name ADAM, was committed to the Muhlenburg Jail on the 24th of July, 1852. Said boy is black; about 16 or 17 years old; 5 feet 8 or 9 inches high; will weigh about 150 lbs. He has *lost a part of the finger next to his little finger on the right hand; also the great toe on his left foot.* This boy says he belongs to Wm. Mosley; that said Mosley was moving to Mississippi from Virginia. He further states that he is lost, and not a runaway. His owner is requested to come forward, prove property, pay expenses, and take him away, or he will be disposed of as the law directs.

S. H. Dempsey, J. M. C.

Greenville, Ky., Oct. 20, 1852:

RUNAWAY SLAVE

A negro man arrested and placed in the Barren County jail, Ky., on the 21st instant, calling himself HENRY, about 22 years old; says he ran away from near Florence, Alabama, and belongs to John Calaway. He is about five feet eight inches high, dark, but not very black, rather thin visage, pointed nose, *no scars perceivable*, rather spare built; says he has been runaway nearly three months. The owner can get him by applying and paying the reward and expenses; if not, he will be proceeded against according to law. This 24th of August, 1852.              Samuel Adwell, Jailer.
Aug. 25, 1852.

In the same paper are two more poor fellows, who probably have been sold to pay jail-fees, before now.

### NOTICE

Taken up by M. H. Brand, as a runaway slave, on the 22d ult., in the city of Covington, Kenton county, Ky., a negro man calling himself CHARLES WARFIELD, about 30 years old, but looks older, about 6 feet high; no particular marks: had no free papers, but he *says he is free,* and *was born in Pennsylvania,* and in *Fayette county.* Said negro was lodged in jail on the said 22d ult., and the owner or owners, if any, are hereby notified to come forward, prove property, and pay charges, and take him away.

C. W. HULL, J. K. C.

August 3, 1852.

### COMMITTED

To the Jail of Graves county, Ky., on the 4th inst., a negro man calling himself DAVE or DAVID. He *says he is free,* but formerly belonged to Samuel Brown, of Prince William county, Virginia. He is of black color, about 5 feet 10 inches high, weighs about 180 lbs.; supposed to be about 45 years old; had on brown pants and striped shirt. He had in his possession an old rifle gun, an old pistol, and some old clothing. He also informs me that he has escaped from the Dyersburg Jail, Tennessee, where he had been confined some eight or nine months. The owner is hereby notified to come forward, prove property, pay charges, &c.

L. B. HOLEFIELD, Jailer G. C.

June 28, 1852.

*Savannah Daily Georgian,* 6th Sept., 1852:

### ARRESTED

ABOUT three weeks ago, under suspicious circumstances, a negro woman, who calls herself PHEBE, or PHILLIS. *Says she is free,* and lately from Beaufort District, South Carolina. Said woman is about 50 years of age, stout in stature, mild-spoken, 5 feet 4 inches high, and weighs about 140 pounds. Having made diligent inquiry by letter, and from what I can learn, said woman is a runaway. Any person owning said slave can get her by making application to me, properly authenticated.

WARING RUSSELL,
County Constable.

Savannah, Oct. 25, 1852.

oct. 26.

### 250 DOLLARS REWARD

RANAWAY from Sparta, Ga., about the first of last year my boy GEORGE. He is a good carpenter, about 35 years: a bright mulatto, tall and quite likely. *He was brought about three years ago from St. Mary's, and had, when he ran away, a wife there, or near there, belonging to a Mr. Holzendorff.* I think he has told me he has been about Macon also. He had, and perhaps still has, a brother in Savannah. *He is very intelligent.* I will give the above reward for his confinement in some jail in the State, so that I can get him. Refer, for any further information, to Rabun & Whitehead, Savannah, Ga.

W. J. SASSNETT.

Oxford, Ga., Aug. 13th, 1852.

From these advertisements, and hundreds of similar ones, one may learn the following things:

1. That the arguments for the enslaving of the *negro* do not apply to a large part of the actual slaves.

2. That they are not, in the estimation of their masters, very stupid.

3. That they are not remarkably contented.

4. That they have no particular reason to be so.

5. That multitudes of men claiming to be free are constantly being sold into slavery.

In respect to the complexion of these slaves, there are some points worthy of consideration. The writer adds the following advertisements, published by Wm. I. Bowditch, Esq., in his pamphlet "Slavery and the Constitution."

From the *Richmond* (Va.) *Whig*:

### 100 DOLLARS REWARD

WILL be given for the apprehension of my negro (?) Edmund Kenney. *He has straight hair, and complexion so nearly white that it is believed a stranger would suppose there was no African blood in him.* He was with my boy Dick a short time since in Norfolk, *and offered him for sale,* and was apprehended, *but escaped under pretence of being a white man!*

ANDERSON BOWLES

January 6, 1836.

From the *Republican Banner and Nashville Whig* of July 14, 1849:

### 200 DOLLARS REWARD

RANAWAY from the subscriber, on the 23d of June last, a bright mulatto woman, named Julia, about 25 years of age. She is of common size, *nearly white*, and very likely. She is a good seamstress, and can read a little. *She may attempt to pass for white,*—dresses fine. She took with her Anna, her child, 8 or 9 years old, and considerably darker than her mother. . . . She once belonged to a Mr. Helm, of Columbia, Tennessee.

I will give a reward of $50 for said negro and child, if delivered to me, or confined in any jail in this state, so I can get them; $100, if caught in any other Slave state, and confined in a jail so that I can get them; and $200, if caught in any Free state, and put in any good jail in Kentucky or Tennessee, so I can get them.

A. W. JOHNSON.

Nashville, July 9, 1849.

The following three advertisements are taken from Alabama papers:

### RANAWAY

From the Subscriber, working on the plantation of Col. H. Tinker, a bright mulatto boy, named Alfred. Alfred is about 18 years old, pretty well grown, *has blue eyes, light flaxen hair, skin disposed to freckle. He will try to pass as free-born.*

Green County, Ala.    S. G. STEWART.

### 100 DOLLARS REWARD

Ran away from the subscriber, a bright mulatto man-slave, named Sam. *Light, sandy hair, blue eyes, ruddy complexion,—is so white as very easily to pass for a free white man.*

EDWIN PECK

Mobile, April 22, 1837.

### RANAWAY

On the 15th of May, from me, a negro woman, named Fanny. Said woman is 20 years old; is rather tall; can read and write, and so forge passes for herself. Carried

away with her a pair of ear-rings,—a Bible with a red cover; is very pious. She prays a great deal, and was, as supposed, contented and happy. *She is as white as most white women, with straight, light hair, and blue eyes, and can pass herself for a white woman.* I will give $500 for her apprehension and delivery to me. She is very intelligent.
Tuscaloosa, May 29, 1845.                                                                            JOHN BALCH.

From the *Newbern* (N. C.) *Spectator*:

### 50 DOLLARS REWARD

Will be given for the apprehension and delivery to me of the following slaves:— Samuel, and Judy his wife, with their four children, belonging to the estate of Sacker Dubberly, deceased.

I will give $10 for the apprehension of *William Dubberly*, a slave belonging to the estate. William is about 19 years old, *quite white, and would not readily be taken for a slave.*
                                                                                                            JOHN J. LANE.

March 13, 1837.

The next two advertisements we cut from the *New Orleans Picayune* of Sept. 2, 1846:

### 25 DOLLARS REWARD

Ranaway from the plantation of Madame Fergus Duplantier, on or about the 27th of June, 1846, a bright mulatto, named Ned, very stout built, about 5 feet 11 inches high, *speaks English and French,* about 35 years old, waddles in his walk. *He may try to pass himself for a white man, as he is of a very clear color, and has sandy hair.* The above re- ward will be paid to whoever will bring him to Madame Duplantier's plantation, Manchac, or lodge him in some jail where he can be conveniently obtained.

### 200 DOLLARS REWARD

Ran away from the subscriber, last November, *a white negro* man, about 35 years old, height about 5 feet 8 or 10 inches, *blue eyes, has a yellow woolly head, very fair skin.*

These are the characteristics of three races. The copper-colored complexion shows the Indian blood. The others are the mixed races of negroes and whites. It is known that the poor remains of Indian races have been in many cases forced into slavery. It is no less certain that while children have sometimes been kidnapped and sold into slavery. Rev. George Bourne, of Virginia, Presbyterian minister, who wrote against slavery there as early as 1816, gives an account of a boy who was stolen from his parents at seven years of age, immersed in a tan-vat to change his complexion, tattooed and sold, and, after a captivity of fourteen years, succeeded in escaping. The tanning process is not necessary now, as a fair skin is no pre- sumption against slavery. There is reason to think that the grandmother of poor Emily Russell was a *white child*, stolen by kidnappers. That kidnappers may steal and sell white children at the South now, is evident from these advertisements.

The writer, within a week, has seen a fugitive quadroon mother, who had with her two children,—a boy of ten months, and a girl of three years. Both were sur- passingly fair, and uncommonly beautiful. The girl had blue eyes and golden hair. The mother and those children were about to be sold for the division of an estate, which was the reason why she fled. When the mind once becomes familiarized with the process of slavery,—of enslaving first black, then Indian, then mulatto, then quadroon, and when blue eyes and golden hair are advertised as properties of *negroes*,—what protection will there be for poor white people, especially as under the present fugitive law they can be carried away without a jury trial?

A Governor of South Carolina openly declared, in 1835, that the laboring population of any country, bleached or unbleached, were a *dangerous element*, unless reduced to slavery. Will not this be the result, then?

## Part IV

### Chapter I

#### The Influence of the American Church on Slavery

There is no country in the world where the religious influence has a greater ascendency than in America. There is no country where the clergy are more powerful. This is the more remarkable, because in America religion is entirely divorced from the state, and the clergy have none of those artificial means for supporting their influence which result from rank and wealth. Taken as a body of men, the American clergy are generally poor. The salaries given to them afford only a bare support, and yield them no means of acquiring property. Their style of living can be barely decent and respectable, and no more. The fact that, under these circumstances, the American clergy are probably the most powerful body of men in the country, is of itself a strong presumptive argument in their favor. It certainly argues in them, as a class, both intellectual and moral superiority.

It is a well-known fact that the influence of the clergy is looked upon by our statesmen as a most serious element in making up their political combinations; and that that influence is so great, that no statesman would ever undertake to carry a measure against which all the clergy of the country should unite. Such a degree of power, though it be only a power of opinion, argument and example, is not without its dangers to the purity of any body of men. To be courted by political partisans is always a dangerous thing for the integrity and spirituality of men who profess to be governed by principles which are not of this world. The possession, too, of so great a power as we have described, involves a most weighty responsibility; since, if the clergy do possess the power to rectify any great national immorality, the fact of its not being done seems in some sort to bring the sin of the omission to their door.

We have spoken, thus far, of the clergy alone; but in America, where the clergyman is, in most denominations, elected by the church, and supported by its voluntary contributions, the influence of the church and that of the clergy are, to a very great extent, identical. The clergyman is the very ideal and expression of the church. They choose him, and retain him, because he expresses more perfectly than any other man they can obtain, their ideas of truth and right. The clergyman is supported, in all cases, by his church, or else he cannot retain his position in it. The fact of his remaining there is generally proof of identity of opinion, since, if he differed very materially from them, they have the power to withdraw from him, and choose another. . . .

In speaking, therefore, of this subject, we shall speak of the church and the clergy as identical, using the word church in the American sense of the word, for that class of men, of all denominations, who are *organized* in bodies distinct from nominal Christians, as professing to be actually controlled by the precepts of Christ.

What, then, is the influence of the church on this great question of slavery? Certain things are evident on the very face of the matter.

1. It has not put an end to it.
2. It has not prevented the increase of it.
3. It has not occasioned the repeal of the laws which forbid education to the slave.
4. It has not attempted to have laws passed forbidding the separation of families and legalizing the marriage of slaves.
5. It has not stopped the internal slave-trade.
6. It has not prevented the extension of this system, with all its wrongs, over new territories.

With regard to these assertions it is presumed there can be no difference of opinion.

What, then, have they done?

In reply to this, it can be stated,

1. That almost every one of the leading denominations have, at some time, in their collective capacity, expressed a decided disapprobation of the system, and recommended that something should be done with a view to its abolition.
2. One denomination of Christians has pursued such a course as entirely, and in fact, to free every one of its members from any participation in slave-holding. We refer to the Quakers. The course by which this result has been effected will be shown by a pamphlet soon to be issued by the poet J. G. Whittier[3], one of their own body.
3. Individual members, in all denominations, animated by the spirit of Christianity, have in various ways entered their protest against it.

It will be well now to consider more definitely and minutely the sentiments which some leading ecclesiastical bodies in the church have expressed on this subject.

It is fair that the writer should state the sources from which the quotations are drawn. Those relating to the action of Southern judicatories are principally from a pamphlet compiled by the Hon. James G. Birney, and entitled "The Church the Bulwark of Slavery." The writer addressed a letter to Mr. Birney, in which she inquired the sources from which he compiled. His reply was, in substance, as follows: That the pamphlet was compiled from original documents, or files of newspapers, which had recorded these transactions at the time of their occurrence. It was compiled and published in England, in 1842, with a view of leading the people there to understand the position of the American church and clergy. Mr. Birney

---

[3]An ardent abolitionist since his conversion to the movement in 1833, John Greenleaf Whittier was at this time a corresponding editor of the *National Era*.

says that, although the statements have long been before the world, he has never known one of them to be disputed; that, knowing the extraordinary nature of the sentiments, he took the utmost pains to authenticate them.

We will first present those of the Southern States.

### 1. *The Presbyterian Church*

HARMONY PRESBYTERY, OF SOUTH CAROLINA.

Whereas, sundry persons in Scotland and England, and others in the north, east and west of our country, have denounced slavery as obnoxious to the laws of God, some of whom have presented before the General Assembly of our church, and the Congress of the nation, memorials and petitions, with the avowed object of bringing into disgrace slave-holders, and abolishing the relation of master and slave: And whereas, from the said proceedings, and the statements, reasonings and circumstances connected therewith, it is most manifest that those persons "know not what they say, nor whereof they affirm;" and with this ignorance discover a spirit of self-righteousness and exclusive sanctity, &c., therefore,

1. *Resolved*, That as the kingdom of our Lord is not of this world, His church, as such, has no right to abolish, alter, or affect any institution or ordinance of men, political or civil, &c.

2. *Resolved*, That slavery has existed from the days of those good old slave-holders and patriarchs, Abraham, Isaac and Jacob (who are now in the kingdom of heaven), to the time when the apostle Paul sent a runaway home to his master Philemon, and wrote a Christian and fraternal letter to this slave-holder, which we find still stands in the canon of the Scriptures; and that slavery has existed ever since the days of the apostle, and does now exist.

3. *Resolved*, That as the relative duties of master and slave are taught in the Scriptures, in the same manner as those of parent and child, and husband and wife, the existence of slavery itself is not opposed to the will of God; and whosoever has a conscience too tender to recognize this relation as lawful is "righteous over much," is "wise above what is written," and has submitted his neck to the yoke of men, sacrificed his Christian liberty of conscience, and leaves the infallible word of God for the fancies and doctrines of men. . . .

The Methodist Church is, in some respects, peculiarly situated upon this subject, because its constitution and book of discipline contain the most vehement denunciations against slavery of which language is capable, and the most stringent requisitions that all members shall be disciplined for the holding of slaves; and these denunciations and requisitions have been reäffirmed by its General Conference.

It seemed to be necessary, therefore, for the Southern Conference to take some notice of this fact, which they did, with great coolness and distinctness, as follows:

### THE GEORGIA ANNUAL CONFERENCE

*Resolved, unanimously*, That, whereas there is a clause in the discipline of our church which states that we are as much as ever convinced of the great evil of *slavery*; and whereas the said clause has been *perverted* by some, and used in such a manner as to produce the impression that the Methodist Episcopal Church believed *slavery* to be a *moral evil*;—

Therefore *Resolved*, That it is the sense of the Georgia Annual Conference that slavery, as it exists in the United States, *is not a moral evil.*

*Resolved*, That we view *slavery* as a civil and domestic institution, and one with which, as ministers of Christ, we have nothing to do, further than to ameliorate the condition of the slave, by endeavoring to impart to him and his master the benign influences of the religion of Christ, and aiding both on their way to heaven.

On motion, it was *Resolved*, unanimously, That the Georgia Annual Conference regard with feelings of profound respect and approbation the dignified course pursued by *our several superintendents*, or bishops, *in suppressing* the attempts that have been made by various individuals to get up and protract an excitement in the churches and country on the subject of *abolitionism*.

*Resolved*, further, That they shall have our cordial and zealous support in sustaining them in the ground they have taken. . . .

Let us now inquire what has, in fact, been the course of the Northern church on this subject. . . .

## *Chapter II*

In the first place, have any of these opinions ever been treated in the church as heresies, and the teachers of them been subjected to the censures with which it is thought proper to visit heresy?

After a somewhat extended examination upon the subject, the writer has been able to discover but one instance of this sort. It may be possible that such cases have existed in other denominations, which have escaped inquiry.

A clergyman in the Cincinnati N. S. Presbytery maintained the doctrine that slave-holding was justified by the Bible, and for persistence in teaching this sentiment was suspended by that presbytery. He appealed to Synod, and the decision was confirmed by the Cincinnati Synod. The New School General Assembly, however, reversed this decision of the presbytery, and restored the standing of the clergyman. The presbytery, on its part, refused to receive him back, and he was received into the Old School Church.

The Presbyterian Church has probably exceeded all other churches of the United States in its zeal for doctrinal opinions. This church has been shaken and agitated to its very foundation with questions of heresy; but, except in this individual case, it is not known that any of these principles which have been asserted by Southern Presbyterian bodies and individuals have ever been discussed in its General Assembly as matters of heresy.

About the time that Smylie's pamphlet came out, the Presbyterian Church was convulsed with the trial of the Rev. Albert Barnes for certain alleged heresies. These heresies related to the federal headship of Adam, the propriety of imputing his sin to all his posterity, and the question whether men have any ability of any kind to obey the commandments of God.

For advancing certain sentiments on these topics, Mr. Barnes was silenced by the vote of the synod to which he belonged, and his trial in the General Assembly on these points was the all-engrossing topic in the Presbyterian Church for some time. The Rev. Dr. L. Beecher went through a trial with reference to similar opinions. During all this time, no notice was taken of the heresy, if such it be, that the right to buy, sell, and hold men for purposes of gain, was expressly given by God; although that heresy was publicly promulgated in the same Presbyterian Church, by Mr. Smylie, and the presbyteries with which he was connected.

If it be accounted for by saying that the question of slavery is a question of *practical morals*, and not of dogmatic theology, we are then reminded that questions of morals of far less magnitude have been discussed with absorbing interest.

The Old School Presbyterian Church, in whose communion the greater part of the slave-holding Presbyterians of the South are found, has never felt called upon to discipline its members for upholding a system which denies legal marriage to all slaves. Yet this church was agitated to its very foundation by the discussion of a question of morals which an impartial observer would probably consider of far less magnitude, namely, whether a man might lawfully marry his deceased wife's sister. For the time, all the strength and attention of the church seemed concentrated upon this important subject. The trial went from Presbytery to Synod, and from Synod to General Assembly; and ended with deposing a very respectable minister for this crime.

Rev. Robert P. Breckenridge, D.D., a member of the Old School Assembly, has thus described the state of the slave population as to their marriage relations: "The system of slavery denies to a whole class of human beings the sacredness of marriage and of home, compelling them to live in a state of concubinage; for in the eye of the law no colored slave-man is the husband of any wife in particular, nor any slave-woman the wife of any husband in particular; no slave-man is the father of any children in particular, and no slave-child is the child of any parent in particular."

Now, had this church considered the fact that three million men and women were, by the laws of the land, obliged to live in this manner, as of equally serious consequence, it is evident, from the ingenuity, argument, vehemence, Biblical research, and untiring zeal, which they bestowed on Mr. McQueen's trial, that they could have made a very strong case with regard to this also. . . .

But, it will be said that it is not becoming for the Christian church to enter into political matters. Again, we ask, what is the Christian church? Is it not an association of republican citizens, each one of whom has his rights and duties as a legal voter?

Now, suppose a law were passed which depreciated the value of cotton or sugar three cents in the pound, would these men consider the fact that they are church-members as any reason why they should not agitate for the repeal of such law? Certainly not. Such a law would be brittle as the spider's web; it would be swept away before it was well made. Every law to which the majority of the community does not assent is, in this country, immediately torn down.

Why, then, does this monstrous system stand from age to age? Because the community CONSENT TO IT. They *reënact* these unjust laws every day, by their silent permission of them.

The kingdom of our Lord Jesus Christ is not of this world, say the South Carolina Presbyteries; therefore, the church has no right to interfere with any civil institution; but yet all the clergy of Charleston could attend in a body to give sanction to the proceedings of the great Vigilance Committee. They could not properly exert the least influence *against* slavery, because it is a civil institution, but they could give the whole weight of their influence in *favor* of it.

Is it not making the kingdom of our Lord Jesus Christ quite as much of this world, to patronize the oppressor, as to patronize the slave?

❦ ❦ ❦

# An Affectionate and Christian Address of Many Thousands of Women of Great Britain and Ireland to Their Sisters the Women of the United States of America

*Uncle Tom's Cabin* sold a million and a half copies in England in its first year of publication and sparked an outpouring of political action. Over half a million women in the British Isles signed this antislavery address to their American counterparts, appealing to "sisters," "wives," and "mothers" to protest slavery's outrages on the Christian family. On May 7, 1853, the address and signatures were presented to Stowe at Stafford House, the Duchess of Sutherland's palatial residence, at an event marking the climax of her triumphal tour of Great Britain.

common origin a common faith and we sincerely believe a common cause urge us at the present moment to address you on the subject of that system of Negro slavery which still prevails so extensively and even under kindly disposed masters with such frightful results in many of the vast regions of the western world.

We will not dwell on the ordinary topics of the progress of civilization on the advance of freedom every where on the rights and requirements of the nineteenth century.—but we appeal to you very seriously to reflect and to ask counsel of God how far such a state of things is in accordance with His Holy Word the inalienable rights of immortal souls and the pure and merciful spirit of the Christian religion.

We do not shut our eyes to the difficulties nay the dangers that might beset the immediate abolition of that long-established system we see and admit the necessity of preparation for so great an event but in speaking of indispensable preliminaries we cannot be silent on those laws of your country which in direct contravention of God's own law 'instituted in the time of man's innocency' deny in effect to the slave, the sanctity of marriage with all its joys rights and obligations which separate at the will of the master the wife from the husband and the children from the parents Nor can we be silent on that awful system which either by statute or by custom interdicts to any race of man or any portion of the human family education in the truths of the Gospel and the ordinances of Christianity.

A remedy applied to these two evils alone would commence the amelioration of their sad condition. We appeal to you then as sisters as wives and as mothers to raise your voices to your fellow-citizens and your prayers to God for the removal of this affliction from the Christian world. We do not say these things in a spirit of self-complacency as though our nation were free from the guilt it perceives in others. We acknowledge with grief and shame our heavy share in this great sin. We acknowledge that our forefathers introduced nay compelled the adoption of slavery in those mighty colonies We humbly confess it before Almighty God and it is because we so deeply feel and so unfeignedly avow our own complicity that we now venture to implore your aid to wipe away our common crime and our common dishonour.

[Connecticut Historical Society, Hartford, Conn.]

❧ ❧ ❧

# An Appeal to Women of the Free States of America, on the Present Crisis in Our Country

Stowe's eloquent "Appeal to Women of the Free States" was published in the *Independent* on February 23, 1854, on the eve of the Senate vote on the Kansas-Nebraska Bill, which repealed the Missouri Compromise and allowed for the spread of slavery in territories, if "popular sovereignty" so decided.

Modeled on the British women's "Affectionate and Christian Address" and envisioning a concerted, worldwide movement of women of all classes rising in a tide against slavery, Stowe's "Appeal" urges American women to live up to the promises of their democratic republic. Her rhetoric rests on two prongs. On the one hand, she invokes "holier feelings, which are peculiar to womanhood." But she also appeals to "the time of our revolutionary struggle" and to America as "a nation specially raised up by God to advance the cause of liberty and religion."

he Providence of God has brought our nation to a crisis of most solemn interest.

A question is now pending in our national legislature, which is most vitally to affect the temporal and eternal interests, not only of ourselves, but of our children, and our children's children for ages yet unborn. Through our nation, it is to affect the interests of liberty and Christianity throughout the whole world.

Of the woes, the injustice, and the misery of slavery, it is not needful to speak. There is but one feeling and one opinion on this among us all. I do not think there is a mother among us all, who clasps her child to her breast, who could ever be made to feel it right that that child should be a slave; not a mother among us all who would not rather lay that child in its grave.

Nor can I believe that there is a woman so unchristian as to think it right to inflict on her neighbor's child what she would think worse than death were it inflicted on her own. I do not think there is a wife who would think it right *her* husband should be sold to a trader, and worked all his life without rights and without wages. I do not believe there is a husband who would think it right that *his* wife should be considered, by law, the property of another man, and not his own. I do not think there is a father or mother who would believe it right, were they forbidden by law to teach their children to read. I do not believe there is a brother who would think it right to have his sister held as property, with no legal defense for her personal honor, by any man living.

All this is inherent in slavery. It is not the abuse of slavery, but the legal nature of it. And there is not a woman in the United States, when the question is fairly put before her, who thinks these things are right.

However ambition and the love of political power may blind the stronger sex, God has given to woman a deeper and a more immovable knowledge, in those holier feelings, which are peculiar to womanhood, and which guard the sacredness of the family state.

But though our hearts have bled over this wrong, there have been many things tending to fetter our hands, to perplex our efforts, and to silence our voice. We have been told that to speak of it, was an invasion of the rights of other States. We have been told of promises and of compacts, and the natural expression of feeling has in many cases been restrained by an appeal to those honorable sentiments which respect the keeping of engagements.

The warm beatings of many hearts have been hushed; our yearnings and sympathies have been repressed, because we have not known what to do; and many have come to turn a deaf ear to the whole tale of sorrow, because unwilling to harrow up the soul with feeling, where action was supposed to be impossible.

But a time has now come, when the subject is arising under quite another aspect.

The question is not now, shall the wrongs of slavery exist, as they have, on their own territories? But shall we permit them to be extended over all the free territories of the United States? Shall the woes and miseries of slavery be extended over a region of fair, free, unoccupied territory, nearly equal, in extent, to the whole of the free States?

Nor is this all; this is not the last thing that is expected or intended. Should this movement be submitted to in silence, should the North consent to this breach of solemn contract on the part of the South, there yet remains one more step to be apprehended, viz: the legalizing of slavery throughout the free States. By a decision of the Supreme Court in the Lemmon case, it may be declared lawful for slave property to be held in the northern free States. Should this come to pass, it is no more improbable that there may be, four years hence, slave depots in New-York city, than it was four years ago, that the South would propose a repeal of the "Missouri Compromise."

Women of the free States! the question is not, shall we remonstrate with slavery on its own soil? but are we willing to receive slavery into the free States and territories of the Union?

Shall the whole power of the United States go into the hands of slavery?

Shall every State in it be thrown open as a slave State? This will be the final result and issue of the question which is now pending. This is the fearful crisis at which we stand. And now, is there any thing which the women of a country can do? Oh women of the free States! what did your brave mothers do in the time of our revolutionary struggle? Did not *liberty* in those days feel the strong impulse of woman's heart?

Never was there a great interest agitating the community, when woman's influence was not felt for good or for evil. At the time when the struggle for the abolition of the slave-trade was convulsing England, women contributed more than any other laborers to that great triumph of humanity. The women and children of England to a great extent refused to receive into their families the sugar raised by the suffering slave. Seventy thousand families refused the use of sugar, as a testimony to their abhorrence of the manner in which it was produced. At that time women were unwearied in passing from house to house, distributing tracts and books, and presenting the subject in families.

One lady alone called on and conversed in this way with more than two thousand families, and others were not behind her in their labors.

The women all over England were associated in corresponding circles for prayer and for labor. Petitions to government were gotten up and signed by women.

During my recent visit in England, I was called to the bedside of an aged mother in Israel, whose prayers and labors on earth are well-nigh ended, but who had borne this sacred cause in her heart from the very commencement. I was never more impressed than when, raised in her bed, with quivering lips and streaming eyes, she lifted her hands solemnly in prayer to God, that he would bless the labors for the cause of the slave in America, and at last bring on the final abolition of slavery through the world.

Women of America! we do not know with what thrilling earnestness the hopes and the eyes of the world are fastened on our country, and with what intenseness they desire that we should take decided ground for universal liberty. This sacred desire is spread through the lower and working classes of other countries, as well as through those in higher ranks.

When I was in England, although I distinctly stated that the raising of money was no part of my object, and, on account of the state of my health, declined to take any responsibility of that kind, yet money was actually pressed upon me unsolicited, from the mere impulse to do something for this cause. Most affecting letters were received from poor working men and women, inclosing small sums in postage-stamps, for this object.

Nor has this feeling been confined to England alone; in France, Switzerland, and Germany, there has been the same deep emotion. A lady in Stuttgard undertook to make a collection for an American anti-slavery fair, and while contributions from all ranks freely flowed in, a poor peasant and his wife in the neighborhood, took down from the walls of their cottage two prints, probably the only superfluities they possessed on earth, and sent them to the collection.

During my stay, I heard from Christians of all denominations, how deeply their souls had been moved in prayer for America, in view of this evil. A Catholic lady from the old town of Orleans wrote of her intention to offer special supplications after the manner of her faith. In a circle of Protestant pastors and Christians in Switzerland, I heard the French language made eloquent in pleadings with God that America might have grace given her to right the cause of the oppressed.

Why all this emotion in foreign lands? Is it not because the whole world has been looking toward America with hope, as a nation specially raised up by God to advance the cause of liberty and religion?

There has been a universal expectation, that the next step taken by America would surely be one which should have a tendency to right this great wrong. Those who are struggling for civil and religious freedom in Europe, speak this word *slavery* in sad whispers, as one names the fault of a revered friend. They can scarce believe the advertisements which American papers bring to them, of slave-sales; of men, women, and children traded like cattle. Scarcely can they trust their eyes, when they read the laws of the slave States, and the decisions of their courts. The advocates of despotism hold these things up to them and say, "See what comes of republican liberty!" Hitherto the answer has been, America is more than half free, and she certainly will, in time, repudiate slavery altogether.

But what can they say now, if, just as the great struggle for human rights is commencing throughout Europe, America opens all her free territories to the most unmitigated despotism? This will be not merely betraying American liberty, but the cause of liberty throughout the world.

And while all nations are moved in view of this subject of American slavery, shall we only be unmoved? Shall even the poor laboring man and woman of Europe be so pressed in view of the wrongs of the slave as to inquire, what can *we* do? and we wives, and mothers, and sisters of America, sit down content to do nothing in such a crisis as this?

What, then, is the duty of American women at this time? The first duty is for each woman, *for herself* thoroughly to understand the subject, and to feel that as mother, wife, sister, or member of society, she is bound to give her influence on the right side.

In the second place, women can make exertions to get up petitions, in their particular districts, to our national legislature. They can take measures to communicate information in their vicinity. They can employ lecturers to spread the subject before the people of their town or village. They can circulate the speeches of our members in Congress, and in many other ways secure a full understanding of the present position of our country.

Above all, it seems to be necessary and desirable that we should make this subject a matter of earnest prayer. The present crisis in the history of the world, is one which calls upon all who believe in an Almighty Guardian and Ruler of nations, to betake themselves to his throne.

A conflict is now commencing between the forces of liberty and despotism throughout the whole world. We, who are Christians, and believe in the sure word of prophecy, know that fearful convulsions and overturnings are predicted, before the coming of Him who is to rule the earth in righteousness. How important in this crisis, that all who believe in prayer should retreat beneath the shadow of the Almighty!

It is a melancholy but unavoidable result of such great encounters of principle, that they always tend to degenerate into sectional and personal bitterness. It is this liability, which forms one of the most solemn and affecting features of the crisis now presented. We are on the eve of a conflict which will try men's souls, and strain, to their utmost tension, the bonds of brotherly union which bind this nation together.

Let us pray that in the agitation of this question between the North and the South, the war of principle may not become a mere sectional conflict, degenerating into the encounter of physical force. Let us raise our hearts to Him who has the power to restrain the wrath of man, that He will avert these consequences, which our sins as a nation have so justly deserved.

And as far as our social influence extends, let us guard against indiscriminate bitterness and vituperation.

Doubtless, there are noble minds at the South, who do not participate in the machinations of their political leaders, whose sense of honor and justice is outraged by this proposition, equally with our own.

While, then, we seek to sustain the cause of free principle unwaveringly, let us hold it also to be our true office, as women, to moderate the acrimony of political contest, remembering that the slaveholder and the slave are alike our brethren, whom the law of God commands us to love as ourselves.

For the sake of both, for the sake of our common country, for the sake of outraged and struggling liberty throughout the world, let every woman of America now do her duty.

# Dred

A TALE OF THE GREAT DISMAL SWAMP

Stowe's second antislavery novel, published in 1856 by Phillips, Sampson, reflects the growing violence and sectional strife as the nation moved closer to Civil War. In the following chapters Stowe introduces her insurrectionary hero, Dred, drawing liberally on historical documents describing the rebellion of Denmark Vesey. Dred attempts to enlist Harry, who is both half brother and slave to Tom Gordon, in a conspiracy to kill the masters. Armed with a rifle and a knowledge of "the wrathful denunciations of the ancient prophets against oppression and injustice," Dred calls for a day of vengeance; his Old Testament imprecations of plague and pestilence and deliverance through physical resistance foreshadow the Civil War. His militancy stands in contrast to the New Testament pacifism of, on the one hand, Uncle Tom, and in this novel, of Milly, modeled on Sojourner Truth.

As in *Uncle Tom's Cabin*, Stowe appeals not only to the Bible but to the Declaration of Independence. Her musings about the effect on the slave of Fourth of July orations on man's "inalienable right to life, liberty, and the pursuit of happiness" recalls Frederick Douglass's famous 1852 oration, "What To the Slave Is the Fourth of July?"

## Chapter XVIII
### Dred

Harry spent the night at the place of Mr. John Gordon, and arose the next morning in a very discontented mood of mind. Nothing is more vexatious to an active and enterprising person than to be thrown into a state of entire idleness; and Harry, after lounging about for a short time in the morning, found his indignation increased by every moment of enforced absence from the scene of his daily labors and interest. Having always enjoyed substantially the privileges of a freeman in the ability to regulate his time according to his own ideas, to come and go, to buy and sell, and transact business unfettered by any felt control, he was the more keenly alive to the degradation implied in his present position.

"Here I must skulk around," said he to himself, "like a partridge in the bushes, allowing everything to run at loose ends, preparing the way for my being found fault with for a lazy fellow, by and by; and all for what? Because my younger brother chooses to come, without right or reason, to domineer over me, to insult

my wife; and because the laws will protect him in it, if he does it! Ah! ah! that 's
it. They are all leagued together! No matter how right I am—no matter how bad
he is! Everybody will stand up for him, and put me down; all because my grandmother was born in Africa, and his grandmother was born in America. Confound
it all, I won't stand it! Who knows what he 'll be saying and doing to Lisette while
I am gone? I 'll go back and face him, like a man! I 'll keep straight about my
business, and, if he crosses me, let him take care! He has n't got but one life, any
more than I have. Let him look out!"

And Harry jumped upon his horse, and turned his head homeward. He struck
into a circuitous path, which led along that immense belt of swampy land, to which
the name of Dismal has been given. As he was riding along, immersed in thought,
the clatter of horses' feet was heard in front of him. A sudden turn of the road brought
him directly facing to Tom Gordon and Mr. Jekyl, who had risen early and started
off on horseback, in order to reach a certain stage-dépôt before the heat of the day.
There was a momentary pause on both sides; when Tom Gordon, like one who knows
his power, and is determined to use it to the utmost, broke out, scornfully:

"Stop, you damned nigger, and tell your master where you are going!"

"You are not my master!" said Harry, in words whose concentrated calmness
conveyed more bitterness and wrath than could have been given by the most violent outburst.

"You d_____d whelp!" said Tom Gordon, striking him across the face twice
with his whip, "take *that*, and *that!* We 'll see if I 'm not your master! There, now,
help yourself, won't you? Is n't that a master's mark?"

It had been the life-long habit of Harry's position to repress every emotion of
anger within himself. But, at this moment, his face wore a deadly and frightful
expression. Still, there was something majestic and almost commanding in the attitude with which he reined back his horse, and slowly lifted his hand to heaven.
He tried to speak, but his voice was choked with repressed passion. At last he said:

"You may be sure, Mr. Gordon, this mark will *never* be forgotten!"

There are moments of high excitement, when all that is in a human being seems
to be roused, and to concentrate itself in the eye and the voice. And, in such moments, *any* man, apparently by virtue of his mere humanity, by the mere awful-
ness of the human soul that is in him, gains power to over-awe those who in other
hours scorn him. There was a minute's pause, in which neither spoke; and Mr.
Jekyl, who was a man of peace, took occasion to touch Tom's elbow, and say:

"It seems to me this is n't worth while—we shall miss the stage." And, as
Harry had already turned his horse and was riding away, Tom Gordon turned
his, shouting after him, with a scornful laugh:

"I called on your wife before I came away, this morning, and I liked her rather
better the second time than I did the first!"

This last taunt flew like a Parthian arrow backward, and struck into the soul
of the bondman with even a keener power than the degrading blow. The sting of
it seemed to rankle more bitterly as he rode along, till at last he dropped the reins
on his horse's neck, and burst into a transport of bitter cursing.

"Aha! aha! it has come nigh *thee*, has it? It toucheth *thee*, and thou faintest!"
said a deep voice from the swampy thicket beside him.

Harry stopped his horse and his imprecations. There was a crackling in the swamp, and a movement among the copse of briers; and at last the speaker emerged, and stood before Harry. He was a tall black man, of magnificent stature and proportions. His skin was intensely black, and polished like marble. A loose shirt of red flannel, which opened very wide at the breast, gave a display of a neck and chest of herculean strength. The sleeves of the shirt, rolled up nearly to the shoulders, showed the muscles of a gladiator. The head, which rose with an imperial air from the broad shoulders, was large and massive, and developed with equal force both in the reflective and perceptive department. The perceptive organs jutted like dark ridges over the eyes, while that part of the head which phrenologists attribute to the moral and intellectual sentiments, rose like an ample dome above them. The large eyes had that peculiar and solemn effect of unfathomable blackness and darkness which is often a striking characteristic of the African eye. But there burned in them, like tongues of flame in a black pool of naphtha, a subtle and restless fire, that betokened habitual excitement to the verge of insanity. If any organs were predominant in the head, they were those of ideality, wonder, veneration, and firmness; and the whole combination was such as might have formed one of the wild old warrior prophets of the heroic ages. He wore a fantastic sort of turban, apparently of an old scarlet shawl, which added to the outlandish effect of his appearance. His nether garments, of coarse negro-cloth, were girded round the waist by a strip of scarlet flannel, in which was thrust a bowie-knife and hatchet. Over one shoulder he carried a rifle, and a shot-pouch was suspended to his belt. A rude game-bag hung upon his arm. Wild and startling as the apparition might have been, it appeared to be no stranger to Harry; for, after the first movement of surprise, he said, in a tone of familiar recognition, in which there was blended somewhat of awe and respect:

"O, it is you, then, Dred! I did n't know that you were hearing me!"

"Have I not heard?" said the speaker, raising his arm, and his eyes gleaming with wild excitement. "How long wilt thou halt between two opinions? Did not Moses refuse to be called the son of Pharaoh's daughter? How long wilt thou cast in thy lot with the oppressors of Israel, who say unto thee, 'Bow down that we may walk over thee'? Shall not the Red Sea be divided? 'Yea,' saith the Lord, 'it shall.' "

"Dred! I know what you mean!" said Harry, trembling with excitement.

"Yea, thou dost!" said the figure. "Yea, thou dost! Hast thou not eaten the fat and drunk the sweet with the oppressor, and hid thine eyes from the oppression of thy people? Have not *our* wives been for a prey, and thou hast not regarded? Hath not our cheek been given to the smiter? Have we not been counted as sheep for the slaughter? But thou saidst, Lo! I knew it not, and didst hide thine eyes! Therefore, the curse of Meroz is upon thee, saith the Lord. And *thou* shalt bow down to the oppressor, and his rod shall be upon thee; and *thy* wife shall be for a prey!"

"Don't talk in that way!—don't!" said Harry, striking out his hands with a frantic gesture, as if to push back the words. "You are raising the very devil in me!"

"Look here, Harry," said the other, dropping from the high tone he at first used to that of common conversation, and speaking in bitter irony, "did your master strike you? It's sweet to kiss the rod, is n't it? Bend your neck and ask to be struck again!—won't you? Be meek and lowly; that's the religion for you! You are a *slave*, and you wear broadcloth, and sleep soft. By and by he will give you a fip to buy salve for those cuts! Don't fret about your wife! Women always like the master better than the slave! Why should n't they? When a man licks his master's foot, his wife scorns him,—serves him right. Take it meekly, my boy! 'Servants, obey your masters.' Take your master's old coats—take your wife when he's done with her—and bless God that brought you under the light of the Gospel! Go! *you* are a slave! But, as for me," he said, drawing up his head, and throwing back his shoulders with a deep inspiration, "*I* am a free man! Free by this," holding out his rifle. "Free by the Lord of hosts, that numbereth the stars, and calleth them forth by their names. Go home—that's all I have to say to you! You sleep in a curtained bed.—I sleep on the ground, in the swamps! You eat the fat of the land. I have what the ravens bring me! But no man whips me!—no man touches *my* wife!—no man says to me, 'Why do ye so?' Go! *you* are a slave!—I am free!" And, with one athletic bound, he sprang into the thicket, and was gone.

The effect of this address on the already excited mind of the bondman may be better conceived than described. He ground his teeth, and clenched his hands.

"Stop!" he cried, "Dred, I will—I will—I'll do as you tell me—I will not be a slave!"

A scornful laugh was the only reply, and the sound of crackling footsteps retreated rapidly. He who retreated struck up, in a clear, loud voice, one of those peculiar melodies in which vigor and spirit are blended with a wild, inexpressible mournfulness. The voice was one of a singular and indescribable quality of tone; it was heavy as the sub-bass of an organ, and of a velvety softness, and yet it seemed to pierce the air with a keen dividing force which is generally characteristic of voices of much less volume. The words were the commencement of a wild camp-meeting hymn, much in vogue in those parts:

> "Brethren, don't you hear the sound?
>     The martial trumpet now is blowing;
> Men in order listing round,
>     And soldiers to the standard flowing."

There was a wild, exultant fulness of liberty that rolled in the note; and, to Harry's excited ear, there seemed in it a fierce challenge of contempt to his imbecility, and his soul at that moment seemed to be rent asunder with a pang such as only those can know who have felt what it is to be a slave. There was an uprising within him, vague, tumultuous, overpowering; dim instincts, heroic aspirations; the will to do, the soul to dare; and then, in a moment, there followed the picture of all society leagued against him, the hopeless impossibility of any outlet to what was burning within him. The waters of a nature naturally noble, pent up, and without outlet, rolled back upon his heart with a suffocating force; and, in his hasty anguish, he cursed the day of his birth. The spasm of his emotion was interrupted by the sudden appearance of Milly coming along the path.

"Why, bless you, Milly," said Harry, in sudden surprise, "where are you going?"

"O, bless you, honey, chile, I 's gwine on to take de stage. Dey wanted to get up de wagon for me; but, bless you, says I, what you s'pose de Lord gin us legs for? I never wants no critturs to tug me round, when I can walk myself. And, den, honey, it 's so pleasant like, to be a walking along in de bush here, in de morning; 'pears like de voice of de Lord is walking among de trees. But, bless you, chile, honey, what 's de matter o' yer face?"

"It 's Tom Gordon, d———n him!" said Harry.

"Don't talk dat ar way, chile!" said Milly; using the freedom with Harry which her years and weight of character had gradually secured for her among the members of the plantation.

"I *will* talk that way! Why should n't I? I am not going to be good any longer."

"Why, 't won't help de matter to be *bad*, will it, Harry? 'Cause you hate Tom Gordon, does you want to act just like him?"

"No!" said Harry, "I won't be like him, but I 'll have my revenge! Old Dred has been talking to me again, this morning. He always did stir me up so that I could hardly live; and I won't stand it any longer!"

"Chile," said Milly, "you take care! Keep clear on him! He 's in de wilderness of Sinai; he is with de blackness, and darkness, and tempest. He han't come to de heavenly Jerusalem. O! O! honey! dere 's a blood of sprinkling dat speaketh better things dan dat of Abel. Jerusalem above is *free*—is *free*, honey; so, don't you mind, now, what happens in *dis* yer time."

"Ah, ah, Aunt Milly! this may do well enough for old women like you; but, stand opposite to a young fellow like me, with good strong arms, and a pair of doubled fists, and a body and soul just as full of fight as they can be; it don't answer to go to telling about a heavenly Jerusalem! We want something here. We 'll have it too! How do you know there is any heaven, any how?

"Know it?" said Milly, her eye kindling, and striking her staff on the ground. "Know it? I knows it by de *hankering arter it* I got in here;" giving her broad chest a blow which made it resound like a barrel. "De Lord knowed what he was 'bout when he made us. When he made babies rooting round, with der poor little mouths open, he made milk, and de mammies for 'em too. Chile, we 's nothing but great babies, dat an't got our eyes opened—rooting round and round; but de Father 'll feed us yet—he will so."

"He 's a long time about it," said Harry, sullenly.

"Well, chile, an't it a long time 'fore your corn sprouts—a long time 'fore it gets into de ears?—but you plants, for all dat. What 's dat to me what I is here?—Shan't I reign with de Lord Jesus?"

"I don't know," said Harry.

"Well, honey, I *does!* Jest so sure as I 's standing on dis yer ground, I knows in a few years I shall be reigning with de Lord Jesus, and a casting my crown at his feet. Dat 's what I knows. Flesh and blood did n't reveal it unto me, but de Spirit of de Father. It 's no odds to me what I does here; every road leads straight to glory, and de glory an't got no end to it!" And Milly uplifted her voice in a favorite stave—

"When we 've been dere ten thousand years,
  Bright shining like de sun,
We 've no less days to sing God's praise
  Than when we first begun."

"Chile," said she to him, solemnly, "I an't a fool. Does ye s'pose dat I thinks folks has any business to be sitting on der cheers all der life long, and working me, and living on my money? Why, I knows dey han't! An't it all wrong, from fust to last, de way dey makes merchandise o' us! Why, I knows it is; but I 's still about it, for de Lord's sake. I don't work for Miss Loo—I works for de Lord Jesus; and he is good pay—no mistake, now I tell you."

"Well," said Harry, a little shaken, but not convinced, "after all, there is n't much use in trying to do any other way. But you 're lucky in feeling so, Aunt Milly; but I can't."

"Well, chile, any way, don't you do nothing rash, and don't you hear *him*. Dat ar way out is through seas of blood. Why, chile, would you turn against Miss Nina? Chile, if they get a going, they won't spare nobody. Don't you start up dat ar tiger; 'cause, I tell ye, ye can't chain him, if ye do!"

"Yes," said Harry, "I see it 's all madness, perfect madness; there 's no use thinking, no use talking. Well, good-morning, Aunt Milly. Peace go with you!" And the young man started his horse, and was soon out of sight.

## Chapter XIX
## The Conspirators

We owe our readers now some words of explanation respecting the new personage who has been introduced into our history; therefore we must go back somewhat, and allude to certain historical events of painful significance.

It has been a problem to many, how the system of slavery in America should unite the two apparent inconsistencies of a code of slave-laws more severe than that of any other civilized nation, with an average practice at least as indulgent as any other; for, bad as slavery is at the best, it may yet be admitted that the practice, as a whole, has been less cruel in this country than in many. An examination into history will show us that the cruelty of the laws resulted from the effects of indulgent practice. During the first years of importation of slaves into South Carolina, they enjoyed many privileges. Those who lived in intelligent families, and had any desire to learn, were instructed in reading and writing. Liberty was given them to meet in assemblies of worship, in class-meetings, and otherwise, without the presence of white witnesses; and many were raised to situations of trust and consequence. The result of this was the development of a good degree of intelligence and manliness among the slaves. There arose among them grave, thoughtful, energetic men, with their ears and eyes open, and their minds constantly awake to compare and reason.

When minds come into this state, in a government professing to be founded on principles of universal equality, it follows that almost every public speech, document, or newspaper, becomes an incendiary publication.

Of this fact the southern slave states have ever exhibited the most singular unconsciousness. Documents containing sentiments most dangerous for slaves to hear have been publicly read and applauded among them. The slave has heard, amid shouts, on the Fourth of July, that his masters held the truth to be self-evident, that all men were born equal, and had an *inalienable right* to life, liberty, and the pursuit of happiness; and that all governments derive their just power from the consent of the governed. Even the mottoes of newspapers have embodied sentiments of the most insurrectionary character.

Such inscriptions as "Resistance to tyrants is obedience to God" stand, to this day, in large letters, at the head of southern newspapers; while speeches of senators and public men, in which the principles of universal democracy are asserted, are constant matters of discussion. Under such circumstances, it is difficult to induce the servant, who feels that he is a man, to draw those lines which seem so obvious to masters, by whom this fact has been forgotten. Accordingly we find that when the discussions for the admission of Missouri as a slave state produced a wave whose waters undulated in every part of the Union, there were found among the slaves men of unusual thought and vigor, who were no inattentive witnesses and listeners. The discussions were printed in the newspapers; and what was printed in the newspapers was further discussed at the post-office door, in the tavern, in the bar-room, at the dinner-party, where black servants were listening behind the chairs. A free colored man in the city of Charleston, named Denmark Vesey, was the one who had the hardihood to seek to use the electric fluid in the cloud thus accumulated. He conceived the hopeless project of imitating the example set by the American race, and achieving independence for the blacks.

Our knowledge of this man is derived entirely from the printed reports of the magistrates who gave an account of the insurrection, of which he was the instigator, and who will not, of course, be supposed to be unduly prejudiced in his favor. They state that he was first brought to the country by one Captain Vesey, a young lad, distinguished for personal beauty and great intelligence, and that he proved, for twenty years, a most faithful slave; but, on drawing a prize of fifteen hundred dollars in the lottery, he purchased his freedom of his master, and worked as a carpenter in the city of Charleston. He was distinguished for strength and activity, and, as the accounts state, maintained such an irreproachable character, and enjoyed so much the confidence of the whites, that when he was accused, the charge was not only discredited, but he was not even arrested for several days after, and not till the proof of his guilt had become too strong to be doubted. His historians go on, with considerable naïveté, to remark:

> It is difficult to conceive *what motive he had to enter into such a plot,* unless it was the one mentioned by one of the witnesses, who said that Vesey had *several children who were slaves,* and that he said, on one occasion, *he wished he could see them free,* as he himself artfully remarked in his defence on his trial.

It appears that the project of rousing and animating the blacks to this enterprise occupied the mind of Vesey for more than four years, during which time he was continually taking opportunities to animate and inspire the spirits of his countrymen. The account states that the speeches in Congress of those opposed to the admission of Missouri into the Union, perhaps garbled and misrepresented, furnished him with ample means for inflaming the minds of the colored population.

"Even while walking in the street," the account goes on to say,

> he was not idle; for, if his companion bowed to a white person, as slaves universally do, he would rebuke him, and observe, 'that all men were born equal, and that he was surprised that any one would degrade himself by such conduct; that he would never cringe to the whites; nor ought any one to, who had the feelings of a man.'* When answered, 'We are slaves,' he would say, sarcastically and indignantly, 'You deserve to remain slaves!' And, if he were further asked, 'What can we do?' he would remark, 'Go and buy a spelling-book, and read the fable of "Hercules and the Wagoner." ' He also sought every opportunity of entering into conversation with white persons, during which conversation he would artfully introduce some bold remark on slavery; and sometimes, when, from the character he was conversing with, he found he might be still bolder, he would go so far that, had not his declarations been clearly proved, they would scarcely have been credited.

But his great instrument of influence was a book that has always been prolific of insurrectionary movements, under all systems of despotism.

> He rendered himself perfectly familiar with all those parts of Scripture which he thought he could pervert to his purpose, and would readily quote them to prove that slavery was contrary to the laws of God, and that slaves were bound to attempt their emancipation, however shocking and bloody might be the consequences; that such efforts would not only be pleasing to the Almighty, but were absolutely enjoined.

Vesey, in the course of time, associated with himself five slave-men of marked character—Rolla, Ned, Peter, Monday, and Gullah Jack. Of these, the account goes on to say:

> In the selection of his leaders, Vesey showed great penetration and sound judgment. Rolla was plausible, and possessed uncommon self-possession; bold and ardent, he was not to be deterred from his purpose by danger. Ned's appearance indicated that he was a man of firm nerves and desperate courage. Peter was intrepid and resolute, true to his engagements, and cautious in observing secrecy where it was necessary; he was not to be daunted nor impeded by difficulties, and, though confident of success, was careful in providing against any obstacles or casualties which might arise, and intent upon discovering every means which might be in their power, if thought of beforehand. Gullah Jack was regarded as a sorcerer, and, as such, feared by the natives of Africa, who believe in witchcraft. He was not only considered invulnerable, but that he could make others so by his charms, and that he could, and certainly would, provide all his followers with arms. He was artful, cruel, bloody; his disposition, in short, was diabolical. His influence among the Africans was inconceivable. Monday was firm, resolute, discreet, and intelligent.
>
> It is a melancholy truth that the general good conduct of all the leaders, except Gullah Jack, was such as rendered them objects least liable to suspicion. Their conduct had secured them, not only the unlimited confidence of their owners, but they had been indulged in every comfort, and allowed every privilege compatible with

*These extracts are taken from the official report.

their situation in the community; and, though Gullah Jack was not remarkable for the correctness of his deportment, he by no means sustained a bad character. But, . . . not only were the leaders of good character, and very much indulged by their owners, but this was very generally the case with all who were convicted, many of them possessing the highest confidence of their owners, *and not one a bad character*.

The conduct and behavior of Vesey and his five leaders during their trial and imprisonment may be interesting to many. When Vesey was tried, he folded his arms, and seemed to pay great attention to the testimony given against him, but with his eyes fixed on the floor. In this situation he remained immovable until the witnesses had been examined by the court, and cross-examined by his counsel, when he requested to be allowed to examine the witnesses himself, which he did. The evidence being closed, he addressed the court at considerable length. When he received his sentence, tears trickled down his cheeks.

Rolla, when arraigned, affected not to understand the charge against him; and when, at his request, it was explained to him, assumed, with wonderful adroitness, astonishment and surprise. He was remarkable throughout his trial for composure and great presence of mind. When he was informed that he was convicted, and was advised to prepare for death, he appeared perfectly confounded, but exhibited no signs of fear.

In Ned's behavior there was nothing remarkable. His countenance was stern and immovable, even while he was receiving sentence of death. From his looks it was impossible to discover or conjecture what were his feelings. Not so with Peter Poyes. In his countenance were strongly marked disappointed ambition, revenge, indignation, and an anxiety to know how far the discoveries had extended. He did not appear to fear personal consequences, for his whole behavior indicated the reverse, but exhibited an evident anxiety for the success of their plan, in which his whole soul was embarked. His countenance and behavior were the same when he received his sentence, and his only words were, on retiring, 'I suppose you 'll let me see my wife and family before I die,' and that in no supplicating tone. When he was asked, a day or two after, 'If it was possible that he could see his master and family murdered, who had treated him so kindly?' he replied to the question only by a smile. In their prison, the convicts resolutely refused to make any confessions or communications which might implicate others; and Peter Poyes sternly enjoined it upon them to maintain this silence—'*Do not open your lips; die silent, as you will see me do!*' and in this resolute silence they met their fate. Twenty-two of the conspirators were executed upon one gallows.

The account says,

That Peter Poyes was one of the most active of the recruiting agents. All the principal conspirators kept a list of those who had consented to join them, and Peter was said, by one of the witnesses, to have had six hundred names on his list; but, so resolutely to the last did he observe his pledge of secrecy to his associates, that, of the whole number arrested and tried, not one of them belonged to his company. In fact, in an insurrection in which thousands of persons were supposed to have been implicated, only thirty-six were convicted.

Among the children of Denmark Vesey was a boy by a Mandingo slave-woman, who was his father's particular favorite. The Mandingos are one of the finest of African tribes, distinguished for intelligence, beauty of form, and an indomitable pride and energy of nature. As slaves, they are considered particularly valuable by those who have tact enough to govern them, because of their great capability and their proud faithfulness; but they resent a government of brute force, and under such are always fractious and dangerous.

This boy received from his mother the name of Dred; a name not unusual among the slaves, and generally given to those of great physical force.

The development of this child's mind was so uncommon as to excite astonishment among the negroes. He early acquired the power of reading, by an apparent instinctive faculty, and would often astonish those around him with things which he had discovered in books. Like other children of a deep and fervent nature, he developed great religious ardor, and often surprised the older negroes by his questions and replies on this subject. A son so endowed could not but be an object of great pride and interest to a father like Denmark Vesey. The impression seemed to prevail universally among the negroes that this child was born for extraordinary things; and perhaps it was the yearning to acquire liberty for the development of such a mind which first led Denmark Vesey to reflect on the nature of slavery, and the terrible weights which it lays on the human intellect, and to conceive the project of liberating a race.

The Bible, of which Vesey was an incessant reader, stimulated this desire. He likened his own position of comparative education, competence, and general esteem among the whites, to that of Moses among the Egyptians; and nourished the idea that, like Moses, he was sent as a deliverer. During the process of the conspiracy, this son, though but ten years of age, was his father's confidant; and he often charged him, though he should fail in the attempt, never to be discouraged. He impressed it upon his mind that he should never submit tamely to the yoke of slavery; and nourished the idea already impressed, that some more than ordinary destiny was reserved for him. After the discovery of the plot, and the execution of its leaders, those more immediately connected with them were sold from the state, even though not proved to have participated. With the most guarded caution, Vesey had exempted his son from suspicion. It had been an agreed policy with them both, that in the presence of others they should counterfeit alienation and dislike. Their confidential meetings with each other had been stolen and secret. At the time of his father's execution, Dred was a lad of fourteen. He could not be admitted to his father's prison, but he was a witness of the undaunted aspect with which he and the other conspirators met their doom. The memory dropped into the depths of his soul, as a stone drops into the desolate depths of a dark mountain lake.

Sold to a distant plantation, he became noted for his desperate, unsubduable disposition. He joined in none of the social recreations and amusements of the slaves, labored with proud and silent assiduity, but, on the slightest rebuke or threat, flashed up with a savage fierceness, which, supported by his immense bodily strength, made him an object of dread among overseers. He was one of those of whom they gladly rid themselves; and, like a fractious horse, was sold from master to master. Finally, an overseer, hardier than the rest, determined on the task of subduing him. In the scuffle that ensued Dred struck him to the earth, a dead man, made his escape to the swamps, and was never afterwards heard of in civilized life.

The reader who consults the map will discover that the whole eastern shore of the Southern States, with slight interruptions, is belted by an immense chain of swamps, regions of hopeless disorder, where the abundant growth and vegetation of nature, sucking up its forces from the humid soil, seems to rejoice in a savage exuberance, and bid defiance to all human efforts either to penetrate or subdue. These wild regions are the homes of the alligator, the mocassin, and the rattle-snake. Evergreen trees, mingling freely with the deciduous children of the forest, form here dense jungles, verdant all the year round, and which afford shelter to numberless birds, with whose warbling the leafy desolation perpetually resounds. Climbing vines, and parasitic plants, of untold splendor and boundless exuberance of growth, twine and interlace, and hang from the heights of the highest trees pennons of gold and purple,—triumphant banners, which attest the solitary majesty of nature. A species of parasitic moss wreaths its abundant draperies from tree to tree, and hangs in pearly festoons, through which shine the scarlet berry and green leaves of the American holly.

What the mountains of Switzerland were to the persecuted Vaudois,[1] this swampy belt has been to the American slave. The constant effort to recover from thence fugitives has led to the adoption, in these states, of a separate profession, unknown at this time in any other Christian land—hunters, who train and keep dogs for the hunting of men, women, and children. And yet, with all the convenience of this profession, the reclaiming of the fugitives from these fastnesses of nature has been a work of such expense and difficulty, that the near proximity of the swamp has always been a considerable check on the otherwise absolute power of the overseer. Dred carried with him to the swamp but one solitary companion—the Bible of his father. To him it was not the messenger of peace and goodwill, but the herald of woe and wrath!

As the mind, looking on the great volume of nature, sees there a reflection of its own internal passions, and seizes on that in it which sympathizes with itself,— as the fierce and savage soul delights in the roar of torrents, the thunder of avalanches, and the whirl of ocean-storms,—so is it in the great answering volume of revelation. There is something there for every phase of man's nature; and hence its endless vitality and stimulating force. Dred had heard read, in the secret meetings of conspirators, the wrathful denunciations of ancient prophets against oppression and injustice. He had read of kingdoms convulsed by plagues; of tempest, and pestilence, and locusts; of the sea cleft in twain, that an army of slaves might pass through, and of their pursuers whelmed in the returning waters. He had heard of prophets and deliverers, armed with supernatural powers, raised up for oppressed people; had pondered on the nail of Jael, the goad of Shamgar, the pitcher and lamp of Gideon; and thrilled with fierce joy as he read how Samson, with his two strong arms, pulled down the pillars of the festive temple, and whelmed his triumphant persecutors in one grave with himself.

In the vast solitudes which he daily traversed, these things entered deep into his soul. Cut off from all human companionship, often going weeks without seeing a human face, there was no recurrence of every-day and prosaic ideas to check

---

[1]A Protestant religious sect of medieval origin, the Vaudois were persecuted and declared heretics for their pre-Reformation beliefs in apostolic simplicity and the priesthood of all believers.

the current of the enthusiasm thus kindled. Even in the soil of the cool Saxon heart the Bible has thrown out its roots with an all-pervading energy, so that the whole frame-work of society may be said to rest on soil held together by its fibres. Even in cold and misty England, armies have been made defiant and invincible by the incomparable force and deliberate valor which it breathes into men. But, when this oriental seed, an exotic among us, is planted back in the fiery soil of a tropical heart, it bursts forth with an incalculable ardor of growth.

A stranger cannot fail to remark the fact that, though the slaves of the South are unable to read the Bible for themselves, yet most completely have its language and sentiment penetrated among them, giving a Hebraistic coloring to their habitual mode of expression. How much greater, then, must have been the force of the solitary perusal of this volume on so impassioned a nature!—a nature, too, kindled by memories of the self-sacrificing ardor with which a father and his associates had met death at the call of freedom; for, none of us may deny that, wild and hopeless as this scheme was, it was still the same in kind with the more successful one which purchased for our fathers a national existence.

A mind of the most passionate energy and vehemence, thus awakened, for years made the wild solitudes of the swamp its home. That book, so full of startling symbols and vague images, had for him no interpreter but the silent courses of nature. His life passed in a kind of dream. Sometimes, traversing for weeks these desolate regions, he would compare himself to Elijah traversing for forty days and nights the solitudes of Horeb; or to John the Baptist in the wilderness, girding himself with camel's hair, and eating locusts and wild honey. Sometimes he would fast and pray for days; and then voices would seem to speak to him, and strange hieroglyphics would be written upon the leaves. In less elevated moods of mind, he would pursue, with great judgment and vigor, those enterprises necessary to preserve existence. The negroes lying out in the swamps are not so wholly cut off from society as might at first be imagined. The slaves of all the adjoining plantations, whatever they may pretend, to secure the good-will of their owners, are at heart secretly disposed, from motives both of compassion and policy, to favor the fugitives. They very readily perceive that, in the event of any difficulty occurring to themselves, it might be quite necessary to have a friend and protector in the swamp; and therefore they do not hesitate to supply these fugitives, so far as they are able, with anything which they may desire. The poor whites, also, who keep small shops in the neighborhood of plantations, are never particularly scrupulous, provided they can turn a penny to their own advantage; and willingly supply necessary wares in exchange for game, with which the swamp abounds.

Dred, therefore, came in possession of an excellent rifle, and never wanted for ammunition, which supplied him with an abundance of food. Besides this, there are here and there elevated spots in the swampy land, which by judicious culture, are capable of great productiveness. And many such spots Dred had brought under cultivation, either with his own hands, or from those of other fugitives, whom he had received and protected. From the restlessness of his nature, he had not confined himself to any particular region, but had traversed the whole swampy belt of both the Carolinas, as well as that of Southern Virginia; residing a few months in one place, and a few months in another. Wherever he stopped, he formed a sort of retreat, where he received and harbored fugitives. On one occasion, he rescued a trembling and bleeding mulatto woman from the dogs of the hunters, who had pursued her into the swamp. This woman he made his wife, and appeared to entertain a very deep affection for her. He made a retreat for her, with more than common ingenuity, in the swamp adjoining the Gordon plantation; and, after that, he was more especially known in that locality. He had fixed his eye upon Harry, as a person whose ability, address, and strength of character, might make him at some day a leader in a conspiracy against whites. Harry, in common with many of the slaves on the Gordon plantation, knew perfectly well of the presence of Dred in the neighborhood, and had often seen and conversed with him. But neither he nor any of the rest of them ever betrayed before any white person the slightest knowledge of the fact.

This ability of profound secrecy is one of the invariable attendants of a life of slavery. Harry was acute enough to know that his position was by no means so secure that he could afford to dispense with anything which might prove an assistance in some future emergency. The low white traders in the neighborhood also knew Dred well; but, as long as they could drive an advantageous trade with him, he was secure from their intervention. So secure had he been, that he had been even known to mingle in the motley throng of a camp-meeting unmolested. Thus much with regard to one who is to appear often on the stage before our history is done.

❦   ❦   ❦

# What Is to Be Done With Them?

On the front page of the August 21, 1862 *Independent*, where her columns appeared irregularly between 1853 and 1862, Stowe addressed the question on many white people's minds: what should be done with the slaves after emancipation? Whereas at the end of *Uncle Tom's Cabin* she sent her black characters to Canada and Liberia, here Stowe explicitly rejects colonization.

As in her "Appeal to Women of the Free States," Stowe builds on widely held national ideologies, in this case, individualism and equal rights, arguing that all citizens, including immigrants and free blacks, will rise to the level of their own ambitions if left alone and treated equally before the law.

any well-meaning people can form no idea of immediate emancipation but one full of dangers and horrors. They imagine the blacks free from every restraint of law, roaming abroad a terror and nuisance to the land. They never seem to have formed the idea that emancipated blacks can be taken care of, and governed, and kept from excesses by the civil law, just like any other free men and women. Let us look at this question a little.

Have not the pauper and prison population of old Europe been shipped liberally over to America, and turned out upon our wharves by thousands, without any other provision for their care and restraint than the ordinary civil code of this country? They have been left to take care of themselves and choose their own ways and places in society; and all this has been done from year to year, while the Old World has been looking on, predicting that such an influx of ignorance and vice would swamp our free institutions. These people came to us cramped by oppression, darkened by ignorance, hardened by vice, brutalized by poverty—the most unfit material, so thought legislators in Europe, to do anything with—and what did we do with them? We?—we let them take their equal chance among us. We simply treated them as equal men and women—free to come and live, trade, work, buy, sell, in our land, as long as they behaved themselves, and liable if they did not behave to be imprisoned and punished like any of the rest of us. A well-conducted foreigner might vote after a suitable time. He was considered to all intents and purposes an American. It was supposed that he had quite as much interest to defend a country where he had all the rights and privileges of a citizen, as any other man in it. And so, though all the world shook its head, and predicted that equal rights and universal suffrage would ruin us, universal suffrage only elevated our foreign population, and did not hurt us. The children of foreign emigrants had rights to free education in our common schools with the children of born Americans. The son of an Irish carman once competed for the gold medal with the son of a Beacon-street gentleman in Boston, and got it. What is the consequence? In one generation the Irishman or German becomes an enthusiastic American.

Has not this war shown that none fight better or braver for a common country than adopted citizens?

They know what liberty and equality are worth, for they have tried the prison-houses of the Old World; and in this war they have been as a wall of fire round about us.

Now, when the question is asked, What shall we do with the black laborers of the South if free—where shall we send them?—one can scarce repress a smile.

We ask, in reply, What will you do *without* them? Do you want to stop raising cotton? And if you don't, do you want to send away the only class of men who know how to raise it?

Here is a climate where a generation of white men must perish of malaria and fevers before they can become acclimated; and here on the soil is a race of hardy peasantry, who appear to have been purposely made and contrived by the Almighty to resist malaria and to delight in the heats that wither the whites—and yet our legislators are gravely pondering the question where they shall ship these laborers, in case they are reduced by God's providence to give them their birthright of liberty!

Send off all the acclimated laborers—send off all the men who know the country—send off all the men who have any experimental knowledge of the cropping of rice and cotton—and send them off simply because they have become freemen?

Is liberty such a bad thing? Is a skillful workman the worse workman because he works for wages and with the hope of doing something for himself?

No; the answer to the question, What shall we do with them? is simply this: Do just what you have done with the oppressed and poor of all nations—give them equal rights, a fair start, and the restraint and protection of just laws, and God and human nature will answer for the rest.

We commend the following passage from Macaulay, which might advantageously be printed in gold letters on our Capitol, where all who run may read:

> Many politicians of our times are in the habit of laying it down as a self-evident proposition, that no people ought to be free till they are fit to use their freedom. The maxim is worthy the fool in the old story who resolved not to go into the water till he had learned to swim. If men are to wait for liberty till they become wise and good in slavery, they may indeed wait for ever.

There is only one cure for the evils which newly acquired freedom produces, and that cure is—FREEDOM.

When a prisoner leaves his cell, he cannot bear the light of day—he is unable to discriminate colors or recognize faces; but the remedy is not remand him into his dungeon, but to accustom him to the rays of the sun.

❦ ❦ ❦

# Will You Take a Pilot?

On August 20, 1862, Horace Greeley's "The Prayer of Twenty Millions" editorial in the influential *New York Tribune* had urged President Lincoln to emancipate the slaves. Unready to take this step, Lincoln responded to Greeley by announcing "My paramount object in this struggle *is* to save the Union, and is *not* either to save or destroy Slavery. If I could save the Union without freeing *any* slave, I would do it; . . . What I do about slavery and the colored race, I do because I believe it helps to save the Union; and what I forbear I forbear because I do *not* believe it would help to save the Union." In her September 11, 1862 essay in the *Independent*, Stowe challenged President Lincoln on this famous utterance and urged emancipation.

nd it was now dark, and Jesus was not come to them. And the sea arose by reason of a great wind that blew. So when they had rowed about five-and-twenty or thirty furlongs, they see Jesus walking on the sea, and drawing nigh unto the ship: and they were afraid.

"But he said unto them, It is I; be not afraid.

"Then they willingly received him into the ship: and immediately the ship was at the land, whither they went."

—In our troubles we have rowed now about five-and-twenty or thirty furlongs, trusting mainly to good oar-strokes and stout arms. Evidently *Jesus* has not yet come to us. We put it to the hearts and consciences of all if things have been conducted in our national councils, and in the broad, general, national feeling, as if he had. There is, doubtless, much faith in him—much respect for him in church and state and army, as there was among the disciples in this ship; but, for the main part, we have considered the management of the ship as a thing we were competent to do without him. Some acts of Congress, some movements of the leaders of affairs, have looked as if we have in dim wise seen Jesus drawing nigh to the ship; and like the disciples of old, there has been a good deal of fear of him. It is a serious thing to take Jesus on board, and give up the management of the ship to him—whether it be the ship of an individual or the ship of state; and there is much shrinking and resistance when the time to do so seems approaching.

For who is this Jesus? Not a man who died eighteen hundred years ago; but a living God, who claims at this moment to be Prince of the kings of the earth—to be the great reigning and working force, who must reign till he hath put all things under his feet.

Since Jesus is our ruler and king, since he is above all other forces, since he has a plan to carry and a purpose to work out in our day, of which our nation and Union and all that we hold important are subservient, it would be as well for us to read over again what he said when he first publicly announced for what he came into our world:

"The Spirit of the Lord is upon me, because he hath anointed me to preach the Gospel to the poor; he hath sent me to heal the broken-hearted, to preach deliverance to the captives, and recovering of sight to the blind, to set at liberty them that are bruised, to preach the acceptable year of the Lord."

There is a resumé of the state policy of the King of kings, full as concise and explicit as the memorable one which the Chief Magistrate of this nation has just given in regard to his—but very different.

The declaration of President Lincoln, we presume, is as honest, as straightforward and explicit as ever a chief magistrate gave:

"My paramount object in this struggle *is* to save the Union, and is *not* either to save or destroy Slavery. If I could save the Union without freeing *any* slave, I would do it; and if I could save it by freeing *all* the slaves, I would do it; and if I could do it by freeing some and leaving others alone, I would also do that. What I do about slavery and the colored race, I do because I believe it helps to save this Union; and what I forbear I forbear because I do *not* believe it would help to save the Union. I shall do *less* whenever I shall believe what I am doing hurts the cause, and I shall do *more* whenever I shall believe doing more will help the cause."

We infer from the declaration of Christ just quoted, that were his policy as King of kings to be stated with equal distinctness, it would run thus:

"My paramount object in this struggle is to set at liberty them that are bruised, and *not* either to save or destroy the Union. What I do in favor of the Union, I do because it helps to free the oppressed; what I forbear, I forbear because it does not help to free the oppressed. I shall do less for the Union whenever it would hurt the cause of the slave, and more when I believe it would help the cause of the slave."

—We ask any thoughtful person to ponder the history of the world since Christ came, and see if there has not been evidence of a mighty working mind which has from age to age been declaring itself clearer and clearer in favor of the poor and oppressed and against the proud and powerful. Nations have been dashed one against each other, as ships lying in harbor are dashed by the upheavings of an earthquake. There have been tumults and blood and agonies and tears; but out of every tumult and agony has come clearer and clearer the recognition of the rights of the poor. Strong is the Lord God that judgeth for them. Their Redeemer is mighty—the Lord of Hosts is his name, and there can be no more doubt in this struggle what the policy of God is than what is the policy of President Lincoln.

If the declared policy of the United States lies directly in the way of that eternal policy declared by Jesus of Nazareth eighteen hundred years ago, so much the worse for it—so much the worse for us. Men may change their minds, but Jesus Christ is the same yesterday, to-day, and for ever. Hath he said it, and shall he not do it? hath he spoken, and shall he not make it good?

But, if our President is a Christian, if he believes that Christ said only what he meant, and no more than what he can do when he declared his policy, his desire to save the Union would lead him as certainly to take it out of the line of injustice and cruelty, as his desire to save a child would lead him to draw it off the track when railroad cars are thundering down upon it.

Let him seriously look abroad on the earth, and ask what means all this shaking and confusion. Is it not all in countries where there exists in one form or other slavery of body or slavery of soul, or both? What means the mustering of Garibaldi against the Pope?—what means the confusion of the French Emperor?—what the low murmurs under the Austrian throne? What power has made it necessary for Russia to consolidate her throne by emancipating all her serfs?—what power menaces and urges us, hedging up our way on the right and the left, and pushing us on to the same result?

Do not things very much look as if Jesus of Nazareth was alive and working out what he came to do? and has he not of old proved a wonderful counselor, a mighty God?

Our President, in formal published documents, has acknowledged that he holds in his hand the tremendous power to free every slave in this land—to put an end to this horror for all generations. If he loves the Union, does he believe in Christ? Does he not believe that Christ has power and will to do what he said?—and when his swift arrows are sent out against oppression and cruelty, shall our armies be held right in the way of them? If they be, there will be many mothers who will weep themselves to stone, like Niobe, whose sons were slain by the arrows of the All-beautiful.

But, alas, our sons will be slain, not because our God was cruel, but because he was good; not because he was angry with *them*, but because our Commander-in-chief would hold them in the very way of God's thunderbolts, in the whistling path of his glittering spear.

On both sides of these armies, there be praying hands—uplifted for and against. Christ is for neither. Our battle is a part of his greater battle—a battle to bring in everlasting righteousness. If we want his strength, we must come on to his ground; but if we stand for that which he has sworn to destroy, down we must go—prayer or no prayer.

474

So, then, knowing who Jesus is, and what he means to do, and what his policy in our affairs, are we ready in this dark storm to receive him into our ship?

It is not the President alone who decides this, it must be the people. He is the exponent of the people, and when their will is sufficiently strong and unanimous, he will hesitate no more. With us, each one, in our prayers, in our words, lies the responsibility, shall Jesus of Nazareth come into our ship?

❦   ❦   ❦

# Playbill from *Uncle Tom's Cabin* Show

*Uncle Tom's Cabin* companies toured the United States, bringing stage versions of *Uncle Tom* to the boards from New York City to the backwoods. *Uncle Tom's Cabin* remained in continuous production for ninety years and played an important role in breaking down lingering Puritan resistance to theater going. As Tom shows were assimilated to the minstrel tradition, they became more sensational, racist, and circuslike. The doubling of characters, especially Topsy, was a popular way for Uncle Tom companies to proclaim the superiority of their productions.

At left: "Stetson's Big Double Spectacular—Uncle Tom's Cabin Co." –Courtesy of Harriet Beecher Stowe Center, Hartford, Connecticut.

PART 3

# Domestic Culture and Politics

# Trials of a Housekeeper

Published in *The Mayflower*, "Trials of a Housekeeper" first appeared in *Godey's Lady's Book* in January 1839, three years after Stowe married and set up house in Walnut Hills, then two miles outside the city of Cincinnati. Like many middle-class white women, Stowe included supervising "help" in her domestic work. This sketch is revealing of both the domestic labor problem in the United States and Stowe's young consciousness.

Addressing "the lords of creation," Stowe combines humorous description with a widely shared insensitivity to the situation of the newly arrived immigrant. The conclusion of the story is striking for its unpolitical use of terms such as *universal emancipation*, *slavery*, and *patriarchal independence*. Like many of her sketches for the Semi-Colon Club, its tone is somewhat uncertain. Yet in her impulse to write about domestic doings, "Trials of a Housekeeper" charts an important direction in Stowe's work.

I have a detail of very homely grievances to present, but such as they are, many a heart will feel them to be heavy—*the trials of a housekeeper*.

"Poh!" says one of the lords of creation, taking his cigar out of his mouth, and twirling it between his two first fingers, "what a fuss these women do make of this simple matter of *managing a family*! I can't see, for my life, as there is anything so extraordinary to be done in this matter of housekeeping: only three meals a day to be got and cleared off, and it really seems to take up the whole of their mind from morning till night. *I* could keep house without so much of a flurry, I know."

Now prithee, good brother, listen to my story, and see how much you know about it. I came to this enlightened West about a year since, and was duly established in a comfortable country residence within a mile and a half of the city, and there commenced the enjoyment of domestic felicity. I had been married about three months, and had been previously *in love* in the most approved romantic way, with all the proprieties of moonlight walks, serenades, sentimental billet-doux, and everlasting attachment.

After having been allowed, as I said, about three months to get over this sort of thing, and to prepare for realities, I was located for life as aforesaid. My family consisted of myself and husband, a female friend as a visiter, and two brothers of my good man, who were engaged with him in business.

I pass over the two or three first days spent in that process of hammering boxes, breaking crockery, knocking things down and picking them up again, which is commonly called getting to housekeeping. As usual, carpets were sewed and stretched, laid down, and taken up to be sewed over; things were reformed, transformed, and conformed, till at last a settled order began to appear. But now came up the great point of all. During our confusion, we had cooked and eaten our meals in a very miscellaneous and pastoral manner, eating now from the top of a barrel, and now from a fireboard laid on two chairs, and drinking, some from teacups, and some from saucers, and some from tumblers, and some from a pitcher big enough to be drowned in, and sleeping, some on sofas, and some on straggling beds and mattresses, thrown down here and there, wherever there was room. All these pleasant barbarities were now at an end: the house was in order; the dishes put up in their places; three regular meals were to be administered in one day, all in an orderly, civilized form; beds were to be made; rooms swept and dusted; dishes washed; knives scoured, and all the et cetera to be attended to. Now for getting "help," as Mrs. Trollope says; and where and how were we to get it? We knew very few persons in the city, and how were we to accomplish the matter? At length the "house of employment" was mentioned, and my husband was despatched thither regularly every day for a week, while I, in the mean time, was very nearly despatched by the abundance of work at home. At length, one evening, as I was sitting completely exhausted, thinking of resorting to the last feminine expedient for supporting life, viz., a good fit of crying, my husband made his appearance, with a most triumphant air, at the door: "There, Margaret, I have got you a couple at last—cook and chambermaid!" So saying, he flourished open the door, and gave to my view the picture of a little, dry, snuffy-looking old woman, and a great staring Dutch girl in a green bonnet with red ribands—mouth wide open, and hands and feet that would have made a Greek sculptor open his mouth too. I addressed forthwith a few words of encouragement to each of this cultivated-looking couple, and proceeded to ask their names, and forthwith the old woman began to snuffle and to wipe her face with what was left of an old silk pocket-handkerchief preparatory to speaking, while the young lady opened her mouth wider, and looked around with a frightened air, as if meditating an escape. After some preliminaries, however, I found out that my old woman was Mrs. Tibbins, and my Hebe's name was Kotterin; also, that she knew much more Dutch than English, and not any too much of either. The old lady was the cook. I ventured a few inquiries: "Had she ever cooked?"

"Yes, ma'am, sartin; she had lived at two or three places in the city."

"I suspect, my dear," said my husband, confidently, "that she is an experienced cook, and so your troubles are over;" and he went to reading his newspaper. I said no more, but determined to wait till morning. The breakfast, to be sure, did not do much honour to the talents of my official; but it was the first time, and the place was new to her. After breakfast was cleared away, I proceeded to give directions for dinner: it was merely a plain joint of meat, I said, to be roasted in the tin oven. The experienced cook looked at me with a stare of entire vacuity: "the tin oven," I repeated, "stands there," pointing to it.

She walked up to it, and touched it with such an appearance of suspicion as if it had been an electrical battery, and then looked round at me with a look of such helpless ignorance that my soul was moved: "I never see one of them things before," said she.

"Never saw a tin oven!" I exclaimed. "I thought you said you had cooked in two or three families."

"They does not have such things as them, though," rejoined my old lady. Nothing was to be done, of course, but to instruct her into the philosophy of the case; and, having spitted the joint, and given numberless directions, I walked off to my room to superintend the operations of Kotterin, to whom I had committed the making of my bed and the sweeping of my room, it never having come into my head that there *could be* be a wrong way of making a bed, and to this day it is a marvel to me how any one could arrange pillows and quilts to make such a nondescript appearance as mine now presented. One glance showed me that Kotterin also was *"just caught,"* and that I had as much to do in her department as in that of my old lady.

Just then the door-bell rang: "Oh, there is the door-bell!" I exclaimed; "run, Kotterin, and show them into the parlour."

Kotterin started to run, as directed, and then stopped, and stood looking round on all the doors, and on me with a wofully puzzled air: "The street-door," said I, pointing towards the entry. Kotterin blundered into the entry, and stood gazing with a look of stupid wonder at the bell ringing without hands, while I went to the door and let in the company before she could be fairly made to understand the connexion between the ringing and the phenomenon of admission.

As dinner-time approached, I sent word into my kitchen to have it set on; but, recollecting the state of the heads of department there, I soon followed my own orders. I found the tin oven standing out in the middle of the kitchen, and my cook seated à la Turk in front of it, contemplating the roast meat with full as puzzled an air as in the morning. I once more explained the mystery of taking it off, and assisted her to get it on to the platter, though somewhat cooled by having been so long set out for inspection. I was standing holding the spit in my hands, when Kotterin, who had heard the door-bell ring, and was determined this time to be in season, ran into the hall, and soon returning, opened the kitchen door, and politely ushered in three or four fashionable-looking ladies, exclaiming, "Here she is." As these were strangers from the city, who had come to make their first call, this introduction was far from proving an eligible one—the look of thunderstruck astonishment with which I greeted their first appearance, as I stood brandishing the spit, and the terrified snuffling and staring of poor Mrs. Tibbins, who again had recourse to her old pocket-handkerchief, almost entirely vanquished their gravity, and it was evident that they were on the point of a broad laugh; so, recovering my self-possession, I apologized, and led the way to the parlour.

Let these few incidents be a specimen of the four mortal weeks that I spent with these *"helps,"* during which time I did almost as much work, with twice as much anxiety, as when there was nobody there; and yet everything went wrong besides. The young gentlemen complained of the patches of starch grimed to their collars, and the streaks of black coal ironed into their dickies, while one week every pocket-handkerchief in the house was starched so stiff that you might as well have carried an earthen plate in your pocket; the tumblers looked muddy; the plates were never washed clean or wiped dry unless I attended to each one; and as to eating and drinking, we experienced a variety that we had not before considered possible.

At length the old woman vanished from the stage, and was succeeded by a knowing, active, capable damsel, with a temper like a steel-trap, who remained with me just one week, and then went off in a fit of spite. To her succeeded a rosy, good-natured, merry lass, who broke the crockery, burned the dinner, tore the clothes in ironing, and knocked down everything that stood in her way about the house, without at all discomposing herself about the matter. One night she took the stopper from a barrel of molasses, and came singing off up stairs, while the molasses ran soberly out into the cellar-bottom all night, till by morning it was in a state of *universal emancipation*. Having done this, and also despatched an entire set of tea-things by letting the waiter fall, she one day made her disappearance.

Then, for a wonder, there fell to my lot a tidy, efficient-trained English girl; pretty, and genteel, and neat, and knowing how to do everything, and with the sweetest temper in the world. "Now," said I to myself, "I shall *rest* from my labours." Everything about the house began to go right, and looked as clean and genteel as Mary's own pretty self. But, alas! this period of repose was interrupted by the vision of a clever, trim-looking young man, who for some weeks could be heard scraping his boots at the kitchen door every Sunday night; and at last Miss Mary, with some smiling and blushing, gave me to understand that she must leave in two weeks.

"Why, Mary," said I, feeling a little mischievous, "don't you like the place?"

"Oh, yes, ma'am."

"Then why do you look for another?"

"I am not going to another place."

"What, Mary, are you going to learn a trade?"

"No, ma'am."

"Why, then, what do you mean to do?"

"I expect to keep house *myself*, ma'am," said she, laughing and blushing.

"Oh ho!" said I, "that is it;" and so, in two weeks, I lost the best little girl in the world: peace to her memory.

After this came an interregnum, which put me in mind of the chapter in Chronicles that I used to read with great delight when a child, where Basha, and Elah, and Tibni, and Zimri, and Omri, one after the other came on to the throne of Israel, all in the compass of half a dozen verses. We had one old woman who stayed a week, and went away with the misery in her tooth; one *young* woman who ran away and got married; one cook, who came at night and went off before light in the morning; one very clever girl, who stayed a month, and then went away because her mother was sick; another, who stayed six weeks, and was taken with the fever herself; and during all this time, who can speak the damage and destruction wrought in the domestic paraphernalia by passing through these multiplied hands?

What shall we do? Shall we go for slavery, or shall we give up houses, have no furniture to take care of, keep merely a gag of meal, a porridge-pot, and a pudding-stick, and sit in our tent door in real patriarchal independence? What shall we do?

🍂 🍂 🍂

# To Sarah Buckingham Beecher, December 17, [1850]

This letter provides an intimate glimpse of Stowe's domestic life just months before she would begin writing *Uncle Tom's Cabin*. Stowe paints in graphic detail the domestic labor of setting up housekeeping after the move from Cincinnati, Ohio, to Brunswick, Maine. The return to New England stimulated Stowe's awareness of regional types, here exemplified by the Yankee John Titcomb, who in his leisurely approach to work foreshadows her Sam Lawson character.

Sarah Buckingham Beecher was the wife of Stowe's brother George Beecher, who committed suicide in 1843. An independently wealthy woman, she occasionally loaned Stowe money.

Brunswick
December 17

Is it really true then that snow is on the ground & Christmas coming & I have not written unto thee most dear Sister?—No I dont believe it—I havent been so naughty—its all a mistake—yes written I must have—and written I have too—in the night watch as I lay on my bed—such beautiful letters—I wish you had only gotten them but by day it has been hurry hurry hurry & drive drive drive—or else the call of a sick room ever since last spring—

I put off writing when your letter first came because I meant to write you a long letter—a full & complete one—& so days slid by—& became weeks—& my little Charlie came————&————&——!!——

—Sarah when I look back I wonder at my self—not that I forgot any one thing that I should remember but that I have remembered *any thing*—From the time that I left Cincinnati with my children to come forth unto a country that I knew not of almost unto the present time it has seemed as if I could scarcely breathe I was so pressed with care——My head dizzy with the whirl of rail roads & steam boats—then ten days sojourn in Boston & a constant toil & hurry in buying my furniture & equipments & then landing at Brunswick in the midst of a drizzly inexorable north east storm & beginning the work of getting to order a deserted damp old house—All day long running from one thing to another—as for example—thus—

Mrs Stowe how shall I make this lounge—what shall I cover the back with first—

(MRS S.)   With the coarse cotton in the closet
(WOMAN)   Mrs. Stowe there isnt any more soap to clean the windows—
(MRS S.)   Where shall I send to get soap?—Here Hatty run up to Mr Fishers & get two bars—

Theres a man below wants to see Mrs. Stowe about the cistern

Before you go down Mrs Stowe just show me how to cover this round end of the lounge

Theres a man up from the depot says a box has come for Mrs. Stowe its coming up to the house will you come down & see about it

Mrs Stowe dont go till you have showed the man how to nail that carpet in the corner—He's nailed it all crooked What shall he do?

The black thread is all used up Mrs Stowe—& what shall I do about putting this gimp on the lounge

Mrs Stowe there has a man come with a lot of pails & tin ware from Furbish will you settle the bill now—

Mrs Stowe here is a letter I have just got from Boston enclosing that bill of lading—wants to know what he shall do with the goods—if you will tell me what to say I will answer it—

Mrs Stowe the meat man is at the door had'nt we better get a little beef steak or something for dinner

Shall Hatty go to Boardmans for some more black thread—

Mrs Stowe this cushion is an inch too wide for the frame What shall we do now—

Mrs Stowe where are the screws of the black walnut bedstead?

Heres a man has brought in these bills for freight Will you settle them now?——

Mrs Stowe I dont understand using this great needle I cant make it go through the cushion—it sticks in the cotton—

Then comes a letter from my husband saying he is sick a bed—& all but dead—dont ever expect to see his family again  wants to know how I shall manage in case I am left a widow—knows we shall get in debt & never get out—wonders at my courage—thinks I am very sanguine—warns me to be prudent as there wont be much to live on in case of his death &c &c. I read the letter & poke it into the stove, & proceed—

Some of my adventures were quite funny—As for example—I had in my kitchen elect no sink cistern or any other water privileges—so I bought at the cotton factory two of the great hogsheads they bring oil in, which here in Brunswick are often used for cisterns & had them brought up in triumph to my yard & was congratulating myself on my energy when lo & behold it was discovered that there was no cellar door except one in the kitchen which was truly a strait & narrow way down a long train of stairs—Hereupon as saith John Bunyan I fell into a muse!—how to get my cisterns into my cellar—In days of chivalry I might have got a knight to make me a breach thro the foundation walls—but that was not to be thought of now—& my oil hogsheads standing disconsolately in the yard seemed to reflect no great credit on my foresight—In this strait I fell upon a real honest yankee cooper whom I besought for the reputation of his craft & mine to take my hogshead to pieces, carry them down in staves & set them up again—which the worthy man actually accomplished one fair summer forenoon to the great astonishment of "us yankees"—When my man came to put up the pump he stared very hard to see my hogsheads thus translated & standing as innocent & quiet as could be in the cellar & when I told him in a very mild quiet way that I got 'em taken to pieces & put together—just as if I had been always in the habit of doing such things—Proff Smyth came down & looked very hard at them & then said "Well nothing can beat a wilful woman"—Then followed diverse negotiations with a very clever—but, (with reverence) somewhat lazy gentleman of jobs who occupyeth a carpenters shop opposite to mine—This same John Titcomb—my very good friend—is a character peculiar to yankee-dom—He is part owner & landlord of the house I rent & connected by birth with all the best families in town—a man of real intelligence—& good educa-tion—a great reader & quite a thinker—Being of an ingenious turn he does paint-ing gilding—staining—upholstery jobs—varnishing—all in addition to his primary trade of carpentry—But he is a man studious of ease—& fully possessed with the idea that man wants but little here below—so he boards himself in his workshop on crackers & herrings washed down with cold water—& spends his time working musing—reading new publications & taking his comfort—In his shop you shall see a joiners bench hammers planes saws gimblets varnish paint—picture frames—fence posts—rare old china—one or two fine portraits of his ancestry—a book case full of books—the tooth of a whale—an old spin-ning wheel & spindle—a ladys parasol frame—a church lamp to be mended—in short Henry says Mr Titcomb's shop is like the ocean there is no end to the curiosities in it—

In all my moving & fussing Mr Titcomb has been my right hand man Whenever a screw was loose—a nail to be driven—a lock mended a pane of glass set—& these cases were manifold he was always on hand—But my sink was no fancy job—& I believe nothing but a very particular friendship would have moved him to undertake it—So this same sink lingered in a precarious state for some weeks—& when I had *nothing else to do*—I used to call & do what I could in the way of enlisting the good mans sympathies in its behalf—

How many times I have been in & seated myself in one of the old rocking chairs—talked first of the news of the day—the rail road—the last proceedings in Congress—the probabilities about the Millenium & thus brought the conversation by little & little round to my sink!———because till the sink was done the pump could not be put up & we could'nt have any rain water—

Sometimes my courage would quite fail to introduce the delicate subject & I would talk of every thing else—turn & get out of the shop & turn back as if a thought had just struck my mind & say

Oh Mr Titcomb about that sink?—
Yes ma'am—I was thinking about going down street this afternoon to look out stuff for it
—Yes sir—if you would be good enough to get it done as soon as possible—we are in great need of it—
I think theres no hurry  I believe we are going to have a dry time now & that you could not catch any water & you wont need a pump at present—

—These negociations extended from the first of June to the first of July & at last my sink was completed—& so also was a new house spout concerning which I had had divers communings with Deacon Dunnin of the Baptist church—Also during this time good Mrs. Mitchell & myself made two sofas—or lounges—a band chair—divers bed spreads pillow cases—pillows—bolsters matrasses—we painted rooms—we revarnished furniture—we—what *didnt* we do?——
Then came on Mr. Stowe—& then came the eighth of July & my little Charley—I was really glad for an excuse to lie in bed for I was full tired I can assure you—Well I was what folks call very comfortable for two weeks when my nurse had to leave me & the very night she left I had an attack of fever & an ague in my breast—& for six weeks after I was never well—the pain in my breast was incessant—& I was miserably in every respect—at last I went to Boston to consult Dr Hoffendahl & there one of my breasts gathered & discharged & after that I began slowly to recover tho very weak—
My baby had scarcely grown at all all this time—the state of my health seemed to keep him feeble—I had not enough for him & his stomach was too weak to bear feeding—My girl also had gone off & left me with an entirely raw Irish hand to cultivate
—About this time a healthy young Irish woman who had lost her babe came to the house & wanted employment I took her in as nurse—& tho she didn't know how to do any thing & was very slack & slovenly yet as the baby throve at the rate of a pound a week all the time upon her milk I have kept her these three months—He is grown a great beautiful boy—as like the one I lost as a twin brother—so like some days that I almost feel sad—
I have had great solicitude about an affection of the tonsils with which he has been troubled—Sometimes he would breathe so loud that he could be heard from one room to another with the door closed—& this disturbed his rest nights so that for several weeks I got very little sleep with him & loss of sleep almost drives me distracted
When I did sleep it was to dream that he was dying of the croup & to wake to hear his hard breathing—that affection seems now to be wearing away he sleeps better—as cold weather comes on my health is firmer & I having discharged the wet nurse as I have enough for him with a little feeding—
Sarah—how little do people realize what it is to bring up a great family!

Another thing that has taken up in its time much of my thoughts was Sister Sarah (Charles wife's) dangerous sickness. She was ill of a large tumour which kept her perfectly helpless for six weeks or more—It was a most immense thing—& discharged dreadfully—We have had her little Nelly here for nearly three months & she tho three years old has always been sick & is almost as helpless & dependent as my baby—so that there are seven under fourteen under my roof—two of them babies—

During this time I have employed my liesure in making up my engagements with newspaper editors—I have written more than anybody or I myself would have thought—I have taught an hour a day in our school—& I have read two hours every evening to the children. The children study Eng history in school & I am reading Scotts historic novels in their order To night I finish the Abbott—shall begin Kenilworth next week—yet I am constantly pursued & haunted by the idea that I dont do any thing—Since I began this note I have been called off at least a dozen times—Once for the fish man to buy a codfish Once to see a man who had brought me some barrels of apples—once to see a book man—then to Mrs Upham to see about a drawing I promised to make for her—then to nurse the baby—then into the kitchen to make a chowder for dinner & now I am at it again for nothing but deadly determination enables me ever to write—it is rowing against wind & tide—

I suppose you think now I have begun I am never going to stop & in truth it looks like it—but the spirit moves now & I must obey—

Christmas is coming & our little household is all alive with preparation every one collecting their little gifts—with wonderful mystery & secrecy—I send my nephew for a New Years a set of flower patterns—The coloured ones are copies—the others are to be coloured by them—If you find on trial that the paper blots when he tries to spread on his colours you can remedy it by pasting over them a thin sizing of isinglass—

How is every body your way—How is William getting along at Chillicothe—have you seen Catherine—Is Agnes yet at Putnam—if so give my love to her Whats become of Mr Ned—or Edward Hale & his little wife—What of Cary Hale—What of Bellinda—the fat funny puss—How are the aunts specially Aunt Ann & how is sister Catharine & Mr Convers—Remember me to all the above named—Convers I learned under his own hand & seal, was married—how does he appear?

Your ready kindness to me in the spring I felt very much—& *why* I did not have the sense to have sent you one line just by way of acknowledgement Im sure I dont know—I felt just as if I had till I awoke & behold I had not—But my dear if my wits are somewhat wool gathering & unsettled my heart is as true as a star—I love you & have thought of you often—

This fall I have felt often *sad*—lonesome—both very unusual feelings with me in these busy days—but the breaking away from my old home & leaving Father & mother & coming to a strange place affected me naturally—In those sad hours my thoughts have often turned to George—& I have thought with encouragement of his blessed state & hoped that I should soon be there too—

I have many warm & kind friends here & have been treated with great attention & kindness—Brunswick is a delightful residence & if you come east next summer you must come to my new house George would delight to go a fishing with the children & see the ships & sail in the sail boats & all that—Give Aunt Harriets love to him & tell him when he gets to be a painter to send me a picture

AFFECTIONATELY YOURS<br>
HStowe

[Beecher-Stowe Collection, Schlesinger Library, Cambridge, Mass.]


❦   ❦   ❦


# What Is a Home?


Stowe's role as a propagandist for the Victorian home emerged full-fledged in the domestic columns she wrote between 1864 and 1866 in the *Atlantic Monthly* under the pseudonym Christopher Crowfield. "What Is a Home?", her column for March 1864, was reprinted in *House and Home Papers* in 1865.

Stowe's advice to homemakers is both practical and profound, rooted in the realities of American middle-class families but pointing beyond to "the New Jerusalem." She advises against furnishings too grand for comfort, yet enshrines woman as the artist of the new Eden. The Christian ideology in which she places the home opens for women a seemingly unlimited sphere of power and influence, yet much of this remains invisible to the family: "So quiet are her operations and movements, that none sees that it is she who holds all things in harmony." Thus Stowe participates in what Jeanne Boydston has called "The Pastoralization of Housework," an idealization of the nineteenth-century middle-class woman's work in the home. But like her sister Catharine Beecher's *Treatise on Domestic Economy*, "What Is a Home?" also elevates the importance of women's domestic work. Jane Tompkins argues that while Stowe endorses conventional ideologies of home and motherhood, she "relocates the center of power in American life, placing it not in the government, nor in the courts of law, nor in the factories, nor in the marketplace, but in the kitchen."


I have shown that a dwelling, rented or owned by a man, in which his own wife keeps house, is not always, or of course, a home. What is it, then, that makes a home? All men and women have the indefinite knowledge of what they want and long for when that word is spoken. "Home!" sighs the disconsolate bachelor, tired of boarding-house fare and buttonless shirts. "Home!"

Selections from pages 55–64, 67–70, and 76–78, *House and Home Papers* (Boston: Ticknor and Fields, 1865).

says the wanderer in foreign lands, and thinks of mother's love, of wife and sister and child. Nay, the word has in it a higher meaning, hallowed by religion; and when the Christian would express the highest of his hopes for a better life, he speaks of his *home* beyond the grave. The word home has in it the elements of love, rest, permanency, and liberty; but besides these it has in it the idea of an education by which all that is purest within us is developed into nobler forms, fit for a higher life. The little child by the home-fireside was taken on the Master's knee when he would explain to his disciples the mysteries of the kingdom.

Of so great dignity and worth is this holy and sacred thing, that the power to create a HOME ought to be ranked above all creative faculties. The sculptor who brings out the breathing statue from cold marble, the painter who warms the canvas into a deathless glow of beauty, the architect who built cathedrals and hung the world-like dome of St. Peter's in mid-air, is not to be compared, in sanctity and worthiness, to the humblest artist, who, out of the poor materials afforded by this shifting, changing, selfish world, creates the secure Eden of a *home*.

A true home should be called the noblest work of art possible to human creatures, inasmuch as it is the very image chosen to represent the last and highest rest of the soul, the consummation of man's blessedness.

Not without reason does the oldest Christian church require of those entering on marriage the most solemn review of all the past life, the confession and repentance of every sin of thought, word, and deed, and the reception of the holy sacrament; for thus the man and woman who approach the august duty of creating a home are reminded of the sanctity and beauty of what they undertake.

In this art of home-making I have set down in my mind certain first principles, like the axioms of Euclid, and the first is,—

*No home is possible without love.*

All business marriages and marriages of convenience, all mere culinary marriages and marriages of mere animal passion, make the creation of a true home impossible in the outset. Love is the jewelled foundation of this New Jerusalem descending from God out of heaven, and takes as many bright forms as the amethyst, topaz, and sapphire of that mysterious vision. In this range of creative art all things are possible to him that loveth, but without love nothing is possible.

We hear of most convenient marriages in foreign lands, which may better be described as commercial partnerships. The money on each side is counted; there is enough between the parties to carry on the firm, each having the appropriate sum allotted to each. No love is pretended, but there is great politeness. All is so legally and thoroughly arranged, that there seems to be nothing left for future quarrels to fasten on. Monsieur and Madame have each their apartments, their carriages, their servants, their income, their friends, their pursuits,—understand the solemn vows of marriage to mean simply that they are to treat each other with urbanity in those few situations where the path of life must necessarily bring them together.

We are sorry that such an idea of marriage should be gaining foothold in America. It has its root in an ignoble view of life,—an utter and pagan darkness as to all that man and woman are called to do in that highest relation where they act as one. It is a mean and low contrivance on both sides, by which all the grand work of home-building, all the noble pains and heroic toils of home-education,—that education where the parents learn more than they teach,—shall be (let us use the expressive Yankee idiom) *shirked*.

It is a curious fact that in those countries where this system of marriages is the general rule there is no word corresponding to our English word *home*. In many polite languages of Europe it would be impossible neatly to translate the sentiment . . . that a man's *house* is not always his *home*.

Let any one try to render the song, "Sweet Home," into French, and one finds how Anglo-Saxon is the very genius of the word. The structure of life, in all its relations, in countries where marriages are matter of arrangement, and not of love, excludes the idea of home.

How does life run in such countries? The girl is recalled from her convent or boarding-school, and told that her father has found a husband for her. No objection on her part is contemplated or provided for; none generally occurs, for the child is only too happy to obtain the fine clothes and the liberty which she has been taught come only with marriage. Be the man handsome or homely, interesting or stupid, still he brings these.

How intolerable such a marriage! we say, with the close intimacies of Anglo-Saxon life in our minds. They are not intolerable, because they are provided for by arrangements which make it possible for each to go his or her several way, seeing very little of the other. The son or daughter, which in due time makes its appearance in this *menage*, is sent out to nurse in infancy, sent to boarding-school in youth, and in maturity portioned and married, to repeat the same process for another generation. Meanwhile, father and mother keep a quiet establishment, and pursue their several pleasures. Such is the system.

Houses built for this kind of life become mere sets of reception-rooms, such as are the greater proportion of apartments to let in Paris, where a hearty English or American family, with their children about them, could scarcely find room to establish themselves. Individual character, it is true, does something to modify this programme. There are charming homes in France and Italy, where warm and noble natures, thrown together, perhaps, by accident, or mated by wise paternal choice, infuse warmth into the coldness of the system under which they live. There are in all states of society some of such domesticity of nature that they will create a home around themselves under any circumstances, however barren. Besides, so kindly is human nature, that Love uninvited before marriage, often becomes a guest after, and with Love always comes a home.

My next axiom is,—

*There can be no true home without liberty.*

The very idea of home is of a retreat where we shall be free to act out personal and individual tastes and peculiarities, as we cannot do before the wide world. We are to have our meals at what hour we will, served in what style suits us. Our hours of going and coming are to be as we please. Our favorite haunts are to be here or there, our pictures and books so disposed as seems to us good, and our whole arrangements the expression, so far as our means can compass it, of our own personal ideas of what is pleasant and desirable in life. This element of liberty, if we think of it, is the chief charm of home. "Here I can do as I please," is the thought with which the tempest-tossed earth-pilgrim blesses himself or herself, turning inward from the crowded ways of the world. This thought blesses the man of business, as he turns from his day's care, and crosses the sacred threshold. It is as restful to him as the slippers and gown and easy-chair by the fireside. Everybody understands him here. Everybody is well content that he should take his ease in his own way. Such is the case in the *ideal* home. That such is not always the case in the real home comes often from the mistakes in the house-furnishing. Much house-furnishing is *too fine* for liberty.

In America there is no such thing as rank and station which impose a sort of prescriptive style on people of certain income. The consequence is that all sorts of furniture and belongings, which in the Old World have a recognized relation to certain possibilities of income, and which require certain other accessories to make them in good keeping, are thrown in the way of all sorts of people.

Young people who cannot expect by any reasonable possibility to keep more than two or three servants, if they happen to have the means in the outset, furnish a house with just such articles as in England would suit an establishment of sixteen. We have seen houses in England having two or three house-maids, and tables served by a butler and two waiters, where the furniture, carpets, china, crystal, and silver were in one and the same style with some establishments in America where the family was hard pressed to keep three Irish servants.

This want of servants is the one thing that must modify everything in American life; it is, and will long continue to be, a leading feature in the life of a country so rich in openings for man and woman that domestic service can be only the stepping-stone to something higher. Nevertheless, we Americans are great travellers; we are sensitive, appreciative, fond of novelty, apt to receive and incorporate into our own life what seems fair and graceful in that of other people. Our women's wardrobes are made elaborate with the thousand elegancies of French toilet,—our houses filled with a thousand knick-knacks of which our plain ancestors never dreamed. Cleopatra did not set sail on the Nile in more state and beauty than that in which our young American bride is often ushered into her new home. Her wardrobe all gossamer lace and quaint frill and crimp and embroidery, her house a museum of elegant and costly gewgaws; and amid the whole collection of elegancies and fragilities, she, perhaps, the frailest.

Then comes the tug of war. The young wife becomes a mother, and while she is retired to her chamber, blundering Biddy rusts the elegant knives, or takes off the ivory handles by soaking in hot water,—the silver is washed in greasy soap-suds, and refreshed now and then with a thump, which cocks the nose of the teapot awry, or makes the handle assume an air of drunken defiance. The fragile China is chipped here and there around its edges with those minute gaps so vexatious to a woman's soul; the handles fly hither and thither in the wild confusion of Biddy's washing-day hurry, when cook wants her to help hang out the clothes. Meanwhile, Bridget sweeps the parlor with a hard broom, and shakes out showers of ashes from the grate, forgetting to cover the damask lounges, and they directly look as rusty and time-worn as if they had come from an auction-store; and all together unite in making such havoc of the delicate ruffles and laces of the bridal outfit and baby-*layette*, that, when the poor young wife comes out of her chamber after her nurse has left her, and, weakened and embarrassed with the demands of the new-comer, begins to look once more into the affairs of her little world, she is ready to sink with vexation and discouragement. Poor little princess! Her clothes are made as princesses wear them, her baby's clothes like a young duke's, her house furnished like a lord's, and only Bridget and Biddy and Polly to do the work of cook, scullery-maid, butler, footman, laundress, nursery-maid, house-maid, and lady's maid. Such is the array that in the Old Country would be deemed necessary to take care of an establishment got up like hers. Everything in it is *too fine*,—not too fine to be pretty, not in bad taste in itself, but too fine for the situation, too fine for comfort or liberty. . . .

If liberty in a house is a comfort to a husband, it is a necessity to children. When we say liberty, we do not mean license. We do not mean that Master Johnny be allowed to handle elegant volumes with bread-and-butter fingers, or that little Miss be suffered to drum on the piano, or practice line-drawing with a pin on varnished furniture. Still it is essential that the family-parlors be not too fine for the family to sit in,—too fine for the ordinary accidents, haps and mishaps, of reasonably well-trained children. The elegance of the parlor where papa and mamma sit and receive their friends should wear an inviting, not a hostile and bristling, aspect to little people. Its beauty and its order gradually form in the little mind a love of beauty and order, and the insensible carefulness of regard.

Nothing is worse for a child than to shut him up in a room which he understands is his, *because* he is disorderly,—where he is expected, of course, to maintain and keep disorder. We have sometimes pitied the poor little victims who show their faces longingly at the doors of elegant parlors, and are forthwith collared by the domestic police and consigned to some attic-apartment, called a play-room, where chaos continually reigns. It is a mistake to suppose, because children derange a well-furnished apartment, that they like confusion. Order and beauty are always pleasant to them as to grown people, and disorder and defacement are painful; but they know neither how to create the one nor to prevent the other,— their little lives are a series of experiments, often making disorder by aiming at some new form of order. Yet, for all this, I am not one of those who feel that in a family everything should bend to the sway of these little people. They are the worst of tyrants in such houses,—still, where children are, though the fact must not appear to them, *nothing must be done without a wise thought of them.*

Here, as in all high art, the old motto is in force, "*Ars est celare artem.*" Children who are taught too plainly by every anxious look and word of their parents, by every family arrangement, by the impressment of every chance guest into the service, that their parents consider their education as the one important matter in creation, are apt to grow up fantastical, artificial, and hopelessly self-conscious. The stars cannot stop in their courses, even for our personal improvement, and the sooner children learn this, the better. The great art is to organize a home which shall move on with a strong, wide, generous movement, where the little people shall act themselves out as freely and impulsively as can consist with the comfort of the whole, and where the anxious watching and planning for them shall be kept as secret from them as possible.

It is well that one of the sunniest and airiest rooms in the house be the children's nursery. It is good philosophy, too, to furnish it attractively, even if the sum expended lower the standard of parlor-luxuries. It is well that the children's chamber, which is to act constantly on their impressible natures for years, should command a better prospect, a sunnier aspect, than one which serves for a day's occupancy of the transient guest. It is well that journeys should be made or put off in view of the interests of the children,—that guests should be invited with a view to their improvement,—that some intimacies should be chosen and some rejected on their account. But it is *not* well that all this should, from infancy, be daily talked out before the child, and he grow up in egotism from moving in a sphere where everything from first to last is calculated and arranged with reference to himself. A little appearance of wholesome neglect combined with real care and never-ceasing watchfulness has often seemed to do wonders in this work of setting human beings on their own feet for the life-journey. . . .

We have heard much lately of the restricted sphere of woman. We have been told how many spirits among women are of a wider, stronger, more heroic mould than befits the mere routine of housekeeping. It may be true that there are many women far too great, too wise, too high, for mere housekeeping. But where is the woman in any way too great or too high, or too wise, to spend herself in creating a home? What can any woman make diviner, higher, better? From such homes go forth all heroisms, all inspirations, all great deeds. Such mothers and such homes have made the heroes and martyrs, faithful unto death, who have given their precious lives to us during these three years of our agony!

Homes are the work of art peculiar to the genius of woman. Man *helps* in this work, but woman leads; the hive is always in confusion without the *queen*-bee. But what a woman must she be who does this work perfectly! She comprehends all, she balances and arranges all; all different tastes and temperaments find in her their rest, and she can unite at one hearthstone the most discordant elements. In her is order, yet an order ever veiled and concealed by indulgence. None are checked, reproved, abridged of privileges by her love of system; for she knows that order was made for the family, and not the family for order. Quietly she takes on herself what all others refuse or overlook. What the unwary disarrange she silently rectifies. Everybody in her sphere breathes easy, feels free; and the driest twig begins in her sunshine to put out buds and blossoms. So quiet are her operations and movements, that none sees that it is she who holds all things in harmony; only, alas, when she is gone, how many things suddenly appear disordered, inharmonious, neglected! All these threads have been smilingly held in her weak hand. Alas, if that is no longer there!

Can any woman be such a housekeeper without inspiration? No. In the words of the old church-service, "Her soul must ever have affiance in God." The New Jerusalem of a perfect home cometh down from God out of heaven. But to make such a home is ambition high and worthy enough for *any* woman, be she what she may.

One thing more. Right on the threshold of all perfection lies *the cross* to be taken up. No one can go over or around that cross in science or in art. Without labor and self-denial neither Raphael nor Michel Angelo nor Newton was made perfect. Nor can man or woman create a true home who is not willing in the outset to embrace life heroically, to encounter labor and sacrifice. Only to such shall this divinest power be given to create on earth that which is the nearest image of heaven.

❦ ❦ ❦

# Servants

Published in *House and Home Papers* in 1865, Stowe's essay "Servants" first appeared in the October 1864 *Atlantic Monthly*, when the sacrifices of the Civil War were underscoring for Stowe "the preciousness of distinctive American ideas."

The promise of greater economic opportunity that drew immigrants from Europe also made it likely that, as servants, they would become "infected with the spirit of democracy" and rebel against condescension or treatment that marked them as inferior. "A servant can never in our country be the mere appendage to another man," Stowe writes; "he must be a fellow citizen."

Stowe's call for "cool contract" arrangements with servants is in keeping with the movement, during this period, toward industrial relationships with domestic help, in contrast to the more familial relationships that characterized the pre–Civil War period. In Stowe's view, such contractual understandings uncoupled domestic service from its oppressive feudal trappings. At the conclusion of her essay she anticipates the call of Charlotte Perkins Gilman (her grandniece) for community laundries. All of these remarks are occasioned by the marriage of Christopher Crowfield's daughter Marianne, who sets up housekeeping and managing servants (as Stowe's daughter Georgiana did in 1864) with no knowledge of what Stowe calls her "profession."

I n the course of my papers various domestic revolutions have occurred. Our Marianne has gone from us with a new name to a new life, and a modest little establishment not many squares off claims about as much of my wife's and Jenny's busy thoughts as those of the proper mistress.

Marianne, as I always foresaw, is a careful and somewhat anxious housekeeper. Her tastes are fastidious; she is made for exactitude: the smallest departures from the straight line appear to her shocking deviations. She had always lived in a house where everything had been formed to quiet and order under the ever-present care and touch of her mother; nor had she ever participated in these cares more than to do a little dusting of the parlor ornaments, or wash the best china, or make sponge-cake or chocolate-caramels. Certain conditions of life had always appeared so to be matters of course that she had never conceived of a house without them. It never occurred to her that such bread and biscuit as she saw at the home-table would not always and of course appear at every table,—that the silver would not always be as bright, the glass as clear, the salt as fine and smooth, the plates and dishes as nicely arranged as she had always seen them, apparently without the thought or care of any one,—for my wife is one of those housekeepers whose touch is so fine that no one feels it. She is never heard scolding or reproving,—never entertains her company with her recipes for cookery or the faults of her servants. She is so unconcerned about receiving her own personal share of credit for the good appearance of her establishment, that even the children of the house have not supposed that there is any particular will of hers in the matter,—it all seems the natural consequence of having very good servants.

One phenomenon they had never seriously reflected on,—that, under all the changes of the domestic cabinet which are so apt to occur in American households, the same coffee, the same bread and biscuit, the same nicely prepared dishes and neatly laid table always gladdened their eyes; and from this they inferred only that good servants were more abundant than most people had supposed. They were somewhat surprised when these marvels were wrought by professedly green hands, but were given to suppose that these green hands must have had some remarkable quickness or aptitude for acquiring. That sparkling jelly, well-flavored ice-creams, clear soups, and delicate biscuits could be made by a raw Irish girl, fresh from her native Erin, seemed to them a proof of the genius of the race; and my wife, who never felt it important to attain to the reputation of a cook, quietly let it pass.

For some time, therefore, after the inauguration of the new household, there was trouble in the camp. Sour bread had appeared on the table,—bitter, acrid coffee had shocked and astonished the palate,—lint had been observed on tumblers, and the spoons had sometimes dingy streaks on the brightness of their first bridal polish,—beds were detected made shockingly awry,—and Marianne came burning with indignation to her mother.

"Such a little family as we have, and two strong girls," said she,—"everything ought to be perfect; there is really nothing to do. Think of a whole batch of bread absolutely sour! and when I gave that away, then this morning another exactly like it! and when I talked to cook about it, she said she had lived in this and that family, and her bread had always been praised as equal to the baker's!"

"I don't doubt she is right," said I. "Many families never have anything but sour bread from one end of the year to the other, eating it unperceiving, and with good cheer; and they buy also sour bread of the baker, with like approbation,—lightness being in their estimation the only virtue necessary in the article."

"Could you not correct her fault?" suggested my wife.

"I have done all I can. I told her we could not have such bread, that it was dreadful; Bob says it would give him the dyspepsia in a week; and then she went and made exactly the same;—it seems to me mere wilfulness."

"But," said I, "suppose, instead of such general directions, you should analyze her proceedings and find out just where she makes her mistake,—is the root of the trouble in the yeast, or in the time she begins it, letting it rise too long?—the time, you know, should vary so much with the temperature of the weather."

"As to that," said Marianne, "I know nothing. I never noticed; it never was my business to make bread; it always seemed quite a simple process, mixing yeast and flour and kneading it; and our bread at home was always good."

"It seems, then, my dear, that you have come to your profession without even having studied it."

My wife smiled, and said,—

"You know, Marianne, I proposed to you to be our family bread-maker for one month of the year before you married."

"Yes, mamma, I remember; but I was like other girls; I thought there was no need of it. I never liked to do such things; perhaps I had better have done it."

"You certainly had," said I; "for the first business of a housekeeper in America is that of a teacher. She can have a good table only by having practical knowledge, and tact in imparting it. If she understands her business practically and experimentally, her eye detects at once the weak spot; it requires only a little tact, some patience, some clearness in giving directions, and all comes right. I venture to say that your mother would have exactly such bread as always appears on our table, and have it by the hands of your cook, because she could detect and explain to her exactly her error."

"Do you know," said my wife, "what yeast she uses?"

"I believe," said Marianne, "it's a kind she makes herself. I think I heard her say so. I know she makes a great fuss about it, and rather values herself upon it. She is evidently accustomed to being praised for her bread, and feels mortified and angry, and I don't know how to manage her."

"Well," said I, "if you carry your watch to a watchmaker, and undertake to show him how to regulate the machinery, he laughs and goes on his own way; but if a brother-machinist makes suggestions, he listens respectfully. So, when a woman who knows nothing of woman's work undertakes to instruct one who knows more than she does, she makes no impression; but a woman who has been trained experimentally, and shows she understands the matter thoroughly, is listened to with respect."

"I think," said my wife, "that your Bridget is worth teaching. She is honest, well-principled, and tidy. She has good recommendations from excellent families, whose ideas of good bread it appears differ from ours; and with a little good-nature, tact, and patience, she will come into your ways."

"But the coffee, mamma,—you would not imagine it to be from the same bag with your own, so dark and so bitter; what do you suppose she has done to it?"

"Simply this," said my wife. "She has let the berries stay a few moments too long over the fire,—they are burnt, instead of being roasted; and there are people who think it essential to good coffee that it should look black, and have a strong, bitter flavor. A very little change in the preparing will alter this."

"Now," said I, "Marianne, if you want my advice, I'll give it to you gratis:— Make your own bread for one month. Simple as the process seems, I think it will take as long as that to give you a thorough knowledge of all the possibilities in the case; but after that you will never need to make any more,—you will be able to command good bread by the aid of all sorts of servants; you will, in other words, be a thoroughly prepared teacher."

"I did not think," said Marianne, "that so simple a thing required so much attention."

"It is simple," said my wife, "and yet requires a delicate care and watchfulness. There are fifty ways to spoil good bread; there are a hundred little things to be considered and allowed for that require accurate observation and experience. The same process that will raise good bread in cold weather will make sour bread in the heat of summer; different qualities of flour require variations in treatment, as also different sorts and conditions of yeast; and when all is done, the baking presents another series of possibilities which require exact attention."

"So it appears," said Marianne, gayly, "that I must begin to study my profession at the eleventh hour."

"Better late than never," said I. "But there is this advantage on your side: a well-trained mind, accustomed to reflect, analyze, and generalize, has an advantage over uncultured minds even of double experience. Poor as your cook is, she now knows more of her business than you do. After a very brief period of attention and experiment, you will not only know more than she does, but you will convince her that you do, which is quite as much to the purpose."

"In the same manner," said my wife, "you will have to give lessons to your other girl on the washing of silver and the making of beds. Good servants do not often come to us; they must be *made* by patience and training; and if a girl has a good disposition and a reasonable degree of handiness, and the housekeeper understands her profession, she may make a good servant out of an indifferent one. Some of my best girls have been those who came to me directly from the ship, with no preparation but docility and some natural quickness. The hardest cases to be managed are not of those who have been taught nothing, but of those who have been taught wrongly,—who come to you self-opinionated, with ways which are distasteful to you, and contrary to the genius of your housekeeping. Such require that their mistress shall understand at least so much of the actual conduct of affairs as to prove to the servant that there are better ways than those in which she has hitherto been trained."

"Don't you think, mamma," said Marianne, "that there has been a sort of reaction against woman's work in our day? So much has been said of the higher sphere of woman, and so much has been done to find some better work for her, that insensibly, I think, almost everybody begins to feel that it is rather degrading for a woman in good society to be much tied down to family affairs."

"Especially," said my wife, "since in these Woman's-Rights Conventions there is so much indignation expressed at those who would confine her ideas to the kitchen and nursery."

"There is reason in all things," said I. "Woman's-Rights Conventions are a protest against many former absurd, unreasonable ideas,—the mere physical and culinary idea of womanhood as connected only with puddings and shirt-buttons, the unjust and unequal burdens which the laws of harsher ages had cast upon the sex. Many of the women connected with these movements are as superior in everything properly womanly as they are in exceptional talent and culture. There is no manner of doubt that the sphere of woman is properly to be enlarged, and that republican governments in particular are to be saved from corruption and failure only by allowing to woman this enlarged sphere. Every woman has rights as a human being first, which belong to no sex, and ought to be as freely conceded to her as if she were a man,—and first and foremost, the great right of doing anything which God and Nature evidently have fitted her to excel in. If she be made a natural orator, like Miss Dickenson[1] or an astronomer, like Mrs. Somerville,[2] or a singer, like Grisi,[3] let not the technical rules of womanhood be thrown in the way of her free use of her powers. Nor can there be any reason shown why a woman's vote in the state should not be received with as much respect as in the family. A state is but an association of families, and laws relate to the rights and immunities which touch woman's most private and immediate wants and dearest hopes; and there is no reason why sister, wife, and mother should be more powerless in the state than in the home. Nor does it make a woman unwomanly to express an opinion by dropping a slip of paper into a box, more than to express that same opinion by conversation. In fact, there is no doubt, that, in all matters relating to the interests of education, temperance, and religion, the state would be a material gainer by receiving the votes of women.

"But, having said all this, I must admit, *per contra*, not only a great deal of crude, disagreeable talk in these conventions, but a too great tendency of the age to make the education of women anti-domestic. It seems as if the world never could advance, except like ships under a head-wind, tacking and going too far, now in this direction, and now in the opposite. Our common-school system now rejects sewing from the education of girls, which very properly used to occupy many hours daily in school a generation ago. The daughters of laborers and artisans are put through algebra, geometry, trigonometry, and the higher mathematics, to the entire neglect of that learning which belongs distinctively to woman. A girl cannot keep pace with her class, if she gives any time to domestic matters; and accordingly she is excused from them all during the whole term of her education. The boy of a family, at an early age, is put to a trade, or the labors of a farm; the father becomes impatient of his support, and requires of him to care for himself. Hence an interrupted education—learning coming by snatches in the winter months or in the intervals of work. As the result, the females in our country towns are commonly, in mental culture, vastly in advance of the males of the same household; but with this comes a physical delicacy, the result of an exclusive use of the brain and a neglect of the muscular system, with great inefficiency in practical domestic duties. The race of strong, hardy, cheerful girls, that used to grow up in country places, and made the bright, neat, New England kitchens of old times,—the girls that could wash, iron, brew, bake, harness a horse and drive him, no less than braid straw, embroider, draw, paint, and read innumerable books,—this race of women, pride of olden time, is daily lessening; and in their stead come

[1]Anna Dickinson (1842–1932), a fearless young orator who won fame during the 1860s, particularly for her support of civil rights for blacks and women.
[2]Mary Fairfax Somerville (1780–1872), one of the foremost women of science of the nineteenth century.
[3]Guilia Grisi, Italian operatic soprano who toured the U. S. in 1854.

the fragile, easily fatigued, languid girls of a modern age, drilled in book-learning, ignorant of common things. The great danger of all this, and of the evils that come from it, is that society by and by will turn as blindly against female intellectual culture as it now advocates it, and, having worked disproportionately one way, will work disproportionately in the opposite direction."

"The fact is," said my wife, "that domestic service is the great problem of life here in America; the happiness of families, their thrift, well-being, and comfort, are more affected by this than by any one thing else. Our girls, as they have been brought up, cannot perform the labor of their own families, as in those simpler, old-fashioned days you tell of; and what is worse, they have no practical skill with which to instruct servants, and servants come to us, as a class, raw and untrained; so what is to be done? In the present state of prices, the board of a domestic costs double her wages, and the waste she makes is a more serious matter still. Suppose you give us an article upon this subject in your 'House and Home Papers.' You could not have a better one."

So I sat down, and wrote thus on

## Servants and Service

Many of the domestic evils in America originate in the fact, that, while society here is professedly based on new principles which ought to make social life in every respect different from the life of the Old World, yet these principles have never been so thought out and applied as to give consistency and harmony to our daily relations. America starts with a political organization based on a declaration of the primitive freedom and equality of all men. Every human being, according to this principle, stands on the same natural level with every other, and has the same chance to rise according to the degree of power or capacity given by the Creator. All our civil institutions are designed to preserve this equality, as far as possible, from generation to generation: there is no entailed property, there are no hereditary titles, no monopolies, no privileged classes,—all are to be as free to rise and fall as the waves of the sea.

The condition of domestic service, however, still retains about it something of the influences from feudal times, and from the near presence of slavery in neighboring States. All English literature, all the literature of the world, describes domestic service in the old feudal spirit and with the old feudal language, which regarded the master as belonging to a privileged class and the servant to an inferior one. There is not a play, not a poem, not a novel, not a history, that does not present this view. The master's rights, like the rights of kings, were supposed to rest in his being born in a superior rank. The good servant was one who, from childhood, had learned "to order himself lowly and reverently to all his betters." When New England brought to these shores the theory of democracy, she brought, in the persons of the first pilgrims, the habits of thought and of action formed in aristocratic communities. Winthrop's Journal, and all the old records of the earlier colonists, show households where masters and mistresses stood on the "right divine" of the privileged classes, howsoever they might have risen up against authorities themselves.

The first consequence of this state of things was a universal rejection of domestic service in all classes of American-born society. For a generation or two, there was, indeed, a sort of interchange of family strength,—sons and daughters engaging in the service of neighboring families, in default of a sufficient working-force of their own, but always on conditions of strict equality. The assistant was to share the table, the family sitting-room, and every honor and attention that might be claimed by son or daughter. When families increased in refinement and education so as to make these conditions of close intimacy with more uncultured neighbors disagreeable, they had to choose between such intimacies and the performance of their own domestic toil. No wages could induce a son or daughter of New England to take the condition of a servant on terms which they thought applicable to that of a slave. The slightest hint of a separate table was resented as an insult; not to enter the front-door, and not to sit in the front-parlor on state-occasions, was bitterly commented on as a personal indignity.

The well-taught, self-respecting daughters of farmers, the class most valuable in domestic service, gradually retired from it. They preferred any other employment, however laborious. Beyond all doubt, the labors of a well-regulated family are more healthy, more cheerful, more interesting, because less monotonous, than the mechanical toils of a factory; yet the girls of New England, with one consent, preferred the factory, and left the whole business of domestic service to a foreign population; and they did it mainly because they would not take positions in families as an inferior laboring-class by the side of others of their own age who assumed as their prerogative to live without labor.

"I can't let you have one of my daughters," said an energetic matron to her neighbor from the city, who was seeking for a servant in her summer vacation; "if you had n't daughters of your own, maybe I would; but my girls ain't going to work so that your girls may live in idleness."

It was vain to offer money. "We don't need your money, ma'am, we can support ourselves in other ways; my girls can braid straw, and bind shoes, but they ain't going to be slaves to anybody."

In the Irish and German servants who took the place of Americans in families, there was, to begin with, the tradition of education in favor of a higher class; but even the foreign population became more or less infected with the spirit of democracy. They came to this country with vague notions of freedom and equality, and in ignorant and uncultivated people such ideas are often more unreasonable for being vague. They did not, indeed, claim a seat at the table and in the parlor, but they repudiated many of those habits of respect and courtesy which belonged to their former condition, and asserted their own will and way in the round, unvarnished phrase which they supposed to be their right as republican citizens. Life became a sort of domestic wrangle and struggle between the employers, who secretly confessed their weakness, but endeavored openly to assume the air and bearing of authority, and the employed, who knew their power and insisted on their privileges. From this cause domestic service in America has had less of mutual kindliness than in old countries. Its terms have been so ill understood and defined that both parties have assumed the defensive; and a common topic of conversation in American female society has often been the general servile war which in one form or another was going on in their different families,—a war as interminable as would be a struggle between aristocracy and common people, undefined by any bill of rights or constitution, and therefore opening fields for endless disputes. In England, the class who go to service *are* a class, and service is a profession; the distance between them and their employers is so marked and defined, and all the customs and requirements of the position are so perfectly understood, that the master or mistress has no fear of being compromised by condescension, and no need of the external voice or air of authority. The higher up in the social scale one goes, the more courteous seems to become the intercourse of master and servant; the more perfect and real the power, the more is it veiled in outward expression,—commands are phrased as requests, and gentleness of voice and manner covers an authority which no one would think of offending without trembling.

But in America all is undefined. In the first place, there is no class who mean to make domestic service a profession to live and die in. It is universally an expedient, a stepping-stone to something higher; your best servants always have something else in view as soon as they have laid by a little money; some form of independence which shall give them a home of their own is constantly in mind. Families look forward to the buying of landed homesteads and the scattered brothers and sisters work awhile in domestic service to gain the common fund for the purpose; your seamstress intends to become a dress-maker, and take in work at her own house; your cook is pondering a marriage with the baker, which shall transfer her toils from your cooking-stove to her own. Young women are eagerly rushing into every other employment, till female trades and callings are all overstocked. We are continually harrowed with tales of the sufferings of distressed needle-women, of the exactions and extortions practised on the frail sex in the many branches of labor and trade at which they try their hands; and yet women will encounter all these chances of ruin and starvation rather than make up their minds to permanent domestic service. Now what is the matter with domestic service? One would think, on the face of it, that a calling which gives a settled home, a comfortable room, rent-free, with fire and lights, good board and lodging, and steady, well-paid wages, would certainly offer more attractions than the making of shirts for tenpence, with all the risks of providing one's own sustenance and shelter.

I think it is mainly from the want of a definite idea of the true position of a servant under our democratic institutions that domestic service is so shunned and avoided in America, that it is the very last thing which an intelligent young woman will look to for a living. It is more the want of personal respect toward those in that position than the labors incident to it which repels our people from it. Many would be willing to perform these labors, but they are not willing to place themselves in a situation where their self-respect is hourly wounded by *the implication of a degree of inferiority which does not follow any kind of labor or service in this country but that of the family.*

There exists in the minds of employers an unsuspected spirit of superiority, which is stimulated into an active form by the resistance which democracy inspires in the working-class. Many families think of servants only as a necessary evil, their wages as exactions, and all that is allowed them as so much taken from the family; and they seek in every way to get from them as much and to give them as little as possible. Their rooms are the neglected, ill-furnished, incommodious ones,—and the kitchen is the most cheerless and comfortless place in the house. Other families, more good-natured and liberal, provide their domestics with more suitable accommodations, and are more indulgent; but there is still a latent spirit of something like contempt for the position. That they treat their servants with so much consideration seems to them a merit entitling them to the most prostrate gratitude; and they are constantly disappointed and shocked at that want of sense of inferiority on the part of these people which leads them to appropriate pleasant rooms, good furniture, and good living as mere matters of common justice.

It seems to be a constant surprise to some employers that servants should insist on having the same human wants as themselves. Ladies who yawn in their elegantly furnished parlors, among books and pictures, if they have not company, parties, or opera to diversify the evening, seem astonished and half indignant that cook and chambermaid are more disposed to go out for an evening gossip than to sit on hard chairs in the kitchen where they have been toiling all day. The pretty chambermaid's anxieties about her dress, the time she spends at her small and not very clear mirror, are sneeringly noticed by those whose toilet-cares take up serious hours; and the question has never apparently occurred to them why a serving-maid should not want to look pretty as well as her mistress. She is a woman as well as they, with all a woman's wants and weaknesses; and her dress is as much to her as theirs to them.

A vast deal of trouble among servants arises from impertinent interferences and petty tyrannical exactions on the part of employers. Now the authority of the master and mistress of a house in regard to their domestics extends simply to the things they have contracted to do and the hours during which they have contracted to serve; otherwise than this, they have no more right to interfere with them in the disposal of their time than with any mechanic whom they employ. They have, indeed, a right to regulate the hours of their own household, and servants can choose between conformity to these hours and the loss of their situation; but, within reasonable limits, their right to come and go at their own discretion, in their own time, should be unquestioned.

If employers are troubled by the fondness of their servants for dancing, evening company, and late hours, the proper mode of proceeding is to make these matters a subject of distinct contract in hiring. The more strictly and perfectly the business matters of the first engagement of domestics are conducted, the more likelihood there is of mutual quiet and satisfaction in the relation. It is quite competent to every housekeeper to say what practices are or are not consistent with the rules of her family, and what will be inconsistent with the service for which she agrees to pay. It is much better to regulate such affairs by cool contract in the outset than by warm altercations and protracted domestic battles.

As to the terms of social intercourse, it seems somehow to be settled in the minds of many employers that their servants owe them and their family more respect than they and the family owe to the servants. But do they? What is the relation of servant to employer in a democratic country? Precisely that of a person who for money performs any kind of service for you. The carpenter comes into your house to put up a set of shelves,—the cook comes into your kitchen to cook your dinner. You never think that the carpenter owes you any more respect than you owe to him because he is in your house doing your behests; he is your fellow-citizen, you treat him with respect, you expect to be treated with respect by him. You have a claim on him that he shall do your work according to your directions,—no more. Now I apprehend that there is a very common notion as to the position and rights of servants which is quite different from this. Is it not a common feeling that a servant is one who may be treated with a degree of freedom by every member of the family which he or she may not return? Do not people feel at liberty to question servants about their private affairs, to comment on their dress and appearance, in a manner which they would feel to be an impertinence, if reciprocated? Do they not feel at liberty to express dissatisfaction with their performances in rude and unceremonious terms, to reprove them in the presence of company, while yet they require that the dissatisfaction of servants shall be expressed only in terms of respect? A woman would not feel herself at liberty to talk to her milliner or her dressmaker in language as devoid of consideration as she will employ towards her cook or chambermaid. Yet both are rendering her a service which she pays for in money, and one is no more made her inferior thereby than the other. Both have an equal right to be treated with courtesy. The master and mistress of a house have a right to require respectful treatment from all whom their roof shelters; but they have no more right to exact it of servants than of every guest and every child, and they themselves owe it as much to servants as to guests.

In order that servants may be treated with respect and courtesy, it is not necessary, as in simpler patriarchal days, that they sit at the family-table. Your carpenter or plumber does not feel hurt that you do not ask him to dine with you, nor your milliner and mantua-maker that you do not exchange ceremonious calls and invite them to your parties. It is well understood that your relations with them are of a mere business character. They never take it as an assumption of superiority on your part that you do not admit them to relations of private intimacy. There may be the most perfect respect and esteem and even friendship between them and you, notwithstanding. So it may be in the case of servants. It is easy to make any person understand that there are quite other reasons than the assumption of personal superiority for not wishing to admit servants to the family privacy. It was not, in fact, to sit in the parlor or at the table, in themselves considered, that was the thing aimed at by New England girls,—these were valued only as signs that they were deemed worthy of respect and consideration, and, where freely conceded, were often in point of fact declined.

Let servants feel, in their treatment by their employers, and in the atmosphere of the family, that their position is held to be a respectable one, let them feel in the mistress of the family the charm of unvarying consideration and good manners, let their work-rooms be made convenient and comfortable, and their private apartments bear some reasonable comparison in point of agreeableness to those of other members of the family, and domestic service will be more frequently sought by a superior and self-respecting class. There are families in which such a state of things prevails; and such families, amid the many causes which unite to make the tenure of service uncertain, have generally been able to keep good permanent servants.

There is an extreme into which kindly disposed people often run with regard to servants, which may be mentioned here. They make pets of them. They give extravagant wages and indiscreet indulgences, and, through indolence and easiness of temper, tolerate neglect of duty. Many of the complaints of the ingratitude of servants come from those who have spoiled them in this way; while many of the longest and most harmonious domestic unions have sprung from a simple, quiet course of Christian justice and benevolence, a recognition of servants as fellow-beings and fellow-Christians, and a doing to them as we would in like circumstances that they should do to us.

The mistresses of American families, whether they like it or not, have the duties of missionaries imposed upon them by that class from which our supply of domestic servants is drawn. They may as well accept the position cheerfully, and, as one raw, untrained hand after another passes through their family, and is instructed by them in the mysteries of good housekeeping, comfort themselves with the reflection that they are doing something to form good wives and mothers for the Republic.

The complaints made of Irish girls are numerous and loud; the failings of green Erin, alas! are but too open and manifest; yet, in arrest of judgment, let us move this consideration: let us imagine our own daughters between the ages of sixteen and twenty-four, untaught and inexperienced in domestic affairs as they commonly are, shipped to a foreign shore to seek service in families. It may be questioned whether as a whole they would do much better. The girls that fill our families and do our house-work are often of the age of our own daughters, standing for themselves, without mothers to guide them, in a foreign country, not only bravely supporting themselves, but sending home in every ship remittances to impoverished friends left behind. If our daughters did as much for us, should we not be proud of their energy and heroism?

When we go into the houses of our country, we find a majority of well-kept, well-ordered, and even elegant establishments where the only hands employed are those of the daughters of Erin. True, American women have been their instructors, and many a weary hour of care have they had in the discharge of this office; but the result on the whole is beautiful and good, and the end of it, doubtless, will be peace.

In speaking of the office of the American mistress as being a missionary one, we are far from recommending any controversial interference with the religious faith of our servants. It is far better to incite them to be good Christians in their own way than to run the risk of shaking their faith in all religion by pointing out to them the errors of that in which they have been educated. The general purity of life and propriety of demeanor of so many thousands of undefended young girls cast yearly upon our shores, with no home but their church, and no shield but their religion, are a sufficient proof that this religion exerts an influence over them not to be lightly trifled with. But there is a real unity even in opposite Christian forms; and the Roman Catholic servant and the Protestant mistress, if alike possessed by the spirit of Christ, and striving to conform to the Golden Rule, cannot help being one in heart, though one go to mass and the other to meeting.

Finally, the bitter baptism through which we are passing, the life-blood dearer than our own which is drenching distant fields, should remind us of the preciousness of distinctive American ideas. They who would seek in their foolish pride to establish the pomp of liveried servants in America are doing that which is simply absurd. A servant can never in our country be the mere appendage to another man, to be marked like a sheep with the color of his owner; he must be a fellow-citizen, with an established position of his own, free to make contracts, free to come and go, and having in his sphere titles to consideration and respect just as definite as those of any trade or profession whatever.

Moreover, we cannot in this country maintain to any great extent large retinues of servants. Even with ample fortunes they are forbidden by the general character of society here, which makes them cumbrous and difficult to manage. Every mistress of a family knows that her cares increase with every additional servant. Two keep the peace with each other and their employer; three begin a possible discord, which possibility increases with four, and becomes certain with five or six. Trained housekeepers, such as regulate the complicated establishments of the Old World, form a class that are not, and from the nature of the case never will be, found in any great numbers in this country. All such women, as a general thing, are keeping, and prefer to keep, houses of their own.

A moderate style of housekeeping, small, compact, and simple domestic establishments, must necessarily be the general order of life in America. So many openings of profit are to be found in this country, that domestic service necessarily wants the permanence which forms so agreeable a feature of it in the Old World.

This being the case, it should be an object in America to exclude from the labors of the family all that can, with greater advantage, be executed out of it by combined labor.

Formerly, in New England, soap and candles were to be made in each separate family; now, comparatively few take this toil upon them. We buy soap of the soap-maker, and candles of the candle-factor. This principle might be extended much further. In France no family makes its own bread, and better bread cannot be eaten than what can be bought at the appropriate shops. No family does its own washing, the family's linen is all sent to women who, making this their sole profession, get it up with a care and nicety which can seldom be equalled in any family.

How would it simplify the burdens of the American housekeeper to have washing and ironing day expunged from her calendar! How much more neatly and compactly could the whole domestic system be arranged! If all the money that each separate family spends on the outfit and accommodations for washing and ironing, on fuel, soap, starch, and the other et ceteras, were united in a fund to create a laundry for every dozen families, one or two good women could do in first rate style what now is very indifferently done by the disturbance and disarrangement of all other domestic processes in these families. Whoever sets neighborhood laundries on foot will do much to solve the American housekeeper's hardest problem.

Finally, American women must not try with three servants to carry on life in the style which in the Old World requires sixteen,—they must thoroughly understand, and be prepared *to teach*, every branch of housekeeping,—they must study to make domestic service desirable, by treating their servants in a way to lead them to respect themselves and to feel themselves respected,—and there will gradually be evolved from the present confusion a solution of the domestic problem which shall be adapted to the life of a new and growing world.

ψ   ψ   ψ

# Selections from *Little Foxes*

In her 1865 "Chimney-Corner" columns for the *Atlantic Monthly*, Stowe chose as her subject seven faults that undermine domestic happiness: Fault-finding, Irritability, Repression, Persistence, Intolerance, Discourtesy, and Exactingness. She used her narrative skill to sketch domestic scenes that, like examples in a preacher's sermon, illustrate her points. These sketches, published in 1865 by J. R. Osgood under the title *Little Foxes*, are particularly sensitive to the jarring of temperaments that occurs within the home as people of very different disposition are thrown together in daily intercourse. Indeed, in their psychological realism they are much more revealing of the home than her idealization of that institution in her first set of papers.

In both "Intolerance" and "Exactingness," her June and September columns, Stowe strives to lessen the burden of unrealistic expectations. She understands how the example of "Mrs. Alexander Exact" sits heavily on the shoulders of less perfect housekeepers, and how parents make their children's lives miserable by casting them in roles for which they are ill suited. Stowe trains her eye on the perfectionist striving of the age, which expressed itself both in high religious expectations and a restless striving for a more perfectly arranged domestic equipage. To the "self-tormented" she counsels self-acceptance. Preaching common sense and acknowledgement of limits, she helps the middle class find the middle way.

## Intolerance

nd what are you going to preach about this month, Mr. Crowfield?"
"I am going to give a sermon on *Intolerance*, Mrs. Crowfield."
"Religious intolerance?"
"No,—domestic and family and educational intolerance,—one of the seven deadly sins on which I am preaching,—one of 'the foxes.'"

People are apt to talk as if all the intolerance in life were got up and expended in the religious world; whereas religious intolerance is only a small branch of the radical, strong, all-pervading intolerance of human nature.

Physicians are quite as intolerant as theologians. They never have had the power of burning at the stake for medical opinions, but they certainly have shown the will. Politicians are intolerant. Philosophers are intolerant, especially those who pique themselves on liberal opinions. Painters and sculptors are intolerant. And housekeepers are intolerant, virulently denunciatory concerning any departures from their particular domestic creed.

Mrs. Alexander Exact, seated at her domestic altar, gives homilies on the degeneracy of modern housekeeping equal to the lamentations of Dr. Holdfast as to the falling off from the good old faith.

"Don't tell me about pillow-cases made without felling," says Mrs. Alexander; "it 's slovenly and shiftless. I would n't have such a pillow-case in my house any more than I 'd have vermin."

"But," says a trembling young housekeeper, conscious of unfelled pillow-cases at home, "don't you think, Mrs. Alexander, that some of these old traditions might be dispensed with? It really is not necessary to do all the work that has been done so thoroughly and exactly,—to double-stitch every wristband, fell every seam, count all the threads of gathers, and take a stitch to every gather. It makes beautiful sewing, to be sure; but when a woman has a family of little children and a small income, if all her sewing is to be kept up in this perfect style, she wears her life out in stitching. Had she not better slight a little, and get air and exercise?"

"Don't tell me about air and exercise! What did my grandmother do? Why, she did all her own work, and made grandfather's ruffled shirts besides, with the finest stitching and gathers; and she found exercise enough, I warrant you. Women of this day are miserable, sickly, degenerate creatures."

"But, my dear Madam, look at poor Mrs. Evans, over the way, with her pale face and her eight little ones."

"Miserable manager," said Mrs. Alexander. "If she 'd get up at five o'clock the year round, as I do, she 'd find time enough to do things properly, and be the better for it."

"But, my dear Madam, Mrs. Evans is a very delicately organized, nervous woman."

"Nervous! Don't tell me! Every woman now-a-days is nervous. She can't get up in the morning, because she 's nervous. She can't do her sewing decently, because she 's nervous. Why, I might have been as nervous as she is, if I 'd have petted and coddled myself as she does. But I get up early, take a walk in the fresh air of a mile or so before breakfast, and come home feeling the better for it. I do all my own sewing,—never put out a stitch; and I flatter myself my things are made as they ought to be. I always make my boys' shirts and Mr. Exact's, and they are made as shirts ought to be,—and yet I find plenty of time for calling, shopping, business, and company. It only requires management and resolution." . . .

Now, in the neighborhood where she lives, Mrs. Alexander Exact is the wonderful woman, the Lady Bountiful, the pattern female. Her cake never rises on one side, or has a heavy streak in it. Her furs never get a moth in them; her carpets never fade; her sweetmeats never ferment; her servants never neglect their work; her children never get things out of order; her babies never cry, never keep one awake o' nights; and her husband never in his life said, "My dear, there 's a button off my shirt." Flies never infest her kitchen, cockroaches and red ants never invade her premises, a spider never had time to spin a web on one of her walls. Everything in her establishment is shining with neatness, crisp and bristling with absolute perfection,—and it is she, the ever-up-and-dressed, unsleeping, wide-awake, omnipresent, never-tiring Mrs. Exact, that does it all.

Besides keeping her household ways thus immaculate, Mrs. Exact is on all sorts of charitable committees, does all sorts of fancy-work for fairs; and what-ever she does is done perfectly. She is a most available, most helpful, most benev-olent woman, and general society has reason to rejoice in her existence.

But, for all this, Mrs. Exact is as intolerant as Torquemada[1] or a locomotive-engine. She has her own track, straight and inevitable; her judgments and opin-ions cut through society in right lines, with all the force of her example and all the steam of her energy, turning out neither for the old nor the young, the weak nor the weary. She cannot, and she will not, conceive the possibility that there may be other sorts of natures than her own, and that other kinds of natures must have other ways of living and doing.

Good and useful as she is, she is terrible as an army with banners to her poor, harassed, delicate, struggling neighbor across the way, who, in addition to an aching, confused head, an aching back, sleepless, harassed nights, and weary, sink-ing days, is burdened everywhere and every hour with the thought that Mrs. Exact thinks all her troubles are nothing but poor management, and that she might do just like her, if she would. With very little self-confidence or self-assertion, she is withered and paralyzed by this discouraging thought. *Is* it, then, her fault that this never-sleeping baby cries all night, and that all her children never could and never would be brought up by those exact rules which she hears of as so effica-cious in the household over the way? The thought of Mrs. Alexander Exact stands over her like a constable; the remembrance of her is grievous; the burden of her opinion is heavier than all her other burdens.

Now the fact is, that Mrs. Exact comes of a long-lived, strong-backed, strong-stomached race, with "limbs of British oak and nerves of wire." The shadow of a sensation of nervous pain or uneasiness never has been known in her family for generations, and her judgments of poor little Mrs. Evans are about as intelligent as those of a good stout Shanghai hen on a humming-bird. Most useful and com-fortable, these Shanghai hens,—and very ornamental, and in a small way useful, these humming-birds; but let them not regulate each other's diet, or lay down schemes for each other's housekeeping. Has not one as much right to its nature as the other?

This intolerance of other people's natures is one of the greatest causes of do-mestic unhappiness. The perfect householders are they who make their house-hold rule so flexible that all sorts of differing natures may find room to grow and expand and express themselves without infringing upon others.

Some women are endowed with a tact for understanding human nature and guiding it. They give a sense of largeness and freedom; they find a place for every

---

[1]Leader of the Spanish Inquisition who developed a reputation for cruelty because of his rigorous enforcement of its procedures.

one, see at once what every one is good for, and are inspired by Nature with the happy wisdom of not wishing or asking of any human being more than that human being was made to give. They have the portion in due season for all: a bone for the dog; catnip for the cat; cuttle-fish and hempseed for the bird; a book or review for their bashful literary visitor; lively gossip for thoughtless Miss Seventeen; knitting for Grandmamma; fishing-rods, boats, and gunpowder, for Young Restless, whose beard is just beginning to grow;—and they never fall into pets, because the canary-bird won't relish the dog's bone, or the dog eat canary-seed, or young Miss Seventeen read old Mr. Sixty's review, or young Master Restless take delight in knitting-work, or old Grandmamma feel complacency in guns and gunpowder.

Again, there are others who lay the foundations of family life so narrow, straight, and strict, that there is room in them only for themselves and people exactly like themselves; and hence comes much misery.

A man and woman come together out of different families and races, often united by only one or two sympathies, with many differences. Their first wisdom would be to find out each other's nature, and accommodate to it as a fixed fact; instead of which, how many spend their lives in a blind fight with an opposite nature, as good as their own in its way, but not capable of meeting their requirements!

A woman trained in an exact, thriving, business family, where her father and brothers bore everything along with true worldly skill and energy, falls in love with a literary man, who knows nothing of affairs, whose life is in his library and his pen. Shall she vex and torment herself and him because he is not a business man? Shall she constantly hold up to him the example of her father and brothers, and how they would manage in this and that case? or shall she say cheerily and once for all to herself,—"My husband has no talent for business; that is not his forte; but then he has talents far more interesting: I cannot have everything; let him go on undisturbed, and do what he can do well, and let me try to make up for what he cannot do; and if there be disabilities come on us in consequence of what we neither of us can do, let us both take them cheerfully"?

In the same manner a man takes out of the bosom of an adoring family one of those delicate, petted singing-birds that seem to be created simply to adorn life and make it charming. Is it fair, after he has got her, to compare her housekeeping, and her efficiency and capability in the material part of life, with those of his mother and sisters, who are strong-limbed, practical women, that have never thought about anything but housekeeping from their cradle? Shall he all the while vex himself and her with the remembrance of how his mother used to get up at five o'clock and arrange all the business of the day,—how she kept all the accounts,—how she saw to everything and settled everything,—how there never were breakdowns or irregularities in her system?

This would be unfair. If a man wanted such a housekeeper, why did he not get one? There were plenty of single women, who understood washing, ironing, clear-starching, cooking, and general housekeeping, better than the little canary-bird which he fell in love with, and wanted for her plumage and her song, for her merry tricks, for her bright eyes and pretty ways. Now he has got his bird, let him keep it as something fine and precious, to be cared for and watched over, and treated according to the laws of its frail and delicate nature; and so treating it, he may many years keep the charms which first won his heart. He may find, too, if he watches and is careful, that a humming-bird can, in its own small, dainty way, build a nest as efficiently as a turkey-gobbler, and hatch her eggs and bring up her young in humming-bird fashion; but to do it, she must be left unfrightened and undisturbed.

But the evils of domestic intolerance increase with the birth of children. As parents come together out of different families with ill-assorted peculiarities, so children are born to them with natures differing from their own and from each other.

The parents seize on their first new child as a piece of special property which they are forthwith to turn to their own account. The poor little waif, just drifted on the shores of Time, has perhaps folded up in it a character as positive as that of either parent; but, for all that, its future course is marked out for it, all arranged and predetermined.

John has a perfect mania for literary distinction. His own education was somewhat imperfect, but he is determined his children shall be prodigies. His firstborn turns out a girl, who is to write like Madame de Staël,—to be an able, accomplished woman. He bores her with literature from her earliest years, reads extracts from Milton to her when she is only eight years old, and is secretly longing to be playing with her doll's wardrobe. He multiplies governesses, spares no expense, and when, after all, his daughter turns out to be only a very pretty, sensible, domestic girl, fond of cross-stitching embroidery, and with a more decided vocation for sponge-cake and pickles than for poetry and composition, he is disappointed and treats her coldly; and she is unhappy and feels that she has vexed her parents, because she cannot be what Nature never meant her to be. If John had taken meekly the present that Mother Nature gave him, and humbly set himself to inquire what it was and what it was good for, he might have had years of happiness with a modest, amiable, and domestic daughter, to whom had been given the instinct to study household good.

But, again, a bustling, pickling, preserving, stocking-knitting, universal-housekeeping woman has a daughter who dreams over her knitting-work and hides a book under her sampler,—whose thoughts are straying in Greece, Rome, Germany,—who is reading, studying, thinking, writing, without knowing why; and the mother sets herself to fight this nature, and to make the dreamy scholar into a driving, thorough-going, exact woman-of-business. How many tears are shed, how much temper wasted, how much time lost, in such encounters!

Each of these natures, under judicious training, might be made to complete itself by cultivation of that which it lacked. The born housekeeper can never be made a genius, but she may add to her household virtues some reasonable share of literary culture and appreciation,—and the born scholar may learn to come down out of her clouds, and see enough of this earth to walk its practical ways without stumbling; but this must be done by tolerance of their nature,—by giving it play and room,—first recognizing its existence and its rights, and then seeking to add to it the properties it wants.

A clever Yankee housekeeper, fruitful of resources, can work with any tools or with no tools at all. If she absolutely cannot get a tack-hammer with a claw on one end, she can take up carpet-nails with an iron spoon, and drive them down with a flat-iron; and she has sense enough not to scold, though she does her work with them at considerable disadvantage. She knows that she is working with tools made for another purpose, and never thinks of being angry at their unhandiness. She might have equal patience with a daughter unhandy in physical things, but acute and skilful in mental ones, if she once had the idea suggested to her.

An ambitious man has a son whom he destines to a learned profession. He is to be the Daniel Webster of the family. The boy has a robust, muscular frame, great physical vigor and enterprise, a brain bright and active in all that may be acquired through the bodily senses, but which is dull and confused and wandering when put to abstract book-knowledge. He knows every ship at the wharf, her build, tonnage, and sailing qualities; he knows every railroad-engine, its power, speed, and hours of coming and going; he is always busy, sawing, hammering, planing, digging, driving, making bargains, with his head full of plans, all relating to something outward and physical. In all these matters his mind works strongly, his ideas are clear, his observation acute, his conversation sensible and worth listening to. But as to the distinction between common nouns and proper nouns, between the subject and the predicate of a sentence, between the relative pronoun and the demonstrative adjective pronoun, between the perfect and the preter-perfect tense, he is extremely dull and hazy. The region of abstract ideas is to him a region of ghosts and shadows. Yet his youth is mainly a dreary wilderness of uncomprehended, incomprehensible studies, of privations, tasks, punishments, with a sense of continual failure, disappointment, and disgrace, because his father is trying to make a scholar and a literary man out of a boy whom Nature made to till the soil or manage the material forces of the world. He might be a farmer, an engineer, a pioneer of a new settlement, a sailor, a soldier, a thriving man of business; but he grows up feeling that his nature is a crime, and that he is good for nothing, because he is not good for what he had been blindly predestined to before he was born.

Another boy is a born mechanic; he understands machinery at a glance; he is all the while pondering and studying and experimenting. But his wheels and his axles and his pulleys are all swept away, as so much irrelevant lumber; he is doomed to go into the Latin School, and spend three or four years in trying to learn what he never can learn well,—disheartened by always being at the tail of his class, and seeing many a boy inferior to himself in general culture who is rising to brilliant distinction simply because he can remember those hopeless, bewildering Greek quantities and accents which he is constantly forgetting,—as, for example, how properispomena become paroxytones when the ultimate becomes long, while paroxytones with a short penult remain paroxytones. Each of this class of rules, however, having about sixteen exceptions, which hold good except in three or four other exceptional cases under them, the labyrinth becomes delightfully wilder and wilder; and the crowning beauty of the whole is, that, when the bewildered boy has swallowed the whole,—tail, scales, fins, and bones,—he then is allowed to read the classics in peace, without the slightest occasion to refer to them again during his college course. . . .

On no subject is there more intolerant judgment, and more suffering from such intolerance, than on the much mooted one of the education of children.

Treatises on education require altogether too much of parents, and impose burdens of responsibility on tender spirits which crush the life and strength out of them. Parents have been talked to as if each child came to them a soft, pulpy mass, which they were to pinch and pull and pat and stroke into shape quite at their leisure,—and a good pattern being placed before them, they were to proceed immediately to set up and construct a good human being in conformity therewith.

It is strange that believers in the divine inspiration of the Bible should have entertained this idea, overlooking the constant and affecting declaration of the great Heavenly Father that *He* has nourished and brought up children and they have rebelled against Him, together with His constant apppeals,—"What could have been done more to my vineyard that I have not done in it? Wherefore, when I looked that it should bring forth grapes, brought it forth wild grapes?" If even God, wiser, better, purer, more loving, admits Himself baffled in this great work, is it expedient to say to human beings that the forming power, the deciding force, of a child's character is in their hands?

Many a poor feeble woman's health has been strained to breaking, and her life darkened, by the laying on her shoulders of a burden of responsibility that never ought to have been placed there; and many a mother has been hindered from using such powers as God has given her, because some preconceived mode of operation has been set up before her which she could no more make effectual than David could wear the armor of Saul.

A gentle, loving, fragile creature marries a strong-willed, energetic man, and by the laws of natural descent has a boy given to her of twice her amount of will and energy. She is just as helpless, in the mere struggle of will and authority with such a child, as she would be in a physical wrestle with a six-foot man.

What then? Has Nature left her helpless for her duties? Not if she understands her nature, and acts in the line of it. She has no power of command, but she has power of persuasion. She can neither bend nor break the boy's iron will, but she can melt it. She has tact to avoid the conflict in which she would be worsted. She can charm, amuse, please, and make willing; and her fine and subtle influences, weaving themselves about him day after day, become more and more powerful. Let her alone, and she will have her boy yet.

But now some bustling mother-in-law or other privileged expounder says to her,—

"My dear, it 's your solemn duty to break that boy's will. I broke my boy's will short off. Keep your whip in sight, meet him at every turn, fight him whenever he crosses you, never let him get one victory, and finally his will will be wholly subdued."

Such advice is mischievous, because what it proposes is as utter an impossibility to the woman's nature as for a cow to scratch up worms for her calf, or a hen to suckle her chickens.

There are men and women of strong, resolute will who are gifted with the power of governing the wills of others. Such persons can govern in this way,—and their government, being in the line of their nature, acting strongly, consistently, naturally, makes everything move harmoniously. Let them be content with their own success, but let them not set up as general education-doctors, or apply their experience to all possible cases.

Again, there are others, and among them some of the loveliest and purest natures, who have no power of command. They have sufficient tenacity of will as respects their own course, but have no compulsory power over the wills of others. Many such women have been most successful mothers, when they followed the line of their own natures, and did not undertake what they never could do.

*Influence* is a slower acting force than authority. It seems weaker, but in the long run it often effects more. It always does better than mere force and authority without its gentle modifying power.

She who obtains an absolute and perfect government over a chld, so that he obeys, certainly and almost mechanically produces effects which are more appreciable in their immediate action on family life; her family will be more orderly, her children in their childhood will do her more credit.

But she who has consciously no power of this kind, whose children are often turbulent and unmanageable, need not despair if she feel that through affection, reason, and conscience, she still retains a strong *influence* over them. If she cannot govern her boy, she can do even a better thing if she can inspire him with a purpose to *govern himself*; for a boy taught to govern himself is a better achievement than a boy merely governed.

If a mother, therefore, is high-principled, religious, affectionate, if she never uses craft or deception, if she governs her temper and sets a good example, let her hold on in good hope, though she cannot produce the discipline of a man-of-war in her noisy little flock, or make all move as smoothly as some other women to whom God has given another and different talent; and let her not be discouraged, if she seem often to accomplish but little in that arduous work of forming human character wherein the great Creator of the world has declared Himself at times baffled.

Family tolerance must take great account of the stages and periods of development and growth in children.

The passage of a human being from one stage of development to another, like the sun's passage across the equator, frequently has its storms and tempests. The change to manhood and womanhood often involves brain, nerves, body, and soul in confusion; the child sometimes seems lost to himself and his parents,—his very nature changing. In this sensitive state come restless desires, unreasonable longings, unsettled purposes; and the fatal habit of indulgence in deadly stimulants, ruining all the life, often springs from the cravings of this transition period.

Here must come in the patience of the saints. The restlessness must be soothed, the family hearth must be tolerant enough to keep there the boy, whom Satan will receive and cherish, if his mother does not. The male element sometimes pours into a boy, like the tides in the Bay of Fundy, with tumult and tossing. He is noisy, vociferous, uproarious, and seems bent only on disturbance; he despises conventionalities, he hates parlors, he longs for the woods, the sea, the converse of rough men, and kicks at constraint of all kinds. Have patience now, let love have its perfect work, and in a year or two, if no deadly physical habits set in, a quiet, well-mannered gentleman will be evolved. Meanwhile, if he does not wipe his shoes, and if he will fling his hat upon the floor, and tear his clothes, and bang and hammer and shout, and cause general confusion in his belongings, do not despair; for if you only get your son, the hat and clothes and shoes and noise and confusion do not matter. Any amount of toleration that keeps a boy contented at home is treasure well expended at this time of life.

One thing not enough reflected on is, that in this transition period between childhood and maturity the heaviest draft and strain of school education occurs. The boy is fitting for the university, the girl going through the studies of the college senior year, and the brain-power, which is working almost to the breaking-point to perfect the physical change, has the additional labor of all the drill and discipline of school.

The girl is growing into a tall and shapely woman, and the poor brain is put to it to find enough phosphate of lime, carbon, and other what not, to build her fair edifice. The bills flow in upon her thick and fast; she pays out hand over hand: if she had only her woman to build, she might get along, but now come in demands for algebra, geometry, music, language, and the poor brain-bank stops payment; some part of the work is shabbily done, and a crooked spine or weakened lungs are the result.[2]

Boarding-schools, both for boys and girls, are for the most part composed of young people in this most delicate, critical portion of their physical, mental, and moral development, whose teachers are expected to put them through one straight, severe course of drill, without the slightest allowance for the great physical facts of their being. No wonder they are difficult to manage, and that so many of them drop, physically, mentally, and morally halt and maimed. It is not the teacher's fault; he but fulfils the parent's requisition, which dooms his child without appeal to a certain course, simply because others have gone through it.

Finally, as my sermon is too long already, let me end with a single reflection. Every human being has some handle by which he may be lifted, some groove in which he was meant to run; and the great work of life, as far as our relations with each other are concerned, is to lift each one by his own proper handle, and run each one in his own proper groove.

## Exactingness

At length I am arrived at my seventh fox,—the last of the domestic quadrupeds against which I have vowed a crusade,—and here opens the chase of him. I call him

---

[2]Stowe is drawing on popular scientific theories in which the physiological demands of puberty and pregnancy were thought to be especially taxing on the body's reserve of phosphates. Such theories were later invoked to discourage women from higher education.

*EXACTINGNESS.*

And having done this, I drop the metaphor, for fear of chasing it beyond the rules of graceful rhetoric, and shall proced to define the trait.

All the other domestic faults of which I have treated have relation to the manner in which the ends of life are pursued; but this one is an underlying, false, and diseased state of conception as to the very ends and purposes of life itself.

If a piano is tuned to exact concert pitch, the majority of voices must fall below it; for which reason, most people indulgently allow their pianos to be tuned a little below this point, in accommodation to the average power of the human voice. Persons of only ordinary powers of voice would be considered absolute monomaniacs, who should insist on having their pianos tuned to accord with any abstract notion of propriety or perfection,—rendering themselves wretched by persistently singing all their pieces miserably out of tune in consequence.

Yet there are persons who keep the requirements of life strained up always at concert pitch, and are thus worn out and made miserable all their days by the grating of a perpetual discord.

There is a faculty of the human mind to which phrenologists have given the name of *Ideality*, which is at the foundation of this exactingness. Ideality is the faculty by which we conceive of and long for perfection; and at a glance it will be seen, that, so far from being an evil ingredient of human nature, it is the one element of progress that distinguishes man's nature from that of the brute. While animals go on from generation to generation, learning nothing and forgetting nothing, practising their small circle of the arts of life no better and no worse from year to year, man is driven by ideality to constant invention and alteration, whence come arts, sciences, and the whole progress of society. Ideality induces discontent with present attainments, possessions, and performances, and hence come better and better ones. So in morals, ideality constantly incites to higher and nobler modes of living and thinking, and is the faculty to which the most effective teachings of the great Master of Christianity are addressed. To be dissatisfied with present attainments, with earthly things and scenes, to aspire and press on to something forever fair, yet forever receding before our steps,—this is the teaching of Christianity, and the work of the Christian.

But every faculty has its own instinctive, wild growth, which, like the spontaneous produce of the earth, is crude and weedy.

Revenge, says Lord Bacon, is a sort of wild justice, obstinacy is untutored firmness,—and so exactingness is untrained ideality; and a vast deal of misery, social and domestic, comes, not of the faculty, but of its untrained exercise.

The faculty which is ever conceiving and desiring something better and more perfect must be modified in its action by good sense, patience, and conscience, or it induces a morbid, discontented spirit, which courses through the veins of individual and family life like a subtle poison.

In a certain neighborhood are two families whose social and domestic *animus* illustrates the difference between ideality and the want of it.

The Daytons are a large, easy-natured, joyous race, hospitable, kindly, and friendly.

Nothing about their establishment is much above mediocrity. The grounds are tolerably kept, the table is tolerably fair, the servants moderately good, and the family character and attainments of the same average level.

Mrs. Dayton is a decent housekeeper, and so her bread be not sour, her butter not frowy, the food abundant, and the table-cloth and dishes clean, she troubles her head little with the niceties and refinements of the *ménage*.

She accepts her children as they come from the hand of Nature, simply opening her eyes to discern what they *are*, never raising the query what she would have had them,—forming no very high expectations concerning them, and well content with whatever develops.

A visitor in the family can easily see a thousand defects in the conduct of affairs, in the management of the children, and in this, that, and the other portion of the household arrangements; but he can see and feel, also, a perfect comfortableness in the domestic atmosphere that almost atones for any defects. He can see that in a thousand respects things might be better done, if the family were not perfectly content to have them as they are, and that each individual member might make higher attainments in various directions, were there not such entire satisfaction with what is already attained.

Trying each other by very moderate standards and measurements, there is great mutual complacency. The oldest boy does not get an appointment in college,—they never expected he would; but he was a respectable scholar, and they receive him with acclamations such as another family would bestow on a valedictorian. The daughters do not profess, as we are told, to draw like artists, but some very moderate performances in the line of the fine arts are dwelt on with much innocent pleasure. They thrum a few tunes on the piano, and the whole family listen and approve. All unite in singing in a somewhat uncultured manner a few psalm-tunes or songs, and take more comfort in them than many amateurs do in their well-drilled performances.

So goes the world with the Daytons; and when you visit them, if you often feel that you could ask more and suggest much improvement, yet you cannot help enjoying the quiet satisfaction which breathes around you.

Now right across the way from the Daytons live the Mores; and the Mores are the very opposites of the Daytons.

Everything about their establishment is brought to the highest point of culture. The carriage-drive never shows a weed, the lawn is velvet, the flower-beds ever-blooming, the fruit-trees and vines grow exactly like the patterns in the best pomological treatises. Within doors the housekeeping is faultless,—all seems to be moving in time and tune,—the table is more than good, it is superlative,— every article is in its way a model,—the children appear to you to be growing up after the most patent-right method, duly trained, snipped, and cultured, like the pear-trees and grape-vines. Nothing is left to accident, or done without much laborious consideration of the best manner of doing it; and the consequences, in the eyes of their simple, unsophisticated neighbors, are very wonderful.

Nevertheless this is not a happy family. All their perfections do not begin to afford them one tithe of the satisfaction that the Daytons derive from their ragged and scrambling performances.

The two daughters, Jane and Maria, had naturally very sweet voices, and when they were little, trilled tunes in a very pleasant and birdlike manner. But now, having been instructed by the best masters, and heard the very first artists, they never sing or play; the piano is shut, and their voices are dumb. If you request a song, they tell you that they never sing now; papa has such an exquisite taste, he takes no interest in any common music; in short, having heard Jenny Lind, Grisi, Alboni, Mario, and others of the tuneful shell, this family have concluded to abide in silence. As to any music that *they* could make, it is n't to be thought of.

For the same reason, the daughters, after attending a quarter or two on the drawing-exercises of a celebrated teacher, threw up their pencils in disgust, and tore up very pretty and agreeable sketches which were the marvel of their good-natured admiring neighbors. If they could draw like Signor Scratchalini, if they could hope to become perfect artists, they tell you, they would have persevered; but they have taken lessons enough to learn that drawing is the labor of a lifetime, and, not having a lifetime to give to it, they resolve to do nothing at all.

They have also, for a similar reason, given up letter-writing. If their chirography were as elegant as Charlotte Cushman's,—if they were perfect mistresses of polite English,—if they were gifted with wit, humor, and fancy, like the first masters of style,—they would take pleasure in epistolary composition, and be good correspondents; but anything short of that is so intolerable, that, except in cases of life and death or urgent business, you cannot get a line out of them. Yet they write very fair, agreeable, womanly letters, and would write much better ones, if they allowed themselves a little more practice.

Mrs. More is devoured by care. She sits with a clouded brow in her elegant, well-regulated house; and when you talk with her, you are surprised to learn that everything in it is in the most dreadful disorder from one end to the other. You ask for particulars, and find that the disorder has relation to exquisite standards of the ways of doing things, derived from observation of life in the most subdivided state of European service,—to all of which she has not as yet been able to raise her domestics. You compliment her on her cook, and she responds, in plaintive accents, "She can do a few things decently, but she is nothing of a cook." You refer with enthusiasm to her bread, her coffee, her muffins and hot rolls, and she listens and sighs. "Yes," she admits, "these are eatable,—not bad; but you should have seen the rolls at a certain *café* in Paris, and the bread at a certain nobleman's in England, where they had a bakery in the castle, and a French baker, who did nothing all the while but to refine and perfect the idea of bread. When she thinks of these things, everything in comparison is so coarse and rough!—but then she has learned to be comfortable." Thus, in every department of housekeeping, to this too well-instructed person,

"Hills peep o'er hills, and Alps on Alps arise."

Not a thing in her wide and apparently beautifully kept establishment is ever done well enough to elicit from her more than a sigh of toleration. "I suppose it must do," she faintly breathes, when poor human nature, having tried and tried again, evidently has got to the boundaries of its capabilities; "you may let it go, Jane; I never expect to be suited."

The poor woman, in the midst of possessions and attainments which excite the envy of her neighbors, is utterly restless and wretched, and feels herself always baffled and unsuccessful. Her exacting nature makes her dissatisfied with herself in everything that she undertakes, and equally dissatisfied with others. In the whole family there is little of that pleasure which comes from the consciousness of mutual admiration and esteem, because each one is pitched to so exquisite a tone that each is afraid to touch another for fear of making discord. They are afraid of each other everywhere. They cannot sing to each other, play to each other, write to each other; they cannot even converse together with any freedom, because each knows that the others are so dismally well informed and critically instructed.

Though all agree in a secret contempt for their neighbors over the way, as living in a most heathenish state of ignorant contentment, yet it is a fact that the elegant brother John will often, on the sly, slip into the Daytons' to spend an evening, and join them in singing glees and catches to their old rattling piano, and have a jolly time of it, which he remembers in contrast with the dull, silent hours at home. Kate Dayton has an uncultivated voice, which often falls from pitch; but she has a perfectly infectious gayety of good-nature, and when she is once at the piano, and all join in some merry troll, he begins to think that there may be something better even than good singing; and then they have dances and charades and games, all in such contented, jolly, impromptu ignorance of the unities of time, place, and circumstance, that he sometimes doubts, where ignorance is such bliss, whether it is n't in truth folly to be wise.

Jane and Maria laugh at John for his partiality to the Daytons, and yet they themselves feel the same attraction. At the Daytons' they somehow find themselves heroines; their drawings are so admired, their singing is so charming to these simple ears, that they are often beguiled into giving pleasure with their own despised acquirements; and Jane, somehow, is very tolerant of the devoted attention of Will Dayton, a joyous, honest-hearted fellow, whom, in her heart of hearts, she likes none the worse for being unexacting and simple enough to think her a wonder of taste and accomplishments. Will, of course, is the farthest possible from the Admirable Crichtons and exquisite Sir Philip Sidneys whom Mrs. More and the young ladies talk up at their leisure, and adorn with feathers from every royal and celestial bird, when they are discussing theoretic possible husbands. He is not in any way distinguished, except for a kind heart, strong native good sense, and a manly energy that has carried him straight into the very heart of many a citadel of life, before which the superior and more refined Mr. John had set himself down to deliberate upon the best and most elegant way of taking it. Will's plain, homely intelligence has often in five minutes disentangled some ethereal snarl in which these exquisite Mores had spun themselves up, and brought them to his own way of thinking by that sort of disenchanting process which honest, practical sense sometimes exerts over ideality.

The fact is, however, that in each of these families there is a natural defect which requires something from the other for completeness. Taking happiness as the standard, the Daytons have it as against the Mores. Taking attainment as the standard, the Mores have it as against the Daytons. A portion of the discontented ideality of the Mores would stimulate the Daytons to refine and perfect many things which might easily be made better, did they care enough to have them so; and a portion of the Daytons' self-satisfied contentment would make the attainments and refinements of the Mores of some practical use in advancing their own happiness.

But between these two classes of natures lies another, to which has been given an equal share of ideality,—in which the conception and the desire of excellence are equally strong, but in which a discriminating common-sense acts like a balance-wheel in machinery. What is the reason that the most exacting idealists never make themselves unhappy about not being able to fly like a bird or swim like a fish? Because common-sense teaches them that these accomplishments are so utterly out of the question that they never arise to the mind as objects of desire. In these well-balanced minds we speak of, common-sense runs an instinctive line all through life between the attainable and the unattainable, and sets the key of desire accordingly.

Common-sense teaches that there is no one branch of human art or science in which perfection is not a point forever receding. A botanist gravely assures us, that to become perfect in the knowledge of one branch of seaweeds would take all the time and strength of a man for a lifetime. There is no limit to music, to the fine arts. There is never a time when the gardener can rest, saying that his garden is perfect. Housekeeping, cooking, sewing, knitting, may all, for aught we know, be pushed on forever, without exhausting the capabilities for better doing.

But while attainment in everything is endless, circumstances forbid the greater part of human beings from attaining in any direction the half of what they see would be desirable; and the difference between the miserable idealist and the contented realist often is, not that both do not see what needs to be done for perfection, but that, seeing it, one is satisfied with the attainable, and the other forever frets and wears himself out on the unattainable.

The principal of a large and complicated public institution was complimented on maintaining such uniformity of cheerfulness amid such a diversity of cares. "I 've made up my mind to be satisfied, when things are done *half* as well as I would have them," was his answer; and the same philosophy would apply with cheering results to the domestic sphere.

There is a saying which one often hears among common people, that such and such a one are persons who never could be happy, unless everything went "*just so*,"—that is, in accordance with their highest conceptions.

When these persons are women, and undertake the sway of a home empire, they are sure to be miserable, and to make others so; for home is a place where by no kind of magic possible to woman can everything be always made to go "just so."

We may read treatises on education,—and very excellent ones there are. We may read very nice stories illustrating home management, in which book-children and book-servants all work into the author's plan with obliging unanimity; but every real child and real servant is an uncompromising fact, whose working into our ideal of life cannot be predicted with any degree of certainty. A husband is another absolute fact, of whose conformity to any ideal conceptions no positive account can be given. So, when a person has the most charming theories of education, the most complete ideals of life, it is often his lot to sit bound hand and foot and see them all trampled under the heel of opposing circumstances.

Nothing is easier than to make an ideal garden. We lay out our grounds, dig, plant, transplant, manure. We read catalogues of roses till we are bewildered with their lustrous glories. We set out plum, pear, and peach, we luxuriate in advance on bushels of choicest grapes, and our theoretic garden is Paradise Regained. But in the actual garden there are cut-worms for every cabbage, squash-bugs for all the melons, slugs and rose-bugs for the roses, curculios for the plums, fire-blight for pears, yellows for peaches, mildew for grapes, and late and early frosts, droughts, winds, and hail-storms here and there for all.

The garden and the family are fair pictures of each other. Both are capable of the most ravishing representations on paper; and the rules and directions for creating beauty and perfection in both can be made so apparently plain that he who runneth may read, and it would seem that a fool need not err therein; and yet the actual results are always halting miles away behind expectation and desire.

It would be an incalculable gain to domestic happiness, if people would begin the concert of life with their instruments tuned to a very low pitch: they who receive the most happiness are generally they who demand and expect the least.

Ideality often becomes an insidious mental and moral disease, acting all the more subtly from its alliances with what is highest and noblest within us. Shall we not aspire to be perfect? Shall we be content with low measures and low standards in anything? To these inquiries there seems of course to be but one answer; yet the individual driven forward in blind, unreasoning aspiration becomes wearied, bewildered, discontented, restless, fretful, and miserable.

An unhappy person can never make others happy. The creators and governors of a home, who are themselves restless and inharmonious, cannot make harmony and peace. This is the secret reason why many a pure, good, conscientious person is only a source of uneasiness in family life. They are exacting, discontented, unhappy; and spread the discontent and unhappiness about them. They are, to begin with, on poor terms with themselves; they do not like themselves; they do not like their own appearance, manners, education, accomplishments; on all these points they try themselves by ideal standards, and find themselves wanting. In morals, in religion, too, the same introverted scrutiny detects only errors and evils, till all life seems to them a miserable, hopeless failure, and they wish they had never been born. They are angry and disgusted with themselves; there is no self-toleration or self-endurance. And persons in a chronic quarrel with themselves are very apt to quarrel with others. That exacting nature which has no patience with one's own inevitable frailties and errors has none for those of others; and thus the great motive by which Christianity enforces tolerance of the faults of others loses its hold. There are people who make no allowances either for themselves or anybody else, but are equally angry and disgusted with both.

Now it is important that those finely strung natures in which ideality largely predominates should begin life by a religious care and restraint of this faculty. As the case often stands, however, religion only intensifies the difficulty, by adding stringency to exaction and censoriousness, driving the subject up with an unremitting strain till the very cords of reason sometimes snap. Yet, properly understood and used, religion is the only cure for the evil of diseased ideality. The Christian religion is the only one that ever proposed to give to all human beings, however various the range of their nature and desires, the great underlying gift of *rest*. Its Author, with a strength of assurance which only supreme Divinity can justify, promises *rest* to all persons, under all circumstances, with all sorts of natures, all sorts of wants, and all sorts of defects. The invitation is as wide as the human race: "Come unto me, all ye that labor and are heavy-laden, and I will give you REST."

Now this is the more remarkable, as this gracious promise is accompanied by the presentation of a standard of perfection which is more ideal and exacting than any other that has ever been placed before mankind,—which, in so many words, sets up absolute perfection as the only true goal of aspiration.

The problem which Jesus proposes to human nature is endless aspiration steadied by endless peace,—a perfectly restful, yet unceasing effort after a good which is never to be attained till we attain a higher and more perfect form of existence. It is because this problem is insolvable by any human wisdom, that He says that they who take His yoke upon them must learn of Him, for He alone can make the perfect yoke easy and its burden light.

The first lesson in this benignant school must lie like a strong, broad foundation under every structure in which we wish to rear a happy life,—and that is, that the full gratification of the faculty of ideality is never to be expected in this present stage of existence, but is to be transferred to a future life. Ideality, with its incessant, restless longings and yearnings, is snubbed and turned out of doors by human philosophy, when philosophy becomes middle-aged and sulky with repeated disappointments,—it is berated as a cheat and a liar,—told to hold its tongue and take itself elsewhere; but Christianity bids it be of good cheer, still to aspire and hope and prophesy, and points to a future where all its dreams shall be outdone by reality.

A full faith in such a perfect future—a perfect faith that God has planted in man no desire which he cannot train to complete enjoyment in that future—gives the mind rest and contentment to postpone for a while gratifications that will certainly come at last.

Such a faith is better even than that native philosophical good sense which restrains the ideal calculations and hopes of some; for it has a wider scope and a deeper power.

We have seen in our time a woman gifted with all those faculties which rejoice in the refinements of society, dispensing the elegant hospitalities of a bountiful home, joyful and giving joy. A sudden reverse has swept all this away, the wealth on which it was based has melted like a fog-bank in a warm morning, and we have seen her with her little family beginning life again in the log-cabin of a Western settlement. We have seen her sitting in the door of the one room that took the place of parlor, bed-room, nursery, and cheerfully making her children's morning toilette by the help of the one tin wash-bowl that takes the place of her well-arranged bathing- and dressing-rooms; and yet, as she twined their curls over her fingers, she had a laugh and a jest and cheerful word for all. The few morning-glories that she was training over her rude porch seemed as much a source of delight to her as her former greenhouse and garden; and the adjustment of the one or two shelves whereon were the half-dozen books left of the library, her husband's private papers, and her own and her children's wardrobe, was entered into daily with a zealous interest as if she had never known a wider sphere.

Such facility of accommodation to life's reverses is sometimes supposed to be merely the result of a hopeful and cheerful temperament; in this case it was purely the work of religion. In early life, this same woman had been the discontented slave of ideality, had sighed with vain longings in the midst of real and substantial comfort, had felt even the creasing of the rose-leaves of her pillow an intolerable annoyance. Now she has resigned herself to the work and toil of life as the soldier does to the duties of the camp, satisfied to do and to bear, enjoying with a free heart the small daily pleasures which spring up like wild-flowers amid daily toils and annoyances, and looking to the end of the campaign for rest and congenial scenes.

This woman has within her the powers and gifts of an artist; but her pencils and her colors are resolutely laid away, and she sits hour after hour darning her children's stockings and turning and arranging a scanty wardrobe which no ingenuity can make more than decent. She was a beautiful musician; but a musical instrument is now a thing of the past; she only lulls her baby to sleep with snatches of the songs which used to form the attraction of brilliant salons. She feels that a world of tastes and talents are lying dormant in her while she is doing the daily work of a nurse, cook, and seamstress; but she remembers WHO took upon Him the form of a servant before her, and she has full faith that her beautiful gifts, like bulbs sleeping under ground, shall come up and blossom again in that fair future which He has promised. Therefore it is that she has no sighs for the present or the past,—no quarrel with her life, or her lot in it; she is in harmony with herself and with all around her; her husband looks upon her as a fair daily miracle, and her children rise up and call her blessed.

But, having laid the broad foundation of faith in a better life, as the basis on which to ground our present happiness, we who are of the ideal nature must proceed to build thereon wisely.

In the first place, we must cultivate the duty of *self-patience* and self-toleration. Of all the religionists and moralists who ever taught, Fénelon is the only one who has distinctly formulated the duty which a self-educator owes to himself. HAVE PATIENCE WITH YOURSELF is a direction often occurring in his writings, and a most important one it is,—because patience with ourselves is essential, if we would have patience with others. Let us look through the world. Who are the people easiest to be pleased, most sunny, most urbane, most tolerant? Are they not persons from constitution and temperament on good terms with themselves,—people who do not ask much of themselves or try themselves severely, and who therefore are in a good humor for looking upon others? But how is a person who is conscious of a hundred daily faults and errors to have patience with himself? The question may be answered by asking, What would you say to a child who fretted, scolded, dashed down his slate, and threw his book on the floor, because he made mistakes in his arithmetic? You would say, of course, "You are but a learner; it is not to be expected that you will not make mistakes; all children do. Have patience." Just as you would talk to that child, talk to yourself. Be reconciled to a lot of inevitable imperfection; be content to try continually, and often to fail. It is the inevitable condition of human existence, and is to be accepted as such. A patient acceptance of mortifications and of defeats of our life's labor is often more efficacious for our moral advancement than even our victories.

In the next place, we must school ourselves not to look with restless desire to degrees of excellence in any department of life which circumstances evidently forbid our attaining. For a woman with plenty of money and plenty of well-trained servants to be content to have fly-specked windows, or littered rooms, or a slovenly-ordered table, is a sin. But in a woman in feeble health, incumbered with a flock of restless little ones, and whose circumstances allow her to keep but one servant, it may be a piece of moral heroism to shut her eyes on many such things, while securing mere essentials to life and health. It may be a virtue in her not to push neatness to such lengths as to wear herself out, or to break down her only servant, and to be resigned to have her tastes and preferences for order, cleanliness, and beauty crossed, as she would resign herself to any other affliction. No purgatory can be more severe to people of a thorough and exact nature than to be so situated that they can only half do everything they undertake; yet such is the fiery trial to which many a one is subjected. Life seems to drive them along without giving them time for anything; everything is ragged, hasty performance, of which the mind most keenly sees and feels the raggedness and hastiness. Even one thing done as it really ought to be done would be a rest and refreshment to the soul; but nowhere, in any department of its undertakings, is there any such thing to be perceived.

But there are cases where a great deal of wear and tear can be saved to the nerves by a considerate making up of one's mind as to how much in certain circumstances had better be undertaken at all. Let the circumstances of life be surveyed, the objects we are pursuing arranged and counted, and see if there are not things here and there that may be thrown out of our plans entirely, that others may be better done.

What if the whole care of expensive table luxuries, like cake and preserves, be thrown out of a housekeeper's budget, in order that the essential articles of cookery may be better prepared? What if ruffling, embroidery, and the entire department of kindred fine arts, be thrown out of her calculations, in providing for the clothing of a family? Many a feeble woman has died of too much ruffling, as she patiently sat up night after night sewing the thread of a precious, invaluable life into elaborate articles which her children were none the healthier or more virtuous for wearing.

Ideality is constantly ramifying and extending the department of the toilette and the needle into a world of work and worry, wherein distracted women wander up and down, seeing no end anywhere. The sewing-machine was announced as a relief to these toils; but has it proved so? We trow not. It only amounts to this,—that now there can be seventy-two tucks on each little petticoat, instead of fifteen, as before, and that twice as many garments are made up and held to be necessary as formerly. The women still sew to the limit of human endurance; and still the old proverb holds good, that woman's work is never done.

In the matter of dress, much wear and tear of spirit and nerves may be saved by not beginning to go in certain directions, well knowing that they will take us beyond our resources of time, strength, and money.

There is one word of fear in the vocabulary of women of our time which must be pondered advisedly,—TRIMMING. In old times a good garment was enough; now-a-days a garment is nothing without trimming. Everything, from the first article that the baby wears up to the elaborate dress of the bride, must be trimmed at a rate that makes the trimming more than the original article. A dress can be made in a day, but it cannot be trimmed under two or three days. Let a faithful, conscientious woman make up her mind how much of all this burden of life she will assume, remembering wisely that there is no end to ideality in anything, and that the only way to deal with many perplexing parts of life is to leave them out altogether.

Mrs. Kirkland, in her very amusing account of her log-cabin experiences,[3] tells us of the great disquiet and inconvenience she had in attempting to arrange in her lowly abode a most convenient clothes-press, which was manifestly too large for the establishment. Having labored with the cumbersome convenience for a great length of time, and with much discomfort, she at last resigned the ordering of it to a brawny-armed damsel of the forest, who began by pitching it out of doors, with the comprehensive remark, that, "where there was n't room for a thing, there was n't."

The wisdom which inspired the remark of this rustic maiden might have saved the lives of many matrons who have worn themselves out in vain attempts to make comforts and conveniences out of things which they had better have thrown out of doors altogether.

True, it requires some judgment to know what, among objects commonly pursued in any department, we really ought to reject; and it requires independence and steadiness to say, "I will not begin to try to do certain things that others are doing, and that, perhaps, they expect of me"; but there comes great leisure and quietness of spirit from the gaps thus made. When the unwieldy clothes-press was once cast out, everything in the log-cabin could have room.

A mother, who is anxiously trying to reconcile the watchful care and training of her little ones with the maintenance of fashionable calls and parties, may lose her life in the effort to do both, and do both in so imperfect a manner as never to give her a moment's peace. But on the morrow after she comes to the serious and Christian resolve, "The training of my children is all that I *can* do well, and henceforth it shall be my *sole* object," there falls into her tumultuous life a Sabbath pause of peace and leisure. It is true that she is still doing a work in which absolute per-

[3]Caroline Kirkland's *A New Home—Who'll Follow?* (1839) describes in realistic detail the rigors of pioneer life in the West.

fection ever recedes; but she can make relative attainments far nearer the standard than before.

Lastly, under the head of ideality let us resolve *to be satisfied with our own past doings, when at the time of doing we used all the light God gave us, and did all in our power.*

The backward action of ideality is often full as tormenting as its forward and prospective movements. The moment a thing is done and over, one would think that good sense would lead us to drop it like a stone in the ocean; but the morbid idealist cannot cut loose from the past.

"Was that, after all, the *best* thing? Would it not have been better so or so?" And the self-tormented individual lies wakeful, during weary night-hours, revolving a thousand possibilities, and conjuring up a thousand vague perhapses. "If I had only done *so* now, perhaps this result would have followed, or that would not"; and as there is never any saying but that so it might have turned out, the labyrinth and the discontent are alike endless.

Now there is grand good sense in the Apostle's direction, "Forgetting the things that are behind, press forward." The idealist should charge himself, as with an oath of God, to let the past alone as an accomplished fact, solely concerning himself with the inquiry, "Did I not do the best I *then* knew how?"

The maxim of the Quietists[4] is, that, when we have acted according to the best light we have, we have expressed the will of God under those circumstances,—since, had it been otherwise, more and different light would have been given us; and with the will of God done by ourselves as by Himself, it is our duty to be content.

Having written thus far in my article, and finding nothing more at hand to add to it, I went into the parlor to read it to Jenny and Mrs. Crowfield. I found the former engaged in the task of binding sixty yards of quilling, (so I think she called it,) which were absolutely necessary for perfecting a dress; and the latter was braiding one of seven little petticoats, stamped with elaborate patterns, which she had taken from Marianne, because that virtuous matron was ruining her eyes and health in a blind push to get them done before October.

Both approved and admired my piece, and I thought of Saint Anthony's preaching to the fishes:—

> The sermon now ended,
> Each turned and descended;
> The pikes went on stealing,
> The eels went on eeling.
>     Much delighted were they,
>     But preferred the old way.

---

[4]Seventeenth-century mystics who believed that perfection lay in the complete passivity of the soul before God, a total absence of self-will.

# Home Decoration

When Catharine Beecher's *A Treatise on Domestic Economy* (1843) was reissued in 1869 under the title *The American Woman's Home*, it included several new chapters written by Harriet Beecher Stowe. In this selection from chapter 6 on "Home Decoration," Stowe exhibits both her love of shaping domestic space and her awareness of Gilded Age temptations to excess. As in all of her domestic writing, her target audience is the middle class.

 aving duly arranged for the physical necessities of a healthful and comfortable home, we next approach the important subject of *beauty* in reference to the decoration of houses. For while the aesthetic element must be subordinate to the requirements of physical existence, and, as a matter of expense, should be held of inferior consequence to means of higher moral growth; it yet holds a place of great significance among the influences which make home happy and attractive, which give it a constant and wholesome power over the young, and contributes much to the education of the entire household in refinement, intellectual development, and moral sensibility.

Here we are met by those who tell us that of course they want their houses handsome, and that, when they get money enough, they intend to have them so, but at present they are too poor, and because they are poor they dismiss the subject altogether, and live without any regard to it.

We have often seen people who said that they could not afford to make their houses beautiful, who had spent upon them, outside or in, an amount of money which did not produce either beauty or comfort, and which, if judiciously applied, might have made the house quite charming.

For example, a man, in building his house, takes a plan of an architect. This plan includes, on the outside, a number of what Andrew Fairservice called "curly-wurlies" and "whigmaliries," which make the house neither prettier nor more comfortable, and which take up a good deal of money. We would venture to say that we could buy the chromo of Bierstadt's "Sunset in the Yo Semite Valley," and four others like it, for half the sum that we have sometimes seen laid out on a very ugly, narrow, awkward porch on the outside of a house. The only use of this porch was to cost money, and to cause every body who looked at it to exclaim as

Pages 84–91, from *An American Woman's Home* (1869).

they went by, "What ever induced that man to put a thing like that on the outside of his house?"

Then, again, in the inside of houses, we have seen a dwelling looking very bald and bare, when a sufficient sum of money had been expended on one article to have made the whole very pretty: and it has come about in this way.

We will suppose the couple who own the house to be in the condition in which people generally are after they have built a house—having spent more than they could afford on the building itself, and yet feeling themselves under the necessity of getting some furniture.

"Now," says the housewife, "I must at least have a parlor-carpet. We must get that to begin with, and other things as we go on." She goes to a store to look at carpets. The clerks are smiling and obliging, and sweetly complacent. The storekeeper, perhaps, is a neighbor or a friend, and after exhibiting various patterns, he tells her of a Brussels carpet he is selling wonderfully cheap—actually a dollar and a quarter less a yard than the usual price of Brussels, and the reason is that it is an unfashionable pattern, and he has a good deal of it, and wishes to close it off.

She looks at it and thinks it is not at all the kind of carpet she meant to buy, but then it is Brussels, and so cheap! And as she hesitates, her friend tells her that she will find it "cheapest in the end—that one Brussels carpet will outlast three or four ingrains," etc., etc.

The result of all this is, that she buys the Brussels carpet, which, with all its reduction in price, is one third dearer than the ingrain would have been, and not half so pretty. When she comes home, she will find that she has spent, we will say eighty dollars, for a very homely carpet whose greatest merit it is an affliction to remember—namely, that it will outlast three ordinary carpets. And because she has bought this carpet she can not afford to paper the walls or put up any window-curtains, and can not even begin to think of buying any pictures.

Now let us see what eighty dollars could have done for that room. We will suppose, in the first place, she invests in thirteen rolls of wall-paper of a lovely shade of buff, which will make the room look sunshiny in the day-time, and light up brilliantly in the evening. Thirteen rolls of good satin paper, at thirty-seven cents a roll, expends four dollars and eighty-one cents. A maroon bordering, made in imitation of the choicest French style, which can not at a distance be told from it, can be bought for six cents a yard. This will bring the paper to about five dollars and a half; and our friends will give a day of their time to putting it on. The room already begins to look furnished.

Then, let us cover the floor with, say, thirty yards of good matting, at fifty cents a yard. This gives us a carpet for fifteen dollars. We are here stopped by the prejudice that matting is not good economy, because it wears out so soon. We humbly submit that it is precisely the thing for a parlor, which is reserved for the reception-room of friends, and for our own dressed leisure hours. Matting is not good economy in a dining-room or a hard-worn sitting-room; but such a parlor as we are describing is precisely the place where it answers to the very best advantage.

We have in mind one very attractive parlor which has been, both for summer and winter, the daily sitting-room for the leisure hours of a husband and wife, and family of children, where a plain straw matting has done service for seven years. That parlor is in a city, and these friends are in the habit of receiving visits from people who live upon velvet and Brussels; but they prefer to spend the money which such carpets would cost on other modes of embellishment; and this parlor has often been cited to us as a very attractive room.

And now our friends, having got thus far, are requested to select some one tint or color which shall be the prevailing one in the furniture of the room. Shall it be green? Shall it be blue? Shall it be crimson? To carry on our illustration, we will choose green, and we proceed with it to create furniture for our room. Let us imagine that on one side of the fireplace there be, as there is often, a recess about six feet long and three feet deep. Fill this recess with a rough frame with four stout legs, one foot high, and upon the top of the frame have an elastic rack of slats. Make a mattress for this, or, if you wish to avoid that trouble, you can get a nice mattress for the sum of two dollars, made of cane-shavings or husks. Cover this with a green English furniture print. The glazed English comes at about twenty-five cents a yard, the glazed French at seventy-five cents a yard, and a nice article of yard-wide French twill (very strong) is from seventy-five to eighty cents a yard.

With any of these cover your lounge. Make two large, square pillows of the same substance as the mattress, and set up at the back. If you happen to have one or two feather pillows that you can spare for the purpose, shake them down into a square shape and cover them with the same print, and you will then have four pillows for your lounge—one at each end, and two at the back, and you will find it answers for all the purposes of a sofa.

It will be a very pretty thing, now, to cut out of the same material as your lounge, sets of lambrequins (or, as they are called, *lamberkins*), a kind of pendent curtain-top . . . to put over the windows, which are to be embellished with white muslin curtains. The cornices to your windows can be simply strips of wood covered with paper to match the bordering of your room, and the lambrequins, made of chintz like the lounge, can be trimmed with fringe or gimp of the same color. The patterns of these can be varied according to fancy, but simple designs are usually the prettiest. A tassel at the lowest point improves the appearance.

The curtains can be made of plain white muslin, or some of the many styles that come for this purpose. If plain muslin is used, you can ornament them with hems an inch in width, in which insert a strip of gingham or chambray of the same color as your chintz. This will wash with the curtains without losing its color, or should it fade, it can easily be drawn out and replaced.

The influence of white-muslin curtains in giving an air of grace and elegance to a room is astonishing. White curtains really create a room out of nothing. No matter how coarse the muslin, so it be white and hang in graceful folds, there is a charm in it that supplies the want of multitudes of other things.

Very pretty curtain-muslin can be bought at thirty-seven cents a yard. It requires six yards for a window.

Let your men-folk knock up for you, out of rough, unplaned boards, some ottoman frames, . . . stuff the tops with just the same material as the lounge, and cover them with the self-same chintz.

Now you have, suppose your selected color to be green, a green lounge in the corner and two green ottomans; you have white muslin curtains, with green lambrequins and borders, and your room already looks furnished. If you have in the house any broken-down arm-chair, reposing in the oblivion of the garret, draw it out—drive a nail here and there to hold it firm—stuff and pad, and stitch the padding through with a long upholsterer's needle, and cover it with the chintz like your other furniture. Presto—you create an easy-chair.

Thus can broken and disgraced furniture reappear, and, being put into uniform with the general suit of your room, take a new lease of life.

If you want a centre-table, consider this—that any kind of table, well concealed beneath the folds of *handsome drapery, of a color corresponding to the general hue of the room*, will look well. Instead of going to the cabinet-maker and paying from thirty to forty dollars upon a little, narrow, cold, marble-topped stand, that gives just room enough to hold a lamp and a book or two, reflect within yourself what a centre-table is made for. If you have in your house a good, broad, generous-topped table, take it, cover it with an ample cloth of green broadcloth. Such a cover, two and a half yards square, of fine green broadcloth, figured with black and with a pattern-border of grape-leaves, has been bought for ten dollars. In a room we wot of, it covers a cheap pine table, such as you may buy for four or five dollars any day; but you will be astonished to see how handsome an object this table makes under its green drapery. Probably you could make the cover more cheaply by getting the cloth and trimming its edge with a handsome border, selected for the purpose; but either way, it will be an economical and useful ornament. We set down our centre-table, therefore, as consisting mainly of a nice broadcloth cover, matching our curtains and lounge.

We are sure that any one with "a heart that is humble" may command such a centre-table and cloth for fifteen dollars or less, and a family of five or six may all sit and work, or read, or write around it, and it is capable of entertaining a generous allowance of books and knick-knacks.

You have now for your parlor the following figures:

| | |
|---|---:|
| Wall-paper and border, . . . . . . . . . . . . . . . . . . . . . . . . . . . . . . . . | $5 50 |
| Thirty yards matting, . . . . . . . . . . . . . . . . . . . . . . . . . . . . . . . . . . . | 15 00 |
| Centre-table and cloth, . . . . . . . . . . . . . . . . . . . . . . . . . . . . . . . . . | 15 00 |
| Muslin for three windows, . . . . . . . . . . . . . . . . . . . . . . . . . . . . . . | 6 75 |
| Thirty yards green English chintz, at 25 cents, . . . . . . . . . . . . . . . . | 7 50 |
| Six chairs, at $2 each, . . . . . . . . . . . . . . . . . . . . . . . . . . . . . . . . . . | 12 00 |
| Total, . . . . . . . . . . . . . . . . . . . . . . . . . . . . . . . . . . . . . . . . . . . . . . | $61 75 |

Subtracted from eighty dollars, which we set down as the price of the cheap, ugly Brussels carpet, we have our whole room papered, carpeted, curtained, and furnished, and we have nearly twenty dollars remaining for pictures.

As a little suggestion in regard to the selection, you can get Miss Oakley's charming little cabinet picture of

"The Little Scrap-Book Maker" for . . . . . . . . . . . . . . . . . . . . . . . . . . . $7 50

Eastman Johnson's "Barefoot Boy," . . . . . . . . . . . . . . . . . . . . . .(Prang)   5 00

Newman's "Blue-fringed Gentians," . . . . . . . . . . . . . . . . . . . .(Prang)   6 00

Bierstadt's "Sunset in the Yo Semite Valley," . . . . . . . . . . . . . .(Prang) 12 00

Here are thirty dollars' worth of really admirable pictures of some of our best American artists, from which you can choose at your leisure. By sending to any leading picture-dealer, lists of pictures and prices will be forwarded to you. These chromos, being all varnished, can wait for frames until you can afford them. Or, what is better, because it is at once cheaper and a means of educating the ingenuity and the taste, you can make for yourselves pretty rustic frames in various modes. Take a very thin board, of the right size and shape, for the foundation or "mat;" saw out the inner oval or rectangular form to suit the picture. Nail on the edge a rustic frame made of branches of hard, seasoned wood, and garnish the corners with some pretty device; such, for instance, as a cluster of acorns; or, in place of the branches of trees, fasten on with glue small pine cones, with larger ones for corner ornaments. Or use the mosses of the wood or ocean shells for this purpose. It may be more convenient to get the mat or inner moulding from a framer, or have it made by your carpenter, with a groove behind to hold a glass. . . . Besides the American and the higher range of German and English chromos, there are very many pretty little French chromos, which can be had at prices from $1 to $5, including black walnut frames.

We have been through this calculation merely to show our readers how much beautiful effect may be produced by a wise disposition of color and skill in arrangement. If any of our friends should ever carry it out, they will find that the buff paper, with its dark, narrow border; the green chintz repeated in the lounge, the ottomans, and lambrequins; the flowing, white curtains; the broad, generous centre-table, draped with its ample green cloth, will, when arranged together, produce an effect of grace and beauty far beyond what any one piece or even half a dozen pieces of expensive cabinet furniture could. The great, simple principle of beauty illustrated in this room is *harmony of color.*

# The True Story of Lady Byron's Life

In "The True Story of Lady Byron's Life," Stowe exposed the dark side of the home: incest. On her second trip to England, in 1856, Stowe had become the confidant of Lady Byron, who revealed the sordid details of Lord Byron's liaison with his half sister, Augusta Leigh. Lady Byron sought Stowe's advice. Should she explain the reasons for her separation from her husband, or continue to bear in silence the blame for the failed marriage? Stowe counseled silence, reminding Lady Byron of the pain that public exposure would entail. Years later, after Lady Byron's death, when yet another unflattering portrayal of Lady Byron appeared, this time in a book by Byron's mistress, the Countess Guiccioli, Stowe told all.

At a time when Elizabeth Cady Stanton and Susan B. Anthony were using popular scandals to call attention to the sexual double standard, Stowe undertook to expose the hypocrisy of Lord Byron and defend the reputation of her friend. She unflinchingly reviewed the history of a relationship in which the much-idealized home was in fact the scene of male cruelty, drunkenness, incest, and the squandering of Lady Byron's inheritance. In spite of Stowe's courageous embrace of these realities—which brought down on her a storm of vituperation and caused the *Atlantic Monthly* a precipitous decline in circulation—she held fast to the Victorian ideology of "pure womanhood."

The reading world of America has lately been presented with a book, which is said to sell rapidly, and which appears to meet with universal favor.

The subject of the book may be thus briefly stated: the mistress of Lord Byron comes before the world for the sake of vindicating his fame from slanders and aspersions cast on him by his wife. The story of the mistress *versus* wife may be summed up as follows:—

Lord Byron, the hero of the story, is represented as a human being endowed with every natural charm, gift, and grace, who by the one false step of an unsuitable marriage wrecked his whole life. A narrow-minded, cold-hearted precisian, without sufficient intellect to comprehend his genius or heart to feel for his temptations, formed with him one of those mere worldly marriages common in high life, and, finding that she could not reduce him to the mathematical proprieties and conventional rules of her own mode of life, suddenly and without warning abandoned him in the most cruel and inexplicable manner.

531

It is alleged that she parted from him in apparent affection and good-humor, wrote him a playful, confiding letter upon the way, but, after reaching her father's house, suddenly and without explanation announced to him that she would never see him again; that this sudden abandonment drew down upon him a perfect storm of scandalous stories, which his wife never contradicted; that she never in any way or shape stated what the exact reasons for her departure had been, and thus silently gave scope to all the malice of thousands of enemies. The sensitive victim was actually driven from England, his home broken up, and he doomed to be a lonely wanderer on foreign shores.

In Italy, under bluer skies and among a gentler people, with more tolerant modes of judgment, the authoress intimates that he found peace and consolation. A lovely young Italian countess falls in love with him, and breaking her family ties for his sake, devotes herself to him, and in blissful retirement with her he finds at last that domestic life for which he was so fitted.

Soothed, calmed, and refreshed, he writes Don Juan, which the world is at this late hour informed was a poem with a high moral purpose, designed to be a practical illustration of the doctrine of total depravity among young gentlemen in high life.

Under the elevating influence of love, he rises at last to higher realms of moral excellence, and resolves to devote the rest of his life to some noble and heroic purpose, becomes the savior of Greece, and dies untimely, leaving a nation to mourn his loss.

The authoress dwells with a peculiar bitterness on Lady Byron's entire *silence* during all these years, as the most aggravated form of persecution and injury. She informs the world that Lord Byron wrote his autobiography with the purpose of giving a fair statement of the exact truth in the whole matter, and that Lady Byron bought up the manuscript of the publisher and insisted on its being destroyed unread, thus inflexibly depriving her husband of his last chance of a hearing before the tribunal of the public.

As a result of this silent, persistent cruelty on the part of a cold, correct, narrow-minded woman, the character of Lord Byron has been misunderstood, and his name transmitted to after ages clouded with aspersions and accusations which it is the object of this book to remove.

Such is the story of Lord Byron's mistress,—a story which is going the length of this American continent and rousing up new sympathy with the poet, and doing its best to bring the youth of America once more under the power of that brilliant, seductive genius from which it was hoped they had escaped. Already we are seeing it revamped in magazine articles, which take up the slanders of the paramour and enlarge on them and wax eloquent in denunciation of the marble-hearted, insensible wife.

All this while it does not appear to occur to the thousands of unreflecting readers that they are listening merely to the story of Lord Byron's mistress and of Lord Byron, and that even by their own showing their heaviest accusation against Lady Byron is that *she has not spoken at all*; her story has never been told.

For many years after the rupture between Lord Byron and his wife, that poet's personality, fate, and happiness, had an interest for the whole civilized world, which we will venture to say was unparalleled. It is within the writer's recollection, how, in the obscure mountain town where she spent her early days, Lord Byron's separation from his wife was for a season the all-engrossing topic.

She remembers hearing her father recount at the breakfast-table the facts as they were given in the public papers, together with his own suppositions and theories of the causes.

Lord Byron's "Fare thee well," addressed to Lady Byron, was set to music and sung with tears by young school-girls, even in this distant America.

Madame de Staël said of this appeal, that she was sure it would have drawn her at once to his heart and his arms: *she* could have forgiven everything; and so said all the young ladies all over the world, not only in England, but in France and Germany,—wherever Byron's poetry appeared in translation.

Lady Byron's obdurate cold-heartedness in refusing even to listen to his prayers or to have any intercourse with him which might lead to reconciliation, was the one point conceded on all sides.

The stricter moralists defended her, but gentler hearts throughout all the world regarded her as a marble-hearted monster of correctness and morality, a personification of the law unmitigated by the gospel.

Literature in its highest walks busied itself with Lady Byron. Wilson, in the character of the Ettrick Shepherd, devotes several eloquent passages to expatiating on the conjugal fidelity of a poor Highland shepherd's wife, who, by patience and prayer and forgiveness, succeeds in reclaiming her drunken husband and making a good man of him; and then points his moral by contrasting with this touching picture the cold-hearted, pharisaical correctness of Lady Byron.

Moore, in his "Life of Lord Byron," when beginning the recital of the series of disgraceful amours which formed the staple of his life in Venice, has this passage:—

> Highly censurable, in point of morality and decorum, as was his course of life while under the roof of Madame * * *, it was (with pain, I am forced to confess) venial in comparison with the strange, headlong career of license to which, when weaned from that connection, he so unrestrainedly and, it may be added, defyingly abandoned himself. Of the state of his mind on leaving England, I have already endeavored to convey some idea, and among the feelings that went to make up that self-centred spirit of resistance which he then opposed to his fate, was an indignant scorn for his own countrymen for the wrongs he thought they had done him. For a time *the kindly sentiments which he still harbored toward Lady Byron, and a sort of vague hope, perhaps, that all would yet come right again*, kept his mind in a mood somewhat more softened and docile, as well as sufficiently under the influence of English opinions to prevent his breaking out into open rebellion against it, as he unluckily did afterward.
>
> *By the failure of the attempted mediation with Lady Byron*, his last link with home was severed; while, notwithstanding the quiet and unobstrusive life which he led at Geneva, there was as yet, he found, no cessation of the slanderous warfare against his character; the same busy and misrepresenting spirit which had tracked his every step at home, having, with no less malicious watchfulness, dogged him into exile.

We should like to know what the misrepresentations and slanders must have been, when this sort of thing is admitted in Mr. Moore's *justification*. It seems to us rather wonderful how anybody, unless it were a person like the Countess

Guiccioli, could misrepresent a life such as even Byron's friend admits he was leading.

During all these years, when he was setting at defiance every principle of morality and decorum, the interest of the female mind all over Europe in the conversion of this brilliant prodigal son was unceasing, and reflects the greatest credit upon the faith of the sex.

Madame de Staël commenced the first effort at evangelization immediately after he left England, and found her catechumen in a most edifying state of humility. He was metaphorically on his knees in penitence, and confessed himself a miserable sinner in the loveliest manner possible. Such sweetness and humility took all hearts. His conversations with Madame de Staël were printed and circulated all over the world, making it to appear that only the inflexibility of Lady Byron stood in the way of his entire conversion.

Lady Blessington, among many others, took him in hand five or six years afterward, and was greatly delighted with his docility and edified by his frank and free confessions of his miserable offences. Nothing now seemed wanting to bring the wanderer home to the fold, but a kind word from Lady Byron. But, when the fair Countess offered to mediate, the poet only shook his head in tragic despair; "he had so many times tried in vain; Lady Byron's course had been from the first that of obdurate silence."

Any one who would wish to see a specimen of the skill of the honorable poet in mystification will do well to read a letter to Lady Byron, which Lord Byron, on parting from Lady Blessington, enclosed for her to read just before he went to Greece. He says:—

> The letter which I enclose *I was prevented from sending, by my despair of its doing any good*. I was perfectly sincere when I wrote it, and am so still. But it is difficult for me to withstand the thousand provocations on that subject which both friends and foes have for seven years been throwing in the way of a man whose feelings were once quick, and whose temper was never patient.

TO LADY BYRON, CARE OF THE HON. MRS. LEIGH, LONDON

Pisa, November, 17, 1821

> I have to acknowledge the receipt of 'Ada's hair,' which is very soft and pretty, and nearly as dark already as mine was at twelve years old, if I may judge from what I recollect of some in Augusta's possession, taken at that age. But it don't curl,—perhaps from its being let grow.
>
> I also thank you for the inscription of the date and name, and I will tell you why;— I believe that they are the only two or three words of your hand-writing in my possession. For your letters I returned, and except the two words, or rather the one word, 'Household,' written twice in an old account-book, I have no other. I burnt your last note, for two reasons: firstly, it was written in a style not very agreeable; and, secondly, I wished to take your word without documents, which are the worldly resources of suspicious people.
>
> I suppose that this note will reach you somewhere about Ada's birthday—the 10th of December, I believe. She will then be six, so that in about twelve more I shall have some chance of meeting her;—perhaps sooner, if I am obliged to go to England by

business or otherwise. Recollect, however, one thing, either in distance or nearness;—every day which keeps us asunder should, after so long a period, rather soften our mutual feelings, which must always have one rallying-point as long as our child exists, which I presume we both hope will be long after either of her parents.

The time which has elapsed since the separation has been considerably more than the whole brief period of our union, and the not much longer one of our prior acquaintance. We both made a bitter mistake; but now it is over, and irrevocably so. For, at thirty-three on my part and a few years less on yours, though it is no very extended period of life, still it is one when the habits and thought are generally so formed as to admit of no modification; and as we could not agree when younger, we should with difficulty do so now.

I say all this, because I own to you, that, notwithstanding everything, I considered our reunion as not impossible for more than a year after the separation;—but then I gave up the hope entirely and forever. But this very impossibility of reunion seems to me at least a reason why, on all the few points of discussion which can arise between us, we should preserve the courtesies of life, and as much of its kindness as people who are never to meet may preserve perhaps more easily than nearer connections. For my own part, I am violent, but not malignant; for only fresh provocations can awaken my resentments. To you, who are colder and more concentrated, I would just hint, that you may sometimes mistake the depth of a cold anger for dignity, and a worse feeling for duty. I assure you that I bear you *now* (whatever I may have done) no resentment whatever. Remember that, *if you have injured me* in aught, this forgiveness is something; and that, if I have *injured you*, it is something more still, if it be true, as the moralists say, that the most offending are the least forgiving.

Whether the offence has been solely on my side, or reciprocal, or on yours chiefly, I have ceased to reflect upon any but two things, viz. that you are the mother of my child, and that we shall never meet again. I think if you also consider the two corresponding points with reference to myself, it will be better for all three.

Yours ever,
Noel Byron.

The artless Thomas Moore introduces this letter in the "Life," with the remark:—

> There are few, I should think, of my readers, who will not agree with me in pronouncing that, if the author of the following letter had not *right* on his side, he had at least most of those good feelings which are found in general to accompany it.

The reader is requested to take notice of the important admission that *the letter was never sent to Lady Byron at all.* It was, in fact, never *intended* for her, but was a nice little dramatic performance, composed simply with the view of acting on the sympathies of Lady Blessington and Byron's numerous female admirers; and the reader will agree with us, we think, that in this point of view it was very neatly done and deserves immortality as a work of high art. For six years he had been plunging into every kind of vice and excess, pleading his shattered domestic joys, and his wife's obdurate heart, as the apology and the impelling cause; filling the air with his shrieks and complaints concerning the slanders which pursued him, while he filled letters to his confidential correspondents with records of new mistresses. During all these years the silence of Lady Byron was unbroken, though Lord Byron not only drew in private on the sympathies of his female admirers, but employed his talents and position as an author in holding her up to contempt and ridicule, before thousands of readers. We shall quote at length his side of the story, which he published in the first Canto of Don Juan, that the reader may see how much reason he had for assuming the injured tone which he did in the letter to Lady Byron quoted above. That letter never was sent to her, and the unmanly and indecent caricature of her, and the indelicate exposure of the whole story on his own side which we are about to quote, were the only communications that could have reached her solitude.

In the following verses, Lady Byron is represented as Donna Inez, and Lord Byron as Don Jose; but the incidents and allusions were so very pointed, that nobody for a moment doubted whose history the poet was narrating.

> "His mother was a learned lady, famed
> For every branch of every science known—
> In every Christian language ever named,
> With virtues equalled by her wit alone:
> She made the cleverest people quite ashamed,
> And even the good with inward envy groaned,
> Finding themselves so very much exceeded
> In their own way, by all the things that she did.
>
> . . . . .
>
> "Her favorite science was the mathematical,
> Her noblest virtue was her magnanimity,
> Her wit (she sometimes tried at wit) was Attic all,
> Her serious sayings darkened to sublimity;
> In short, in all things she was fairly what I call
> A prodigy,—her morning-dress was dimity,
> Her evening, silk, or in the summer, muslin
> And other stuffs, with which I won't stay puzzling.
>
> . . . . .
>
> "Some women use their tongues,—she looked a lecture,
> Each eye a sermon, and her brow a homily,
> And all in all sufficient self-director,
> Like the lamented late Sir Samuel Romilly;
>
> . . . . .
>
> "In short she was a walking calculation—
> Miss Edgeworth's novels stepping from their covers,
> Or Mrs. Trimmer's books on education,
> Or Cœleb's wife set out in quest of lovers.
> Morality's prim personification,
> In which not envy's self a flaw discovers.
> To others' share 'let female errors fall,'
> For she had not even one,—the worst of all.
>
> "O, she was perfect, past all parallel
> Of any modern female saint's comparison;
> So far above the cunning powers of hell
> Her guardian angel had given up his garrison;
> Even her minutest motions went as well

As those of the best time-piece made by Harrison.
In virtues nothing earthly could surpass her
Save thine 'incomparable oil,' Macassar.

"Perfect she was, but as perfection is
Insipid in this naughty world of ours,—

    •   •   •   •   •

Don-Jose like a lineal son of Eve
Went plucking various fruits without her leave.

"He was a mortal of the careless kind,
With no great love for learning or the learn'd,
Who chose to go where'er he had a mind,
And never dreamed his lady was concerned;
The world, as usual, wickedly inclined
To see a kingdom or a house o'erturned,
Whispered he had a mistress, some said *two*,
But for domestic quarrels *one* will do.

"Now Donna Inez had, with all her merit,
A great opinion of her own good qualities,
Neglect indeed requires a saint to bear it,
And such indeed she was in her moralities;
But then she had a devil of a spirit,
And sometimes mixed up fancies with realities,
And let few opportunities escape,
Of getting her liege lord into a scrape.

"This was an easy matter with a man
Oft in the wrong, and never on his guard,
And even the wisest, do the best they can,
Have moments, hours, and days so unprepared,
That you might 'brain them with their lady's fan,'
And sometimes ladies hit exceeding hard,
And fans turn into falchions in fair hands,
And why and wherefore no one understands.

"'T is a pity learned virgins ever wed
With persons of no sort of education;
Or gentlemen, who, though well-born and bred,
Grow tired of scientific conversation.
I don't choose to say much upon this head;
I'm a plain man, and in a single station,
But oh! ye lords of ladies intellectual,
Inform us truly, have they not henpecked you all?

    •   •   •   •   •

"Don Jose and the Donna Inez led
For some time an unhappy sort of life,
Wishing each other not divorced, but dead;
They lived respectably as man and wife,
Their conduct was exceedingly well-bred,

> And gave no outward sign of inward strife,
> Until at length the smothered fire broke out,
> And put the business past all kind of doubt.
>
> "For Inez called some druggists and physicians,
> And tried to prove her loving lord was *mad*;
> But as he had some lucid intermissions,
> She next decided he was only *bad*.
> Yet when they asked her for her depositions,
> No sort of explanation could be had,
> Save that her duty both to man and God
> Required this conduct, which seemed very odd.
>
> "She kept a journal where his faults were noted,
> And opened certain trunks of books and letters,
> All which might, if occasion served, be quoted.
> And then she had all Seville for abettors,
> Besides her good old grandmother (who doted);
> The hearers of her case became repeaters,
> Then advocates, inquisitors, and judges,
> Some for amusement, others for old grudges.
>
> "And then this best and meekest woman bore
> With such serenity her husband's woes;
> Just as the Spartan ladies did of yore,
> Who saw their spouses killed, and nobly chose
> Never to say a word about them more.
> Calmly she heard each calumny that rose,
> And saw *his* agonies with such sublimity,
> That all the word exclaimed, 'What magnanimity!' "

This is the longest and most elaborate version of his own story that Byron ever published; but he busied himself with many others, projecting at one time a Spanish Romance, in which the same story is related in the same transparent manner; but this he was dissuaded from printing. The booksellers, however, made a good speculation in publishing what they called his domestic poems,—that is, poems bearing more or less relation to this subject.

Every person with whom he became acquainted, with any degree of intimacy, was made familiar with his side of the story. Moore's biography is from first to last, in its representations, founded upon Byron's communicativeness and Lady Byron's silence; and the world at last settled down to believing that the account so often repeated and never contradicted must be substantially a true one.

The true history of Lord and Lady Byron has long been perfectly understood in many circles in England, but the facts were of a nature that could not be made public. While there was a young daughter living, whose future might be prejudiced by its recital, and while there were other persons on whom the disclosure of the real truth would have been crushing as an avalanche, Lady Byron's only course was the perfect silence in which she took refuge, and those sublime works of charity and mercy to which she consecrated her blighted earthly life.

But the time is now come when the truth may be told. All the actors in the scene have disappeared from the stage of mortal existence, and passed, let us have faith to hope, into a world where they would desire to expiate their faults by a late publication of the truth.

No person in England, we think, would as yet take the responsibility of relating the true history which is to clear Lady Byron's memory. But, by a singular concurrence of circumstances, all the facts of the case, in the most undeniable and authentic form, were at one time placed in the hands of the writer of this sketch, with authority to make such use of them as she should judge best. Had this melancholy history been allowed to sleep, no public use would have been made of them; but the appearance of a popular attack on the character of Lady Byron calls for a vindication, and the true story of her married life will, therefore, now be related.

Lord Byron has described, in one of his letters, the impression left upon his mind by a young person whom he met one evening in society, and who attracted his attention by the simplicity of her dress, and a certain air, of singular purity and calmness, with which she surveyed the scene around her.

On inquiry, he was told that this young person was Miss Milbanke, an only child, and one of the largest heiresses in England.

Lord Byron was fond of idealizing his experiences in poetry, and the friends of Lady Byron had no difficulty in recognizing the portrait of Lady Byron, as she appeared at this time of her life, in his exquisite description of Aurora Raby.

> "There was
> Indeed a certain fair and fairy one,
> Of the best class, and better than her class,—
> Aurora Raby, a young star who shone
> O'er life, too sweet an image for such glass,
> A lovely being scarcely formed or moulded,
> A rose with all its sweetest leaves yet folded.
>
> •   •   •   •   •
>
> "Early in years, and yet more infantine
> In figure, she had something of sublime
> In eyes which sadly shone, as seraphs' shine.
> All youth, but with an aspect beyond time;
> Radiant and grave, as pitying man's decline;
> Mournful, but mournful of another's crime,
> She looked as if she sat by Eden's door,
> And grieved for those who could return no more.
>
> •   •   •   •   •
>
> "She gazed upon a world she scarcely knew,
> As seeking not to know it; silent, lone,
> As grows a flower, thus quietly she grew,
> And kept her heart serene within its zone.
> There was awe in the homage which she drew;
> Her spirit seemed as seated on a throne,
> Apart from the surrounding world, and strong
> In its own strength, most strange in one so young!"

Some idea of the course which their acquaintance took, and of the manner in which he was piqued into thinking of her is given in a stanza or two.

"The dashing and proud air of Adeline
Imposed not upon her; she saw her blaze
Much as she would have seen a glow-worm shine;
Then turned unto the stars for loftier rays.
Juan was something she could not divine,
Being no sibyl in the new world's ways;
Yet she was nothing dazzled by the meteor,
Because she did not pin her faith on feature.

"His fame, too, for he had that kind of fame
Which sometimes plays the deuce with womankind,
A heterogeneous mass of glorious blame,
Half virtues and whole vices being combined;
Faults which attract because they are not tame;
Follies tricked out so brightly that they blind;
These seals upon her wax made no impression,
Such was her coldness or her self-possession.

     •   •   •   •   •

"Aurora sat with that indifference
Which piques a *preux* chevalier,—as it ought.
Of all offences that 's the worst offence,
Which seems to hint you are not worth a thought.

     •   •   •   •   •

"To his gay nothings, nothing was replied,
Or something which was nothing, as urbanity
Required. Aurora scarcely looked aside,
Nor even smiled enough for any vanity.
The Devil was in the girl! Could it be pride?
Or modesty, or absence, or inanity?

     •   •   •   •   •

"Juan was drawn thus into some attentions,
Slight, but select, and just enough to express,
To females of perspicuous comprehensions,
That he would rather make them more than less.
Aurora at the last (so history mentions,
Though probably much less a fact than guess)
So far relaxed her thoughts from their sweet prison,
As once or twice to smile, if not to listen.

     •   •   •   •   •

"But Juan had a sort of winning way,
A proud humility, if such there be,
Which showed such deference to what females say,
As if each charming word were a decree.
His tact, too, tempered him from grave to gay,
And taught him when to be reserved or free.

He had the art of drawing people out,
Without their seeing what he was about.

"Aurora—who, in her indifference,
Confounded him in common with the crowd
Of flatterers, though she deemed he had more sense
Than whispering foplings, or than witlings loud—
Commenced (from such slight things will great commence)
To feel that flattery which attracts the proud,
Rather by deference than compliment,
And wins even by a delicate dissent.

"And then he had good looks; that point was carried
*Nem. con.* amongst the women, . . . .
Now though we know of old that looks deceive,
And always have done somehow, these good looks
make more impression than the best of books.

"Aurora, who looked more on books than faces,
Was very young, although so very sage,
Admiring more Minerva than the Graces,
Especially upon a printed page.
But virtue's self, with all her tightest laces,
Has not the natural stays of strict old age;
And Socrates, that model of all duty,
Owned to a penchant, though discreet, for beauty."

The presence of this high-minded, thoughtful, unworldly woman is described through two cantos of the wild, rattling "Don Juan," in a manner that shows how deeply the poet was capable of being affected by such an appeal to his higher nature.

For instance, when Don Juan sits silent and thoughtful amid a circle of persons who are talking scandal, the poet says:—

" 'T is true he saw Aurora look as though
She approved his silence; she perhaps mistook
Its motive for that charity we owe,
But seldom pay, the absent.
• • • • •
"He gained esteem where it was worth the most,
And certainly Aurora had renewed
In him some feelings he had lately lost
Or hardened; feelings which, perhaps ideal,
Are so divine that I must deem them real.

"The love of higher things and better days,
The unbounded hope and heavenly ignorance
Of what is called the world and the world's ways,
The moments when we gather from a glance
More joy than from all future pride or praise,

Which kindled manhood, but can ne'er entrance
The heart in an existence of its own
Of which another's bosom is the zone.

"And full of sentiment sublime as billows
Heaving between this world and worlds beyond,
Don Juan, when the midnight hour of pillows
Arrived, retired to his. . . . ."

In all these descriptions of a spiritual, unworldly nature, acting on the spiritual and unworldly part of his own nature, every one who ever knew Lady Byron intimately must have recognized the model from which he drew and the experience from which he spoke, even though nothing was further from his mind than to pay this tribute to the woman he had injured, and though, before these lines, which showed how truly he knew her real character, had come one stanza of ribald, vulgar caricature, designed as a slight to her.

"There was Miss Millpond, smooth as summer's sea,
That usual paragon, an only daughter,
Who seemed the cream of equanimity
'Till skimmed,—and then there was some milk and water.
With a slight shade of blue too, it might be
Beneath the surface; but what did it matter?
Love's riotous, but marriage should have quiet,
And, being consumptive, live on a milk diet."

The result of Byron's intimacy with Miss Milbanke and the enkindling of his nobler feelings was an offer of marriage, which she, though at the time deeply interested in him, declined with many expressions of friendship and interest. In fact, she already loved him, but had that doubt of her power to be to him all that a wife should be, which would be likely to arise in a mind so sensitively constituted and so unworldly. They however continued a correspondence as friends; on her part the interest continually increased, on his the transient rise of better feelings was choked and overgrown by the thorns of base, unworthy passions.

From the height at which he might have been happy as the husband of a noble woman, he fell into the depths of a secret adulterous intrigue with a blood relation, so near in consanguinity that discovery must have been utter ruin and expulsion from civilized society.

From henceforth, this damning guilty secret became the ruling force in his life, holding him with a morbid fascination, yet filling him with remorse and anguish and insane dread of detection. Two years after his refusal by Miss Milbanke, his various friends, seeing that for some cause he was wretched, pressed marriage upon him.

Marriage has often been represented as the proper goal and terminus of a wild and dissipated career, and it has been supposed to be the appointed mission of good women to receive wandering prodigals, with all the rags and disgraces of their old life upon them, and put rings on their hands and shoes on their feet, and introduce them, clothed and in their right minds, to an honorable career in society.

Marriage was therefore universally recommended to Lord Byron by his numerous friends and well-wishers; and so he determined to marry, and in an hour of reckless desperation, sat down and wrote proposals to two ladies. One was declined. The other, which was accepted, was to Miss Milbanke. The world knows well that he had the gift of expression, and will not be surprised that he wrote a very beautiful letter, and that the woman who had already learned to love him fell at once into the snare.

Her answer was a frank, outspoken avowal of her love for him, giving herself to him heart and hand. The good in Lord Byron was not so utterly obliterated that he could receive such a letter without emotion, or practise such unfairness on a loving, trusting heart without pangs of remorse. He had sent the letter in mere recklessness; he had not seriously expected to be accepted, and the discovery of the treasure of affection which he had secured was like a vision of lost heaven to a soul in hell.

But, nevertheless, in his letters written about the engagement, there are sufficient evidences that his self-love was flattered at the preference accorded him by so superior a woman and one who had been so much sought. He mentions with an air of complacency that she has employed the last two years in refusing five or six of his acquaintance; that he had no idea she loved him, admitting that it was an old attachment on his part; he dwells on her virtues with a sort of pride of ownership. There is a sort of childish levity about the frankness of these letters, very characteristic of the man who skimmed over the deepest abysses with the lightest jests. Before the world, and to his intimates, he was acting the part of the successful *fiancé*, conscious all the while of the deadly secret that lay cold at the bottom of his heart.

When he went to visit Miss Milbanke's parents, as her accepted lover, she was struck with his manner and appearance; she saw him moody and gloomy, evidently wrestling with dark and desperate thoughts, and anything but what a happy and accepted lover should be. She sought an interview with him alone, and told him that she had observed that he was not happy in the engagement, and magnanimously added that, if on review he found he had been mistaken in the nature of his feelings, she would immediately release him, and they should remain only friends.

Overcome with the conflict of his feelings, Lord Byron fainted away. Miss Milbanke was convinced that his heart must really be deeply involved in an attachment with reference to which he showed such strength of emotion, and she spoke no more of a dissolution of the engagement.

There is no reason to doubt that Byron was, as he relates in his Dream, profoundly agonized and agitated, when he stood before God's altar, with the trusting young creature whom he was leading to a fate so awfully tragic; yet it was not the memory of Mary Chaworth, but another guiltier and more damning memory that overshadowed that hour.

The moment the carriage doors were shut upon the bridegroom and the bride, the paroxysm of remorse and despair—unrepentant remorse and angry despair— broke forth upon her gentle head.

"You might have saved me from this, madam! you had all in your own power when I offered myself to you first. Then you might have made me what you pleased; but now you will find that you have married a *devil!*"

In Miss Martineau's Sketches, recently published, is an account of the termination of this wedding journey, which brought them to one of Lady Byron's ancestral country-seats, where they were to spend the honeymoon.

Miss Martineau says:—

> At the altar she did not know that she was a sacrifice; but before sunset of that winter day she knew it, if a judgment may be formed from her face and attitude of despair when she alighted from the carriage on the afternoon of her marriage-day. It was not the traces of tears which won the sympathy of the old butler who stood at the open door. The bridegroom jumped out of the carriage and walked away. The bride alighted, and came up the steps alone, with a countenance and frame agonized and listless with evident horror and despair. The old servant longed to offer his arm to the young, lonely creature, as an assurance of sympathy and protection. From this shock she certainly rallied, and soon. The pecuniary difficulties of her new home were exactly what a devoted spirit like hers was fitted to encounter. Her husband bore testimony, after the catastrophe, that a brighter being, a more sympathizing and agreeable companion, never blessed any man's home. When he afterward called her cold and mathematical, and over-pious, and so forth, it was when public opinion had gone against him, and when he had discovered that her fidelity and mercy, her silence and magnanimity, might be relied on, so that he was at full liberty to make his part good, as far as she was concerned.
>
> Silent she was even to her own parents, whose feelings she magnanimously spared. She did not act rashly in leaving him, though she had been most rash in marrying him.

Not all at once did the full knowledge of the dreadful reality into which she had entered come upon the young wife. She knew vaguely, from the wild avowals of the first hours of their marriage, that there was a dreadful secret of guilt, that Byron's soul was torn with agonies of remorse, and that he had no love to give to her in return for a love which was ready to do and dare all for him. Yet bravely she addressed herself to the task of soothing and pleasing and calming the man whom she had taken "for better or for worse."

Young and gifted, with a peculiar air of refined and spiritual beauty; graceful in every movement, possessed of exquisite taste; a perfect companion to his mind in all the higher walks of literary culture, and with that infinite pliability to all his varying, capricious moods which true love alone can give; bearing in her hand a princely fortune, which with a woman's uncalculating generosity was thrown at his feet,—there is no wonder that she might feel for a while as if she could enter the lists with the very Devil himself, and fight with a woman's weapons for the heart of her husband.

There are indications scattered through the letters of Lord Byron which, though brief indeed, showed that his young wife was making every effort to accommodate herself to him, and to give him a cheerful home. One of the poems that he sends to his publisher about this time, he speaks of as being copied by her. He had always the highest regard for her literary judgments and opinions, and this little incident shows that she was already associating herself in a wifely fashion with his aims as an author.

The poem copied by her, however, has a sad meaning which she afterwards learned to understand only too well.

> There's not a joy the world can give like that it takes away,
> When the glow of early thought declines in feeling's dull decay;
> 'T is not on youth's smooth cheek the blush alone that fades so fast,
> But the tender bloom of heart is gone e'er youth itself be past.

> "Then the few whose spirits float above the wreck of happiness
> Are driven o'er the shoals of guilt or ocean of excess;
> The magnet of their course is gone, or only points in vain
> The shore to which their shivered sail shall never stretch again."

Only a few days before she left him forever, Lord Byron sent Murray manuscripts, in Lady Byron's handwriting, of the Siege of Corinth and Parisina, and wrote:—

> I am very glad that the handwriting was a favorable omen of the *morale* of the piece; but you must not trust to that, for my copyist would write out anything I desired, in all the ignorance of innocence.

There were lucid intervals in which Lord Byron felt the charm of his wife's mind and the strength of her powers. "Bell, you could be a poet too, if you only thought so," he would say. There were summer hours in her stormy life, the memory of which never left her, when Byron was as gentle and tender as he was beautiful; when he seemed to be possessed by a good angel, and then for a little time all the ideal possibilities of his nature stood revealed.

The most dreadful men to live with are those who thus alternate between angel and devil. The buds of hope and love called out by a day or two of sunshine are frozen again and again till the tree is killed.

But there came an hour of revelation,—an hour when, in a manner which left no kind of room for doubt, Lady Byron saw the full depth of the abyss of infamy which her marriage was expected to cover, and understood that she was expected to be the cloak and the accomplice of this infamy.

Many women would have been utterly crushed by such a disclosure; some would have fled from him immediately, and exposed and denounced the crime. Lady Byron did neither. When all the hope of womanhood died out of her heart, there arose within her, stronger, purer, and brighter, that immortal kind of love such as God feels for the sinner,—the love of which Jesus spoke and which holds the one wanderer of more account than the ninety and nine that went not astray. She would neither leave her husband nor betray him, nor yet would she for one moment justify his sin; and hence came two years of convulsive struggle, in which sometimes, for a while, the good angel seemed to gain ground, and then the evil one returned with sevenfold vehemence.

Lord Byron argued his case with himself and with her, with all the sophistries of his powerful mind. He repudiated Christianity as authority, asserted the right of every human being to follow out what he called "the impulses of nature."

Subsequently he introduced into one of his dramas the reasoning by which he justified himself in incest.

In the drama of Cain, Adah the sister and the wife of Cain thus addresses him:—

"Cain! walk not with this spirit,
Bear with what we have borne, and love me—I Love thee.
LUCIFER.  More than thy mother and thy sire?
ADAH.  I do. Is that a sin too?
LUCIFER.  No, not yet; It one day will be in your children.
ADAH.  What! Must not my daughter love her brother Enoch?
LUCIFER.  Not as thou lovest Cain.
ADAH.  O, my God! Shall they not love and bring forth things that love
Out of their love? have they not drawn their milk
Out of this bosom? was not he, their father,
Born of the same sole womb, in the same hour
With me? did we not love each other? and
In multiplying our being multiply
Things which will love each other as we love Them?—
And as I love thee, my Cain! go not
Forth with this spirit, he is not of ours.
LUCIFER.  The sin I speak of is not of my making,
And cannot be a sin in you,—whate'er
It seems in those who will replace ye in Mortality.
ADAH.  What is the sin which is not
Sin in itself? can circumstance make sin
Of virtue? if it doth, we are the slaves
Of—"

Lady Byron, though slight and almost infantine in her bodily presence, had the soul, not only of an angelic woman, but of a strong, reasoning man. It was the writer's lot to know her at a period when she formed the personal acquaintance of many of the very first minds of England; but, among all with whom this experience brought her in connection, there was none who impressed her so strongly as Lady Byron. There was an almost supernatural power of moral divination, a grasp of the very highest and most comprehensive things, that made her lightest opinions singularly impressive. No doubt this result was wrought out in a great degree from the anguish and conflict of these two years, when, with no one to help or counsel her but Almighty God, she wrestled and struggled with fiends of darkness for the redemption of her husband's soul.

She followed him through all his sophistical reasonings with a keener reason. She besought and implored, in the name of his better nature, and by all the glorious things that he was capable of being and doing; and she had just power enough to convulse and shake and agonize, but not power enough to subdue.

One of the first of living writers, in the novel of "Romola,"[1] has given, in her masterly sketch of the character of Tito, the whole history of the conflict of a woman like Lady Byron with a nature like that of her husband. She has described a being full of fascinations and sweetnesses, full of generosities and of good-natured impulses; a nature that could not bear to give pain, or to see it in others, but entirely destitute of any firm moral principle; she shows how such a being, merely by yielding step by step to the impulses of passion, and disregarding the claims of truth and right, becomes involved in a fatality of evil, in which deceit, crime, and cruelty are a necessity, forcing him to persist in the basest ingratitude to the father who has done all for him, and hard-hearted treachery to the high-minded wife who has given herself to him wholly.

There are few scenes in literature more fearfully tragic than the one between Romola and Tito, when he finally discovers that she knows him fully, and can be deceived by him no more. Some such hour always must come for strong, decided natures irrevocably pledged, one to the service of good and the other to the slavery of evil. The demoniac cried out: "What have I to do with thee, Jesus of Nazareth? Art thou come to torment me before the time?" The presence of all-pitying purity and love was a torture to the soul possessed by the demon of evil.

These two years, in which Lady Byron was with all her soul struggling to bring her husband back to his better self, were a series of passionate convulsions.

During this time, such was the disordered and desperate state of his worldly affairs, that there were ten executions for debt levied on their family establishment; and it was Lady Byron's fortune each time which settled the account.

Toward the last she and her husband saw less and less of each other, and he came more and more decidedly under evil influences and seemed to acquire a sort of hatred of her.

Lady Byron once said significantly to a friend who spoke of some causeless dislike in another: "My dear, I have known people to be hated for no other reason than because they impersonated conscience."

The biographers of Lord Byron and all his apologists are careful to narrate how sweet, and amiable, and obliging he was to everybody who approached him; and the saying of Fletcher, his man-servant, that *"anybody* could do anything with my Lord, except my Lady," has often been quoted.

The reason of all this will now be evident. "My Lady," was the only one fully understanding the deep and dreadful secrets of his life who had the courage resolutely and persistently and inflexibly to plant herself in his way and insist upon it that, if he went to destruction, it should be in spite of her best efforts.

He had tried his strength with her fully. The first attempt had been to make her an accomplice by sophistry; by destroying her faith in Christianity, and confusing her sense of right and wrong, to bring her into the ranks of those convenient women who regard the marriage tie only as a friendly alliance to cover license on both sides.

When her husband described to her the continental latitude,—the good-humored marriage, in which complaisant couples mutually agreed to form the cloak

[1]George Eliot, *Romola* (1863).

for each other's infidelities,—and gave her to understand that in this way alone she could have a peaceful and friendly life with him, she answered him simply: "I am too truly your friend to do this."

When Lord Byron found that he had to do with one who would not yield, who knew him fully, who could not be blinded and could not be deceived, he determined to rid himself of her altogether.

It was when the state of affairs between herself and her husband seemed darkest and most hopeless, that the only child of this union was born. Lord Byron's treatment of his wife during the sensitive period that preceded the birth of this child, and during her confinement, was marked by paroxysms of unmanly brutality, for which the only possible charity on her part was the supposition of insanity. Moore sheds a significant light on this period, by telling us that about this time Byron was often drunk day after day with Sheridan. There had been insanity in the family, and this was the plea which Lady Byron's love put in for him. She regarded him as, if not insane, at least so nearly approaching the boundaries of insanity as to be a subject of forbearance and tender pity and she loved him with that love resembling a mother's, which good wives often feel when they have lost all faith in their husbands' principles, and all hopes of their affections. Still she was in heart and soul his best friend, true to him with a truth which he himself could not shake.

In the verses addressed to his daughter, Lord Byron speaks of her as

> "The child of love, though born in bitterness,
> And nurtured in convulsion."

A day or two after the birth of this child, Lord Byron came suddenly into Lady Byron's room, and told her that her mother was dead. It was an utter falsehood, but it was only one of the many nameless injuries and cruelties by which he expressed his hatred of her. A short time after her confinement, she was informed by him, in a note, that as soon as she was able to travel she must go,—that he could not and would not longer have her about him; and, when her child was only five weeks old, he carried this threat of expulsion into effect.

Here we will insert briefly Lady Byron's own account—the only one she ever gave to the public—of this separation. The circumstances under which this brief story was written are affecting.

Lord Byron was dead. The whole account between him and her was closed forever in this world. Moore's "Life" had been prepared, containing simply and solely Lord Byron's own version of their story. Moore sent this version to Lady Byron, and requested to know if she had any remarks to make upon it. In reply, she sent a brief statement to him,—the first and only one that had come from her during all the years of the separation, and which appears to have mainly for its object the exculpation of her father and mother from the charge made by the poet of being the instigators of the separation.

In this letter she says, with regard to their separation:—

The facts are: I left London for Kirby Mallory, the residence of my father and mother, on the 15th of January, 1816. LORD BYRON HAD SIGNIFIED TO ME IN WRITING,

JANUARY 6TH, HIS ABSOLUTE DESIRE THAT I SHOULD LEAVE LONDON ON THE EARLIEST DAY THAT I COULD CONVENIENTLY FIX. It was not safe for me to undertake the fatigue of a journey sooner than the 15th. Previously to my departure it had been strongly impressed upon my mind that Lord Byron was under the influence of insanity. This opinion was derived, in a great measure, from the communications made me by his nearest relatives and personal attendant, who had more opportunity than myself for observing him during the latter part of my stay in town. It was even represented to me that he was in danger of destroying himself.

*With the concurrence of his family,* I had consulted Dr. Baillie as a friend, January 8th, respecting the supposed malady. On acquainting him with the state of the case, and with Lord Byron's desire that I should leave London, Dr. Baillie thought that my absence might be advisable as an experiment, assuming the fact of mental derangement; for Dr. Baillie, not having had access to Lord Byron, could not pronounce a positive opinion on that point. He enjoined that, in correspondence with Lord Byron, I should avoid all but light and soothing topics. Under these impressions I left London, determined to follow the advice given by Dr. Baillie. Whatever might have been the conduct of Lord Byron toward me from the time of my marriage, yet, supposing him to be in a state of mental alienation, it was not for *me,* nor for any person of common humanity, to manifest at that moment a sense of injury.

Nothing more than this letter from Lady Byron is necessary to substantiate the fact that she did not *leave* her husband, but *was driven* from him,—driven from him that he might give himself up to the guilty infatuation that was consuming him, without being tortured by her imploring face and by the silent power of her presence and her prayers.

For a long time before this she had seen little of him. On the day of her departure she passed by the door of his room, and stopped to caress his favorite spaniel, which was lying there; and she confessed to a friend the weakness of feeling a willingness even to be something as humble as that poor little creature, might she only be allowed to remain and watch over him. She went into the room where he and the partner of his sins were sitting together, and said, "Byron, I come to say good by," offering at the same time her hand.

Lord Byron put his hands behind him, retreated to the mantel-piece, and, looking round on the two that stood there with a sarcastic smile, said, "When shall we three meet again?" Lady Byron answered, "In Heaven, I trust;" and those were her last words to him on earth.

Now, if the reader wishes to understand the real talents of Lord Byron for deception and dissimulation, let him read, with this story in his mind, the "Fare thee well," which he addressed to Lady Byron through the printer:—

> "Fare thee well, and if forever,
>   Still forever fare thee well.
> Even though unforgiving, never
>   'Gainst thee shall my heart rebel.
>
> Would that breast were bared before thee,
>   Where thy head so oft hath lain,
> While that placid sleep came o'er thee
>   Thou canst never know again.

> Though my many faults defaced me,
> Could no other arm be found
> Than the one which once embraced me
> To inflict a cureless wound?"

The reaction of society against him at the time of the separation from his wife was something which he had not expected, and for which, it appears, he was entirely unprepared. It broke up the guilty intrigue, and drove him from England. He had not courage to meet or endure it. The world, to be sure, was very far from suspecting what the truth was, but the tide was setting against him with such vehemence as to make him tremble every hour lest the whole should be known; and henceforth it became a warfare of desperation to make his story good, no matter at whose expense.

He had tact enough to perceive at first that the assumption of the pathetic and the magnanimous, and general confessions of faults, accompanied with admissions of his wife's goodness, would be the best policy in his case. In this mood he thus writes to Moore:—

> The fault was not in my choice (unless in choosing at all), for I do not believe and I must say it, in the very dregs of all this bitter business, that there ever was a better, or even a brighter, a kinder, or a more amiable, agreeable being than Lady Byron. I never had, nor can have, any reproach to make her while with me. Where there is blame, it belongs to myself.

As there must be somewhere a scapegoat to bear the sin of the affair, Lord Byron wrote a poem called "A Sketch," in which he lays the blame of stirring up strife on a friend and former governess of Lady Byron's, but in this sketch he introduces the following just eulogy on Lady Byron:—

> "Foiled was perversion by that youthful mind
> Which flattery fooled not, baseness could not blind,
> Deceit infect not, near contagion soil,
> Indulgence weaken, nor example spoil,
> Nor mastered science tempt her to look down
> On humbler talents with a pitying frown,
> Nor genius swell, nor beauty render vain,
> Nor envy ruffle to retaliate pain,
> Nor fortune change, pride raise, nor passion bow
> Nor virtue teach austerity,—till now.
> Serenely purest of her sex that live,
> But wanting one sweet weakness,—to forgive.
> Too shocked at faults her soul can never know,
> She deemed that all could be like her below.
> Foe to all vice, yet hardly virtue's friend,
> For virtue pardons those she would amend."

In leaving England, Lord Byron first went to Switzerland, where he conceived and in part wrote out the tragedy of "Manfred." Moore speaks of his domestic misfortunes, and the sufferings which he underwent at this time, as having an influence in stimulating his genius, so that he was enabled to write with a greater power.

Anybody who reads the tragedy of "Manfred" with this story in his mind will see that it is true.

The hero is represented as a gloomy misanthrope, dwelling with impenitent remorse on the memory of an incestuous passion which has been the destruction of his sister for this life and the life to come; but which, to the very last gasp, he despairingly refuses to repent of, even while he sees the fiends of darkness rising to take possession of his departing soul. That Byron knew his own guilt well, and judged himself severely, may be gathered from passages in this poem, which are as powerful as human language can be made. For instance, this part of the "Incantation," which Moore says was written at this time:—

> "Though thy slumber may be deep,
> Yet thy spirit shall not sleep;
> There are shades which will not vanish,
> There are thoughts thou canst not banish;
> By a power to thee unknown,
> Thou canst never be alone;
> Thou art rapt as with a shroud,
> Thou art gathered in a cloud;
> And forever shalt thou dwell
> In the spirit of this spell.
>
> .     .     .     .     .
>
> "From thy false tears I did distil
> An essence which had strength to kill;
> From thy own heart I then did wring
> The black blood in its blackest spring;
> From thy own smile I snatched the snake,
> For there it coiled as in a brake;
> From thy own lips I drew the charm
> Which gave all these their chiefest harm;
> In proving every poison known
> I found the strongest was thine own.
>
> "By thy cold breast and serpent smile,
> By thy unfathomed gulfs of guile,
> By that most seeming virtuous eye,
> By thy shut soul's hypocrisy,
> By the perfection of thine art
> Which passed for human thine own heart,
> By thy delight in others' pain,
> And by thy brotherhood of Cain,
> I call upon thee! and compel
> Thyself to be thy proper hell!"

Again, he represents Manfred as saying to the old Abbot, who seeks to bring him to repentance:—

> "Old man, there is no power in holy men,
> Nor charm in prayer, nor purifying form
> Of penitence, nor outward look, nor fast,
> Nor agony, nor, greater than all these,
> The innate tortures of that deep despair,
> Which is remorse without the fear of hell,
> But all in all sufficient to itself,
> Would make a hell of heaven, can exorcise
> From out the unbounded spirit the quick sense
> Of its own sins, wrongs, sufferance, and revenge
> Upon itself; there is no future pang
> Can deal that justice on the self-condemned
> He deals on his own soul."

And when the Abbot tells him,

> "All this is well,
> For this will pass away, and be succeeded
> By an auspicious hope, which shall look up
> With calm assurance to that blessed place
> Which all who seek may win, whatever be
> Their earthly errors,"

he answers,

> "It is too late."

Then the old Abbot soliloquizes:—

> "This should have been a noble creature; he
> Hath all the energy which would have made
> A goodly frame of glorious elements,
> Had they been wisely mingled; as it is,
> It is an awful chaos,—light and darkness,
> And mind and dust, and passions and pure thoughts
> Mixed, and contending without end or order."

The world can easily see, in Moore's biography, what, after this, was the course of Lord Byron's life,—how he went from shame to shame, and dishonor to dishonor, and used the fortune which his wife brought him in the manner described in those private letters which his biographer was left to print. Moore, indeed, says Byron had made the resolution not to touch his lady's fortune, but adds that it required more self-command than he possessed to carry out so honorable a purpose.

Lady Byron made but one condition with him. She had him in her power, and she exacted that the unhappy partner of his sins should not follow him out of England, and that the ruinous intrigue should be given up. Her inflexibility on this point kept up that enmity which was constantly expressing itself in some publication or other, and which drew her and her private relations with him before the public.

The story of what Lady Byron did with the portion of her fortune which was reserved to her is a record of noble and skillfully administered charities. Pitiful and wise and strong, there was no form of human suffering or sorrow that did not find with her refuge and help. She gave not only systematically, but also impulsively.

Miss Martineau claims for her the honor of having first invented practical schools, in which the children of the poor were turned into agriculturists, artisans, seamstresses, and good wives for poor men. While she managed with admirable skill and economy permanent institutions of this sort, she was always ready to relieve suffering in any form. The fugitive slaves, William and Ellen Crafts, escaping to England, were fostered by her protecting care.

In many cases, where there was distress or anxiety from poverty among those too self-respecting to make their sufferings known, the delicate hand of Lady Byron ministered to the want with a consideration which spared the most refined feelings.

As a mother, her course was embarrassed by peculiar trials. The daughter inherited from the father not only brilliant talents, but a restlessness and morbid sensibility which might be too surely traced to the storms and agitations of the period in which she was born. It was necessary to bring her up in ignorance of the true history of her mother's life, and the consequence was that she could not fully understand that mother.

During her early girlhood, her career was a source of more anxiety than of comfort. She married a man of fashion, ran a brilliant course as a gay woman of fashion, and died early of a lingering and painful disease.

In the silence and shaded retirement of the sick-room, the daughter came wholly back to her mother's arms and heart; and it was on that mother's bosom that she leaned, as she went down into the dark valley. It was that mother who placed her weak and dying hand in that of her Almighty Saviour.

To the children left by her daughter she ministered with the faithfulness of a guardian angel; and it is owing to her influence that those who yet remain are among the best and noblest of mankind.

The person whose relation with Byron had been so disastrous, also, in the latter years of her life, felt Lady Byron's loving and ennobling influences, and in her last sickness and dying hours looked to her for consolation and help.

There was an unfortunate child of sin, born with the curse upon her, over whose wayward nature Lady Byron watched with a mother's tenderness. She was the one who could have patience when the patience of every one else failed; and though her task was a difficult one, from the strange, abnormal propensities to evil in the object of her cares, yet Lady Byron never faltered and never gave over, till death took the responsibility from her hands.

During all this trial, strange to say, her belief that the good in Lord Byron would finally conquer was unshaken.

To a friend who said to her, "O, how could you love him!" she answered, briefly, "My dear, there was the angel in him." It is in us all.

It was in this angel that she had faith. It was for the deliverance of this angel from degradation and shame and sin that she unceasingly prayed. She read every work that Byron wrote,—read it with a deeper knowledge than any human being but herself could possess. The ribaldry and the obscenity and the insults, with which he strove to make her ridiculous in the world, fell at her pitying feet unheeded.

When he broke away from all this unworthy life to devote himself to a manly enterprise for the redemption of Greece, she thought that she saw the beginning of an answer to her prayers. Even although one of his latest acts concerning her was to repeat to Lady Blessington the false accusation which made Lady Byron the author of all his errors, she still had hopes, from the one step taken in the right direction.

In the midst of these hopes came the news of his sudden death. On his deathbed, it is well known that he called his confidential English servant to him, and said to him, "Go to my sister—tell her—go to Lady Byron—you will see her and say"—

Here followed twenty minutes of indistinct mutterings, in which the names of his wife, daughter, and sister frequently occurred. He then said, "Now I have told you all."

"My Lord," replied Fletcher," I have not understood a word your Lordship has been saying."

"Not understand me!" exclaimed Lord Byron with a look of the utmost distress, "what a pity!—then it is too late—all is over!" He afterwards, says Moore, tried to utter a few words, of which none were intelligible except "my sister—my child."

When Fletcher returned to London, Lady Byron sent for him, and walked the room in convulsive struggles to repress her tears and sobs, while she over and over again strove to elicit something from him which should enlighten her upon what that last message had been; but in vain,—the gates of eternity were shut in her face, and not a word had passed to tell her if he had repented.

For all that, Lady Byron never doubted his salvation. Ever before her, during the few remaining years of her widowhood, was the image of her husband, purified and ennobled, with the shadows of earth forever dissipated, the stains of sin forever removed,—"the angel in him," as she expressed it, "made perfect, according to its divine ideal."

Never has more divine strength of faith and love existed in woman. Out of the depths of her own loving and merciful nature, she gained such views of the Divine love and mercy as made all hopes possible. There was no soul of whose future Lady Byron despaired. Such was her boundless faith in the redeeming power of love.

After Byron's death, the life of this delicate creature—so frail in body that she seemed always hovering on the brink of the eternal world, yet so strong in spirit and so unceasing in her various ministries of mercy—was a miracle of mingled weakness and strength.

To talk with her seemed to the writer of this sketch the nearest possible approach to talking with one of the spirits of the just made perfect.

She was gentle, artless, approachable as a little child, with ready, outflowing sympathy for the cares and sorrows and interests of all who approached her, with a naïve and gentle playfulness, that adorned, without hiding, the breadth and strength of her mind, and, above all, with a clear, divining, moral discrimination, never mistaking wrong for right in the slightest shade, yet with a mercifulness that made allowance for every weakness and pitied every sin.

There was so much of Christ in her, that to have seen her seemed to be to have drawn near to heaven. She was one of those few whom absence cannot estrange from friends, whose mere presence in this world seems always a help to every generous thought, a strength to every good purpose, a comfort in every sorrow.

Living so near the confines of the spiritual world, she seemed already to see into it. Hence the words of comfort which she addressed to a friend who had lost a son:—

"Dear friend, remember, as long as our loved ones are in *God's* world, they are in *ours*."

It has been thought by some friends who have read the proof-sheets of the foregoing, that the author should state more specifically her authority for these statements.

The circumstances which led the writer to England at a certain time originated a friendship and correspondence with Lady Byron, which was always regarded as one of the greatest acquisitions of that visit.

On the occasion of a second visit to England, in 1856, the writer received a note from Lady Byron, indicating that she wished to have some private, confidential conversation upon important subjects, and inviting her for that purpose to spend a day with her at her country-seat near London.

The writer went and spent a day with Lady Byron alone, and the object of the invitation was explained to her. Lady Byron was in such a state of health that her physicians had warned her that she had very little time to live. She was engaged in those duties and retrospections which every thoughtful person finds necessary, when coming deliberately and with open eyes to the boundaries of this mortal life.

At that time there was a cheap edition of Byron's works in contemplation, intended to bring his writings into circulation among the masses, and the pathos arising from the story of his domestic misfortunes was one great means relied on for giving it currency.

Under these circumstances, some of Lady Byron's friends had proposed the question to her, *whether she had not a responsibility to society for the truth*; whether *she did right* to allow these writings to gain influence over the popular mind, by giving a silent consent to what she knew to be utter falsehoods.

Lady Byron's whole life had been passed in the most heroic self-abnegation and self-sacrifice, and she had now to consider whether one more act of self-denial was not required of her before leaving this world,—namely, to declare the absolute truth, no matter at what expense to her own feelings.

For this reason it was her desire to recount the whole history to a person of another country, and entirely out of the sphere of personal and local feelings which might be supposed to influence those in the country and station in life where the events really happened, in order that she might be helped by such a person's views in making up an opinion as to her own duty.

The interview had almost the solemnity of a death-bed avowal. Lady Byron stated the facts which have been embodied in this article, and gave to the writer a paper containing a brief memorandum of the whole, with the dates affixed.

We have already spoken of that singular sense of the reality of the spiritual world which seemed to encompass Lady Byron during the last part of her life, and which made her words and actions seem more like those of a blessed being detached from earth than of an ordinary mortal. All her modes of looking at things, all her motives of action, all her involuntary exhibitions of emotion were so high above any common level, and so entirely regulated by the most unworldly causes, that it would seem difficult to make the ordinary world understand exactly how the thing seemed to lie before her mind. What impressed the writer more strongly than anything else was Lady Byron's perfect conviction that her husband was now a redeemed spirit; that he looked back with pain and shame and regret on all that was unworthy in his past life; and that, if he could speak or could act in the case, he would desire to prevent the farther circulation of base falsehoods, and of seductive poetry, which had been made the vehicle of morbid and unworthy passions.

Lady Byron's experience had led her to apply the powers of her strong philosophical mind to the study of mental pathology, and she had become satisfied that the solution of the painful problem which first occurred to her as a young wife was, after all, the true one,—namely, that Lord Byron had been one of those unfortunately constituted persons in whom the balance of nature is so critically hung that it is always in danger of dipping towards insanity, and that in certain periods of his life he was so far under the influence of mental disorder as not to be fully responsible for his actions.

She went over, with a brief and clear analysis, the history of his whole life as she had thought it out during the lonely musings of her widowhood. She dwelt on the ancestral causes that gave him a nature of exceptional and dangerous susceptibility. She went through the mismanagements of his childhood, the history of his schooldays, the influence of the ordinary school course of classical reading on such a mind as his. She sketched boldly and clearly the internal life of the young men of the time as she with her purer eyes had looked through it, and showed how habits, which with less susceptible fibre and coarser strength of nature were tolerable for his companions, were deadly to him, unhinging his nervous system, and intensifying the dangers of ancestral proclivities. Lady Byron expressed the feeling, too, that the Calvinistic theology, as heard in Scotland, had proved in his case, as it often does in certain minds, a subtle poison. He never could either disbelieve or become reconciled to it, and the sore problems it proposes embittered his spirit against Christianity.

"The worst of it is, I *do believe*," he would often say with violence, when he had been employing all his powers of reason, wit, and ridicule upon these subjects.

Through all this sorrowful history was to be seen, not the care of a slandered woman to make her story good, but the pathetic anxiety of a mother who treasures every particle of hope, every intimation of good, in the son whom she cannot cease to love. With indescribable resignation, she dwelt on those last hours, those words addressed to her never to be understood till repeated in eternity.

But all this she looked upon as forever past; believing that, with the dropping of the earthly life, these morbid impulses and influences ceased, and that higher nature which he often so beautifully expressed in his poems became the triumphant one.

While speaking on this subject her pale, ethereal face became luminous with a heavenly radiance; there was something so sublime in her belief in the victory of love over evil, that faith with her seemed to have become sight. She seemed so clearly to perceive the divine ideal of the man she had loved and for whose salvation she had been called to suffer and labor and pray, that all memories of his past unworthiness fell away and were lost.

Her love was never the doting fondness of weak women; it was the appreciative and discriminating love by which a higher nature recognized godlike capabilities under all the dust and defilement of misuse and passion; and she never doubted that the love, which in her was so strong that no injury or insult could shake it, was yet stronger in the God who made her capable of such a devotion, and that in Him it was accompanied by power to subdue all things to itself.

The writer was so impressed and excited by the whole scene and recital that she begged for two or three days to deliberate, before forming any opinion. She took the memorandum with her, returned to London and gave a day or two to the consideration of the subject. The decision which she made was chiefly influenced by her reverence and affection for Lady Byron. She seemed so frail, she had suffered so much, she stood at such a height above the comprehension of the coarse and common world, that the author had a feeling that it would almost be like violating a shrine, to ask her to come forth from the sanctuary of a silence where she had so long abode and plead her cause. She wrote to Lady Byron that while this act of justice did seem to be called for, and to be in some respects most desirable, yet, as it would involve so much that was painful to her, the writer considered that Lady Byron would be entirely justifiable in leaving the truth to be disclosed after her death, and recommended that all the facts necessary should be put in the hands of some person, to be so published.

Years passed on. Lady Byron lingered four years after this interview, to the wonder of her physicians and all her friends.

After Lady Byron's death the writer looked anxiously, hoping to see a memoir of the person whom she considered the most remarkable woman that England has produced in the century. No such memoir has appeared on the part of her friends; and the mistress of Lord Byron has the ear of the public, and is sowing far and wide unworthy slanders, which are eagerly gathered up and read by an undiscriminating community.

There may be family reasons in England which prevent Lady Byron's friends from speaking; but Lady Byron has an American name and an American existence, and reverence for pure womanhood is, we think, a national characteristic of the American; and, so far as this country is concerned, we feel that the public should have this refutation of the slanders of the Countess Guiccioli's book.

# SUGGESTIONS FOR FURTHER READING

❦

## Books

Ammons, Elizabeth, ed. *Critical Essays on Harriet Beecher Stowe*. Boston: G. K. Hall, 1980.

Beecher, Catharine. *A Treatise on Domestic Economy*. [1841]. New York: Schocken Books, 1977.

Bibb, Henry. *The Narrative of the Life and Adventures of Henry Bibb, Written by Himself*. In *Puttin' on Ole Massa*, edited by Gilbert Osofsky. New York: Harper & Row, Publishers, 1969.

Boydston, Jeanne, Mary Kelley, and Anne Margolis. *The Limits of Sisterhood: The Beecher Sisters on Women's Rights and Woman's Sphere*. Chapel Hill: University of North Carolina Press, 1988.

Buell, Lawrence. *New England Literary Culture: From Revolution Through Renaissance*. Cambridge: Cambridge University Press, 1986.

Cott, Nancy F. *The Bonds of Womanhood: "Woman's Sphere" in New England, 1780–1835*. New Haven and London: Yale University Press, 1977.

Crozier, Alice. *The Novels of Harriet Beecher Stowe*. New York: Oxford University Press, 1969.

Fetterley, Judith and Marjorie Pryse, eds. *American Women Regionalists, 1850–1910*. New York: W. W. Norton, 1992.

Foster, Charles H. *The Rungless Ladder: Harriet Beecher Stowe and New England Puritanism*. Durham, N. C.: Duke University Press, 1954.

Gossett, Thomas F. *"Uncle Tom's Cabin" and American Culture*. Dallas: Southern Methodist University Press, 1985.

Hedrick, Joan D. *Harriet Beecher Stowe: A Life*. New York: Oxford University Press, 1994.

Jacobs, Harriet [Linda Brent, pseud.]. *Incidents in the Life of a Slave Girl, Written by Herself*. Edited by Lydia Maria Child [Boston: for the author, 1861], edited and introduced by Jean Fagan Yellin. Cambridge, Mass.: Harvard University Press, 1987.

McDowell, Deborah E. and Arnold Rampersad, eds. *Slavery and the Literary Imagination*. Baltimore and London: The Johns Hopkins University Press, 1989.

Stowe, Charles Edward. *Life of Harriet Beecher Stowe, Compiled from her Letters and Journals*. Boston: Houghton, Mifflin and Co., 1889.

Sundquist, Eric J., ed. *New Essays on "Uncle Tom's Cabin"*. Cambridge: Cambridge University Press, 1986.

*The Writings of Harriet Beecher Stowe*. Cambridge, Mass.: Riverside Press, 1896. 16 volumes.

## Articles

Boydston, Jeanne. "The Pastoralization of Housework." In *Home and Work: Housework, Wages, and the Ideology of Labor in the Early Republic*, by Jeanne Boydston. New York and Oxford: Oxford University Press, 1990.

Brown, Gillian. "Getting in the Kitchen with Dinah: Domestic Politics in *Uncle Tom's Cabin*." *American Quarterly* 36:4 (Fall, 1984):503–523.

Tompkins, Jane. "Sentimental Power: *Uncle Tom's Cabin* and the Politics of Literary History." In *Sensational Designs: The Cultural Work of American Fiction, 1790–1850*. New York: Oxford University Press, 1985.

Welter, Barbara. "The Cult of True Womanhood, 1820–1860." *American Quarterly* 18:2 (Summer, 1966):151–174.